DEVELOPING MANAGERIAL SKILLS IN ORGANIZATIONAL BEHAVIOR

Exercises, Cases, and Readings

Lisa A. Mainiero and **Cheryl L. Tromley**

Fairfield University

Prentice Hall
Englewood Cliffs, New Jersey 07632

Library of Congress Cataloging-in-Publication Data

Mainiero, Lisa A.
    Developing managerial skills in organizational behavior:
  exercises, cases & readings / by Lisa A. Mainiero and Cheryl L. Tromley.
    Bibliography.
    Includes index.
    ISBN 0-13-204504-4
    1. Organizational behavior.   2. Organizational behavior—Case studies.
  3. Organizational behavior—Problems, exercises, etc.
  I. Tromley, Cheryl L.   II. Title.
  HD58.7.M325 1989
  302.3′5—dc19   88–13125
                                                                  CIP

Editorial/production supervision and
    interior design: Fred Dahl
Manufacturing buyer: Edward O'Dougherty

© 1989 by Prentice-Hall, Inc.
A Division of Simon & Schuster
Englewood Cliffs, New Jersey 07632

Printed in the United States of America
10   9   8   7   6   5   4   3   2   1

ISBN   0-13-204504-4

Prentice-Hall International (UK) Limited, *London*
Prentice-Hall of Australia Pty. Limited, *Sydney*
Prentice-Hall Canada Inc., *Toronto*
Prentice-Hall Hispanoamericana, S.A., *Mexico*
Prentice-Hall of India Private Limited, *New Delhi*
Prentice-Hall of Japan, Inc., *Tokyo*
Prentice-Hall of Southeast Asia Pte. Ltd., *Singapore*
Editora Prentice-Hall do Brasil, Ltda., *Rio de Janeiro*

To **David M. Mangini** and **Arnold W. Shaw,**
without whose love, support, and patience
we could not have successfully accomplished
this task.

Contents

CHAPTER 6

Group and Intergroup Behavior, *265*

CHAPTER 7

Organization Design, Structure, and Environment, *318*

CHAPTER 8

Organizational Culture and Planned Change, *382*

Index, *447*

Preface

"So what?" "That's only common sense!" "What does this have to do with my job?" These are some of the comments often heard in graduate level Organizational Behavior courses across the country. We have found that management students insist on action-oriented, skill-building, directly relevant classroom experiences. In short, they want "bang for their buck." Our students asked for exercises, readings, and cases that would help them improve their skills. This book is an attempt to fulfill that request.

Developing Managerial Skills in Organizational Behavior: Exercises, Cases, and Readings, is a collection of new and classic readings in organizational behavior, coupled with action-oriented, skill-building experiential exercises and cases. While targeted for a graduate level management audience, it also is appropriate for advanced undergraduates. The book is organized into eight chapters that cover a range of topics from "Managerial Work" to "Organizational Culture and Planned Change." Each chapter is an integrated package, combining:

1. *Readings* that present the concepts and theories.
2. Experiential *exercises* that give students the opportunity to practice their skills.
3. *Cases* that allow students to apply the concepts and theories to a management situation.
4. A *memo* in which students apply the concepts and theories to their own experience.

Readings. We selected readings that contribute to students' conceptual knowledge and support their skill development, and tried to remain especially sensitive to their relationship with the cases and exercises. Among the selections are "classic" articles and readings that we thought would soon become classic (that is, well-known and well received). In the end, our notion of what constitutes a classic may not be the same as others'—"classic," it seems, is in the eye of the beholder. Ultimately, we chose the readings based on what we wanted our students to learn.

Note: We have sought, in the original material included in this book, to ensure the absence of sexist or outdated language. Unfortunately, this type of language sometimes appears in the older, now classic, readings. Because removal of this language was beyond our control due to copyright restrictions, we sincerely hope that our readers will understand and accept the context in which the articles were written.

Experiential Exercises. The experiential exercises are of three basic types:

1. *Self-assessment exercises* give students the opportunity to analyze their attitudes, behaviors, and perceptions, as well as to diagnose skill weaknesses and build future strengths.

2. *Skill practice exercises* provide students with an opportunity to practice their management skills in the relative safety of the classroom, and analyze the experience as a way to build strengths for future management situations.

3. *Theory application exercises* bring the theories to life so that students can use the concepts rather than simply read about them.

The mix of exercises is flexible so that they can be easily tailored to fit varying time limits and pedagogical needs. Many of the exercises have three or more parts that can be used separately or as a package. For example, students may be asked to: (1) diagnose their skills through the use of a self-assessment questionnaire, (2) practice their skills during a role play or group experience, and (3) develop an action plan that relates what they have learned to their ongoing management experiences.

Integrative Cases. Cases have been included to give students the opportunity to integrate and use the theories and concepts from the readings in solving typical managerial problems. We have found that management students appreciate the opportunity to explore problem situations from a safe distance and do some "Monday morning quarterbacking." There is a wide mix of cases. Some have never been published, and others are well-known and widely used. Still others are based on news events, such as the NASA/Challenger disaster, or on popular theories that have captured the attention of managers, such as Thomas Peters and Robert Waterman's *In Search of Excellence.*

Memos. Each chapter concludes with a brief written assignment that closes the learning loop by giving students the occasion to apply what they have learned to their own experiences. For example, in the chapter on "Leadership and Decision Making," students are asked to reflect on transformational or charismatic leaders they have known, and to specify their characteristics and actions. Some memos are written as an actual on-the-job assignment for students to reflect on the material in the chapter as it applies to their own management experience.

We have sought to provide instructors with complete and clear teaching notes for the experiential exercises and cases. The teaching notes include:

1. Teaching objectives.

2. Time requirements.

3. Procedural instructions.

4. Teaching guidelines that include information on what to expect, how to teach the exercise, and discussion points.

5. A wrap-up section that offers suggestions for concluding the exercise or case.

Whenever possible, we have provided a direct tie-in to the readings in each chapter so that the instructor will assign particular readings in conjunction with each exercise to make the learning experience as integrative as possible. These teaching notes are found in a separate supplement to this book, available from the publisher.

We would like to thank several colleagues: all our Yale professors who taught us the value of the experiential method, especially J. Richard Hackman, Victor Vroom, and Dennis Perkins; our friends, colleagues and fellow alumni of the Yale doctoral program in Organizational Behavior who reviewed the readings selections; our direct contributors to the book, namely John Viega of the University of Connecticut, Judi Babcock of Rhode Island College, and Bonita Betters-Reed of Simmons College, who provided original experiential exercises and cases; our anonymous reviewers who provided helpful suggestions in the direction and focus of the book as well as specific hints on conducting the exercises; Alison Reeves, our editor at Prentice-Hall and Eileen Moran, the Prentice-Hall sales representative; R. Keith Martin, Dean of the School of Business at Fairfield University who provided monetary support for copying and supplies; Nancy Haag and the library staff at the Fairfield University Nyselius Library who provided support in terms of finding references that eluded us; Lynn Lenotti, who typed all the permissions forms for each chapter; Kathy Hanlon, who typed the teaching notes; and especially our students who taught us what we should be teaching them in courses of this type. Without the help, support, patience and guidance of all of these individuals, our task would have been made much more difficult, and we gratefully express our thanks to all.

CHAPTER ONE

Managerial Work

INTRODUCTION

What is managerial work? What do managers do? If you are currently a manager, have been one in the past, or hope to be one in the future, you probably think you know the answer to these questions. Some people might say that managerial work involves finance, strategic planning, marketing, or manufacturing. They would be right in part. Some managers spend part of their time involved in tasks related to these areas. But if they are truly managers, none of these activities is their major responsibility. What all managers have in common is that they manage and interact with people.

Maybe you would say that managers spend their time planning, organizing, directing, and controlling. If you did, your response would fit comfortably in the traditional normative framework, which prescribed what managers *should* do to be effective. This framework was developed in 1916 by Henri Fayol and is an idea on which much traditional management education is founded. From this perspective, managerial work is orderly, systematic, direct, static, and rigid. However, you will probably find that this description does not match your own experience as a manager.

One of the unfortunate effects of this perspective is that many managers have a realistic picture of what managerial work actually involves or ought to involve. If you are one of these managers, you could find yourself in the untenable position of trying to live up to ideals that are unattainable in the "real world" of management.

READINGS

In the first article, "Managerial Work: Analysis from Observation," Henry Mintzberg explodes some of the myths upon which many of us base our ideas about managerial work. Based on his research, he describes six characteristics of managerial work that present a clear picture of how managers actually spend their time. Managers have a heavy workload comprised predominantly of current, specific, and ad-hoc issues. Their work is accomplished at an unrelenting pace and is characterized by variety, fragmentation, and brevity. Mintzberg also shows that managers typically portray a variety of roles in the course of performing their jobs. He introduces a typological framework to illustrate the distinct components of managerial work.

The second reading, "The Human Side of Enterprise," by Douglas McGregor is considered a classic. It examines the assumptions that managers hold about people and identifies the impact these assumptions have on the behavior and attitudes of subordinates.

In this article McGregor presents the assumptions associated with Theory X and Theory Y approaches to management. A manager who holds Theory X assumptions takes the "conventional view" that employees are tools to be used, are basically unwilling to work in the best interests of the company, cannot handle responsibility, and must be tightly controlled, prodded, and punished to get their work done.

By contrast, managers who hold Theory Y assumptions believe that employees are inherently ready to work and accept responsibility, do a good job, and work in the best interests of the company. In addition, they believe that management's responsibility is to create the conditions that will allow employees to develop their full potential and to encourage them to attain their own goals by working toward the goals of the organization.

In "Putting Excellence into Management," Thomas Peters presents the eight attributes, made famous in the book *In Search of Excellence,* that characterize excellence in management:

1. A bias toward action.

2. Simple form and lean staff.

3. Continued contact with customers.

4. Productivity improvement via people.

5. Operational autonomy to encourage entrepreneurship.

6. Stress on one key business value.

7. Emphasis on doing what they know best.

8. Simultaneous loose-tight controls.

Peters argues against management formulas and for simplicity. If effective management can improve organizational performance, putting excellence into management could have dramatic results.

These three readings examine some of the basic considerations of managerial work including what it is, what assumptions we bring to it, how these assumptions influence our behavior and the behavior of those we manage, and what effective or excellent management entails.

EXERCISES AND CASES

The three exercises in this chapter will give you the opportunity to apply the ideas presented in the readings. The first exercise, "Understanding Your Philosophy of Management," is based on McGregor's article, "The Human Side of Enterprise." You will fill out a questionnaire that will help you identify the assumptions that you make about subordinates. By understanding your philosophy of management and some of the consequences associated with it, you will be in a better position to bring about the results you desire.

In the second exercise, "Motivational Styles," you will identify how, as a manager, you typically motivate your subordinates. Motivational style is an important part of managerial behavior. As mentioned previously, the major responsibility of most managers is managing people, and *effectively* managing people means effectively motivating them.

The final exercise, "In Search of Excellence Worksheet," will help you understand how Peters' eight attributes of excellent management can be applied in organizational settings. You will have the opportunity to explore the implications and critically assess these principles. This exercise is an opportunity for you to practice the skill of critical assessment and develop an in-depth understanding of these popular principles.

MEMO

In the memo, "Managerial Work," you will analyze the roles—following Mintzberg—that you routinely fulfill in your present position and develop a plan for improving the fit between how you spend your time and the demands of your job. The relative amount of attention which you, as a manager, devote to each of these roles will depend on your level in the organization, as well as on the structure and demands of your company and job. Matching the demands of your current job and the roles that you fulfill is the first step in what should become an ongoing process.

By the time you finish this chapter you will understand the characteristics of managerial work, your place in the managerial world, your philosophy of management, and your motivational style. You will have begun the process of self-assessment and skill development that will continue throughout this term. You will also better understand some of the ways you can become a more effective manager. Through this knowledge, you will develop a framework with which to organize the information and experiences that will follow.

Managerial Work: Analysis from Observation

Henry Mintzberg

The progress of management science is dependent on our understanding of the manager's working processes. A review of the literature indicates that this understanding is superficial at best. Empirical study of the work of five managers

Reprinted by permission of Henry Mintzberg, "Managerial Work: Analysis from Observation," *Management Science*, Vol. 18, Number 2, 1971. Copyright 1971 by The Institute of Management Sciences.

(supported by those research findings that are available) led to the following description: Managers perform the basic roles which fall into three groupings. The interpersonal roles describe the manager as figurehead, external liaison, and leader; the information processing roles describe the manager as the nerve center of his organization's information system; and the decision-making roles suggest that the manager is at the heart of the system by which organizational resource allocation, improvement, and disturbance decisions are made. Because of the huge burden of responsibility for the operation of these systems, the manager is called upon to perform his work at an unrelenting pace, work that is characterized by variety, discontinuity and brevity. Managers come to prefer issues that are current, specific, and ad hoc, and that are presented in verbal form. As a result, there is virtually no science in managerial work. The management scientist has done little to change this. He has been unable to understand work which has never been adequately described, and he has poor access to the manager's information, most of which is never documented. We must describe managerial work more precisely, and we must model the manager as a programmed system. Only then shall we be able to make a science of management.

What do managers do? Ask this question and you will likely be told that managers plan, organize, coordinate, and control. Since Henri Fayol (9) first proposed these words in 1916, they have dominated the vocabulary of management. (See, for example, [8], [12], [17].) How valuable are they in describing managerial work? Consider one morning's work of the president of a large organization:

As he enters his office at 8:23, the manager's secretary motions for him to pick up the telephone, "Jerry, there was a bad fire in the plant last night, about $30,000 damage. We should be back in operation by Wednesday. Thought you should know."

At 8:45, a Mr. Jamison is ushered into the manager's office. They discuss Mr. Jamison's retirement plans and his cottage in New Hampshire. Then the manager presents a plaque to him commemorating his thirty-two years with the organization.

Mail processing follows: An innocent-looking letter, signed by a Detroit lawyer, reads: "A group of us in Detroit has decided not to buy any of your products because you used that anti-flag, anti-American pinko, Bill Lindell, upon your Thursday night TV show." The manager dictates a restrained reply.

The 10:00 meeting is scheduled by a professional staffer. He claims that his superior, a high-ranking vice-president of the organization, mistreats his staff, and that if the man is not fired, they will all walk out. As soon as the meeting ends, the manager rearranges his schedule to investigate the claim and to react to this crisis.

Which of these activities may be called planning, and which may be called organizing, coordinating, and controlling? Indeed, what do words such as "coordinating" and "planning" mean in the context of real activity? In fact, these four words do not describe the actual work of managers at all; they describe certain vague objectives of managerial work ". . . they are just ways of indicating what we need to explain." [1, p. 537]

Other approaches to the study of managerial work have developed, one dealing with managerial decision-making and policy-making processes, another with the manager's interpersonal activities. (See, for example, [2] and [10].) And some empirical researchers, using the "diary" method, have studied, what might be called, managerial "media"—by what means, with whom, how long, and where managers spend their time.[1] But in no part of this literature is the actual content of managerial work systematically and meaningfully described.[2] Thus, the question posed at the start—what do managers do?—remains essentially unanswered in the literature of management.

This is indeed an odd situation. We claim to teach management in schools of both business and public administration; we undertake major research programs in management; we find a growing segment of the management science community concerned with the problems of senior management. Most of these people—the planners, information and control theorists, systems analysts, etc.—are attempting to analyze and change working habits that they themselves do not understand. Thus, at a conference called at M.I.T. to assess the impact of the computer on the manager, and attended by a number of America's foremost management scientists, a participant found it necessary to comment after lengthy discussion [20, p. 198]:

I'd like to return to an earlier point. It seems to me that until we get into the question of what the top manager does or what the functions

1. Carlson [6] carried out the classic study just after World War II. He asked nine Swedish managing directors to record on diary pads details of each activity in which they engaged. His method was used by a group of other researchers, many of them working in the U.K. (See [4], [5], [15], [25].)

2. One major project, involving numerous publications, took place at Ohio State University and spanned three decades. Some of the vocabulary used followed Fayol. The results have generated little interest in this area. (See, for example, [13]).

are that define the top management job, we're not going to get out of the kind of difficulty that keeps cropping up. What I'm really doing is leading up to my earlier question which no one really answered. And that is: Is it possible to arrive at a specification of what constitutes the job of a top manager?

His question was not answered.

RESEARCH STUDY ON MANAGERIAL WORK

In late 1966, I began research on this question, seeking to replace Fayol's words by a set that would more accurately describe what managers do. In essence, I sought to develop by the process of induction a statement of managerial work that would have empirical validity. Using a method called "structured observation," I observed for one-week periods the chief executives of five medium to large organizations (a consulting firm, a school system, a technology firm, a consumer goods manufacturer, and a hospital).

Structured as well as unstructured (i.e., anecdotal) data were collected in three "records". In the *chronology record,* activity patterns throughout the working day were recorded. In the *mail record,* for each of 890 pieces of mail processed during the five weeks, were recorded its purpose, format and sender, the attention it received and the action it elicited. And, recorded in the *contact record,* for each of the 368 verbal interactions, were the purpose, the medium (telephone call, scheduled or unscheduled meeting, tour), the participants, the form of initiation, and the location. It should be noted that all categorizing was done during and after observation so as to ensure that the categories reflected only the work under observation. [19] contains a fuller description of this methodology and a tabulation of the results of the study.

Two sets of conclusions are presented below. The first deals with certain characteristics of managerial work, as they appeared from analysis of the numerical data (e.g., How much time is spent with peers? What is the average duration of meetings? What proportion of contacts are initiated by the manager himself?). The second describes the basic content of managerial work in terms of ten roles. This description derives from an analysis of the data on the recorded *purpose* of each contact and piece of mail.

The liberty is taken of referring to these findings as descriptive of managerial, as opposed to chief executive, work. This is done because many of the findings are supported by studies of other types of managers. Specifically, most of the conclusions on work characteristics are to be found in the combined results of a group of studies of foremen [11], [16], middle managers [4], [5], [15], [25], and chief executives [6]. And although there is little useful material on managerial roles, three studies do provide some evidence of the applicability of the role set. Most important, Sayles' empirical study of production managers [24] suggests that at least five of the ten roles are performed at the lower end of the managerial hierarchy. And some further evidence is provided by comments in Whyte's study of leadership in a street gang [26] and Neustadt's study of three U.S. presidents [21]. (Reference is made to these findings where appropriate.) Thus, although most of the illustrations are drawn from my study of chief executives, there is some justification in asking the reader to consider when he sees the terms "manager" and his "organization" not only "presidents" and their "companies", but also "foremen" and their "shops", "directors" and their "branches", "vice-presidents" and their "divisions". The term *manager* shall be used with reference to all those people in charge of formal organizations or their subunits.

SOME CHARACTERISTICS OF MANAGERIAL WORK

Six sets of characteristics of managerial work derive from analysis of the data of this study. Each has a significant bearing on the manager's ability to administer a complex organization.

Characteristic 1. The Manager Performs a Great Quantity of Work at an Unrelenting Pace

Despite a semblance of normal working hours, in truth managerial work appears to be very taxing. The five men in this study processed an average of thirty-six pieces of mail each day, participated in eight meetings (half of which were scheduled), engaged in five telephone calls, and took one tour. In his study of the foremen, Guest [11] found that the number of activities per day averaged 583, with no real break in the pace.

Free time appears to be very rare. If by chance a manager has caught up with the mail, satisfied the callers, dealt with all the disturbances, and avoided scheduled meetings, a subordinate will likely show up to usurp the available time. It seems that the manager cannot expect to have much time for leisurely reflection during office hours. During "off" hours, our chief executives spent much time on work-related reading. High-level managers appear to be able to escape neither from an environment which recognizes the power and status of their positions nor from their own minds which have been trained to search continually for new information.

Characteristic 2. Managerial Activity is Characterized by Variety, Fragmentation, and Brevity

There seems to be no pattern to managerial activity. Rather, variety and fragmentation appear to be characteristic, as successive activities deal with issues that differ greatly both in type and in content. In effect the manager must be prepared to shift moods quickly and frequently.

A typical chief executive day may begin with a telephone call from a director who asks a favor (a "status request"); then a subordinate calls to tell of a strike at one of the facilities (fast movement of information, termed "instant communication"); this is followed by a relaxed scheduled event at which the manager speaks to a group of visiting dignitaries (ceremony); the manager returns to find a message from a major consumer who is demanding the renegotiation of a contract (pressure); and so on. Throughout the day, the managers of our study encountered this great variety of activity. Most surprisingly, the significant activities were interspersed with the trivial in no particular pattern.

Furthermore, these managerial activities were characterized by their brevity. Half of all the activities lasted less than nine minutes and only ten percent exceeded one hour's duration. Guest's foremen averaged 48 seconds per activity, and Carlson [6] stressed that his chief executives were unable to work without frequent interruption.

In my own study of chief executives, I felt that the managers demonstrated a preference for tasks of short duration and encouraged interruption. Perhaps the manager becomes accustomed to variety, or perhaps the flow of "instant communication" cannot be delayed. A more plausible explanation might be that the manager becomes conditioned by his workload. He develops a sensitive appreciation for the opportunity cost of his own time. Also, he is aware of the ever present assortment of obligations associated with his job—accumulations of mail that cannot be delayed, the callers that must be attended to, the meetings that require his participation. In other words, no matter what he is doing, the manager

is plagued by what he must do and what he might do. Thus, the manager is forced to treat issues in an abrupt and superficial way.

Characteristic 3. Managers Prefer Issues That are Current, Specific, and Ad Hoc

Ad hoc operating reports received more attention than did routine ones; current, uncertain information—gossip, speculation, hearsay—which flows quickly was preferred to historical, certain information; "instant communication" received first consideration; few contacts were held on a routine or "clocked" basis; almost all contacts concerned well-defined issues. The managerial environment is clearly one of stimulus-response. It breeds, not reflective planners, but adaptable information manipulators who prefer the live, concrete situation, men who demonstrate a marked action-orientation.

Characteristic 4. The Manager Sits Between His Organization and a Network of Contacts

In virtually every empirical study of managerial time allocation, it was reported that managers spent a surprisingly large amount of time in horizontal or lateral (nonline) communications. It is clear from this study and from that of Sayles [24] that the manager is surrounded by a diverse and complex web of contacts which serves as his self-designed external information system. Included in this web can be clients, associates and suppliers, outside staff experts, peers (managers of related or similar organizations), trade organizations, government officials, independents (those with no relevant organizational affiliation), and directors or superiors. (Among these, directors in this study and superiors in other studies did *not* stand out as particularly active individuals.)

The managers in this study received far more information than they emitted, much of it coming from contacts, and more from subordinates who acted as filters. Figuratively, the manager appears as the neck of an hourglass, sifting information into his own organization from its environment.

Characteristic 5. The Manager Demonstrates a Strong Preference for the Verbal Media

The manager has five media at his command—mail (documented), telephone (purely verbal), unscheduled meeting (informal face-to-face), scheduled meeting (formal face-to-face), and tour (observation). Along with all the other empirical studies of work characteristics, I found a strong predominance of verbal forms of communication.

Mail. By all indications, managers dislike the documented form of communication. In this study, they gave cursory attention to such items as operating reports and periodicals. It was estimated that only thirteen percent of the input mail was of specific and immediate use to the managers. Much of the rest dealt with formalities and provided general reference data. The managers studied initiated very little mail, only twenty-five pieces in the five weeks. The rest of the outgoing mail was sent in reaction to mail received—a reply to a request, an acknowledgment, some information forwarded to a part of the organization. The managers appeared to dislike this form of communication, perhaps because the mail is a relatively slow and tedious medium to use.

Telephone and Unscheduled Meetings. The less formal means of verbal communication—the telephone, a purely verbal form, and the unscheduled meeting, a face-to-face form—were used frequently (two-thirds of the contracts in the study) but for brief encounters (average duration of six and twelve minutes respectively). They were used primarily to deliver requests and to transmit pressing information to those outsiders and subordinates who had informal relationships with the manager.

Scheduled Meetings. These tended to be of long duration, averaging sixty-eight minutes in this study, and absorbing over half the managers' time. Such meetings provided the managers with their main opportunities to interact with large groups and to leave the confines of their own offices. Scheduled meetings were used when the participants were unfamiliar to the manager (e.g., students who request that he speak at a university), when a large quantity of information had to be transmitted (e.g., presentation of a report), when ceremony had to take place, and when complex strategy-making or negotiation had to be undertaken. An important feature of the scheduled meeting was the incidental, but by no means irrelevant, information that flowed at the start and end of such meetings.

Tours. Although the walking tour would appear to be a powerful tool for gaining information in an informal way, in this study tours accounted for only three percent of the managers' time.

In general, it can be concluded that the man-

ager uses each medium for particular purposes. Nevertheless, where possible, he appears to gravitate to verbal media since these provide greater flexibility, require less effort, and bring faster response. It should be noted here that the manager does not leave the telephone or the meeting to get back to work. Rather, communication is his work, and these media are his tools. The operating work of the organization—producing a product, doing research, purchasing a part—appears to be undertaken infrequently by the senior manager. The manager's productive output must be measured in terms of information, a great part of which is transmitted verbally.

Characteristic 6. Despite the Preponderance of Obligations, the Manager Appears to be Able to Control His Own Affairs

Carlson suggested in his study of Swedish chief executives that these men were puppets, with little control over their own affairs. A cursory examination of our data indicates that this is true. Our managers were responsible for the initiation of only thirty-two percent of their verbal contacts and a smaller proportion of their mail. Activities were also classified as to the nature of the managers' participation, and the active ones were outnumbered by the passive ones (e.g., making requests vs. receiving requests). On the surface, the manager is indeed a puppet, answering requests in the mail, returning telephone calls, attending meetings initiated by others, yielding to subordinates' requests for time, reacting to crises.

However, such a view is misleading. There is evidence that the senior manager can exert control over his own affairs in two significant ways: (1) It is he who defines many of his own long-term commitments, by developing appropriate information channels which later feed him information, by initiating projects which later demand his time, by joining committees or outside boards which provide contacts in return for his services, and so on. (2) The manager can exploit situations that appear as obligations. He can lobby at ceremonial speeches; he can impose his values on his organization when his authorization is requested; he can motivate his subordinates whenever he interacts with them; he can use the crisis situation as an opportunity to innovate.

Perhaps these are two points that help distinguish successful and unsuccessful managers. All managers appear to be puppets. Some decide who will pull the strings and how, and they then take advantage of each move that they are forced to make.

Others, unable to exploit this high-tension environment, are swallowed up by this most demanding of jobs.

THE MANAGER'S WORK ROLES

In describing the essential content of managerial work, one should aim to model managerial activity, that is, to describe it as a set of programs. But an undertaking as complex as this must be preceded by the development of a useful typological description of managerial work. In other words, we must first understand the distinct components of managerial work. At the present time we do not.

In this study, 890 pieces of mail and 368 verbal contacts were categorized as to purpose. The incoming mail was found to carry acknowledgements, requests and solicitations of various kinds, reference data, news, analytical reports, reports on events and on operations, advice on various situations, and statements of problems, pressures, and ideas. In reacting to mail, the managers acknowledged some, replied to the requests (e.g., by sending information), and forwarded much to subordinates (usually for their information). Verbal contacts involved a variety of purposes. In 15% of them activities were scheduled, in 6% ceremonial events took place and a few involved external board work. About 34% involved requests of various kinds, some insignificant, some for information, some for authorization of proposed actions. Another 36% essentially involved the flow of information to and from the manager, while the remainder dealt specifically with issues of strategy and with negotiations. (For details, see [19].)

In this study, each piece of mail and verbal contact categorized in this way was subjected to one question: Why did the manager do this? The answers were collected and grouped and regrouped in various ways (over the course of three years) until a typology emerged that was felt to be satisfactory. While an example, presented below, will primarily explain this process to the reader, it must be remembered that (in the words of Bronowski [3, p. 62]): "Every induction is a speculation and it guesses at a unity which the facts present but do not strictly imply."

Consider the following sequences of two episodes: A chief executive attends a meeting of an external board on which he sits. Upon his return to his organization, he immediately goes to the office of a subordinate, tells of a conversation he had with a fellow board member, and concludes with the statement: "It looks like we shall get the contract."

The purposes of these two contacts are clear—to attend an external board meeting, and to give current information (instant communication) to a subordinate. But why did the manager attend the meeting? Indeed, why does he belong to the board? And why did he give this particular information to his subordinate?

Basing analysis on this incident, one can argue as follows: The manager belongs to the board in part so that he can be exposed to special information which is of use to his organization. The subordinate needs the information but has not the status which would give him access to it. The chief executive does. Board memberships bring chief executives in contact with one another for the purpose of trading information.

Two aspects of managerial work emerge from this brief analysis. The manager serves in a "liaison" capacity because of the status of his office, and what he learns here enables him to act as "disseminator" of information into his organization. We refer to these as *roles*—organized sets of behaviors belonging to identifiable offices or positions [23]. Ten roles were chosen to capture all the activities observed during this study.

All activities were found to involve one or more of three basic behaviors—interpersonal contact, the processing of information, and the making of decisions. As a result, our ten roles are divided into three corresponding groups. Three roles—labelled *figurehead, liaison,* and *leader*—deal with behavior that is essentially interpersonal in nature. Three others—*nerve center, disseminator,* and *spokesman*—deal with information-processing activities performed by the manager. And the remaining four—*entrepreneur, disturbance handler, resource allocator,* and *negotiator*—cover the decision-making activities of the manager. We describe each of these roles in turn, asking the reader to note that they form a *gestalt,* a unified whole whose parts cannot be considered in isolation.

The Interpersonal Roles

Three roles relate to the manager's behavior that focuses on interpersonal contact. These roles derive directly from the authority and status associated with holding managerial office.

Figurehead. As legal authority in his organization, the manager is a symbol, obliged to perform a number of duties. He must preside at ceremonial events, sign legal documents, receive visitors, make himself available to many of those who feel, in the words of one of the men studied, "that the only way to get something done is to get to the top." There is evidence that this role applies at other levels as well. Davis [7, pp. 43–44] cites the case of the field sales manager who must deal with those customers who believe that their accounts deserve his attention.

Leader. Leadership is the most widely recognized of managerial roles. It describes the manager's relationship with his subordinates—his attempts to motivate them and his development of the milieu in which they work. Leadership actions pervade all activity—in contrast to most roles, it is possible to designate only a few activities as dealing exclusively with leadership (these mostly related to staffing duties). Each time a manager encourages a subordinate, or meddles in his affairs, or replies to one of his requests, he is playing the *leader* role. Subordinates seek out and react to these leadership clues, and, as a result, they impart significant power to the manager.

Liaison. As noted earlier, the empirical studies have emphasized the importance of lateral or horizontal communication in the work of managers at all levels. It is clear from our study that this is explained largely in terms of the *liaison* role. The manager establishes his network of contacts essentially to bring information and favors to his organization. As Sayles notes in his study of production supervisors [24, p. 258], "The one enduring objective [of the manager] is the effort to build and maintain a predictable, reciprocating system of relationships . . ."

Making use of his status, the manager reacts with a variety of peers and other people outside his organization. He provides time, information, and favors in return for the same from others. Foremen deal with staff groups and other foremen; chief executives join boards of directors, and maintain extensive networks of individual relationships. Neustadt notes this behavior in analyzing the work of President Roosevelt [21, p. 150]:

> His personal sources were the product of a sociability and curiosity that reached back to the other Roosevelt's time. He had an enormous acquaintance in various phases of national life and at various levels of government; he also had his wife and her variety of contacts. He extended his acquaintanceships abroad; in the war years Winston Churchill, among others, became a "personal source". Roosevelt quite deliberately exploited these relationships and mixed them up to widen his own range of information. He changed his sources as his interests changed, but no one

who ever had interested him was quite forgotten or immune to sudden use.

The Informational Roles

A second set of managerial activities relate primarily to the processing of information. Together they suggest three significant managerial roles, one describing the manager as a focal point for a certain kind of organizational information, the other two describing relatively simple transmission of this information.

Nerve Center. There is indication, both from this study and from those by Neustadt and Whyte, that the manager serves as the focal point in his organization for the movement of nonroutine information. Homans, who analyzed Whyte's study, draws the following conclusions [26, p. 187]:

> Since interaction flowed toward [the leaders], they were better informed about the problems and desires of group members than were any of the followers and therefore better able to decide on an appropriate course of action. Since they were in close touch with other gang leaders, they were also better informed than their followers about conditions in Cornerville at large. Moreover, in their positions at the focus of the chains of interaction, they were better able than any follower to pass on to the group decisions that had been reached.

The term *nerve center* is chosen to encompass those many activities in which the manager receives information.

Within his own organization, the manager has legal authority that formally connects him — and only him—to *every* member. Hence, the manager emerges as *nerve center* of internal information. He may not know as much about any one function as the subordinate who specializes in it, but he comes to know more about his total organization than any other member. He is the information generalist. Furthermore, because of the manager's status and its manifestation in the *liaison* role, the manager gains unique access to a variety of knowledgeable outsiders including peers who are themselves *nerve centers* of their own organizations. Hence, the manager emerges as his organization's *nerve center* of external information as well.

As noted earlier, the manager's nerve center information is of a special kind. He appears to find it most important to get his information quickly and informally. As a result, he will not hesitate to bypass formal information channels to get it, and he is prepared to deal with a large amount of gossip, hearsay, and opinion which has not yet become substantiated fact.

Disseminator. Much of the manager's information must be transmitted to subordinates. Some of this is of a *factual* nature, received from outside the organization or from other subordinates. And some is of a *value* nature. Here, the manager acts as the mechanism by which organizational influencers (owners, governments, employee groups, the general public, etc., or simply the "boss") make their preferences known to the organization. It is the manager's duty to integrate these value positions, and to express general organizational preferences as a guide to decisions made by subordinates. One of the men studied commented: "One of the principal functions of this position is to integrate the hospital interests with the public interests." Papandreou describes this duty in a paper published in 1952, referring to management as the "peak coordinator" [22].

Spokesman. In his *spokesman* role, the manager is obliged to transmit his information to outsiders. He informs influencers and other interested parties about his organization's performance, its policies, and its plans. Furthermore, he is expected to serve outside his organization as an expert in its industry. Hospital administrators are expected to spend some time serving outside as public experts on health, and corporation presidents, perhaps as chamber of commerce executives.

The Decisional Roles

The manager's legal authority requires that he assume responsibility for all of his organization's important actions. The *nerve center* role suggests that only he can fully understand complex decisions, particularly those involving difficult value tradeoffs. As a result, the manager emerges as the key figure in the making and interrelating of all significant decisions in his organization, a process that can be referred to as *strategy-making.* Four roles describe the manager's control over the strategy-making system in his organization.

Entrepreneur. The *entrepreneur* role describes the manager as initiator and designer of much of the controlled change in his organization. The manager looks for opportunities and potential problems which may cause him to initiate action. Action takes the form of *improvement projects*—the marketing of a new product, the strengthening of a weak department, the purchasing of new equipment, the reorganization of formal structure, and so on.

The manager can involve himself in each improvement project in one of three ways: (1) He may *delegate* all responsibility for its design and approval, implicitly retaining the right to replace that subordinate who takes charge of it. (2) He may delegate the design work to a subordinate, but retain the right to *approve* it before implementation. (3) He may actively *supervise* the design work himself.

Improvement projects exhibit a number of interesting characteristics. They appear to involve a number of subdecisions, consciously sequenced over long periods of time and separated by delays of various kinds. Furthermore, the manager appears to supervise a great many of these at any one time— perhaps fifty to one hundred in the case of chief executives. In fact, in his handling of improvement projects, the manager may be likened to a juggler. At any one point, he maintains a number of balls in the air. Periodically, one comes down, receives a short burst of energy, and goes up again. Meanwhile, an inventory of new balls waits on the sidelines and, at random intervals, old balls are discarded and new ones added. Both Lindblom [2] and Marples [18] touch on these aspects of strategy-making, the former stressing the disjointed and incremental nature of the decisions, and the latter depicting the sequential episodes in terms of a stranded rope made up of fibres of different lengths each of which surfaces periodically.

Disturbance Handler. While the *entrepreneur* role focuses on voluntary change, the *disturbance handler* role deals with corrections which the manager is forced to make. We may describe this role as follows: The organization consists basically of specialist operating programs. From time to time, it experiences a stimulus that cannot be handled routinely, either because an operating program has broken down or because the stimulus is new and it is not clear which operating program should handle it. These situations constitute disturbances. As generalist, the manager is obliged to assume responsibility for dealing with the stimulus. Thus, the handling of disturbances is an essential duty of the manager.

There is clear evidence for this role both in our study of chief executives and in Sayles' study of production supervisors [24, p. 162]:

The achievement of this stability, which is the manager's objective, is a never-to-be-attained ideal. He is like a symphony orchestra conductor, endeavoring to maintain a melodious performance in which contributions of the various instruments are coordinated and sequenced, patterned and paced, while the orchestra members are having various personal difficulties, stage hands are moving music stands, alternating excessive heat and cold are creating audience and instrument problems, and the sponsor of the concert is insisting on irrational changes in the program.

Sayles goes further to point out the very important balance that the manager must maintain between change and stability. To Sayles, the manager seeks "a dynamic type of stability" (p. 162). Most disturbances elicit short-term adjustments which bring back equilibrium; persistent ones require the introduction of long-term structural change.

Resource Allocator. The manager maintains ultimate authority over his organization's strategy-making system by controlling the allocation of its resources. By deciding who will get what (and who will do what), the manager directs the course of his organization. He does this in three ways:

1. *In scheduling his own time,* the manager allocates his most precious resource and thereby determines organizational priorities. Issues that receive low priority do not reach the *nerve center* of the organization and are blocked for want of resources.

2. In designing the organizational structure and in carrying out many improvement projects, the manager *programs the work of his subordinates.* In other words, he allocates their time by deciding what will be done and who will do it.

3. Most significantly, the manager maintains control over resource allocation by the requirement that he *authorize all significant decisions* before they are implemented. By retaining this power, the manager ensures that different decisions are interrelated— that conflicts are avoided, that resource constraints are respected, and that decisions complement one another.

Decisions appear to be authorized in one of two ways. Where the costs and benefits of a proposal can be quantified, where it is competing for specified resources with other known proposals, and where it can wait for a certain time of year, approval for a proposal is sought in the context of a formal *budgeting* procedure. But these conditions are most often not met—timing may be crucial, nonmonetary costs may predominate, and so on. In these cases, approval is sought in terms of an *ad hoc request for authorization.* Subordinate and manager meet (perhaps informally) to discuss one proposal alone.

Authorization choices are enormously complex ones for the manager. A myriad of factors must be considered (resource constraints, influencer preferences, consistency with other decisions, feasibility, payoff, timing, subordinate feelings, etc.). But the fact that the manager is authorizing the decision rather than supervising its design suggests that he has little time to give to it. To alleviate this difficulty, it appears that managers use special kinds of *models* and *plans* in their decision-making. These exist only in their minds and are loose, but they serve to guide behavior. Models may answer questions such as, "Does this proposal make sense in terms of the trends that I see in tariff legislation?" or "Will the EDP department be able to get along with marketing on this?" Plans exist in the sense that, on questioning, managers reveal images (in terms of proposed improvement projects) of where they would like their organizations to go: "Well, once I get these foreign operations fully developed, I would like to begin to look into a reorganization," said one subject of this study.

Negotiator. The final role describes the manager as participant in negotiation activity. To some students of the management process [8, p. 343], this is not truly part of the job of managing. But such distinctions are arbitrary. Negotiation is an integral part of managerial work, as this study notes for chief executives and as that of Sayles made very clear for production supervisors [24, p. 131]: "Sophisticated managers place great stress on negotiations as a way of life. They negotiate with groups who are setting standards for their work, who are performing support activity for them, and to whom they wish to 'sell' their services."

The manager must participate in important negotiation sessions because he is his organization's legal authority, its *spokesman* and its *resource allocator.* Negotiation is resource trading in real time. If the resource commitments are to be large, the legal authority must be present.

These ten roles suggest that the manager of an organization bears a great burden of responsibility. He must oversee his organization's status system; he must serve as a crucial informational link between it and its environment; he must interpret and reflect its basic values; he must maintain the stability of its operations; and he must adapt it in a controlled and balanced way to a changing environment.

MANAGEMENT AS A PROFESSION AND AS A SCIENCE

Is management a profession? To the extent that different managers perform one set of basic roles, management satisfies one criterion for becoming a profession. But a profession must require, in the words of the Random House Dictionary, "knowledge of some department of learning or science." Which of the ten roles now requires specialized learning? Indeed, what school of business or public administration teaches its students how to disseminate information, allocate resources, perform as figurehead, make contacts, or handle disturbances? We simply know very little about teaching these things. The reason is that we have never tried to document and describe in a meaningful way the procedures (or programs) that managers use.

The evidence of this research suggests that there is as yet no science in managerial work—that managers do not work according to procedures that have been prescribed by scientific analysis. Indeed, except for his use of the telephone, the airplane, and the dictating machine, it would appear that the manager of today is indistinguishable from his predecessors. He may seek different information, but he gets much of it in the same way—from word-of-mouth. He may make decisions dealing with modern technology but he uses the same intuitive (that is, nonexplicit) procedures in making them. Even the computer, which has had such a great impact on other kinds of organizational work, has apparently done little to alter the working methods of the general manager.

How do we develop a scientific base to understand the work of the manager? The description of roles is a first and necessary step. But righter forms of research are necessary. Specifically, we must attempt to model managerial work—to describe it as a system of programs. First, it will be necessary to decide what programs managers actually use. Among a great number of programs in the manager's repertoire, we might expect to find a time scheduling program, an information disseminating program, and a disturbance-handling program. Then, researchers will have to devote a considerable amount of effort to studying and accurately describing the content of each of these programs—the information and heuristics used. Finally, it will be necessary to describe the interrelationships among all of these programs so that they may be combined into an integrated descriptive model of managerial work.

When the management scientist begins to understand the programs that managers use, he can begin to design meaningful systems and provide help for the manager. He may ask: Which managerial activities can be fully reprogrammed (i.e., automated)? Which cannot be reprogrammed because they require human responses? Which can be partially reprogrammed to operate in a man-machine system? Perhaps scheduling, information collecting, and resource allocating activities lend themselves to varying degrees of reprogramming. Management will emerge as a science to the extent that such efforts are successful.

IMPROVING THE MANAGER'S EFFECTIVENESS

Fayol's fifty year old description of managerial work is no longer of use to us. And we shall not disentangle the complexity of managerial work if we insist on viewing the manager simply as a decision-maker or simply as a motivator of subordinates. In fact, we are unlikely to overestimate the complexity of the manager's work, and we shall make little headway if we take overly simple or narrow points of view in our research.

A major problem faces today's manager. Despite the growing size of modern organizations and the growing complexity of their problems (particularly those in the public sector), the manager can expect little help. He must design his own information system, and he must take full charge of his organization's strategy-making system. Furthermore, the manager faces what might be called the *dilemma of delegation*. He has unique access to much important information but he lacks a formal means of disseminating it. As much of it is verbal, he cannot spread it around in an efficient manner. How can he delegate a task with confidence when he has neither the time nor the means to send the necessary information along with it?

Thus, the manager is usually forced to carry a great burden of responsibility in his organization. As organizations become increasingly large and complex, this burden increases. Unfortunately, the man cannot significantly increase his available time or significantly improve his abilities to manage. Hence, in the large, complex bureaucracy, the top manager's time assumes an enormous opportunity cost and he faces the real danger of becoming a major obstruction in the flow of decisions and information.

Because of this, as we have seen, managerial work assumes a number of distinctive characteristics. The quantity of work is great; the pace is unrelenting; there is great variety, fragmentation, and brevity in the work activities; the manager must concentrate on issues that are current, specific, and ad hoc, and to do so, he finds that he must rely on verbal forms of communications. Yet it is on this man that the burden lies for designing and operating strategy-making and information processing systems that are to solve his organization's (and society's) problems.

The manager can do something to alleviate these problems. He can learn more about his own roles in his organization, and he can use this information to schedule his time in a more efficient manner. He can recognize that only he has much of the information needed by his organization. Then, he can seek to find better means of disseminating it into the organization. Finally, he can turn to the skills of his management scientists to help reduce his workload and to improve his ability to make decisions.

The management scientist can learn to help the manager to the extent he can develop an understanding of the manager's work and the manager's information. To date, strategic planners, operations researchers, and information system designers have provided little help for the senior manager. They simply have had no framework available by which to understand the work of the men who employed them, and they have had poor access to the information which has never been documented. It is folly to believe that a man with poor access to the organization's true *nerve center* can design a formal management information system. Similarly, how can the long-range planner, a man usually uninformed about many of the *current* events that take place in and around his organization, design meaningful strategic plans? For good reason, the literature documents many manager complaints of naive planning and many planner complaints of disinterested managers. In my view, our lack of understanding of managerial work has been the greatest block to the progress of management science.

The ultimate solution to the problem—to the overburdened manager seeking meaningful help—must derive from research. We must observe, describe, and understand the real work of managing; then and only then shall we significantly improve it.

REFERENCES

1. Braybrooke, David, "The Mystery of Executive Success Re-examined," *Administrative Science Quarterly,* Vol. 8 (1964), pp. 533–560.

2. _____and Lindblom, Charles E., *A Strategy of Decision,* Free Press, New York, 1963.

3. Bronowski, J., "The Creative Process," *Scientific American,* Vol. 199 (September 1958), pp. 59–65.

4. Burns, Tom, "The Directions of Activity and Communications in a Departmental Executive Group," *Human Relations,* Vol. 7 (1954), pp. 73–97.

5. _____, "Management in Action," *Operational Research Quarterly,* Vol. 8 (1957), pp. 45–60.

6. Carlson, Sune, *Executive Behavior,* Strömbergs, Stockholm, 1951.

7. Davis, Robert T., *Performance and Development of Field Sales Managers,* Division of Research, Graduate School of Business Administration, Harvard University, Boston, 1957.

8. Drucker, Peter F., *The Practice of Management,* Harper and Row, New York, 1954.

9. Fayol, Henri, *Administration industrielle et générale,* Dunods, Paris, 1950 (first published 1916).

10. Gibb, Cecil A., "Leadership," Chapter 31 in Gardner Lindzey and Elliot A. Aronson (editors), *The Handbook of Social Psychology,* Vol. 4, Second edition, Addison-Wesley, Reading, Mass., 1969.

11. Guest, Robert H., "Of Time and the Foreman," *Personnel,* Vol. 32 (1955-56), pp. 478–486.

12. Gulick, Luther H., "Notes on the Theory of Organization," in Luther Gulick and Lyndall Urwick (editors), *Papers on the Science of Administration,* Columbia University Press, New York, 1937.

13. Hemphill, John K., *Dimensions of Executive Positions,* Bureau of Business Research Monograph Number 98, The Ohio State University, Columbus, 1960.

14. Homans, George C., *The Human Group,* Harcourt, Brace, New York, 1950.

15. Horne, J.H. and Lupton, Tom, "The Work Activities of Middle Managers—An Exploratory Study," *The Journal of Management Studies,* Vol. 2 (February 1965), pp. 14–33.

16. Kelly, Joe, "The Study of Executive Behavior by Activity Sampling," *Human Relations,* Vol. 17 (August 1964), pp. 277–287.

17. Mackenzie, R. Alex, "The Management Process in 3D," *Harvard Business Review* (November-December 1969), pp. 80–87.

18. Marples, D.L., "Studies of Managers—A Fresh Start?," *The Journal of Management Studies,* Vol. 4 (October 1967), pp. 282–299.

19. Mintzberg, Henry, "Structured Observation as a Method to Study Managerial Work," *The Journal of Management Studies,* Vol. 7 (February 1970), pp. 87–104.

20. Myers, Charles A. (Editor), *The Impact of Computers on Management,* The M.I.T. Press, Cambridge, Mass., 1967.

21. Neustadt, Richard E., *Presidential Power: The Politics of Leadership,* The New American Library, New York, 1964.

22. Papandreou, Andreas G., "Some Basic Problems in the Theory of the Firm," in Bernard F. Haley (editor), *A Survey of Contemporary Economics,* Vol. II, Irwin, Homewood, Illinois, 1952, pp. 183–219.

23. Sarbin, T.R. and Allen, V.L., "Role Theory," in Gardner Lindzey and Elliot A. Aronson (editors), *The Handbook of Social Psychology,* Vol. I, Second edition, Addison-Wesley, Reading, Mass., 1968, pp. 488–567.

24. Sayles, Leonard R., *Managerial Behavior: Administration in Complex Enterprises,* McGraw-Hill, New York, 1964.

25. Stewart, Rosemary, *Managers and Their Jobs,* Macmillan, London, 1967.

26. Whyte, William F., *Street Corner Society,* 2nd edition, University of Chicago Press, Chicago, 1955.

The Human Side of Enterprise

Douglas Murray McGregor

It has become trite to say that industry has the fundamental know-how to utilize physical science and technology for the material benefit of mankind, and that we must now learn how to utilize the social sciences to make our human organizations truly effective.

To a degree, the social sciences today are in a position like that of the physical sciences with respect to atomic energy in the thirties. We know that past conceptions of the nature of man are inadequate and, in many ways, incorrect. We are becoming quite certain that, under proper conditions, unimagined resources of creative human energy could become available within the organizational setting.

We cannot tell industrial management how to apply this new knowledge in simple, economic ways. We know it will require years of exploration, much costly development research, and a substantial amount of creative imagination on the part of management to discover how to apply this growing knowledge to the organization of human effort in industry.

This article is based on an address by Dr. McGregor before the Fifth Anniversary Convocation of the MIT School of Industrial Management. Reprinted, by permission of the publisher, from *Management Review,* November, 1957. Copyright © 1957 American Management Association, New York. All rights reserved.

MANAGEMENT'S TASK: THE CONVENTIONAL VIEW

The conventional conception of management's task in harnessing human energy to organizational requirements can be stated broadly in terms of three propositions. In order to avoid the complications introduced by a label, let us call this set of propositions "Theory X":

1. Management is responsible for organizing elements of productive enterprise—money, materials, equipment, people—in the interest of economic ends.

2. With respect to people, this is a process of directing their efforts, motivating them, controlling their actions, modifying their behavior to fit the needs of the organization.

3. Without this active intervention by management, people would be passive—even resistant—to organizational needs. They must therefore be persuaded, rewarded, punished, controlled—their activities must be directed. This is management's task. We often sum it up by saying that management consists of getting things done through other people.

Behind this conventional theory there are several additional beliefs—less explicit, but widespread:

4. The average man is by nature indolent—he works as little as possible.

5. He lacks ambition, dislikes responsibility, prefers to be led.

6. He is inherently self-centered, indifferent to organizational needs.

7. He is by nature resistant to change.

8. He is gullible, not very bright, the ready dupe of the charlatan and the demagogue.

The human side of economic enterprise today is fashioned from propositions and beliefs such as these. Conventional organizational structures and managerial policies, practices, and programs reflect these assumptions.

In accomplishing its task—with these assumptions as guides—management has conceived of a range of possibilities.

At one extreme, management can be "hard" or "strong." The methods for directing behavior involve coercion and threat (usually disguised), close supervision, tight controls over behavior. At the other extreme, management can be "soft" or "weak." The methods for directing behavior involve being permissive, satisfying people's demands, achieving harmony. Then they will be tractable, accept direction.

This range has been fairly completely explored during the past half century, and management has learned some things from the exploration. There are difficulties in the "hard" approach. Force breeds counter-forces: restriction of output, antagonism, militant unionism, subtle but effective sabotage of management objectives. This "hard" approach is especially difficult during times of full employment.

There are also difficulties in the "soft" approach. It leads frequently to the abdication of management—to harmony, perhaps, but to indifferent performance. People take advantage of the soft approach. They continually expect more, but they give less and less.

Currently, the popular theme is "firm but fair." This is an attempt to gain the advantages of both the hard and the soft approaches. It is reminiscent of Teddy Roosevelt's "speak softly and carry a big stick."

IS THE CONVENTIONAL VIEW CORRECT?

The findings which are beginning to emerge from the social sciences challenge this whole set of beliefs about man and human nature and about the task of management. The evidence is far from conclusive, certainly, but it is suggestive. It comes from the laboratory, the clinic, the schoolroom, the home, and even to a limited extent from industry itself.

The social scientist does not deny that human behavior in industrial organization today is approximately what management perceives it to be. He has, in fact, observed it and studied it fairly extensively. But he is pretty sure that this behavior is *not* a consequence of man's inherent nature. It is a consequence rather of the nature of industrial organizations, of management philosophy, policy, and practice. The conventional approach of Theory X is based on mistaken notions of what is cause and what is effect.

Perhaps the best way to indicate why the conventional approach of management is inadequate is to consider the subject of motivation.

PHYSIOLOGICAL NEEDS

Man is a wanting animal—as soon as one of his needs is satisfied, another appears in its place. This process is unending. It continues from birth to death.

Man's needs are organized in a series of levels—a hierarchy of importance. At the lowest level, but pre-eminent in importance when they are thwarted, are his *physiological needs*. Man lives for bread alone, when there is no bread. Unless the circumstances are unusual, his needs for love, for status, for recognition are inoperative when his stomach has been empty for a while. But when he eats regularly and adequately, hunger ceases to be an important motivation. The same is true of the other physiological needs of man—for rest, exercise, shelter, protection from the elements.

A satisfied need is not a motivator of behavior! This is a fact of profound significance that is regularly ignored in the conventional approach to the management of people. Consider your own need for air: Except as you are deprived of it, it has no appreciable motivating effect upon your behavior.

SAFETY NEEDS

When the physiological needs are reasonably satisfied, needs at the next higher level begin to dominate man's behavior—to motivate him. These are called *safety needs*. They are needs for protection against danger, threat, deprivation. Some people mistakenly refer to these as needs for security. However, unless man is in a dependent relationship where he fears arbitrary deprivation, he does not demand security. The need is for the "fairest possible break." When he is confident of this, he is more than willing to take risks. But when he feels threatened or dependent, his greatest need is for guarantees, for protection, for security.

The fact needs little emphasis that, since every industrial employee is in a dependent relationship, safety needs may assume considerable importance. Arbitrary management actions, behavior which arouses uncertainty with respect to continued employment or which reflects favoritism or discrimination, unpredictable administration of policy—these can be powerful motivators of the safety needs in the employment relationship *at every level,* from worker to vice president.

SOCIAL NEEDS

When man's physiological needs are satisfied and he is no longer fearful about his physical welfare, his *social needs* become important motivators of his behavior—needs for belonging, for association, for acceptance by his fellows, for giving and receiving friendship and love.

Management knows today of the existence of these needs, but it often assumes quite wrongly that they represent a threat to the organization. Many studies have demonstrated that the tightly knit, cohesive work group may, under proper conditions, be far more effective than an equal number of separate individuals in achieving organizational goals.

Yet management, fearing group hostility to its own objectives, often goes to considerable lengths to control and direct human efforts in ways that are inimical to the natural "groupiness" of human beings. When man's social needs—and perhaps his safety needs, too—are thus thwarted, he behaves in ways which tend to defeat organizational objectives. He becomes resistant, antagonistic, uncooperative. But this behavior is a consequence, not a cause.

EGO NEEDS

Above the social needs—in the sense that they do not become motivators until lower needs are reasonably satisfied—are the needs of greatest significance to management and to man himself. They are the *egoistic needs,* and they are of two kinds:

1. Those needs that relate to one's self-esteem—needs for self-confidence, for independence, for achievement, for competence, for knowledge.

2. Those needs that relate to one's reputation—needs for status, for recognition, for appreciation, for the deserved respect of one's fellows.

Unlike the lower needs, these are rarely satisfied; man seeks indefinitely for more satisfaction of these needs once they have become important to him. But they do not appear in any significant way until physiological, safety, and social needs are all reasonably satisfied.

The typical industrial organization offers few opportunities for the satisfaction of these egoistic needs to people at lower levels in the hierarchy. The conventional methods of organizing work, particularly in mass-production industries, give little heed to these aspects of human motivation. If the practices of scientific management were deliberately calculated to thwart these needs, they could hardly accomplish this purpose better than they do.

SELF-FULFILLMENT NEEDS

Finally—a capstone, as it were, on the hierarchy of man's needs—there are what we may call the *needs for self-fulfillment.* These are the needs for realizing one's own potentialities, for continued self-development, for being creative in the broadest sense of that term.

It is clear that the conditions of modern life give only limited opportunity for these relatively weak needs to obtain expression. The deprivation most people experience with respect to other lower-level needs, and the needs for self-fulfillment remain dormant.

MANAGEMENT AND MOTIVATION

We recognize readily enough that a man suffering from a severe dietary deficiency is sick. The deprivation of physiological needs has behavioral consequences. The same is true—although less well recognized—of deprivation of higher-level needs. The man whose needs for safety, association, independence, or status are thwarted is sick just as surely as the man who has rickets. And his sickness will have behavioral consequences. We will be mistaken if we attribute his resultant passivity, his hostility, his refusal to accept responsibility to his inherent "human nature." These forms of behavior are *symptoms* of illness—of deprivation of his social and egoistic needs.

The man whose lower-level needs are satisfied is not motivated to satisfy those needs any longer. For practical purposes they exist no longer. Management often asks, "Why aren't people more productive? We pay good wages, provide good working conditions, have excellent fringe benefits and steady employment. Yet people do not seem to be willing to put forth more than minimum effort."

The fact that management has provided for these physiological and safety needs has shifted the motivational emphasis to the social and perhaps to the egoistic needs. Unless there are opportunities *at work* to satisfy these higher-level needs, people will be deprived; and their behavior will reflect this deprivation. Under such conditions, if management continues to focus its attention on physiological needs, its efforts are bound to be ineffective.

People *will* make insistent demands for more money under these conditions. It becomes more important than ever to buy the material goods and services which can provide limited satisfaction of the thwarted needs. Although money has only limited value in satisfying many higher-level needs, it can become the focus of interest if it is the *only* means available.

THE CARROT-AND-STICK APPROACH

The carrot-and-stick theory of motivation (like Newtonian physical theory) works reasonably well under certain circumstances. The *means* for satisfying man's physiological and (within limits) his safety needs can be provided or withheld by management. Employment itself is such a means, and so are wages, working conditions, and benefits. By these means the individual can be controlled so long as he is struggling for subsistence.

But the carrot-and-stick theory does not work at all once man has reached an adequate subsistence level and is motivated primarily by higher needs. Management cannot provide a man with self-respect, or with the respect of his fellows, or with the satisfaction of needs for self-fulfillment. It can create such conditions that he is encouraged and enabled to seek such satisfactions for *himself,* or it can thwart him by failing to create those conditions.

But this creation of conditions is not "control." It is not a good device for directing behavior. And so management finds itself in an odd position. The high standard of living created by our modern technological know-how provides quite adequately for the satisfaction of physiological and safety needs. The only significant exception is where management practices have not created confidence in a "fair break"—and thus where safety needs are thwarted. But by making possible the satisfaction of low-level needs, management has deprived itself of the ability to use as motivators the devices on which conventional theory has taught it to rely—rewards, promises, incentives, or threats and other coercive devices.

The philosophy of management by direction and control—*regardless of whether it is hard or soft*—is inadequate to motivate because the human needs on which this approach relies are today unimportant motivators of behavior. Direction and control are essentially useless in motivating people whose important needs are social and egoistic. Both the hard and the soft approach fail today because they are simply irrelevant to the situation.

People, deprived of opportunities to satisfy at work the needs which are now important to them, behave exactly as we might predict—with indolence, passivity, resistance to change, lack of responsibility, willingness to follow the demagogue, unreasonable demands for economic benefits. It would seem that we are caught in a web of our own weaving.

A NEW THEORY OF MANAGEMENT

For these and many other reasons, we require a different theory of the task of managing people based on more adequate assumptions about human nature and human motivation. I am going to be so bold as to suggest the broad dimensions of such a theory. Call it "Theory Y," if you will.

1. Management is responsible for organizing the elements of productive enterprise—money, materials, equipment, people—in the interest of economic ends.

2. People are *not* by nature passive or resistant to organizational needs. They have become so as a result of experience in organizations.

3. The motivation, the potential for development, the capacity for assuming responsibility, the readiness to direct behavior toward organizational goals are all present in people. Management does not put them there. It is a responsibility of management to make it possible for people to recognize and develop these human characteristics for themselves.

4. The essential task of management is to arrange organizational conditions and methods of operation so that people can achieve their own goals *best* by directing *their own* efforts toward organizational objectives.

This is a process primarily of creating opportunities, releasing potential, removing obstacles, encouraging growth, providing guidance. It is what Peter Drucker has called "management by objectives" in contrast to "management by control." It does *not* involve the abdication of management, the absence of leadership, the lowering of standards, or the other characteristics usually associated with the "soft" approach under Theory X.

SOME DIFFICULTIES

It is no more possible to create an organization today which will be a full, effective application of this theory than it was to build an atomic power plant in 1945. There are many formidable obstacles to overcome.

The conditions imposed by conventional organization theory and by the approach of scientific management for the past half century have tied men to limited jobs which do not utilize their capabilities, have discouraged the acceptance of responsibility, have encouraged passivity, have eliminated meaning from work. Man's habits, attitudes, expectations—his whole conception of membership in an industrial organization—have been conditioned by his experience under these circumstances.

People today are accustomed to being directed, manipulated, controlled in industrial organizations and to finding satisfaction for their social, egoistic, and self-fulfillment needs away from the job. This is true of much of management as well as of workers. Genuine "industrial citizenship"—to borrow again a term from Drucker—is a remote and unrealistic idea, the meaning of which has not even been considered by most members of industrial organizations.

Another way of saying this is that Theory X places exclusive reliance upon external control of human behavior, while Theory Y relies heavily on self-control and self-direction. It is worth noting that this difference is the difference between treating people as children and treating them as mature adults. After generations of the former, we cannot expect to shift to the latter overnight.

STEPS IN THE RIGHT DIRECTION

Before we are overwhelmed by the obstacles, let us remember that the application of theory is always slow. Progress is usually achieved in small steps. Some innovative ideas which are entirely consistent with Theory Y are today being applied with some success.

Decentralization and Delegation

These are ways of freeing people from the too-close control of conventional organization, giving them a degree of freedom to direct their own activities, to assume responsibility, and, importantly, to satisfy their egoistic needs. In this connection, the flat organization of Sears, Roebuck and Company provides an interesting example. It forces "management by objectives," since it enlarges the number of people reporting to a manager until he cannot direct and control them in the conventional manner.

Job Enlargement

This concept, pioneered by I.B.M. and Detroit Edison, is quite consistent with Theory Y. It encourages the acceptance of responsibility at the bottom of the organization; it provides opportunities for satisfying social and egoistic needs. In fact, the reorganization of work at the factory level offers one of the more challenging opportunities for innovation consistent with Theory Y.

Participation and Consultative Management

Under proper conditions, participation and consultative management provide encouragement to people to direct their creative energies toward organizational objectives, give them some voice in decisions that affect them, provide significant opportunities for the satisfaction of social and egoistic needs. The Scanlon Plan is the outstanding embodiment of these ideas in practice.

Performance Appraisal

Even a cursory examination of conventional programs of performance appraisal within the ranks of management will reveal how completely consistent they are with Theory X. In fact, most such programs tend to treat the individual as though he were a product under inspection on the assembly line.

A few companies—among them General Mills, Ansul Chemical, and General Electric—have been experimenting with approaches which involve the individual in setting "targets" or objectives *for himself,* and in a *self*-evaluation of performance semiannually or annually. Of course, the superior plays an important leadership role in this process—one, in fact, which demands substantially more competence than the conventional approach. The role is, however, considerably more congenial to many managers than the role of "judge" or "inspector" which is usually forced upon them. Above all, the individual is encouraged to take a greater responsibility for planning and appraising his own contribution to organizational objectives; and the accompanying effects on egoistic and self-fulfillment needs are substantial.

APPLYING THE IDEAS

The not infrequent failure of such ideas as these to work as well as expected is often attributable to the fact that a management has "bought the idea" but applied it within the framework of Theory X and its assumptions.

Delegation is not an effective way of exercising management by control. Participation becomes a farce when it is applied as a sales gimmick or a device for kidding people into thinking they are important. Only the management that has confidence in human capacities and is itself directed toward organizational objectives rather than toward the preservation of personal power can grasp the implications of this emerging theory. Such management will find and apply successfully other innovative ideas as we move slowly toward the full implementation of a theory like Y.

THE HUMAN SIDE OF ENTERPRISE

It is quite possible for us to realize substantial improvements in the effectiveness of industrial organizations during the next decade or two. The social sciences can contribute much to such developments; we are only beginning to grasp the implications of the growing body of knowledge in these fields. But if this conviction is to become a reality instead of a pious hope, we will need to view the process much as we view the process of releasing the energy of the atom for constructive human ends—as a slow, costly, sometimes discouraging approach toward a goal which would seem to many to be quite unrealistic.

The ingenuity and the perseverance of industrial management in the pursuit of economic ends have changed many scientific and technological dreams into commonplace realities. It is now becoming clear that the application of these same talents to the human side of enterprise will not only enhance substantially these materialistic achievements, but will bring us one step closer to "the good society."

Putting Excellence into Management

Thomas J. Peters

What makes for excellence in the management of a company? Is it the use of sophisticated management techniques such as zero-based budgeting, management by objectives, matrix organization, and sector, group, or portfolio management? Is it greater use of computers to control companies that continue to grow even larger in size and more diverse in activities? Is it a battalion of specialized MBAs, well-versed in the techniques of strategic planning?

Probably not. Although most well-run companies use a fair sampling of all these tools, they do not use them as substitutes for the basics of good management. Indeed, McKinsey & Co., a management consultant concern, has studied management practices at thirty-seven companies that are often used as examples of well-run organizations and has found that they have eight common attributes. None of those attributes depends on "modern" management tools or gimmicks. In fact, none of them requires high technology, and none of them costs a cent to implement. All that is needed is time, energy, and a willingness on the part of management to think rather than to make use of management formulas.

The outstanding performers work hard to keep things simple. They rely on simple organizational structures, simple strategies, simple goals, and simple communications. The eight attributes that characterize their managements are:

☐ A bias toward action.
☐ Simple form and lean staff.
☐ Continued contact with customers.
☐ Productivity improvement via people.
☐ Operational autonomy to encourage entrepreneurship.

Reprinted from July 21, 1980 issue of *Business Week* by special permission. Copyright © 1980 by McGraw-Hill, Inc.

☐ Stress on one key business value.

☐ Emphasis on doing what they know best.

☐ Simultaneous loose-tight controls.

Although none of these sounds startling or new, most are conspicuously absent in many companies today. Far too many managers have lost sight of the basics—service to customers, low-cost manufacturing, productivity improvement, innovation, and risk-taking. In many cases, they have been seduced by the availability of MBAs, armed with the "latest" in strategic planning techniques. MBAs who specialize in strategy are bright, but they often cannot implement their ideas, and their companies wind up losing the capacity to act. At Standard Brands, Inc., for example, Chairman F. Ross Johnson discovered this the hard way when he brought a handful of planning specialists into his consumer products company. "The guys who were bright [the strategic planners] were not the kinds of people who could implement programs," he lamented to *Business Week*. Two years later, he removed the planners.

Another consumer products company followed a similar route, hiring a large band of young MBAs for the staffs of senior vice-presidents. The new people were assigned to build computer models for designing new products. Yet none of the products could be manufactured or brought to market. Complained one line executive, "The models incorporated eighty-three variables in product planning, but we were being killed by just one—cost."

Companies are being stymied not only by their own staffs but often by their structure. McKinsey studied one company where the new-product process required 223 separate committees to approve an idea before it could be put into production. Another company was restructured recently into 200 strategic business units—only to discover that it was impossible to implement 200 strategies. And even at General Electric Co., which is usually cited for its ability to structure itself according to its management needs, an executive recently complained, "Things become bureaucratic with astonishing speed. Inevitably when we wire things up, we lose vitality." Emerson Electric Co., with a much simpler structure than GE, consistently beats its huge competitor on costs—manufacturing its products in plants with fewer than 600 employees.

McKinsey's study focused on ten well-managed companies: International Business Machines, Texas Instruments, Hewlett-Packard, 3M, Digital Equipment, Procter & Gamble, Johnson & Johnson,

McDonald's, Dana, and Emerson Electric. On the surface, they have nothing in commmon. There is no universality of product line: Five are in high technology, one is in packaged goods, one makes medical products, one operates fast-food restaurants, and two are relatively mundane manufacturers of mechanical and electrical products. But each is a hands-on operator, not a holding company or a conglomerate. And while not every plan succeeds, in the day-to-day pursuit of their businesses these companies succeed far more often than they fail. And they succeed because of their management's almost instinctive adherence to the eight attributes.

BIAS TOWARD ACTION

In each of these companies, the key instructions are *do it, fix it, try it*. They avoid analyzing and questioning products to death, and they avoid complicated procedures for developing new ideas. Controlled experiments abound in these companies. The attitude of managment is to "get some data, do it, then adjust it," rather than to wait for a perfect overall plan. The companies tend to be tinkerers rather than inventors, making small steps of progress rather than conceiving sweeping new concepts. At McDonald's Corp., for example, the objective is to do the little things regularly and well.

Ideas are solicited regularly and tested quickly. Those that work are pushed fast; those that don't are discarded just as quickly. At 3M Co., the management never kills an idea without trying it out; it just goes on the back burner.

These managements avoid long, complicated business plans for new projects. At 3M, for example, new product ideas must be proposed in less than five pages. At Procter & Gamble Co., one-page memos are the rule, but every figure in a P & G memo can be relied on unfailingly.

To ensure that they achieve results, these companies set a few well-defined goals for their managers. At Texas Instruments Inc., for one, a typical goal would be a set date for having a new plant operating or for having a designated percent of a sales force call on customers in a new market. A TI executive explained, "We've experimented a lot, but the bottom line for any senior manager is the maxim that more than two objectives is no objective."

These companies have learned to focus quickly on problems. One method is to appoint a "czar" who has responsibility for one problem across the company. At Digital Equipment Corp. and Hewlett-Packard Co., for example, there are software czars, because customer demand for programming has become the key issue for the future growth of those companies. Du Pont Co., when it discovered it was spending $800 million a year on transportation, set up a logistics czar. Other companies have productivity czars or energy czars with the power to override a manufacturing division's autonomy.

Another tool is the task force. But these companies tend to use the task force in an unusual way. Task forces are authorized to fix things, not to generate reports and paper. At Digital Equipment, TI, HP, and 3M, task forces have a short duration, seldom more than ninety days. Says a Digital Equipment executive, "When we've got a big problem here, we grab ten senior guys and stick them in a room for a week. They come up with an answer and implement it." All members are volunteers, and they tend to be senior managers rather than junior people ordered to serve. Management espouses the busy-member theory: "We don't want people on task forces who want to become permanent task force members. We only put people on them who are so busy that their major objective is to get the problem solved and to get back to their main jobs." Every task force at TI is disbanded after its work is done, but within three months the senior operations committee formally reviews and assesses the results. TI demands that the managers who requested and ran the task force justify the time spent on it. If the task force turns out to have been useless, the manager is chided publicly, a painful penalty in TI's peer-conscious culture.

SIMPLE FORM AND LEAN STAFF

Although all ten of these companies are big—the smallest, McDonald's, has sales in excess of $1.9 billion—they are structured along "small is beautiful" lines. Emerson Electric, 3M, J & J and HP are divided into small entrepreneurial units that—although smaller than economies of scale might suggest—manage to get things done. No HP division, for example, ever employs more than 1,200 people. TI, with ninety product customer centers, keeps each notably autonomous.

Within the units themselves, activities are kept to small, manageable groups. At Dana Corp., small teams work on productivity improvement. At the high-technology companies, small autonomous teams, headed by a product "champion," shepherd ideas through the corporate bureaucracy to ensure that they quickly receive attention from the top.

Staffs are also kept small to avoid bureaucracies. Fewer than 100 people help run Dana, a $3 billion corporation. Digital Equipment and Emerson are also noted for small staffs.

CLOSENESS TO THE CUSTOMER

The well-managed companies are customer driven—not technology driven, not product driven, not strategy driven. Constant contact with the customer provides insights that direct the company. Says one executive, "Where do you start? Not by poring over abstract market research. You start by getting out there with the customer." In a study of two fast-paced industries (scientific instruments and component manufacturing), Eric Von Hippel, associate professor at Massachusetts Institute of Technology, found that 100% of the major new product ideas—and 80% of the minor new product variations—came directly from customers.

At both IBM and Digital Equipment, top management spends at least thirty days a year conferring with top customers. No manager at IBM holds a staff job for more than three years, except the legal, finance, and personnel departments. The reason: IBM believes that staff people are out of the mainstream because they do not meet with customers regularly.

Both companies use customer-satisfaction surveys to help determine management's compensation. Another company spends 12% of its research and development budget on sending engineers and scientists out to visit customers. One R & D chief spends two months each year with customers. At Lanier Business Products Inc., another fast growing company, the twenty most senior executives make sales calls every month.

Staying close to the customer means sales and service overkill. "Assistants to" at IBM are assigned to senior executives with the sole function of processing customer complaints within twenty-four hours. At Digital Equipment, J & J, IBM, and 3M, immense effort is expended to field an extraordinarily well-trained sales force. Caterpillar Tractor Co., another company considered to have excellent management, spends much of its managerial talent on efforts to make a reality of its motto, "twenty-four-hour parts delivery anywhere in the world."

These companies view the customer as an integral element of their businesses. A bank officer who started his career as a J & J accountant recalls that he was required to make customer calls even though he was in a financial department. The reason:

to ensure that he understood the customer's perspective and could handle a proposal with empathy.

PRODUCTIVITY IMPROVEMENT
VIA CONSENSUS

One way to get productivity increases is to install new capital equipment. But another method is often overlooked. Productivity can be improved by motivating and stimulating employees. One way to do that is to give them autonomy. At TI, shop floor teams set their own targets for production. In the years since the company has used this approach, executives say, workers have set goals that required them to stretch but that are reasonable and attainable.

The key is to motivate all the people involved in each process. At 3M, for example, a team that includes technologists, marketers, production people, and financial types is formed early in a new product venture. It is self-sufficient and stays together from the inception to the national introduction. Although 3M is aware that this approach can lead to redundancy, it feels that the team spirit and motivation make it worthwhile.

Almost all these companies use "corny" but effective methods to reward their workers. Badges, pins, and medals are all part of such recognition programs. Outstanding production teams at TI are invited to describe their successes to the board, as a form of recognition. Significantly, the emphasis is never only on monetary awards.

AUTONOMY TO ENCOURAGE
ENTREPRENEURSHIP

A company cannot encourage entrepreneurship if it holds its managers on so tight a leash that they cannot make decisions. Well-managed companies authorize their managers to act like entrepreneurs. Dana, for one, calls this method the "store manager" concept. Plant managers are free to make purchasing decisions and to start productivity programs on their own. As a result, these managers develop unusual programs with results that far exceed those of a division or corporate staff. And the company has a grievance rate that is a fraction of the average reported by the United Auto Workers for all the plants it represents.

The successful companies rarely will force their managers to go against their own judgment. At 3M, TI, IBM, and J & J, decisions on product promotion are not based solely on market potential. An important factor in the decision is the zeal and drive of the volunteer who champions a product. Explains one executive at TI, "In every instance of a new product failure, we had forced someone into championing it involuntarily."

The divisional management is generally responsible for replenishing its new product array. In these well-managed companies, headquarters staff may not cut off funds for divisional products arbitrarily. What is more, the divisions are allowed to reinvest most of their earnings in their own operations. Although this flies in the face of the product-portfolio concept, which dictates that a corporate chief milk mature divisions to feed those with apparently greater growth potential, these companies recognize that entrepreneurs will not be developed in corporations that give the fruits of managers' labor to someone else.

Almost all these companies strive to place new products into separate startup divisions. A manager is more likely to be recognized—and promoted—for pushing a hot new product out of his division to enable it to stand on its own than he is for simply letting his own division get overgrown.

Possibly most important at these companies, entrepreneurs are both encouraged and honored at all staff levels. TI, for one, has created a special group of "listeners"—138 senior technical people called "individual contributors"—to assess new ideas. Junior staff members are particularly encouraged to bring their ideas to one of these individuals for a one-on-one evaluation. Each "contributor" has the authority to approve substantial startup funds ($20,000 to $30,000) for product experimentation. TI's successful Speak'n'Spell device was developed this way.

IBM's Fellows Program serves a similar purpose, although it is intended to permit proven senior performers to explore their ideas rather than to open communication lines for bright comers. Such scientists have at their beck and call thousands of IBM's technical people. The Fellows tend to be very skilled gadflies, people who can shake things up—almost invariably for the good of the company.

The operating principle at well-managed companies is to do one thing well. At IBM, the all-pervasive value is customer service. At Dana it is productivity improvement. At 3M and HP, it is new product development. At P & G it is product quality. At McDonald's it is customer service—quality, cleanliness, and value.

STRESS ON A KEY BUSINESS VALUE

At all these companies, the values are pursued with an almost religious zeal by the chief executive officers. Rene McPherson, now dean of Stanford University's Graduate School of Business but until recently Dana's CEO, incessantly preached cost reduction and productivity improvement—and the company doubled its productivity in seven years. Almost to the day when Thomas Watson, Jr., retired from IBM he wrote memos to the staff on the subject of calling on customers—even stressing the proper dress for the call. TI's ex-chairman Patrick Haggerty made it a point to drop in at a development laboratory on his way home each night when he was in Dallas. And in another company, where competitive position was the prime focus, one division manager wrote 700 memos to his subordinates one year, analyzing competitiors.

Such single-minded focus on a value becomes a culture for the company. Nearly every IBM employee has stories about how he or she took great pains to solve a customer's problem. New product themes even dominate 3M and HP lunchroom conversations. Every operational review at HP focuses on new products, with a minimum amount of time devoted to financial results or projections—because President John Young has made it clear that he believes that proper implementation of new-product plans automatically creates the right numbers. In fact, Young makes it a point to start new employees in the new-product process and keep them there for a few years as part of a "socialization" pattern. "I don't care if they do come from the Stanford Business School," he says. "For a few years they get their hands dirty, or we are not interested." At McDonald's, the company's values are drummed into employees at Hamburger U., a training program every employee goes through.

As the employees who are steeped in the corporate culture move up the ladder, they become role models for newcomers, and the process continues. It is possibly best exemplified by contrast. American Telephone & Telegraph Co., which recently began to develop a marketing orientation, has been hamstrung in its efforts because of a lack of career telephone executives with marketing successes. When Archie J. McGill was hired from IBM to head AT&T's marketing, some long-term employees balked at his leadership because he "wasn't one of them," and so was not regarded as a model.

Another common pitfall for companies is the sending of mixed signals to line managers. One company has had real problems introducing new products despite top management's constant public stress on innovation—simply because line managers perceived the real emphasis to be on cost-cutting. They viewed top management as accountants who refused to invest or to take risks, and they consistently proposed imitative products. At another company, where the CEO insisted that his major thrust was new products, an analysis of how he spent his time over a three-month period showed that no more than 5 percent of his efforts were directed to new products. His stated emphasis therefore was not credible. Not surprisingly, his employees never picked up the espoused standard.

Too many messages, even when sincerely meant, can cause the same problem. One CEO complained that no matter how hard he tried to raise what he regarded as an unsatisfactory quality level he was unsuccessful. But when McKinsey questioned his subordinates, they said, "Of course he's for quality, but he's for everything else, too. We have a theme a month here." The outstanding companies, in contrast, have one theme and stick to it.

STICKING TO WHAT THEY KNOW BEST

Robert W. Johnson, the former chairman of J & J, put it this way: "Never acquire any business you don't know how to run." Edward G. Harness, CEO at P & G, says, "This company has never left its base." All the successful companies have been able to define their strengths—marketing, customer contact, new product innovation, low-cost manufacturing—and then build on them. They have resisted the temptation to move into new businesses that look attractive but require corporate skills they do not have.

SIMULTANEOUS LOOSE-TIGHT CONTROLS

While this may sound like a contradiction, it is not. The successful companies control a few variables tightly, but allow flexibility and looseness in others. 3M uses return on sales and number of employees as yardsticks for control. Yet it gives management lots of leeway in day-to-day operations. When McPherson became president of Dana, he threw out all the company's policy manuals and substituted a one-page philosophy statement and a control system that required divisions to report costs and revenues on a daily basis.

IBM probably has the classic story about flexible controls. After the company suffered well-publicized and costly problems with its System 360 computer several years ago—problems that cost hundreds of millions of dollars to fix—Watson ordered Frank T. Cary, then a vice-president, to incorporate a system of checks and balances in new-product testing. The system made IBM people so cautious that they stopped taking risks. When Cary became president of IBM, one of the first things he did to reverse that attitude was to loosen some of the controls. He recognized that the new system would indeed prevent such an expensive problem from ever happening again, but its rigidity would also keep IBM from ever developing another major system.

By sticking to these eight basics, the successful companies have achieved better-than-average growth. Their managements are able not only to change but also to change quickly. They keep their sights aimed externally at their customers and competitors, and not on their own financial reports.

Excellence in management takes brute perseverance—time, repetition, and simplicity. The tools include plant visits, internal memos, and focused systems. Ignoring these rules may mean that the company slowly loses its vitality, its growth flattens, and its competitiveness is lost.

Exercise: Understanding Your Philosophy of Management

PURPOSE

The purpose of this exercise is to help you understand your philosophy of management. By the time you finish this exercise, you will:

1. Identify your basic assumptions about subordinates.

2. Learn how strongly you hold these assumptions.

3. Develop a basis for understanding the consequences of your assumptions.

INTRODUCTION

Many people have a story to tell about a job in which they were productive and satisfied. Equally often, people have a story about a job in which they were unproductive and dissatisfied. While many factors may have contributed to these experiences, a common thread is usually the treatment these individuals received from their bosses. If you ever had a boss who caused you to feel dissatisfied with your job, you probably swore that when you achieved a position of authority you would treat your subordinates differently. Unfortunately, events do not always unfold the way we plan.

Managers vary widely in their attitudes and behaviors toward subordinates. These attitudes and behaviors are based on the assumptions that managers hold about people in general, employees of a company in particular, and the role of

---

This exercise is based on the ideas presented in D. M. McGregor, "The Human Side of Enterprise," *Management Review,* 1957, November, 22–28, 88–92.

management. These assumptions, in turn, form the basis of a philosophy of management that can affect subordinates' satisfaction and productivity.

Managers' assumptions about people arise from a complex mix of personality and experience. They shape the attitudes toward subordinates that we bring to our first job. During the course of our experiences at work, our assumptions and attitudes are modified by our interactions with subordinates, superiors, and peers. These interactions all occur in the context of an organizational culture with norms about how we should treat subordinates.

This process takes place continually over our working lives. It is so subtle that we are often unaware that it is occurring. The result is that we may find, to our dismay, that we sometimes treat our subordinates in precisely the way we had sworn not to do. Why? Most of us are relatively unaware of our assumptions about subordinates and how these assumptions may have changed. Therefore, understanding your assumptions and attitudes can be the first step in becoming the manager that you want to be.

INSTRUCTIONS

1. Read the directions and complete the Philosophy of Management Questionnaire.

2. Transfer your responses to the Scoring Key.

3. Find your score.

4. Read the descriptions provided and interpret your score.

5. Participate in a class discussion.

PHILOSOPHY OF MANAGEMENT QUESTIONNAIRE

Directions: Carefully read each of the following statements and decide how strongly you agree or disagree with each according to the scale provided. Indicate your response in the space provided beside each statement.

1	2	3	4	5	6	7
STRONGLY DISAGREE	DISAGREE	SLIGHTLY DISAGREE	NEITHER AGREE NOR DISAGREE	SLIGHTLY AGREE	AGREE	STRONGLY AGREE

_____ 1. Employees should be involved in setting their goals.

_____ 2. Employees need something beyond enough money and a secure job.

_____ 3. Most people resist change.

_____ 4. Managers should guide rather than control.

_____ 5. Most people do not like to work.

_____ 6. The average person is easily deceived.

_____ 7. Groups of employees spell trouble for the organization.

_____ 8. People enjoy having greater variety in their work.

_____ 9. Managers should try to achieve harmony in their departments at all costs.

_____ 10. The organization should provide employees with the opportunity to gain self-confidence and realize their potentials.

_____ 11. The average employee does not care about the organization's needs or goals.

_____ 12. People enjoy being creative.

_____ 13. Good wages, working conditions, fringe benefits, and steady employment are enough to satisfy most people.

_____ 14. The average employee dislikes responsibility.

_____ 15. People need to feel a sense of achievement and competence.

_____ 16. Employees can learn to direct their own activities.

_____ 17. The fewer tasks employees' jobs entail, the more productive they will be.

_____ 18. It is management's responsibility to develop an employee's capacity for responsibility.

_____ 19. Employees are basically children and should be treated that way.

_____ 20. Groups are a natural and positive outgrowth of human interaction.

_____ 21. Managers should set goals for employees.

_____ 22. Managers should closely supervise subordinates' behavior.

_____ 23. People naturally try to increase their knowledge.

_____ 24. Most employees do not work any harder than they have to.

_____ 25. Recognition and appreciation may make employees work harder than money.

_____ 26. Management philosophy, policy, and practice can influence the productivity of employees.

_____ 27. Employees are adults capable of self-direction and self-control.

_____ 28. Employees are happiest when they do not have to think about their jobs.

_____ 29. People are not naturally passive.

_____ 30. Groups tend to make people more resistant, antagonistic, and uncooperative.

_____ 31. People want to develop their talents and abilities to their fullest extent.

_____ 32. Employees need to be directed and controlled.

_____ 33. Employees can be motivated to work in the best interest of the organization.

_____ 34. Managers should create opportunities for people to realize their full potential.

_____ 35. Most people have very little ambition.

_____ 36. A main responsibility of management is to get subordinates to accept direction.

_____ 37. Managers should strive to help employees become self-directed.

_____ 38. When employees are unproductive, it is because they are basically lazy.

_____ 39. Groups can often be more effective than individuals at performing organizational tasks.

_____ 40. Most employees want to be told what to do.

_____ 41. People will learn things only if they are forced to.

_____ 42. In general, employees care about how well they perform their jobs.

_____ 43. People need independence.

_____ 44. Employees are primarily motivated by money.

_____ 45. Managers should exercise tight control over their departments.

_____ 46. People enjoy assuming responsibility.

_____ 47. Managers should try to keep tight, cohesive groups of employees from forming.

_____ 48. Employees should have a voice in the decisions that affect them.

SCORING

Directions: Transfer each of your answers from the questionnaire to the scoring key below. The numbers on the scoring key correspond to the numbers next to each statement of the questionnaire. For example, if you answered 6 to statement 3, you would put a 6 in the first row of Column 2. When you have completed the scoring key, add up all your scores in Columns 1 and 2. Next, subtract your Column 2 total from your Column 1 total. Place an *X,* on the scale provided, corresponding to this score.

Column 1	Column 2
1. _____	3. _____
2. _____	5. _____
4. _____	6. _____
8. _____	7. _____
10. _____	9. _____
12. _____	11. _____
15. _____	13. _____
16. _____	14. _____
18. _____	17. _____
20. _____	19. _____
23. _____	21. _____
25. _____	22. _____
26. _____	24. _____
27. _____	28. _____
29. _____	30. _____
31. _____	32. _____
33. _____	35. _____
34. _____	36. _____
37. _____	38. _____
39. _____	40. _____
42. _____	41. _____
43. _____	44. _____
46. _____	45. _____
48. _____	47. _____

Column 1 total _____

Column 2 total _____

Column 1 total − Column 2 total = _____

144	124	104	84	64	44	24	0	−24	−44	−64	−84	−104	−124	−144

STRONG
THEORY Y

STRONG
THEORY X

INTERPRETATION

Directions: Read the following descriptions to get an indication of your management philosophy and how strongly you hold the assumptions associated with it. Read McGregor's article, "The Human Side of Enterprise," to learn more about your management philosophy and some of the consequences of the related assumptions.

☐ If your score falls between + 144 and 0, your management philosophy is based on Theory Y assumptions. The closer you fall to 144, the more strongly you hold these assumptions and the fewer Theory X assumptions you hold. The closer your score is to 0, the more your management philosophy reflects a mix of Theory Y and Theory X assumptions.

☐ If your score falls between 0 and – 144, your management philosophy is based on Theory X assumptions. The closer you fall to – 144, the more strongly you hold these assumptions, and the fewer Theory Y assumptions you hold. The closer your score is to 0, the more your management philosophy reflects a mix of Theory X and Theory Y assumptions.

Theory Y

You believe that:

☐ Management should create conditions that enable and encourage employees to attain their own goals by working toward the goals of the organization.

☐ Employees are inherently ready to accept responsibility, do a good job, and work in the best interests of the company.

☐ It is management's responsibility to create the conditions that will allow employees to develop their fullest potential.

Theory X

You believe that:

☐ Management's only responsibility is to improve the company's "bottom line."

☐ The employees of an organization are tools to be used to meet this goal.

☐ People are basically unwilling to work in the best interests of the company, cannot handle responsibility, and must be tightly controlled, prodded, and punished to get their work done.

DISCUSSION QUESTIONS

1. What do the results of this questionnaire tell you about your philosophy of management?

2. What are some of the consequences of your assumptions? Have you seen any evidence of these consequences in your job?

3. Which philosophy of management characterizes your boss in his or her interactions with you as a subordinate? Which philosophy of management characterizes top management at your company? What impact has this had on you?

4. Is it likely, in your opinion, that people can learn to change their philosophy of management? Which changes would you like to make? Why?

REFERENCE

McGregor, D. M. "The Human Side of Enterprise," *Management Review,* 1957, November, 22–28, 88–92.

Exercise: Motivational Styles

PURPOSE

The purpose of this exercise is to provide you with an opportunity to explore your management style. By the time you finish this exercise, you will:

1. Identify your motivational style.

2. Observe different management styles in action.

3. Determine ways in which you can become an effective motivator of people.

INTRODUCTION

Managers exercise different styles of management when motivating their subordinates. Some managers are task-masters, cracking the whip at every possible opportunity. Others are more lenient with subordinates, allowing them the chance to set their own pace. This is the difference, as described by McGregor, between Theory X management and Theory Y management. The type of motivational style that is exercised by a manager has a direct impact on how subordinates relate to the manager. Some subordinates respond positively to a "cracking the whip" style, while others resent such an approach.

The "Motivational Styles Inventory" was developed by John Veiga of the University of Connecticut. Used with permission of the author. The idea for Part II of this exercise was originally presented by J. Veiga and J. Yanouzas at the Eastern Academy of Management Convention, Boston, 1987.

This is a two-part exercise. In Part I, you will complete a questionnaire thatdetermines your likely motivational style. In Part II, you will participate in a group observation in which others will provide you with feedbacck about your motivational approach to subordinates.

INSTRUCTIONS

Part I

1. Complete the Motivational Styles Questionnaire.

2. Score your results as indicated.

3. Decide if you agree with your score. Does your profile accurately describe you?

Part II

1. Form groups of six.

2. On the worksheet provided, select a production task.

3. When it is your turn to be the manager, select two members of your group to serve as your subordinates for the production task you have chosen.

4. While the remaining group members serve as observers, show your "subordinates" how to complete the task you have selected.

5. Listen to the feedback offered by other group members concerning your motivational style. To what extent does it match your questionnaire results?

6. Observe other group members until each group member has had a chance to "motivate" subordinates in your group.

7. Participate in a class discussion.

MOTIVATIONAL STYLE INVENTORY

Directions: Each question consists of an incomplete sentence and three possible phrases that complete the sentence. You are to score each phrase as follows: Rate the phrase a 3 if it *best* characterizes your management style and/or beliefs, a 2 if the phrase is the next best, and a 1 is the phrase is *least* like you. Be sure to rate all three phrases—*no ties.* Place your ratings in the column marked "Your Rating."

		Your Rating	Scoring A	B	C
1.	In establishing performance goals for others, I:				
	a. trust my people to set their own pace.	___			___
	b. try to encourage goals that challenge and stretch.	___	___		
	c. leave little doubt about what I expect.	___		___	
2.	When people come to me with personal problems, I:				
	a. try to act like a sounding board, let them grapple with the problem, then help them explore alternatives.	___	___		
	b. try to fix things if I can; otherwise I stay out of such problems.	___		___	
	c. try to act like a good friend.	___			___
3.	In making work assignments, I:				
	a. ask people what their preferences are and strive for a good match.	___			___
	b. rely on my own judgment and then tell the individuals involved what's expected.	___		___	
	c. try to get people to experiment with new areas and provide the necessary support while they learn.	___	___		
4.	When discipline is necessary, I:				
	a. try to make sure the person realizes that it's nothing personal.	___		___	
	b. try to encourage the individual to develop ways to avoid the need for future disciplinary action.	___			___
	c. let the individual know how disappointed I am and what I will and will not tolerate in the future.	___		___	
5.	The work climate I seek to create emphasizes:				
	a. stimulating excitement and enthusiasm toward achieving goals.	___	___		
	b. warmth and support.	___	___		
	c. that people won't be asked to do more than I can do.	___		___	
6.	In developing employee potential, I:				
	a. provide encouragement and help people remove barriers to experimentation.	___	___		
	b. try to create a friendly and supportive climate.	___			___
	c. think you have to be realistic and accept that some people can't be developed further.	___		___	

7. I believe a good manager should promote values that:
   a. emphasize caring and trust among subordinates.   _____   _____
   b. serve to make others stronger both individually   _____ _____
      and collectively.
   c. place organizational goals ahead of any individual's _____   _____
      needs or desires.

8. When I discuss work assignments with subordinates I:
   a. make sure that they understand how their part   _____ _____
      fits into the picture.
   b. try to be sensitive to their feelings and deal with   _____   _____
      their concerns.
   c. try to be as detailed as I can, so that there won't   _____   _____
      be any excuses for not doing what I've told them.

9. As a manager, I strive to:
   a. set the example for everyone to follow.   _____   _____
   b. contribute to the organization by helping my   _____ _____
      subordinates gain a sense of purpose and personal
      power.
   c. be valued by others as someone who can be   _____   _____
      counted on for support and understanding.

10. As a manager I:
    a. want people to like me.   _____   _____
    b. get overzealous and end up running over some   _____ _____
       people.
    c. try to create enthusiasm for high performance   _____ _____
       goals.

11. A good leader:
    a. maintains tight control and follows up regularly on   _____   _____
       subordinates.
    b. seeks to help others feel in control and powerful.   _____ _____
    c. promotes harmony and trust among subordinates.   _____   _____

12. As a leader, I:
    a. seek my followers' loyalty.   _____   _____
    b. seek my followers' friendship and understanding.   _____   _____
    c. seek to help my followers to do the best they can.   _____ _____

13. Performance evaluations should:
    a. not damage the person's self-esteem in any way.   _____   _____
    b. make clear what the person must do.   _____ _____
    c. get the individual to take personal responsibility for   _____ _____
       achieving some small step towards improvement.

14. When delegating, a manager should:
    a. follow up regularly to insure the individual is   _____   _____
       staying on track.
    b. try to insure, whenever possible, that the   _____ _____
       individuals develop and grow from the experience.
    c. try to make sure no one feels manipulated into   _____   _____
       simply doing more work.

15. When subordinates fail to deliver after I have discussed with them the need to do better, I am inclined to:

    a. ignore it, if possible, assuming that they already feel bad and will try even harder the next time.   _____   _____

    b. call them on it immediately and demand an explanation.   _____   _____

    c. see what we can learn from the failure so as to minimize it happening again.   _____   _____

Column totals   ☐   ☐   ☐

                                                     A   B   C

SCORING

Directions: Transpose each rating directly across to the A, B, or C column marked next to each rating. Then total your ratings for each of the three columns. The bar chart below can be developed into a profile of your motivational style. To do so, shade in the area in each bar to correspond with each of your column totals. For example, if your total for column A is 38 then you would shade in the area up to 38 on that bar. (You will have to approximate the location of your score if it is not printed on the bar.) The percentiles along the left column provide you with a way to compare yourself to other managers who have completed the inventory. For example, a score of 42 on Column A means that about 80 percent of all managers score *lower* than you on this dimension and about 20 percent score *higher* than you.

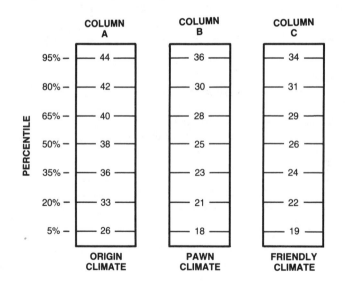

INTERPRETATION

Managers vary widely on the kind of motivational climate their actions tend to create. Generally, however, these actions contribute to one of three climates:

1. A climate that tends to create "origins"—measured by Column A.

2. A climate that tends to create "pawns"—measured by Column B.

3. A climate that tends to emphasize friendly relations—measured by Column C.

The higher your score on each of these dimensions, the greater the tendency for you to create the climate described. Here is a more complete description of each of these climates:

☐ *A creates an "origin" climate:* The tendency for your management practices and beliefs is to create a motivational climate that enhances the development of *origins*. That is, people feel in control of their surroundings, feel personally energized, feel they can have impact on their environment, are uplifted and made more powerful by your actions.

☐ *B creates a "pawn" climate:* The tendency for your management practices and beliefs is to create a motivational climate that makes others feel like *pawns*. That is, people do not feel in control, feel constrained by rules and procedures, feel they have little control over their organizational fate, feel they are not growing or developing in their jobs, rely on the boss to tell them what to do and when to do it.

☐ *C creates a "friendly" climate:* The tendency for your management practices and beliefs is to create a motivational climate that stresses friendship and warmth between superior and subordinate as the *primary* goal—even if it means that organizational goals will be sacrificed or made secondary. Underlying this climate is the manager's desire to be nurturing and reassuring.

Of course, the major question is, "Which climate is the most effective?" Research on employee motivation suggests that the origin climate is the one that managers should strive to create whenever possible. Clearly, the extent to which your actions work against creating such a climate—and thereby produce an overly pawnish climate—the less effective you are in motivating others.

Moreover, while having a friendly climate is often desirable, such a climate can be dysfunctional if a manager places greater emphasis on being liked than on getting subordinates to do their best. Hence, the ideal motivational profile would be a high score on creating an origin climate, a low score on creating a pawn climate, and a low to moderate score on creating a friendly climate.

PART II: MOTIVATIONAL STYLE OBSERVATION

Directions: Select one of the six tasks described below. Then select two members of your group to serve as your "subordinates." Your job is to motivate these subordinates to successfully perform the task you have chosen in the way in which you think it should be accomplished. The remaining group members will serve as observers. It will be the observer's duty to provide feedback to each "manager" about his or her motivational style. Remember to record your observations on the Observation Sheet provided.

Tasks

In the manager role, you will need to manage your subordinates to do one of the following tasks:

1. Drawing concentric circles on the board.
2. Building a house of cards.
3. Creating paper airplanes.
4. Measuring the dimensions of desks and chairs.
5. Drawing a picture of a horse.
6. Creating notepads out of scratch paper.

How to Use the Observation Sheet

In observing each manager's style, does the manager:

Origin

☐ Energize subordinates to create their own style, be creative and innovative in completing tasks?

☐ Allow subordinates to feel that they are in control of the task, rather than being controlled by the manager?

☐ Encourage subordinates to grow and develop from the learning that takes place by performing the tasks?

Pawn

☐ Force subordinates to conform to the manager's rules and regulations?

☐ Cause subordinates to feel they are not in control of the task?

☐ Encourage the reliance of subordinates on the manager's every direction, rule, and deadline in completing the task?

Friendly

☐ Suggest that the manager wants to be liked and accepted by subordinates?

☐ Imply that the manager is more concerned with employee morale than performance?

☐ Encourage the pursuit of friendly cooperation to the exclusion of emphasizing standards, goals, and deadlines?

OBSERVATION SHEET

Manager 1: _____

Most likely motivational style: _____

Evidence: _____

_____

_____

_____

_____

_____

Manager 2: _____

Most likely motivational style:_____

Evidence: _____

_____

_____

_____

_____

_____

Manager 3: _____

Most likely motivational style: _____

Evidence: _____

_____

_____

_____

_____

_____

Manager 4: _____

Most likely motivational style: _____

Evidence: _____

_____

_____

_____

_____

_____

Manager 5: _____

Most likely motivational style: _____

Evidence: _____

_____

_____

_____

_____

Manager 6: _____

Most likely motivational style: _____

Evidence: _____

_____

_____

_____

_____

DISCUSSION QUESTIONS

1. To what extent did your questionnaire results match the feedback given by group members about your management style?

2. If differences exist, which results do you think represent a truer picture of yourself as a motivator of people? Why or why not?

3. To what extent do the motivational styles illustrated in this exercise parallel McGregor's discussion of Theory X and Theory Y management philosophies?

4. What is the motivational style of your boss?

Exercise: In Search of Excellence Worksheet

PURPOSE

The purpose of this exercise is to help you identify and use the principles advocated by Peters and Waterman in their book, *In Search of Excellence.* By the time you complete this exercise, you will:

1. Rate your company and your university on these principles.

2. Understand the managerial implications of these principles.

3. Critically assess the appropriateness of these principles to organizational settings.

INTRODUCTION

In their book, Thomas Peters and Robert Waterman developed eight characteristics of successful, excellent organizations. They developed these principles after years of researching management philosophies, structures, and the concept of innovation. By studying companies such as IBM, Hewlett-Packard, Johnson Bros., 3M, Digital Equipment Corporation, Emerson Electric, and others, the authors were able to develop recommendations that suggest some of the characteristics for effective management and organizational practices.

The "In Search of Excellence" principles have been used by many corporations as a way to determine the relative "health" of their companies. In companies where innovation is being blocked, these principles can be used to revitalize the organization. In addition, because these principles implicitly emphasize the importance of a human resource approach in managing others, their application relates closely to management style and philosophy.

INSTRUCTIONS

1. Read the article by Peters, "Putting Excellence into Management."

2. Rate your company on the eight *In Search of Excellence* principles.

3. Complete the first column of the chart provided by:
   a. Checking the boxes corresponding to the criterion that apply to your particular firm.

This exercise is based on an earlier version entitled, "In Search of Excellence Worksheet" by Dorothea Hai in *Organizational Behavior: Experiences and Cases* (New York: West Publishing Co. 1986). The reading insert included in the exercise, "Who's Excellent Now?" is reprinted from *Business Week,* November 5, 1984, by special permission. Copyright© by McGraw-Hill, Inc.

b. Give an example showing why each criterion is characteristic of your company. This should be done prior to the class session.

4. In groups of four to seven members, share your responses to the charts.

5. As a group, rate your university on the eight *In Search of Excellence* principles using the second column of the chart.

6. Participate in a brief class discussion.

7. Read the insert excerpted from *Business Week*.

8. Participate in a full class discussion.

PETERS AND WATERMAN'S EIGHT CHARACTERISTICS

	Where You Work Now or Did Work	*Your University*
1. *A Bias for Action:* A preference for doing something—anything rather than sending a question through cycles and cycles of analyses and committee reports.		
2. *Staying Close to the Customer:* Then learning his or her preferences and catering to them.		
3. *Autonomy and Entrepreneurship:* Breaking the corporation into small companies and encouraging them to think.		
4. *Productivity Through People:* Creating in all employees the awareness that their best efforts are essential and that they will share in the rewards of the company's success.		
5. *Hands-on, Value-Driven:* Insisting that executives keep in touch with the firm's essential business and employees.		
6. *Stick-to-the-Knitting:* Remaining with the business the company knows best.		
7. *Simple Form, Lean Staff:* Few administrative layers, few people at the upper levels.		
8. *Simultaneous Loose-Tight Properties:* Fostering a climate in which there is dedication to the central values of the company, combined with tolerance for all employees who accept those values.		

Who's Excellent Now?
Some of the Best-Seller's Picks
Haven't Been Doing So Well Lately

Not long after *In Search of Excellence* zoomed to the top of the best-seller list, co-author Thomas J. Peters gave a speech to a division of Hewlett-Packard Co., one of the star companies in the book. After the speech, as Peters recalls, the division's manager told him: " 'What we should do is call you in to give a speech once a quarter. So we can remember what it was that we were when we were really a great company. And to remind us how damned hard it is to maintain some of those traits once you get big.' "

Judging from Hewlett-Packard's current difficulties, the manager knew what he was talking about. The turmoil and product-development problems plaguing HP—the third-largest computer maker after International Business Machines Corp. and Digital Equipment Corp.—hardly make it look like one of America's most innovative, best-run companies. Although its earnings are still strong, HP has stumbled badly in the critical microcomputer and superminicomputer markets.

THE EIGHT ATTRIBUTES OF EXCELLENCE

1. *Bias for Action*: A preference for doing something—anything—rather than sending an idea through endless cycles of analyses and committee reports.

2. *Staying Close to the Customer*: Learning his preferences and catering to them.

3. *Autonomy and Entrepreneurship*: Breaking the corporation into small companies and encouraging them to think independently and competitively.

4. *Productivity Through People*: Creating in all employees the awareness that their best efforts are essential and that they will share in the rewards of the company's success.

5. *Hands-on, Value-Driven*: Insisting that executives keep in touch with the firm's essential business and promote a strong corporate culture.

6. *Stick to the Knitting*: Remaining with the businesses the company knows best.

7. *Simple Form, Lean Staff*: Few administrative layers, few people at the upper levels.

8. *Simultaneous Loose-Tight Properties*: Fostering a climate where there is dedication to the central values of the company combined with tolerance for all employees who accept those values.

DISENCHANTMENT

To regain its stride, HP is being forced to abandon attributes of excellence for which it was praised. Its technology-driven, engineering-oriented culture, in which decentralization and innovation were a religion and entrepreneurs were the gods, is giving way to a marketing culture and growing centralization. The continuing exodus of disenchanted managers—12 have left in just the last six months—tells the story. "The time spent in coordinating meetings has increased by an order of magnitude in the last four years," sighs André Schwager, a former HP general manager who left in September. "It's clear that the culture is beginning to change."

Hewlett-Packard is not the only "excellent company" that is not looking so excellent these days. According to studies by *Business Week,* management consultants McKinsey & Co., and Standard & Poor's Compustat Services Inc., at least 14 of the 43 "excellent" companies highlighted by Peters and co-author Robert H. Waterman Jr. in their book just two years ago have lost their luster (table, page 43).

If judged on their performance during the last decade, Delta Air Lines, Walt Disney Productions, Eastman Kodak, and Texas Instruments would not pass the financial tests for excellence laid down in the book. In more recent years, nine others—Atari, Avon, Caterpillar Tractor (page 44), Chesebrough-Pond's, DEC, Fluor, Levi Strauss, Revlon, and Dart & Kraft's Tupperware International—have suffered significant earnings declines that stem from serious business problems, management problems, or both. While most outsiders still view them as well-managed and in robust financial health, other members of the elite have been humbled by blunders: Johnson & Johnson in high-technology medical equipment, Dana in financial services, and 3M in office automation.

It is far too early to determine whether these troubles are only temporary. For example, Delta Air Lines Inc., which has to contend with deregulation, and Texas Instruments Inc., which sustained a staggering loss in 1983 because of its foray into home computers, are reporting strong earnings this year.

Even so, it comes as a shock that so many companies have fallen from grace so quickly—and it also raises some questions. Were these companies so excellent in the first place? Are the eight attributes of excellence the only eight attributes of excellence? Does adhering to them make a difference?

NEW LESSONS

Not surprisingly, critics question whether there was any new lesson to be learned from the book in the first place. Management writer Peter F. Drucker, for one, dismisses *In Search of Excellence* as "a book for juveniles" and as nothing more than a reaction to the last recession, when "a great many American managers [became] convinced that if things become too complicated, you can't run them."

In their own defense, Peters and Waterman argue that their intent was to address those qualities of good management that too many managers had ignored. That *Excellence* has so far sold nearly 2.8 million copies in the U.S.—and hundreds of thousands of copies abroad—proves that it struck a responsive nerve in U.S. and even foreign managers. Indeed, it is important to recall the context in which the book appeared: Japan was conquering many of the markets that U.S. companies had dominated. And it was becoming increasingly evident that there was too much analysis-paralysis, too much bureaucracy, too little innovation, and too little attention being paid to customers and employees at too many American companies.

The book's basic message was that U.S. companies could regain their competitive edge by paying more attention to people—customers and employees—and by sticking to the skills and values they know best. And when virtually all eyes were turned to Japan for the answer, the book showed there were worthy models of management in our own backyard.

Then why have so many of the excellent companies fallen? "There's no real reason to have ever expected that all of these companies would have done well forever and ever," says Peters. Adds Waterman: "If you're big, you've got the seeds of your own destruction in there." The excellent companies, Peters and Wateraman contend, just seemed to be big corporations that were "losing less fast."

Clearly, several of the 43 companies, including Revlon Inc. and Atari Inc., should never have made anyone's list of well-managed companies. Charles Revson, the late founder of Revlon, was an entrepreneurial and marketing genius. But even those who still worship him admit he was no great manager.

LOVE OF NUMBERS

Atari, the company that rose and fell with the video-game boom and collapse—and stuck Warner Communications Inc. with hundreds of millions of dollars in losses—managed to break almost all of the eight commandments of excellence. Out-of-control management and bloated fiefdoms—not autonomy, entrepreneurship, and a simple and lean form—were hallmarks at that company, whose payroll zoomed from a few hundred to 7,000 and back to a few hundred in just seven years. Atari was so out of touch with its market that it failed to realize its customers were losing interest in video-game players and switching to home computers—a fatal oversight.

At several companies, a love for product, customers, and entrepreneurship gave way to a love for numbers. This helps explain why Chesebrough-Pond's Inc. stalled in 1981, when sales in its core health and beauty businesses slowed and some of its vaunted acquisitions—notably Bass shoes and Prince tennis rackets—ran into trouble. This was also the case at Revlon under Michel C. Bergerac. The ITT Corp. alumnus installed some of the so-called modern management techniques that Revlon needed. But former executives and industry experts say an overemphasis on numbers has dulled much of Revlon's marketing pizazz.

Peters argues that it is virtually impossible to score a perfect 10 on all eight attributes of excellence. Several excellent companies that fell by the wayside overstressed some attributes and ignored others. Disney Productions' employees were so devoted to clean-taste values established by its founder that it lost its creative flair and failed to respond to changes in moviegoers' tastes. Employees were so wedded to the legacy that many protested the making of *Splash,* one of the company's first efforts in recent years to make a truly contemporary film—and one that turned out to be a hit.

In most instances, the transgressors ran amok by walking away from the principles that had been key to their earlier successes. A slew of companies— TI, Revlon, Fluor, Avon, Johnson & Johnson, Dana, and 3M—did not "stick to their knitting" and are paying the price. Fluor Corp. made the mistake of paying a staggering $2.3 billion for St. Joe Minerals Corp. in 1981—right before metals prices collapsed. Instead of helping Fluor ride out the rough times in its mainstay engineering-construction business, St. Joe has added to Fluor's financial woes. Its earnings plummeted to $27.7 million last year from $158.9 million in 1981. Its stock, which was trading at 71 right before its acquisition, is now hovering around 18.

WHEN STRICTNESS HURTS

In the *Harvard Business Review,* consultant Daniel T. Carroll attacked *Excellence* for ignoring the importance of such factors as proprietary technology, government policy, and national culture. The *Business Week* and McKinsey studies suggest that the criticism is well-founded. Of the 14 excellent companies that had stumbled, 12 were inept in adapting to a fundamental change in their markets. Their experiences show that strict adherence to the eight commandments—which do not emphasize reacting to broad economic and business trends—may actually hurt a company.

For example, Delta Air Lines, which had flourished by maintaining a low debt and exploiting a close-knit culture to keep costs low, failed to see that deregulation had changed its world. The Atlanta-based carrier was slow in recognizing the importance of computers to keep tabs on ticket prices in different markets. Consequently, Delta first failed to meet competitors' lower prices. Then it overreacted. The result: an $86.7 million loss in its fiscal year ended June, 1983, and a brand-new computer system.

Staying close to the customer can backfire on a company when a market shifts dramatically, leaving the company close to the wrong customer. This is what happened to Avon Products Inc. and to Dart & Kraft's Tupperware unit when the housewives to whom they catered began to pursue careers. Similarly, DEC and HP—companies run by engineers for customers who are engineers—have stumbled in trying to sell to customers without a technical background.

FRUSTRATION

Hewlett-Packard's famed innovative culture and decentralization spawned such enormously successful products as its 3000 minicomputer, the handheld scientific calculator, and the new ThinkJet nonimpact printer. But when a new climate required its fiercely autonomous divisions to cooperate in product development and marketing, HP's passionate devotion to the "autonomy and entrepreneurship"

that Peters and Waterman advocate became a hindrance.

To its astonishment, HP found itself frustrated in trying to move into such new high-growth, high-tech markets as superminicomputers, engineering work stations, personal computers and office automation. Two years after its rollout, the HP 9000 work station that was developed in a $100 million crash effort still lacks competitive software, and HP has been outstripped by a crowd of startups. HP's response: centralizing.

One major lesson from all this is that the excellent companies of today will not necessarily be the excellent companies of tomorrow. But the more important lesson is that good management requires much more than following any one set of rules. *In Search of Excellence* was a response to an era when management put too much emphasis on number-crunching. But companies can also get into trouble by overemphasizing Peters' and Waterman's principles. Says Waterman: "The book has been so popular that people have taken it as a formula for success rather than what it was intended to be. We were writing about the art, not the science of management."

THE "EXCELLENT COMPANIES" CITED BY PETERS AND WATERMAN

Allen-Bradley	International Business
Amdahl	Machines
Atari	Johnson & Johnson
Avon Products	K mart
Bechtel Group	Levi Strauss
Boeing	Marriott
Bristol-Myers	M&M Mars
Caterpillar Tractor	Maytag
Chesebrough-Pond's	McDonald's
Dana	Merck
Data General	National Semiconductor
Delta Air Lines	Procter & Gamble
Digital Equipment	Raychem
Dow Chemical	Revlon
Du Pont	Schlumberger
Eastman Kodak	Standard Oil (Indiana)
Emerson Electric	Texas Instruments
Fluor	3M
Frito-Lay	Tupperware International
Hewlett-Packard	Wal-Mark Stores
Hughes Aircraft	Walt Disney Productions
Intel	Wang Laboratories

Data: *In Search of Excellence.*

WHY SOME OF THE "EXCELLENT" COMPANIES HAVE STUMBLED
THE COMMANDMENTS OF EXCELLENCE THEY BROKE

	Bias for Action	Staying Close to the Customer	Autonomy and Entrepreneurship	Productivity Through People	Hands-on, Value-Driven	Stick to the Knitting	Simple Form, Lean Staff	Simultaneous Loose-Tight Properties
Atari (b)(c)	✓	✓	✓	✓	✓		✓	✓
Avon Products (c)		✓		✓		✓		
Caterpillar Tractor (c)	✓			✓				
Chesebrough-Pond's (c)	✓		✓	✓				
Delta Air Lines (a)(c)		✓						
Digital Equipment (c)	✓		✓					
Disney Productions (a)(c)		✓	✓					
Eastman Kodak (a)		✓		✓				
Fluor (c)					✓			
Hewlett-Packard (c)								
LeviStrauss (c)		✓		✓				
Revlon (c)	✓	✓	✓	✓	✓	✓		
Tupperware (b)(c)		✓		✓				
Texas Instruments (a)	✓	✓	✓			✓	✓	✓

(a) Did not pass Peters' and Waterman's financial-criteria hurdle in 1974-83.

(b) Not tested against financial criteria because they were not included in Compustat's data base.

(c) Difficulty adapting to fundamental change in market.

Data: BW, Standard & Poor's Compustat Services Inc., McKinsey & Co.

DISCUSSION QUESTIONS

1. To what extent do you agree with the criticisms of the *In Search of Excellence* principles advocated by the authors of the *Business Week* excerpts in this exercise?

2. Which principles were characteristic of your organization? Your university?

3. What implications do these principles have for a human resource approach to management in the organizations studied? Are Peters and Waterman advocating Theory Y or Theory X management?

4. To what extent is it realistic to assume that companies can follow these principles effectively for the long run?

Peters, Thomas, and Robert Waterman. *In Search of Excellence: Lessons from America's Best Companies.* New York: Harper and Row, 1982.

Memo: Managerial Work

The purpose of this memo is to help you understand what roles you routinely fulfill in your current position and to improve the fit between how you spend your time and the demands of your job. Think about your job and review the following role descriptions.

Interpersonal Roles

1. *Figurehead:* Acting as a representative of the organization by performing symbolic duties, such as presiding at ceremonial events and receiving visitors.

2. *Leader:* Interacting with subordinates, including but not limited to motivating, directing, guiding, staffing, helping, encouraging, evaluating.

3. *Liaison:* Establishing and maintaining a network of contacts and relationships outside the organization to bring favors and information to the organization.

Informational Roles

1. *Nerve Center:* Collecting information from formal and informal channels both inside and outside the organization.

2. *Disseminator:* Integrating and transmitting information collected to subordinates.

3. *Spokesperson:* Integrating and transmitting information collected to outsiders and serving, outside of the organization, as an industry expert.

Decisional Roles

1. *Entrepreneur:* Seeking, initiating, and designing improvement projects.

2. *Disturbance Handler:* Making short-term adjustments and long-term structural changes to maintain the equilibrium of the organization.

The role descriptions are based on those presented in H. Mintzberg, "Managerial Work: Analysis from Observation," *Management Science,* 1971, Vol. 18, 97–110.

3. *Resource Allocator:* Controlling allocation of own and subordinates' time, as well as authorizing all significant decisions.

4. *Negotiator:* Negotiating with factors in the external environment such as suppliers, banks, customers, clients, and the government.

Now answer the following questions:

1. Which roles do you spend the most time fulfilling in the day-to-day course of doing your job? The least time?

2. Which roles are most important to the successful performance of your job? Least important?

3. Are you focusing your energy on the roles that are most important to the successful performance of your job?

4. On which roles are you spending too much time? Too little time?

5. What are the consequences of spending too much or too little time on the roles you have identified?

6. Which roles would your boss say are the most important to the successful performance of your job?

7. Do you and your boss agree or disagree? Why?

Use this analysis to formulate a plan for improving the fit between how you spend your time and the demands of your job.

1. What steps will you have to take to enable you to spend less or more time on the roles you just identified (such as improving your skills, delegating authority, taking time from other activities, getting additional resources)?

2. What support and resources will you need from your boss?

3. What obstacles might you encounter?

4. How do you plan to overcome these obstacles?

5. What are the potential consequences—both the positive and negative—for you, your boss, the rest of your work group, and your company?

CHAPTER TWO

Interpersonal Relations, Communication And Conflict

INTRODUCTION

As mentioned in Chapter One, a manager's major responsibility is managing people. In addition, Mintzberg's research shows that most of the roles fulfilled by managers in the course of doing their job involve interacting with others. Managers depend on superiors, subordinates, and peers for information, resources, and cooperation. For example, it has been estimated that managers get only 20 to 40% of their information in written form. The remaining 60 to 80% comes from other people through face-to-face encounters or over the telephone. Thus, developing and maintaining effective interpersonal relationships is an important component of managerial success.

There is sometimes a tendency to discount the importance of interpersonal skills for managerial success, but do not fall into that trap. Technical skills are important, but no manager, no matter how technically competent, will be successful without knowing how to manage interpersonal relations.

One of the skills that is critical to managerial success is the ability to communicate effectively. Managers must know how to get the information they need from others and to make others understand them.

READINGS

In the first article, "Defensive Communication," Jack Gibb explores ways to improve communication by decreasing defensiveness. We commonly think about improving our communication with people in order to improve our interpersonal relationship with them. Gibb takes the opposite view by asserting that it is the interpersonal relationship that must be changed to improve communication. The type of change that he explores in this article is reducing the degree of defensiveness. People respond defensively to a perceived threat. When this happens it creates defensiveness in the other party and an increasingly destructive circular pattern develops. Defensiveness creates distortion in communication and the way to overcome this is to create a supportive climate. Gibb presents six pairs of defensive and supportive categories, along with explanations and examples. By following his guidelines you will be able to reduce the defensiveness in your relationships and improve the quality of your communication.

In "Managing Interpersonal Conflict," James Ware and Louis Barnes explore the nature, sources, determinants, and dynamics of interpersonal conflict, as well as approaches to managing conflict. Many managers ignore interpersonal conflict because they are afraid of the consequences of trying to deal with it. However, conflict is an organizational reality and the ability to effectively manage conflict is crucial for managerial success.

Because there is no single best way to manage interpersonal conflict, an analysis of the situation is usually a necessary first step. Once you understand the situation, you will be in a position to decide whether to manage the conflict, withdraw from it, or smooth it over. If you decide to manage the conflict, the authors present three basic options: bargaining, controlling, and confrontation. This article will help you feel less uncomfortable the next time you are confronted with a situation involving interpersonal conflict. You will understand the dynamics of the situation and the options available to you.

John Gabarro and John Kotter, in "Managing Your Boss," discuss how to improve one particular kind of relationship, the one with your boss. They argue that effective management involves not only managing subordinates, but also managing superiors. They emphasize the notion that boss and subordinate are mutually dependent. To improve your relationship with your boss, you must understand your own and your boss' strengths, weaknesses, work styles, and needs. Once you have this information you can develop a mutually productive and effective way of working together. This article is especially interesting because it is rare to think of the importance of "managing up." Gabarro and Kotter suggest that it is just as important to effective management as "managing down."

Interpersonal relations is a vast area to attempt to cover in one chapter and with three readings. Within our space limitations we selected readings that we felt would provide you with a solid foundation on which to build your skills. Gibb deals with a critical but often ignored aspect of communication. Ware and Barnes explore the anxiety-laden area of conflict management. Finally, Gabarro and Kotter alert us to the importance of managing our relationship with our boss. The information in these articles will provide the groundwork for the exercises and case that follow.

EXERCISES AND CASES

The first exercise, "Giving and Receiving Feedback," will help you develop skills in a specific kind of communication—feedback—which is especially critical for managerial success. Much of the interpersonal conflict that Ware and Barnes see as an organizational reality could be avoided if the misunderstandings that sometimes lead to it could be eliminated. One avenue for decreasing misunderstanding is feedback.

It is important to learn how to tell subordinates, superiors, and peers about the effect of their communication and behavior. For this communication to have the desired results it must be accurately understood. This involves creating and maintaining a supportive climate. As Gibb reported in his article, a defensive climate leads to distorted communication and thus feedback that is difficult or impossible to use.

Knowing how to receive feedback is an equally important and often neglected skill. We are often unaware of the impact of our behavior on others. Only through feedback are we able to collect the information that allows us to be more certain our behavior is having the effect we desire.

Feedback is often a source of anxiety for managers. The purpose of this exercise is to reduce anxiety and increase your feedback skills. To that end you will:

1. Evaluate how you normally give and receive feedback.

2. Learn the guidelines for effective feedback.

3. Practice giving and receiving feedback in a performance appraisal role play.

The second exercise, "Developing Conflict Resolution Skills," will give you the opportunity to understand how you normally resolve conflict and practice using effective conflict-resolution skills. As already stated, managers are often uneasy in conflict situations, and they may tend to avoid or ignore the situation rather than resolve it. This strategy may work to reduce anxiety in the short run, but it can lead to worse problems in the long term. The first step in improving your conflict-resolution skills is understanding how you typically approach conflict situations. The next step is to practice alternative conflict-resolution skills. This exercise is an opportunity for you to begin this process.

The "Bob Knowlton" case illustrates how *not* to manage the relationship with your boss. This case, in which poor communication and conflict resolution led to disaster, clearly illustrates how important the development of interpersonal skills is to managerial success. We may never see the consequences of poor communication, or we may see it and not understand its antecedents, but this does not make it any less destructive. By the time you finish this case you should be more aware of the importance of expending the effort to create and maintain successful interpersonal relations. Do not discount their importance; they can be the difference between success and failure as a manager.

MEMO

The memo to your boss will enable you to apply what you have learned about interpersonal relations to your own situation. You are asked to analyze your relationship and develop a plan for improvement. By completing this plan you may find a way to improve one of your most important organizational relationships and begin using what you have learned to increase your success as a manager.

By the time you finish this chapter you will have had an opportunity to practice using two of the most vital interpersonal skills: communication and conflict resolution. You will also have an idea of your current strengths and weaknesses in this area so that you will know what you already do well and what you need to improve.

Defensive Communication

Jack R. Gibb

One way to understand communication is to view it as a people process rather than as a language process. If one is to make fundamental improvement in communication, he must make changes in interpersonal relationships. One possible type of alteration—and the one with which this paper is concerned—is that of reducing the degree of defensiveness.

DEFINITION AND SIGNIFICANCE

Defensive behavior is defined as that behavior which occurs when an individual perceives threat or anticipates threat in the group. The person who behaves defensively even though he also gives some attention to the common task, devotes an appreciable portion of his energy to defending himself. Besides talking about the topic, he thinks about how he appears to others, how he may be seen more favorably, how he may win, dominate, impress, or escape punishment, and/or how he may avoid or mitigate a perceived or an anticipated attack.

Such inner feelings and outward acts tend to create similarly defensive postures in others; and, if unchecked, the ensuing circular response becomes increasingly destructive. Defensive behavior, in short, engenders defensive listening, and this in turn produces postural, facial, and verbal cues which raise the defense level of the original communicator.

Defense arousal prevents the listener from concentrating upon the message. Not only do defensive communicators send off multiple value, motive, and affect cues, but also defensive recipients distort what they receive. As a person becomes more and more defensive, he becomes less and less able to perceive accurately the motives, the values, and the emotions of the sender. The writer's analyses of tape recorded discussions revealed that increases in defensive behavior were correlated positively with losses in efficiency in communication. Specifically, distortions became greater when defensive states existed in the groups.

The converse, moreover, also is true. The more "supportive" or defense reductive the climate the less the receiver reads into the communication distorted loadings which arise from projections of his own anxieties, motives, and concerns. As defenses are reduced, the receivers become better able to concentrate upon the structure, the content, and the cognitive meanings of the message.

CATEGORIES OF DEFENSIVE AND SUPPORTIVE COMMUNICATION

In working over an eight-year period with recordings of discussions occurring in varied settings, the writer developed the six pairs of defensive and supportive categories presented in Table 1. Behavior which a listener perceives as possessing any of the characteristics listed in the left-hand column arouses defensiveness, whereas that which he interprets as having any of the qualities designated as supportive reduces defensive feelings.[1] The degree to which these reactions occur depends upon the personal level of defensiveness and upon the general climate in the group at the time.

Evaluation and Description

Speech or other behavior which appears evaluative increases defensiveness. If by expression, manner of speech, tone of voice, or verbal content the sender seems to be evaluating or judging the listener, then the receiver goes on guard. Of course, other factors may inhibit the reaction. If the listener thought that the speaker regarded him as an equal and was being open and spontaneous, for example, the evaluativeness in a message would be neutralized and perhaps not even perceived. This same principle applies equally to the other five categories of potentially defense-producing climates. The six sets are interactive.[2]

Because our attitudes toward other persons are frequently, and often necessarily, evaluative,

---

[1]J. R. Gibb, "Defense Level and Influence Potential in Small Groups," in L. Petrullo and B. M. Bass (eds.), *Leadership and Interpersonal Behavior* (New York: Holt, Rinehart and Winston, Inc., 1961), pp.66–81.

[2]J. R. Gibb, "Sociopsychological Processes of Group Instruction," in N. B. Henry (ed.), *The Dynamics of Instructional Groups* (Fifty-ninth Yearbook of the National Society for the Study of Education, Part II, 1960), pp. 115–135.

Reprinted by permission of the International Communication Association from the *Journal of Communication,* 1961, Vol. 11, pp. 141–148.

TABLE I

Categories of Behavior Characteristic of Supportive and Defensive Climates in Small Groups

Defensive Climates	Supportive Climates
1. Evaluation	1. Description
2. Control	2. Problem orientation
3. Strategy	3. Spontaneity
4. Neutrality	4. Empathy
5. Superiority	5. Equality
6. Certainty	6. Provisionalism

expressions which the defensive person will regard as nonjudgmental are hard to frame. Even the simplest question usually conveys the answer that the sender wishes or implies the response that would fit into his value system. A mother, for example, immediately following an earth tremor that shook the house, sought for her small son with the question: "Bobby, where are you?" The timid and plaintive "Mommy, I didn't do it" indicated how Bobby's chronic mild defensiveness predisposed him to react with a projection of his own guilt and in the context of his chronic assumption that questions are full of accusation.

Anyone who has attempted to train professionals to use information-seeking speech with neutral affect appreciates how difficult it is to teach a person to say even the simple "who did that?" without being seen as accusing. Speech is so frequently judgmental that there is a reality base for the defensive interpretations which are so common.

When insecure, group members are particularly likely to place blame, to see others as fitting into categories of good or bad, to make moral judgments of their colleagues, and to question the value, motive, and affect loadings of the speech which they hear. Since value loadings imply a judgment of others, a belief that the standards of the speaker differ from his own causes the listener to become defensive.

Descriptive speech, in contrast to that which is evaluative, tends to arouse a minimum of uneasiness. Speech acts which the listener perceives as genuine requests for information or as material with neutral loadings is descriptive. Specifically, presentations of feelings, events, perceptions, or processes which do not ask or imply that the receiver change behavior or attitude are minimally defense producing. The difficulty in avoiding overtone is illustrated by the problems of news reporters in writing stories about unions, communists, Negroes, and religious activities without tipping off the "party" line of the newspaper.

One can often tell from the opening words in a news article which side the newspaper's editorial policy favors.

Control and Problem Orientation

Speech which is used to control the listener evokes resistance. In most of our social intercourse someone is trying to do something to someone else— to change an attitude, to influence behavior, or to restrict the field of activity. The degree to which attempts to control produce defensiveness depends upon the openness of the effort, for a suspicion that hidden motives exist heightens resistance. For this reason attempts of nondirective therapists and progressive educators to refrain from imposing a set of values, a point of view, or a problem solution upon the receivers meet with many barriers. Since the norm is control, noncontrollers must earn the perceptions that their efforts have no hidden motives. A bombardment of persuasive "messages" in the fields of politics, education, special causes, advertising, religion, medicine, industrial relations, and guidance has bred cynical and paranoidal responses in listeners.

Implicit in all attempts to alter another person is the assumption by the change agent that the person to be altered is inadequate. That the speaker secretly views the listener as ignorant, unable to make his own decisions, uninformed, immature, unwise, or possessed of wrong or inadequate attitudes is a subconscious perception which gives the latter a valid base for defensive reactions.

Methods of control are many and varied. Legalistic insistence on detail, restrictive regulations and policies, conformity norms, and all laws are among the methods. Gestures, facial expressions, other forms of nonverbal communication, and even such simple acts as holding a door open in a particular manner are means of imposing one's will upon another and hence are potential sources of resistance.

Problem orientation, on the other hand, is the antithesis of pesuasion. When the sender communicates a desire to collaborate in defining a mutual problem and in seeking its solution, he tends to create the same problem orientation in the listener; and, of greater importance, he implies that he has no predetermined solution, attitude, or method to impose. Such behavior is permissive in that it allows the receiver to set his own progress—or to share with the sender in doing so. The exact methods of attaining permissiveness are not known, but they must involve a constellation of cues and they certainly go beyond mere verbal assurances that the communicator has no hidden desires to exercise control.

Strategy and Spontaneity

When the sender is perceived as engaged in a strategem involving ambiguous and multiple motivations, the receiver becomes defensive. No one wishes to be a guinea pig, a role player, or an impressed actor, and no one likes to be the victim of some hidden motivation. That which is concealed, also, may appear larger than it really is with the degree of defensiveness of the listener determining the perceived size of the suppressed element. The intense reaction of the reading audience to the material in the *Hidden Persuaders* indicates the prevalance of defensive reactions to multiple motivations behind strategy. Group members who are seen as "taking a role," as feigning emotion, as toying with their colleagues, as withholding information, or as having special sources of data are especially resented. One participant once complained that another was "using a listening technique" on him!

A large part of the adverse reaction to much of the so-called human relations training is a feeling against what are perceived as gimmmicks and tricks to fool or to "involve" people, to make a person think he is making his own decision, or to make the listener feel that the sender is genuinely interested in him as a person. Particularly violent reactions occur when it appears that someone is trying to make a strategem appear spontaneous. One person has reported a boss who incurred resentment by habitually using the gimmick of "spontaneously" looking at his watch and saying, "My gosh, look at the time—I must run to an appointment." The belief was that the boss would create less irritation by honestly asking to be excused.

Similarly, the deliberate assumption of guilelessness and natural simplicity is especially resented. Monitoring the tapes of feedback and evaluation sessions in training groups indicates the surprising extent to which members perceive the strategies of their colleagues. This perceptual clarity may be quite shocking to the strategist, who usually feels that he has cleverly hidden the motivational aura around the "gimmick."

This aversion to deceit may account for one's resistance to politicians who are suspected of behind-the-scenes planning to get his vote, to psychologists whose listening apparently is motivated by more than the manifest or content-level interest in his behavior, or to the sophisticated, smooth, or clever person whose "oneupmanship" is marked with guile. In training groups the role-flexible person frequently is resented because his changes in behavior are perceived as strategic maneuvers.

In contrast, behavior which appears to be spontaneous and free of deception is defense reductive. If the communicator is seen as having a clean id, as having uncomplicated motivations, as being straightforward and honest, and as behaving spontaneously in response to the situation, he is likely to arouse minimal defense.

Neutrality and Empathy

When neutrality in speech appears to the listener to indicate a lack of concern for his welfare, he becomes defensive. Group members usually desire to be perceived as valued persons, as individuals of special worth, and as objects of concern and affection. The clinical, detached, person-is-an-object-of-study attitude on the part of many psychologist-trainers is resented by group members. Speech with low affect that communicates little warmth or caring is in such contrast with the affect-laden speech in social situations that it sometimes communicates rejection.

Communication that conveys empathy for the feelings and respect for the worth of the listener, however, is particularly supportive and defense reductive. Reassurance results when a message indicates that the speaker identifies himself with the listener's problems, shares his feelings, and accepts his emotional reactions at face value. Abortive efforts to deny the legitimacy of the receiver's emotions by assuring the receiver that he need not feel bad, that he should not feel rejected, or that he is overly anxious, though often intended as support giving, may impress the listener as lack of acceptance. The combination of understanding and empathizing with the other person's emotions with no accompanying effort to change him apparently is supportive at a high level.

The importance of gestural behavioral cues in communicating empathy should be mentioned. Apparently spontaneous facial and bodily evidences of concern are often interpreted as especially valid evidence of deep-level acceptance.

Superiority and Equality

When a person communicates to another that he feels superior in position, power, wealth, intellectual ability, physical characteristics, or other ways, he arouses defensiveness. Here, as with the other sources of disturbance, whatever arouses feelings of inadequacy causes the listener to center upon the affect loading of the statement rather than upon the cognitive elements. The receiver then reacts by not hearing the message, by forgetting it, by competing with the sender, or by becoming jealous of him.

The person who is perceived as feeling superior communicates that he is not willing to enter into a shared problem-solving relationship, that he probably does not desire feedback, that he does not require help, and/or that he will be likely to try to reduce the power, the status, or the worth of the receiver.

Many ways exist for creating the atmosphere that the sender feels himself equal to the listener. Defenses are reduced when one perceives the sender as being willing to enter into participative planning with mutual trust and respect. Differences in talent, ability, worth, appearance, status, and power often exist, but the low defense communicator seems to attach little importance to these distinctions.

Certainty and Provisionalism

The effects of dogmatism in producing defensiveness are well known. Those who seem to know the answers, to require no additional data, and to regard themselves as teachers rather than as co-workers tend to put others on guard. Moreover, in the writer's experiment, listeners often perceived manifest expressions of certainty as connoting inward feelings of inferiority. They saw the dogmatic individual as needing to be right, as wanting to win an argument rather than solve a problem, and as seeing his ideas as truths to be defended. This kind of behavior often was associated with acts which others regarded as attempts to exercise control. People who were right seemed to have low tolerance for members who were "wrong"—i.e., who did not agree with the sender.

One reduces the defensiveness of the listener when he communicates that he is willing to experiment with his own behavior, attitudes, and ideas. The person who appears to be taking provisional attitudes, to be investigating issues rather than taking sides on them, to be problem solving rather than debating, and to be willing to experiment and explore tends to communicate that the listener may have some control over the shared quest or the investigation of the ideas. If a person is genuinely searching for information and data, he does not resent help or company along the way.

CONCLUSION

The implications of the above material for the parent, the teacher, the manager, the administrator, or the therapist are fairly obvious. Arousing defensiveness interferes with communication and thus makes it difficult—and sometimes impossible—for anyone to convey ideas clearly and to move effectively toward the solution of therapeutic, educational, or managerial problems.

Managing Interpersonal Conflict

James P. Ware
Louis B. Barnes

> *History is largely the record of conflict.*
> Kenneth Boulding

Dealing with conflict that involves oneself or one's bosses, peers, or subordinates is a task that few managers enjoy. Whether the conflict is openly hostile or subtly covert, strong personal feelings may be involved. Furthermore, there are often valid points of view on both sides, and the process of finding an acceptable solution can be mentally exhausting and emotionally draining. Yet the ability to productively manage such conflict is clearly critical to managerial success. Interpersonal differences often become sharpest when we perceive the organizational stakes to be high, but almost all organizations also include their share of petty issues blown into major conflicts. The problem for a concerned manager is to build upon human differences of opinion while not letting them jeopordize overall performance, satisfaction, and growth.

The purpose of this reading is to explore the nature and sources of interpersonal conflict, to understand its determinants and dynamics, and to discuss several specific approaches to managing conflict—whether as an adversary or as a third-party mediator.

SOME ASSUMPTIONS AND DEFINITIONS

Several basic assumptions and definitions are key to the ideas that will be expressed here. To help the following discussion, these are noted below:

Interpersonal conflict typically involves a relationship that has a sequence of conditions and events tending toward aggressive behavior and disorder. However, conflict can also be viewed in terms of its background conditions, the perceptions of the involved parties, their feelings, their actual behavior, and the consequences or outcomes of their behavior.

Conflict is an organizational reality that is inherently neither good nor bad in and of itself. It can be destructive, but it can also play a productive role both within a person and between persons. The problems usually arise when potential conflict is either unrealistically suppressed or when it escalates beyond control of the adversaries or third-party intermediaries. Whereas most managers seek to reduce conflict because of its negative repercussions, some seek to use it for its positive effects on creativity, motivation, and performance. The management of conflict usually entails maintaining a delicate balance between these positive and negative attributes.

There is no "one best way" for managing interpersonal conflict, either as an involved adversary or as a third party. Rather, there are a number of strategies and tactics involving the external conditions, differing perceptions, internal feelings, behavior, and outcomes. In addition, the relationships of the involved parties (for examples, superiors and subordinates, peers, etc.) and their past histories as adversaries, allies, or relatively neutral third parties pose another key variable. The relative power of the involved parties is another consideration in deciding whether to withdraw from the conflict, compromise, work toward controlling a conflict within certain boundaries, seek constructive confrontations, force conflict into a win/lose pattern, smooth it over with friendly acts, or try to enact a variety of other subtle or forceful approaches.

Conflict as an involved participant is emotionally very different from conflict as a relatively objective third party. Indeed, as we will see, one strength of involving third parties lies in their potential to add an objective perspective to the perceptions, feelings, and behavior of the involved adversaries. In this reading, we view the management of conflict from the vantage point of both the biased adversary and the outside third party who might be a boss, colleague, friend, or even subordinate. Each of these roles poses its own distinct strengths and weaknesses.

QUESTIONS ON CONFLICT MANAGEMENT

A manager often becomes concerned with conflict when it leads to negative outcomes in individual or organizational productivity, satisfaction, or growth. In analyzing conflict management, he or she might start with these consequences or outcomes, partly with the idea of looking at both the positive and negative sides of the coin. A second area of examination is the behavior patterns manifested by the involved parties. A third entails the different feelings and perceptions. And a fourth looks for the underlying and background conditions that help to initiate and perpetuate the conflict. It is important for a manager, either as a participant or a third party, to appreciate that any of these four areas may be an appropriate action point for dealing with conflict. With regard to these four areas, a manager might post the following questions:

1. What are the important personal and organizational outcomes or consequences of the conflict as they currently exist? What of future outcomes?

2. What are the behavior patterns that seem to characterize the conflict? How do these patterns highlight the substantive issues, perceptions, and underlying causes of the conflict?

3. What are the substantive issues involved? To what extent are they colored by one-sided perceptions? To what extent are the perceptions further colored by feelings and involvement? Where in the

organization is there potential for relative objectivity on the part of a third party?

4. What are the apparent underlying and background conditions leading to the conflict feelings, perceptions, behavior, and outcomes?

Question 1: Outcome Considerations

We have already suggested that conflicts generally have both positive and negative consequences. An increased awareness of both kinds of outcomes complicates the diagnosis, but can lead to significantly more effective intervention decisions. Examples of both positive and negative consequences are briefly discussed below.

Positive Outcomes. The competitive nature of conflict can increase the motivation and creativity of the participants. A manufacturing manager who gets angry at being pushed around by a sales vice president may respond by trying harder to produce a workable production schedule ("just to show him I can do it"). The same competitive dynamics—the urge to win—often leads to innovative breakthroughs, because of the effort and willingness to consider new approaches. Interpersonal conflicts frequently clarify persistent, underlying organizational problems. Furthermore, intense conflict can force attention to basic issues and, therefore, lead to productive resolution of long-standing difficulties, since the problems can no longer be smoothed over or easily avoided.

Conflict involvement can also sharpen an individual's approaches to bargaining, influence, and competitive problem solving. In addition, the participants often increase their own understanding of personal values and positions on important issues. Conflict often forces a manager to clarify an idea more effectively to explain it to someone who clearly disagrees with it.

Thus, conflicts are often functional, or at least can lead to functional outcomes, for the organization and for one or both of the individuals involved. In addition, however, there are often negative consequences, and conflict can escalate to a level where the negative outcomes clearly outweigh the positive ones.

Negative Outcomes. Interpersonal conflicts are often unpleasant emotional experiences—a subordinate who suppresses anger with a boss; a pair of managers who exchange angry words with each other; two colleagues who avoid each other because of previous tensions, and jeopardize a department's

productivity as a result; two other associates who "play games" by not sharing relevant and important information. All of these pattterns penalize the organization and have an emotional impact on the people involved. The organizational landscape is littered with managers who could not get along with their bosses, colleagues, or subordinates. Put one way, this might mean that they were not good "people managers," but put another way we could say that the firm had failed to develop effective procedures for dealing with the outcomes of conflict.

When a person is engaged in conflict, these negative outcomes spill out as emotions of anger, frustration, fear of failure, and a sense of personal inadequacy. Careers can be sidetracked or ruined. The stress of conflict relationships can make life miserable for the people involved, disrupt patterns of work, and consume an inordinate amount of time for those involved as well as for those affected or indirectly concerned. The direct loss of productivity is but one negative business outcome; the danger of continued poor decisionmaking because of withheld information is yet another. The irony is that those parties determined to "win" their own limited battles often cause major losses for themselves and the organization in the final analysis.

Short-term negative outcomes can also lead to patterns of worsening relationships unless some remedial action is taken, and both the involved and third-party managers have the problem of deciding when the time has come for action. While on rare occasions managers deliberately maintain tensions for their positive outcomes, most managers seek to change the situation before the schisms become too great. Before they can take appropriate steps, though, they ususally need to understand the behavior taking place.

Question 2: Behavior Patterns

As we noted above, interpersonal conflicts tend to develop patterns. That is, the two parties engage in open conflict over a particular issue, then separate or gather forces before coming together and going at each other again. Often an organizational procedure like budgeting, scheduling, or work assignments precipitates the conflict and serves as part of the background. Sometimes an apparently trivial issue sets one party against another. There may even be periods of time when two people seem to work relatively well together or are effectively buffered from each other. Then, once again, some event or change in circumstances sets them off. While these triggering events are not always predictable, there is often a pattern to them that can be identified. Poor listening, one-upmanship, power plays for resources, perceived insults, and overcontrolling comments can all serve to kindle the fires of distorted perceptions and feelings. The initial triggering behaviors can set in motion reactions and reciprocal behaviors that then begin a conflict cycle. Careful attention to when and how a conflict arises is an important part of developing a conflict management strategy.

It is equally important to note the way the conflict principals express their differences. When the conflict is open and active, the behaviors are usually obvious: shouts, sulking, continued insults, heated debate, unwillingness to listen, hardening of positions, and so on. However, when conflict is latent, the signs are not so evident. The behavior is usually more subtle: writing memos to avoid face-to-face contact; delaying decisions to block the other party; interacting only through subordinates or third parties; avoiding direct exchanges; and changing times of daily arrivals and departures to avoid meeting. The list could go on and on. Detecting such suppressed conflict requires great sensitivity but is also highly important since many conflicts are expressed indirectly.

Developing an understanding of behavior patterns in a particular conflict situation is an important prelude to planning the way to manage the conflict. If particular events trigger open conflict, those events can sometimes be stopped or actively constrained. This kind of understanding can also lead participants or third parties to make more effective role choices as to when and where to enter the conflict. Finally, as noted earlier, the patterns of conflict can provide important clues to the underlying reasons for the conflict.

Question 3: Substantive Issues, Perceptions, and Feelings

Most conflicts include two distinctively different kinds of issues. *Substantive* issues involve disagreements over policies, procedures, decisions, use of resources, roles and responsibilities, or other organizational practices. *Emotional* issues, in contrast, involve the distorted perceptions and feelings that two people can feel about each other and about the substantive issues over which they are contending. Because our social customs and the norms of most organizations discourage the open expression of negative personal feelings, intense emotional conflicts are often expressed and rationalized as substantive

issues. In fact, we often seek out substantive disagreements on trivial issues to provide justification for what has become basically an emotional conflict with another individual.

This tendency to distort and magnify differences means that conflicts often escalate rapidly in intensity and importance. Each person builds a grievance list of real and perceived problems. We seek support wherever we can find it, repeatedly citing our evidence to justify our feelings as a means of gaining sympathy. Worse yet, we attribute all kinds of negative motives and intentions to the other person while thinking of ourselves as the injured "good guy."

Conflicts also escalate because each time two people interact they try to "score points," and each interaction then becomes part of the history of the conflict. Any time one person perceives that he or she has lost a round, the effort to win the next one becomes that much more intense.

A product manager and an inventory control manager had to meet regularly to review and update product-line sales forecasts. Their interests conflicted somewhat since the product manager wanted to minimize unit costs and avoid stockouts, while the inventory control manager wanted to minimize total purchasing costs and inventory levels. When their forecasts became inaccurate, the two managers had several substantive disagreements over the forecasting procedures and their divergent goals. Gradually, however, the two managers lost sight of each other's different basic assumptions and organizational needs. They began to personalize their differences. Each felt threatened and attacked by the other, and these feelings intensified each time they interacted. Their growing distrust and lack of respect spilled over into personal antagonism, with each manager perceiving ulterior motives and unpleasant personality traits in the other. It got even worse with personal threats, name calling, and accusations of stupidity, self-interest, and dishonesty. Thus, a legitimate set of substantive differences was transformed into the vicious cycle of a heated emotional battle. Most of us have seen or been in such situations.

Some managers involved in a conflict dispute are determined to work it out with the other party by themselves through bargaining, control procedures, confrontation, or other forms of negotiation. Still other managers perceive the conflict as something to avoid, withdraw from, or smooth over as though it were not there. Colleagues and bosses are probably less reluctant to take the first approach than subordinates, who may feel forced to fall back upon the second approach, and all parties may prefer a third-party mediator. One's choice has much to do with one's own tolerance for conflict and the uncertainties that surround it. With experience, a manager can get a sense of how much to "trust" his or her perceptions and feelings during such stressful times. Even though there is evidence that some degree of stress may indeed be a productive motivator, most people have difficulty remaining open-minded and flexible during periods of very high stress. In addition, performance shortcomings may challenge one's assumptions about personal abilities and self-concept. The most natural response is then to look outward for a scapegoat—for example, "If only they would give me more accurate sales forecasts, then I wouldn't be stuck with all this excess inventory." It is much easier to change my perception about someone else's ability ("She just doesn't know how to forecast") or motives ("He's deliberately feeding me false data to make me look bad") than it is to admit personal failure or the need for help. This scapegoating tendency is another personal characteristic that contributes to escalation in conflict situations.

The advantage of having a third party trusted by both adversaries is that those more objective perceptions and feelings can serve as a reality check for both adversaries. If the third party can help work out a procedure for coping with the conflict, that may be a major step toward further agreement or resolution. A boss acting as a third party has the added power of being able to arbitrate or tip the power imbalance one way or the other, but even this apparent advantage can have negative effects in the long run if the boss is perceived as "taking sides" too often. One of the hardest, yet most important, challenges for the third party is to stay in touch with the perceptions and feelings of the two adversaries while at the same time keeping his or her own views separate, thereby dealing with the conflict *relationship* rather than being pulled into a single point of view.

Question 4: Underlying and Background Conditions

The underlying causes of interpersonal conflict are just as numerous and varied as the ways in which conflicts are expressed. Indeed, several of the more common reasons that conflicts develop have already been identified. The difficulty of assessing the factors that "really" cause or reinforce a particular conflict is that there are ususally multiple factors involved. Separation of the primary causes is often almost impossible, since most serious conflicts have reached a point of being self-reinforcing. That is, they have such a powerful history and have become so personalized that their original sources are almost irrelevant to the current level of conflict. Nevertheless, any attempt to understand a conflict must consider the kinds of factors behind the two people's actions. Management of the conflict then means changing the situational factors surrounding it or the ways in which the two people respond to the situation and to each other.

For discussion purposes, we divide these causal factors into two categories: situational or external characteristics and personal/internal characteristics. Keep in mind, however, that these distinctions are somewhat arbitrary, and are treated here as more distinctive than they usually are in fact.

Situational External Characteristics. This category includes all external conditions surrounding the two people—the pressures of time and deadlines; competition for budgetary funds, staff, organizational influence, and other scarce resources; performance pressures from bosses, peers, and other departments; promotion opportunities; and the organizational rules and procedures that affect their interaction.

We have previously seen the way interdepartmental conflict in complex organizations works. When two people from different departments (such as the market analyst and inventory control manager described above) must interact, they often represent and reflect their own reference group's differences in goals, values, and priorities. Thus, interdepartmental conflict frequently becomes interpersonal conflict unless the two representatives can rise above the special interest of the groups they represent.

But even two people from the same department can be put into competition for scarce resources, whether it be budgetary funds, subordinates, control over key procedures and decisions, office space, or the boss's time or job. The pressures to perform can make the personal stakes so high that individual managers become highly inflexible and defensive. These stakes are particularly important when middle managers are placed in competition for promotion opportunities that stress individual responsibilities and rewards. Since most organizations reward managers who are "winners" both formally (promotions and salary increases) and informally (influence, status, credibility), the social pressues to compete and win can be extremely intense.

Personal/Internal Factors. The personal goals, styles, and abilities of two people in conflict can also have a powerful effect on their behavior and their relationship. Personal career goals and ambitions can develop in response to the organizational pressures just described. However, people often experience feelings of rivalry and interpersonal competition even when there is little *external* basis for such emotions. Sometimes, of course, there is actually a poor fit between a person and the job requirements, and his or her poor performance may indeed create serious problems for someone else. More frequently, however, conflict erupts and escalates because one manager perceives another to be actively blocking a personally important goal. Whether that perception is accurate or not is almost irrelevant. The resulting feelings of anger, frustration, and anxiety contribute to the emotional escalation of conflict in ways such as those we saw earlier. These kinds of feelings are particularly strong among ambitious, competitive, achievement-oriented individuals.

In addition, we often hear of bad "chemistry" between two people. If they have very different personal values, styles, or basic assumptions that affect their work habits, they are likely to disagree over the ways to accomplish important tasks. For example, consider the tensions between a aggressive, high-energy manager and a careful, methodical analyst; or between a talkative, easygoing plant manager and a quiet, reserved manufacturing manager. Sometimes personal styles are complementary, but sometimes they become basically incompatible. When the people involved feel strongly about their ways of doing things, conflict is almost inevitable.

One of the most critical personal characteristics that feeds a conflict is one's capacity for coping with stress. When personal and organizational stakes are high, we tend to develop "short fuses" and become intolerant of others' mistakes or even of their legitimate needs. When two people are under extreme pressure and must interact frequently, it is very difficult for them to avoid blaming each other for the problems they experience.

By the time external conditions of a situation become fueled by each person's internal anxieties and stress levels, it is easy to see how conflict can surface into the areas of perceptions, feelings, and behavior. Faced with these realities, and with the outcomes of a conflict situation, either as an adversary or an onlooker, a manager is faced with a series of action choices. The first is whether to avoid or try to manage the conflict. Although the choice may seem clear-cut on paper (that is, managers should manage), it seems fair to say that most managers are better at conflict avoidance, or smoothing over than they are at conflict management. The skills and strength for managing a conflict, either as an involved participant or as a third party, do not come easily for most people. At the same time, it is important to note that there are times when avoidance or smoothing over negative outcomes and stress can make sense in the short term—and even in the long term if satisfaction is valued more highly than performance or growth. This is true in many family situations and in some family businesses. But in other situations where management is trying to optimize the balance of the three outcomes—performance, satisfaction, and growth—there is probably a greater need for managing the conflict.

MANAGING CONFLICT

If a manager chooses to try to manage and not to withdraw from or smooth over a conflict situation, he or she must first evaluate where he or she is in the situation. Am I an adversary or a third party? Boss or subordinate? Representative or free agent? With power and dependencies or, relatively speaking, without them? Any of these roles poses its own set of demands and choices. Some of these demands and choices also depend upon one's personal attributes, for example: How do *I* feel about using what power I have in this fashion? Am I willing to take on this conflict? In this section, we wish to briefly discuss three general approaches to conflict management and to raise several questions that a manager might ask before taking one of these or still another approach.[1]

The three approaches can be roughly categorized as (1) bargaining, (2) controlling, and (3) confrontation. Bargaining behavior is probably most prevalent under conditions of required interdependence and an approximate balance of power. Controlling behavior is more apt to be used when one party (including the third party) has relatively high power

---

[1]Ideas in this section are drawn from various sources, including Richard Walton, *Interpersonal Peacemaking,* Boston: Addison-Wesley, 1969; Louis R. Pondy, "Organizational Conflict: Concepts and Models," *Administrative Science Quarterly,* vol. 12, no. 2, Sept. 1967, pp. 296–320; and Robert R. Blake and Jane S. Mouton, *The New Managerial Grid,* Houston: Gulf Publishing, 1978.

but where the interdependence requirements are more flexible. Confrontation behavior may be used under either of the above conditions but seems to depend more upon the personal attributes of the involved parties and the assumptions they make about the setting and time pressures. During our discussion of each of these approaches below, we make the assumption that the acting manager "understands" the conflict situation in terms of the outcomes and consequences, the behavior, the perceptions and feelings as they relate to the substantive issues, and the underlying/background conditions. Each of these dimensions offers an entry point for either an adversary or a third-party mediator, but the choice of an approach heavily depends upon the individual's position, skills, and personal preferences.

Option 1: Bargaining

For a manager involved as adversary or mediator in a conflict situation, the only rational approach often appears to be negotiation or bargaining with the other party on the substantive isssues. The assumption behind this is usually that the conflict has involved a win/lose game in which one party would gain or lose at the other's expense. However, if two parties come to the bargaining table in a union-management fashion, they would each then signal that they wished to consider and seek new ways to resolve or compromise the conflict. The alternative presumably means win/lose warfare or withdraw into a stalemate.

The advantage of a bargaining approach is that the goal of compromise is a step beyond the goal of conflict. In approaching such negotiations, the two parties, with or without a third-party mediator, usually prepare to lose as well as to win some points. The goal is to obtain an acceptable solution in a rational way for public consumption. At the same time, many bargaining situations involve games such as bluffing, behind-the-scenes negotiations, an attempt to marshal outside power sources, a tendency to overstate one's initial demands, and the heavy use of legalistic procedures since these preserve the appearance of a rational process. Each bargaining tactic can involve risks as well as rewards. Another problem with a bargaining approach is that the parties often place a higher premium on acceptable compromises than on sound solutions. A manager who engages in a bargaining approach, either as a party in conflict or as a third party, can lose sight of the organization's well-being and become consumed in the limited goals of reaching an acceptable solution.

Option 2: Controlling

Four general ways can be used to control interpersonal conflict. These usually appear when there is a power imbalance, for example, when one party can exert pressures to make them happen. Conflict control can also be used temporarily until the crisis is concluded or conditions improve enough to permit bargaining or confrontation. Other times, two adversaries will tire of the controls or a third party appears who gains the trust of the two adversaries. The four controlling behaviors open to either adversaries or mediators are (1) prevention of interaction or reduction of its frequency; (2) structuring the forms and patterns of interaction; (3) reduction or alteration of the external situational pressures; and (4) personal counseling to help the two parties accept and deal with the process and realities of the conflict. This fourth approach involves a kind of third-party help different from mediation, and can also be used with bargaining and confrontation approaches. We now examine each of the controlling approaches more closely.

Prevention of Interaction or Reduction of Its Frequency. This strategy is often useful when emotions are high. It controls conflict by reducing the possibility of triggering events. If the two people are physically separated and no longer need to interact with each other, then there is little opportunity for them to express differences. While the differences continue to exist, the intense feelings are likely to dissipate without recurring conflict episodes, or at least to settle sufficiently to permit other approaches.

There are many ways to reduce or eliminate interaction, some of which have already been suggested. Sometimes operating procedures can be modified to eliminate the necessity for two people to work together. If that option is impossible, perhaps peers or subordinates can substitute for one or both parties; however, if the conflict stems from an underlying conflict of interest, it is just as likely to flare up in the new pair. One or both of the people could be transferred to a new job or even to a new physical location.

Several of these options are relatively expensive and time-consuming. However, they may be useful if there is no other way to work out the differences, or if the mutual hostility has reached such a level that a confrontation would be either impossible or inordinately long and drawn out. Keep in mind, however, that separation of the two parties may create more serious long-term problems or only delay an eventual necessary confrontation. When adversaries are separated, their hostilities sometimes merely go underground and may become more rather than less intense because of the absence of any opportunity to express them. When that happens the eventual confrontation may be even more serious, as the suppressed emotions finally are released. At times like this, the trusted third parties can help to judge whether reducing interaction makes sense.

Structuring Forms of Interaction. Often the separation options listed above simply are not feasible. When the two parties must continue to interact, the conflict can be controlled by imposing clear limitations on their behavior. These procedures can be as specific and narrow as the parties wish. For example, they might specify the time and place of meetings, the allowable discussion topics, the specific information to be provided by each individual, or even the types of questions or comments that are not allowed. Alternatively, the imposed procedures might specify or imply new channels of communication: meetings could be replaced by memos, messages, or telephone calls. These new forms of structured interaction are often limited only by the imaginations of the involved parties.

The way in which these ground rules are established depends greatly on the specific situation, and on the relationships between the involved people. A manager can generally impose these kinds of procedures on subordinates or other adversaries with less organizational authority. In the absence of a clear mandate from above, the ground rules are often arrived at by negotiation, mutual agreement, or the help of a third party.

This approach permits the continued exchange of vital information but seeks to prevent the exchange of hostile judgmental emotions that would interfere with necessary communication. Similar to physical separation, this strategy should be considered temporary. Here again the suppression of strong emotions can easily lead to move violent and destructive flareups subsequently. Once again, too, involved adversaries may find that their own perspectives need the objectivity of outsiders to reduce distortion in making judgments on when to use and when to abandon this approach.

Reduction or Alteration of External Pressures. Instead of focusing on the interactions that characterize the conflict, a strategy of changing the conditions that fuel it is often more effective. When the diagnosis of the conflict suggests that situational factors are largely responsible, dealing with those factors directly can control the conflict, or even eliminate it completely. Of course, the factors to be changed depend on the specific circumstances, each manager's power to affect the critical factors, and the organizational consequences of the changes (sometimes a change that might control the conflict would not be appropriate for other, more important reasons). Situational factors that could be changed include extension of deadlines, addition of new project personnel, modification of organizational policies or allowances of temporary exceptions, arrangement of periodic informational meetings, an increase in budget allocations, and protection of the principals from harassment by peers or even organizational superiors. Sometimes these mechanisms are in the hands of one of the adversaries and can be acted upon. Sometimes they need actions from outside or above the conflict.

Personal Counseling. In contrast to the other control strategies, this approach does not address the conflict itself, but focuses on the way the two people react to it. The underlying assumption here is that providing counseling, reassurance, and emotional support helps make the conflict more tolerable. In addition, the process of ventilating feelings about an "enemy" to a colleague or friend usually releases builtup tensions, and may become a first step toward personally discovering new ways to deal directly with the conflict. Alternatively, discussion of the problem with a third party can lead an individual to invent new procedures or personal goals that make him or her less dependent on the other party, thus reducing the inherent stress in the conflict.

As noted above, control of a conflict situation by oneself or a third party is a useful short-term strategy, because either the situation or the parties can often be changed. Where this is unlikely, though, or when interdependence needs are high, managers may do well to think about ways in which to constructively confront the conflict.

Option 3: Confrontation

As with the other approaches to managing conflict, a manager, either as adversary or mediator, has choices in confronting a conflict. One major choice lies in his or her intent. Is the intent to confront the differences in a constructive, getting-beyond-the-conflict manner or is it to confront differences in a way that is more destructive and attacking than integrative? The problem with adversarial confrontation is that even though one adversary wants to be constructive, the other adversary may perceive the initial attempt as an attack. Consequently, constructive confrontation must almost always begin with a serious and well-communicated attempt to *understand* and *explore* the other party's perceptions and feelings. Of course, this process can be aided by a third party who helps to build an exploratory climate while going beyond the initial temptations to support one of the two adversaries. But the important point to remember is that a constructive confrontation does not usually begin with a confrontation. It begins with an attempt to understand. Once a climate of exploration has been introduced, constructive confrontation has the advantage of conveying the possibility of a win/win solution. It seeks an information exchange of data—substance as well as perceptions and feelings—that provides new definitions of the problem and new motives for a common solution. These processes require skill and patience, but more than that they often require persistence and an active effort to help each party listen to the other while constantly looking for ways to move beyond the deadlock. This is true for adversaries *and* mediators. Each operates under considerable stress at times, but a crucial expression is often the simple question of "What if...?" as a way of searching for new action alternatives.

At the same time, confrontation behavior can walk a narrow tightrope initially while the two adversaries seek to release their emotions and feelings. Once again, a third party can help to legitimate these expressions while also channeling or policing the ways in which negative or hostile feelings are expressed. For example, the third party—or even one of the adversaries—may suggest that the parties agree to express and explore feelings that result from the actual behavior of each adversary rather than venting feelings based upon inference and speculation of the other's motives and perceptions. Without such ground rules for the expression of feelings, confrontation can easily become more destructive than constructive. With them, it is usually easier to move to new stages of information exchange and problem solving.

SOME RELEVANT ACTION QUESTIONS

In line with taking action to help manage a conflict instead of to avoid it, smooth it over, or use power to suppress it, an involved *or* third-party manager might well pause and raise the following questions. These questions are probably more important when considering a confrontation strategy, which is potentially both the most difficult and the most rewarding, but they also apply to the other approaches.

1. *To what extent is there a productive level of tension and motivation in the conflict relationship? Or has the conflict become highly destructive in nature?* If conflict resolution is to be successful, there typically must be enough stress in the situation for the participants to desire a resolution but not so much that they are unable to deal with the issues or each other. Insufficient tension may require someone to call attention to the personal or organizational outcomes that make the latent conflict dangerous or dysfunctional. Excessive tension may require cooling-off steps or temporary controlling measures.

By the same token, interpersonal conflict often persists because only one party is motivated to do something about it. When this happens, little can be done until the tension level is again high enough so that *both* adversaries at least *say* that they want to work toward a resolution. Such stated motivation can at least serve as a starting point.

2. *What are the balances of status and power postitions between the two or three parties?* The balance-of-power configurations can play a major part in determining appropriate paths to conflict resolutions or avoidance in a given situation. For example, there may be less chance for successful resolution when one party in a two-party relationship is much more powerful or influential than the other. It is often harder to secure third-party involvement in such situations as well, particularly when the power imbalance involves a superior and a subordinate. At the same time, those are also the times when third-party mediation can be most helpful, in that the third party can help to rebalance the power equation. Conflict resolution advantages are clearly on the side of the higher-status person, whether that person be an adversary or a third party.

3. *To what extent are there time and flexibility resources available?* Conflict resolution in almost any form can require considerable time, new procedures, offsite meetings, outside help, painful adjustments, restructuring of relationships, and tolerance for uncertainties. As conflict conditions develop and change, so might the participant needs for time and resources. It may indeed be easier to change situational or external variables, such as new procedures, than to change the internal perceptions of *all* parties in the

conflict arena, particularly those who are reference group members or advocates standing behind the two adversaries. Under these conditions, active counseling by a number of managers may help provide new perspectives throughout the conflict arena. In other words, changing the feelings and perceptions of the two adversaries may not be enough if their reference groups do not allow them to let go of the conflict. To work on all involved parties will take more time.

CONCLUSION

Interpersonal conflict can be both a constructive and a destructive force within an organization. More importantly to recognize, though, is the fact that such conflict is almost inevitable in any human organization. A manager's first choice is whether to ignore or avoid such realities, or whether to find ways to manage the complexities of conflict. The first alternative is quite often easier in the short run but

more costly in the long run. At the same time, the management of conflict requires some understanding of its outcomes, its destructive behavior and reciprocity patterns, the perceptions and feelings that drive the behavior, and the underlying and background conditions that help to perpetuate the conflict. Each of these approaches provides entry points for managing conflict in bargaining, controlling, or confronting fashions—separately or in combination with each other. While these action approaches are rough in concept, they help a manager to explore his or her options in dealing with the realities of a conflict situation. Almost every manager has ample opportunity to view such situations as both an outsider and as an involved adversary. While this reading may capture some issues in interpersonal conflict, it cannot capture the emotional qualities that pervade such situations. Fortunately, most readers can do that for themselves. If not, they may be in the most difficulty in the future.

Managing Your Boss

John J. Gabarro

John P. Kotter

To many the phrase *managing your boss* may sound unusual or suspicious. Because of the traditional top-down emphasis in organizations, it is not obvious why you need to manage relationships upward—unless, of course, you would do so for personal or political reasons. But in using the expression *managing your boss,* we are not referring to political maneuvering or apple polishing. Rather, we are using the term to mean the process of consciously working with your superior to obtain the best possible results for you, your boss, and the company.

Recent studies suggest that effective managers take time and effort to manage not only relationships with their subordinates but also those with their

bosses.[1] These studies show as well that this aspect of management, essential though it is to survival and advancement, is sometimes ignored by otherwise talented and aggressive managers. Indeed, some managers who actively and effectively supervise subordinates, products, markets, and technologies, nevertheless assume an almost passive reactive stance vis-à-vis their bosses. Such a stance practically always hurts these managers and their companies.

If you doubt the importance of managing your relationship with your boss or how difficult it is to do so effectively, consider for a moment the following sad but telling story:

Frank Gibbons was an acknowledged manufacturing genius in his industry and, by any profitability standard, a very effective executive. In 1973, his strengths propelled him into the position of vice president of manufacturing for the second largest and most profitable company in its industry. Gibbons was not, however, a good manager of people. He knew this, as did others in his company and his industry. Recognizing this weakness, the president made sure that those who reported to Gibbons were good at

Reprinted by permission of *Harvard Business Review.* "Managing Your Boss" by J. J. Gabarro and J. P. Kotter, 58(1). Copyright © 1980 by the President and Fellows of Harvard College; all rights reserved.

1. See, for example, John J. Gabarro, "Socialization at the Top: How CEOs and Their Subordinates Develop Interpersonal Contracts," *Organizational Dynamics,* Winter 1979; and John P. Kotter, *Power in Management,* AMACOM, 1979.

working with people and could compensate for his limitations. The arrangement worked well.

In 1975, Philip Bonnevie was promoted into a position reporting to Gibbons. In keeping with the previous pattern, the president selected Bonnevie because he had an excellent track record and a reputation for being good with people. In making that selection, however, the president neglected to notice that, in his rapid rise through the organization, Bonnevie himself had never reported to anyone who was poor at managing subordinates. Bonnevie has always had good-to-excellent bosses. He had never been forced to manage a relationship with a difficult boss. In retrospect, Bonnevie admits he had never thought that managing his boss was a part of his job.

Fourteen months after he started working for Gibbons, Bonnevie was fired. During that same quarter, the company reported a net loss for the first time in seven years. Many of those who were close to these events say that they don't really understand what happened. This much is known, however: while the company was bringing out a major new product— a process that required its sales, engineering, and manufacturing groups to coordinate their decisions very carefully—a whole series of misunderstandings and bad feelings developed between Gibbons and Bonnevie.

For example, Bonnevie claims Gibbons was aware of and had accepted Bonnevie's decision to use a new type of machinery to make the new product; Gibbons swears he did not. Furthermore, Gibbons claims he made it clear to Bonnevie that introduction of the product was too important to the company in the short run to take any major risks.

As a result of such misunderstandings, planning went awry: a new manufacturing plant was built that could not produce the new product designed by engineering, in the volume desired by sales, at a cost agreed on by the executive committee. Gibbons blamed Bonnevie for the mistake. Bonnevie blamed Gibbons.

Of course, one could argue that the problem here was caused by Gibbon's inability to manage his subordinates. But one can make just as strong a case that the problem was related to Bonnevie's inability to manage his boss. Remember, Gibbons was not having difficulty with any other subordinates. Moreover, given the personal price paid by Bonnevie (being fired and having his reputation within the industry severely tarnished), there was little consolation in saying the the problem was that Gibbons was poor at managing subordinates. Everyone already knew that.

We believe that the situation could have turned out differently had Bonnevie been more adept at understanding Gibbons and at managing his relationship with him. In this case, an inability to manage upward was unusually costly. The company lost $2 to $5 million, and Bonnevie's career was, at least temporarily, disrupted. Many less costly cases like this probably occur regularly in all major corporations, and the cumulative effect can be very destructive.

MISREADING THE BOSS-SUBORDINATE RELATIONSHIP

People often dismiss stories like the one we just related as being merely cases of personality conflict. Because two people can on occasion be psychologically or temperamentally incapable of working together, this can be an apt description. But more often, we have found, a personality conflict is only a part of the problem—sometimes a very small part.

Bonnevie did not just have a different personality from Gibbons, he also made or had unrealistic assumptions and expectations about the very nature of boss-subordinate relationships. Specifically, he did not recognize that his relationship to Gibbons involved *mutual dependence* between two *fallible* human beings. Failing to recognize this, a manager typically either avoids trying to manage his or her relationship with a boss or manages it ineffectively.

Some people behave as if their bosses were not very dependent on them. They fail to see how much the boss needs their help and cooperation to do his or her job effectively. These people refuse to acknowledge that the boss can be severely hurt by their actions and needs cooperation, dependability, and honesty from them.

Some see themselves as not very dependent on their bosses. They gloss over how much help and information they need from the boss in order to perform their own jobs well. This superficial view is particularly damaging when a manager's job and decisions affect other parts of the organization, as was the case in Bonnevie's situation. A manager's immediate boss can play a critical role in linking the manager to the rest of the organization, in making sure the manager's priorities are consistent with organizational needs, and in securing the resources the manager needs to perform well. Yet some managers need to see themselves as practically self-sufficient, as not needing the critical information and resources a boss can supply.

Many managers, like Bonnevie, assume that the boss will magically know what information or help their subordinates need and provide it to them.

Certainly, some bosses do an excellent job of caring for their subordinates in this way, but for a manager to expect that from all bosses is dangerously unrealistic. A more reasonable expectation for managers to have is that modest help will be forthcoming. After all, bosses are only human. Most really effective managers accept this fact and assume primary responsibility for their own careers and development. They make a point of seeking the information and help they need to do a job instead of waiting for their bosses to provide it.

In light of the foregoing, it seems to us that managing a situation of mutual dependence among fallible human beings requires the following:

☐ That you have a good understanding of the other person and yourself, especially regarding strengths, weaknesses, work styles, and needs.

☐ That you use this information to develop and manage a healthy working relationship—one which is compatible with both persons' work styles and assets, is characterized by mutual expectations, and meets the most critical needs of the other person. And that is essentially what we have found highly effective managers doing.

UNDERSTANDING THE BOSS & YOURSELF

Managing your boss requires that you gain an understanding of both the boss and his context as well as your own situation and needs. All managers do this to some degree, but many are not thorough enough.

The Boss's World

At a minimum, you need to appreciate your boss's goals and pressures, his or her strengths and weaknesses. What are your boss's organizational and personal objectives, and what are the pressures on him, especially those from his boss and others at his level? What are your boss's long suits and blind spots? What is his or her preferred style of working? Does he or she like to get information through memos, formal meetings, or phone calls? Does your boss thrive on conflict or try to minimize it?

Without this information, a manager is flying blind when dealing with his boss, and unnecessary conflicts, misunderstandings, and problems are inevitable.

Goals & Pressures. In one situation we studied, a top-notch marketing manager with a superior performance record was hired into a company as a vice president "to straighten out the marketing and sales problems." The company, which was having financial difficulties, had been recently acquired by a larger corporation. The president was eager to turn it around and gave the new marketing vice president free rein—at least initially. Based on his previous experience, the new vice president correctly diagnosed that greater market share was needed and that strong product management was required to bring that about. As a result, he made a number of pricing decisions aimed at increasing high-volume business.

When margins declined and the financial situation did not improve, however, the president increased pressure on the new vice president. Believing that the situation would eventually correct itself as the company gained back market share, the vice president resisted the pressure.

When by the second quarter margins and profits had still failed to improve, the president took direct control over all pricing decisions and put all items on a set level of margin, regardless of volume. The new vice president began to find himself shut out by the president, and their relationship deteriorated. In fact, the vice president found the president's behavior bizarre. Unfortunately, the president's new pricing scheme also failed to increase margins, and by the fourth quarter both the president and the vice president were fired.

What the new vice president had not known until it was too late was that improving marketing and sales had been only *one* of the president's goals. His more immediate goal had been to make the company more profitable—quickly.

Nor had the new vice president known that his boss was invested in this short-term priority for personal as well as business reasons. The president had been a strong advocate of the acquisition within the parent company, and his personal credibility was at stake.

The vice president made three basic errors. He took information supplied to him at face value, he made assumptions in areas where he had no information, and—most-damaging—he never actively tried to clarify what his boss's objectives were. As a result, he ended up taking actions that were actually at odds with the president's priorities and objectives.

Managers who work effectively with their bosses do not behave this way. They seek out information about the boss's goals and problems and pressures. They are alert for opportunities to question the boss and others around him to test their assumptions. They pay attention to clues in the boss's behavior. Although it is imperative they do this when they begin working with a new boss, effective managers also do this on an ongoing basis because they recognize that priorities and concerns change.

Strengths, Weaknesses & Work Styles. Being sensitive to a boss's work style can be crucial, especially when the boss is new. For example, a new president who was organized and formal in his approach replaced a man who was informal and intuitive. The new president worked best when he had written reports. He also preferred formal meetings with set agendas.

One of his division managers realized this need and worked with the new president to identify the kinds and frequency of information and reports the president wanted. This manager also made a point of sending background information and brief agendas for their discussions. He found that with this type of preparation their meetings were very useful. Moreover, he found that with adequate preparation his new boss was even more effective at brainstorming problems than his more informal and intuitive predecessor had been.

In contrast, another division manager never fully understood how the new boss's work style differed from that of his predecessor. To the degree that he did sense it, he experienced it as too much control. As a result, he seldom sent the new president the background information he needed, and the president never felt fully prepared for meetings with the manager. In fact, the president spent much of his time when they met trying to get information that he felt he should have had before his arrival. The boss experienced these feelings as frustrating and inefficient, and the subordinate often found himself thrown off guard by the questions that the president asked. Ultimately, this division manager resigned.

The difference between the two division managers just described was not so much one of ability or even adaptability. Rather, the difference was that one of the men was more sensitive to his boss's work style than the other and to the implications of his boss's needs.

You & Your Needs

The boss is only one-half of the relationship. You are the other half, as well as the part over which you have more direct control. Developing an effective working relationship requires, then, that you know your own needs, strengths and weaknesses, and personal style.

Your Own Style. You are not going to change either your basic personality structure or that of your boss. But you can become aware of what it is about you that impedes or facilitates working with your boss and, with that awareness, take actions that make the relationship more effective.

For example, in one case we observed, a manager and his superior ran into problems whenever they disagreed. The boss's typical response was to harden his position and overstate it. The manager's reaction was then to raise the ante and intensify the forcefulness of his argument. In doing this, he channeled his anger into sharpening his attacks on the logical fallacies in his boss's assumptions. His boss in turn would become even more adamant about holding his original position. Predictably, this escalating cycle resulted in the subordinate avoiding whenever possible any topic of potential conflict with his boss.

In discussing this problem with his peers, the manager discovered that his reaction to the boss was typical of how he generally reacted to counterarguments—but with a difference. His response would overwhelm his peers, but not his boss. Because his attempts to discuss this problem with his boss were unsuccessful, he concluded that the only way to change the situation was to deal with his own instinctive reactions. Whenever the two reached an impasse, he would check his own impatience and suggest that they break up and think about it before getting together again. Usually when they renewed their discussion, they had digested their differences and were more able to work them through.

Gaining this level of self-awareness and acting on it are difficult but not impossible. For example, by reflecting over his past experiences, a young manager learned that he was not very good at dealing with difficult and emotional issues where people were involved. Because he disliked those issues and realized that his instinctive responses to them were seldom very good, he developed a habit of touching base with his boss whenever such a problem arose. Their discussions always surfaced ideas and approaches the manager had not considered. In many cases, they also identified specific actions the boss could take to help.

Dependence on Authority Figures. Although a superior-subordinate relationship is one of mutual dependence, it is also one in which the subordinate is typically more dependent on the boss than the other way around. This dependence inevitably results in the subordinate feeling a certain degree of frustration, sometimes anger, when his actions or options are constrained by his boss's decisions. This is a normal part of life and occurs in the best of relationships. The way in which a manager handles these frustrations largely depends on his or her predisposition toward dependence on authority figures.

Some people's instinctive reaction under these circumstances is to resent the boss's authority and to rebel against the boss's decisions. Sometimes a person will escalate a conflict beyond what is appropriate. Seeing the boss almost as an institutional enemy, this type of manager will often, without being conscious of it, fight with the boss just for the sake of fighting. His reactions to being constrained are usually strong and sometimes impulsive. He sees the boss as someone who, by virtue of his role, is a hindrance to progress, an obstacle to be circumvented or at best tolerated.

Psychologists call this pattern of reactions counterdependent behavior. Although a counterdependent person is difficult for most superiors to manage and usually has a history of strained relationships with superiors, this sort of manager is apt to have even more trouble with a boss who tends to be directive or authoritarian. When the manager acts on his or her negative feelings, often in subtle and nonverbal ways, the boss sometimes *does* become the enemy. Sensing the subordinate's latent hostility, the boss will lose trust in the subordinate or his judgment and behave less openly.

Paradoxically, a manager with this type of predisposition is often a good manager of his own people. He will often go out of his way to get support for them and will not hesitate to go to bat for them.

At the other extreme are managers who swallow their anger and behave in a very compliant fashion when the boss makes what they know to be a poor decision. These managers will agree with the boss even when a disagreement might be welcome or when the boss would easily alter his decision if given more information. Because they bear no relationship to the specific situation at hand, their responses are as much an overreaction as those of counterdependent managers. Instead of seeing the boss as an enemy, these people deny their anger—the other extreme—and tend to see the boss as if he or she were an all-wise parent who should know best, should take responsibility for their careers, train them in all they need to know, and protect them from overly ambitious peers.

Both counterdependence and overdependence lead managers to hold unrealistic views of what a boss is. Both views ignore that most bosses, like everyone else, are imperfect and fallible. They don't have unlimited time, encyclopedic knowledge, or extrasensory perception; nor are they evil enemies. They have their own pressures and concerns that are sometimes at odds with the wishes of the subordinate—and often for good reason.

Altering predispositions toward authority, especially at the extremes, is almost impossible without intensive psychotherapy (psychoanalytic theory and research suggest that such predispositions are deeply rooted in a person's personality and upbringing). However, an awareness of these extremes and the range between them can be very useful in understanding where your own predispositions fall and what the implications are for how you tend to behave in relation to your boss.

If you believe, on the one hand, that you have some tendencies toward counterdependence, you can understand and even predict what your reactions and overreactions are likely to be. If, on the other hand, you believe you have some tendencies toward overdependence, you might question the extent to which your overcompliance or inability to confront real differences may be making both you and your boss less effective.

DEVELOPING & MANAGING THE RELATIONSHIP

With a clear understanding of both your boss and yourself, you can—usually—establish a way of working together that fits both of you, that is characterized by unambiguous mutual expectations, and that helps both of you to be more productive and effective. We have already outlined a few things such a relationship consists of, which are itemized in the *Exhibit,* and here are a few more.

Compatible Work Styles

Above all else, a good working relationship with a boss accommodates differences in work style. For example, in one situation we studied, a manager (who had a relatively good relationship with his superior) realized that during meetings his boss would often become inattentive and sometimes brusque. The subordinate's own style tended to be discursive and exploratory. He would often digress from the topic at hand to deal with background factors, alternative approaches, and so forth. His boss, instead, preferred to discuss problems with a minimum of background detail and became impatient

Make sure you understand your boss and his context, including:

His goals and objectives

The pressures on him

His strengths, weaknesses, blind spots

His preferred work style

Assess yourself and your needs, including:

Your own strengths and weaknesses

Your personal style

Your predisposition toward dependence on authority figures

Develop and maintain a relationship that:

Fits both your needs and styles

Is characterized by mutual expectations

Keeps your boss informed

Is based on dependability and honesty

Selectively uses your boss's time and resources

and distracted whenever his subordinate digressed from the immediate issue.

Recognizing this difference in style, the manager became terser and more direct during meetings with his boss. To help himself do this, before meetings with the boss he would develop brief agendas that he used as a guide. Whenever he felt that a disgression was needed, he explained why. This small shift in his own style made these meetings more effective and far less frustrating for them both.

Subordinates can adjust their styles in response to their bosses' preferred method for receiving information. Peter Drucker divides bosses into "listeners" and "readers." Some bosses like to get information in report form so that they can read and study it. Others work better with information and reports presented in person so that they can ask questions. As Drucker points out, the implications are obvious. If your boss is a listener, you brief him in person, then follow it up with a memo. If your boss is a reader, you cover important items or proposals in a memo or report, *then* discuss them with him.

Other adjustments can be made according to a boss's decision-making style. Some bosses prefer to be involved in decisions and problems as they arise. These are high-involvement managers who like to

keep their hands on the pulse of the operation. Usually their needs (and your own) are best satisfied if you touch base with them on an ad hoc basis. A boss who has a need to be involved will become involved one way or another, so there are advantages to including him at your initiative. Other bosses prefer to delegate—they don't want to be involved. They expect you to come to them with major problems and inform them of important changes.

Creating a compatible relationship also involves drawing on each other's strengths and making up for each other's weaknesses. Because he knew that his boss—the vice president of engineering—was not very good at monitoring his employees' problems, one manager we studied made a point of doing it himself. The stakes were high: the engineers and technicians were all union members, the company worked on a customer-contract basis, and the company had recently experienced a serious strike.

The manager worked closely with his boss, the scheduling department, and the personnel office to ensure that potential problems were avoided. He also developed an informal arrangement through which his boss would review with him any proposed changes in personnel or assignment policies before taking action. The boss valued his advice and credited his subordinate for improving both the performance of the division and the labor-management climate.

Mutual Expectations

The subordinate who passively assumes that he or she knows what the boss expects is in for trouble. Of course, some superiors will spell out their expectations very explicitly and in great detail. But most do not. And although many corporations have systems that provide a basis for communicating expectations (such as formal planning processes, career planning reviews, and performance appraisal reviews), these systems never work perfectly. Also, between these formal reviews expectations invariably change.

Ultimately, the burden falls on the subordinate to find out what the boss's expectations are. These expectations can be both broad (regarding, for example, what kinds of problems the boss wishes to be informed about and when) as well as very specific (regarding such things as when a particular project should be completed and what kinds of information the boss needs in the interim).

Getting a boss who tends to be vague or nonexplicit to express his expectations can be difficult. But effective managers find ways to get that information. Some will draft a detailed memo covering key aspects of their work and then send it to their bosses for approval. They then follow this up with a face-to-face discussion in which they go over each item in the memo. Their discussion often surfaces virtually all of the boss's relevant expectations.

Other effective managers will deal with an inexplicit boss by initiating an ongoing series of informal discussions about "good management" and "our objectives." Still others find useful information more indirectly through those who used to work for the boss and through the formal planning systems in which the boss makes commitments to his superior. Which approach you choose, of course, should depend on your understanding of your boss's style.

Developing a workable set of mutual expectations also requires that you communicate your own expectations to the boss, find out if they are realistic, and influence the boss to accept the ones that are important to you. Being able to influence the boss to value your expectations can be particularly important if the boss is an overachiever. Such a boss will often set unrealistically high standards that need to be brought into line with reality.

A Flow of Information

How much information a boss needs about what a subordinate is doing will vary significantly depending on the boss's style, the situation he is in, and the confidence he has in the subordinate. But it is not uncommon for a boss to need more information than the subordinate would naturally supply or for the subordinate to think the boss knows more than he really does. Effective managers recognize that they probably underestimate what the boss needs to know and make sure they find ways to keep him informed through a process that fits his style.

Managing the flow of information upward is particularly difficult if the boss does not like to hear about problems. Although many would deny it, bosses often give off signals that they want to hear only good news. They show great displeasure—usually nonverbally—when someone tells them about a problem. Ignoring individual achievement, they may even evaluate more favorably subordinates who do not bring problems to them.

Nevertheless—for the good of the organization, boss, and subordinate—a superior needs to hear about failures as well as successes. Some subordinates deal with a good-news-only boss by finding indirect ways to get the necessary information to him,

such as a management information system in which there is no messenger to be killed. Others see to it that potential problems, whether in the form of good surprises or bad news, are communicated immediately.

Dependability & Honesty

Few things are more disabling to a boss than a subordinate on whom he cannot depend, whose work he cannot trust. Almost no one is intentionally undependable, but many managers are inadvertently so because of oversight or uncertainty about the boss's priorities. A commitment to an optimistic delivery date may please a superior in the short term but be a source of displeasure if not honored. It's difficult for a boss to rely on a subordinate who repeatedly slips deadlines. As one president put it (describing a subordinate): "When he's great, he's terrific, but I can't depend on him. I'd rather he be more consistent even if he delivered fewer peak successes—at least I could rely on him."

Nor are many managers intentionally dishonest with their bosses. But it is so easy to shade the truth a bit and play down concerns. Current concerns often become future surprise problems. It's almost impossible for bosses to work effectively if they cannot rely on a fairly accurate reading from their subordinates. Because it undermines credibility, dishonesty is perhaps the most troubling trait a subordinate can have. Without a basic level of trust in a subordinate's word, a boss feels he has to check all of a subordinate's decisions, which makes it difficult to delegate.

Good Use of Time & Resources

Your boss is probably as limited in his store of time, energy, and influence as you are. Every request you make of him uses up some of these resources. For this reason, common sense suggests drawing on these resources with some selectivity. This may sound obvious, but it is surprising how many managers use up their boss's time (and some of their own credibility) over relatively trivial issues.

In one instance, a vice president went to great lengths to get his boss to fire a meddlesome secretary in another department. His boss had to use considerable effort and influence to do it. Understandably, the head of the other department was not pleased. Later, when the vice president wanted to tackle other more important problems that required changes in the scheduling and control practices of the other department, he ran into trouble. He had used up many of his own as well as his boss's blue chips on the relatively trivial issue of getting the secretary fired, thereby making it difficult for him and his boss to meet more important goals.

WHOSE JOB IS IT?

No doubt, some subordinates will resent that on top of all their other duties, they also need to take time and energy to manage their relationships with their bosses. Such managers fail to realize the importance of this activity and how it can simplify their jobs by eliminating potentially severe problems. Effective managers recognize that this part of their work is legitimate. Seeing themselves as ultimately responsible for what they achieve in an organization, they know they need to establish and manage relationships with everyone on whom they are dependent, and that includes the boss.

Exercise: Giving and Receiving Feedback

PURPOSE

This exercise is designed to give you the opportunity to practice giving and receiving feedback in a typical job situation—the performance appraisal. By the time you finish this exercise you will:

1. Understand the guidelines for giving and receiving maximally useful feedback.

2. Practice using these guidelines to give and receive feedback.

3. Identify your strengths and weaknesses in this skill.

4. Develop an action plan identifying additional sources of information.

INTRODUCTION

The ability to give and receive feedback is a critical component of managerial success.

Giving Feedback

The basic task of a manager is managing people. As a result, managers spend a significant portion of their time providing subordinates with information about their performance. Giving feedback usually occurs in two contexts:

☐ Structured performance appraisal.

☐ Day-to-day interaction.

The guidelines for giving and receiving feedback in this exercise are based in part on those presented in C. R. Mill, "Feedback: The Art of Giving and Receiving Help," in L. Porter and C. R. Mill (eds.), *The Reading Book for Human Relations Training* (NTL Institute, 1976).

Knowing how to provide this information in a form that can be easily understood and used is a critical managerial skill.

It is equally important to be able to communicate with peers and superiors about the effects their behavior is having on us. Conflicts and misunderstandings seem endemic to organizational life. Many of these problems can be minimized or avoided with the increased use of effective feedback.

Receiving Feedback

We usually think about feedback skills in terms of giving feedback to others. However, learning how to receive feedback is an equally important skill. We are often woefully ignorant of the impact our behavior has on others. What we intend is often not the outcome. How many times have you been surprised to find out, years after the fact, that something you did was misinterpreted, often with negative consequences? By learning how to receive feedback and to elicit it when it is needed, you will be able to increase the likelihood of having the impact you desire.

Feedback—whether positive or negative, whether given or received—is often a source of anxiety for managers. The many and varied reasons for this anxiety are often rooted in a natural fear of hurting or being hurt. While it would be unrealistic to say this fear can be eliminated entirely, it is possible to reduce the anxiety many managers' experience through knowledge and practice. This exercise is an opportunity for you to begin to learn the vital skills of giving and receiving feedback.

INSTRUCTIONS

This a four-part exercise. In Part I you will evaluate how you normally give and receive feedback. In Part II you will have the opportunity to practice giving and receiving feedback in an organizational role-play. In Part III you will give and receive feedback about the feedback skills you displayed in Part II. In Part IV you will compare your perceptions from Part I with the feedback you received in Part III and develop an action plan.

Part I

1. Read the directions and complete the Feedback Skills Self-Assessment Questionnaire.

2. Find your score.

3. Read the Guidelines for Effective Feedback.

4. Compare your self-assessment results with the guidelines.

5. List your strengths and weaknesses on Action Plan I.

Part II

1. Read the directions and complete the Performance Appraisal Role-Play.

2. Complete the Performance Appraisal Role-Play Feedback Form.

Part III

1. Using the Performance Appraisal Role-Play Feedback Form give your role-play partner feedback about the feedback skills he or she displayed during the role-play.

2. Receive feedback from your role-play partner about the feedback skills you displayed during the role-play.

3. Enter this information on Action Plan II.

Part IV

1. Complete Action Plan III.

2. Participate in a class discussion.

PART 1: FEEDBACK SKILLS SELF-ASSESSMENT

FEEDBACK SKILLS SELF-ASSESSMENT QUESTIONNAIRE

Directions: The following self-assessment questionnaire contains two sections: (1) giving feedback and (2) receiving feedback. Complete each section according to the instructions provided. Be honest with yourself. Unless you decide otherwise, no one else will see this evaluation. This is an opportunity for you to assess your own strengths and weaknesses; an opportunity for you to determine what you are already doing well and what you need to improve.

Section 1: Giving Feedback

Think back to a time when you gave someone feedback about their behavior. For each of the following pairs, check the statement that most closely matches what you *normally* do when you give feedback to someone else:

When I give feedback to someone else I:

1. a. Describe the behavior. _____(a)
   b. Evaluate the behavior. _____(b)

2. a. Focus on the feeings that the behavior evokes. _____(a)
   b. Tell the person what they should be doing differently. _____(b)

3. a. Give specific instances of the behavior. _____(a)
   b. Generalize. _____(b)

4. a. Deal only with behavior that the person can control. _____(a)
   b. Sometimes focus on something the person can do nothing about. _____(b)

5. a. Tell the person as soon as possible after the behavior. _____(a)
   b. Sometimes wait too long. _____(b)

6. a. Focus on the effect the behavior has on me. _____(a)
   b. Try to figure out why the individual did what they did. _____(b)

7. a. Balance negative feedback with positive feedback. _____(a)
   b. Sometimes focus only on the negative. _____(b)

8. a. Do some soul searching to make sure that the reason I am giving
      the feedback is to help the other person or to strengthen our relationship. _____(a)
   b. Sometimes give feedback to punish, win, or dominate the other person. _____(b)

Section 2: Receiving Feedback

Think back to a time when someone gave you feedback about your behavior. For each of the following pairs, check the statement that most closely matches what you *normally* do when someone gives you feedback.

1. a. I sometimes ask for feedback about my behavior. _____(a)
   b. I rarely elicit feedback about my behavior. _____(b)

When someone else gives me feedback I:

2. a. Listen carefully and concentrate on understanding what is being said. _____(a)
   b. Let my mind wander, interrupt, or spend my time trying to formulate a response. _____(b)

3. a. Check to make sure I've understood what the person means. _____(a)
   b. Just assume that I understand. _____(b)

4. a. Ask for examples and clarification. _____(a)
   b. Try to justify my behavior and defend myself. _____(b)

5. a. Ask additional people for input when the feedback doesn't agree
      with my perceptions. _____(a)
   b. Discount feedback that doesn't agree with my perceptions. _____(b)

FEEDBACK SKILLS SELF-ASSESSMENT SCORING KEY

Directions: On the scoring key below indicate:

1. How many (a) responses you checked for giving feedback.
2. How many (b) responses you checked for giving feedback.
3. How many (a) responses you checked for receiving feedback.
4. How many (b) responses you checked for receiving feedback.

Scoring Key

Giving Feedback		Receiving Feedback	
(a)	(b)	(a)	(b)
_____	_____	_____	_____

INTERPRETATION

The (a) responses are your self-perceived strengths, and the (b) responses are your self-perceived weaknesses. By looking at the proportion of your (a) and (b) responses, you will be able to see an overview of:

1. How effective you feel you are when giving and receiving feedback.

2. Where you feel your strengths and weaknesses lie. That is, do your strengths and/or weaknesses involve giving or receiving feedback?

GUIDELINES FOR EFFECTIVE FEEDBACK

Directions: Review the following guidelines. Each guideline corresponds in order to one of the questions in the Self-Assessment Questionnaire.

☐ Compare each of your responses to the corresponding guideline. You will note that each guideline begins with two code words (such as *Descriptive and Evaluative*). One of these code words corresponds to a strength (in this case, *Descriptive*) and one corresponds to weakness (*Evaluative*). Each of these code words is also labeled as either (a) or (b), corresponding to the (a) or (b) responses in the Self-Assessment Questionnaire. (page 76)

☐ For each (a) alternative that you checked in the Self-Assessment Questionnaire, circle the corresponding code word in Action Plan I, Part 1: Self-Assessment.

☐ Follow the same procedure for all of your (b) responses.

Example: If you checked *1. a. Describe the behavior* in Section 1 (giving feedback) of the Self-Assessment Questionnaire, go to guideline *1* in *Section 1: Giving Feedback* of the Guidelines for Effective Feedback. The code word corresponding to your response is *(a) Descriptive.* Circle *Descriptive* in the *Strength (a)—Giving* section of Action Plan I.

Section 1: Giving Feedback

1. (a) *Descriptive,* (b) *Evaluative*
Effective feedback describes the behavior rather than evaluates it. For example, it is more effective to say, "You have interrupted me ten times during this meeting" than "You're a loudmouthed, inconsiderate jerk." The descriptive statement describes only the behavior ("you did . . ."). The evaluative statement attacks the individual ("you are . . . "). While no one likes to hear that they have repeatedly interrupted you, they will be less defensive to a valid description than to a personal attack.

2. (a) *Feelings evoked,* (b) *Do it differently*
Effective feedback focuses on the feelings that the behavior evokes in the person giving the feedback: it is not a demand to change. For example, it is more effective to say, "When you interrupt me it makes me feel like you don't care about what I have to say" than "You have to stop interrupting people." The latter may be what you feel, but effective feedback does not demand change. Helpful feedback is given so the person can better understand the effect that their behavior has on you. It is up to the person receiving the feedback to decide what to do about it, if anything.

3. (a) *Specific,* (b) *General*
Effective feedback gives specific examples of the behavior rather than general ones. For example, it is more effective to say, "You have interrupted me ten times during this meeting" than "You always interrupt people." The more specific the feedback, the easier it is for the person receiving the feedback to understand exactly what you mean, to believe what you say, and to develop a plan for change.

4. (a) *Controllable, (b) Uncontrollable*
Effective feedback concerns behavior the individual can do something about. Telling someone about something over which they have no control will only frustrate them and create resentment. For example, saying, "Your voice really gets on my nerves" is not helpful feedback.

5. (a) *Timely,* (b) *Late*
Feedback is most effective when it is given as soon as possible after the occurrence. Of course, "as soon as possible" must be considered in light of your state of mind and with deference to the feeling of the individual to whom you wish to give the feedback. It is not a good idea to give feedback when you are angry, when it might embarrass the receiver, or when the receiver is particularly vulnerable.

6. (a) *Effect,* (b) *Analyze*

Effective feedback focuses on the effect the behavior has on you. Analyzing the reasons for an individual's behavior is beyond the boundary of feedback; it belongs in a psychologist's office. It is most helpful to assume that the target of our feedback had good intentions.

7. (a) *Positive and negative,* (b) *Negative only*

Effective feedback can be both positive and negative. Both are important. Yet there is a tendency to think of feedback in only negative terms. People are more likely to take negative feedback seriously if they believe that their positive behavior is also observed and acknowledged. People are also more likely to believe the positive feedback you give them if they know you are being honest with them in general; sometimes being honest involves negative feedback. The ideal is to find a balance between the two. This does *not* mean that every time you give someone negative feedback you must also strain to find something positive to say. It *does* mean that over time there should be a balance. During a structured feedback situation, such as performance appraisal, there should be a balance during the session.

8. (a) *Help,* (b) *Punish*

Before you give feedback you should be honest with yourself about your motivation. As much as we would all like to deny it, we are human with human emotions and weaknesses. Remember, feedback is not a demand to change, nor should it ever be done to punish, win, or dominate the other person. You should only give feedback if you can honestly tell yourself that your motivation is to help the other person or strengthen your relationship.

Section 2: Receiving Feedback

1. (a) *Elicit,* (b) *Wait*

Because people may not always be willing to take the risk to tell you about how your behavior is affecting them, you may get this valuable information only if you ask. This does not mean that you should ask everyone you meet about how they feel about you. It does mean that, when you have a question about how a behavior has been received—the more specific the better—you should take the chance and ask.

2. (a) *Listen,* (b) *Wander*

To be effective, feedback must be heard and understood. For this to happen it is important that you concentrate on what is being said to you. This may take some effort. Our minds tend to wander, and it is common to spend the time trying to formulate an appropriate response. Listening is the stage where communication most commonly breaks down. Therefore, when someone is giving you feedback—whether you think they are right or wrong—listen carefully and concentrate on understanding what is being said.

3. (a) *Check,* (b) *Assume*

When you receive feedback, make sure that what you understand is what the giver means. We all hear things through a variety of different filters, which can distort meaning and cause misunderstanding. To avoid this, rephrase the feedback and ask the person giving you the feedback whether that is what was meant.

4. (a) *Clarify,* (b) *Justify*

One of the most common errors people make when receiving feedback is justifying, explaining, or defending their behavior. This is counterproductive. In the first place, your reasons are really irrelevant. What you should be interested in is the effect your behavior is having on the other person: your motivation will not change that effect. In the second place, justifying, explaining, and defending often makes people reluctant to give you feedback in the future because they may feel that they are wasting their time. What you should do is ask questions to maximize your understanding. These questions may involve the clarification of points that are not clear to you or a request for specific examples. If you ask these questions, it is important not to be challenging or defensive. For example, it is a good idea to say, "It would help me understand what you mean if you could give me an example." It is not helpful to say, "I don't think I do that. Give me a specific time when I did what you are talking about."

5. (a) *Ask Others,* (b) *Discount*

At times you will receive feedback that it is inconsistent with your perceptions of your behavior. When this happens, it is easy to discount what you have heard. However, we are often the worst judge of the effects of our behavior on others. Rather than just automatically discounting incongruous feedback, you should elicit additional feedback from others. This is an especially good time to actively seek feedback.

ACTION PLAN I

Part 1: Self-Assessment

Strength (a): Giving	Weakness (b): Giving
Descriptive	Evaluative
Feeling Evoked	Do it differently
Specific	General
Controllable	Uncontrollable
Timely	Late
Effect	Analyze
Positive and negative	Negative only
Help	Punish
Strength (a): Receiving	**Weakness (b): Receiving**
Elicit	Wait
Listen	Wander
Check	Assume
Clarify	Justify
Ask others	Discount

PART II: PERFORMANCE APPRAISAL ROLE-PLAY

Directions: In Part II you will have the opportunity to practice giving and receiving feedback in a typical organizational situation—the performance appraisal. You will be playing two roles. In one you will provide feedback; in the other you will receive feedback.

Choose someone else in the class as a partner. This should be someone with whom you feel relatively comfortable with but need not be someone you know well.

With your partner, decide who will be the first to give and receive feedback. Whoever gives feedback first will play the role of Patrick/Patricia (Pat) Simmons. The person receiving feedback will play the role of Alexander/Alexandra (Alex) Thompson.

Both of you should read the General Information section. The individual portraying Pat Simmons should also read the role description entitled "Role of Pat Simmons: Alex Thompson Performance Appraisal." The individual portraying Alex Thompson should read the role description entitled "Role of Alex Thompson." You may elaborate on these roles as much as you like. For example, you may want to make up specific examples of behavior. **Note: Do not read any roles that are not yours.**

You will have 20 minutes to complete the performance appraisal. When you finish, you should fill out the Performance Appraisal Role-Play Feedback Form. On this form you will indicate how effectively your partner in the role-play gave or received feedback. That is, the person who portrayed Simmons should evaluate how effectively the person who portrayed Thompson received feedback. The person who portrayed Thompson should evaluate how effectively the person who portrayed Simmons gave feedback. You should evaluate your partner on the dimensions presented in the feedback guidelines. The code words are provided on the form, but if you have any questions refer to the guidelines. For each dimension about which you have information, indicate the behavior and its effect on you. For example, for *Justify* the *Behavior* could be "tried to blame production department for late delivery" and the *Impact on You* could be "felt like you can't handle responsibility." You may not have information about all of the dimensions.

When you have completed the Performance Appraisal Role-Play Feedback Form, switch roles for the next 20-minute performance appraisal. The person who played Pat Simmons will play Samuel/Samantha (Sam) Reynolds and should read that role description. The person who played Alex Thompson will be playing Pat Simmons and should read the description entitled "Role of Pat Simmons: Sam Reynolds' Performance Appraisal."

When you finish the performance appraisal, complete the Performance Appraisal Role-Play Feedback Form.

PERFORMANCE APPRAISAL ROLE-PLAY FEEDBACK FORM
GIVING FEEDBACK

	Behavior	*Impact on You*
Descriptive		
Evaluative		
Feeling evoked		
Do it differently		
Specific		
General		
Controllable		
Uncontrollable		
Effect		
Analyze		
Positive and negative		
Negative only		
Help		
Punish		

PERFORMANCE APPRAISAL ROLE-PLAY FEEDBACK FORM
RECEIVING FEEDBACK

	Behavior	*Impact on You*
Elicit		
Wait		
Listen		
Wander		
Check		
Assume		
Clarify		
Justify		

Plastimold, Inc. is a major force in the packaging industry. They are currently the largest manufacturer of plastic containers in the United States. Plastimold employs 3,500 employees at one location in New England. Last year they had $175 million in sales.

The Industrial Plastics division produces disposal and storage containers for the chemical industry, holding tanks, and other components for the automotive industry and specialized shipping and product handling containers for the aerospace industry.

The Consumer Plastics division, which is almost twice as large as the Industrial division, produces plastic containers for a range of consumer products including food products, toiletries, pharmaceuticals, soaps, detergents, cleansers, soft drinks, alcoholic beverages, and motor oil. See Figure 1 for Plastimold's organization chart.

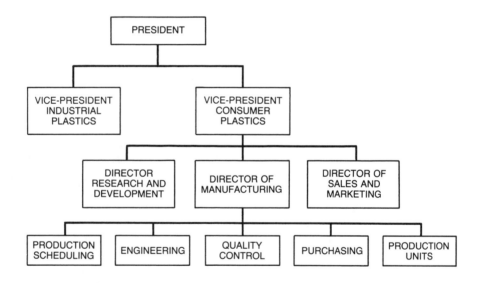

Figure 1. Organization Chart, Plastimold, Inc.

Pat Simmons is the head of the engineering department. This department is responsible for the product and tool design. They also "troubleshoot" all production problems. Five section chiefs report directly to Simmons (see Figure 2). Simmons is about to give a yearly performance appraisal to two of the section chiefs, Alex Thompson and Sam Reynolds. Both section chiefs are senior engineers whose duties are both technical and supervisory. Six draftsmen and one junior engineer report directly to each of them.

Alex Thompson has a degree in mechanical engineering from an Ivy League university and has twelve years of experience in the industry. Alex was hired by Plastimold three years ago.

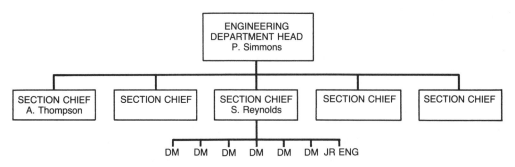

Figure 2. Organization Chart, Department of Engineering

Sam Reynolds has been with Plastimold for twenty-one years. He/she started out as a draftsman and received his/her degree in mechanical engineering by attending school at night. Sam was promoted to section chief four years ago.

Role of Pat Simmons:
Alex Thompson Performance Appraisal

You are about to meet Alex Thompson. You are very pleased with Alex's technical performance. He/she has the most productive section in the department. The designs Alex's section produces are top-drawer. Production rarely finds any problems with them, and as a result Alex spends less time than any other section head troubleshooting design problems in the production units. In fact, you have been giving Alex's section the overflow that the other sections haven't been able to complete. On occasion you have even asked Alex to consult with other section heads who were having technical problems.

In spite of this you are concerned about Alex's relationship with his/her subordinates and the other section heads as well as his/her attitude toward you.

Alex seems to go through draftsmen like water. The section has almost twice the turnover of any other section, and the Personnel Department is having trouble replacing all of the draftsmen who have quit. You have received some complaints about Alex's management style. You think that this might be related to the low morale and high turnover that seem to characterize the section.

According to the interviews Personnel conducted with the draftsmen who quit, Alex is always on their backs. He/she doesn't trust them to do anything on their own and is constantly checking and criticizing their work. As one departing draftsmen put it, "Alex was always on me, every line I drew. Plus, I could do a thousand things exactly right and then make one small inconsequential mistake, and you'd think I had just bombed the plant. I just can't stand being treated like an incompetent fool anymore." Another draftsman said, "Alex is constantly pressuring us to do more, get more done, do it better. We all work very hard, but Alex either doesn't realize that or doesn't care. Nothing we do is ever good enough."

Alex's fellow section chiefs are also displeased by his/her behavior. They say Alex is arrogant and acts like he/she is the only one who knows how to do the job.

You are also becoming increasingly uncomfortable with Alex's attitude toward you. Sometimes you wonder who the boss is. Alex frequently usurps your authority and ignores your directives.

Role of Alex Thompson

You feel pretty good about your upcoming performance appraisal. Your section is the most productive in the consumer engineering department. You rarely have to spend time correcting problems once your designs are in production. You know the same cannot be said for the other section heads. You can't figure out why they don't fire some of them. It seems to you they spend as much time fixing mistakes as they do designing products. Pat often has to have you go pull their fat out of the fire. They aren't even grateful for all your effort. In fact they act resentful, as if you were intruding or something, rather than helping them out of a tight spot.

You don't know what Pat expects from you and you resent all the extra work he/she heaps on you. You feel you're being punished for being the most productive department. Everytime you get a little ahead Pat dumps someone else's work on you. Sometimes you feel like you're doing everyone's else's work in addition to your own. Plus, Pat often doesn't know as much as you do about the technical end of the job, and you're often forced to do his/her work as well as your own and the rest of the section chiefs'.

You also feel as though you're doing such a good job against incredible odds. The draftsmen that the Personnel Department sends you are not as qualified as they should be. You feel as though you spend all your time redoing their designs. You've often said that you might as well do it yourself. Not only that, but they are an unreliable bunch. By the time you get them broken in to your way of doing things, they up and leave for another job. People just aren't as reliable as they used to be.

Role of Pat Simmons:
Sam Reynolds' Performance Appraisal

You are about to meet with Sam Reynolds. Sam has a great relationship with his/her subordinates and the other section heads. You also find Sam easy to work with. He/she is always eager to comply with your wishes and supports your goals for the department.

Sam's section has the lowest turnover in the department. The draftsmen and junior engineer who work for Sam are always singing his/her praises. They say that they like the way Sam delegates responsibility to them. It makes them feel like he/she trusts them. Sam's style seems to be to coach and guide rather than tightly control. Sam also wants his/her people to get ahead. He/she has even encouraged two of the draftsmen who report to him/her to go back to school for their engineering degrees.

Sam's section appears to work like a team. Whenever you go into his/her section, you see people talking together and trying to help each other out.

You've never seen any real conflict in Sam's section, there's always a nice relaxed atmosphere. Sam really seems to have a talent for keeping things running smoothly.

However, you have some questions about Sam's technical performance. He/she has the least productive section in the department. Sam spends too much of his/her time in the production units trying to iron out problems with his/her section's designs. In the past year you have had to give another section head work that Sam should have been able to complete.

You feel that Sam may not be supervising his/her staff closely enough. Too many mistakes are getting by him/her. You also wonder if Sam may not be carrying this relaxed atmosphere a little too far. Sometimes it seems like Sam's section spends as much time talking as working.

Sam also spends a lot of time talking with the other section heads and the people in production. It is not uncommon for you to find him/her standing around one of the production units talking with one of his/her old cronies. Maybe Sam's not spending enough time on the nuts and bolts.

Role of Sam Reynolds

You feel pretty confident about your upcoming performance appraisal. Your section is working well together and morale is high. You have a good relationship with Pat as well as your subordinates, the other section heads, and the people in production. In fact, just last week you were able to save the department about two weeks in down time because of the relationship that you've established with the production department.

Some of the other section heads don't seem to understand the importance of maintaining a good relationship with the other parts of the company. You've been around long enough to know that the way you get things done around here is through the people you know, not the things you know.

It's not that you don't know your job, you do. Your designs are innovative and creative. Because of this you sometimes have to spend a little extra time in the production units ironing out difficulties. Your designs are not just stock drawings reworked for a different job. Sometimes that takes a little extra time but you think it's worth it. One of the reasons that you can take those kinds of risks is that you have such a good relationship with the people in production.

You remember what it was like to be a draftsman. They're a pretty creative bunch and you try to let them have the room to exercise their talents. Often they have come up with ideas that saved the company a lot of money and resulted in a better product. You believe that your section is a team and should operate that way. You believe in involving your subordinates in all of the decisions that affect them. You are always open to suggestions, and you give people the opportunity to make mistakes. You figure that is the only way that they will learn.

You have a good relationship with the other section heads. You've helped them out with your contacts in the production units and they've helped you out when you had problems. All in all everyone gets along pretty well.

PART III: FEEDBACK

Directions: In Part III you will give your partner feedback about how effectively he/ she gave and received feedback in Part II and you will receive feedback from your partner. Using the Performance Appraisal Role-Play Feedback Form, spend ten minutes giving your partner the feedback that you have noted. You will then switch and your partner will give you feedback.

Be sure to observe the guidelines for effective feedback when you are giving and receiving feedback. A helpful way to phrase your feedback is to say, for example, "When you tried to blame production for the late delivery, it made me feel as though you can't handle the responsibility I've given you."

If there is anything about which you specifically want feedback, such as any potential weaknesses you identified in Part I, you should share them with your partner at this time. However, your partner is not limited to these areas.

While your partner is giving you feedback, make notes of your strengths and weaknesses on Action Plan II. The code words are provided for your convenience. One useful way to keep track of the feedback you are receiving is to circle the code word involved and make a note of the example in the space provided.

ACTION PLAN II

Part III: Performance Appraisal Role-Play Feedback

Strength (a): Giving	Weakness (b) Giving
Descriptive	Evaluative
Feeling evoked	Do it differently
Specific	General
Controllable	Uncontrollable
Effect	Analyze
Postive and negative	Negative only
Help	Punish
Strength (a): Receiving	Weakness (b): Receiving
Elicit	Wait
Listen	Wander
Check	Assume
Clarify	Justify

PART IV: ACTION PLAN III

Directions:

1. Compare you self-assessment with the feedback you received in Part III.

2. Define areas of agreement and disagreement for both giving and receiving feedback.

3. Indicate this information in your action plan in the space provided.

4. Determine the areas about which you want additional feedback. This need not be limited only to those areas about which there was disagreement.

5. Identify the person or persons from whom you intend to illicit this additional feedback.

ACTION PLAN III

Giving Feedback:	
Parts I & III Agree: Strength	Where Can I Get Additional Information?
Parts I & III Agree: Weakness	Where Can I Get Additional Information
Parts I & III Disagree	Where Can I Get Additional Information?
Receiving Feedback	
Parts I & III Agree: Strength	Where Can I Get Additional Information?
Parts I & III Agree: Weakness	Where Can I Get Additional Information?
Parts I & III: Disagree	Where Can I Get Additional Information?

DISCUSSION QUESTIONS

1. How much agreement was there between Part I and Part III? Where do you plan to get additional information about those skills for which there was disagreement?

2. What was the most difficult guideline for effective feedback for you to put into practice? Why?

3. Which of your relationships (subordinate, superior, peer) could benefit most from the increased use of effective feedback? Why?

□ In which of your relationships do you think it will be hardest to increase your use of effective feedback? Why?

REFERENCES

Mill, C.R. "Feedback: The Art of Giving and Receiving Help."
In L. Porter and C.R. Mill (eds.), *The Reading Book for Human Relations Training.* NTL Institute, 1976.

Exercise: Developing Conflict-Resolution Skills

PURPOSE

The purpose of this exercise is to help you to identify your personal conflict-resolution style. By the time you complete this exercise, you will:

1. Identify your personal style of conflict resolution.

2. Determine the potential dysfunctional outcomes associated with particular styles of conflict resolution.

3. Understand the confrontational method and how it works as a method of conflict resolution.

INTRODUCTION

Conflict management is a vital part of effective managerial performance. As managers portray the roles of "disturbance handler" and "negotiator," many situations require them to resolve conflicts effectively and productively.

However, most managers find that handling conflicts productively can be a difficult proposition. Rather than solving the conflict directly, those people who are involved in the conflict are typically labeled as "troublemakers." Managers are more likely to dismiss such individuals as having personality deficiencies that contribute to poor performance on the job rather than find a way to resolve the conflict. When confronted with a problem, managers need to guard against the tendency to assume that bad behaviors imply bad persons. Instead, managers should learn productive ways in which conflicts can be objectively resolved.

The table on "A Comparison of Five Conflict Management Approaches" originally appeared in Chapter 8, "Managing Conflict," in David Whetten and Kim Cameron, *Developing Management Skills* (Glenview, IL: Scott Foresman and Co., 1984). Used with permission.

INSTRUCTIONS

In Part I of this exercise, you will complete a questionnaire that will help you understand your own conflict-resolution style. In Part II, you will learn how to productively confront conflict through a role-play practice session that will help you to improve your conflict-management skills.

Part I

1. Complete the conflict-resolution questionnaire that follows.

2. Score the questionnaire to determine your style of conflict-resolution.

3. Read "Conflict-Resolution Styles."

4. Participate in a class discussion. Your instructor will provide a worksheet with confrontational responses to the situations described in the questionnaire.

Part II

1. Choose a partner for the role-play session. One individual should play the role of Mike, the manager, while the other individual portrays the role of Janet, the sales manager.

2. Utilize confrontational methods to resolve the conflict. Your instructor will ask you to report on your solution.

3. Participate in a class discussion.

PART I: CONFLICT STYLES QUESTIONNAIRE

Directions: Rank order the following responses on a 1-4 scale, with number 1 indicating your most likely response to the situation and 4 indicating your least likely response to the situation. Try to consider how you would actually react if faced with the situation described, rather than how you think you *should* react.

1. One of your subordinates has recently been asking for a raise. Money is available within the budget for exceptional performers, but in your opinion this subordinate does not fall into that category. You would be most likely to:

_____a. Tell him/her that you do not feel that his/her recent performance warrants a raise.

_____b. Avoid the discussion.

_____c. Compromise by saying that you will grant a raise but for a smaller percentage than requested.

_____d. Tell him/her that you would like to grant the raise, but your hands are tied.

2. George is a valued technical expert in your department, but lately he has been telling everyone what to do in their jobs. His opinion is respected in his area of expertise, but his recent behavior is causing much resentment. You would be most likely to:

_____a. Assume the situation will resolve itself shortly.

_____b. Tell George to back off—he's causing more problems than he's worth.

_____c. Tell your subordinates that George is a valued employee but at the same time tell George that he should only concentrate on areas where he can make an appropriate contribution.

_____d. Remind everyone that George is a valued employee and the group should be like a family.

3. One of your peers has recently accepted a new project that crosses your area. He/she has visited your department and asked for help from your subordinates. At first you agreed to lend your people, but it is now becoming excessive. You would be most likely to:

_____a. Tell him/her to use his/her own people on the project.

_____b Assume the problem will resolve itself when the project is completed in a few months.

_____c. Tell him/her he/she can have your people only for a limited time and only if he/she agrees to an exchange with some of his/her employees to do the work in your department.

_____d. Let him/her continue using your people; after all, your department does have the necessary expertise.

4. You have had a service order into the Purchasing Department for the past three months, and you should have received your equipment by now. The equipment is not urgent, however. You call the Purchasing Department, only to find that the equipment had never been ordered. This is a situation that has occurred previously with this department. You would be most likely to:

_____a. Accept the response as being "par for the course."

_____b. Tell them you are furious and that you will take this matter to their boss immediately.

_____c. Compromise by saying if they can get you the equipment in a few weeks, you won't call their boss.

_____d. Understand their pressures and let them know you will give them a second chance.

5. Your boss has just given you another new project to work on over the next few months. You feel you are already overburdened and just can't take on any more work. You would be most likely to:

_____a. Resignedly accept the project; after all, you don't want any hard feelings between you and your boss.

_____b. Decide not to work on the project and hope your boss forgets about it.

_____c. Suggest to your boss that you are willing to work on the project if your workload is reduced in other areas.

_____d. Tell your boss you just can't do it and that he/she is being unfair by requesting this extra work.

6. You gave a coveted work assignment to one of your subordinates who has recently shown much promise, but your top performer has been acting hurt since the situation occurred. You would be most likely to:

_____a. Force the issue with your top performer by asking him/her to tell you what is bothering him/her.

_____b. Ignore the problem.

_____c. Let your top performer know he/she is still a valued employee.

_____d. Have your top performer work with your other employee on the project to provide whatever assistance is needed.

7. Your boss has just given you an assignment that would require you to work over the weekend. In his/her mind, it is a top priority assignment and should be accomplished quickly and efficiently. You feel that more time is necessary for you to do your best, and your don't particularly want to work over the weekend. You would be most likely to:

_____a. Negotiate time off on Monday for having worked the weekend.

_____b. Tell your boss that you are unwilling to work the weekend and that you don't feel the project is really that urgent.

_____c. Decide not to work the weekend on you own but work early next week on the project. If your boss questions you, you can pretend that there was too much to do over the weekend and you are still working.

_____d. Accept the assignment so as not to cause conflict between you and your boss.

8. Being part of an internal auditing team, you've discovered a misappropriation of funds in another department. The head of this department has been with the company for many years and is considered a valued employee. You would be most likely to:

_____a. Say nothing.

_____b. Tell your superior immediately.

_____c. Confront him/her with your knowledge, but allow him/her to replace the money.

_____d. Assume that he/she must have financial difficulties at home and that he/she will soon change his/her behavior.

9. You have just given an important assignment to a group of young promising executives. While they have never handled such an assignment, you firmly believe they have the skills to do the job well. The members of a more experienced group, who have a long history of service to the company, resent your decision and have started to slack off on the job. You would be most likely to:

_____a. Tell them to go back and redo the work more carefully.

_____b. Say nothing, because they have always done their work well in the past. Assume they will come around.

_____c. Give the assignment to the more experienced group.

_____d. Give the more experienced group part of a different coveted assignment.

10. You are the controller of a manufacturing firm. You have recently adopted the policy of restrained purchasing because of budget constraints. The Purchasing Department, however, continues to produce an excessive number of requisitions for purchases that is throwing your budget calculations off balance. You would be most likely to:

_____a. Ignore the situation.

_____b. Refuse to honor the most recent purchase orders.

_____c. Tell the head of Purchasing that, although you understand his/her needs, you cannot accommodate him/her during the present fiscal year, but might be able to do something for him/her in the budget next year.

_____d. Assume that Purchasing must be in a crisis situation, and allocate more monies to their budget fund from other departmental allocations.

SCORING KEY

Directions: To determine your most likely conflict-resolution style, write in your rank for each response. Then total the numbers in each column to determine your particular conflict-resolution style.

Forcing	*Avoiding*	*Accommodating*	*Compromising*
1a _____	1b _____	1d _____	1c _____
2b _____	2a _____	2d _____	2c _____
3a _____	3b _____	3d _____	3c _____
4b _____	4a _____	4d _____	4c _____
5d _____	5b _____	5a _____	5c _____
6a _____	6b _____	6c _____	6d _____
7b _____	7c _____	7d _____	7a _____
8b _____	8a _____	8d _____	8c _____
9a _____	9b _____	9c _____	9d _____
10b _____	10a _____	10d _____	10c _____

Totals

_____   _____   _____   _____

INTERPRETATION

Total your scores in each column. Your *lowest* total represents your likely method of conflict-resolution. Then read "Conflict-Resolution Styles" to learn more about your particular style of conflict resolution.

Conflict-Resolution Styles

Managers' responses to interpersonal confrontations fall into four categories: forcing, accommodating, avoiding, and compromising.

☐ The *forcing* response is an attempt to satisfy your own needs at the expenses of others. Forcing involves the use of formal authority, physical threats, intimidation, or even majority rule.

☐ *Accommodating* satisfies another person's concerns while neglecting your own. Individuals who respond to conflict situations by using an accommodating style frequently find they are being taking advantage of by allowing other parties to get their way.

☐ The *avoiding* style characterizes individuals who neglect the interests of both parties by postponing a decision on the conflict. This is often the response of managers who are not well prepared emotionally to handle a conflict situation; they seem to believe by ignoring the situation and postponing a decision, the conflict will go away.

☐ Finally, *compromising* involves asking both parties to make a sacrifice to achieve a mutually workable solution to the problem. Those who use the compromising style may be able to find a way to solve the problem on a short-term basis, but in the long run they may find that their original compromise breeds latent hostility and frustration.

Each confrontational style has its own distinct effect:

☐ *Forcing* creates hostility and resentment against those who use the style because those who feel closed out of a decision process will naturally react against that decision.

☐ *Accommodating* leads to a situation in which the individual preserves harmonious relationships at the expense of his or her own rights in the conflict situation.

☐ *Avoiding* causes frustration and anger because individuals who must wait for a decision waste time and energy until their problem is resolved.

☐ *Compromising* offers only partial satisfaction to both parties since it forces each party to give up something to gain something in the interchange. Someone wins, and someone loses—a "win-lose" method.

As indicated by the Ware and Barnes reading, "Managing Interpersonal Conflict," we should employ an open confrontational response to conflict situations. Confrontation is an attempt to fully address and redress the concerns of both parties—it is often referred to as the "problem-solving"or collaborative method of conflict resolution. The intent of the confrontational method is to find solutions to the root causes of the conflict that are satisfactory to both parties. In this way, a "win-win" solution can be achieved.

The following table offered by Whetten and Cameron (1984) describes the typical methods and outcomes associated with the styles of conflict resolution:

A COMPARISON OF FIVE CONFLICT MANAGEMENT APPROACHES

Approach	Objective	Your Posture	Supporting Rationale	Likely Outcome
Forcing	Get your way.	"I know what's right. Don't question my judgment or authority."	It is better to risk causing a few hard feelings than to abandon a position you are committed to.	You feel vindicated, but other party feels defeated and possibly humiliated.
Avoiding	Avoid having to deal with conflict.	"I'm neutral on that issue." Let me think about it.	Disagreements are inherently bad because they create tension.	Interpersonal problems don't get resolved, causing long-term frustration manifested in variety of ways.
Compromising	Reach an agreement quickly.	"Let's search for a mutually agreeable solution."	Prolonged conflicts distract people from their work and engender bitter feelings.	Participants become conditioned to seek expedient, rather than effective, solutions.
Accommodating	Don't upset the other person.	"How can I help you feel good about this encounter? My position isn't so important that it is worth risking bad feelings between us."	Maintaining harmonious relationships should be our top priority.	Other person is likely to take advantage of you.
Collaborating	Solve the problem together.	"This is my position, what is yours?" "I'm committed to finding the best possible solution."	The positions of both parties are equally important (though not necessarily equally valid). Equal emphasis should be placed on the quality of the outcome and the fairness of the decision-making process.	The problem is most likely resolved. Also, both parties are committed to the solution and satisfied that they have been treated fairly.

PART II: ROLE-PLAY EXERCISE ON MANAGING CONFLICT

Directions: The purpose of this role play is to have you practice confrontational conflict-resolution skills. Choose a partner with whom you will work during this exercise. One individual will play the owner/entrepreneur, Mike; the other will play the sales manager, Janet. You may read both roles as preparation for the role play.

Practice confrontational methods of conflict resolution as a way to mediate the conflict. To prepare for your discussion, think about what you want to achieve in the role-play session. What will you give up? What do you want to gain in return? How would you like to see the conflict resolved? Determine tentative answers to these questions:

1. What is the source of the conflict?

2. Which emotions may surface?

3. How can the conflict be resolved in a way that meets each person's objectives?

4. What is the root cause of this conflict? What is really at stake?

5. Is there a superordinate goal that both parties hold in common as a way to resolve the conflict?

Your instructor will ask you to report on your solution.

Role of Mike, Owner/Entrepreneur

You hear the phone ring, but you are unsure if you really want to answer it. It could be Janet, the last person that you want to talk to today. Instead, you wait until it stops ringing and call your sister. Things couldn't be worse, as far as you're concerned.

You tell your sister what has been troubling you. Just as soon as you returned from vacation, everything seems to have fallen apart. Sales were down during the months of November and December, but you never expected it to be this bad. Now you have to decide if you are going to put in more money to keep the business going or simply shut it down altogether. Janet really put a knife in your back in that regard.

You thought she was motivated and happy in her job. She was, it seems, until two months ago. She came to the office every day in a sour mood, complaining that because of the time of year, she couldn't make her sales quotas. She also started complaining about having to do promotion and sales training on top of her regular sales job. After you spoke to her, it seemed that she understood that in a fledgling business it is necessary to do several jobs at once—all employees have to pull more than their weight. But now you're not sure that she really understood.

Just before vacation, she stormed into the office, saying she had to have more money to hire salespeople. You explained that this just wasn't realistic at the present time; there just wasn't any money to go around. She stormed out. Afterwards, you received a call from her husband who said that she was just having a difficult time, and was upset because she needed to feel appreciated and supported in her work. You tried to do what you could, but, with all the details involved in running a start-up entrepreneurial business, there just wasn't enough time to give her the kind of attention that she needed.

You like Janet and think that she is a motivated, competent, and effective worker. You have really grown to depend on her. But lately she has been creating havoc in the office with her sour moods. In a small office, when one person is having a bad day, everyone suffers. You're not sure how much of this the office can take.

You were confident that Janet would come around to your way of thinking and become more realistic about the business. But you were shocked and surprised—and a little hurt—when on Tuesday, Janet submitted her resignation. This was after two other salespeople quit, and two of the delivery men said that they could no longer support their deliveries.

Because Janet was contributing so much to the business, her departure will send everything into a spin. You need to get her back, even on a temporary six-week basis, just to help you train someone else. You would even be willing to give her more money in her base salary for a short period as an inducement.

Might as well give her a call to set up an appointment to discuss keeping her on—even if just a few weeks.

Role of Janet, Sales Manager

Well I've had it. No more. I'm not going to be taken advantage of any longer. I know I can make a lot more money elsewhere, and that's what I'm going to do. I'm not going to stand for this treatment any longer.

I really believed in the business. That's why I took a chance and thought it would be a lot more worthwhile to get involved in a small entrepreneurial business of this type—you know, see it grow, right from the start. But Mike won't capitalize the business the way it should be capitalized. He's such a tightwad. And then he goes and takes a vacation for a week, clear across the country! If things were really that bad, he would have stayed here. He wouldn't have been able to afford the trip.

I tried my best in November and December, but it was just a bad time of year. There was nothing I could do, really. And Mike wanted me to train new salespeople and do promotion at the same time! It was impossible—especially for the pay I was getting. Because I was on a part commission/part base salary, my pay really dipped when sales went down. In six months, when my husband goes back to school, I'm going to have to be the primary breadwinner in our family. I can't accept this low-level pay—and backslides—for this kind of treatment.

The problem is that Mike won't let go of the money. I wanted to hire two terrific salespeople in December, but they wanted more than he could offer. So I lost them. And his business will suffer without good salespeople. Now that I'm leaving, who knows what will happen!

Over the past few months, things have really been lousy. He just doesn't seem to care—or even notice—how much of myself I put into his business. That's what he's always saying: that it's *his* business, that *he's* the one who has to make the bottom line decisions. I have really sacrificed, right along with him, for the past year. But if he's always going to fight with me, what's the use?

I really thought that, when I told him I wanted to quit, it would make him realize how much he needed me—how valuable I am to his business. He treats me like a piece of furniture. I have a lot of good ideas, and if he would just listen to them, I know he could make a go of the business. But he's so stubborn and so tightfisted I'm not sure it would work.

Would I go back? I don't know. Maybe if he begged—and loosened up the purse strings a little. I just don't know if it's worth it. The phone is ringing—could that be Mike?

The Setting

Mike has asked Janet to come into the office for a discussion. Janet has just arrived, and both are ready to share their perspectives.

DISCUSSION QUESTIONS

1. What sources of conflict contributed to the conflict between Mike and Janet?

2. How did you resolve the conflict? Was it restored successfully to both parties' mutual satisfaction?

3. What are the differences between compromising and confrontation? Why are these differences so important?

4. Are conflict styles a function of personality or an adaptation to the situation? Explain.

REFERENCES

David A. Whetten and Kim S. Cameron. *Developing Management Skills.* Glenview, IL.: Scott Foresman and Company, 1984. Chapter 8.

Case: Bob Knowlton

PURPOSE

The Bob Knowlton case highlights a classic management dilemma—a misunderstanding between a subordinate and his boss. By the time you finish this case assignment, you will:

1. Understand how miscommunication and poor conflict resolution can affect real organizational situations.

2. Diagnose the problems associated with managing your boss.

3. Learn how to diagnose organizational situations to gain the appropriate skills for similar situations you may encounter as a manager.

INTRODUCTION

The Bob Knowlton case illustrates how poor interpersonal communications, misjudgments, and poor conflict-resolution skills can significantly affect workplace situations. In the case, a new player, Simon Fester is introduced as an unknown to Bob Knowlton, causing misjudgments and misperceptions. A conflict arises that ultimately leads to Bob Knowlton's resignation. As you read the case, keep in mind the readings by Gibb, "Defensive Communication," by Ware and Barnes, "Managing Interpersonal Conflict," and by Gabarro and Kotter, "Managing Your Boss."

INSTRUCTIONS

1. Read all three articles in the chapter as preparation for this case.

2. Read the Bob Knowlton case. Answer these questions:

a. What attitudes, misjudgments, assumptions, and misperceptions are generated on the part of the three key individuals in the case?

b. How could this conflict have been easily resolved?

3. Participate in a class discussion.

Bob Knowlton

Bob Knowlton was sitting alone in the conference room of the laboratory. The rest of the group had gone. One of the secretaries had stopped and talked for a while about her husband's coming induction into the Army, and had finally left. Bob, alone in the laboratory, slid a little further down in his chair, looking with satisfaction at the results of the first test run of the new photon unit.

He liked to stay after the others had gone. His appointment as project head was still new enough to give him a deep sense of pleasure. His eyes were on the graphs before him, but in his mind he could hear Dr. Jerrold, the head of the laboratory, saying again, "There's one thing about this place that you can bank on. The sky is the limit for the person who can produce!" Knowlton felt again the tingle of happiness

and embarrassment. Well, dammit, he said to himself, he had produced. He wasn't kidding anybody. He had come to the Simmons Laboratories 2 years ago. During a routine testing of some rejected Clanson components, he had stumbled onto the idea of the photon correlator, and the rest had just happened. Jerrold has been enthusiastic; a separate project had been set up for further research and development of the device, and he had gotten the job of running it. The whole sequence of events still seemed a little miraculous to Knowlton.

He shrugged out of the reverie and bent determinedly over the sheets when he heard someone come into the room behind him. He looked up expectantly; Jerrold often stayed late himself, and now and then dropped in for a chat. This always made the day's end especially pleasant for Bob. It wasn't Jerrold. The man who had come in was a stranger. He was tall, thin, and rather dark. He wore steel-rimmed glasses and had on a very wide leather belt with a large brass buckle. His wife remarked later that it was the kind of belt the pilgrims must have worn.

The stranger smiled and introduced himself, "I'm Simon Fester. Are you Bob Knowlton?" Bob said yes, and they shook hands. "Doctor Jerrold said I might find you in. We were talking about your work, and I'm very much interested in what you are doing." Bob waved to a chair.

Fester didn't seem to belong in any of the standard categories of visitors: customer, visiting fireman, stockholder. Bob pointed to the sheets on the table. "There are the preliminary results of a test we're running. We've got a new gadget by the tail and we're trying to understand it. It's not finished, but I can show you the section that we're testing."

He stood up, but Fester was deep in the graphs. After a moment, he looked up with an odd grin. "These look like plots of a Jennings surface. I've been playing around with some autocorrelation functions of surfaces—you know that stuff." Bob, who had no idea what he was referring to, grinned back and nodded, and immediately felt uncomfortable. "Let me show you the monster," he said, and led the way to the work room.

After Fester left, Knowlton slowly put the graphs away, feeling vaguely annoyed. Then, as if he had made a decision, he quickly locked up and took the long way out so that he would pass Jerrold's office. But the office was locked. Knowlton wondered whether Jerrold and Fester had left together.

The next morning, Knowlton dropped into Jerrold's office, mentioned that he had talked with Fester, and asked who he was. "Sit down for a minute," Jerrold said, "I want to talk to you about him. What do you think of him?" Knowlton replied truthfully that he thought Fester was very bright and probably very competent. Jerrold looked pleased.

"We're taking him on," he said. "He's had a very good background in a number of laboratories, and he seems to have ideas about the problems we're tackling here." Knowlton nodded in agreement, instantly wishing that Fester would not be placed with him.

"I don't know yet where he will finally land," Jerrold continued, "but he seems interested in what you are doing. I thought he might spend a little time with you by way of getting started." Knowlton nodded thoughtfully. "If his interest in your work continues, you can add him to your group."

"Well, he seemed to have some good ideas even without knowing exactly what we are doing," Knowlton answered. "I hope he stays; we'd be glad to have him."

Knowlton walked back to the laboratory with mixed feelings. He told himself that Fester would be good for the group. He was no dunce, he'd produce. Knowlton thought again of Jerrold's promise when he had promoted him—"the person who produces gets ahead in this outfit." The words seemed to carry the overtones of a threat now.

The next day, Fester didn't appear until mid-afternoon. He explained that he had had a long lunch with Jerrold, discussing his place in the laboratory. "Yes," said Knowlton, "I talked with Jerry this morning about it, and we both thought you might work with us for a while." Fester smiled in the same knowing way that he had smiled when he mentioned the Jennings surfaces, "I'd like to," he said.

Knowlton introduced Fester to the other members of the laboratory. Fester and Link, the mathematician of the group, hit it off well together, and spent the rest of the afternoon discussing a method of analysis of patterns that Link had been worrying over for the last month.

It was 6:30 when Knowlton left the laboratory that night. He had waited almost eagerly for the end of the day to come—when everyone would be gone and he could sit in the quiet rooms, relax, and think it over. "Think what over?" he asked himself. He didn't know. Shortly after 5 p.m. everyone had gone except Fester, and what followed was almost a duel. Knowlton was annoyed that he was being cheated out of his quiet period, and finally resentfully determined that Fester should leave first.

Fester was reading at the conference table, and Knowlton was sitting at his desk in the little glass-enclosed cubicle that he used during the day when he needed to be undisturbed. Fester was carefully studying the last year's progress reports. The time dragged. Knowlton doodled on a pad, the tension growing inside him. What the hell did Fester think he was going to find in the reports?

Knowlton finally gave up and they left the laboratory together. Fester took several reports with him to study in the evening. Knowlton asked him if he thought the reports gave a clear picture of the laboratory's activities.

"They're excellent," Fester answered with obvious sincerity. "They're not only good reports; what they report is damn good, too!" Knowlton was surprised at the relief he felt, and grew almost jovial as he said goodnight.

Driving home, Knowlton felt more optimistic

about Fester's presence in the laboratory. He had never fully understood the analysis that Link was attempting. If there was anything wrong with Link's approach, Fester would probably spot it. "And if I'm any judge," he murmured, "he won't be especially diplomatic about it."

He described Fester to his wife, who was amused by the broad leather belt and the brass buckle. "It's the kind of belt that pilgrims must have worn," she laughed.

"I'm not worried about how he holds his pants up," Knowlton laughed with her. "I'm afraid that he's the kind that just has to make like a genius twice each day. And that can be pretty rough on the group."

Knowlton had been asleep for several hours when he was abruptly awoken by the telephone. He realized it had rung several times. He swung off the bed muttering about damn fools and telephones. It was Fester. Without any excuses, apparently oblivious of the time, he plunged into an excited recital of how Link's patterning problems could be resolved.

Knowlton covered the mouthpiece to answer his wife's stage-whispered "Who is it?" "It's the genius," replied Knowlton.

Fester, completely ignoring that it was 2 a.m., proceeded excitedly to start in the middle of an explanation of a completely new approach to certain photon laboratory problems that he had stumbled onto while analyzing past experiments. Knowlton managed to put some enthusiasm in his own voice and stood there, half-dazed and very uncomfortable, listening to Fester talk endlessly about what he had discovered. It was probably not only a new approach but also an analysis that showed the inherent weakness of the previous experiment and how experimentation along that line would certainly have been inconclusive. The following day Knowlton spent the entire morning with Fester and Link, the mathematician, the morning meeting having been called off so that Fester's work of the previous night could be gone over intensively. Fester was very anxious that this be done and Knowlton was not too unhappy to suspend the meeting for reasons of his own.

For the next several days, Fester sat in the back office that had been turned over to him and did nothing but read the progress reports of the work that had been done in the last 6 months. Knowlton felt apprehensive about the reaction that Fester might have to some of his work. He was a little surprised at his own feelings. He had always been proud (although he had put on a convincingly modest face) of the way in which new ground in the study of photon-measuring devices had been broken in his group. Now he wasn't

sure, and it seemed to him that Fester might easily show that the line of research they had been following was unsound or even unimaginative.

The next morning, as was the custom in Bob's group, the members of the laboratory, including the secretaries, sat around the conference table. Bob always prided himself on the fact that the work of the laboratory was guided and evaluated by the group as a whole, and he was fond of repeating that it was not a waste of time to include secretaries in such meetings. Often, what started out as a boring recital of fundamental assumptions to a naive listener, uncovered new ways of regarding these assumptions that would not have occurred to the researcher who had long ago accepted them as a necessary basis for his or her work.

These group meetings also served Bob in another sense. He admitted to himself that he would have felt far less secure if he had had to direct the work out of his own mind, so to speak. With the group meeting as the principle of leadership, it was always possible to justify the exploration of blind alleys because of the general educative effect on the team. Fester was there. Lucy Jones and Martha Smith, the laboratory secretaries, were there. Link was sitting next to Fester, their conversation concerning Link's mathematical study apparently continuing from yesterday. The other members, Bob Davenport, George Thurlow, and Arthur Oliver, were waiting quietly.

Knowlton, for reasons that he didn't quite understand, proposed for discussion this morning a problem that all of them had spent considerable time on previously, with the conclusion that a solution was impossible, that there was no feasible way to treat it in an experimental fashion. When Knowlton proposed the problem, Davenport remarked that there was hardly any use in reviewing it again, that he was satisfied that there was no way to approach the problem with the equipment and the physical capacities of the laboratory.

This statement had the effect of a shot of adrenalin on Fester. He said he would like to know about the problem in detail, and walking to the blackboard, began to write the "factors" as various members of the group began to discuss the problem and simultaneously list the reasons for its abandonment.

Very early in the description of the problem, it was evident that Fester would disagree about the impossibility of attacking it. The group realized this and finally the descriptive materials and their recounting of the reasoning that had led to its abandonment dwindled away. Fester began his statement which, as it proceeded, might well have been prepared the previous night although Knowlton knew this was impossible. He could not help being impressed with the organized, logical way that Fester was presenting ideas that must have occurred to him only a few minutes before.

Fester had some things to say, however, that left Knowlton with a mixture of annoyance, irritation and, at the same time, a rather smug feeling of superiority over Fester in at least one area. Fester thought that the way the problem had been analyzed was really typical of group thinking and, with an air of sophistication that made it difficult for a listener to dissent, he proceeded to comment on the American emphasis on team ideas, satirically describing the ways in which they had led to a "high level of mediocrity."

During this time, Knowlton observed that Link stared studiously at the floor, and he was very conscious of Thurlow's and Davenport's glances toward him at several points during Fester's speech. Inwardly, Knowlton couldn't help feeling that this was one point at least in which Fester was off on the wrong foot. The whole laboratory, following Jerry's lead, talked if not practiced the theory of small research teams as the basic organization for effective research. Fester insisted that the problem could be approached and that he would like to study it for a while himself.

Knowlton ended the morning session by remarking that the meetings would continue and that the very fact that a supposedly insoluble experimental problem was now going to receive another chance was another indication of the value of such meetings. Fester immediately remarked that he was not all averse to meetings for the purpose of informing the group of the progress of its members—that the point he wanted to make was that creative advances were seldom accomplished in such meetings, that they were made by the individual "living with" the problem closely and continuously, a sort of personal relationship to it.

Knowlton went on to say to Fester that he was very glad that Fester had raised these points and that he was sure the group would profit by reexamining the basis on which they had been operating. Knowlton agreed that individual effort was probably the basis for making the major advances, but that he considered the group meetings useful primarily because of the effect they had on keeping the group together and on helping the weaker members of the group keep up with the members who were able to advance more easily and quickly in the analysis of problems.

It was clear as days went by and meetings continued as they did, that Fester came to enjoy them because of the pattern that the meetings assumed. It became typical for Fester to hold forth and it was unquestionably clear that he was more brilliant, better prepared on the various subjects that were germane to the problems being studied, and more capable of progress than anyone there. Knowlton grew increasingly disturbed as he realized that his leadership of the group had been, in fact, taken over.

Whenever the subject of Fester was mentioned in occasional meetings with Jerrold, Knowlton would comment only on Fester's ability and obvious capacity for work. Somehow he never felt that he could mention his own discomforts, not only because they revealed a weakness on his part but also because it was quite clear that Jerrold himself was considerably impressed with Fester's work and with the contacts he had with him outside the photon laboratory.

Knowlton now began to feel that perhaps the intellectual advantages that Fester had brought to the group did not quite compensate for what he felt were evidences of a breakdown in the cooperative spirit that he had seen in the group before Fester's coming. More and more of the morning meetings were skipped. Fester's opinion of the abilities of other group members, with the exception of Link, was obviously low. At times, during the morning meetings or in smaller discussions, he had been on the point of rudeness, refusing to pursue an argument when he claimed it was based on the other person's ignorance of the facts involved. His impatience with others led him to make similar remarks to Jerrold. Knowlton inferred this from a conversation with Jerrold in which Jerrold asked whether Davenport and Oliver were going to be continued on; and his failure to mention Link led Knowlton to believe that this was the result of private conversations between Fester and Jerrold.

It was not difficult for Knowlton to make a quite convincing case on whether the brilliance of Fester was sufficient compensation for the beginning of the breakup of the group. He took the opportunity to speak privately with Davenport and Oliver, and it was quite clear that both were uncomfortable because of Fester. Knowlton didn't press the discussion beyond the point of hearing them in one way or anther say that they did feel awkward and that it was sometimes difficult for them to understand the arguments Fester advanced, but often embarrassing to ask him to provide the background on which his arguments were based. Knowlton did not interview Link.

About 6 months after Fester came to the

photon laboratory, a meeting was scheduled in which the sponsors of the research would visit the laboratory to get an idea of the work and its progress. It was customary at these meetings for project heads to present the research being conducted in their groups. The members of each group were invited to other meetings, which were held later in the day and open to all, but the special meetings were usually attended only by project heads, the head of the laboratory, and the sponsors.

As the time for the special meeting approached, it seemed to Knowlton that he must avoid the presentation at all cost. He felt that he could not trust himself to present the ideas and work that Fester had advanced, because of his apprehension as to whether he could present them in sufficient detail and answer questions correctly. On the other hand, he did not feel he could ignore these newer lines of work and present only the material that he had done or had been started before Fester's arrival. He also felt that it would not be beyond Fester at all, in his blunt and undiplomatic way (if he were present at the meeting, that is) to comment on his own presentation and reveal the inadequacy that Knowlton felt he had. It also seemed quite clear that it would not be easy to keep Fester from attending the meeting, even though he was not on the administrative level that was invited.

Knowlton found an opportunity to speak to Jerrold and raised the question. He remarked to Jerrold that, with the meetings coming up and with the interest in the work and with the contributions that Fester had been making, Fester would probably like to attend these meetings, but that there was a question of the feelings of the others in the group if Fester alone were invited. Jerrold dismissed this very lightly by saying that he didn't think the group would fail to understand Fester's rather different position, and that he thought Fester by all means should be invited. Knowlton then immediately agreed, adding that Fester should present the work because much of it had been done by him and that, as Knowlton put it, this would be an opportune way to recognize Fester's contributions and to reward him since he was eager to be recognized as a productive member of the laboratory. Jerrold agreed and so the matter was decided.

Fester's presentation was very successful and in some ways dominated the meeting. He attracted the interest and attention of many in attendance, and a long discussion followed his presentation. Later in the evening, with the entire laboratory staff present, a small circle of people formed about Fester in the cocktail period before the dinner. One of them was Jerrold himself, and a lively discussion took place

concerning the application of Fester's theory. All of this disturbed Knowlton and his reaction and behavior were characteristic. He joined the circle, praised Fester to Jerrold and to the others, and remarked on the brilliance of the work.

Without consulting anyone, Knowlton began to take an interest in the possibility of a job elsewhere. After a few weeks he found that a new laboratory of considerable size was being organized in a nearby city, and that his training would enable him to secure a project-head job equivalent to his present one, with slightly more money.

He immediately accepted it and notified Jerrold by a letter, which he mailed on a Friday night to Jerrold's home. The letter was quite brief and Jerrold was stunned. The letter merely said he had found a better position; that there were personal reasons why he didn't want to appear at the laboratory anymore; and that he would be glad to return at a later time from where he would be some 40 miles away, to assist if there was any mixup at all in the past work. It also mentioned that he felt sure that Fester could supply any leadership for the group, and that his decision to leave so suddenly was based on some personal problems; he hinted at problems of health in his family, his mother and father. All of this was fictitious, of course. Jerrold took it at face value but still felt that this was very strange behavior and quite unaccountable since he had always felt his relationship with Knowlton had been warm and that Knowlton was satisfied and, as a matter of fact, quite happy and productive.

Jerrold was considerably disturbed, because he had already decided to place Fester in charge of another project that was going to be set up very soon. He had been wondering how to explain to Knowlton, in light of the obvious help and value Knowlton was getting from Fester and the high regard in which he held him. He had, as a matter of fact, considered the possibility that Knowlton could add to his staff another person with Fester's kind of background and training, which had proven so valuable.

Jerrold did not make any attempt to meet Knowlton. In a way, he felt aggrieved about the situation. Fester, too, was surprised at the suddenness of Knowlton's departure and when Jerrold asked him whether he had reasons to prefer to stay with the photon group instead of the impending Air Force project, he chose the Air Force project and went on to that job the following week. The photon laboratory was hard hit. The leadership of the laboratory was temporarily given to Link until someone could be hired to take charge.

DISCUSSION QUESTIONS

1. To what extent did Bob Knowlton contribute to his downfall? Was Bob a captive of his own assumptions and perceptions?

2. Diagnose the relationship between Bob Knowlton and his boss. Where did the relationship go wrong? How could it have been salvaged?

3. To what extent did the lack of communication among the three players in the case, and the type of evaluative or ambiguous communication that did occur, contribute to the problems associated with the case?

4. What is Bob's preferred style of conflict resolution? How did his style of conflict resolution contribute to his problems?

Memo: Interpersonal Relations

Write a letter to your boss (present or past), analyzing your relationship and outlining a plan for improvement. Your analysis should include:

1. Your boss's strengths, weaknesses, priorities, goals, working style, expectations, and assumptions.

2. Your strengths, weaknesses, priorities, goals, working styles, expectations, and assumptions.

3. Areas of potential or actual conflict.

4. The patterns that characterize your communication. Is it defensive or supportive? Be specific.

5. Environmental stress, uncertainty, and pressure.

6. How your boss is dependent on you, how you are dependent on your boss, and what implications this has for your relationship.

Your plan for improving your relationship should:

1. Be specific.

2. Include steps to maximize the strengths of your relationship and minimize the weaknesses—including, but not limited to, adaptations you plan to make and information you need from your boss.

3. Include a mechanism to monitor and maintain your relationship on an ongoing basis.

CHAPTER THREE

Motivation, Job Design, And Rewards

INTRODUCTION

One of the questions most frequently asked by managers is, "How can I motivate my subordinates to become more productive in their jobs?" What makes the difference between an effective manager and an average manager is the manager's ability to motivate subordinates to perform. As a result, motivation and performance are topics of universal concern to managers in all types of organizations. Achieving a better understanding of motivational processes can be the key to managerial success.

What is motivation? Motivation is defined by most theorists as "the will to perform." When employees are motivated to perform, they are able to put effort into the task at hand. Effort is one of the key determinants of motivation.

The question many managers face is, "How can I get my subordinates to put added effort into their work?" Although there has been a great deal written about the subject of motivation, there is no "cookbook" answer to these questions. What we do know is that motivation arises from a complex interaction of personality traits and situational determinants. People can be motivated from their own internal ambitions to perform well on the job, but if the tasks they perform in their jobs are not sufficiently challenging or interesting, they will be less willing to be productive.

Managers can therefore do two things to motivate their subordinates:

1. Manage subordinates to bring out the needs, drives, and ambitions of each individual and tie performance to the achievement of individual goals.

2. Create the proper conditions for motivation to occur through job design and task assignments. This means that managers must be sensitive to the needs of their employees and support their achievements on the job. Managers also must carefully examine the job design and reward systems of the organization to determine whether or not employee motivation is fully supported.

READINGS

Many managers believe that the way to motivate subordinates is to pay them well. For years, there has been a debate concerning the relationship of extrinsic rewards, such as pay, to motivation.

The first article, "One More Time . . . How Do You Motivate Employees?" by Frederick Herzberg, addresses this problem. It describes a key difference between the factors that contribute to satisfaction or dissatisfaction and those that influence motivational processes—the job context versus the job content. *Job context* is defined as the factors that are outside the control of the individual's job, such as pay, working conditions, managerial style, benefits, and other such factors. *Job content* factors are those that are part of the job over which the employee has some control. Opportunities for recognition, visibility, achievement, and challenge through well-designed job tasks take place in this category. Herzberg argues that the job context factors contribute to employee satisfaction or dissatisfaction, but that motivation is enhanced only by job content.

What Herzberg is saying is that motivation is *not* determined by pay or other contextual factors—only job challenge. Pay, as a contextual factor, only contributes to the extent to which an employee is satisfied or dissatisfied on the job. At best, it is a short-term motivator. Contextual factors cannot sustain motivation; only job content factors can. This theory, being counterintuitive, has touched off a debate on this subject that continues even today.

Other researchers have examined the ways in which jobs are designed to determine ways to enhance motivation and productivity. The second article in the chapter is "Designing Work for Individuals and Groups" by J. Richard Hackman. This article describes the Job Characteristics Model of motivation, which suggests that a well designed job may enhance employee motivation. Motivation may increase when employees achieve three critical psychological states: (1) experienced meaningfulness, (2) experienced responsibility, and (3) knowledge of results. Five job characteristics contribute to motivation: (1) skill variety, (2) task identity, (3) task significance, (4) autonomy, and (5) feedback from the job.

The third article, "On the Folly of Rewarding A, While Hoping for B" by Steven Kerr, describes how organizational systems often reward employees for undesirable behaviors, rather than positive ones. As we know, the feedback and reinforcement process is critical to sustain employee motivation. But many corporate policies and procedures unknowingly serve as a means to depress rather than support employee motivation. Sometimes, as Kerr argues, companies actually reward undesirable behaviors. When employees feel that they are not being rewarded for a job well done, they become dissatisfied. They wonder, "What's the use?" Achieving congruence between corporate reward systems and employee performance is vital to ensure increased motivation and organizational effectiveness.

Taken together, these three articles represent key themes on motivational processes at work. The articles presented in this chapter characterize some of the most important facets of motivational processes in organizations. Due to space limitations, we could not include many other theories, such as expectancy theory, reinforcement theory, and equity theory. However, we believe that the themes presented in the three readings chosen are the most workable. For example, managers can make direct changes in subordinate motivation by redesigning their jobs.

EXERCISES AND CASES

To help you practice your motivational skills, three exercises and one case are included. The first exercise, "A Job Redesign Project," asks you to apply the

Hackman and Oldham motivational theory to your own job, as well as the jobs of your subordinates. Hackman and Oldham present several job redesign principles. By understanding how jobs can be better designed to enhance motivation, you may be able to increase the productivity of your work group.

The second exercise is a case entitled, "Plant Democracy at National Foods." This case is based on a now famous social science experiment that occurred at the General Foods-Topeka dog food production plant. In this production plant, an entirely new system of factory work design was developed. It is called *semiautonomous work teams* and is based on the ideas of Herzberg, Hackman and Oldham, and Richard Walton, a professor of business administration at Harvard University. Each unit was responsible for a small "chunk" of the production process. In this way, motivation was increased by providing real responsibility, meaningfulness, and decision-making autonomy to the production teams. This design represents the "wave of the future" for factory shop-floor work design—the case describes the issues.

The third exercise, "Making Rewards Work," focuses on the role of rewards in motivational processes. In this exercise, three case vignettes are used to describe, as Kerr maintains, the ways in which organizational systems sometimes discourage rather than reward appropriate employee behavior. The exercise will provide you with an opportunity to identify ways to use rewards to motivate employees rather than discourage them.

MEMO

Finally, the memo assignment, "Motivation, Job Design and Rewards," asks you to think about the material learned in this chapter and apply it to your job. How effective is the current design of your job? Is your job meeting your internal needs for friendship, status, and for security? What rewards do you seek? By considering these questions, you will develop a better understanding of what motivates you and what type of job you will find most rewarding.

By the time you finish this chapter, you will have a better understanding of motivational processes, the role of job design, and reward systems. You will also begin to practice using these motivational theories to improve your performance as a manager.

One More Time: How Do You Motivate Employees?

Frederick Herzberg

FOREWORD

KITA—the externally imposed attempt by management to "install a generator" in the employee—

has been demonstrated to be a total failure, the author says. The absence of such "hygiene" factors

Reprinted by permission of *Harvard Business Review*. "One More Time: How Do You Motivate Employees?"

by Frederick Herzberg, 46(1). Copyright © 1968 by the President and Fellows of Harvard College; all rights reserved.

as good supervisor-employee relations and liberal fringe benefits can make a worker unhappy, but their presence will not make him want to work harder. Essentially meaningless changes in the tasks that workers are assigned to do have not accomplished the desired objective either. The only way to motivate the employee is to give him challenging work in which he can assume responsibility.

Frederick Herzberg, who is Professor and Chairman of the Psychology Department at Case Western Reserve University, has devoted many years to the study of motivation in the United States and abroad. He is the author of *Work and the Nature of Man* (World Publishing Company, 1966).

How many articles, books, speeches, and workshops have pleaded plaintively, "How do I get an employee to do what I want him to do?"

The psychology of motivation is tremendously complex, and what has been unraveled with any degree of assurance is small indeed. But the dismal ratio of knowledge to speculation has not dampened the enthusiasm for new forms of snake oil that are constantly coming on the market, many of them with academic testimonials. Doubtless this article will have no depressing impact on the market for snake oil, but since the ideas expressed in it have been tested in many corporations and other organizations, it will help—I hope—to redress the imbalance in the aforementioned ratio.

'MOTIVATING' WITH KITA

In lectures to industry on the problem, I have found that the audiences are anxious for quick and practical answers, so I will begin with a straightforward, practical formula for moving people.

What is the simplest, surest, and most direct way of getting someone to do something? Ask him? But if he responds that he does not want to do it, then that calls for a psychological consultation to determine the reason for his obstinacy. Tell him? His response shows that he does not understand you, and now an expert in communication methods has to be brought in to show you how to get through to him. Give him a monetary incentive? I do not need to remind the reader of the complexity and difficulty involved in setting up and administering an incentive system. Show him? This means a costly training program. We need a simple way.

Every audience contains the "direct action" manager who shouts, "Kick him!" And this type of manager is right. The surest and least circumlocuted way of getting someone to do something is to kick him in the pants—give him what might be called the KITA.

There are various forms of KITA, and here are some of them:

☐ *Negative Physical KITA.* This is a literal application of the term and was frequently used in the past. It has, however, three major drawbacks: (1) it is inelegant; (2) it contradicts the precious image of benevolence that most organizations cherish; and (3) since it is a physical attack, it directly stimulates the autonomic nervous system, and this often results in negative feedback—the employee may just kick you in return. These factors give rise to certain taboos against negative physical KITA.

The psychologist has come to the rescue of those who are no longer permitted to use negative physical KITA. He has uncovered infinite sources of psychological vulnerabilities and the appropriate methods to play tunes on them. "He took my rug away"; "I wonder what he meant by that"; "The boss is always going around me"—these symptomatic expressions of ego sores that have been rubbed raw are the result of application of:

☐ *Negative Psychological KITA.* This has several advantages over negative physical KITA. First, the cruelty is not visible; the bleeding is internal and comes much later. Second, since it affects the higher cortical centers of the brain with its inhibitory powers, it reduces the possibility of physical backlash. Third, since the number of psychological pains that a person can feel is almost infinite, the direction and site possibilities of the KITA are increased many times. Fourth, the person administering the kick can manage to be above it all and let the system accomplish the dirty work. Fifth, those who practice it receive some ego satisfaction (oneupmanship), whereas they would find drawing blood abhorrent. Finally, if the employee does complain, he can always be accused of being paranoid, since there is no tangible evidence of an actual attack.

Now, what does negative KITA accomplish? If I kick you in the rear (physically or psychologically), who is motivated? *I* am motivated; *you* move! Negative KITA does not lead to motivation, but to movement. So:

□ *Positive KITA.* Let us consider motivation. If I say to you, "Do this for me or the company, and in return I will give you a reward, an incentive, more status, a promotion, all the quid pro quos that exist in the industrial organization," am I motivating you? The overwhelming opinion I receive from management people is, "Yes, this is motivation."

I have a year-old Schnauzer. When it was a small puppy and I wanted it to move, I kicked it in the rear and it moved. Now that I have finished its obedience training, I hold up a dog biscuit when I want the Schnauzer to move. In this instance, who is motivated—I or the dog? The dog wants the biscuit, but it is I who want it to move. Again, I am the one who is motivated, and the dog is the one who moves. In this instance all I did was apply KITA frontally; I exerted a pull instead of a push. When industry wishes to use such positive KITAs, it has available an incredible number and variety of dog biscuits (jelly beans for humans) to wave in front of the employee to get him to jump.

Why is it that managerial audiences are quick to see that negative KITA is *not* motivation, while they are almost unanimous in their judgment that positive KITA *is* motivation? It is because negative KITA is rape, and positive KITA is seduction. But it is infinitely worse to be seduced than to be raped; the latter is an unfortunate occurrence, while the former signifies that you were a party to your own downfall. This is why positive KITA is so popular: it is a tradition; it is in the American way. The organization does not have to kick you; you kick yourself.

Myths About Motivation

Why is KITA not motivation? If I kick my dog (from the front or the back), he will move. And when I want him to move again, what must I do? I must kick him again. Similarly, I can charge a man's battery, and then recharge it, and recharge it again. But it is only when he has his own generator that we can talk about motivation. He then needs no outside stimulation. He *wants* to do it.

With this in mind, we can review some positive KITA personnel practices that were developed as attempts to instill "motivation":

1. *Reducing time spent at work*—This represents a marvelous way of motivating people to work—getting them off the job! We have reduced (formally and informally) the time spent on the job over the last 50 or 60 years until we are finally on the way to the "6½-day weekend." An interesting variant of this approach is the development of off-hour recreation programs. The philosophy here seems to be that those who play together, work together. The fact is that motivated people seek more hours of work, not fewer.

2. *Spiraling wages*—Have these motivated people? Yes, to seek the next wage increase. Some medievalists still can be heard to say that a good depression will get employees moving. They feel that if rising wages don't or won't do the job, perhaps reducing them will.

3. *Fringe benefits*—Industry has outdone the most welfare-minded of welfare states in dispensing cradle-to-the-grave succor. One company I know of had an informal "fringe benefit of the month club" going for a while. The cost of fringe benefits in this country has reached approximately 25% of the wage dollar, and we still cry for motivation.

People spend less time working for more money and more security than ever before, and the trend cannot be reversed. These benefits are no longer rewards; they are rights. A 6-day week is inhuman, a 10-hour day is exploitation, extended medical coverage is a basic decency, and stock options are the salvation of American initiative. Unless the ante is continuously raised, the psychological reaction of employees is that the company is turning back the clock.

When industry began to realize that both the economic nerve and the lazy nerve of their employees had insatiable appetites, it started to listen to the behavioral scientists who, more out of a humanist tradition than from scientific study, criticized management for not knowing how to deal with people. The next KITA easily followed.

4. *Human relations training*—Over 30 years of teaching and, in many instances, of practicing psychological approaches to handling people have resulted in costly human relations programs and, in the end, the same question: How do you motivate workers? Here, too, escalations have taken place. Thirty years ago it was necessary to request, "Please don't spit on the floor." Today the same admonition requires three "please"s before the employee feels that his superior has demonstrated the psychologically proper attitudes toward him.

The failure of human relations training to produce motivation led to the conclusion that the supervisor or manager himself was not psychologically true to himself in his practice of interpersonal decency. So an advanced form of human relations KITA, sensitivity training, was unfolded.

5. *Sensitivity training*—Do you really, really understand yourself? Do you really, really, really trust the other man? Do you really, really, really, really cooperate? The failure of sensitivity training is now being explained, by those who have become opportunistic exploiters of the technique, as a failure to really (five times) conduct proper sensitivity training courses.

With the realization that there are only temporary gains from comfort and economic and interpersonal KITA, personnel managers concluded that the fault lay not in what they were doing, but in the employee's failure to appreciate what they were doing. This opened up the field of communications, a whole new area of "scientifically" sanctioned KITA.

6. *Communications*—The professor of communications was invited to join the faculty of management training programs and help in making employees understand what management was doing for them. House organs, briefing sessions, supervisory instruction on the importance of communication, and all sorts of propaganda have proliferated until today there is even an International Council of Industrial Editors. But no motivation resulted, and the obvious thought occurred that perhaps management was not hearing what the employees were saying. That led to the next KITA.

7. *Two-way communication*—Management ordered morale surveys, suggestion plans, and group participation programs. Then both employees and management were communicating and listening to each other more than ever, but without much improvement in motivation.

The behavioral scientists began to take another look at their conceptions and their data, and they took human relations one step further. A glimmer of truth was beginning to show through in the writings of the so-called higher-order-need psychologists. People, so they said, want to actualize themselves. Unfortunately, the "actualizing" psychologists got mixed up with the human relations psychologists, and a new KITA emerged.

8. *Job participation*—Though it may not have been the theoretical intention, job participation often became a "give them the big picture" approach. For example, if a man is tightening 10,000 nuts a day on an assembly line with a torque wrench, tell him he is building a Chevrolet. Another approach had the goal of giving the employee a *feeling* that he is determining, in some measure, what he does on his job. The goal was to provide a *sense* of achievement rather than a substantive achievement in his task. Real

achievement, of course, requires a task that makes it possible.

But still there was no motivation. This led to the inevitable conclusion that the employees must be sick, and therefore to the next KITA.

9. *Employee counseling*—The initial use of this form of KITA in a systematic fashion can be credited to the Hawthorne experiment of the Western Electric Company during the early 1930s. At that time, it was found that the employees harbored irrational feelings that were interfering with the rational operation of the factory. Counseling in this instance was a means of letting the employers unburden themselves by talking to someone about their problems. Although the counseling techniques were primitive, the program was large indeed.

The counseling approach suffered as a result of experiences during World War II, when the programs themselves were found to be interfering with the operation of the organizations; the counselors had forgotten their role of benevolent listeners and were attempting to do something about the problems that they heard about. Psychological counseling, however, has managed to survive the negative impact of World War II experiences and today is beginning to flourish with renewed sophistication. But, alas, many of these programs, like all the others, do not seem to have lessened the pressure of demands to find out how to motivate workers.

Since KITA results only in short-term movement, it is safe to predict that the cost of these programs will increase steadily and new varieties will be developed as old positive KITAs reach their satiation points.

HYGIENE VS. MOTIVATORS

Let me rephrase the perennial question this way: How do you install a generator in an employee? A brief review of my motivation-hygiene theory of job attitudes is required before theoretical and practical suggestions can be offered. The theory was first drawn from an examination of events in the lives of engineers and accountants. At least 16 other investigations, using a wide variety of populations (including some in the Communist countries), have since been completed, making the original research one of the most replicated studies in the field of job attitudes.

The findings of these studies, along with corroboration from many other investigations using different procedures, suggest that the factors involved in producing job satisfaction (and motivation) are separate and distinct from the factors that lead to job dissatisfaction. Since separate factors need to be considered, depending on whether job satisfaction or job dissatisfaction is being examined, it follows that these two feelings are not opposites of each other. The opposite of job satisfaction is not job dissatisfaction but, rather, *no* job satisfaction; and, similarly, the opposite of job dissatisfaction.

Stating the concept presents a problem in semantics, for we normally think of satisfaction and dissatisfaction as opposites—i.e., what is not satisfying must be dissatisfying, and vice versa. But when it comes to understanding the behavior of people in their jobs, more than a play on words is involved.

Two different needs of man are involved here. One set of needs can be thought of as stemming from his animal nature—the built-in drive to avoid pain from the environment, plus all the learned drives which become conditioned to the basic biological needs. For example, hunger, a basic biological drive, makes it necessary to earn money, and then money becomes a specific drive. The other set of needs relates to that unique human characteristic, the ability to achieve and, through achievement, to experience psychological growth. The stimuli for the growth needs are tasks that induce growth; in the industrial setting, they are the *job content*. Contrariwise, the stimuli inducing pain-avoidance behavior are found in the *job environment*.

The growth or *motivator* factors that are intrinsic to the job are: achievement, recognition for achievement, the work itself, responsibility, and growth or advancement. The dissatisfaction-avoidance or *hygiene* (KITA) factors that are extrinsic to the job include: company policy and administration, supervision, interpersonal relationships, working conditions, salary, status, and security.

A composite of the factors that are involved in causing job satisfaction and job dissatisfaction, drawn from samples of 1,685 employees, is shown in *Exhibit I*. The results indicate that motivators were the primary cause of satisfaction, and hygiene factors the primary cause of unhappiness on the job. The employees, studied in 12 different investigations, included lower-level supervisors, professional women, agricultural administrators, men about to retire from management positions, hospital maintenance personnel, manufacturing supervisors, nurses, food handlers, military officers, engineers, scientists, housekeepers, teachers, technicians, female assemblers, accountants, Finnish foremen, and Hungarian engineers.

They were asked what job events had occurred in their work that had led to extreme satisfaction or extreme dissatisfaction on their part. Their responses are broken down in the exhibit into percentages of total "positive" job events and of total "negative" job events. (The figures total more than 100% on both the "hygiene" and "motivators" sides because often at least two factors can be attributed to a single event; advancement, for instance, often accompanies assumption of responsibility.)

To illustrate, a typical response involving achievement that had a negative effect for the employee was, "I was unhappy because I didn't do the job successfully." A typical response in the small number of positive job events in the Company Policy and Administration grouping was, "I was happy because the company reorganized the section so that I didn't report any longer to the guy I didn't get along with."

As the lower right-hand part of the exhibit shows, of all the factors contributing to job satisfaction, 81% were motivators. And of all the factors contributing to the employees' dissatisfaction over their work, 69% involved hygiene elements.

Eternal Triangle

There are three general philosophies of personnel management. The first is based on organizational theory, the second on industrial engineering, and the third on behavioral science.

The organizational theorist believes that human needs are either so irrational or so varied and adjustable to specific situations that the major function of personnel management is to be as pragmatic as the occasion demands. If jobs are organized in a proper manner, he reasons, the result will be the most efficient job structure, and the most favorable job attitudes will follow as a matter of course.

The industrial engineer holds that man is mechanistically oriented and economically motivated and his needs are best met by attuning the individual to the most efficient work process. The goal of personnel management therefore should be to concoct the most appropriate incentive system and to design the specific working conditions in a way that facilitates the most efficient use of the human machine. By structuring jobs in a manner that leads to the most efficient operation, the engineer believes that he can obtain the optimal organization of work and the proper work attitudes.

The behavioral scientist focuses on group sentiments, attitudes of individual employees, and the

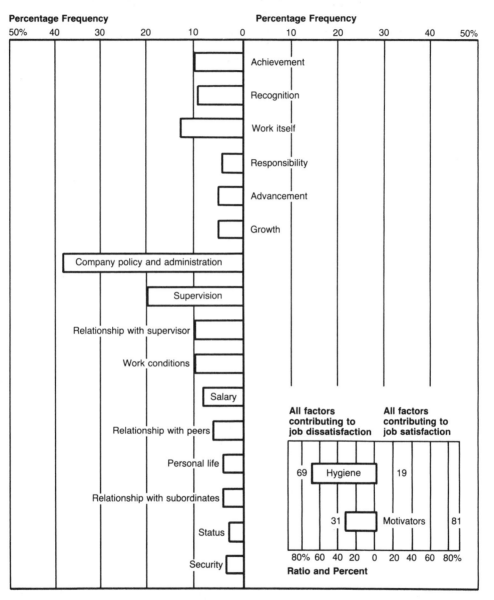

Factors characterizing 1,844 events on the job that led to *extreme dissatisfaction*

Factors characterizing 1,753 events on the job that led to *extreme satisfaction*

Percentage Frequency

50% 40 30 20 10 0 10 20 30 40 50%

- Achievement
- Recognition
- Work itself
- Responsibility
- Advancement
- Growth
- Company policy and administration
- Supervision
- Relationship with supervisor
- Work conditions
- Salary
- Relationship with peers
- Personal life
- Relationship with subordinates
- Status
- Security

All factors contributing to job dissatisfaction

All factors contributing to job satisfaction

| 69 | Hygiene | 19 |
| 31 | Motivators | 81 |

80% 60 40 20 0 20 40 60 80%

Ratio and Percent

organization's social and psychological climate. According to his persuasion, he emphasizes one or more of the various hygiene and motivator needs. His approach to personnel management generally emphasizes some form of human relations education, in the hope of instilling healthy employee attitudes and an organizational climate which he considers to be felic-itous to human values. He believes that proper attitudes will lead to efficient job and organizational structure.

There is always a lively debate as to the overall effectiveness of the approaches of the organizational theorist and the industrial engineer. Manifestly they have achieved much. But the nagging question for the behavioral scientist has been: What is the cost in human problems that eventually cause more expenses to the organization—for instance, turnover, absenteeism, errors, violation of safety rules, strikes, restriction of output, higher wages, and greater fringe benefits? On the other hand, the behavioral scientist is hard put to document much manifest improvement in personnel management, using his approach.

The three philosophies can be depicted as a triangle, as is done in *Exhibit II,* with each persuasion claiming the apex angle. The motivation-hygiene theory claims the same angle as industrial engineering, but for opposite goals. Rather than rationalizing the work to increase efficiency, the theory suggests that work be *enriched* to bring about effective utilization of personnel. Such a systematic attempt to motivate employees by manipulating the motivator factors is just beginning.

The term *job enrichment* describes this embryonic movement. An older term, job enlargement, should be avoided because it is associated with past failures stemming from a misunderstanding of the problem. Job enrichment provides the opportunity for the employee's psychological growth, while job enlargement merely makes a job structurally bigger. Since scientific job enrichment is very new, this article only suggests the principles and practical steps that have recently emerged from several successful experiments in industry.

EXHIBIT II
'Triangle' of Philosophies of Personnel Management.

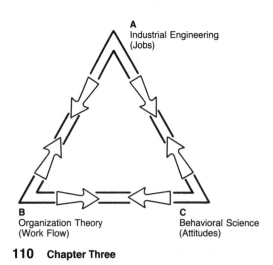

A
Industrial Engineering
(Jobs)

B
Organization Theory
(Work Flow)

C
Behavioral Science
(Attitudes)

Job Loading

In attempting to enrich an employee's job, management often succeeds in reducing the man's personal contribution, rather than giving him an opportunity for growth in his accustomed job. Such an endeavor, which I shall call horizontal job loading (as opposed to vertical loading or providing motivator factors), has been the problem of earlier job enlargement programs. This activity merely enlarges the meaninglessness of the job. Some examples of this approach, and their effect, are:

☐ Challenging the employee by increasing the amount of production expected of him. If he tightens 10,000 bolts a day, see if he can tighten 20,000 bolts a day. The arithmetic involved shows that multiplying zero by zero still equals zero.

☐ Adding another meaningless task to the existing one, usually some routine clerical activity. The arithmetic here is adding zero to zero.

☐ Rotating the assignments of a number of jobs that need to be enriched. This means washing dishes for a while, then washing silverware. The arithmetic is substituting one zero for another zero.

☐ Removing the most difficult parts of the assignment in order to free the worker to accomplish more of the less challenging assignments. This traditional industrial engineering approach amounts to subtraction in the hope of accomplishing addition.

These are common forms of horizontal loading that frequently come up in preliminary brainstorming sessions on job enrichment. The principles of vertical loading have not all been worked out as yet, and they remain rather general, but I have furnished seven useful starting points for consideration in *Exhibit III.*

A Successful Application

An example from a highly successful job enrichment experiment can illustrate the distinction between horizontal and vertical loading of a job. The subjects of this study were the stockholder correspondents employed by a very large corporation. Seemingly, the task required of these carefully selected and highly trained correspondents was quite complex and challenging. But almost all indexes of performance and job attitudes were low, and exit interviewing confirmed that the challenge of the job existed merely as words.

EXHIBIT III
Principles of Vertical Job Loading.

Principle	Motivators Involved
A. Removing some controls while retaining accountability	Responsibility and personal achievement
B. Increasing the accountability of individuals for own work	Responsibility and recognition
C. Giving a person a complete natural unit of work (module, division, area, and so on)	Responsibility, achievement, and recognition
D. Granting additional authority to an employee in his activity, job freedom	Responsibility, achievement, and recognition
E. Making periodic reports directly available to the worker himself rather than to the supervisor	Internal recognition
F. Introducing new and more difficult tasks not previously handled	Growth and learning
G. Assigning individals specific or specialized tasks, enabling them to become experts	Responsibility, growth and advancement

A job enrichment project was initiated in the form of an experiment with one group, designated as an achieving unit, having its job enriched by the principles described in *Exhibit III*. A control group continued to do its job in the traditional way. (There were also two "uncommitted" groups of correspondents formed to measure the so-called Hawthorne Effect—that is, to gauge whether productivity and attitudes toward the job changed artificially merely because employees sensed that the company was paying more attention to them in doing something different or novel. The results for these groups were substantially the same as for the control group, and for the sake of simplicity I do not deal with them in this summary.) No changes in hygiene were introduced for either group other than those that would have been made anyway, such as normal pay increases.

The changes for the achieving unit were introduced in the first two months, averaging one per week of the seven motivators listed in *Exhibit III*. At the end of six months the members of the achieving unit were found to be outperforming their counterparts in the control group, and in addition indicated a marked increase in their liking for their jobs. Other results showed that the achieving group had lower absenteeism and, subsequently, a much higher rate of promotion.

Exhibit IV illustrates the changes in performance, measured in February and March, before the study period began, and at the end of each month of the study period. The shareholder service index represents quality of letters, including accuracy of information, and speed of response to stockholders' letters of inquiry. The index of a current month was averaged into the average of the two prior months, which means that improvement was harder to obtain if the indexes of the previous months were low. The "achievers" were performing less well before the six-month period started, and their performance service index continued to decline after the introduction of the motivators, evidently because of uncertainty over their newly granted responsibilities. In the third month, however, performance improved, and soon the members of this group had reached a high level of accomplishment.

EXHIBIT IV
Shareholder Service Index in Company Experiment
[Three-Month Cumulative Average]

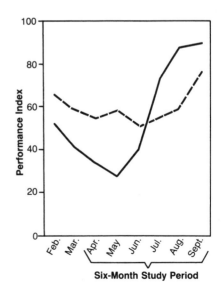

Exhibit V shows the two groups' attitudes toward their job, measured at the end of March, just before the first motivator was introduced, and again at the end of September. The correspondents were asked 16 questions, all involving motivation. A typical one was, "As you see it, how many opportunities do you feel that you have in your job for making worthwhile contributions?" The answers were scaled from 1 to 5, with 80 as the maximum possible score. The achievers became much more positive about their job, while the attitude of the control unit remained about the same (the drop is not statistically significant).

How was the job of these correspondents restructured? *Exhibit VI* lists the suggestions made that were deemed to be horizontal loading, and the actual vertical loading changes that were incorporated in the job of the achieving unit. The capital letters under "Principle" after "Vertical loading" refer to the corresponding letters in *Exhibit III*. The reader will note that the rejected forms of horizontal loading correspond closely to the list of common manifestations of the phenomenon on page 113, left column.

EXHIBIT V

Changes in Attitudes Toward Tasks in Company Experiment.
[Changes in Mean Scores over Six-Month Period

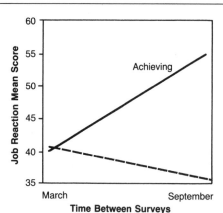

STEPS TO JOB ENRICHMENT

Now that the motivator idea has been described in practice, here are the steps that managers should take in instituting the principle with their employees.

1. Select those jobs in which (a) the investment in industrial engineering does not make changes too costly, (b) attitudes are poor, (c) hygiene is becoming very costly, and (d) motivation will make a difference in performance.

2. Approach these jobs with the conviction that they can be changed. Years of tradition had led managers to believe that the content of the jobs is sacrosanct and the only scope of action that they have is in ways of stimulating people.

3. Brainstorm a list of changes that may enrich the jobs, without concern for their practicality.

4. Screen the list to eliminate suggestions that involve hygiene, rather than actual motivation.

5. Screen the list for generalities, such as "give them more responsibility," that are rarely followed in practice. This might seem obvious, but the motivator words had never left industry; the substance has just been rationalized and organized out. Words like "responsibility," "growth," "achievement," and "challenge," for example, have been elevated to the lyrics of the patriotic anthem for all organizations. It is the old problem typified by the pledge of allegiance of the flag being more important than contributions to the country—of following the form, rather than the substance.

6. Screen the list to eliminate any *horizontal* loading suggestions.

7. Avoid direct participation by the employees whose jobs are to be enriched. Ideas they have expressed previously certainly constitute a valuable source for recommended changes, but their direct involvement contaminates the process with human relations *hygiene* and, more specifically, gives them only a *sense* of making a contribution. The job is to be changed, and it is the content that will produce the motivation, not attitudes about being involved or the challenge inherent in setting up a job. That process will be over shortly, and it is what the employees will be doing from then on that will determine their motivation. A sense of participation will result only in short-term movement.

8. In the initial attempts at job enrichment, set up a controlled experiment. At least two equivalent groups should be chosen, one an experimental unit in which the motivators are systematically introduced over a period of time, and the other one a control group in which no changes are made. For both groups, hygiene should be allowed to follow its natural course for the duration of the experiment. Pre- and post-installation tests of performance and

job attitudes are necessary to evaluate the effectiveness of the job enrichment program. The attitude test must be limited to motivator items in order to divorce the employee's view of the job he is given from all the surrounding hygiene feelings that he might have.

9. Be prepared for a drop in performance in the experimental group the first few weeks. The changeover to a new job may lead to a temporary reduction in efficiency.

10. Expect your first-line supervisors to experience some anxiety and hostility over the changes you are making. The anxiety comes from their fear that the changes will result in poorer performance for their unit. Hostility will arise when the employees start assuming what the supervisors regard as their own responsibility for performance. The supervisor without checking duties to perform may then be left with little to do.

After a successful experiment, however, the supervisor usually discovers the supervisory and managerial functions he has neglected, or which were never his because all his time was given over to checking the work of his subordinates. For example, in the R&D division of one large chemical company I know of, the supervisors of the laboratory assistants were theoretically responsible for their training and evaluation. These functions, however, had come to be performed in a routine, unsubstantial fashion. After the job enrichment program, during which the supervisors were not merely passive observers of the assistants' performance, the supervisors actually were devoting their time to reviewing performance and administering thorough training.

What has been called an employee-centered style of supervision will come about not through education of supervisors, but by changing the jobs that they do.

CONCLUDING NOTE

Job enrichment will not be a one-time proposition, but a continuous management function. The

EXHIBIT VI

Enlargement vs. Enrichment of Correspondents' Tasks in Company Experiment.

Horizontal Loading Suggestions (Rejected)	Vertical Loading Suggestions (Adopted)	Principle
Firm quotas could be set for letters to be answered each day, using a rate which would be hard to reach	Subject matter experts were appointed within each unit for other members of the unit to consult with before seeking supervisory help. (The supervisor had been answering all specialized and difficult questions.)	G
The women could type the letters themselves, as well as compose them, or take on any other clerical functions.	Correspondents signed their own names on letters. (The supervisor had been signing all letters.)	B
All difficult or complex inquiries could be channeled to a few women so that the remainder could achieve high rates of output. Thes jobs could be exchanged from time to time.	The work of the more experienced correspondents was proofread frequently by supervisors and was done at the correspondents' desks, dropping verification from 100% to 10%. (Previously, all correspondents' letters had been checked by the supervisor.)	A
The women could be rotated through units handling different customers, and then sent back to their own units.	Production was discussed, but only in terms such as "a full day's work is expected." As time went on, this was no longer mentioned. (Before, the group had been constantly reminded of the number of letters that needed to be answered.)	D
	Outgoing mail went directly to the mailroom without going over supervisors' desks. (The letters had always been routed through the supervisors.)	A
	Correspondents were encouraged to answer letters in a more personalized way. (Reliance on the form-letter approach had been standard practice.)	C
	Each correspondent was held personally responsible for the quality and accuracy of letters. (This responsibility had been the province of the supervisor and the verifier.)	B, E

initial changes, however, should last for a very long period of time. There are a number of reasons for this:

☐ The changes should bring the job up to the level of challenge commensurate with the skill that was hired.

☐ Those who have still more ability eventually will be able to demonstrate it better and win promotion to higher-level jobs.

☐ The very nature of motivators, as opposed to hygiene factors, is that they have a much longer-term effect on employees' attitudes. Perhaps the job will have to be enriched again, but this will not occur as frequently as the need for hygiene.

Not all jobs can be enriched, nor do all jobs need to be enriched. If only a small percentage of the time and money that is now devoted to hygiene, however, were given to job enrichment efforts, the return in human satisfaction and economic gain would be one of the largest dividends that industry and society have ever reaped through their efforts at better personnel management.

The argument for job enrichment can be summed up quite simply: If you have someone on a job, use him. If you can't use him on the job, get rid of him, either via automation or by selecting someone with lesser ability. If you can't use him and you can't get rid of him, you will have a motivation problem.

Designing Work for Individuals And for Groups

J. Richard Hackman

As yet there are no simple or generally accepted criteria for a well-designed job, nor is a single technology acknowledged as the proper way to go about redesigning work. Moreover, it often is unclear in specific circumstances whether work should be structured to be performed by individual employees, or whether it should be designed to be carried out by a *group* of employees working together.

The first part of this selection reviews one current model for work design that focuses on the individual performer. In the second part, discussion turns to a number of issues that must be dealt with when work is designed for interacting teams of employees.

DESIGNING WORK FOR INDIVIDUALS

A model specifying how job characteristics and individual differences interact to affect the satisfaction, motivation, and productivity of individuals at work has been proposed by Hackman and Oldham

Reprinted with permission from J. R. Hackman, E. E. Lawler III, and L. W. Porter (eds.), *Perspectives on Behavior on Organizations* (New York: McGraw-Hill Book Company, 1977).

(1976). The model is specifically intended for use in planning and carrying out changes in the design of jobs. It is described below, and then is used as a guide for a discussion of diagnostic procedures and change principles that can be used in redesigning the jobs of individuals.

The Job Characteristics Model

The basic job characteristics model is shown in Figure 19-1. As illustrated in the figure, five core job dimensions are seen as creating three critical psychological states which, in turn, lead to a number of beneficial personal and work outcomes. The links among the job dimensions, the psychological states, and the outcomes are shown to be moderated by the strength of individuals' growth needs. The major classes of variables in the model are reviewed briefly below.

Psychological States. The three following psychological states are postulated as critical in affecting a person's motivation and satisfaction on the job:

1. Experienced meaningfulness: The person must experience the work as generally important, valuable, and worthwhile.

FIGURE 19-1

The Job Characteristics Model of Work Motivation.

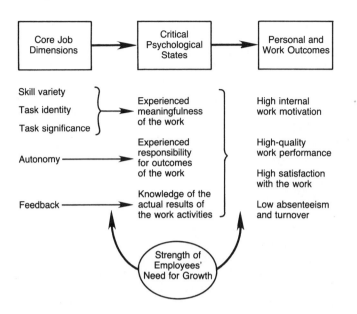

2. Experienced responsibility: The individual must feel personally responsible and accountable for the results of the work he or she performs.

3. Knowledge of results: The individual must have understanding, on a fairly regular basis, of how effectively he or she is performing the job.

The more these three conditions are present, the more people will feel good about themselves when they perform well. Or, following Hackman and Lawler (1971), the model postulates that internal rewards are obtained by individuals when they *learn* (knowledge of results) that they *personally* (experienced responsibility) have performed well on a task that they *care about* (experienced meaningfulness). These internal rewards are reinforcing to the individual, and serve as incentives for continued efforts to perform well in the future. When the persons do not perform well, they do not experience a reinforcing state of affairs, and may elect to try harder in the future so as to regain the rewards that good performance brings. The net result is a self-perpetuating cycle of positive work motivation powered by self-generated rewards, that is predicted to continue until one or more of the three psychological states is no longer present—or until the individual no longer values the internal rewards that derive from good performance.

Job Dimensions. Of the five job characteristics shown in Figure 19-1 as fostering the emergence of the psychological states, three contribute to the experienced meaningfulness of the work, and one each contributes to experienced responsibility and to knowledge of results.

The three job dimensions that contribute to a job's *meaningfulness* are:

1. *Skill variety* The degree to which a job requires a variety of different activities in carrying out the work, which involve the use of a number of different skills and talents of the person.

When a task requires a person to engage in activities that challenge or stretch his or her skills and abilities, that task almost invariably is experienced as meaningful by the individual. Many parlor games, puzzles, and recreational activities, for example, achieve much of their fascination because they tap and test the intellective or motor skills of the people who do them. When a job draws upon several skills of an employee, that individual may find the job to be of very high personal meaning—even if, in any absolute sense, it is not of great significance or importance.

2. *Task identity* The degree to which the job requires completion of a "whole" and identifiable

piece of work—that is, doing a job from beginning to end with a visible outcome.

If an employee assembles a complete product or provides a complete product of service he or she should find the work more meaningful than if he or she were responsible for only a small part of the whole job—other things (such as skill variety) being equal.

3. *Task significance* The degree to which the job has a substantial impact on the lives or work of other people—whether in the immediate organization or in the external environment.

When individuals understand that the results of their work may have a significant effect on the well-being of other people, the experienced meaningfulness of the work usually is enhanced. Employees who tighten nuts on aircraft brake assemblies, for example, are more likely to perceive their work as meaningful than are workers who fill small boxes with paper clips—even though the skill levels involved may be comparable.

The job characteristic predicted to prompt feelings of personal *responsibility* for the work outcomes is autonomy. "Autonomy" is defined as the degree to which the job provides substantial freedom, independence, and discretion to the individual in scheduling the work and in determining the procedures to be used in carrying it out.

To the extent that autonomy is high, work outcomes will be viewed by workers as depending substantially on their *own* efforts, initiatives, and decisions, rather than on the adequacy of instructions from the boss or on a manual of job procedures. In such circumstances, individuals should feel a strong personal responsibility for the successes and failures that occur on the job.

The job characteristic that fosters *knowledge of results* is "feedback," which is defined as the degree to which carrying out the work activities required by the job results in the individual's obtaining direct and clear information about the effectiveness of his or her performance.

It often is useful to combine the scores of a job on the five dimensions described above into a single index reflecting the overall potential of the job to prompt self-generated work motivation on the part of job incumbents. Following the model diagrammed in Figure 19-1, a job high in motivating potential must be high on at least one (and hopefully more) of the three dimensions that lead to experienced meaningfulness, *and* high on autonomy and feedback as well—thereby creating conditions for all three of the critical psychological states to be present. Arithmetically, scores of

jobs on the five dimensions are combined as follows to meet this criterion:

Motivating potential score (MPS) =

$$\left(\frac{\substack{\text{skill} \\ \text{variety}} + \substack{\text{task} \\ \text{identity}} + \substack{\text{task} \\ \text{significance}}}{3} \right)$$

$$\times \text{ autonomy} \times \text{ job feedback}$$

As can be seen from the formula, a near-zero score of a job on either autonomy or feedback will reduce the overall MPS to near-zero; whereas a near-zero score on one of the three job dimensions that contribute to experienced meaningfulness cannot, by itself, do so.

Strength of the Individual's Need for Growth. The strength of a person's need for growth is postulated to moderate how people react to complex, challenging work at two points in the model shown in Figure 19-1: first, at the link between the objective job dimensions and the psychological states, and again between the psychological states and the outcome variables. The first link means that persons with a high need for growth are more likely (or better able) to *experience* the psychological states when an objective job is enriched than persons with a low need for growth. The second link means that individuals with a high need for growth will respond more positively to the psychological states, when they are present, than persons with a low need for growth.

Outcome Variables. Also shown in Figure 19-1 are several outcomes that are affected by the level of self-generated motivation experienced by people at work. Of special interest as an outcome variable is internal work motivation (Lawler & Hall, 1970; Hackman & Lawler, 1971), because it taps directly the contingency between effective performance and self-administered affective rewards. Typically questionnaire items measuring internal work motivation include: (1) I feel a great sense of personal satisfaction when I do this job well; (2) I feel bad and unhappy when I discover that I have performed poorly on this job; and (3) My own feelings are *not* affected much one way or the other by how well I do on this job (reversed scoring).

Other outcomes listed in Figure 19-1 are the quality of work performance, job satisfaction (especially satisfaction with opportunities for personal growth and development on the job), absenteeism, and turnover. All these outcomes are predicted to be affected positively by a job high in motivating potential.

Validity of the Job Characteristics Model

Empirical testing of the job characteristics model of work motivation is reported in detail elsewhere (Hackman & Oldham, 1976). In general, results are supportive, as suggested by the following overview:

1. People who work on jobs high on the core job characteristics are more motivated, satisfied, and productive than people who work on jobs that score low on these characteristics. The same is true for absenteeism, although less strongly so.

2. Responses to jobs high in objective motivating potential are more positive for people who have strong needs for growth than for people with weak needs for growth. The moderating effect of an individual's need for growth occurs both at the link betweeen the job dimensions and the psychological states and at the link between the psychological states and the outcome measures, as shown in Figure 19-1. (This moderating effect is not, however, obtained for absenteeism.)

3. The job characteristics operate *through* the psychological states in influencing the outcome variables, as predicted by the model, rather than influencing the outcomes directly. Two anomalies have been identified, however: (1) results involving the feedback dimension are in some cases less strong than for those obtained for the other dimensions (perhaps in part because individuals receive feedback at work from many sources—not just the job), and (2) the linkage between autonomy and experienced responsibility does not operate exactly as specified by the model in affecting the outcome variables (Hackman & Oldham, 1976).

Diagnostic Use of the Model

The job characteristics model was designed so that each major class of variables (objective job characteristics, mediating psychological states, strength of the individual's need for growth, and work motivation and satisfaction) can be directly measured in actual work situations. Such measurements are obtained using the Job Diagnostic Survey (JDS), which is described in detail elsewhere (Hackman &

Oldham, 1975). The major intended uses of the JDS are (1) to diagnose existing jobs before planned work redesign, and (2) to evaluate the effects of work redesign—for example, to determine which job dimensions did and did not change, to assess the impact of the changes on the motivation and satisfaction of employees, and to test for any possible alterations after the change in the need for growth of people whose jobs were redesigned.

In the paragraphs to follow, several steps are presented that might be followed by a change agent in carrying out a diagnosis using the JDS.

Step 1: Are Motivation and Satisfaction Really Problems? Sometimes organizations undertake job enrichment or work redesign to improve work motivation and satisfaction when in fact the real problem with work performance lies elsewhere—for example, in the equipment or technology of the job. It is important, therefore, to examine the level of employees' motivation and satisfaction at an early stage in a job diagnosis. If motivation and satisfaction are problems, and are accompanied by documented problems in work performance, absenteeism, or turnover as revealed by independent organizational indices, the change agent would continue to step 2. If not, the agent presumably would look to other aspects of the work situation (e.g., the technology, the workflow) to identify and understand the reasons for the problem which gave rise to the diagnostic activity.

Step 2: Is the Job Low in Motivating Potential? To answer this question, the change agent would examine the Motivating Potential Score of the target job, and compare it with the MPS scores of other jobs to determine whether or not the *job itself* is a probable cause of the motivational problems documented in step 1. If the job turns out to be low on MPS, he would continue to step 3; if it scores high, he would look for other reasons for the motivational difficulties (e.g., the pay plan, the nature of supervision, and so on).

Step 3: What Specific Aspects of the Job Are Causing the Difficulty? This step involves examination of the job on each of the five core job dimensions, to pinpoint the specific strengths and weaknesses of the job as it currently exists. It is useful at this stage to construct a profile of the target job, to make visually apparent where improvements need to be made. An illustrative profile for two jobs (one "good" job and one job needing improvement) is shown in Figure 19-2.

Job A is an engineering maintenance job, and is high on all of the core dimensions; the MPS of this job is very high: 260.[1] Job enrichment would not be recommended for this job; if employees working on the job are unproductive and unhappy, the reasons probably have little to do with the design of the work itself.

FIGURE 19-2
JDS Profile of a "Good" Job and a "Bad" Job.

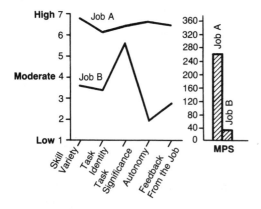

Job B, on the other hand, has many problems. This job involves the routine and repetitive processing of checks in a bank. The MPS of 30—which is quite low—would be even lower if it were not for the moderately high task significance of the job. (Task signifiance is moderately high because the people are handling large amounts of other people's money, and their efforts potentially have important consequences for the unseen clients.) The job provides the individuals with very little direct feedback about how effectively they are performing; the employees have little autonomy in how they go about doing the job; and the job is moderately low in both skill variety and task identity.

For Job B, then, there is plenty of room for improvement, and many avenues to consider in planning job changes. For still other jobs, the avenues for change may turn out to be considerably more specific: for example, feedback and autonomy may be reasonably high, but one or more of the core dimensions which contribute to the experienced meaningfulness of the work (i.e., skill variety, task identity, and task significance) may be low. In such a case, attention would turn to ways to increase the standing of the job on these latter three dimensions.

---

[1]MPS scores can range from 1 to 343. The average is about 125.

Step 4: How Ready Are the Employees for Change? Once it has been documented that there is need for improvement in the focal job, and the particularly troublesome aspects of the job have been identified, then it is appropriate to begin planning the specific action steps which will be taken to enrich the job. An important factor in such planning is determining the strength of the employees' needs for growth, since employees whose needs for growth are strong should respond more readily to job enrichment than employees whose needs are weak. The measure of the need for growth provided by the JDS can be helpful in identifying which employees should be among the first to have jobs changed (i.e., those whose needs for growth are strong), and how such changes should be introduced (e.g., perhaps with more caution for individuals whose needs for growth are weak).

Step 5: What Special Problems and Opportunities Are Present in the Existing Work System? Before undertaking actual job changes, it is always advisable to search for any special roadblocks that may exist in the organizational unit as it currently exists, and for special opportunities that may be built upon in the change program.

Frequently of special importance in this regard in this level of *satisfaction* employees currently experience with various aspects of their organizational life. For example, the JDS provides measures of satisfaction with pay, job security, co-workers, and supervision. If the diagnosis reveals high dissatisfaction in one or more of these areas, then it may be very difficult to initiate and maintain a successful job redesign project (Oldham, 1976; Oldham, Hackman & Pearce, 1976). On the other hand, if satisfaction with supervision is especially high, then it might be wise to build an especially central role for supervisors in the initiation and management of the change process.

Other examples could be given as well. The point is simply that such supplementary measures (especially those having to do with aspects of employee satisfaction) may be helpful in highlighting special problems and opportunities that deserve explicit recognition and attention as part of the diagnosis of an existing work system.

Principles for Enriching Jobs

The core job dimensions specified in the job-characteristics model are tied directly to a set of action principles for redesigning jobs (Hackman,

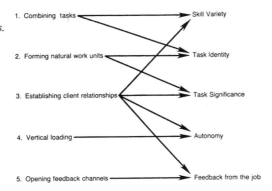

FIGURE 19–3
Principles for Changing Jobs.

1. Combining tasks → Skill Variety
2. Forming natural work units → Task Identity
3. Establishing client relationships → Task Significance
4. Vertical loading → Autonomy
5. Opening feedback channels → Feedback from the job

Oldham, Janson & Purdy, 1975; Walters & Associates, 1975). As shown in Figure 19-3, these principles specify what types of changes in jobs are most likely to lead to improvements in each of the five core job dimensions, and thereby to an increase in the motivating potential of the job as a whole.

Principle 1: Forming Natural Work Units. A critical step in the design of any job is the decision about how the work is to be distributed among the people who do it. Consider, for example, a typing pool—consisting of one supervisor and ten typists— that does all the typing for one division of an organization. Jobs are delivered in rough draft or dictated form to the supervisor, who distributes them as evenly as possibly among the typists. In such circumstances the individual letters, reports, and other tasks performed by a given typist in one day or week are randomly assigned. There is no basis for identifying with the work or the person or department for whom it is performed, or for placing any personal value upon it.

By contrast, creating natural units of work increases employees' "ownership" of the work, and therefore improves the chances that employees will view it as meaningful and important rather than as irrelevant and boring. In creating natural units of work, one must first identify what the basic work items are. In the typing pool example, that might be "pages to be typed." Then these items are grouped into natural and meaningful categories. For example, each typist might be assigned continuing responsibility for all work requested by a single department or by several smaller departments. Instead of typing one section of a large report, the individual will type the entire piece of work, with the knowledge of exactly what the total outcome of the work is. Furthermore, over a period of time the typists will develop a growing sense of how the work affects co-workers or customers who receive the completed product. Thus,

as shown in Figure 19-3, forming natural units of work increases two of the core job dimensions that contribute to experienced meaningfulness—task identity and task significance.

It is still important that work be distributed so that the system as a whole operates efficiently, of course, and workloads must be arranged so that they are approximately equal among employees. The principle of natural work units simply requires that these traditional criteria be supplemented so that, insofar as possible, the tasks that arrive at an employee's work station form an identifiable and meaningful whole.

Principle 2: Combining Tasks. The very existence of a pool made up entirely of persons whose sole function is typing, reflects a fractionalization of jobs that sometimes can lead to such hidden costs as high absenteeism and turnover, extra supervisory time, and so on. The principle of combining tasks is based on the assumption that such costs often can be reduced by simply taking existing and fractionalized tasks and putting them back together again to form a new and larger module of work. At the Medfield, Massachusetts plant of Corning Glass Works, for example, the job of assembling laboratory hotplates was redesigned by combining a number of previously separate tasks. After the change, each hotplate was assembled from start to finish by one operator, instead of going through several separate operations performed by different people.

Combining tasks (like forming natural work units) contributes in two ways to experienced meaningfulness of the work. First, task identity is increased. The hotplate assembler, for example, can see and identify with a finished product ready for shipment—rather than a nearly invisible junction of solder. Moreover, as more tasks are combined into a single worker's job, the individual must use a greater variety of skills in performing the job, further increasing the meaningfulness of the work.

Principle 3: Establishing Relationships with Clients. By establishing direct relationships between workers and their clients, jobs often can be improved in three ways. First, feedback increases because additional opportunities are created for the employees to receive direct praise or criticism of their work outputs. Second, skill variety may increase, because of the need to develop and exercise one's interpersonal skills in managing and maintaining the relationship with the client. Finally, autonomy will increase to the degree that individuals are given real personal responsibility for deciding how to manage their relationships with the people who receive the outputs of their work.

Creating relationships with clients can be viewed as a three-step process: (1) identification of who the client actually is; (2) establishing the most direct contact possible between the worker and the client; and (3) establishing criteria and procedures so that the client can judge the quality of the product or service received and relay his judgments directly back to the worker. Especially important (and, in many cases, difficult to achieve) is identification of the specific criteria by which the work output is assessed by the client—and ensuring that both the worker and the client understand these criteria and agree with them.

Principle 4: Vertical Loading. In vertical loading, the intent is to partially close the gap between the "doing" and the "controlling" aspects of the job. Thus, when a job is vertically loaded, responsibilities and controls that formerly were reserved for management are given to the employee as part of the job. Among ways this might be achieved are the following:

☐ Giving the job incumbents responsibility for deciding on work methods, and for advising or helping train less experienced workers.

☐ Providing increased freedom in time management, including decisions about when to start and stop work, when to take a break, and how to assign work priorities.

☐ Encouraging workers to do their own trouble-shooting and manage work crises, rather than calling immediately for a supervisor.

☐ Providing workers with increased knowledge of the financial aspects of the job and the organization, and increased control over budgetary matters that affect their own work.

When a job is vertically loaded, it inevitably increases in *autonomy*. And, as shown in Figure 19-1,

this should lead to increased feelings of personal responsibility and accountability for the work outcomes.

Principle 5: Opening Feedback Channels. In virtually all jobs there are ways to open channels of feedback to individuals to help them learn not only how well they are performing their jobs, but also whether their performance is improving, deteriorating, or remaining at a constant level. While there are various sources from which information about performance can come, it usually is advantageous for workers to learn about their performance *directly as they do the job*—rather than from management on an occasional basis.

Feedback provided by the job itself is more immediate and private than feedback provided by its supervisor, and can also increase workers' feelings of personal control over their work. Moreover, it avoids many of the potentially disruptive interpersonal problems which can develop when workers can find out how they are doing only by means of direct messages or subtle cues from the boss.

Exactly what should be done to open channels for feedback from the job varies from job to job and organization to organization. In many cases, the changes involve simply removing existing blocks which isolate the individual from naturally occurring data about performance, rather than generating entirely new feedback mechanisms. For example:

Establishing direct relationships with clients (discussed above) often removes blocks between the worker and natural external sources of data about the work.

Quality control in many organizations often eliminates a natural source of feedback, because all quality checks are done by people other than the individuals responsible for the work. In such cases, feedback to the workers, if there is any, may be belated and diluted. By placing most quality-control functions in the hands of workers themselves, the quantity and quality of data available to them about their own performance will dramatically increase.

Tradition and established procedure in many organizations dictate that records about performance be kept by a supervisor and transmitted up (not down) the organizational hierarchy. Sometimes supervisors even check the work and correct any errors themselves. The worker who made the error never knows it occurred and is therefore denied the very information which can enhance both internal work motivation and the technical adequacy of his performance. In many cases, it is possible to provide standard summaries of performance records directly to the workers (and perhaps also to their superiors), thereby giving employees personally and regularly the data they need to improve their effectiveness.

Computers and other automated machines sometimes can be used to provide individuals with data now blocked from them. Many clerical operations, for example, are now performed on computer consoles. These consoles often can be programmed to provide the clerk with immediate feedback in the form of a CRT display or a printout indicating that an error has been made. Some systems even have been programmed to provide the operator with a positive feedback message when a period of error-free performance has been sustained.

Conclusion. The principles for redesigning jobs reviewed above, while illustrative of the kinds of changes that can be made to improve the jobs of individuals in organizations, obviously are not exhaustive. They were selected for attention here because of the links (Figure 19-3) between the principles and the core job dimensions in the motivational model presented earlier. Other principles for enriching jobs (which, although often similar to those presented here, derive from alternative conceptual frameworks) are presented by Ford (1969), Glaser (1975), Herzberg (1974), and Katzell and Yankelovich (1975, chap. 6).

DESIGNING WORK FOR TEAMS

Often it is easier or more appropriate, given the nature of the work to be done and the organizational circumstances under which it is to be done, to design work for interacting teams rather than for individuals working alone. In such cases, the ultimate aim generally is similar to that sought when individual job enrichment is carried out: that is, to improve the quality of the work experience of the people involved, and simultaneously to increase the quality and quantity of the work produced. The difference is that the work is defined and implemented as a *group* task, rather than as an interconnected set of individual tasks. Because of this, a larger chunk of work can be included within the boundaries of the task, thereby increasing the intrinsic meaningfulness of the work. Moreover, the possibility is increased for the development of close, socially satisfying work relationships among team members. Such relationships are highly valued by many people, but difficult or impossible to achieve by means of redesign of individual jobs in such

work settings as assembly lines, where individual work stations may be fixed and so widely separated that meaningful social interaction with others is (for all practical purposes) precluded.

Until relatively recently, most work design for teams has been carried out from the perspective of sociotechnical systems theory, and has involved the creation of autonomous or semi-autonomous work groups. Specific arrangements (e.g., how the group task itself is designed, the size and composition of the work group, the nature of the reward system) have varied from project to project, but the following attributes are characteristic of most autonomous work groups:[2]

1. A "whole" task for the group, in which the mission of the group is sufficiently identifiable and significant that members find the work of the group meaningful.

2. Workers who each have a number of the skills required for completion of the group task, thereby increasing the flexibility of the group in carrying out the task. When individuals do not have a robust repertoire of skills initially, procedures are developed to encourage cross-training among members.

3. Autonomy for the group to make decisions about the methods by which the work is carried out, the scheduling of various activities, the assignment of different individuals to different tasks, and (sometimes) the selection of new group members.

4. Compensation based on the performance of the group as a whole, rather than on the contributions of individual group members.

It should be emphasized that these four ingredients are simply summary statements of the kinds of changes that often are made when work is redesigned for interacting teams. They do not represent the only way to design work for groups, nor are these ingredients necessarily the most appropriate ones for any given instance. Therefore, it may be useful to step back from specific change principles and attempt to identify the major *general* criteria for the design of work for teams—and then to explore alternative strategies for attempting to achieve those criteria.

_____

[2]See, for example, Bucklow (1966), Davis (1966, p. 44). Davis and Trist (1974), Gulowsen (1972) pp. 375-378), and Trist, Higgin, Murray, and Pollock (1963, chap. 9).

Design Criteria for Interacting Work Groups

The two criteria listed below appear to be the minimum requirements for the design of interacting work teams if high productivity by the team and the satisfaction of its members are to be achieved simultaneously.

1. The team itself should be a cohesive group, in which members feel committed to the goals of the group, and in which they can experience significant personal satisfaction through their interactions with teammates.

In a highly cohesive group, members greatly value the rewards (usually interpersonal) that fellow members can provide. This means that the quality of the social experience of members in cohesive groups is likely to be high rather than low. It also means that cohesive groups usually have a considerable leverage in enforcing member compliance with group norms. That is, since members of cohesive groups strongly value the rewards controlled by their peers, they are especially likely to engage in behavior that is congruent with group norms. Failure to do so can result in those rewards being made unavailable to them (e.g., being "frozen out") or can lead other group members to negatively sanction their actions (Hackman, 1976).

The problem is that while cohesive groups have been shown to generate a high degree of uniformity of behavior in terms of group norms, the *direction* of those norms is unrelated to the level of cohesiveness of the group (Berkowitz, 1954; Schachter, Ellertson, McBride, & Gregory, 1951; Seashore, 1954). Sometimes highly cohesive groups enforce a norm of low performance; at other times they encourage and support members' efforts toward high performance. Relatively little is known about what factors determine whether group norms will encourage high or low performance (e.g., Lawler & Cammann, 1972; Vroom, 1969, pp. 226-227). It is necessary, therefore, to propose an additional criterion for the design of work teams in organizations.

2. The environment of the work group, including its task, must be such that the group norms that emerge and are enforced are consistent with the two aims of high productivity and satisfying interpersonal relationships.

Approaches to Work Design for Interacting Groups

Meeting the two design criteria identified above requires, at minimum, attention to (1) the composition and dynamics of the group itself, (2) reward contingencies in the organizational environment, and (3) the structure of the group task. These matters are explored below.

Design and Maintenance of the Group qua Group. It is important that members of an interacting work team be able to experience themselves as part of a group that is *psychologically meaningful* to them. Usually this requires that the group be moderately small (usually less than fifteen members, although apparently successful autonomous work groups of larger size have been reported), and that members occupy a single workplace (or at least contiguous workplaces with easy access to one another). Merely calling a set of people a "group" for reasons other than the nature of their relationships with each other (e.g., a set of flight attendants who have the same supervisor but who literally fly all over the country and rarely see one another) does not meet the conditions for creation of an effective work team.

Moreover, while reasonably close and meaningful interpersonal relationships can be important to the success of interacting work teams, group process interventions (e.g., "team building") that focus *exclusively* on relationships among group members—or on the social climate of the group as a whole—should be used with caution. Direct interpersonal interventions can be quite powerful in altering social behavior in a group, and for this reason they may be very useful in increasing the capability and willingness of members to share with one another special skills that are needed for work on the group task. Yet research also shows that when such interventions are used alone, the group's task effectiveness rarely is enhanced (and often suffers) as a result (cf. Hackman & Morris, 1975; Herold, in press). Thus, while process interventions can be of great use as part of a broader intervention package aimed at creating effective work teams, total reliance on such interventions appears inappropriate if the goal is to work toward simultaneous improvement of the social experience of the members *and* their collective task productivity.

Design of Environmental Contingencies. The way the organizational environment of the group is arranged can affect whether or not it is in the best interest of group members to work together effectively and, indeed, whether or not it is *possible* for them to do so. Especially important in this regard are the compensation system and the role of the first-line supervisor.

In almost every case in which autonomous work groups have been successfully created in organizations, pay systems have been arranged so that members were paid on a basis of the performance of the group as a whole, rather than in terms of the level of performance of individual employees. Moving to a group-based compensation system increases the chances that internal cooperation and cohesiveness will increase as members work together to obtain the group-level rewards. Moreover, dysfunctional group interaction that grows from the fear (or the fact) of pay inequities among members should diminish when compensation is tied directly to the output of the group as a whole. It should be noted, however, that simply moving to a group-level compensation system does *not* eliminate the possibility of less than optimal productivity norms. When group members mistrust management, for example, norms enforcing low productivity may emerge to protect the group against possible changes of performance standards by management. Thus, while group-level compensation plans play an important part in the design of work for interacting teams, they in no way guarantee high group productivity.

Also critical to the design of work for teams is the new role that first-line supervisors play under such arrangements. In many applications, the supervisor moves from having day-to-day (even minute-to-minute) responsibility for the work behavior and productivity of individual employees to a role that primarily involves managing the *boundaries* of the group—not what goes on within those boundaries (Taylor, 1971). Thus, the supervisor assists the group in liaison with other groups, and may serve as the advocate of the group in discussion with higher management, but routine decision-making about the work and management of work crises is left to the group. Under such conditions, group members should experience substantially more ownership of their work activities and output, thereby creating the conditions required for members to experience collective responsibility for—and commitment to—their shared task.

Design of the Group Task. One of the greatest determinants of whether a group develops a norm of high or low productivity is the design of the group task itself. What task characteristics are likely to prompt high group commitment to effective performance? As a start, the five core dimensions used in the job characteristics model of individual work motivation would seem useful (i.e., skill variety, task identity, task significance, autonomy, and feedback).

There is no reason why such dimensions could not be applied to the analysis of group tasks just as they are to individual tasks.

If group tasks were designed to be high on these or similar job dimensions, then an increase in the task-relevant motivation of group members would be expected—and, over time, group norms about productivity should become consistent with the increased motivation of individual group members. Yet, such positive outcomes should come about only (1) if the individual group members identify with and feel commitment to the group as a whole (it is, after all, a *group* task), and (2) if the internal process of the group facilitates and reinforces (rather than impairs) concerted action toward shared group goals.

The core job dimensions have little to offer toward the creation of these two conditions. How, for example, could a group task be designed so that all members see it as providing high autonomy—and therefore experience substantial *personal* responsibility for the outcomes of the *group?* Moreover, given that it is now well documented that how group tasks are designed affects not only the motivation of group members, but also the patterns of social interaction that develop among them (Hackman & Morris, 1975), how can group tasks be structured so that they prompt task-effective rather than dysfunctional interaction among members?

Such questions have no simple answers. And while task design *per se* potentially can contribute to their solution, the issues raised also are affected by the environmental contingencies that are operative, and by the design and composition of the group itself. Thus, once again, it must be concluded that no single approach can create an effective design for work to be done by interacting teams. Instead, such a goal requires simultaneous use of a number of different handles for change—some of which have to do with the group, some with the task, and some with the broader organizational contexts.

Group versus Individual Task Design: Which When?

Choices for designing work for individuals or for groups are complex, and in many cases depend on factors idiosyncratic to a given situation. In general, however, a group-based design seems indicated when one or more of the following conditions is present:

1. When the product, service, or technology is such that meaningful individual work is not realistically possible (e.g., when a large piece of heavy

equipment is being produced). In such cases it often is possible for a group to take autonomous reponsibility for an entire product or service—while the only possible job design for individuals would involve small segments of the work (cf. Walton, 1975).

2. When the technology or physical work setting is such that high interdependence among workers is required. For example, Susman (1970) has suggested that one effect of increased automation (especially in continuous process production) is to increase interdependence among workers. The creation of autonomous work groups under such circumstances would seem to be a rather natural extension of the imperatives of the technology itself. When, on the other hand, there are no required interdependencies (e.g., telephone installers who operate their own trucks, coordinating only with a foreman or dispatcher), then there would seem to be no real basis on which meaningful work teams could be formed, and enrichment of individual jobs might be a better alternative.

3. When individuals have strong social needs—and the enrichment of individual jobs would run significant risk of breaking up existing groups of workers that provide social satisfactions to their members. In such cases, designing work for teams would capitalize on the needs of employees, whereas individual-oriented job enrichment might require that individuals give up important social satisfactions to obtain a better job (Reif & Luthans, 1972).

4. When the overall motivating potential of employees' jobs would be expected to be *considerably* higher if the work were arranged as a group task rather than as a set of individual tasks. Probably in most cases the standing of a job on the core dimensions would increase if the job were designed as a group task, simply because a larger piece of work can be done by a group than by an individual. This should not, however, automatically tilt the decision toward group work design—there are numerous interpersonal factors that must be attended to in effectively designing work for interacting groups. Sometimes the risk or effort required to deal with such factors may make it more appropriate to opt for individual task design, even though a group task might be expected to be somewhat better *as a task* than would be any of the individual tasks.

Cautions in Designing Work for Groups

In conclusion, three caveats about the design of work for groups are suggested:

1. Existing evidence suggests that the work must provide group members with *substantial* autonomy if they are to experience high responsibility for it. Just as "pseudo-participation" in organizations may be worse than no participation at all, so it is that autonomous work groups should not be formed unless there is reasonable assurance that the result will not be a potentially frustrating state of "pseudo-autonomy." This, of course, requires careful attention to issues of management and supervision, to ensure that managers are both willing and able to provide the group with sufficient real autonomy to carry out the proposed group task (cf. Gulowsen, 1972).

2. The needs of employees who will make up the groups must be carefully attended to, because work in interacting teams on a complex task will not be satisfying or motivating to all people. Optimally, the need of group members for both social interaction and growth should be rather high. If the social needs of group members are high but their needs for growth are low, then there is risk that the group members will use the group soley as a source of social satisfaction. Even if the task were very high in objective motivating potential, members might find the group so much more involving than the task that productivity would suffer. When, on the other hand, members have a high need for growth but low needs for social interaction, then it might be better to consider designing the work for individuals, if technology permits. If employees have both low social needs and low needs for growth, then prospects for creating teams in which members work together effectively and productively on a challenging task would appear very dim indeed.

3. Finally, it should be noted that virtually all of the above discussion has focused on characteristics of groups and of tasks that are likely to generate high *motivation* to perform the task effectively. For some group tasks, the level of motivation (or effort) of group members is not critical to the success of the group; instead, the effectiveness of the performance varies simply with the level of knowledge and skill of the members, or with the peformance strategies utilized by the group (cf. Hackman & Morris, 1975). In such circumstances, the attributes of the group, the task, and the environment that would be required for a high degree of group effectiveness would be quite different from those proposed here.

REFERENCES

Berkowitz, L. Group standards, cohesiveness and productivity. *Human Relations*, 1954, 7, 509-519.

Bucklow, M. A new role for the work group. *Administrative Science Quarterly, 1966,* **11,** 59-78.

Davis, L. E. The design of jobs. *Industrial Relations,* 1966, **6,** 21-45.

Davis, L. E., & Trist, E. L. Improving the quality of work life: Sociotechnical case studies. In J. O'Toole (Ed.), *Work and the quality of life.* Cambridge, Mass.: MIT Press, 1974.

Ford, R. N. *Motivation through the work itself.* New York: American Management Association, 1969.

Glaser, E. M. *Improving the quality of worklife . . . And in the process, improving productivity.* Los Angeles: Human Interaction Research Institute, 1975.

Gulowsen, J. A measure of work group autonomy. In L. E. Davis & J. C. Taylor (Eds.), *Design of jobs.* Middlesex, England: Penguin, 1972.

Hackman, J. R. Group influences on individuals in organizations. In M. D. Dunnette (Ed.), *Handbook of industrial and organizational psychology.* Chicago: Rand McNally, 1976.

Hackman, J. R., & Lawler, E. E. Employee reactions to job characteristics. *Journal of Applied Psychology Monograph,* 1971, **55,** 259-286.

Hackman, J. R., & Morris, C. G. Group tasks, group interaction process, and group performance effectiveness: A review and proposed integration. In L. Berkowitz (Ed.), *Advances in experimental social psychology* (Vol. 8). New York: Academic Press, 1975.

Hackman, J. R., & Oldham, G. R. Development of the Job Diagnostic Survey. *Journal of Applied Psychology,* 1975, **60,** 159-170.

Hackman, J. R., & Oldham, G. R. Motivation through the design of work: Test of a theory. *Organizational Behavior and Human Performance,* 1976, **16,** 250-279.

Hackman, J. R., Oldham, G., Janson, R., & Purdy, K. A new strategy for job enrichment. *California Management Review, 1975,* **17** (4), 57-71.

Herold, D. M. Group effectiveness as a function of task-appropriate interaction processes. In J. L. Livingstone (Ed.), *Managerial accounting: The behavioral foundations.* Columbus, Ohio: Grid Publishers, in press.

Herzberg, F. The wise old Turk. *Harvard Business Review,* 1974, **52,** 70-80.

Katzell, R. A., Yankelovich, D., et al. *Work, productivity and job satisfaction.* New York: The Psychological Corporation, 1975.

Lawler, E. E., & Cammann, C. What makes a work group successful? In A. J. Marrow (Ed.), *The failure of success.* New York: Amacom, 1972.

Lawler, E. E., & Hall, D. T. The relationship of job characteristics to job involvement, satisfaction and intrinsic motivation. *Journal of Applied Psychology,* 1970, **54,** 305-312.

Oldham, G. R. Job characteristics and internal motivation: The moderating effect of interpersonal and individual variables. *Human Relations,* 1976, **29,** 559-569.

Oldham, G. R., Hackman, J. R., & Pearce, J. L. Conditions under which employees respond positively to enriched work. *Journal of Applied Psychology,* 1976, **61,** 395-403.

Reif, W. E., & Luthans, F. Does job enrichment really pay off? *California Management Review,* 1972, **15,** 30-37.

Schachter, S., Ellertson, N., McBride, D., & Gregory, D. An experimental test of cohesiveness and productivity. *Human Relations,* 1951, **4,** 229-238.

Seashore, S. *Group cohesiveness in the industrial work group.* Ann Arbor: University of Michigan, 1954.

Susman, G. I. The impact of automation on work group autonomy and task specialization. *Human Relations,* 1970, **23,** 567-577.

Taylor, J. C. Some effects of technology in organizational change. *Human Relations,* 1971, **24,** 105-123.

Trist, E. L., Higgin, G. W., Murray, H., & Pollock, A. B. *Organizational choice.* London: Tavistock, 1963.

Vroom, V. H. Industrial social psychology. In G. Lindzey & E. Aronson (Eds.), *Handbook of social psychology* (2d ed.). Reading, Mass.: Addison-Wesley, 1969.

Walters, R. W., & Associates. *Job enrichment for results.* Reading, Mass.: Addison-Wesley, 1975.

Walton, R. E. From Hawthorne to Topeka and Kalmar. In E. L. Cass & F. G. Zimmer (Eds.), *Man and work in society.* New York: Van Nostrand-Reinhold, 1975.

On the Folly of Rewarding A, While Hoping for B

Steven Kerr

Whether dealing with monkeys, rats, or human beings, it is hardly controversial to state that most organisms seek information concerning what activities are rewarded, and then seek to do (or at least pretend to do) those things, often to the virtual exclusion of activities not rewarded. The extent to which this occurs of course will depend on the perceived attractiveness of the rewards offered, but neither operant nor expectancy theorists would quarrel with the essence of this notion.

Nevertheless, numerous examples exist of reward systems that are fouled up in that behaviors which are rewarded are those which the rewarder is trying to *discourage,* while the behavior he desires is not being rewarded at all.

In an effort to understand and explain this phenomenon, this paper presents examples from society, from organizations in general, and from profit making firms in particular. Data from a manufacturing company and information from an insurance firm are examined to demonstrate the consequences of such reward systems for the organizations involved, and possible reasons why such reward systems continue to exist are considered.

SOCIETAL EXAMPLES

Politics

Official goals are "purposely vague and general and do not indicate . . . the host of decisions that must be made among alternative ways of achieving official goals and the priority of multiple goals . . ." (8, p. 66). They usually may be relied on to offend absolutely no one, and in this sense can be considered high acceptance, low quality goals. An example might be "build better schools." Operative goals are higher in quality but lower in acceptance, since they specify where the money will come from, what alternative goals will be ignored, etc.

The American citizenry supposedly wants its candidates for public office to set forth operative goals, making their proposed programs "perfectly clear," specifying sources and uses of funds, etc.

However, since operative goals are lower in acceptance, and since aspirants to public office need acceptance (from at least 50.1 percent of the people), most politicians prefer to speak only of official goals, at least until after the election. They of course would agree to speak at the operative level if "punished" for not doing so. The electorate could do this by refusing to support candidates who do not speak at the operative level.

Instead, however, the American voter typically punishes (withholds support from) candidates who frankly discuss where the money will come from, rewards politicians who speak only of official goals, but hopes that candidates (despite the reward system) will discuss the issues operatively. It is academic whether it was moral for Nixon, for example, to refuse to discuss his 1968 "secret plan" to end the Vietnam war, his 1972 operative goals concerning the lifting of price controls, the reshuffling of his cabinet, etc. The point is that the reward system made such refusal rational.

It seems worth mentioning that no manuscript can adequately define what is "moral" and what is not. However, examination of costs and benefits, combined with knowledge of what motivates a particular individual, often will suffice to determine what for him is "rational."[1] If the reward system is so designed that it is irrational to be moral, this does not necessarily mean that immorality will result. But is this not asking for trouble?

War

If some oversimplification may be permitted, let it be assumed that the primary goal of the organization (Pentagon, Luftwaffe, or whatever) is to win. Let it be assumed further that the primary goal of most individuals on the front lines is to get home alive. Then there appears to be an important conflict in goals—personally rational behavior by those at the bottom will endanger goal attainment by those at the top.

---

[1]In Simon's (10, pp. 76-77) terms, a decision is "subjectively rational" if it maximizes an individual's valued outcomes so far as his knowledge permits. A decision is "personally rational" if it is oriented toward the individual's goals.

Reprinted with permission from the *Academy of Management Journal,* 1975, Vol. 18, pp. 769-783.

But not necessarily! It depends on how the reward system is set up. The Vietnam war was indeed a study of disobedience and rebellion, with terms such as "fragging" (killing one's own commanding officer) and "search and evade" becoming part of the military vocabulary. The difference in subordinates' acceptance of authority between World War II and Vietnam is reported to be considerable, and veterans of the Second World War often have been quoted as being outraged at the mutinous actions of many American soldiers in Vietnam.

Consider, however, some critical differences in the reward system in use during the two conflicts. What did the GI in World War II want? To go home. And when did he get to go home? When the war was won! If he disobeyed the orders to clean out the trenches and take the hills, the war would not be won and he would not go home. Furthermore, what were his chances of attaining his goal (getting home alive) if he obeyed the orders compared to his chances if he did not? What is being suggested is that the rational soldier in World War II, *whether patriotic or not,* probably found it expedient to obey.

Consider the reward system in use in Vietnam. What did the man at the bottom want? To go home. And when did he get to go home? When his tour of duty was over! This was the case *whether or not* the war was won. Furthermore, concerning the relative chance of getting home alive by obeying orders compared to the chance if they were disobeyed, it is worth noting that a mutineer in Vietnam was far more likely to be assigned rest and rehabilitation (on the assumption that fatigue was the cause) than he was to suffer any negative consequence.

In his description of the "zone of indifference," Barnard stated that "a person can and will accept a communication as authoritative only when at the time of his decision, he believes it to be compatible with his personal interests as a whole" (1, p. 165). In light of the reward system used in Vietnam, would it not have been personally irrational for some orders to have been obeyed? Was not the military implementing a system which *rewarded* disobedience, while *hoping* that soldiers (despite the reward system) would obey orders?

Medicine

Theoretically, a physician can make either of two types of error, and intuitively one seems as bad as the other. A doctor can pronounce a patient sick when he is actually well, thus causing him needless anxiety and expense, curtailment of enjoyable foods and activities, and even physical danger by subjecting him to needless medication and surgery. Alternately, a doctor can label a sick person well, and thus avoid treating what may be a serious, even fatal ailment. It might be natural to conclude that physicians seek to minimize both types of error.

Such a conclusion would be wrong.[2] It is estimated that numerous Americans are presently afflicted with iatrogenic (physician *caused*) illnesses (9). This occurs when the doctor is approached by someone complaining of a few stray symptoms. The doctor classifies and organizes these symptoms, gives them a name, and obligingly tells the patient what further symptoms may be expected. This information often acts as a self-fulfilling prophecy, with the result that from that day on the patient for all practical purposes is sick.

Why does this happen? Why are the physicians so reluctant to sustain a type 2 error (pronouncing a sick person well) that they will tolerate many type 1 errors? Again, a look at the reward system is needed. The punishments for a type 2 error are real: guilt, embarrassment, and the threat of lawsuit and scandal. On the other hand, a type 1 error (labeling a well person sick) "is sometimes seen as sound clinical practice, indicating a healthy conservative approach to medicine" (9, p. 69). Type 1 errors also are likely to generate increased income and a stream of steady customers who, being well in a limited physiological sense, will not embarrass the doctor by dying abruptly.

Fellow physicians and the general public therefore are really *rewarding* type 1 errors and at the same time *hoping* fervently that doctors will try not to make them.

GENERAL ORGANIZATIONAL EXAMPLES

Rehabilitation Centers and Orphanages

In terms of the prime beneficiary classification (2, p. 42) organizations such as these are supposed to exist for the "public-in-contact," that is, clients. The orphanage therefore theoretically is interested in placing as many children as possible in good homes. However, often orphanages surround themselves with so many rules concerning adoption that it is nearly impossible to pry a child out of the place.

---

[2]In one study (4) of 14,867 films for signs of tuberculosis, 1,216 positive readings turned out to be clinically negative; only 24 negative readings proved clinically active, a ratio of 50 to 1.

Orphanages may deny adoption unless the applicants are a married couple, both of the same religion as the child, without history of emotional or vocational instability, with a specified minimum income and a private room for the child, etc.

If the primary goal is to place children in good homes, then the rules ought to constitute means toward that goal. Goal displacement results when these "means become ends-in-themselves that displace the original goals" (2, p. 229).

To some extent these rules are required by law. But the influence of the reward system on the orphanage's management should not be ignored. Consider, for example, that the:

1. Number of children enrolled often is the most important determinant of the size of the allocated budget.

2. Number of children under the director's care also will affect the size of his staff.

3. Total organizational size will determine largely the director's prestige at the annual conventions, in the community, etc.

Therefore, to the extent that staff size, total budget, and personal prestige are valued by the orphanage's executive personnel, it becomes rational for them to make it difficult for children to be adopted. After all, who wants to be the director of the smallest orphanage in the state?

If the reward system errs in the opposite direction, paying off only for placements, extensive goal displacement again is likely to result. A common example of vocational rehabilitation in many states, for example, consists of placing someone in a job for which he has little interest and few qualifications, for two months or so, and then "rehabilitating" him again in another position. Such behavior is quite consistent with the prevailing reward system, which pays off for the number of individuals placed in any position for 60 days or more. Rehabilitation counselors also confess to competing with one another to place relatively skilled clients, sometimes ignoring persons with few skills who would be harder to place. Extensively disabled clients find that counselors often prefer to work with those whose disabilities are less severe.[3]

Universities

Society *hopes* that teachers will not neglect their teaching responsibilities but *rewards* them al-

most entirely for research and publications. This is most true at the large and prestigious universities. Cliches such as "good research and good teaching go together" notwithstanding, professors often find that they must choose between teaching and research oriented activities when allocating their time. Rewards for good teaching usually are limited to outstanding teacher awards, which are given to only a small percentage of good teachers and which usually bestow little money and fleeting prestige. Punishments for poor teaching also are rare.

Rewards for research and publications, on the other hand, and punishments for failure to accomplish these, are commonly administered by universities at which teachers are employed. Furthermore, publication oriented resumés usually will be well received at other universities, whereas teaching credentials, harder to document and quantify, are much less transferable. Consequently it is rational for university teachers to concentrate on research, even if to the detriment of teaching and at the expense of their students.

By the same token, it is rational for students to act based upon the goal displacement which has occurred within universities concerning what they are rewarded for. If it is assumed that a primary goal of a university is to transfer knowledge from teacher to student, then grades become identifiable as a means toward that goal, serving as motivational, control, and feedback devices to expedite the knowledge transfer. Instead, however, the grades themselves have become much more important for entrance to graduate school, successful employment, tuition refunds, parental respect, etc., than the knowledge or lack of knowledge they are supposed to signify.

It therefore should come as no surprise that information has surfaced in recent years concerning fraternity files for examinations, term paper writing services, organized cheating at the service academies, and the like. Such activities constitute a personally rational response to a reward system which pays off for grades rather than knowledge.

BUSINESS RELATED EXAMPLES

Ecology

Assume that the president of XYZ Corporation is confronted with the following alternatives:

1. Spend $11 million for antipollution equipment to keep from poisoning fish in the river adjacent to the plant; or

---

[3]Personal interviews conducted during 1972-1973.

2. Do nothing, in violation of the law, and assume a one in ten chance of being caught, with a resultant $1 million fine plus the necessity of buying the equipment.

Under this not unrealistic set of choices it requires no linear program to determine that XYZ Corporation can maximize its probabilities by flouting the law. Add the fact that XYZ's president is probably being rewarded (by creditors, stockholders, and other salient parts of his task environment) according to criteria totally unrelated to the number of fish poisoned, and his probable course of action becomes clear.

Evaluation of Training

It is axiomatic that those who care about a firm's well-being should insist that the organization get fair value for its expenditures. Yet it is commonly known that firms seldom bother to evaluate a new GRID, MBO, job enrichment program, or whatever, to see if the company is getting its money's worth. Why? Certainly it is not because people have not pointed out that this situation exists; numerous practitioner oriented articles are written each year to just this point.

The individuals (whether in personnel, manpower planning, or wherever) who normally would be responsible for conducting such evaluations are the same ones often charged with introducing the change effort in the first place. Having convinced top management to spend the money, they usually are quite animated afterwards in collecting arigorous vignettes and anecdotes about how successful the program was. The last thing many desire is a formal, systematic, and revealing evaluation. Although members of top management may actually *hope* for such systematic evaluation, their reward systems continue to *reward* ignorance in this area. And if the personnel department abdicates its responsibility, who is to step into the breach? The change agent himself? Hardly! He is likely to be too busy collecting anecdotal "evidence" of his own, for use with his next client.

Miscellaneous

Many additional examples could be cited of systems which in fact are rewarding behaviors other than those supposedly desired by the rewarder. A few of these are described briefly below.

Most coaches disdain to discuss individual accomplishments, preferring to speak of teamwork, proper attitude, and a one-for-all spirit. Usually, however, rewards are distributed according to individual performance. The college basketball player who feeds his teammates instead of shooting will not compile impressive scoring statistics and is less likely to be drafted by the pros. The ballplayer who hits to right field to advance the runners will win neither the batting nor home run titles, and will be offered smaller raises. It therefore is rational for players to think of themselves first, and the team second.

In business organizations where rewards are dispensed for unit performance or for individual goals achieved, without regard for overall effectiveness, similar attitudes often are observed. Under most Management by Objectives (MBO) systems, goals in areas where quantification is difficult often go unspecified. The organization therefore often is in a position where it *hopes* for employee effort in the areas of team building, interpersonal relations, creativity, etc., but it formally *rewards* none of these. In cases where promotions and raises are formally tied to MBO, the system itself contains a paradox in that it "asks employees to set challenging risky goals, only to face smaller paychecks and possibly damaged careers if these goals are not accomplished" (5, p. 40).

It is *hoped* that administrators will pay attention to long run costs and opportunities and will institute programs which will bear fruit later on. However, many organizational reward systems pay off for short run sales and earnings only. Under such circumstances it is personally rational for officials to sacrifice long term growth and profit (by selling off equipment and property, or by stifling research and development) for short term advantages. This probably is more pertinent in the public sector, with the result that many public officials are unwilling to implement programs which will not show benefits by election time.

As a final, clear-cut example of a fouled-up reward system, consider the cost-plus contract or its next of kin, the allocation of next year's budget as a direct function of this year's expenditures. It probably is conceivable that those who award such budgets and contracts really hope for economy and prudence in spending. It is obvious, however, that adopting the proverb "to him who spends shall more be given," rewards not economy, but spending itself.

TWO COMPANIES' EXPERIENCES

A Manufacturing Organization

A midwest manufacturer of industrial goods had been troubled for some time by aspects of its organizational climate it believed dysfunctional. For research purposes, interviews were conducted with many employees and a questionnaire was administered on a companywide basis, including plants and offices in several American and Canadian locations. The company strongly encouraged employee participation in the survey, and made available time and space during the workday for completion of the instrument. All employees in attendance during the day of the survey completed the questionnaire. All instruments were collected directly by the researcher, who personally administered each session. Since no one employed by the firm handled the questionnaire, and since respondent names were not asked for, it seems likely that the pledge of anonymity given was believed.

A modified version of the Expect Approval scale (7) was included as part of the questionnaire. The instrument asked respondents to indicate the degree of approval or disapproval they could expect if they performed each of the described actions. A seven point Likert scale was used, with one indicating that the action would probably bring strong disapproval and seven signifying likely strong approval.

Although normative data for this scale from studies of other organizations are unavailable, it is possible to examine fruitfully the data obtained from this survey in several ways. First, it may be worth noting that the questionnaire data corresponded closely to information gathered through interviews. Futhermore, as can be seen from the results summarized in Table 1, sizable differences between various work units, and between employees at different job levels within the same work unit, were obtained. This suggests that response bias effects (social desirability in particular loomed as a potential concern) are not likely to be severe.

Most importantly, comparisons between scores obtained on the Expect Approval scale and a statement of problems which were the reason for the survey revealed that the same behaviors which managers in each division thought dysfunctional were those which lower level employees claimed were rewarded. As compared to job levels 1 to 8 Division B (see Table 1), those in Division A claimed a much higher acceptance by management of "conforming" activities. Between 31 and 37 percent of Division A employees at levels 1-8 stated that going along with the majority agreeing with the boss, and staying on everyone's good side brought approval; only once (level 5-8 responses to one of the three items) did a majority suggest that such actions would generate disapproval.

Furthermore responses from Division A workers at levels 1-4 indicate that behaviors geared toward risk avoidance were as likely to be rewarded as to be punished. Only at job levels 9 and above was it apparent that the reward system was positively reinforcing behaviors desired by top management. Overall, the same "tendencies toward conservatism and apple-polishing at the lower levels" which divisional management had complained about during the interviews were those claimed by subordinates to be the most rational course of action in light of the existing reward system. Management apparently was not getting the behaviors it was *hoping* for, but it certainly was getting the behaviors it was perceived by subordinates to be *rewarding*.

An Insurance Firm

The Group Health Claims Division of a large eastern insurance company provides another rich illustration of a reward system which reinforces behaviors not desired by top management.

Attempting to measure and reward accuracy in paying surgical claims, the firm systematically keeps track of the number of returned checks and letters of complaint received from policyholders. However, underpayments are likely to provoke cries of outrage from the insured, while overpayments often are accepted in courteous silence. Since it often is impossible to tell from the physician's statement which of two surgical procedures, with different allowable benefits, was performed, and since writing for clarifications will interfere with other standards used by the firm concerning "percentage of claims paid within two days of receipt," the new hire in more than one claims section is soon acquainted with the informal norm: "When in doubt, pay it out!"

The situation would be even worse were it not for the fact that other features of the firm's reward system tend to neutralize those described. For example, annual "merit" increases are given to all employees, in one of the following three amounts:

1. If the worker is "outstanding" (a select category, into which no more than two employees per section may be placed): 5 percent

2. If the worker is "above average" (normally all workers not "outstanding" are so rated): 4 percent

3. If the worker commits gross acts of negligence and irresponsibility for which he might be discharged in many other companies: 3 percent.

TABLE 1

Summary of Two Divisions' Data Relevant to Conforming and Risk-Avoidance
Behaviors (Extent to Which Subjects Expect Approval)

Dimension	Item	Division and Sample	Total Responses	1, 2, or 3 Disapproval	4	Percentage of Workers Responding 5, 6, or 7 Approval
Risk Avoidance	Making a risky decision based on the best information available at the time, but which turns out wrong.	A, levels 1-4 (lowest)	127	61	25	14
		A, levels 5-8	172	46	31	23
		A, levels 9 and above	17	41	30	30
		B, levels 1-4 (lowest)	31	58	26	16
		B, levels 5-8	19	42	42	16
		B, levels 9 and above	10	50	20	30
	Setting extremely high and challenging standards and goals, and then narrowly failing to make them.	A, levels 1-4	122	47	28	25
		A, levels 5-8	168	33	26	41
		A, levels 9+	17	24	6	70
		B, levels 1-4	31	48	23	29
		B, levels 5-8	18	17	33	50
		B, levels 9+	10	30	0	70
	Setting goals which are extremely easy to make and then making them.	A, levels 1-4	124	35	30	35
		A, levels 5-8	171	47	27	26
		A, levels 9+	17	70	24	6
		B, levels 1-4	31	58	26	16
		B, levels 5-8	19	63	16	21
		B, levels 9+	10	80	0	20
Conformity	Being a "yes man" and always agreeing with the boss.	A, levels 1-4	126	46	17	37
		A, levels 5-8	180	54	14	31
		A, levels 9+	17	88	12	0
		B, levels 1-4	32	53	28	19
		B, levels 5-8	19	68	21	11
		B, levels 9+	10	80	10	10
	Always going along with the majority.	A, levels 1-4	125	40	25	35
		A, levels 5-8	173	47	21	32
		A, levels 9+	17	70	12	18
		B, levels 1-4	31	61	23	16
		B, levels 5-8	19	68	11	21
		B, levels 9+	10	80	10	10
	Being careful to stay on the good side of everyone, so that everyone agrees that you are a great guy.	A, levels 1-4	124	45	18	37
		A, levels 5-8	173	45	22	33
		A, levels 9+	17	64	6	30
		B, levels 1-4	31	54	23	23
		B, levels 5-8	19	73	11	16
		B, levels 9+	10	80	10	10

Now, since (a) the difference between the 5 percent theoretically attainable through hard work and the 4 percent attainable merely by living until the review date is small and (b) since insurance firms seldom dispense much of a salary increase in cash (rather, the worker's insurance benefits increase, causing him to be further overinsured), many employees are rather indifferent to the possibility of obtaining the extra one percent reward and therefore tend to ignore the norm concerning indiscriminant payments.

However, most employees are not indifferent to the rule which states that, should absences or latenesses total three or more in any six-month period, the entire 4 or 5 percent due at the next "merit" review must be forfeited. In this sense the firm may be described as *hoping* for performance, while *rewarding* attendance. What it gets, of course, is attendance. (If the absence-lateness rule appears to the reader to be stringent, it really is not. The company counts "times" rather than "days" absent, and a ten-day absence therefore counts the same as one lasting two days. A worker in danger of accumulating a third absence within six months merely has to remain ill (away from work) during his second absence until his first absence is more than six months old. The limiting factor is that at some point his salary ceases, and his sickness benefits take over. This usually is sufficient to get the younger workers to return, but for those with 20 or more years' service, the company provides sickness benefits of 90 percent of normal salary, tax-free! Therefore. . . .)

CAUSES

Extremely diverse instances of systems which reward behavior A although the rewarder apparently hopes for behavior B have been given. These are useful to illustrate the breadth and magnitude of the phenomenon, but the diversity increases the difficulty of determining commonalities and establishing causes. However, four general factors may be pertinent to an explanation of why fouled up reward systems seem to be so prevelant.

Fascination with an "Objective" Criterion

It has been mentioned elsewhere that:

Most "objective" measures of productivity are objective only in that their subjective elements are a) determined in advance, rather than coming into play at the time of the formal evaluation, and

b) well concealed on the rating instrument itself. Thus industrial firms seeking to devise objective rating systems first decide, in an arbitrary manner, what dimensions are to be rated, . . . usually including some items having little to do with organizational effectiveness while excluding others that do. Only then does Personnel Division churn out official-looking documents on which all dimensions chosen to be rated are assigned point values, categories, or whatever (6, p. 92).

Nonetheless, many individuals seek to establish simple, quantifiable standards against which to measure and reward performance. Such efforts may be successful in highly predictable areas within an organization, but are likely to cause goal displacement when applied anywhere else. Overconcern with attendance and lateness in the insurance firm and with number of people placed in the vocational rehabilitation division may have been largely responsible for the problems described in those organizations.

Overemphasis on Highly Visible Behaviors

Difficulties often stem from the fact that some parts of the task are highly visible while other parts are not. For example, publications are easier to demonstrate than teaching, and scoring baskets and hitting home runs are more readily observable than feeding teammates and advancing base runners. Similarly, the adverse consequences of pronouncing a sick person well are more visible than those sustained by labeling a well person sick. Team-building and creativity are other examples of behaviors which may not be rewarded simply because they are hard to observe.

Hypocrisy

In some of the instances described the rewarder may have been getting the desired behavior, notwithstanding claims that the behavior was not desired. This may be true, for example, of management's attitude toward apple-polishing in the manufacturing firm (a behavior which subordinates felt was rewarded, despite management's avowed dislike of the practice). This also may explain politicians' unwillingness to revise the penalties for disobedience of ecology laws, and the failure of top management to devise reward systems which would cause systematic evaluation of training and development programs.

Emphasis on Morality or Equity Rather than Efficiency

Sometimes consideration of other factors prevents the establishment of a system which rewards behaviors desired by the rewarder. The felt obligation of many Americans to vote for one candidate or another, for example, may impair their ability to withhold support from politicians who refuse to discuss the issues. Similarly, the concern for spreading the risks and costs of wartime military service may outweigh the advantage to be obtained by commiting personnel to combat until the war is over.

It should be noted that only with respect to the first two causes are reward systems really paying off for other than desired behaviors. In the case of the third and fourth causes the system *is* rewarding behaviors desired by the rewarder, and the systems are fouled up only from the standpoints of those who believe the rewarder's public statements (cause 3), or those who seek to maximize efficiency rather than other outcomes (cause 4).

CONCLUSIONS

Modern organization theory requires a recognition that the members of organizations and society possess divergent goals and motives. It therefore is unlikely that managers and their subordinates will seek the same outcomes. Three possible remedies for this potential problem are suggested.

Selection

It is theoretically possible for organizations to employ only those individuals whose goals and motives are wholly consonant with those of management. In such cases the same behaviors judged by subordinates to be rational would be perceived by management as desirable. State-of-the-art reviews of selection techniques, however, provide scant grounds for hope that such an approach would be successful (for example, see 12).

Training

Another theoretical alternative is for the organization to admit those employees whose goals are not consonant with those of management and then, through training, socialization, or whatever, alter employee goals to make them consonant. However, research on the effectiveness of such training programs, though limited, provides further grounds for pessimism (for example, see 3).

Altering the Reward System

What would have been the result if:

1. Nixon had been assured by his advisors that he could not win re-election except by discussing the issues in detail?

2. Physicians' conduct was subject to regular examination by review boards for type 1 errors (calling healthy people ill) and to penalties (fines, censure, etc.) for errors of either type?

3. The President of XYZ Corportion had to choose between (a) spending $11 million dollars for antipollution equipment, and (b) incurring a fifty-fifty chance of going to jail for five years?

Managers who complain that their workers are not motivated might do well to consider the possibility that they have installed reward systems which are paying off for behaviors other than those they are seeking. This, in part, is what happened in Vietnam, and this is what regularly frustrates societal efforts to bring about honest politicians, civic-minded managers, etc. This certainly is what happened in both the manufacturing and the insurance companies.

A first step for such managers might be to find out what behaviors currently are being rewarded. Perhaps an instrument similar to that used in the manufacturing firm could be useful for this purpose. Chances are excellent that these managers will be surprised by what they find—that their firms are not rewarding what they assume they are. In fact, such undesirable behavior by organizational members as they have observed may be explained largely by the reward systems in use.

This is not to say that all organizational behavior is determined by formal rewards and punishments. Certainly it is true that in the absence of formal reinforcement some soldiers will be patriotic, some presidents will be ecology minded, and some orphanage directors will care about children. The point, however, is that in such cases the rewarder is not *causing* the behaviors desired but is only a fortunate bystander. For an organization to *act* upon its members, the formal reward system should positively reinforce desired behaviors, not constitute an obstacle to be overcome.

It might be wise to underscore the obvious fact that there is nothing really new in what has been said.

In both theory and practice these matters have been mentioned before. Thus in many states Good Samaritan laws have been installed to protect doctors who stop to assist a stricken motorist. In states without such laws it is commonplace for doctors to refuse to stop, for fear of involvement in a subsequent lawsuit. In college basketball additional penalties have been instituted against players who foul their opponents deliberately. It has long been argued by Milton Friedman and others that penalties should be altered so as to make it irrational to disobey the ecology laws, and so on.

By altering the reward system the organization escapes the necessity of selecting only desirable people or of trying to alter undesirable ones. In Skinnerian terms (as described in 11, p. 704), "As for responsibility and goodness—as commonly defined— no one . . . would want or need them. They refer to a man's behaving well despite the absence of positive reinforcement that is obviously sufficent to explain it. Where such reinforcement exists, 'no one needs goodness.' "

REFERENCES

1. Barnard, Chester I. *The Functions of the Executive* (Cambridge, Mass.: Harvard University Press, 1964).

2. Blau, Peter M., and W. Richard Scott. *Formal Organizations* (San Francisco: Chandler, 1962).

3. Fiedler, Fred E. "Predicting the Effects of Leadership Training and Experience from the Contingency Model," *Journal of Applied Psychology*, Vol. 56 (1972), 114-119.

4. Garland, L. H. "Studies of the Accuracy of Diagnostic Procedures," *American Journal Roentgenological, Radium Therapy Nuclear Medicine*, Vol. 82 (1959), 25-38.

5. Kerr, Steven. "Some Modifications in MBO as an OD Strategy," *Academy of Management Proceedings*, 1973, pp. 39-42.

6. Kerr, Steven. "What Price Objectivity?" *American Sociologist*, Vol. 8 (1973), 92-93.

7. Litwin, G. H., and R. A. Stringer, Jr. *Motivation and Organizational Climate* (Boston: Harvard University Press, 1968).

8. Perrow, Charles. "The Analysis of Goals in Complex Organizations," in A. Etzioni (Ed.), *Readings on Modern Organizations* (Englewood Cliffs, N.J.: Prentice-Hall, 1969).

9. Scheff, Thomas J. "Decision Rules, Types of Error, and Their Consequences in Medical Diagnosis," in F. Massarik and P. Ratoosh (Eds.), *Mathematical Explorations in Behavioral Science* (Homewood, Ill.: Irwin, 1965).

10. Simon, Herbert A. *Administrative Behavior* (New York: Free Press, 1957).

11. Swanson, G. E. "Review Symposium: Beyond Freedom and Dignity," *American Journal of Sociology*, Vol. 78 (1972), 702-705.

12. Webster, E. *Decision Making in the Employment Interview* (Montreal: Industrial Relations Center, McGill University, 1964).

Exercise: A Job Redesign Project

PURPOSE

The purpose of this exercise is to give you the opportunity to learn and use the principles of job design. By the time you complete this exercise, you will:

1. Understand the Hackman and Oldham (1976) model of job redesign.

2. Diagnose the "Motivating Potential Score" of your current job.

3. Practice applying job redesign principles.

INTRODUCTION

According to Herzberg (1968), motivation in the workplace is associated with the *job content*, while dissatisfaction is associated with *job context* factors. Hackman and Oldham (1976), in their theory of job redesign, expanded upon this idea and identified five job characteristics that they felt contributed to motivation: (1) skill variety, (2) task identity, (3) task significance, (4) autonomy, and (5) feedback from the job itself. The more a job evidenced these characteristics, the greater the motivation on the part of the jobholder. By measuring these five job characteristics, the relative "motivating potential" of the job could therefore be determined.

This exercise asks you to participate in a job redesign process. First, you will complete the original "Job Diagnostic Survey" to assess the motivating potential of your job. Next, you will evaluate your level of satisfaction and dissatisfaction, as well as your internal work motivation and growth need strength. Finally, those jobs in the class with the lowest Motivating Potential Scores (MPS) will serve as the targets of a job redesign program.

INSTRUCTIONS

1. Read the article by Hackman, "Designing Work for Individuals and Groups."

2. Complete Part I of the Job Diagnostic Survey as directed by your instructor to assess the motivating potential of your job. Work on Part I only.

3. Score your results to determine the Motivating Potential Score of your job.

4. Complete Part II of the Job Diagnostic Survey to determine your level of satisfaction, internal work motivation, and Growth Need Strength.

The Job Diagnostic Survey is used with permission from Richard Hackman and Greg Oldham, *Work Design* (Reading, Mass: Addison-Wesley, 1980).

5. As directed by your instructor, identify the three lowest MPS-scored jobs in the class.

6. In small groups of 4 to 6 people, focus on these jobs and attempt to redesign them according to the principles in Part III.

7. *Option:* Retake the Job Diagnostic Survey with one of your subordinates' jobs in mind.

8. In groups, discuss ways in which your subordinates' jobs can be altered to enhance motivation.

PART I: THE JOB DIAGNOSTIC SURVEY

Directions: On the following pages, you will find several different kinds of questions about your job. Specific instructions are given at the start of each section. Please read them carefully, but move through the entire questionnaire quickly. The questions are designed to obtain your perceptions of your job and your reactions to it.

PART I: THE JOB DIAGNOSTIC SURVEY (SHORT FORM)

SECTION ONE

Directions: This part of the questionnaire asks you to describe your job, as *objectively* as you can. Please do *not* use this part of the questionnaire to show how much you like or dislike your job. Questions about that will come later. Instead, try to make your descriptions as accurate and as objective as you possibly can.

A sample question is given below:

1. To what extent does your job require you to work with mechanical equipment?

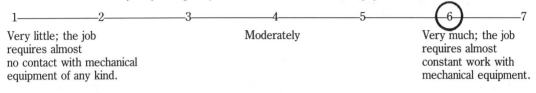

| 1 | 2 | 3 | 4 | 5 | 6 | 7 |

Very little; the job
requires almost
no contact with mechanical
equipment of any kind.

Moderately

Very much; the job
requires almost
constant work with
mechanical equipment.

You are to *circle* the number which is the most accurate description of your job. If, for example, your job requires you to work with mechanical equipment a good deal of the time—but also requires some paperwork—you might circle the number six, as was done in the example above.

If you do not understand these instructions, please ask for assistance. If you do understand them, turn the page and begin.

1. To what extent does your job require you to *work closely with other people* (either "clients" or people in related jobs in your own organization)?

1————————2————————3————————4————————5————————6————————7

Very little; dealing with other people is not at all necessary in doing the job.	Moderately; some dealing with others is necessary.	Very much; dealing with other people is an absolutely essential and crucial part of doing the job.

2. How much *autonomy* is there in your job? That is, to what extent does your job permit you to decide *on your own* how to go about doing the work?

1————————2————————3————————4————————5————————6————————7

Very little; the job gives me almost no personal "say" about how and when the work is done.	Moderate autonomy; many things are standardized and not under my control, but I can make some decisions about the work.	Very much; the job gives me almost complete responsibility for deciding how and when the work is done.

3. To what extent does your job involve a *"whole" and identifiable piece of work?* That is, is the job a complete piece of work that has an obvious beginning and end? Or is it only a small *part* of the overall piece of work, which is finished by other people or by automatic machines?

1————————2————————3————————4————————5————————6————————7

My job is only a tiny part of the overall piece of work; the results of my activities cannot be seen in the final product of service.	My job is a moderate-sized "chunk" of the overall piece of work; my own contribution can be seen in the final outcome.	My job involves doing the whole piece of work, from start to finish; the results of my activities are easily seen in the final product or service.

4. How much *variety* is there in your job? That is, to what extent does the job require you to do many different things at work, using a variety of your skills and talents?

1————————2————————3————————4————————5————————6————————7

Very little; the job requires me to do the same routine things over and over again.	Moderate variety.	Very much; the job requires me to do many different things, using a number of different skills and talents.

5. In general, how *significant or important* is your job? That is, are the results of your work likely to significantly affect the lives or well-being of other people?

1————————2————————3————————4————————5————————6————————7

Not very significant; the outcomes of my work are *not* likely to have important effects on other people	Moderately significant.	Highly significant; the outcomes of my work can affect other people in very important ways.

6. To what extent do *managers or co-workers* let you know how well you are doing on your job?

1————————2————————3————————4————————5————————6————————7

Very little; people
almost never let me
know how well I am
doing.

Moderately;
sometimes people
may give me "feedback";
other times they may not.

Very much; managers
or co-workers provide
me with almost
constant "feedback" about
how well I am doing.

7. To what extent does *doing the job itself* provide you with information about your work peformance? That is, does the actual *work itself* provide clues about how well you are doing—aside from any "feedback" co-workers or supervisors may provide?

1————————2————————3————————4————————5————————6————————7

Very little; the
job itself is set
up so I could work
forever without
finding out how well
I am doing.

Moderately; sometimes
doing the job
provides "feedback" to
me; sometimes it
does not.

Very much; the job
is set up so that I
get almost constant
"feedback" as I work
about how well I am doing.

Directions: Listed below are a number of statements that could be used to describe a job. You are to indicate whether each statement is an *accurate* or an *inaccurate* description of *your* job.

Once again, please try to be as objective as you can in deciding how accurately each statement describes your job—regardless of whether you like or dislike your job.

Write a number in the blank beside each statement, based on the following scale:

How accurate is the statement in describing your job?

1	2	3	4	5	6	7
Very Inaccurate	Mostly Inaccurate	Slightly Inaccurate	Uncertain	Slightly Accurate	Mostly Accurate	Very Accurate

_____ 1. The job requires me to use a number of complex or high-level skills.

_____ 2. The job requires a lot of cooperative work with other people.

_____ 3. The job is arranged so that I do *not* have the chance to do an entire piece of work from beginning to end.

_____ 4. Just doing the work required by the job provides many chances for me to figure out how well I am doing.

_____ 5. The job is quite simple and repetitive.

_____ 6. The job can be done adequately by a person working alone—without talking or checking with other people.

_____ 7. The supervisors and co-workers on this job almost *never* give me any feedback about how well I am doing my work.

_____ 8. In this job, alot of other people can be affected by how well the work gets done.

_____ 9. The job denies me any chance to use my personal initiative or judgment in carrying out the work.

_____10. Supervisors often let me know how well they think I am performing the job.

_____11. The job provides me the chance to completely finish the pieces of work I begin.

_____12. The job itself provides very few clues about whether or not I am performing well.

_____13. The job gives me considerable opportunity for independence and freedom in how I do the work.

_____14. The job itself is *not* very significant or important in the broader scheme of things.

SECTION THREE

Directions: Now please indicate how you personally feel about your job. Each of the statements below is something that a person might say about his or her job. You are to indicate your own, personal *feelings* about your job by marking how much you agree with each of the statements.

Write a number in the blank for each statement, based on this scale:

How much do you agree with the statement?

1	2	3	4	5	6	7
Disagree Strongly	Disagree	Disagree Slightly	Neutral	Agree Slightly	Agree	Agree Strongly

_____1. My opinion of myself goes up when I do this job well.

_____2. Generally speaking, I am very satisfied with this job.

_____3. I feel a great sense of personal satisfaction when I do this job well.

_____4. I frequently think of quitting my job.

_____5. I feel bad and unhappy when I discover that I have performed poorly on this job.

_____6. I am generally satisfied with the kind of work I do in this job.

_____7. My own feelings generally are *not* affected much one way or the other by how well I do on this job.

SCORING KEY

The Short Form of the Job Diagnostic Survey (JDS) measures several characteristics of jobs, the reactions of the respondents to their jobs, and the growth need strength of the respondents. Some of the scales tapped by the JDS are not included in the Short Form; others are measured with fewer items. The scales measuring the objective job dimensions are, however, identical with those in the JDS.

Each variable measured by the JDS Short Form is listed below, along with (a) a one- or two-sentence description of the variable, and (b) a list of the questionnaire items that are averaged to yield a summary score for the variable.

I. *Job Dimensions:* Objective characteristics of the job itself.

A. *Skill Variety:* The degree to which a job requires a variety of different activities in carrying out the work, which involve the use of a number of different skills and talents of the employee.

Average the following items:
Section One #4 _____
Section Two #1 _____
#5 (reversed scoring—that is, subtract the number entered by the respondent from 8) $8 - \underline{\hspace{1cm}} = \dfrac{\underline{\hspace{1cm}}}{3}$

B. *Task Identity:* The degree to which the job requires the completion of a "whole" and identifiable piece of work—that is, doing a job from beginning to end with a visible outcome.

Average the following items:
Section One #3 _____
Section Two #11 _____
#3 (reversed scoring) $8 - \underline{\hspace{1cm}} = \dfrac{\underline{\hspace{1cm}}}{3}$

C. *Task Significance:* The degree to which the job has a substantial impact on the lives or work of other people—whether in the immediate organization or in the external environment.

Average the following items:
Section One #5 _____
Section Two #8 _____
#14 (reversed scoring) $8 - \underline{\hspace{1cm}} = \dfrac{\underline{\hspace{1cm}}}{3}$

D. *Autonomy:* The degree to which the job provides substantial freedom, independence, and discretion to the employee in scheduling his or her work and determining the procedures to be used in carrying it out.

Average the following items:
Section One #2 _____
Section Two #13 _____
#9 (reversed scoring) $8 - \underline{\hspace{1cm}} = \dfrac{\underline{\hspace{1cm}}}{3}$

E. *Feedback from the Job Itself:* The degree to which carrying out the work activities required by the job results in the employee's information about the effectiveness of his or her performance.

Average the following items:
Section One #7 _____
Section Two #4 _____
#12 (reversed scoring) $8 - \underline{\hspace{1cm}} = \dfrac{\underline{\hspace{1cm}}}{3}$

F. *Feedback from Agents:* The degree to which the employee receives information about his or her performance effectiveness from supervisors or from co-workers. (This construct is *not* a job characteristic per se; it is included only to provide information supplementary to construct E above.)

Average the following items:
Section One #6 _____
Section Two #10
#7 (reversed scoring) $8 -$ _____ $= \dfrac{_____}{3}$

G. *Dealing with Others:* The degree to which the job requires the employee to work closely with other people (whether other organization members or organizational "clients").

Average the following items:
Section One #1 _____
Section Two #2 _____
#6 (reversed scoring) $8 -$ _____ $= \dfrac{_____}{3}$

II. *Motivating Potential Score:* A score reflecting the potential of a job for eliciting positive internal work motivation on the part of employees (especially those with high desire for Growth Need Satisfaction) is given below:

$$\text{Motivating Potential Score (MPS)} = \frac{\text{Skill variety} + \text{Task identity} + \text{Task significance}}{3} \times \text{Autonomy} \times \text{Feedback from the job}$$

My MPS score_____

Analysis of Part I

For diagnostic purposes:

☐ A score higher than 200 is a job in good shape with high motivating potential.

☐ A score lower than 100 means that the job would benefit from redesign.

☐ A score between 100 and 200 suggests possibilities in either direction.

PART II: THE JOB DIAGNOSTIC SURVEY

Directions: Now that you have identified the Motivating Potential Score of your job, it is important to assess your level of satisfaction with it, your degree of internal work motivation, and your Growth Need Strength. These indices, taken together with your job's MPS, determine whether or not you are a candidate for job redesign.

PART II: THE JOB DIAGNOSTIC SURVEY (SHORT FORM)

SECTION FOUR

Directions: Now please indicate how *satisfied* you are with each aspect of your job listed below. Once again, write the appropriate number in the blank beside each statement.

How satisfied are you with this aspect of your job?

1	2	3	4	5	6	7
Extremely Dissatisfied	Dissatisfied	Slightly Dissatisfied	Neutral	Slightly Satisfied	Satisfied	Extremely Satisfied

_____ 1. The amount of job security I have.

_____ 2. The amount of pay and fringe benefits I receive.

_____ 3. The amount of personal growth and development I get in doing my job.

_____ 4. The people I talk to and work with on my job.

_____ 5. The degree of respect and fair treatment I receive from my boss.

_____ 6. The feeling of worthwhile accomplishment I get from doing my job.

_____ 7. The chance to get to know other people while on the job.

_____ 8. The amount of support and guidance I receive from my supervisor.

_____ 9. The degree to which I am fairly paid for what I contribute to this organization.

_____10. The amount of independent thought and action I can exercise in my job.

_____11. How secure things look for me in the future in this organization.

_____12. The chance to help other people while at work.

_____13. The amount of challenge in my job.

_____14. The overall quality of the supervision I receive on my work.

SECTION FIVE

Directions: Listed below are a number of characteristics that could be present on any job. People differ about how much they would like to have each one present in their own jobs. We are interested in learning *how much you personally would like* to have each one present in your job.

Using the following scale, please indicate the *degree* to which you *would like* to have each characteristic present in your job. (*Note:* The numbers on this scale are different from those used in previous scales.)

4	5	6	7	8	9	10
Would like having this only a moderate amount (or less)			Would like having this very much			Would like having this *extremely* much

_____ 1. High respect and fair treatment from my supervisor.

_____ 2. Stimulating and challenging work.

_____ 3. Chances to exercise independent thought and action in my job.

_____ 4. Great job security.

_____ 5. Very friendly co-workers.

_____ 6. Opportunities to learn new things from my work.

_____ 7. High salary and good fringe benefits.

_____ 8. Opportunities to be creative and imaginative in my work.

_____ 9. Quick promotions.

_____10. Opportunities for personal growth and development in my job.

_____11. A sense of worthwhile accomplishment in my work.

III. *Affective Responses to the Job:* The private, affective reactions or feelings an employee gets from working on his or her job.

   A. *General Satisfaction:* An overall measure of the degree to which the employee is satisfied and happy in his or her work.

     Average the following items from Section Three: #2

                #6   8 - _____ = _____

                #4 (reversed scoring)   3⌐

   B. *Internal Work Motivation:* The degree to which the employee is self-motivated to perform effectively on the job.

     Average the following items from Section Three: #1

                #3

                #5   8 - _____ = _____

                #7 (reversed scoring)   4⌐

   C. *Specific Satisfactions:* These short scales tap several specific aspects of the employee's job satisfaction.

     1. "Pay" satisfaction. Average items #2 and #9 of Section Four.

               _____ + _____ = 2⌐_____

     2. "Security" satisfaction. Average items #1 and #11 of Section Four.

               _____ + _____ = 2⌐_____

     3. "Social" satisfaction. Average items #4, #7, and #12 of Section Four.

               _____ + _____ + _____ = 3⌐_____

     4. "Supervisory" satisfaction. Average items #5, #8, and #14 of Section Four.

               _____ + _____ + _____ = 3⌐_____

     5. "Growth" satisfaction. Average items #3, #6, #10, and #13 of Section Four.

               _____ + _____ + _____ + _____ = 2⌐_____

IV. *Individual Growth Need Strength:* This scale taps the degree to which an employee has strong or weak desire to obtain "growth" satisfactions from his or her work. Average items #2, #3, #6, #8, #10, #11 from Section Five. Before averaging, subtract 3 from each item score; this will result in a summary scale ranging from one to seven.

   _____ + _____ + _____ + _____ + _____ + _____

   – 3

   _____ + _____ + _____ + _____ + _____ + _____ = 6⌐_____

       Analysis of Part II

        For diagnostic purposes:

         ☐ *The GNS:* A score higher than 5 suggests you are ready for a redesign. A score lower than 3 suggests you may not be responsive. An in-between score suggests that you could move in either direction.

         ☐ *Internal work motivation:* A score higher than 4 suggests a high level of internal work motivation; anything lower suggests a lack of internal work motivation.

         ☐ *Satisfactions:* Scores higher than 4 suggest higher levels of satisfaction. Scores lower than 4 suggest there is room for change.

PART III: JOB REDESIGN

Directions: Post your Motivating Potential Scores on the chalkboard, with a shortened or abbreviated title describing the job next to each score. Examine the variety of MPS scores in the class. Which are the highest scores and why? Which are the lowest?

Take the three lowest MPS scores in the classroom as candidates for job redesign. Form three groups. Each group should include one of the lowest MPS-scored jobs in the class. Interview the low MPS jobholders to determine:

- ☐ The interdependencies associated with the job.
- ☐ The level of task identity.
- ☐ Task significance.
- ☐ Skill variety.
- ☐ Autonomy.
- ☐ Feedback.

Examine the growth satisfaction scores, the internal work motivation score, and the Growth Need Strength score to get a sense of the potential for redesign. The individual may be a candidate for job redesign if:

- ☐ The MPS score is low.
- ☐ The GNS and internal work motivation scores are high.

Identify ways in which the job could be redesigned according to the principles of job redesign in the Hackman (1977) article.

THE JOB CHARACTERISTICS MODEL: PRINCIPLES FOR REDESIGN

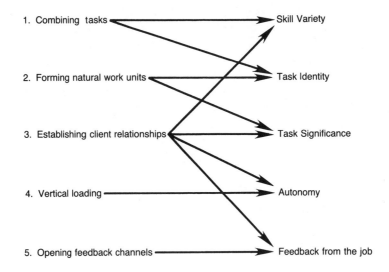

Diagnostic Questions for Redesign

1. Are motivation and satisfaction really problematic?

2. Is the job low in motivating potential?

3. What specific aspects of the job are causing the difficulty?

4. How "ready" are employees for change?

Option: Retake the Job Diagnostic Survey with one of your subordinate's jobs in mind. Consider what can be done to redesign the job, if needed. In groups, describe the problematic jobs that you supervise, and identify ways in which those jobs can be redesigned to increase motivation.

Subordinate's Job MPS score:_____

Ways in Which Subordinate Jobs Could be Improved

1. _____

2. _____

3. _____

4. _____

5. _____

6. _____

DISCUSSION QUESTIONS

1. To what extent do power, politics, and "turf" issues influence the degree to which jobs can be redesigned?

2. What implications does job redesign have for delegation activities by the manager?

3. What unintended consequences may occur when new procedures are introduced in one area, and similar changes are not effected in other corresponding areas or departments?

4. How can you use the information you obtained in this exercise directly as a way to improve subordinates' motivation at work?

REFERENCES

Herzberg, Frederick. "One More Time . . . How Do You Motivate Employees?" *Harvard Business Review.* January-February, 1986.

Hackman, J. Richard, and Greg Oldham. "Development of the Job Diagnostic Survey," *Journal of Applied Social Psychology,* 1975, 159-170.

Case: Plant Democracy at National Foods

PURPOSE

This case introduces you to the concept of semiautonomous work teams and demonstrates some of the unintended effects of job redesign programs. By the time you finish this case assignment, you will:

1. Understand the concept of semiautonomous work teams.

2. Identify the positive aspects of job redesign programs and their productivity benefits.

3. Determine the conditions that can have a negative effect on job redesign programs.

This case is reprinted from John F. Veiga and John N. Yanouzas, *The Dynamics of Organization Theory* (New York: West Publishers, 1984), pp. 405-408. It is based largely on the experience of General Foods Corporation as reported in "Stonewalling Plant Democracy," *Business Week,* March 28, 1977, 78-87. Used with permission.

INTRODUCTION

The Hackman (1977) article, "Designing Work for Individuals and Groups," introduces the idea of semiautonomous work teams, which represents a radical change in how work is designed. As an alternative to the standard assembly line concept, these teams typically are responsible for a "chunk" of the work that is managed by the project team. Workers on each team make their own job assignments, interview prospective employees, schedule coffee breaks, determine pay raises, and generally manage themselves and their work. In this way, workers are motivated by the challenge of the job itself—the actual work about which they have some control. At the same time, some of the demotivating aspects of routine assembly line work are eliminated.

The following case represents a history of the job redesign changes that occurred at the National Food Company. Semiautonomous teams were used in the redesign to improve productivity and minimize turnover. As you read the case, which has four parts, consider how successful you think the redesign efforts may be for each portion of the case.

INSTRUCTIONS

1. Read the article by Hackman, "Designing Work for Individuals and Groups."

2. Read Part I of the case, "Plant Democracy at National Foods." Complete the analysis questions at the end of this section.

3. Read Part II of the case. Complete the analysis estimates at the end of this section.

4. Read Part III of the case. How close were your estimates of production costs, turnover, and absenteeism?

5. Read Part IV of the case. Complete the discussion questions at the end of the case.

PART I

The opening of a new pet food processing plant at Omaha, Nebraska, gave the National Food Company (NF) an opportunity to design its organization structure in a manner that incorporates modern design principles. Utilizing the design principles of (1) *participation*, an attempt to distribute power throughout the organization and (2) *autonomy*, creation of independent work teams, NF designed a new factory system aimed at overcoming problems that beset other food processing plants. The specific goals of the new factory system, according to T. K. Nunley, manager of organizational development at

NF, included maximum machine utilization, minimum waste, low distribution costs, low productivity costs, and low absenteeism and turnover. Many of the functions traditionally the prerogatives of management were designed to be performed by the workers. The aim of the new system was to have workers make job assignments, interview prospective employees, schedule coffee breaks, and decide on pay raises. Having workers perform these duties was NF's way of attempting "to balance the needs of the people with the needs of the business," according to Nunley.

1. If you were asked by Nunley to react to his design ideas and goals, what would you tell him? Why?

2. Do you think a new structure alone will create the behaviors and outcomes that Nunley expects? Discuss.

Do not read until you have completed the analysis questions for Part I.

PART II

The factory system designed by a NF task force working with a professor from Harvard Business School eliminated some layers of management and supervisory personnel and assigned three areas of responsibility to self-managing work teams—processssing, packaging, and shipping. Each of the shift teams has seven to fourteen members who decide how to share authority and responsibility for a variety of tasks. For example, a processing team not only handles the actual pet food manufacturing, but also is responsible for unloading raw materials, maintaining equipment, inspecting for quality control, engineering how the work should be performed, and deciding on the size of pay raises for team members.

Work is directed by a team leader described as a "coach," rather than a supervisor or foreman. Work is made less boring by allowing team members to rotate between monotonous and interesting jobs. Pay is determined by the number of tasks each member masters and performs. The teams make necessary management decisions. To reduce perceived hierarchical status differences, NF removed some of the traditional management symbols. For example, there is now a common entrance for employees and management, and reserved parking spaces for management have been eliminated.

Analysis Questions

1. Estimate the efficiency of the factory system designed by the NF task force with respect to:

a. Production costs per unit:	_____Higher	_____Unchanged	_____Lower
b. Employee turnover:	_____Higher	_____Unchanged	_____Lower
c. Absenteeism due to lost time because of accidents	_____Higher	_____Unchanged	_____Lower

Do not read until you have completed the analysis questions for Part II.

PART III

The new factory system installed at the Omaha plant of NF was heralded as a model for the future and Nunley, who proclaims it as being "very successful," indicated that NF is applying a similar system at another dog food plant in St. Louis and at a coffee plant in Maryland. Reports indicate that NF may eventually install a similar system at two plants in Mexico and among white-collar workers at the headquarters organization in Stamford, Connecticut. Even the former manager of NF's Omaha and Milwaukee plants, James T. Lyman, who was a critic of the new system, admits, "Based on both the economic results and the quality of working life, it can be considered a success."

There remains little doubt that NF has met many of its goals. Unit costs are 6 percent less than in other plants using a traditional factory sytem. This, says Nunley, should amount to a savings of over $1.2 million in one year. Employee turnover is only 7 percent and the plant has not experienced a lost time accident in three and one-half years.

Analysis Questions

1. How close were your estimates of production costs, turnover, and absenteeism due to lost time for accidents? How can you explain the differences?

2. Is this outcome what you expected? Why, or why not?

Do not read until you have completed the analysis questions for Part III.

PART IV

Management analysts and former employees of the Omaha plant reveal a story that is somewhat different from the one released by National Foods. Critics say that after the initial euphoria, the new factory system, confronted by indifference and open hostility from some of the NF managers and staff specialists, has been modified several times.

"The system fell apart. It didn't work in practice," says one former manager. Another ex-employee adds, "It was both successful and unsuccessful. From an economic point of view, it was an absolute success, but from a human and organizational standpoint, it created a power struggle. It was much too threatening to both managers and staff specialists." He predicts that the plant will eventually be switched to a more traditional factory system.

The major problem was not that workers cannot manage their own work, as much as that some management and staff personnel felt their own positions were threatened by the workers' good performance. A management analyst suggested that the system, built around the team concept, was not compatible with NF's bureaucracy. NF's attorneys, fearing reaction from the National Labor Relations Board, opposed the concept of allowing team members to make pay raise decisions. Staff specialists feared the loss of prestige and even their positions, because the teams were doing some of their work. Personnel managers objected because the team members made hiring decisions and performed some of the other personnel functions like screening, training, and so on. Engineers resented engineering work being done by the team members. Quality control personnel saw an erosion of their functions since team members were responsible for some quality control work.

Another ex-employee, who was enthusiastic about the new system when it was first installed, saw it deteriorate. "Creating a new system is one thing, maintaining it is different," she claims. "There were pressures almost from the beginning, and not because of failures. The basic reason was power. The new arrangement contradicted corporate policy. People like stable states. This system has to be changing otherwise it will die. Why allow worker discretion to make changes and then turn around and freeze the system?"

The ex-plant manager felt that any time a structural change is made, one should not be surprised by unanticipated consequences.

If you have industrial engineers who have been designing work based on traditional principles for many years, they get anxious and threatened when they are thrown into a plant where the workers are doing job design. The personnel people are also threatened by the loss of functions they have performed in the past, and on top of that the personnel people must deal with a whole new set of problems such as the power struggle, peer complaints about pay raise decisions, etc. Controllers want someone from their own fraternity in the system, and so on. Plant democracy does not eliminate problems, all it does is create a new set of problems. As a result, pressures build up, the system starts to fragment, and when you fragment it, you also degrade it.

Consequently critics point out, there has been a slow "stiffening and tightening" in the Omaha system, such as more job classifications, more supervision, less participation, and so on. NF has added seven management positions to the plant including a plant industrial engineer, a controller and a manufacturing service manager. NF claims that the additions were due to plant expansion, but critics believe that it was more due to the "tightening up" of the system. A management analyst suggests that the modifications have caused a slight decrease in quality, a buildup of minor problems because of fewer team meetings, and increased competition between shifts.

Another problem area is pay. As the new system was implemented, team members who were voting on pay raise decisions began to feel peer pressure and stress. "You work with one person for several years and you get to be pretty good friends. Then it is difficult to be objective in deciding on pay raises," says one worker. "Moreover, the equal-pay-for-equal-work principle begins to break down."

Managers at the Omaha plant feel that their careers at NF have been jeopardized by getting involved in the new system. Along with the ex-plant manager, another manager who has since departed, says. "They felt we had created something that the corporate management couldn't handle, so their guys were sent in and we were forced out. By being involved in the new system at Omaha, I ruined my career at National Foods." Such skepticism exists even with some of the managers who have remained at the Omaha plant, and it affects all the work teams. One team member said, "Every time we make a mistake, I wonder if Stamford thinks that maybe it could have been avoided if the plant were operated by a traditional system." But even so, he adds, "This is the best place I've ever worked."

DISCUSSION QUESTIONS

1. What went wrong at the National Foods plant? Why were the job redesign changes rendered less effective over time?

2. In your opinion, will the forces in the Omaha system continue to effect the implementation of future change?

3. What specific action steps would you recommend to the headquarters of National Foods to stop the redesign effort from eroding further?

4. Based upon the case, what would you recommend to the management of any firm that is considering plant redesign?

REFERENCES

For additional information on the original General Foods case in Topeka, Kansas, see R. Walton, "How to Counter Alienation in the Plant," *Harvard Business Review,* 1972, 50 (6), 70-81, and R. E. Walton, "Work Innovation at Topeka: After 6 Years," *Journal of Applied Behavioral Science,* 1977, 13, 422-233.

Exercise: Making Rewards Work

PURPOSE

The purpose of this exercise is to help you understand how rewards affect behavior in organizations. By the time you finish this exercise you will:

1. Understand how rewards are misused in many organizations.

2. Determine how the misuse of rewards can adversely affect organizational effectiveness.

3. Identify ways to improve the use of organizational rewards.

INTRODUCTION

Despite the confusion and contradictions often accompanying a discussion of rewards, one finding is clear: People tend to repeat the actions for which they are rewarded. Unfortunately, as Kerr (1975) points out, all too often the behaviors for which people are rewarded in organizations are not the behaviors that lead to organizational effectiveness.

As a manager you will be called on to determine the behaviors for which your subordinates will be rewarded. You will decide whether they are promotable and what their raises will be. Because of this, you will be able to influence whether or not your subordinates' behavior works for or against the goals of the organization.

This exercise is an opportunity for you to evaluate rewarded behavior and determine if and how the reward structure should be changed. It is an opportunity for you to see how easily and insidiously the reward structure can become an enemy rather than an ally of organizational effectiveness.

INSTRUCTIONS

1. Read the three descriptions of organizational reward situations and answer the following questions:

- What are the goals of the organization?
- Which behaviors are being rewarded?
- Are the rewarded behaviors consistent with the organization's goals?
- What are the consequences of the reward structure for the organization?
- How should the reward structure be changed to more closely align it with the organization's goals?
- What are the barriers to changing the reward structure? How can they be overcome?

2. Participate in class discussion.

THE ERD

The Ecological Resource Department (ERD) is charged with protecting the environment. When the Protected Wetlands Act (PWA) was passed each state had a specified period of time to determine which areas were wetlands and therefore deserving of protection. One Midwestern state, with a large number of inland lakes (which are often surrounded by wetlands), did not have time to survey the entire state. Instead it declared all property within 1,000 yards of any inland lake to be wetlands. This ruling meant that anyone who wanted to develop any of this property needed the approval of the ERD.

Gordon Henry had owned 356 acres of lakefront property for 20 years. Some of the property was low and wet, but an ecologist (who had been instrumental in writing the PWA) surveyed the property and determined that the wetlands on Gordon's property were insignificant and artificial. They were insignificant because they did not provide a habitat for the water fowl that the PWA was intended to protect. They were considered artificial because a road that had been built across the property acted as a dam for the natural drainage of water. In addition, the streams, which normally drained the property, had become clogged with fallen trees and other debris.

When Gordon died, his heirs could not afford the taxes and insurance on the property. They decided to develop it by selling single-family homesites of over 10 acres each. They filed a permit application with the ERD to fill four of the 356 acres. The ERD refused the application citing irrevocable harm to the environment as their reason; no amount of expert testimony would sway them.

This Midwestern state also has a Timbering Act providing that the state cannot inhibit people from cutting trees on their land—including clear cutting or strip timbering. On appeal, in an effort to sway the ERD, Gordon's daughter told them that if they were not allowed to fill the four acres and thus develop their land for sale, they would be forced to clear cut the timber from the entire 356 acres. The ERD responded by saying that they had no jurisdiction over timbering but that they did over filling and the permit would not be granted.

The Whistle Blower

Jeremy Armstrong worked for a large government defense contractor that made various types of ammunition for the armed forces. This company had a policy of strict quality control that was continually reinforced in the company's in-house newsletter, annual report, employee handbook, frequent press releases, and posters throughout the factory. Jeremy, the personnel director, did not actually participate in the manufacturing process, but he was proud of his company's commitment to quality.

Jeremy began to hear some disturbing rumors concerning the falsification of test results. Eventually, a group of workers came to him and reported that their supervisor had repeatedly ordered them to reduce by 50 percent the number of bullets they reported as misfires. They asked for his help and he agreed. Jeremy was uncertain about how to proceed, but on Friday he called the legal department at the national headquarters. They asked for the names of the workers who had filed the complaint, and Jeremy gave them the information with the assurance that the names of the workers as well as his own would be kept confidential. They further assured him that the matter would be fully investigated.

When Jeremy returned to work on Monday, he was shocked to find the factory in turmoil. He was called into the plant manager's office as soon as he arrived and was informed that the president of the company had called to say that he had blown the whistle. Jeremy also was told that the supervisor whom he had accused had been informed of his and the workers' identities. The supervisor was left in his position and, according to reliable sources, destroyed any evidence that could have been used against him. Two weeks later Jeremy was told that the supervisor had been promoted to a position at national headquarters and that the workers who had blown the whistle would be suspended for a month without pay for falsifying the test results.

The New Member

Lynn Seeley was finishing her MBA at Harvard Business School. She was in the top 10 percent of her class and had several promising job offers from which to choose. She was especially intrigued by an offer as assistant to the president of a small electronics firm—New Frontier. Lynn spent two days at New Frontier. During that time she learned that the company was about to launch a new product that was expected to double the company's revenues within the year. She was also shown several other equally promising products that were near completion.

Les Snyder, New Frontier's founder and president, told Lynn that he was interested in hiring someone who could take charge of the day-to-day operation of the business so he could return to his real interest, which was research and development. Les also said that he felt that, with the growth the company was experiencing, there was a need for someone with a business background and a fresh perspective at the helm. He was concerned that he did not have the knowledge to effectively guide the company any longer because, although revenues had been growing, profits had been shrinking. Les said that he was prepared to pay her top dollar because she would be assuming so much responsibility. When he proposed a figure Lynn was happily surprised to find that it was 20 percent higher than her other offers. Lynn was excited by the opportunities at New Frontier as well as the salary. She turned down her other offers and accepted the position.

When Lynn arrived for her first day at work, Les called her into his office and told her to spend the next couple of weeks becoming familiar with the company. He told her that he was going to rely on her to use what she had learned in business school to make the company's operation as up-to-date as its technology. What Lynn observed during this orientation period both distressed and challenged her. The company's accounting department was out of date; there was no coordinated marketing or sales effort and no strategic orientation. No one at New Frontier seemed to know or care what the rest of the industry was doing, and they did not even know if there was a market for their products—including the new product that was about to be launched. Lynn was excited by the potential she saw in the company and was determined to turn the operation into a well coordinated and highly profitable venture. Lynn spent the weekend working at home on a detailed proposal to turn New Frontier into the highly effective and profitable company that she knew it could be.

On Monday Lynn presented her proposal to Les. Les glanced at it briefly, saying that he would consider it and get back to her. During the next week Les did not mention the proposal. Whenever Lynn tried to bring it up Les would change the subject. Other things also began to bother her. Les was spending all of his time in his office running the business and no time in the lab. He included her in all of the decisions he made, but, although he continually told her how much he valued her insight and initiative, he never followed any of her advice. Lynn became increasingly frustrated by her lack of impact and Les's reluctance to turn over any of the responsibility to her.

DISCUSSION QUESTIONS

1. How has the reward structure of your organization influenced your behavior in your organization?

2. Does the reward structure of your organization reinforce behaviors that are consistent or inconsistent with its goals? How?

3. How could the reward structure of your organization be changed to increase the congruence between organizational rewards and organizational goals?

4. How can you distinguish what is actually rewarded from what the organization claims to want?

REFERENCES

Kerr, S. "On the Folly of Rewarding A While Hoping for B," *Academy of Management Review,* 1975, Vol. 18, 769-783.

Memo: Motivation, Job Design, and Rewards

Following is a list of some attributes of work that people find rewarding. Because people prefer different things, space has been provided for you to customize your list. Circle the ten job attributes that would be the most rewarding to you. Rank order the ten selections from most to least important.

_____Feeling of achievement	_____Respect of others
_____Recognition	_____Good salary
_____Responsibility	_____Freedom and flexibility
_____Opportunity for advancement	_____Participation in decisions
_____Opportunity for growth	_____Challenge
_____Pleasant working conditions	_____Feedback on performance
_____Friendships	_____Using valued skills
_____Status	_____Completing a job from start to finish
_____Security	
_____Feelings of self-esteem	_____Lots of free time

_____Autonomy _____ _____
_____Doing something important _____ _____ _____

1. Are there any similarities among the job attributes that you selected as most important to you? Among those you did not select?

2. Are internal or external rewards more important to you?

3. What kind of job would provide you with all ten of your initial selections? Write a brief description of it. Be specific. For example, describe the skills you would be using, the tasks performed by you, your boss, your subordinates, your peers, as well as whether you would work alone or in a group. Where do you think you could find such a job?

4. How closely does your current job conform to what you have just described?

5. Which of the characteristics you selected are absolutely essential to your job satisfaction? Which could you be satisfied without? Write a brief description of a job that would provide you with only the characteristics that you identified as absolutely essential.

6. Does your current job provide you with the characteristics that are absolutely essential to your satisfaction? Which are missing?

Keep this information to use as data when you do the career development exercises in Chapter Six.

CHAPTER FOUR

Leadership and Decision Making

INTRODUCTION

How would you describe an effective leader? There are as many aspects as there are answers to this deceptively simple question. Everyone wants to know how to become a better leader, but few people really understand what effective leadership *is*. Students intuitively understand that effective leadership is a vital aspect of management. In fact, many would argue that leadership is the essence of effective management practices.

However, although we all know effective leaders when we see them in action, learning how to become one is a difficult task. Few valid prescriptions for effective leadership exist. Effective leadership seems to involve more than just "charisma"; it requires an understanding of the situation and the decision-making practices that apply to the situation. Leadership also requires flexibility in personal style—both decision-making styles and leadership styles—to adapt to the requirements of varying management situations and decision problems.

Historically, research in this area first linked effective leadership to individual traits, assuming that one central "leadership personality profile" would emerge. When this approach was unsuccessful, leader behaviors were examined to determine which styles of leader interaction with subordinates were not effective. Currently, contingency approaches to leadership, which focus on the situational conditions the leader faces, contribute the most to our understanding of effective leadership practices.

Leadership, in other words, is a very complex phenomenon. Everybody seems to have a different theory of leadership. Defining the essence of leadership is problematic at best.

There is limited agreement, however, on one aspect of leadership. That is, leadership seems to involve learning how to make effective decisions. A leader is someone who is able to size up a situation quickly (often in the absence of information), define a direction to pursue, and mobilize subordinates' energies toward the achievement of a particular goal. In other words, leaders must make decisions on the direction to follow. It often is the role of the leader to make decisions on strategy and the task accomplishment.

READINGS

The three articles in this chapter deal with leadership and decision-making practices.

The first article, "A Normative Model of Leadership Style" by Victor H. Vroom and Philip Yetton, examines the intersection of leadership and decision-making practices. These authors maintain that one of the most difficult aspects of leadership is determining under what conditions to allow subordinates to participate in decisions. Vroom and Yetton examine this dilemma carefully, presenting five styles of leadership based on three central categories—autocratic (AI, AII), consultative (CI, CII), or group (GI)—as a means to characterize leadership and decision-making practices. Vroom and Yetton suggest three decision criteria:

1. The quality of the decision.

2. The level of subordinates' acceptance.

3. The amount of time available.

They have developed a decision tree to help managers determine when and under what conditions subordinate participation in decision making is recommended.

The second article, "Leadership: Good, Better, Best" by Bernard Bass, identifies the necessary behaviors and characteristics for effective leadership. In this article, Bass describes the differences between transactional and transformational leadership. Bass argues that *transformational leaders* capture the fragile essence of leadership by inspiring others, by developing and showing consideration towards subordinates, and by providing intellectual stimulation. *Transactional leaders,* on the other hand, set up contingent reinforcement practices that create a no-win situation for subordinates—and for the leader. Bass further identifies the characteristics of charismatic leaders, maintaining that "charisma" is what separates an ordinary leader from an effective one.

The third article, "The Science of Muddling Through" by Charles Lindblom, concerns methods and modes of decision-making practices. Two methods of decision making are proposed: the root method and the branch method. The *root method* involves a comprehensive means-end analysis; the *branch method* assumes relativistic comparisons across particular decision-making outcomes. The root method is the method most commonly advocated but it is not adaptable to complex policy decisions, many of which are made by managers. Lindblom argues that most managerial decision-making practices, especially those concerning the adoption of policy, produce satisfactory rather than optimal solutions.

Because the study of leadership is so complex and intensive, we could not present readings that address each and every dimension of effective leadership. We chose to focus on those models that were "actionable" and realistic in their use. By concentrating on the intersection of leadership and decision-making practices, we hope students will gain greater appreciation of the need to diagnose a situation before taking leadership action.

EXERCISES AND CASES

The three exercises in the chapter will help you build skills in leadership and decision-making.

The first exercise, "Leadership and Decision-Making: Applying the Vroom and Yetton Model," allows you to determine the range of participative behavior that should be used in different leadership situations. In this exercise, you will have an opportunity to use the Vroom and Yetton decision tree to determine the appropriate leadership style to different management decisions. By understanding the conditions under which a leader should adopt participatory behaviors, compared with the conditions under which a leader should make decisions alone, you will be better able to assess this dimension in your own leadership practices.

The second exercise, a case entitled "The Man Who Killed Braniff," analyzes the downfall of one corporate executive as a result of his management practices. The case describes the leadership and decision-making style of Harding Lawrence and the role his style played in the "death" of Braniff airlines. Therefore, this case best illustrates how *not* to be an effective transformational leader. What should this leader have done to transform the situation? By understanding what went wrong in this case, you will be able to determine what *not* to do when presented with a leadership dilemma.

"Vanatin: Group Ethics and Decision Making" is a group experience providing an opportunity for you to participate in a management decision that has serious ethical and moral repurcussions. As a manager, you have to consider at all times the ethics of decision-making situations. Frequently, managers must choose between the profit-making motive and pressures for corporate social responsibility. Managers often complain that they are "caught between a rock and a hard place," because doing what is good for the company may not always be good for society at large. This exercise gives you an opportunity to see how you might react when confronted with an ethical decision. As Lindblom says, "Do the ends always justify the means?" Not necessarily—especially when ethical and moral issues are concerned.

MEMO

Finally, the memo assignment, "Leadership and Decision Making," asks you to consider leaders you have known. Which leaders have been effective managers? To what extent did they allow subordinate participation in decisions affecting them? Were they transformational leaders? How can you improve your own leadership skills to become a better decision maker and leader? The memo will help you develop an action plan to improve your leadership and decision-making skills.

By the time you finish this chapter, you will have a better understanding of effective leadership practices in organizations. You will also have gained experience in making decisions and determining the range of participative behavior required for effective management practice. You will also have had the opportunity to reflect on different methods of decision making, as well as the ethical and moral consequences of key management decisions.

A Normative Model of Leadership Style

Victor H. Vroom

Philip Yetton

INTRODUCTION

One of the most persistent and controversial issues in the study of management concerns the issue of participation in decision making by subordinates. Traditional models of the managerial process have been autocratic in nature. The manager makes decisions on matters within his area of freedom, issues orders or directives to his subordinates, and monitors their performance to ensure conformity with these directives. Scientific management, from its early developments in time and motion study to its contemporary manifestations in linear and heuristic programming, has contributed to this centralization of decision making in organizations by focusing on the development of methods by which managers can make more rational decisions, substituting objective measurements and empirically validated methods for casual judgments.

Most social psychologists and other behavioral scientists who have turned their attention toward the implications of psychological and social processes for the practice of management have called for greater participation by subordinates in the problem-solving and decision-making process. Pointing to evidence of restriction of output and lack of involvement under traditional managerial systems, they have argued for greater influence in decision making on the part of those who are held responsible for decision execution.

The empirical evidence provides some, but not overwhelming, support for beliefs in the efficacy of participative management. Field experiments on rank-and-file workers by Coch and French,[1] Bavelas,[2] and Strauss[3] indicate that impressive increases in productivity can be brought about by giving workers an opportunity to participate in decision making and goal setting. In addition, several correlational field studies[4] indicate positive relationships between the amount of influence which supervisors afford their subordinates in decisions which affect them and individual or group performance. On the other hand, in an experiment conducted in a Norwegian factory, French et al.[5] found no significant differences in production between workers who did and workers who did not participate in decisions regarding introduction of changes in work methods; and in a recent laboratory experiment, Sales and Rosen[6] found no significant differences between groups exposed to democratic and autocratic supervision. To complicate the picture further, Morse and Reimer[7] compared the effects of two programs of change, each of which was introduced in two divisions of the clerical operations of a large insurance company. One of the programs involved increased participation in decision making by rank-and-file workers, while the other involved increased hierarchical control. The results show a significant increase in productivity under both programs, with the hierarchically controlled program producing the greater increase.

Reconciliation of these discrepant findings is not an easy task. It is made complex by different

Abridged from Victor H. Vroom and Philip Yetton, *Leadership and Decision Making* (Pittsburgh: University of Pittsburgh Press, 1973), by permission of the publisher and authors. © 1973 by the University of Pittsburgh Press.

Reprinted by permission from H. J. Leavitt, L. R. Pondy and D. M. Boje (Eds.), *Readings in Managerial Psychology,* 3rd ed. Chicago: University of Chicago Press, 1980.

1. L. Coch and J. R. P. French, Jr., "Overcoming Resistance to Change." *Human Relations* 1 (1948): 512–32.

2. Reported in J. R. P. French, Jr., "Field Experiments: Changing Group Productivity," in J. G. Miller, Ed., *Experiments in Social Process: A Symposium on Social Psychology* (New York: McGraw-Hill, 1950), pp. 79–96.

3. Reported in W. F. Whyte, *Money and Motivation* (New York: Harper, 1955).

4. D. Katz, N. Maccoby, and Nancy C. Morse, *Productivity, Supervision and Morale in an Office Situation* (Ann Arbor: University of Michigan, Institute for Social Research, 1950); V. H. Vroom, *Some Personality Determinants of the Effects of Participation* (Englewood Cliffs, N.J.: Prentice-Hall, 1960).

5. J. R. P. French, Jr., J. Israel, and D. As, "An Experiment on Participation in a Norwegian Factory," *Human Relations* 13 (1960): 3–9.

6. S. M. Sales and N. A. Rosen, "A Laboratory Investigation of the Effectiveness of Two Industrial Supervisory Patterns" (unpublished manuscript, Cornell University, 1965).

7. Nancy C. Morse and E. Reimer, "The Experimental Change of a Major Organizational Variable," *Journal of Abnormal Social Psychology* 52 (1956): 120–29.

empirical interpretations of the term "participation"[8] and by great differences in the situations in which it is applied. It appears highly likely that an increase in participation of subordinates in decision making may increase productivity under some circumstances but decrease productivity under other circumstances. Identification of the situational conditions which determine the efficacy of participative management requires the specification of the decision-making processes which it entails and of the various mechanisms by which it may influence the extent to which the formal objectives of the organization are attained.

The conclusion appears inescapable that participation in decision making has consequences which vary from one situation to another. Given the potential importance of this conclusion for the study of leadership and its significance to the process of management, it appears to be critical for social scientists to begin to develop some definitions of the circumstances under which participation in decision making may contribute to or hinder organizational effectiveness. These could then be translated into guidelines of potential value to managers in choosing the leadership styles to fit the demands of the situations which they encounter.

In this chapter, one approach to dealing with this important problem will be described. A normative model is developed which is consistent with existing empirical evidence concerning the consequences of participation and which purports to specify a set of rules which should be used in determining the form and amount of participation in decision making by subordinates to be used in different classes of situations.

BASIC ASSUMPTIONS

1. The normative model should be constructed in such a way as to be of potential value to managers or leaders in determining which leadership styles they should employ in each of the various situations that they encounter in carrying out their formal leadership roles. Consequently, it should deal with behaviors which are within their repertoire and their control.

2. There are a number of discrete social processes by which organizational problems can be translated into solutions and these processes vary in terms of the potential amount of participation by subordinates in the problem-solving process.

The term "participation" has been used in a number of different ways. Perhaps the most influential definitions have been those of French et al.[9] and Vroom,[10] who define participation as a process of joint decision making by two or more parties. The amount of participation of any individual is the amount of influence he has on the decisions and plans agreed upon. Given the existence of a property such as participation which varies from high to low, it should be possible to define leadership styles or behaviors which represent clear alternative processes for making decisions which can be related to the amount of participation each process affords the managers' subordinates.

A taxonomy of leadership style created for normative purposes should distinguish among methods which are likely to have different outcomes but should not be so elaborate that leaders are unable to determine which style they are employing in any given instance. The taxonomy to be used in the normative model is shown in table 1.

It should be noted that the styles are arranged in two columns corresponding to their applicability to problems which involve the entire group or some subset of it (hereafter called group problems) or a single subordinate (hereafter called individual problems). If a problem or decision clearly affects only one subordinate, the leader would choose among the methods shown in the right-hand column; if it had potential effects on the entire group (or subset of it), he would choose among the methods shown in the left-hand column. The styles in both columns are arranged from top to bottom in terms of the opportunity for subordinates to influence the solution to the problem. (The principle behind the numbering system is as follows: The letters A, C, G, and D stand for autocratic, consultative, group, and delegation. The numerals I and II denote variations on the basic decision processes.)

3. No single leadership style is applicable to all situations; the function of a normative model should be to provide a framework for the analysis of situational requirements which can be translated into prescriptions of leadership styles.

The fact that the most effective leadership method or style is dependent on the situation is

8. G. Strauss, "Some Notes on Power Equalization," in H. J. Leavitt, ed., *The Social Science of Organizations* (Englewood Cliffs, N.J.: Prentice-Hall, 1963), pp. 39–84.

9. French, Israel, and As, "An Experiment on Participation."

10. Vroom, *Some Personality Determinants.*

becoming widely recognized by behavioral scientists interested in problems of leadership and administration. A decision-making process which is optimal for a quarterback on a football team making decisions under severe time constraints is likely to be far from optimal when used by a dean introducing a new curriculum to be implemented by his faculty. Even the advocates of participative management have noted this "situational relativity" of leadership styles. Thus, Argyris writes:

> No one leadership style is the most effective. Each is probably effective under a given set of conditions. Consequently, I suggest that effective leaders are those who are capable of behaving in many different leadership styles, depending on the requirements of reality as they and others perceive it. I call this "reality-centered" leadership.[11]

It is necessary to go beyond noting the importance of situational factors and begin to move toward a roadmap or normative model which attempts to prescribe the most appropriate leadership style for different kinds of situations. The most comprehensive treatment of situational factors as determinants of the effectiveness and efficiency of participation in decision making is found in the work of Tannenbaum and Schmidt.[12] They list and discuss a large number of variables including attributes of the manager, his subordinates, and the situation, which ought to enter into the manager's decision about the degree to which he should share his power with his subordinates. But they do not go beyond this inventory of variables to show how these might be combined and translated into different forms of actions.

4. The most appropriate unit for the analysis of the situation is the particular problem to be solved and the context in which the problem occurs.

While it is becoming widely recognized that different situations require different leadership methods, there is less agreement concerning the appropriate units for the analysis of the situation. One approach is to assume that the situations which interact with or condition the choice and effectiveness of different leadership styles correspond to the environment of the system. Alternatively, one might assume that the critical features of the situation concern the role of the leader, including his relations with his subordinates.

The approach taken here is to utilize the properties of the problem to be solved as the most critical situational dimensions for determining the appropriate form or amount of participation. Different prescriptions would be made for a given leader for different problems within a given role. It should be noted that constructing a normative model with the problem rather than the role or any organizational differences as the unit of analysis does not rule out the possibility that different roles and organizations may involve different distributions of problem types and which in aggregate may require different modal styles or levels of participation.

5. The leadership method used in response to one situation should not constrain the method or style used in other situations.

This assumption is necessary to make possible the construction of a normative model founded on problem differences. It may seem inconsistent with the view, first proposed by McGregor,[13] that consistency in leadership style is desirable because it enables subordinates to predict or anticipate their superiors' behavior and to adapt to it. However, predictability does not preclude variability. There are many variable phenomena which can be predicted quite well because the rules or processes which govern them are understood. The antithesis of predictability is randomness and, if McGregor is correct, a normative model to regulate choices among alternative leadership styles should be deterministic rather than stochastic. The model developed here is deterministic; the normatively prescribed style for a given problem type is a constant.

CONCEPTUAL AND EMPIRICAL BASIS OF THE MODEL

A model designed to regulate, in some rational way, choices among the leadership styles shown in table 1 should be based on sound empirical evidence concerning the likely consequences of the styles. The more complete the empirical base of knowledge, the

11. C. Argyris, *Interpersonal Competence and Organizational Effectiveness* (Homewood, Ill.: Irwin-Dorsey, 1962), p. 81.

12. R. Tannenbaum and W. H. Schmidt, "How to Choose a Leadership Pattern," *Harvard Business Review* 36 (1958): 95–101.

13. D. McGregor, "Getting Effective Leadership in the Industrial Organization," *Advanced Management* 9 (1944): 148–53.

TABLE 1
Decision Methods for Group and Individual Problems.

Group Problems	Individual Problems
AI You solve the problems or make the decision yourself, using information available to you at that time.	**AI** You solve the problem or make the decision yourself, using information available to you at that time.
AII You obtain the necessary information from subordinates, then decide on the solution to the problem yourself. You may or may not tell subordinates what the problem is in getting the information from them. The role played by your subordinates in making the decision is clearly one of providing the necessary information to you, rather than generating or evaluating alternative solutions.	**AII** You obtain necessary information from the subordinate, then decide on solution to problem yourself. You may or may not tell the subordinate what the problem is in getting the information from him. The role played by the subordinate in making the decision is clearly one of providing the necessary information to you, rather than generating or evaluating alternative solutions.
CI You share the problem with relevant subordinates individually, getting their ideas and suggestions without bringing them together as a group. Then you make the decision which may or may not reflect your subordinates' influence.	**CI** You share the problem with the subordinate, getting his ideas and suggestions, then you make the decision which may or may not reflect your subordinate's influence.
CII You share the problem with your subordinates as a group, collectively obtaining their ideas and suggestions. Then, you make the decision which may or not reflect your subordinates' influence.	
GII You share the problem with your subordinates as a group. Together you generate and evaluate alternatives and attempt to reach agreement (consensus) on a solution.	**GI** You share the problem with your subordinate and together you analyze the problem and arrive at a mutually agreeable solution.
	DI You delegate the problem to your subordinate, providing him with any relevant information that you possess, but giving him responsibility for solving the problem by himself. You may or may not request him to tell you what solution he has reached.

greater the certainty with which one can develop the model and the greater will be its usefulness. In this section we will restrict ourselves to the development of a model concerned only with group problems and, hence, will use only the methods shown in the left-hand column of table 1. To aid in this analysis, it is important to distinguish three classes of outcomes which bear on the ultimate effectiveness of decisions. These are:

1. The quality or rationality or the decision.

2. The acceptance of commitment on the part of subordinates to execute the decision effectively.

3. The amount of time required to make the decision.

The evidence regarding the effects of participation on each of these outcomes or consequences has been reviewed elsewhere.

The results suggest that allocating problem-solving and decision-making tasks to entire groups as compared with the leader or manager in charge of the groups, requires a greater investment of man hours but produces higher acceptance of decisions and a higher probability that the decisions will be executed efficiently. Differences between these two methods in quality of decisions and in elapsed time are inconclusive and probably highly variable.

. . . It would be naïve to think that group decision making is always more "effective" than autocratic decision making, or vice versa; the relative effectiveness of these two extreme methods depends both on the weights attached to quality, acceptance, and time variables and on differences in amounts of these outcomes resulting from these methods, neither of which is invariant from one situation to another. The critics and proponents of participative management would do well to direct their efforts toward identifying the properties of situations in which different decision-making approaches are effective rather than wholesale condemnation or deification of one approach.[14]

Stemming from this review, an attempt has been made to identify these properties of the situation or problem which will be the basic elements in the model. These problem attributes are of two types: (1) those which specify the importance of quality and acceptance for a particular problem (see A and D below) and (2) those which, on the basis of available evidence, have a high probability of moderating the effects of participation on each of these outcomes (see B, C, E, G, and H below). The following are the problem attributes used in the present form of the model.

A. The importance of the quality of the decision.

B. The extent to which the leader possesses sufficient information/expertise to make a high-quality decision by himself.

C. The extent to which subordinates, taken collectively, have the necessary information to generate a high-quality decision.

D. The extent to which the problem is structured.

E. The extent to which acceptance or commitment on the part of subordinates is critical to the effective implementation of the decision.

F. The prior probability that the leader's autocratic decision will receive acceptance by subordinates.

G. The extent to which subordinates are motivated to attain the organizational goals as represented in the objectives explicit in the statement of the problem.

H. The extent to which subordinates are likely to be in disagreement over preferred solutions.

Table 2 shows the same eight problem attributes expressed in the form of questions which might be used by a leader in diagnosing a particular problem before choosing his leadership style. In phrasing the questions, technical language has been held to a minimum. Furthermore, the questions have been phrased in yes-no form, translating the continuous variables defined above into dichotomous variables. For example, instead of attempting to determine how important the decision quality is to the effectiveness of the decision (attribute A), the leader is asked in the first question to judge whether there is any quality component to the problem. Similarly, the difficult task of specifying exactly how much information the leader possesses that is relevant to the decision (attribute B) is reduced to a simple judgment by the leader concerning whether he has sufficient information to make a high-quality decision.

TABLE 2
Problem Attributes.

A. If decision were accepted, would it make a difference?

B. Do I have sufficient information to make a high-quality decision?

C. Do subordinates have sufficient additional information to result in a high-quality decision?

D. Do I know exactly what information is needed, who possesses it, and how to collect it?

E. Is acceptance of decision by subordinates critical to effective implementation?

F. If you were to make the decision by yourself, is it certain that it would be accepted by your subordinates?

G. Can subordinates be trusted to base solutions on organizational considerations?

H. Is conflict among subordinates likely in preferred solutions?

Expressing what are obviously continuous variables in dichotomous form greatly simplifies the problem of developing a model incorporating these attributes which can be used by leaders. It sidesteps the problem of scaling each problem attribute and

---

14. V. H. Vroom, "Industrial Social Psychology," in G. Lindsey and E. Aronson, eds., *Handbook of Social Psychology* (Reading, Mass.: Addison-Wesley, 1970), chap. 5, pp. 239–40.

reduces the complexities of the judgments required of leaders.

It has been found that managers can diagnose a situation quite quickly and accurately by answering this set of eight questions concerning it. But how can such responses generate a prescription concerning the most effective leadership style or decision process? What kind of normative model of participation in decision making can be built from this set of problem attributes?

A NORMATIVE MODEL OF LEADERSHIP STYLES

Let us assume that you are a manager faced with a concrete problem to be solved. We will also assume that you have judged that this problem could potentially affect more than one of your subordinates. Hence, it is what we have defined as a group problem, and you have to choose among the five decision processes (AI, AII, CI, CII, GII) shown at the left side of table 1.

On a priori grounds any one of these five decision processes could be called for. The judgments you have made concerning the status of each of the problem's attributes can be used to define a set of feasible alternatives. This occurs through a set of rules which eliminate decision processes from the feasible set under certain specifiable conditions.

The rules are intended to protect both the quality and acceptance of the decision. In the present form of the model, there are three rules which protect decision quality and four which protect acceptance. The seven rules are presented here both as verbal statements and the more formal language of set theory. In the set theoretic formulation, the letters refer to the problem attributes as stated in question form in table 2. $\bar{A}$ signifies that the answer to question A for a particular problem is yes; A signifies that the answer to that question is no; $\cap$ signifies intersection; $\Rightarrow$ signifies "implies"; and $\bar{A}\bar{I}$ signifies not AI. Thus $A \cap \bar{B} \Rightarrow AI$ may be read as follows; when both the answer to question A is yes and the answer to question B is no, AI is eliminated from the feasible set.

1. *The Information Rule.* If the leader does not possess enough information or expertise to solve the problem by himself, AI is eliminated from the feasible set. (Its use risks a low-quality decision.) (A $\cap \bar{B} \Rightarrow \bar{A}\bar{I}$)

2. *The Trust Rule.* If the subordinates cannot be trusted to base their efforts to solve the problems on organizational goals, GII is eliminated from the

feasible set. (Alternatives which eliminate the leader's final control over the decision reached may jeopardize the quality of the decision.) (A $\cap \bar{G} \Rightarrow \bar{G}\bar{I}\bar{I}$)

3. *The Unstructured Problem Rule.* If the leader lacks the necessary information or expertise to solve the problem by himself, and if the problem is unstructured, i.e., he does not know exactly what information is needed and where it is located, the method used must provide not only for him to collect the information but to do so in an efficient and effective manner. Methods which involve interaction among all subordinates with full knowledge of the problem are likely to be both more efficient and more likely to generate a high-quality solution to the problem. Under these conditions, AI, AII, and CI are eliminated from the feasible set. (AI does not provide for him to collect the necessary information, and AII and CI represent more cumbersome, less effective, and less efficient means of bringing the necessary information to bear on the solution of the problem than methods which do permit those with the necessary information to interact.) (A $\cap \bar{B} \cap \bar{D} \Rightarrow \bar{A}\bar{I}$, $\bar{A}\bar{I}\bar{I}$, $\bar{C}\bar{I}$)

4. *The Acceptance Rule.* If the acceptance of the decision by subordinates is critical to effective implementation and if it is not certain that an autocratic decision made by the leader would receive th' acceptance, AI and AII are eliminated from feasible set. (Neither provides an opportunit' subordinates to participate in the decision ar risk the necessary acceptance.) (E $\cap$ F $\Rightarrow$

5. *The Conflict Rule.* If the accept decision is critical, and an autocratic d certain to be accepted, and subordinat be in conflict or disagreement over solution, AI, AII, and CI are el' feasible set. (The method used ir should enable those in disagre' differences with full knowle' cordingly, under these cor which involve no interar relationships and theref' those in conflict to eliminated from the risk of leaving som the necessary (Ē $\cap$ F̄ $\cap$ H̄

6. *The* is unimportan' certain to res' CI, and CII ar

method used should maximize the probability of acceptance as this is the only relevant consideration in determining the effectiveness of the decision. Under these circumstances AI, AII, CI, and CII which create less acceptance or commitment than GII are eliminated from the feasible set. To use them is to run the risk of getting less than the needed acceptance of the decision.) $(\bar{A} \cap E \cap \bar{F} \Rightarrow \bar{A}\bar{I}, \bar{A}\bar{I}\bar{I}, \bar{C}\bar{I}, \bar{C}\bar{I}\bar{I})$

7. *The Acceptance Priority Rule.* If acceptance is critical, not assured by an autocratic decision and if subordinates can be trusted, AI, AII, CI, and CII are eliminated from the feasible set. (Methods which provide equal partnership in the decision-making process can provide greater acceptance without risking decision quality. Use of any method other than GII results in an unnecessary risk that the decision will not be fully accepted or receive the necessary commitment on the part of subordinates.) $(A \cap E \cap \bar{F} \cup G \Rightarrow \bar{A}\bar{I}, \bar{A}\bar{I}\bar{I}, \bar{C}\bar{I}, \bar{C}\bar{I}\bar{I})$

Application of these rules to a problem is aided by their pictorial representation in the form of a decision tree. Figure 1 shows a simple decision tree which serves this purpose.

The problem attributes are arranged along the top of the figure. To apply the rules to a particular problem one starts at the left-hand side and works toward the right, asking oneself the question immediately above any box that is encountered. When a terminal node is reached, the number designates the problem type which in turn designates a set of methods which remains feasible after the rules have been applied.[15] It can be seen that this method of representing the decision tree generates fourteen problem types. Problem type is a nominal variable designating classes of problems generated by the aths which lead to the terminal nodes. Thus, all oblems which have no quality requirements and in ich acceptance is not critical are defined as type 1; problems which have no quality requirement in h acceptance is critical but the prior probability of tance of the leader's decision is high are defined e 2; and so on.

he feasible set for each of the fourteen types is shown in table 3. It can be seen that e some problem types for which only one emains in the feasible set, others for which

le 2 has not been applied to problem types 4, 14. This rule eliminates GII from the feasible nswer to question G is no. Thus, we can ariants of each of these types.

Four

TABLE 3
Problem Types and the Feasible Set of Leadership Styles.

Problem Type	Acceptable Methods
1	AI, AII, CI, CII, GII
2	AI, AII, CI, CII, GII
3	GII
4	AI, AII, CI, CII, GII*
5	AI, AII, CI, CII, GII*
6	GII
7	CII
8	CI, CII
9	AII, CI, CII, GII*
10	AII, CI, CII, GII*
11	CII, GII*
12	GII
13	CII
14	CIII, GII*

*Within the feasible set only when the answer to question G is yes.

two methods remain feasible, and still others for which five methods remain feasible. It should be recalled that the feasible set is defined as the set of methods which remains after all those which violate rules designated to protect the quality and acceptance of the decision have been excluded.

CHOOSING AMONG ALTERNATIVES IN THE FEASIBLE SET

When more than one method remains in the feasible set, there are a number of alternative decision rules which might dictate the choice among them. One, which will be examined in greatest depth, utilizes the number of man-hours used in solving the problem as the basis for choice. Given a set of methods with equal likelihood of meeting both quality and acceptance requirements for the decision, it chooses that method which requires the least investment in man-hours. This is deemed to be the method furthest to the left within the feasible set. Thus, if AI, AII, CI, CII, and GII are all feasible as in problem types 1 and 2, AI would be the method chosen. This decision rule acts to minimize man-hours subject to quality and acceptance constraints.

This decision rule for choosing among alternatives in the feasible set results in the prescription of each of the five decision processes in some situations. AI is prescribed for four problem types (1, 2, 4, and 5); AII is prescribed for two problem types (9 and

10); CI is prescribed for only one problem type (8); CII is prescribed for four problem types (7, 11, 13, and 14); and GII is prescribed for three problem types (3, 6, and 12). The relative frequency with which the five decision processes would be prescribed for any leader would, of course, be dependent on the distribution of problem types in his role.

SHORT-TERM VERSUS LONG-TERM MODELS

The model described above seeks to protect, if relevant, the quality of the decision, to create any necessary acceptance of the decision, and to expend the least number of man-hours in the process. In view of its attention to conditions surrounding the making and implementation of a particular decision rather than any long-term considerations, it could be termed a short-term model.

It seems likely, however, that the leadership methods which may be optimal for short-term results may be different from those which would be optimal when executed over a longer period of time. Consider a leader who has been uniformly pursuing an autocratic style (AI or AII) and, perhaps as a consequence, has subordinates who cannot be trusted to pursue organizational goals (attribute G) and who have little additional knowledge or experience to bring to bear on the decisions to be made (attribute C). An examination of the structure of the time-minimizing model reveals that with few exceptions, the leader would be instructed by the model to continue his present autocratic style.

It appears likely, however, that the use of more participative methods would, in time, change the status of these problem attributes (i.e., increase the extent to which subordinates would have information relevant to the solution of problems in the future and increase the extent to which their goals are congruent with those of the organization) so as to develop ultimately a more effective problem-solving system. In the example given above, an autocratic approach would be indicated to maximize short-run benefits but a higher degree of participation might maximize performance aggregated over a longer period.

A promising approach to the development of a long-term model is one which places less weight on man-hours as the basis for choice of method within the feasible set. Given a long-term orientation one would be interested in the trade-off between man-hours in problem solving and team development, both of which increase with participation. Viewed in these terms, the time minimizing model places maximum relative weight on man-hours and no weight on development and hence chooses the style furthest to the left within the feasible set. A model which places less weight on man-hours and more weight on development would, if these assumptions are correct, choose a style further to the right within the feasible set.

SUMMARY

In this chapter, a normative model of leadership style was developed. The model attempts to deal with the complexities of the processes involved in leadership by specifying (1) a set of alternatives among which a choice is to be made, (2) the general nature of the processes which they affect, (3) the principal variables governing the effects of the alternatives on each process, and (4) explicit rules for decision making based on estimates of the outcome of each process.

Some might argue that it is premature for social scientists to attempt to be prescriptive. Our knowledge is too little and the issues too complex to warrant explicit normative models dealing with matters such as leadership style. It is also true, however, that leaders are facing daily the task of selecting decision-making processes which in turn reflect their leadership style. Is it likely that a model which requires them to deal analytically with the forces impinging upon them and which is consistent with admittedly imperfect research base would produce less rational choices than those which they do make? The criterion for social ability is not perfection but improvement over present practice.

Furthermore, social scientists are increasingly having an influence not only on people's leadership style but also on such matters as job design, training methods, and compensation systems. Too frequently, in the view of the present authors, their prescriptions for action, whether it be job enrichment, sensitivity training, or group decision making, are not based on a systematic analysis of the situation in a manner which would point to the costs and benefits of available alternatives.

Perhaps the most convincing argument for the development of normative models is the fact that in developing and using them their weaknesses can be identified. Insofar as these weaknesses stem from lack of basic knowledge, this deficiency can be remedied through further research. A strong case can be made for the continued interplay between the worlds of practice and social science on the basis of their mutual contributions to one another.

FIGURE 1
Problem Types.

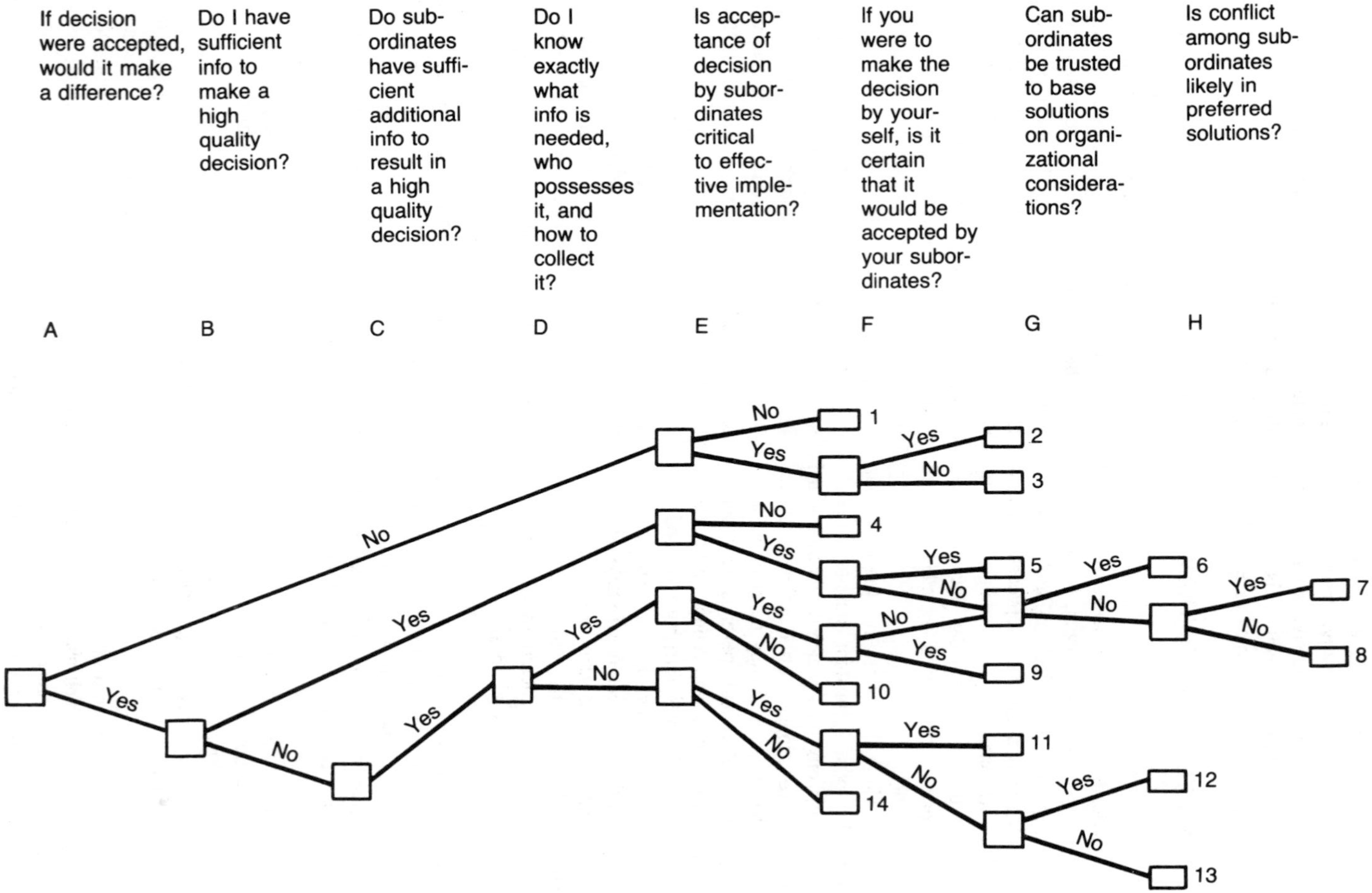
If decision were accepted, would it make a difference?
Do I have sufficient info to make a high quality decision?
Do subordinates have sufficient additional info to result in a high quality decision?
Do I know exactly what info is needed, who possesses it, and how to collect it?
Is acceptance of decision by subordinates critical to effective implementation?
If you were to make the decision by yourself, is it certain that it would be accepted by your subordinates?
Can subordinates be trusted to base solutions on organizational considerations?
Is conflict among subordinates likely in preferred solutions?
A
B
C
D
E
F
G
H
Yes
No
1
2
3
4
5
6
7
8
9
10
11
12
13
14

Leadership: Good, Better, Best

Bernard M. Bass

What does Lee Iacocca have that many other executives lack? Charisma. What would have happened to Chrysler without him? It probably would have gone bankrupt. Here are two more questions: How much does business and industry encourage the emergence of leaders like Iacocca? And how much effort has organizational psychology put into research on charismatic leadership? The answers are that business and industry have usually discouraged charismatic leadership and that, for the most part, organizational psychology has ignored the subject. It has been customary to see leadership as a method of getting subordinates to meet job requirements by handing out rewards or punishments.

Take a look at Barry Bargainer. Barry considers himself to be a good leader. He meets with subordinates to clarify expectations—what is required of them and what they can expect in return. As long as they meet his expectations, Barry doesn't bother them.

Cynthia Changer is a different kind of leader. When facing a crisis, Cynthia inspires her team's involvement and participation in a "mission." She solidifies it with simple words and images and keeps reminding her staff about it. She has frequent one-to-one chats with each of her employees at his or her work station. She is a consultant, coach, teacher, and mother figure.

Barry Bargainer, a transactional leader, may inspire a reasonable degree of involvement, loyalty, commitment, and performance from his subordinates. But Cynthia Changer, using a transformational approach, can do much more.

The first part of this article contrasts transactional and transformational leadership styles and the results that are obtained when managers select each approach. The second section reports on surveys of personnel in the military and in industry and examines factors in both approaches to leadership, as they emerged from the survey results. Transformational leadership is presented as a way to augment transactional approaches to management, since it is often more effective in achieving higher levels of improvement and change among employees.

Reprinted with permission of The Free Press, a Division of Macmillan, Inc., from *Leadership and Performance Beyond Expectations* by Bernard M. Bass. Copyright © 1985 by The Free Press.

A NEW PARADIGM

For half a century, leadership research has been devoted to studying the effects of democratic and autocratic approaches. Much investigative time has gone into the question of who should decide—the leader or the led. Equally important to research has been the distinction between task orientation and relations orientation. Still another issue has been the need of the leader to "initiate structure" for subordinates and to be considerate of them. At the same time, increasing attention has been paid to the ability to promote change in individuals, groups, and organizations.

The need to promote change and deal with resistance to it has, in turn, put an emphasis on democratic, participative, relations-oriented, and considerate leadership. Contingent rewards have been stressed in training and research with somewhat limited results.

In the past, we have mostly considered how to marginally improve and maintain the quantity or quality of performance, how to substitute one goal for another, how to shift attention from one action to another, how to reduce resistance to particular actions, or how to implement decisions. But higher-order changes are also possible. Increases in effort and the rate at which a group's speed and accuracy improve can sometimes be accelerated. Such higher-order changes also may involve larger shifts in attitudes, beliefs, values, and needs. Quantum leaps in performance may result when a group is roused out of its despair by a leader with innovative or revolutionary ideas and a vision of future responsibilities. Leaders may help bring about a radical shift in attention. The context may be changed by leaders. They may change what the followers see as figure and what they see as ground or raise the level of maturity of their needs and wants. For example, followers' concerns may be elevated from their need for recognition and achievement.

The lower order of improvement—changes in degree or marginal improvement—can be seen as the result of leadership that is an exchange process: a *transaction* in which followers' needs are met if their performance measures up to their explicit or implicit contracts with their leader. But higher-order improvement calls for *transformational* leadership.

There is a great deal of difference between the two types of leadership.

TRANSACTIONAL LEADERSHIP IN ACTION

Transactional leaders like Barry Bargainer recognize what actions subordinates must take to achieve outcomes. Transactional leaders clarify these role and task requirements for their subordinates so that they are confident in exerting necessary efforts. Transactional leaders also recognize subordinates' needs and wants and clarify how they will be satisfied if necessary efforts are made. (See Exhibit 1.) This approach is currently stressed in leadership training, and it is good as far as it goes; however, the transactional approach has numerous shortcomings.

First, even after training, managers do not fully utilize transactional leadership. Time pressures, poor appraisal methods, doubts about the efficacy of positive reinforcement, leader and subordinate discomfort with the method, and lack of management skills are all partly responsible. How reinforcements are scheduled, how timely they are, and how variable or consistent they are all mediate the degree of their influence.

Some leaders, practicing management by exception, intervene only when things go wrong. In this instance, the manager's discomfort about giving negative feedback is even more self-defeating. When supervisors attribute poor performance to lack of ability, they tend to "pull their punches" by distorting feedback so that it is more positive than it should be.

Another common problem occurs when supervisors say and actually believe they are giving feedback to their subordinates, who feel they are not receiving it. For example, Barry Bargainer may meet with his group of subordinates to complain that things are not going well. Barry thinks he is giving negative feedback while his subordinates only hear Barry grumbling about conditions. Barry may give Henry a pat on the back for a job he thinks has been done well. Henry may feel that he knows he did a good job, and it was condescending for Barry to mention it.

People differ considerably in their preference for external reinforcement or self-reinforcement. Task-oriented and experienced subordinates generally are likely to be self-reinforcing. They may say: "If I have done something well, I know it without other people telling me so," and "As long as I think I have done something well, I am not too concerned about what other people think I have done."

Subordinates and supervisors attach differing importance to various kinds of feedback. Many subordinates attach more importance than do supervisors to their own success or failure with particular tasks, and to their own comparisons with the work of others. Subordinates are also likely to attach more importance than do supervisors to co-workers' comments about their work. Supervisiors tend to put the most weight on their own comments to their subordinates, and to recommendations for rewards they, as supervisors, can make, such as raises, promotions, and more interesting assignments.

Transactional leadership often fails because the leaders lack the reputation for being able to deliver

EXHIBIT 1
Transactional Leadership (L = Leader; F = Follower).

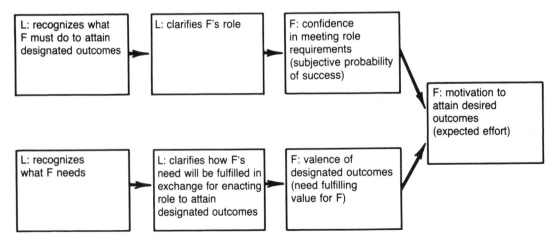

rewards. Transactional leaders who fulfill the self-interested expectations of their subordinates gain and maintain the reputation for being able to deliver pay, promotions, and recognition. Those that fail to deliver lose their reputation and are not considered to be effective leaders.

Transactional leadership may be abandoned by managers when noncontingent rewards (employees are treated well, regardless of performance) will work just as well to boost performance. For example, in a large, nonprofit organization, a study by Phillip Podsakoff et al. showed that contingent rewards (those given only if performance warrants them) did contribute to employee performance, but noncontingent rewards were correlated almost as strongly with performance as contingent rewards.

Noncontingent rewards may provide a secure situation in which employees' self-reinforcement serves as a consequence for good performance (for example, IBM's straight salaries for all employees). An employee's feeling of obligation to the organization for providing noncontingent rewards fuels his or her effort to perform at least adequately. The Japanese experience is exemplary; in the top third of such Japanese firms as Toyota, Sony, and Mitsubishi, employees and the companies feel a mutual sense of lifetime obligation. Being a good family member does not bring immediate pay raises and promotions, but overall family success will bring year-end bonuses. Ultimately, opportunities to advance to a higher level and salary will depend on overall meritorious performance.

When the contingent reinforcement used is aversive (reinforcement that recipients prefer to avoid), the success of the transactional leader usually plummets. In the same not-for-profit organization studied by Podsakoff et al., neither contingent reprimand, disapproval, nor punishment had any effect on performance or overall employee satisfaction. The same results have been observed in other organizations. Contingent approval and disapproval by results-oriented leaders did improve subordinates' understanding of what was expected of them but failed to have much effect on motivation or performance. In general, reprimand may be useful in highlighting what not to do, but usually it does not contribute to positive motivation, particularly when subordinates are expected to be innovative and creative.

Even when it is based solely on rewards, transactional leadership can have unintended consequences. When expounding on the principles of leadership, Vice Admiral James B. Stockdale argued that people do not like to be programmed:

. . . You cannot persuade (people) to act in their own self-interest all of the time. A good leader appreciates contrariness.

. . . some men all of the time and all of the men some of the time knowingly will do what is clearly to their disadvantage if only because they do not like to be suffocated by carrot-and-stick coercion. I will not be a piano key. I will not bow to the tyranny of reason.

In working subtly against transactional leadership, employees may take short-cuts to complete the exchange of reward for compliance. For instance, quality may suffer if the leader does not monitor it as closely as he or she does the quantity of output. The employee may begin to react defensively rather than adequately; in some cases, reaction formation, withdrawal, hostility, or "game playing" may result.

THE ALTERNATIVE: ADD TRANSFORMATIONAL LEADERSHIP TO THE MANAGER-EMPLOYEE RELATIONSHIP

James McGregor Burns, the biographer of Franklin D. Roosevelt and of John F. Kennedy, was the first to contrast transactional with transformational leadership. The transformational leader motivates us to do more than we originally expected to do. Such a transformation can be achieved in the following ways:

1. Raising our level of consciousness about the importance and value of designated outcomes and ways of reaching these outcomes.

2. Getting us to transcend our own self-interests for the sake of the team, organization, or larger polity.

3. Raising our need level on Abraham Maslow's hierarchy from, say, the need for security to the need for recognition, or expanding our portfolio of needs by, for example, adding the need for self-actualization to the need for recognition.

Cynthia Changer is a transformational leader; Barry Bargainer is not. Exhibit 2 is a model of transformational leadership that starts with a current level of effort based on a follower's current level of confidence and desire for designated outcomes. A transactional leader contributes to such confidence and desire by clarifying what performance is required and how needs will be satisfied as a consequence.

EXHIBIT 2
Transformational Leadership (L = Leader; F = Follower).

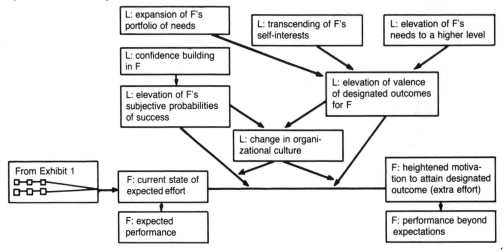

The transformational leader induces additional effort by directly increasing the follower's confidence as well as by elevating the level of outcomes through expanding his or her transcendental interests and level or breadth of needs in Maslow's hierarchy.

The need for more transformational leaders in business and industry was illustrated in an in-depth interview survey of a representative national sample of 845 working Americans. The survey found that while most employees liked and respected their managers, they felt their managers really didn't know how to motivate employees to do their best. Although 70% endorsed the work ethic, only 23% said they were working as hard as they could in their jobs. Only 9% agreed that their performance was motivated by transaction; most reported that there actually was little connection between how much they earned and the level of effort they put into the job.

REPORT ON A STUDY OF TRANSFORMATIONAL LEADERSHIP

I set out to find evidence of transformational leadership and its effects at various levels in industrial and military organizations, *not just at the top.*

I defined transformational leadership for 70 senior executives. Then, I asked them to describe in detail a transformational leader whom they had encountered at any time during their career. All respondents claimed to have known at least one such person. Most cited a former immediate supervisor or higher-level manager in the organization. A few mentioned family members, consultants, or counselors.

This transformational leader induced respondents to work ridiculous hours *and to do more than they ever expected to do.* Respondents reported that they aimed to satisfy the transformational leader's expectations and to give the leader all the support asked of them. They wanted to emulate the leader. The transformational leader increased their awareness of and promoted a higher quality of performance and greater innovativeness. Such a leader convinced followers to extend themselves and to develop themselves further. Total commitment to and belief in the organization emerged as consequences of belief in the leader and heightened self-confidence.

Many respondents (all were male) indicated that the transformational leader they could identify in their own careers was like a benevolent father who remained friendly and treated the respondent as an equal despite the leader's greater knowledge and experience. The leader provided a model of integrity and fairness and also set clear and high standards of performance. He encouraged followers with advice, help, support, recognition, and openness. He gave followers a sense of confidence in his intellect, yet was a good listener. He gave followers autonomy and encouraged their self-development. He was willing to share his greater knowledge and expertise with them. Yet he could be formal and firm and would reprimand followers when necessary. Most respondents, however, were inclined to see the transforming leader as informal and accessible. Such a leader could be counted on to stand up for his subordinates. Along with the heightened and changed motivation and awareness, frequent reactions of followers to the transforming leader included trust, strong liking, admiration, loyalty, and respect.

In conducting a second survey, I used the descriptions from the first to create a questionnaire of 73 behavioral items. Responses to each item were on a five-point frequency scale. A total of 176 senior U. S. Army officers completed the questionnaire describing the behavior of their immediate superiors. Five factors emerged from a statistical factor analysis of the data. Two dealt with transactional leadership, the exchange relationship between superior and subordinate: contingent reward, by which subordinates earned benefits for compliance with the leader's clarification of the paths toward goals, and management by exception, by which the leader gave negative feedback for failure to meet agreed-upon standards. Three of the factors dealt with transformational leadership—the broadening and elevating of goals and of subordinates' confidence in their ability to go beyond expectations. These factors were (1) charismatic leadership (leaders aroused enthusiasm, faith, loyalty, and pride and trust in themselves and their aims); (2) individualized consideration (leaders maintained a developmental and individualistic orientation toward subordinates); and (3) intellectual stimulation (leaders enhanced the problem-solving capabilities of their associates). An interesting sidelight was that more transformational leadership was observed (by respondents) in combat units than in support units.

As expected, the three transformational factors were more highly correlated with perceived unit effectiveness than were the two transactional factors. Parallel results were obtained for subordinates' satisfaction with their leader. Charismatic, considerate, and intellectually stimulating leaders were far more satisfying to work for than were those who merely practiced the transactions of contingent reinforcement. I obtained similar results from a survey of 256 business managers, 23 educational administrators, and 45 professionals. Moreover, in these latter samples, respondents reported that they made greater efforts when leaders were charismatic, individualizing, and intellectually stimulating. Contingent reward was also fairly predictive of extra effort, but management by exception was counterproductive. Further analysis of the data by my colleague, David Waldman, supported the model shown in Exhibit 2. The analysis demonstrated that when a leader displayed transformational abilities and engaged in transactional relationships, extra effort made by subordinates was above and beyond what could be attributed to transactional factors alone.

TRANSACTIONAL FACTORS: CONTINGENT REINFORCEMENT AND MANAGEMENT-BY-EXCEPTION

According to our questionnaire surveys, positive and aversive contingent reinforcement are the two ways managers in organized settings engage in transactional leadership to influence employee performance. Ordinarily, contingent reward takes two forms: praise for work well done and recommendations for pay increases, bonuses, and promotion. In addition, this kind of reward can take the form of commendations for effort or public recognition and honors for outstanding service.

Contingent punishment can take several forms as a reaction to a deviation from norms—when, for example, production falls below agreed-upon standards or quality falls below acceptable levels. The manager may merely call attention to the derivation. Being told of one's failure to meet standards may be sufficient punishment to change behavior. Being told why one has failed can be helpful, particularly to the inexperienced or inexpert subordinate, especially if the negative feedback is coupled with further clarification about what kind of performance is expected. While other penalties—such as fines, suspensions without pay, loss of leader support, or discharge—may be imposed, these are less frequently used and are less likely to promote effectiveness.

When the manager, for one reason or another, chooses to intervene only when failures, breakdowns, and deviations occur, he or she is practicing management by exception. The rationale of those who use this practice is, "If it ain't broke, don't fix it!" The research studies I have completed with military officers, business executives, professionals, and educational administrators generally indicate that as a steady diet, management by exception can be counterproductive. But contingent rewards yield a fairly good return in terms of subordinate effort and performance. Nevertheless, in the aggregate, there will be additional payoff when the transformational factors appear in a leader's portfolio.

Charismatic and Inspirational Leadership

Charisma is not exclusively the province of world-class leaders or a few generals or admirals. It is to be found to some degree in industrial and military leaders throughout organizations. Furthermore, charisma is the most important component in the larger concept of transformational leadership. In my study I found that many followers described their military or industrial leader as someone who made everyone enthusiastic about assignments, who inspired loyalty to the organization, who commanded respect from everyone, who had a special gift of seeing what was really important, and who had a sense of mission that excited responses. Followers had complete faith in the leaders with charisma, felt proud to be associated with them, and trusted their capacity to overcome any obstacle. Charismatic leaders served as symbols of success and accomplishment for their followers.

Charisma is one of the elements separating the ordinary manager from the true leader in organizational settings. The leader attracts intense feelings of love (and sometimes hatred) from his or her subordinates. They want to identify with the leader. Although feelings about ordinary managers are bland, relations are smoother and steadier. Like most intimate relationships, the relations between the charismatic leader and his or her followers tend to be more turbulent.

There may be a scarcity of charismatic leaders in business and industry because managers lack the necessary skills. On the other hand, managers who have the skills may not recognize opportunity or may be unwilling to risk what is required to stand out so visibly among their peers. More charismatic leaders potentially exist in organizational settings; furthermore, they may be necessary to an organization's success.

The ability to inspire—arouse emotions, animate, enliven, or even exalt—is an important aspect of charisma. Inspirational leadership involves the arousal and heightening of motivation among followers. Followers can be inspired by a cold, calculating, intellectual discourse, the brilliance of a breakthrough, or the beauty of an argument. Yet it is the followers' emotions that ultimately have been aroused. Followers may hold an intellectual genius in awe and reverence, but the inspirational influence on them is emotional.

Consider the specific leadership behaviors Gary Yukl used to illustrate what he meant by inspirational leadership:

> My supervisor held a meeting to talk about how vital the new contract is for the company and said he was confident we could handle it if we all did our part. My boss told us we were the best design group he had ever worked with and he was sure that this new product was going to break every sales record in the company.

The inspiring supervisor was not dispassionate. The supervisor talked about how *vital* the new contract was to the company. He said he was *confident* in his people. He told them they were the *best* group he had *ever* worked with. He was sure the product would *break every record.*

In summary, as a consequence of his or her self-confidence, absence of inner conflict, self-determination, and requisite abilities, a leader will be held in high esteem by followers, particularly in times of trouble. He or she can generally inspire them by emotional support and appeals that will transform their level of motivation beyond original expectations. Such a leader can sometimes also inspire followers by means of intellectual stimulation. The charismatic leader can do one or the other, or both.

Individualized Consideration

The transformational leader has a developmental orientation toward followers. He evaluates followers' potential both to perform their present job and to hold future positions of greater responsibility. The leader sets examples and assigns tasks on an individual basis to followers to help significantly alter their abilities and motivations as well as to satisfy immediate organizational needs.

Delegating challenging work and increasing subordinate responsibilities are particularly useful approaches to individualized development. As General Omar Bradley pointed out, there is no better way to develop leadership than to give an individual a job involving responsibility and let him work it out. A survey of 208 chief executives and senior officers by Charles Margerison reported that important career influences on them before age 35 included being "stretched" by immediate bosses and being given leadership experience, overall responsibility for important tasks, and wide experience in many functions.

The transformational leader will consciously or unconsciously serve as a role model for subordinates. For example, in the Margerison survey, the executives attributed their own successful development as managers to having had early on in their careers managers who were models.

Managerial training supports the idea that managers profit from role models. What may be different in what I propose, however, is that the transformational leader emphasizes *individualism.* Personal influence and the one-to-one superior-subordinate relationship is of primary importance to the development of leaders. An organizational culture of individualism, even of elitism, should be encouraged; an organization should focus attention on identifying prospective leaders among subordinates.

Individualized attention is viewed as especially important by the new military commander of a unit. The commander is expected to learn the names of all those in the units at least two levels below his and to become familiar with their jobs. *Military leaders need to avoid treating all subordinates alike.* They must discover what best motivates each individual soldier or sailor and how to employ him most effectively. They must be generous in the use of their time. But as General Eugene Meyer notes, the leaders' interest must be genuine.

Individualized consideration implies that seniors maintain face-to-face contact or at least frequent telephone contact with juniors. The Intel Corporation accepted the fact that recently graduated engineers are more up to date on the latest advances in technology than are experienced executives of greater power and status in the firm. Therefore, the firm has consciously encouraged frequent contact and open communication between the recent college graduates and the senior executives through leveling arrangements. Senior executives and junior professionals are all housed in small, unpretentious, accessible offices that share common facilities. The organization stresses that influence is based on knowledge rather than power. In other well-managed firms, "walk-around management" promotes individual contact and communication between those low and high in the hierarchy.

In another study of a high-tech company, Rudi Klauss and Bernard Bass found that project engineers were most influenced by and gained most of their information relevant to decision making from informal contact and individual discussion rather than from written documentation. This company did not believe that the aggregated data from management information systems were the most important inputs for decision making. Rather, two-thirds to three-quarters of the total work time of managers was spent in oral communication. It was the immediate, timely tidbits of gossip, speculation, opinion, and relevant facts that was most influential, not generalized reports reviewing conditions over a recent period of time. Individualized attention of superior to subordinate provided this opportunity for inputs of current and timely information.

Managers are most likely to make face-to-face contact with colleagues at their same organizational level (or by telephone for such colleagues at a distance physically). For superiors and subordinates, written memos are more frequently used. Yet regular, face-to-face debriefing sessions to disseminate important information from superior to subordinate will provide a better basis for organizational decision making and make the superior better equipped to deal with the erratic flow of work and demands on his or her time and the speed that decision making often requires. Unfortunately, unless personal contact becomes a matter of policy (such as walk-around management), communications from superior to subordinate are more likely to be on paper—or now, no doubt, increasingly on computer—rather than face-to-face.

Individualized consideration is reflected when a manager keeps each employee fully informed about what is happening and why—preferably in a two-way conversation rather than a written memo. Employees come to feel that they are on the inside of developments and do not remain bystanders. Sudden changes of plan are less likely to surprise them. If the interaction is two-way, employees have the opportunity to ask questions to clarify understanding. At the same time, managers learn first-hand their subordinates' concerns.

Individualized consideration is also demonstrated when the senior executive or professional takes time to serve as mentor for the junior executive or professional. A mentor is a trusted counselor who accepts a guiding role in the development of a younger or less experienced member of the organization. The mentor uses his or her greater knowledge, experience, and status to help develop his or her protégé and not simply to pull the protégé up the organizational ladder on the mentor's coattails. This relationship is different from one in which a manager is supportive or provides advice when asked for it. Compared with the formal, distant relationship most often seen between a high-level executive and a junior somewhere down the line, the mentor is paternalistic or maternalistic and perhaps is a role model for the junior person.

A follow-up of 122 recently promoted people in business indicated that two-thirds had had mentors. This popularity of mentoring in business, government, and industry reflects the current interest on the part of both individuals and organizations in the career development of the individual employee.

Intellectual Stimulation

The statement, "These ideas have forced me to rethink some of my own ideas, which I had never questioned before," sums up the kind of intellectual stimulation that a transformational leader can provide. Intellectual stimulation can lead to other comments like, "She enables me to think about old problems in new ways," or "He provides me with new ways of looking at things that used to be a puzzle for me."

Intellectual stimulation arouses in followers the awareness of problems and how they may be solved. It promotes the hygiene of logic that is compelling and convincing. It stirs the imagination and generates thoughts and insights. It is not the call to immediate action aroused by emotional stimulation. This intellectual stimulation is seen in a discrete leap in the followers' conceptualization, comprehension, and discernment of the nature of the problems they face and their solutions.

Executives should and can play a role as transforming leaders to the degree that they articulate what they discern, comprehend, visualize, and conceptualize to their colleagues and followers. They should articulate what they see as the opportunities and threats facing their organization (or unit within it) and the organization's strengths, weaknesses, and comparative advantages. Leadership in complex organizations must include the ability to manage the problem-solving process in such a way that important problems are identified and solutions of high quality are found and carried out with the full commitment of organization members.

The intellectual component may be obscured by surface considerations. Accused of making snap decisions, General George Patton commented: "I've been studying the art of war for 40-odd years . . . [A] surgeon who decides in the course of an operation to change its objective is not making a snap decision but one based on knowledge, experience, and training. So am I."

The importance of a leader's technical expertise and intellectual power, particularly in high-performing systems, often is ignored in comparison with the attention paid to his or her interpersonal competence. Where would Polaroid be without Edwin Land? What kind of corporation would Occidental Petroleum be without Armand Hammer?

In this intellectual sphere, we see systematic differences between transformational and transactional leaders. The transformational leader may be less willing to accept the status quo and more likely to seek new ways of doing things while taking maximum advantage of opportunities. Transactional managers will focus on what can clearly work, will keep time constraints in mind, and will do what seems to be most efficient and free of risk.

What may intellectually separate the two kinds of leaders is that transformational leaders are likely to be more proactive than reactive in their thinking, more creative, novel, and innovative in their ideas,

and less inhibited in their ideational search for solutions. Transactional leaders may be equally bright, but their focus is on how best to keep running the system for which they are responsible; they react to problems generated by observed deviances and modify conditions as needed while remaining ever mindful of organizational constraints.

TRANSFORMATIONAL LEADERSHIP: BENEVOLENT OR MALEVOLENT?

Charismatic leadership, individualized consideration, and intellectual stimulation have been clearly seen in the moving and shaking that took place between 1982 and 1984 in a number of firms, such as General Electric, Campbell Soup, and Coca Cola. In each instance, the transformation could be attributed to a newly appointed chief. These transformational leaders were responsible for iconoclastic changes of image, increased organizational flexibility, and an upsurge of new products and new approaches. In each case, the transformational leadership of John F. Welch, Jr. of General Electric, Gordon McGovern of Campbell Soup, and Roberto Goizueta of Coca Cola paid off in invigoration and revitalization of their firms and an acceleration in business success.

Clearly, heads may be broken, feelings hurt, and anxieties raised with the advent of transformational leaders such as Welch, McGovern, or Goizueta. "Business as usual" is no longer tolerated. Such transformations may be moral or immoral.

For James Burns, transformational leadership is moral if it deals with true needs and is based on informed choice. The moral transformational leader is one who is guided by such universal ethical principles as respect for human dignity and equal rights. The leadership mobilizes and directs support for "more general and comprehensive values that express followers' more fundamental and enduring needs" (*Leadership*, Harper, 1978). Moral leadership helps followers to see the real conflict between competing values, the inconsistencies between espoused values and behavior, the need for realignments in values, and the need for changes in behavior or transformations of institutions. Burns argued that if the need levels elevated by transformational leaders were not authentic, then the leadership was immoral.

The well-being of organizational life will be better served in the long run by moral leadership. That is, transformations that result in the fulfillment of real needs will prove to be more beneficial to the organization than transformations that deal with manufactured needs and group delusions. Organizational leaders should subscribe to a code of ethics that is accepted by their society and their profession.

The ethical transformational leader aims toward and succeeds in promoting changes in a firm— changes that strengthen firm viability, increase satisfaction of owners, managers, employees, and customers, and increase the value of the firm's products. But transformational leaders can be immoral if they create changes based on false images that cater to the fantasies of constituencies. Firms can be driven into the ground by such leaders. A transformational leader can lull employees and shareholders alike with false hopes and expectations while he or she is preparing to depart in a golden parachute after selling out the company's interests.

Whether transformational or transactional leadership will take hold within an organization will depend to some extent on what is happening or has happened outside of it. Welch, McGovern, and Goizueta all came into power to transform firms that were in danger of failing to keep pace with changes in the marketplace. Transformational leadership is more likely to emerge in times of distress and rapid change.

The personalities of followers will affect a leader's ability to be transformational. Charisma is a two-way process. A leader is seen as charismatic if he or she has followers who imbue him or her with extraordinary value and personal power. This is more easily done when subordinates have highly dependent personalities. On the other hand, subordinates who pride themselves on their own rationality, skepticism, independence, and concern for rules of law and precedent are less likely to be influenced by a charismatic leader or the leader who tries to use emotional inspiration. Subordinates who are egalitarian, self-confident, and high in status are likely to resist charismatic leaders.

WHICH KIND OF LEADERSHIP SHOULD MANAGERS USE?

Managers need to appreciate what kind of leadership is expected of them. Current leadership training and management development emphasize transactional leadership, which is good as far as it goes, but clearly has its limits. Transactional leaders will let their subordinates know what is expected of them and what they can hope to receive in exchange for fulfilling expectations. Clarification makes subordinates confident that they can fulfill expectations and achieve mutually valued outcomes. But subordinates' confidence and the value they place on potential outcomes can be further increased, through transformational leadership. Leadership, in other words, can become an inspiration to make extraordinary efforts.

Charismatic leadership is central to the transformational leadership process. Charismatic leaders have great referent power and influence. Followers want to identify with them and to emulate them. Followers develop intense feelings about them, and above all have trust and confidence in them. Transformational leaders may arouse their followers emotionally and inspire them to extra effort and greater accomplishment. As subordinates become competent with the mainly transformational leader's encouragement and support, contingent reinforcement may be abandoned in favor of self-reinforcement.

Clearly, there are situations in which the transformational approach may not be appropriate. At the same time, organizations need to draw more on the resources of charismatic leaders, who often can induce followers to aspire to and maintain much higher levels of productivity than they would have reached if they had been operating only through the transactional process.

The Science of "Muddling Through"

Charles E. Lindblom

Suppose an administrator is given responsibility for formulating policy with respect to inflation. He might start by trying to list all related values in order of

Reprinted by permission of the author from *Public Administration Review*, 1959, 19(2), pp. 79–88.

importance, e.g., full employment, reasonable business profit, protection of small savings, prevention of a stock market crash. Then all possible policy outcomes could be rated as more or less efficient in attaining a maximum of these values. This would of course require a prodigious inquiry into values held by members of society and an equally prodigious set of calculations on how much of each value is equal to how much of each other value. He could then proceed to outline all possible policy alternatives. In a third step, he would undertake systematic comparison of his multitude of alternatives to determine which attains the greatest amount of values.

In comparing policies, he would take advantage of any theory available that generalized about classes of policies. In considering inflation, for example, he would compare all policies in the light of the theory of prices. Since no alternatives are beyond his investigation, he would consider strict central control and the abolition of all prices and markets on the one hand and elimination of all public controls with reliance completely on the free market on the other, both in the light of whatever theoretical generalizations he could find on such hypothetical economies.

Finally, he would try to make the choice that would in fact maximize his values.

An alternative line of attack would be to set as his principal objective, either explicitly or without conscious thought, the relatively simple goal of keeping prices level. This objective might be compromised or complicated by only a few other goals, such as full employment. He would in fact disregard most other social values as beyond his present interest, and he would for the moment not even attempt to rank the few values that he regarded as immediately relevant. Were he pressed, he would quickly admit that he was ignoring many related values and many possible important consequences of his policies.

As a second step, he would outline those relatively few policy alternatives that occurred to him. He would then compare them. In comparing his limited number of alternatives, most of them familiar from past controversies, he would not ordinarily find a body of theory precise enough to carry him through a comparison of their respective consequences. Instead he would rely heavily on the record of past experience with small policy steps to predict the consequences of similar steps extended into the future.

Moreover, he would find that the policy alternatives combined objectives or values in different ways. For example, one policy might offer price level stability at the cost of some risk of unemployment; another might offer less price stability but also less risk of unemployment. Hence, the next step in his approach—the final selection—would combine into one the choice among values and the choice among instruments for reaching values. It would not, as in the first method of policy-making, approximate a more mechanical process of choosing the means that

best satisfied goals that were previously clarified and ranked. Because practitioners of the second approach expect to achieve their goals only partially, they would expect to repeat endlessly the sequence just described, as conditions and aspirations changed and as accuracy of prediction improved.

BY ROOT OR BY BRANCH

For complex problems, the first of these two approaches is of course impossible. Although such an approach can be described, it cannot be practiced except for relatively simple problems and even then only in a somewhat modified form. It assumes intellectual capacities and sources of information that men simply do not possess, and it is even more absurd as an approach to policy when the time and money that can be allocated to a policy problem is limited, as is always the case. Of particular importance to public administrators is the fact that public agencies are in effect usually instructed not to practice the first method. That is to say, their prescribed functions and constraints—the politically or legally possible—restrict their attention to relatively few values and relatively few alternative policies among the countless alternatives that might be imagined. It is the second method that is practiced.

Curiously, however, the literatures of decision-making, policy formulation, planning, and public administration formalize the first approach rather than the second, leaving public administrators who handle complex decisions in the position of practicing what few preach. For emphasis I run some risk of overstatement. True enough, the literature is well aware of limits on man's capacities and of the inevitability that policies will be approached in some such style as the second. But attempts to formalize rational policy formulation—to lay out explicitly the necessary steps in the process—usually describe the first approach and not the second.[1]

The common tendency to describe policy formulation even for complex problems as though it followed the first approach has been strengthened by the attention given to, and successes enjoyed by, operations research, statistical decision theory, and systems analysis. The hallmarks of these procedures,

---

[1]James G. March and Herbert A. Simon similarly characterize the literature. They also take some important steps, as have Simon's recent articles, to describe a less heroic model of policy-making. See *Organizations* (John Wiley and Sons, 1958), p. 137.

typical of the first approach, are clarity of objective, explicitness of evaluation, a high degree of comprehensiveness of overview, and, wherever possible, quantification of values for mathematical analysis. But these advanced procedures remain largely the appropriate techniques of relatively small-scale problem-solving where the total number of variables to be considered is small and value problems restricted. Charles Hitch, head of the Economics Division of RAND Corporation, one of the leading centers for application of these techniques, has written:

I would make the empirical generalization from my experience at RAND and elsewhere that operations research is the art of sub-optimizing, i.e., of solving some lower-level problems, and that difficulties increase and our special competence diminishes by an order of magnitude with every level of decision making we attempt to ascend. The sort of simple explicit model which operations researchers are so proficient in using can certainly reflect most of the significant factors influencing traffic control on the George Washington Bridge, but the proportion of the relevant reality which we can represent by any such model or models in studying, say, a major foreign-policy decision, appears to be almost trivial.[2]

Accordingly, I propose in this paper to clarify and formalize the second method, much neglected in the literature. This might be described as the method of *successive limited comparisons*. I will contrast it with the first approach, which might be called the rational-comprehensive method.[3] More impressionistically and briefly—and therefore generally used in this article—they could be characterized as the branch method and root method, the former continually building out from the current situation, step-by-step and by small degrees; the latter starting from fundamentals anew each time, building on the past only as experience is embodied in a theory, and always prepared to start completely from the ground up.

Let us put the characteristics of the two methods side by side in simplest terms.

Rational-Comprehensive (Root)

1a. Clarification of values or objectives distinct from and usually prerequisite to empirical analysis of alternative policies.

2a. Policy-formulation is therefore approached through means-end analysis: First the ends are isolated, then the means to achieve them are sought.

3a. The test of a "good" policy is that it can be shown to be the most appropriate means to desired ends.

4a. Analysis is comprehensive; every important relevant factor is taken into account.

5a. Theory is often heavily relied upon.

Successive Limited Comparisons (Branch)

1b. Selection of value goals and empirical analysis of the needed action are not distinct from one another but are closely intertwined.

2b. Since means and ends are not distinct, means-end analysis is often inappropriate or limited.

3b. The test of a "good" policy is typically that various analysts find themselves directly agreeing on a policy (without their agreeing that it is the most appropriate means to an agreed objective).

4b. Analysis is drastically limited:
  i) Important possible outcomes are neglected.
  ii) Important alternative potential policies are neglected.
  iii) Important affected values are neglected.

5b. A succession of comparisons greatly reduces or eliminates reliance on theory.

Assuming that the root method is familiar and understandable, we proceed directly to clarification of its alternative by contrast. In explaining the second, we shall be describing how most administrators do in fact approach complex questions, for the root method, the "best" way as a blueprint or model, is in fact not workable for complex policy questions, and adminis-

---

[2]"Operations Research and National Planning—A Dissent," 5 *Operations Research* 718 (October, 1957). Hitch's dissent is from particular points made in the article to which his paper is a reply; his claim that operations research is for low-level problems is widely accepted.

For examples of the kind of problems to which operations research is applied, see C. W. Churchman, R. L. Ackoff and E. L. Arnoff, *Introduction to Operations Research* (John Wiley and Sons, 1957); and J. F. McCloskey and J. M. Coppinger (eds.), *Operations Research for Management*, Vol. II, (The Johns Hopkins Press, 1956).

[3]I am assuming that administrators often make policy and advise in the making of policy and am treating decision-making and policy-making as synonymous for purposes of this paper.

trators are forced to use the method of successive limited comparisons.

INTERTWINING EVALUATION AND EMPIRICAL ANALYSIS (1b)

The quickest way to understand how values are handled in the method of successive limited comparisons is to see how the root method often breaks down in *its* handling of values or objectives. The idea that values should be clarified, and in advance of the examination of alternative policies, is appealing. But what happens when we attempt it for complex social problems? The first difficulty is that on many critical values or objectives, citizens disagree, congressmen disagree, and public administrators disagree. Even where a fairly specific objective is prescribed for the administrator, there remains considerable room for disagreement on sub-objectives. Consider, for example, the conflict with respect to locating public housing, described in Meyerson and Banfield's study of the Chicago Housing Authority[4]—disagreement which occurred despite the clear objective of providing a certain number of public housing units in the city. Similarly conflicting are objectives in highway location, traffic control, minimum wage administration, development of tourist facilities in national parks, or insect control.

Administrators cannot escape these conflicts by ascertaining the majority's preference, for preferences have not been registered on most issues; indeed, there often *are* no preferences in the absence of public discussion sufficient to bring an issue to the attention of the electorate. Furthermore, there is a question of whether intensity of feeling should be considered as well as the number of persons preferring each alternative. By the impossibility of doing otherwise, administrators often are reduced to deciding policy without clarifying objectives first.

Even when an administrator resolves to follow his own values as a criterion for decisions, he often will not know how to rank them when they conflict with one another, as they usually do. Suppose, for example, that an administrator must relocate tenants living in tenements scheduled for destruction. One objective is to empty the buildings fairly promptly, another is to find suitable accommodation for persons displaced, another is to avoid friction with residents in other areas in which a large influx would be unwel-

come, another is to deal with all concerned through persuasion if possible, and so on.

How does one state even to himself the relative importance of these partially conflicting values? A simple ranking of them is not enough; one needs ideally to know how much of one value is worth sacrificing for some of another value. The answer is that typically the administrator chooses—and must choose—directly among policies in which these values are combined in different ways. He cannot first clarify his values and then choose among policies.

A more subtle third point underlies both the first two. Social objectives do not always have the same relative values. One objective may be highly prized in one circumstance, another in another circumstance. If, for example, an administrator values highly both the dispatch with which his agency can carry through its projects *and* good public relations, it matters little which of the two possibly conflicting values he favors in some abstract or general sense. Policy questions arise in forms which put to administrators such a question as: Given the degree to which we are or are not already achieving the values of dispatch and the values of good public relations, is it worth sacrificing a little speed for a happier clientele, or is it better to risk offending the clientele so that we can get on with our work? The answer to such a question varies with circumstances.

The value problem is, as the example shows, always a problem of adjustments at a margin. But there is no practicable way to state marginal objectives or values except in terms of particular policies. That one value is preferred to another in one decision situation does not mean that it will be preferred in another decision situation in which it can be had only at great sacrifice of another value. Attempts to rank or order values in general and abstract terms so that they do not shift from decision to decision end up by ignoring the relevant marginal preference. The significance of this third point thus goes very far. Even if all administrators had at hand an agreed set of values, objectives, and constraints, and an agreed ranking of these values, objectives, and constraints, their marginal values in actual choice situations would be impossible to formulate.

Unable consequently to formulate the relevant values first and then choose among policies to achieve them, administrators must choose directly among alternative policies that offer different marginal combinations of values. Somewhat paradoxically, the only practicable way to disclose one's relevant marginal values even to oneself is to describe the policy one chooses to achieve them. Except roughly and vaguely,

---

[4]Martin Meyerson and Edward C. Banfield, *Politics, Planning and the Public Interest* (The Free Press, 1955).

I know of no way to describe—or even to under-stand—what my relative evaluations are for, say, freedom and security, speed and accuracy in governmental decisions, or low taxes and better schools than to describe my preferences among specific policy choices that might be made between the alternatives in each of the pairs.

In summary, two aspects of the process by which values are actually handled can be distinguished. The first is clear: evaluation and empirical analysis are intertwined; that is, one chooses among values and among policies at one and the same time. Put a little more elaborately, one simultaneously chooses a policy to attain certain objectives and chooses the objectives themselves. The second aspect is related but distinct: the administrator focuses his attention on marginal or incremental values. Whether he is aware of it or not, he does not find general formulations of objectives very helpful and in fact makes specific marginal or incremental comparisons. Two policies, X and Y, confront him. Both promise the same degree of attainment of objectives a, b, c, d, and e. But X promises him somewhat more of f than does Y, while Y promises him somewhat more of g than does X. In choosing between them, he is in fact offered the alternative of a marginal or incremental amount of f at the expense of a marginal or incremental amount of g. The only values that are relevant to his choice are these increments by which the two policies differ; and when he finally chooses between the two marginal values, he does so by making a choice between policies.[5]

As to whether the attempt to clarify objectives in advance of policy selection is more or less rational than the close intertwining of marginal evaluation and empirical analysis, the principal difference established is that for complex problems the first is impossible and irrelevant, and the second is both possible and relevant. The second is possible because the administrator need not try to analyze any values except the values by which alternative policies differ and need not be concerned with them except as they differ marginally. His need for information on values or objectives is drastically reduced as compared with the root method; and his capacity for grasping, comprehending, and relating values to one another is not strained beyond the breaking point.

---

[5]The line of argument is, of course, an extension of the theory of market choice, especially the theory of consumer choice, to public policy choices.

RELATIONS BETWEEN MEANS AND ENDS (2B)

Decision-making is ordinarily formalized as a means-ends relationship: means are conceived to be evaluated and chosen in the light of ends finally selected independently of and prior to the choice of means. This is the means-ends relationship of the root method. But it follows from all that has just been said that such a means-end relationship is possible only to the extent that values are agreed upon, are reconcilable, and are stable at the margin. Typically, therefore, such a means-ends relationship is absent from the branch method, where means and ends are simultaneously chosen.

Yet any departure from the means-ends relationship of the root method will strike some readers as inconceivable. For it will appear to them that only in such a relationship is it possible to determine whether one policy choice is better or worse than another. How can an administrator know whether he has made a wise or foolish decision if he is without prior values or objectives by which to judge his decisions? The answer to this question calls up the third distinctive difference between root and branch methods: how to decide the best policy.

THE TEST OF "GOOD" POLICY (3B)

In the root method, a decision is "correct," "good," or "rational" if it can be shown to attain some specified objective, where the objective can be specified without simply describing the decision itself. Where objectives are defined only through the marginal or incremental approach to values described above, it is still sometimes possible to test whether a policy does in fact attain the desired objectives; but a precise statement of the objectives takes the form of a description of the policy chosen or some alternative to it. To show that a policy is mistaken one cannot offer an abstract argument that important objectives are not achieved; one must instead argue that another policy is more to be preferred.

So far, the departure from customary ways of looking at problem-solving is not troublesome, for many administrators will be quick to agree that the most effective discussion of the correctness of policy does take the form of comparison with other policies that might have been chosen. But what of the situation in which administrators cannot agree on values or objectives, either abstractly or in marginal terms? What then is the test of "good" policy? For the root method, there is no test. Agreement on objectives failing, there is no standard of "correctness." For the method of successive limited comparisons, the test is agreement on policy itself, which remains possible even when agreement on values is not.

It has been suggested that continuing agreement in Congress on the desirability of extending old age insurance stems from liberal desires to strengthen the welfare programs of the federal government and from conservative desires to reduce union demands for private pension plans. If so, this is an excellent demonstration of the ease with which individuals of different ideologies often can agree on concrete policy. Labor mediators report a similar phenomenon: the contestants cannot agree on criteria for settling their disputes but can agree on specific proposals. Similarly, when one administrator's objective turns out to be another's means, they often can agree on policy.

Agreement on policy thus becomes the only practicable test of the policy's correctness. And for one administrator to seek to win the other over to agreement on ends as well would accomplish nothing and create quite unnecessary controversy.

If agreement directly on policy as a test for "best" policy seems a poor substitute for testing the policy against its objectives, it ought to be remembered that objectives themselves have no ultimate validity other than that they are agreed upon. Hence agreement is the test of "best" policy in both methods. But where the root method requires agreement on what elements in the decision constitute objectives and on which of these objectives should be sought, the branch method falls back on agreement wherever it can be found.

In an important sense, therefore, it is not irrational for an administrator to defend a policy as good without being able to specify what it is good for.

NON-COMPREHENSIVE ANALYSIS (4B)

Ideally, rational-comprehensive analysis leaves out nothing important. But it is impossible to take everything important into consideration unless "important" is so narrowly defined that analysis is in fact quite limited. Limits on human intellectual capacities and on available information set definite limits to man's capacity to be comprehensive. In actual fact, therefore, no one can practice the rational-comprehensive method for really complex problems, and every administrator faced with a sufficiently complex problem must find ways drastically to simplify.

An administrator assisting in the formulation of agricultural economic policy cannot in the first place be competent on all possible policies. He cannot even comprehend one policy entirely. In planning a soil bank program, he cannot successfully anticipate the impact of higher or lower farm income on, say, urbanization—the possible consequent loosening of family ties, possible consequent eventual need for revisions in social security and further complications for tax problems arising out of new federal responsibilities for social security and municipal responsibilities for urban services. Nor, to follow another line of repercussions, can he work through the soil bank program's effects on prices for agricultural products in foreign markets and consequent implications for foreign relations, including those arising out of economic rivalry between the United States and the U.S.S.R.

In the method of successive limited comparisons, simplification is systematically achieved in two principal ways. First, it is achieved through limitation of policy comparisons to those policies that differ in relatively small degree from policies presently in effect. Such a limitation immediately reduces the number of alternatives to be investigated and also drastically simplifies the character of the investigation of each. For it is not necessary to undertake fundamental inquiry into an alternative and its consequences; it is necessary only to study those respects in which the proposed alternative and its consequences differ from the status quo. The empirical comparison of marginal differences among alternative policies that differ only marginally is, of course, a counterpart to the incremental or marginal comparison of values discussed above.[6]

Relevance as Well as Realism

It is a matter of common observation that in Western democracies public administrators and policy analysts in general do largely limit their analyses to incremental or marginal differences in policies that are chosen to differ only incrementally. They do not do so, however, solely because they desperately need some way to simplify their problems; they also do so in order to be relevant. Democracies change

---

[6]A more precise definition of incremental policies and a discussion of whether a change that appears "small" to one observer might be seen differently by another is to be found in my "Policy Analysis," 48 *American Economic Review* 298 (June, 1958).

their policies almost entirely through incremental adjustments. Policy does not move in leaps and bounds.

The incremental character of political change in the United States has often been remarked. The two major political parties agree on fundamentals; they offer alternative policies to the voters only on relatively small points of difference. Both parties favor full employment, but they define it somewhat differently; both favor the development of water power resources, but in slightly different ways; and both favor unemployment compensation, but not the same level of benefits. Similarly, shifts of policy within a party take place largely through a series of relatively small changes, as can be seen in their only gradual acceptance of the idea of governmental responsibility for support of the unemployed, a change in party positions beginning in the early 30's and culminating in a sense in the Employment Act of 1946.

Party behavior is in turn rooted in public attitudes, and political theorists cannot conceive of democracy's surviving in the United States in the absence of fundamental agreement on potentially disruptive issues, with consequent limitation of policy debates to relatively small differences in policy.

Since the policies ignored by the administrator are politically impossible and so irrelevant, the over-simplification of analysis achieved by concentrating on policies that differ only incrementally is not a capricious kind of simplification. In addition, it can be argued that, given the limits on knowledge within which policy-makers are confined, simplifying by limiting the focus to small variations from present policy makes the most of available knowledge. Because policies being considered are like present and past policies, the administrator can obtain information and claim some insight. Non-incremental policy proposals are therefore typically not only politically irrelevant but also unpredictable in their consequences.

The second method of simplification of analysis is the practice of ignoring important possible consequences of possible policies, as well as the values attached to the neglected consequences. If this appears to disclose a shocking shortcoming of successive limited comparisons, it can be replied that, even if the exclusions are random, policies may nevertheless be more intelligently formulated than through futile attempts to achieve a comprehensiveness beyond human capacity. Actually, however, the exclusions, seeming arbitrary or random from one point of view, need be neither.

Achieving a Degree of Comprehensiveness

Suppose that each value neglected by one policy-making agency were a major concern of at least one other agency. In that case, a helpful division of labor would be achieved, and no agency need find its task beyond its capacities. The shortcomings of such a system would be that one agency might destroy a value either before another agency could be activated to safeguard it or in spite of another agency's efforts. But the possibility that important values may be lost is present in any form of organization, even where agencies attempt to comprehend in planning more than is humanly possible.

The virtue of such a hypothetical division of labor is that every important interest or value has its watchdog. And these watchdogs can protect the interests in their jurisdiction in two quite different ways: first, by redressing damages done by other agencies; and, second, by anticipating and heading off injury before it occurs.

In a society like that of the United States in which individuals are free to combine to pursue almost any possible common interest they might have and in which government agencies are sensitive to the pressures of these groups, the system described is approximated. Almost every interest has its watchdog. Without claiming that every interest has a sufficiently powerful watchdog, it can be argued that our system often can assure a more comprehensive regard for the values of the whole society than any attempt at intellectual comprehensiveness.

In the United States, for example, no part of government attempts a comprehensive overview of policy on income distribution. A policy nevertheless evolves, and one responding to a wide variety of interests. A process of mutual adjustment among farm groups, labor unions, municipalities and school boards, tax authorities, and government agencies with responsibilities in the fields of housing, health, highways, national parks, fire, and police accomplishes a distribution of income in which particular income problems neglected at one point in the decision processes become central at another point.

Mutual adjustment is more pervasive than the explicit forms it takes in negotiation between groups; it persists through the mutual impacts of groups upon each other even where they are not in communication. For all the imperfections and latent dangers in this ubiquitous process of mutual adjustment, it will often accomplish an adaptation of policies to a wider range of interests than could be done by one group centrally.

Note, too, how the incremental pattern of policy-making fits with the multiple pressure pattern. For when decisions are only incremental—closely related to known policies, it is easier for one group to anticipate the kind of moves another might make and easier too for it to make correction for injury already accomplished.[7]

Even partisanship and narrowness, to use pejorative terms, will sometimes be assets to rational decision-making, for they can doubly insure that what one agency neglects, another will not; they specialize in personnel to distinct points of view. The claim is valid that effective rational coordination of the federal administration, if possible to achieve at all, would require an agreed set of values[8]—if "rational" is defined as the practice of the root method of decision-making. But a high degree of administrative coordination occurs as each agency adjusts its policies to the concerns of the other agencies in the process of fragmented decision-making I have just described.

For all the apparent shortcomings of the incremental approach to policy alternatives with its arbitrary exclusion coupled with fragmentation, when compared to the root method, the branch method often looks far superior. In the root method, the inevitable exclusion of factors is accidental, unsystematic, and not defensible by any argument so far developed, while in the branch method the exclusions are deliberate, systematic, and defensible. Ideally, of course, the root method does not exclude; in practice it must.

Nor does the branch method necessarily neglect long-run considerations and objectives. It is clear that important values must be omitted in considering policy, and sometimes the only way long-run objectives can be given adequate attention is through the neglect of short-run considerations. But the values omitted can be either long-run or short-run.

SUCCESSION OF COMPARISONS (5B)

The final distinctive element in the branch method is that the comparisons, together with the policy choice, proceed in a chronological series.

---

[7]The link between the practice of the method of successive limited comparisons and mutual adjustment of interests in a highly fragmented and decision-making process adds a new facet to pluralist theories of government and administration.

[8]Herbert Simon, Donald W. Smithburg, and Victor A. Thompson, *Public Administration* (Alfred A. Knopf, 1950), p. 434.

Policy is not made once and for all; it is made and re-made endlessly. Policy-making is a process of successive approximation to some desired objectives in which what is desired itself continues to change under reconsideration.

Making policy is at best a very rough process. Neither social scientists, nor politicians, nor public administrators yet know enough about the social world to avoid repeated error in predicting the consequences of policy moves. A wise policy-maker consequently expects that his policies will achieve only part of what he hopes and at the same time will produce unanticipated consequences he would have preferred to avoid. If he proceeds through a *succession* of incremental changes, he avoids serious lasting mistakes in several ways.

In the first place, past sequences of policy steps have given him knowledge about the probable consequences of further similar steps. Second, he need not attempt big jumps toward his goals that would require predictions beyond his or anyone else's knowledge, because he never expects his policy to be a final resolution of a problem. His decision is only one step, one that if successful can quickly be followed by another. Third, he is in effect able to test his previous predictions as he moves on to each further step. Lastly, he often can remedy a past error fairly quickly—more quickly than if policy proceeded through more distinct steps widely spaced in time.

Compare this comparative analysis of incremental changes with the aspiration to employ theory in the root method. Man cannot think without classifying, without subsuming one experience under a more general category of experiences. The attempt to push categorization as far as possible and to find general propositions which can be applied to specific situations is what I refer to with the word "theory." Where root analysis often leans heavily on theory in this sense, the branch method does not.

The assumption of root analysts is that theory is the most systematic and economical way to bring relevant knowledge to bear on a specific problem. Granting the assumption, an unhappy fact is that we do not have adequate theory to apply to problems in any policy area, although theory is more adequate in some areas—monetary policy, for example—than in others. Comparative analysis, as in the branch method, is sometimes a systematic alternative to theory.

Suppose an administrator must choose among a small group of policies that differ only incrementally from each other and from present policy. He might aspire to "understand" each of the alternatives—for example, to know all the consequences of each aspect of each policy. If so, he would indeed require theory. In fact, however, he would usually decide that, *for policy-making purposes,* he need know, as explained above, only the consequences of each of those aspects of the policies in which they differed from one another. For this much more modest aspiration, he requires no theory (although it might be helpful, if available), for he can proceed to isolate probable differences by examining the differences in consequences associated with past differences in policies, a feasible program because he can take his observations from a long sequence of incremental changes.

For example, without a more comprehensive social theory about juvenile delinquency than scholars have yet produced, one cannot possibly understand the ways in which a variety of public policies—say on education, housing, recreation, employment, race relations, and policing—might encourage or discourage delinquency. And one needs such an understanding if he undertakes the comprehensive overview of the problem prescribed in the models of the root method. If, however, one merely wants to mobilize knowledge sufficient to assist in a choice among a small group of similar policies—alternative policies on juvenile court procedures, for example—he can do so by comparative analysis of the results of similar past policy moves.

THEORISTS AND PRACTITIONERS

This difference explains—in some cases at least—why the administrator often feels that the outside expert or academic problem-solver is sometimes not helpful and why they in turn often urge more theory on him. And it explains why an administrator often feels more confident when "flying by the seat of his pants" than when following the advice of theorists. Theorists often ask the administrator to go the long way round to the solution of his problems, in effect ask him to follow the best canons of the scientific method, when the administrator knows that the best available theory will work less well than more modest incremental comparisons. Theorists do not realize that the administrator is often in fact practicing a systematic method. It would be foolish to push this explanation too far, for sometimes practical decision-makers are pursuing neither a theoretical approach nor successive comparisons, nor any other systematic method.

It may be worth emphasizing that theory is sometimes of extremely limited helpfulness in policy-making for at least two rather different reasons. It is

greedy for facts; it can be constructed only through a great collection of observations. And it is typically insufficiently precise for application to a policy process that moves through small changes. In contrast, the comparative method both economizes on the need for facts and directs the analyst's attention to just those facts that are relevant to the fine choices faced by the decision-maker.

With respect to precision of theory, economic theory serves as an example. It predicts that an economy without money or prices would in certain specified ways misallocate resources, but this finding pertains to an alternative far removed from the kind of policies on which administrators need help. On the other hand, it is not precise enough to predict the consequences of policies restricting business mergers, and this is the kind of issue on which the administrators need help. Only in relatively restricted areas does economic theory achieve sufficient precision to go far in resolving policy questions; its helpfulness in policy-making is always so limited that it requires supplementation through comparative analysis.

SUCCESSIVE COMPARISON AS A SYSTEM

Successive limited comparisons is, then, indeed a method or system; it is not a failure of method for which administrators ought to apologize. None the less, its imperfections, which have not been explored in this paper, are many. For example, the method is without a built-in safeguard for all relevant values, and it also may lead the decision-maker to overlook excellent policies for no other reason than that they are not suggested by the chain of successive policy steps leading up to the present. Hence, it ought to be said that under this method, as well as under some of the most sophisticated variants of the root method—operations research, for example—policies will continue to be as foolish as they are wise.

Why then bother to describe the method in all the above detail? Because it is in fact a common method of policy formulation, and is, for complex problems, the principal reliance of administrators as well as of other policy analysts.[9] And because it will

<hr />

[9]Elsewhere I have explored this same method of policy formulation as practiced by academic analysts of policy ("Policy Analysis," 48 *American Economic Review* 298 [June, 1958]). Although it has been here presented as a method for public administrators, it is no less necessary to analysts more removed from immediate policy questions, despite their tendencies to describe their own analytical

be superior to any other decision-making method available for complex problems in many circumstances, certainly superior to a futile attempt at superhuman comprehensiveness. The reaction of the public administrator to the exposition of method doubtless will be less a discovery of a new method than a better acquaintance with an old. But by becoming more conscious of their practice of this method, administrators might practice it with more skill and know when to extend or constrict its use. (That they sometimes practice it effectively and sometimes not may explain the extremes of opinion on "muddling through," which is both praised as a highly sophisticated form of problem-solving and denounced as no method at all. For I suspect that in so far as there is a system in what is known as "muddling through," this method is it.)

One of the noteworthy incidental consequences of clarification of the method is the light it throws on the suspicion an administrator sometimes entertains that a consultant or adviser is not speaking relevantly and responsibly when in fact by all ordinary objective evidence he is. The trouble lies in the fact that most of us approach policy problems within a framework given by our view of a chain of successive policy choices made up to the present. One's thinking about appropriate policies with respect, say, to urban traffic control is greatly influenced by one's knowledge of the incremental steps taken up to the present. An administrator enjoys an intimate knowledge of his past sequences that "outsiders" do not share, and his thinking and that of the "outsider" will consequently be different in ways that may puzzle both. Both may appear to be talking intelligently, yet each may find the other unsatisfactory. The relevance of the policy chain of succession is even more clear when an American tries to discuss, say, antitrust policy with a Swiss, for the chains of policy in the two countries are strikingly different and the two individuals consequently have organized their knowledge in quite different ways.

If this phenomenon is a barrier to communication, an understanding of it promises an enrichment of intellectual interaction in policy formulation. Once the source of difference is understood, it will sometimes be stimulating for an administrator to seek out a policy analyst whose recent experience is with a policy chain different from his own.

This raises again a question only briefly discussed above on the merits of like-mindedness among government administrators. While much of organization theory argues the virtues of common values and agreed organizational objectives, for complex problems in which the root method is inapplicable, agencies will want among their own personnel two types of diversification: administrators whose thinking is organized by reference to policy chains other than those familiar to most members of the organization and, even more commonly, administrators whose professional or personal values or interests create diversity of view (perhaps coming from different specialties, social classes, geographical areas) so that, even within a single agency, decision-making can be fragmented and parts of the agency can serve as watchdogs for other parts.

---

efforts as though they were the rational-comprehensive method with an especially heavy use of theory. Similarly, this same method is inevitably resorted to in personal problem-solving, where means and ends are sometimes impossible to separate, where aspirations or objectives undergo constant development, and where drastic simplification of the complexity of the real world is urgent if problems are to be solved in the time that can be given to them. To an economist accustomed to dealing with the marginal or incremental concept in market processes, the central idea in the method is that both evaluation and empirical analyses are incremental. Accordingly I have referred to the method elsewhere as "the incremental method."

Exercise: Leadership and Decision Making: Applying the Vroom and Yetton Model

PURPOSE

The purpose of this exercise is to help you become more aware of the conditions that lead to effective participation. By the time you finish this exercise, you will:

1. Apply the Vroom and Yetton (1972) model to different decision-making situations.

2. Diagnose the conditions under which participative (GII), versus autocratic (AI, AII) and consultative (CI, CII), leadership styles should be employed.

3. Understand how to determine leadership style decisions with your own group of subordinates.

INTRODUCTION

Leadership and the decision-making process in management jobs are inexorably intertwined. Managers make decisions every day regarding problems that must be effectively handled. Some of those decisions may require the acceptance of subordinates for their successful implementation. Other decisions may have far reaching consequences. Depending on the type of decision to be made, managers must determine whether or not to employ a participative leadership style. Some decisions require subordinate participation; others do not.

Victor H. Vroom and Philip Yetton (1972) developed a normative model of leadership and decision-making practices that describes the conditions under which leaders or managers should: (1) engage in participative decision making with subordinates or (2) utilize a more autocratic or directive style. This exercise presents their theory, and asks you to apply this theory to a variety of cases that illustrate a decision-making problem.

INSTRUCTIONS

1. Read the article by Vroom and Yetton, "A Normative Model of Leadership Style."

2. Review the four case situations. Which leadership style do *you* think is best to employ in each situation?

This exercise originally appeared in Douglas T. Hall, Donald D. Bowen, Roy J. Lewicki, Francine S. Hall (eds.), *Experiences in Management and Organizational Behavior,* 2nd ed., as "Choosing a Leadership Style: Applying the Vroom and Yetton Model" (New York: John Wiley & Sons, 1982).

3. Follow the decision tree to determine your response.

4. In small groups of four to seven people, determine your answers to the four situations.

5. Report your answers when instructed to do so.

6. Participate in a class discussion.

CASE I

You are general foreman in charge of a large gang laying an oil pipeline. It is now necessary to estimate your expected rate of progress in order to schedule material deliveries to the next field site.

You know the nature of the terrain you will be traveling and have the historical data needed to compute the mean and variance in the rate of speed over that type of terrain. Given these two variables, it is a simple matter to calculate the earliest and latest times at which materials and support facilities will be needed at the next site. It is important that your estimate be reasonably accurate. Underestimates result in idle foremen and workers, and an overestimate results in tying up materials for a period of time before they are to be used.

Progress has been good, and your five foremen and other members of the gang stand to receive substantial bonuses if the project is completed ahead of schedule.

CASE II

You are supervising the work of 12 engineers. Their formal training and work experiences are very similar, permitting you to use them interchangeably on projects. Yesterday your manager informed you that a request had been received from an overseas affiliate for four engineers to go abroad on extended loan for a period of six to eight months. For a number of reasons, he argued and you agreed that this request should be met from your group.

All your engineers are capable of handling this assignment, and from the standpoint of present and future projects there is no particular reason why any one should be retained over any other. The problem is somewhat complicated by the fact that the overseas assignment is in what is generally regarded in the company as an undesirable location.

CASE III

You are the head of a staff unit reporting to the vice-president of finance. He has asked you to provide a report on the firm's current portfolio to include recommendations for changes in the selection criteria currently employed. Doubts have been raised about the efficiency of the existing system in the current market conditions, and there is considerable dissatisfaction with prevailing rates of return.

You plan to write the report, but at the moment you are quite perplexed about the approach to take. Your own specialty is the bond market, and it is clear to you that a detailed knowledge of the equity market, which you lack, would greatly enhance the value of the report. Fortunately, four members of your staff are specialists in different segments of the equity market. Together, they possess a vast amount of knowledge about the intricacies of investment. However, they seldom agree on the best way to achieve anything when it comes to the stock market. Although they are obviously conscientious as well as knowledgeable, they have major differences when it comes to investment philosophy and strategy.

You have six weeks before the report is due. You have already begun to familiarize yourself with the firm's current portfolio and have been provided by management with a specific set of constraints that any portfolio must satisfy. Your immediate problem is to come up with some alternatives to the firm's present practices and select the most promising for detailed analysis in your report.

CASE IV

You are on the division manager's staff and work on a wide variety of problems of both an administrative and technical nature. You have been given the assignment of developing a universal method to be used in each of the five plants in the division for manually reading equipment registers, recording the readings, and transmitting the scorings to a centralized information system. All plants are located in a relatively small geographical region.

Until now there has been a high error rate in the reading and/or transmittal of the data. Some locations have considerably higher error rates than others, and the methods used to record and transmit the data vary between plants. It is probable, therefore, that part of the error variance is a function of specific local conditions rather than anything else, and

FIGURE 1
Decision Process Flow Chart.

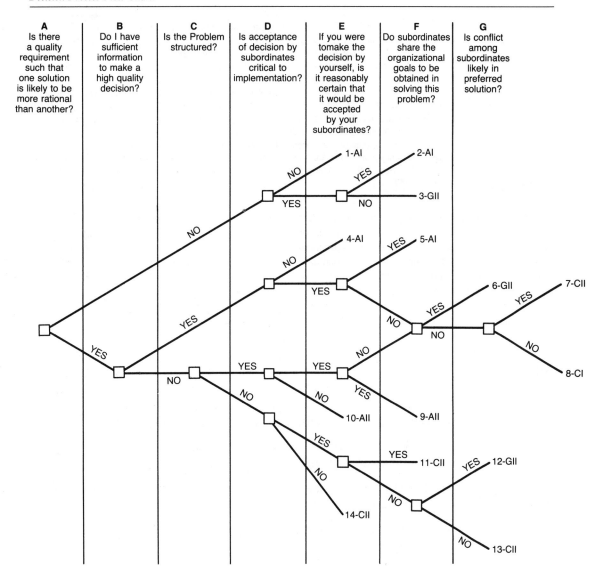

A	B	C	D	E	F	G
Is there a quality requirement such that one solution is likely to be more rational than another?	Do I have sufficient information to make a high quality decision?	Is the Problem structured?	Is acceptance of decision by subordinates critical to implementation?	If you were tomake the decision by yourself, is it reasonably certain that it would be accepted by your subordinates?	Do subordinates share the organizational goals to be obtained in solving this problem?	Is conflict among subordinates likely in preferred solution?

1-AI

2-AI

3-GII

4-AI

5-AI

6-GII

7-CII

8-CI

9-AII

10-AII

11-CII

12-GII

13-CII

14-CII

TABLE 1

Types of Management Decision Styles.

AI You solve the problem or make the decision yourself, using information available to you at that time.

AII You obtain the necessary information from your subordinate(s), then decide on the solution to the problem yourself. You may or may not tell your subordinates what the problem is in getting the information from them. The role played by your subordinates in making the decision is clearly one of providing the necessary information to you, rather than generating or evaluating alternative solutions.

CI You share the problem with relevant subordinates individually, getting their ideas and suggestions without bringing them together as a group. Then *you* make the decision which may or may not reflect your subordinates' influence.

CII You share the problem with your subordinates as a group, collectively obtaining their ideas and suggestions. Then *you* make the decision which may or may not reflect your subordinates' influence.

GII You share a problem with your subordinates as a group. Together you generate and evaluate alternatives and attempt to reach agreement (consensus) on a solution. Your role is much like that of chairman. You do not try to influence the group to adopt "your" solution and you are willing to accept and implement any solution which has the support of the entire group.

this will complicate the establishment of any system common to all plants. You have the information on error rates but no information on the local practices that generate these errors or on the local conditions that necessitate the different practices.

Everyone would benefit from an improvement in the quality of the data as they are used in a number of important decisions. Your contacts with the plants are through the quality-control supervisors who are responsible for collecting the data. They are a conscientious group committed to doing their jobs well, but are highly sensitive to interference on the part of the higher management in their own operations. Any solution that does not receive the active support of the various plant supervisors is unlikely to reduce the error rate significantly.

DISCUSSION QUESTIONS

1. Where does your preferred strategy fall on the leadership and decision-making continuum: autocratic, consultative, or participative?

2. Which "errors" do you commonly make in your leadership decisions: quality, acceptance, or time?

3. What factors may account for differences in how people diagnose leadership situations?

4. How useful is this theory in making decisions on how to lead your group of subordinates in actual leadership situations?

Case: The Man Who Killed Braniff

PURPOSE

The "Man Who Killed Braniff" describes the impact Harding Lawrence had on Braniff Airlines as its chief executive. By the time you finish this case assignment you will:

1. Understand the impact a leader's style can have on an organization.

2. Use the theories of leadership and decision making presented in this chapter to understand events that affected the survival of a major organization.

3. Determine the effect that a different style of leadership and decision making would have had on the survival of Braniff Airlines.

INTRODUCTION

This case presents the facts behind a major news story. It describes the leadership and decision-making style of Harding Lawrence and the role that style played in the "death" of Braniff Airlines. Keep the articles in this chapter—Vroom and Yetton (1980), Bass (1983), and Lindblom (1959)—in mind as you read and analyze the case.

INSTRUCTIONS

1. Read "The Man Who Killed Braniff."

2. Analyze the case using the theories of leadership and decision making presented in this chapter.

3. Participate in a class discussion.

Byron Harris

It was a gray June morning in 1979. Under the taupe concrete spars and crossbars of the Braniff International terminal at the Dallas-Fort Worth Regional Airport (DFW), hundreds of people had gathered on the apron of the runway. It was a bizarre corporate festivity, a combination diplomatic ceremony and high school halftime. A band played. Twenty ticket agents in designer uniforms had been pressed into service as flag bearers. They carried 12-foot poles with foreign flags and marched in choreographed patterns. Their faces wore a variety of expressions, from amusement to lock-jawed company loyalty to irritation at being forced to participate in the spectacle.

The occasion was the inauguration of Braniff air service from DFW to the European continent. After speeches by local dignitaries, the stars of the show, three Boeing 747 jets, were introduced. They flew over the field a few hundred feet off the ground, circling back over the crowd again and again. A rented

Reprinted with permission from the July issue of *Texas Monthly*. Copyright © 1982 by Texas Monthly.

film crew recorded the pageantry, and all retired to the terminal.

In a VIP lounge, champagne flowed and strudel was served. An accordion player mingled with the crowd. Harding Lawrence, the Braniff chief executive, moved serenely among the guests, nodding here, touching an elbow there. It was his special day. His planes would now fly not only to London but also to Frankfurt, Paris, Brussels, and Amsterdam. So calm was Lawrence that, uncharacteristically, he was talking to the press. He even admitted that there was a cloud on Braniff's horizon. "The problem we have, of course, is the price of petroleum products," he said to a television reporter. "Jet fuel is about 55¢ a gallon, and that's awfully expensive." The reporter was accustomed to the airline industry's cries of concern over fuel prices. What he wasn't used to came at the end of the interview when Lawrence nodded benignly and said, "God bless you."

It takes a man with a special kind of self-image to bestow a blessing on a reporter after an interview. But Lawrence had always been extraordinary—he stood out as a showman even in a business where executives were known for their flamboyance. He was the spitting image of a captain of industry: gray hair, bushy salt-and-pepper eyebrows, a gravelly voice that exuded self-confidence. Lawrence *was* his airline, and vice versa. When he took it over in 1965, Braniff was an obscure regional carrier that had barely entered the jet age. Lawrence immediately expanded the jet fleet. He bought routes to South America from Pan American Grace Airways. He painted his planes exotic colors, dressed his stewardesses in uniforms designed by Pucci, and then had them actually take off parts of those outfits after the planes were airborne, in what was promoted as the "air strip." Lawrence's Braniff was flashy and au courant, and it made money. In 1974, the airline earned an 18.2% return on equity, the best in the industry. By 1978, it had become the nation's seventh-largest carrier, with a 19.6% return on equity, double the industry average.

But just as the airline's fortunes had risen on the wings of Lawrence's vision, so they fell. By the end of 1980, when Lawrence was forced out, Braniff was losing nearly $6 million a week, consumed by the very flair that had propelled it to greatness. Less than 16 months later the airline went out of business, bankrupted by monstrous debt and a skittish public. Texas was obsessed with the drama of those last months—the acrimonious fare wars, the desperate selling off of routes, the celebrity ad campaigns, all the financial gymnastics that sustained the illusion that the company was still salvageable. For a while, the day-to-day headlines even obscured the truth: that Braniff's demise was a certainty long before Lawrence Harding left, as much a certainty as that his genius was the seed of its success and his ego the seed of its destruction.

A ONE-MAN AIR SHOW

The identification of an airline with one man was not unique to Braniff and Harding Lawrence, although they may have been its most extreme embodiment. It was a historical part of the airline industry. TWA, originally Transcontinental Air Transport, hired Charles Lindbergh to survey its early routes and called itself the Lindbergh Line. Juan Trippe started Pan Am as a mail carrier after failing to establish a passenger line on Long Island with nine used Navy biplanes. The airline grew in a large part because of Trippe's extraordinary skill at securing foreign routes. Eastern carved its identity under the tutelage of Eddie Rickenbacker, the top U.S. flying ace in World War I, who was referred to by Eastern's employees simply as "the captain." Continental was

founded by a young pilot named Robert Six in 1934. He borrowed $90,000 from his father-in-law and converted a small Western mailcarrier into a passenger airline. Six, who is 6' 4" tall, built his airline on the strength of his personality and his physical presence. He was the only one of the early pioneers still in the business when he retired this spring. His chief assistant until 1965 was Harding Lawrence.

Both Lawrence's genius and his ego were honed in the adolescence of the airline industry. He was born in 1920 in Perkins, Oklahoma. During World War II, he helped run an Army Air Force pilot training school in Terrell, east of Dallas. He hired on with Pioneer Airlines after the war, working at Houston's Hobby Field in the hanger next to that of another rising star: Lamar Muse of Trans-Texas Airways. Muse, who went on to pilot Southwest Airlines and Muse Air, remembers Lawrence vividly. "He was convinced he was a brilliant man," says Muse. "He was very smart and very astute." Lawrence stayed with Pioneer after it merged with Continental, ascending rapidly through the ranks to the number two spot under Robert Six. When Braniff, which had toddled along on the fringes of the industry for 37 years, went looking for a president in 1965, it looked to Continental.

From the day of Lawrence's arrival, Braniff was a one-man show. He was a master salesman, a persuader, above all a consummate actor who, according to staff members, often appeared to be rendering his own thespian interpretation of what an executive ought to be. Sometimes he would test his persuasive powers just to see how far he could go with them; at the height of his form he could talk people into believing things they knew to be untrue. Dave Stamey, a former Braniff vice-president, tells a story similar to those told by others who worked for Lawrence. "He could sit here in this chair, look out the window, and convince you it was raining, even though the sun was shining," Stamey says. "He'd say it was climatic aberration, or that it was a seasonal variation, or that the angle of the sun was refracting the light, making the rain invisible. Even though all your experience told you it wasn't raining, when you went outside you'd put your raincoat on."

Sometimes, say the executives who worked closely with him over the years, Lawrence didn't seem to know where the actor stopped and the real person began. But the real person had acumen as well as charm. Revenue passenger miles, available seat miles, break-even load factors, all these data were in his brain, evolving into a matrix of facts and figures that reflected the airline's health from day to day. In addition to being an "operations guy," he was a big thinker, a maestro of creative marketing. He was a brilliant man, his executives say, a brilliant man whose skills were rewarded. After three years as president, he became chairman of Braniff Airways in 1968 and chairman and chief executive officer to its parent company, Braniff International, in 1973.

That noteworthy year was marred only by Lawrence's pleading guilty to making illegal contributions to Richard Nixon's reelection campaign, a $40,000 indiscretion made in Braniff's name for which he was fined $1,000. The $40,000 was a fraction of a slush fund that Braniff used principally to pay kickbacks to travel agents in South America. The Civil Aeronautics Board, which investigated and even made noises about taking away some of Braniff's routes, described the fund as holding more than $641,000; Lawrence described it as less than $1 million. Whatever the amount, the CAB backed down in 1976, letting Braniff off with a $300,000 fine. In those days it seemed that nothing could keep Lawrence from leaving the airline in triumph at retirement age. No one foresaw the economic turns that would prove Braniff's mortal enemies. But the airline's biggest enemy had been there all along. It was Harding Lawrence himself.

THE TERROR OF FLIGHT 6

Lawrence the enemy won notoriety on Braniff's Flight 6, an early-evening run from DFW to La Guardia. Lawrence's wife, Mary Wells, lived in New York City, where she ran her advertising agency, Wells, Rich, Greene, so he spent his workdays in Dallas and commuted to New York for weekends. Flight 6 was a Boeing 727. Lawrence always sat in seat 6B of first class. He demanded it. If another passenger had somehow been assigned to 6B, that passenger would have to be coaxed out of his seat by the ticket agent—and God help the agent for making the oversight in the first place.

Hell hath no fury like the wrath Lawrence could unleash on an employee who did not meet his standards. After all, he *was* the airline. A slip in the airline's service was a personal insult to him. His tantrums on Flight 6 are legend. On one flight a stewardess served him an entire selection of condiments with his meal instead of asking him which ones he preferred. He slammed his fist into the plate splattering food on the surrounding seats of the first-class cabin. "Don't you *ever* assume what I want!" he screamed.

Another time he arrived at the plane in what the flight attendant describes as a state of inebriation. Shortly after takeoff he began yelling orders and shouting profanity, she says. As the flight progressed he became more intoxicated, continued to swear, and threatened the whole crew with dismissal. He broke a wine glass over his dinner tray. He charged that the attendants had used the wrong plates for dessert. Gradually, other passengers began leaving the cabin for the quieter coach section. The tirade continued: he complained repeatedly that the attendants were mixing his drink wrong. He was drinking Scotch on the rocks.

"On several occasions flight attendants came to me in tears, fearful of losing their jobs," says Ed Clements, former director of flight attendant services at Braniff. "I was sickened by what he was doing to the employees." Clements says few of the incidents were reported in writing because the women were afraid they'd suffer reprisals. And he says Lawrence abused his flight privileges as well as the cabin crews. On transatlantic flights, Clements says, Lawrence would commonly block the first two rows on one side of the coach section in addition to taking his two complimentary seats in first class. This was so he and his wife could lie down and sleep on their way to London. The practice often left six passengers in Dallas, for the planes to London regularly flew full.

The transatlantic flights were not without incident either. On one flight Lawrence dumped a trayful of food onto a stewardess's lap because it had gotten cold while he was away from his seat. On another he overturned a champagne bucket that was being used to store fruit. On a third he threw a dinner roll at a flight attendant. Stories about these displays spread rapidly through the employee ranks. By the late 1970s Lawrence's appearance on an aircraft was likely to arouse two emotions in the crew: fear and hatred. Workers went to great lengths to prevent a tantrum. Row six in first class would be made spotless before Lawrence's arrival: even windows on his aisle would be washed. Flight attendants would study their service manuals before takeoff. The rest of the plane might be a mess, coach service might suffer, but Lawrence's service would be up to par.

Inevitably, perhaps, dissatisfied employees meant dissatisfied customers. Marketing surveys showed that Braniff was not popular with many of the people who flew on it. While an ostentatious, entrepreneurial customer was attracted to the airline's first-class service, many of the passengers who flew in coach chose Braniff because there was no other airline that flew at the time of day they had to travel.

Although Braniff was Dallas's hometown airline, it did not enjoy great goodwill there. Says Hal Salfen, a Braniff vice-president from 1971 to 1973, "People hated Braniff. That's absolutely true. The employees had the attitude that they were doing you a favor to get you on the plane."

THURSDAY, BLOODY THURSDAY

If Lawrence was a terror in the air, he cut just as wide a swath through his executives on the ground. Thursdays were dreaded by vice presidents, for on Thursday the big boss held his top-level staff meeting. The executives grouped around a large table, Lawrence at the head. The focus of attention would shift from man to man (no more than two women were ever listed among the corporate officers) as each gave a report on his department. The process would go smoothly for the first few reports, then a snag would develop. A computer was down, say, or traffic had been slower than expected over the previous weekend. Suddenly the bearer of bad tidings would find himself stopped in midsentence.

"Why is the computer down?" Lawrence would ask. Then, "Why didn't you fix it?" Then, "When will it be fixed?" or "Why didn't you tell me this sooner?" Then, "How will this affect projected revenue?" The volume would rise as the questions went on, until the unlucky executive found Lawrence standing beside him, yelling, "I pay you a good salary and I expect you to do your job! Why don't you do it?" Leaning forward, Lawrence would stop with his bushy eyebrows just inches from the malefactor's face, his eyes, which sometimes appeared to be solid brown, devoid of pupils, boring in. And finally would come the growled question, "Why don't you get *on the team*?"

When the meeting ended, recalls one staff member, the victim would have to be "shoveled into his seat and wheeled down the hall." In some cases the sufferer would have invited the explosion by falling down on his job. But often the outbursts were simply a chance for the chief to flex his muscles—Lawrence had to have his sacrificial lamb every Thursday. For the top-level staff, the lesson of these episodes had little to do with Braniff's computer problems, traffic projections, or other facets of running the company. Smart executives simply learned not to give Lawrence bad news.

Thursdays evolved their own ritual, in which details such as where one sat became urgent matters of self-preservation. No one wanted to be "downwind" of an executive who was to be sacrificed: some of the invective might splatter. Early on a Thursday,

the phone lines at Braniff headquarters would begin to buzz as executives asked each other the question: who is going to give Harding bad news today? Shortly before the meeting was to begin, a decorous scramble for chairs ensued—after the lamb had selected his seat.

A few stubborn souls would brave the machine-gun fire and persist in the delivery of a report even if its contents were unfavorable. One of these was Ed Acker, president of the airline under Lawrence from 1970 to 1975 and now chairman of Pan Am, who was widely known for his ability to handle the big boss. "Nobody gave Harding bad news," he says, "because nobody *wanted* to give him bad news." The point recurs in other descriptions of the Lawrence regime. Many of his executives were weak, untrained as managers, selected haphazardly from the airline's ranks by Lawrence himself. Appointed to their positions through his magnanimity, they were reluctant to displease him. In addition, they were often unsure of their own abilities. Their insecurity, combined with Lawrence's natural tendency toward management by intimidation, created a climate that was at best paralytic.

"They started out as strong customers," says Neal Robinson, a veteran of the Lawrence years, now executive vice-president of U.S. Telephone. "They were very serious about themselves and their jobs. But the constant pounding from Harding over the years sapped them of the will to fight."

The result was a group that could carry out decisions once they were made but generally deferred to Lawrence on policymaking, no matter how flawed the policies he made might be. By the late 1970s the company's managerial structure resembled a pyramid with an illusory base, the chief executive floating above an ineffectual management corps. Braniff lacked what management analysts call infrastructure, the network of people who transmit information and make decisions, giving the company internal direction. The big boss didn't get all the information he needed, and his ego often prevented him from trusting what his subordinates did tell him. He flew the airline by the seat of his pants. For a while, though, it was quite an air show. The 1978 balance sheet showed a profit of $45.2 million, the company's largest ever.

Much of Braniff's success, however, was as attributable to good fortune as to shrewdness. Between 1973 and 1975, for example, many airlines were laboring to pay for widebodied jets—DC-10s, L-1011s and 747s—that were flying nearly empty or were mothballed because passenger traffic had not grown as fast as they had expected. (There are still more than 100 747s and DC-10s for sale on the world market.) Braniff was widely congratulated in the press for having sagaciously decided not to buy the big jets, for taking the conservative road when others took chances. But the truth is that when other airlines were ordering those planes in 1969 and 1970, Braniff didn't have the money to buy them. "It was sheer-ass luck," says one former vice-president. And by the end of 1978, record profits notwithstanding, that luck was running out.

FLYING TOO HIGH

That year was a watershed for the entire industry. On October 24, the Airline Deregulation Act became law. Over a short period of time, it started phasing out regulation of routes and fares, the two elements that had shaped the industry since its beginning. Airlines had been rigidly regulated by the Civil Aeronautics Board since 1938. Until deregulation, the CAB decided where individual airlines would be allowed to fly by awarding route authorities. These pearls were parceled out after hearings and deliberations that often took years. Airlines vying for routes had to present detailed arguments as to why they, and not their competitors, should be allowed to fly from one city to another. This protracted process conditioned executives like Lawrence to think of routes as commodities of immense value. In a world where routes were scarce, they must be procured and protected at any cost.

The CAB's first move in implementing deregulation was to open dormant routes—those for which authority had been granted but which were not being flown—on a first-come, first-served basis. The airlines dispatched representatives to the CAB in Washington to snap up these windfalls. Press accounts of the event describe lawyers in pin-striped suits queued up all day, briefcases in hand, outside the CAB office. At night they would turn over their places to paid stand-ins who bedded down in sleeping bags on the sidewalks.

The frenzy was prompted partly by the airlines' uncertainty as to how far deregulation would go. Braniff, which had decided to seize every route it could get its hands on, applied for more than 300 of them in one day. The airline had nowhere near the resources to fly all those routes; the strategy was to take the most suitable ones and incorporate them into the existing system, to establish Braniff's presence in new markets before the CAB changed its mind and went back to parceling out routes the old way. The

flaw in the strategy was fundamental. The reason the routes were dormant was that other carriers had found them unprofitable. That didn't dissuade Lawrence, however. He insisted that routes that had failed for other carriers would work for Braniff if properly integrated into the system.

To Lawrence, the decision transcended considerations of short-term profit and loss; it was a matter of survival. He foresaw the deregulated industry as one with a few large airlines and several small ones, but few middle-sized competitors. And in this he may have been right. For Braniff, Lawrence believed, it was grow or be eaten, so he made the airline bigger. On December 15, 1978, Braniff began service on 32 routes to 16 new cities. It was now making runs such as Memphis to Orlando, Kansas City to Philadelphia—flights that other airlines had found they couldn't make money on. Meanwhile, most carriers were either expanding cautiously or waiting to see how deregulation developed. "Lawrence was off on a trip that boggled the minds of most people in this business," says Morten Beyer, president of Avmark, a Washington-based aviation consulting firm. "From a business standpoint he was off his rocker. You should dominate the markets you're in, but the Braniff expansion was helter-skelter. They did not support their DFW operations. If they had done that, they might have succeeded."

Lawrence's empire building was approved by a board of directors that had for years been a rubber stamp for his proposals. Company records indicate that the board members may have regarded their positions as honors rather than duties. In 1978 six of the eleven outside directors of the company—those who were not Braniff officers—attended less than 75% of the board's meetings and committee meetings. But if the board seemed to lack diligence in reviewing Lawrence's plans, it was not acting any differently from most airline boards of the day. Moreover, Lawrence's past success was a convincing reason to let him have his way.

His way took money. New stations had to be opened, personnel to be moved to new cities, new employees to be hired. A new Boeing 727 cost $12 million, a 747 more than $45 million. According to the 1978 annual report, Braniff planned to spend $925.2 million on 41 new aircraft through 1981. Some experts say that to service the new routes properly, the company would have had to spend even more than that on planes, well over $1 billion. Airline analysts stress that a route is in essence a business in itself. Although part of a larger system, it must be conceived, executed, staffed, advertised and sold as a trip between two cities. By the end of 1978 Braniff was on the verge of adding four cities in Europe and four in the Pacific on top of the 16 new cities in the U.S. It was starting 24 new businesses in less than 12 months.

That the board acquiesced in this decision is no less surprising than that the company was able to borrow money to do it. Even though Braniff had earned $45.2 million in 1978, it still had long-term debt and lease obligations of $423 million, and its current liabilities exceeded its assets by $14 million. In the short term, Braniff was $14 million in the hole. The proposed spending spree meant that the company's debt-to-equity ratio would climb astronomically. Still, in 1978 Lawrence was able to secure credit from Boeing and $100 million in insurance company and bank loans.

How did he do it? It was the Lawrence charm, the acting skill, and the ability to persuade, aided considerably by the past record of success. "He had them mesmerized," says one insider, "and he had himself convinced he could do it too." At age 58, he wanted to establish Braniff as a worldwide airline before he retired. The plans were going forward: applications were filed to fly to a dozen additional destinations in Latin America and to Bahrain in the Middle East, Peking, Shanghai, Canton, Bangkok, Djakarta, and New Delhi. With just a few more links, Braniff would girdle the globe!

FORT LAWRENCE

Meanwhile, back in Dallas, another of Lawrence's dreams was consuming more than $70 million. Lawrence conceived Braniff Place, on the outskirts of DFW, as the gemstone of the airline. Not only would it house the company's world headquarters—its executive offices and training facilities—but when completed in 1978 it would also be a 113-room hotel for Braniff employees. It would include an employee recreation center with a nine-hole, par-three golf course, a swimming pool, saunas, and tennis and hand-ball courts.

The complex was as unconventional as Lawrence himself. The design was Mediterranean: four brilliant white terraced buildings, flanked by raised earthen shoulders, set beside a man-made lake. A sunken parking lot was rimmed with blue tile and centered around a fountain. The buildings made a glittering monument to Lawrence, but they looked better than they functioned. Lawrence had selected a California firm as the architect and a Texas company as the interior designer. He insisted on overseeing

the minutest construction details himself. Communication between the three was cumbersome; hundreds of change orders were necessary. The complex was funded in 1976 with $35 million in DFW Airport bonds, but in 1978 Braniff had to go back for more bonds totaling $36 million to cover cost overruns and equipment.

Executive offices were to have gardens on the terraces outside their windows, so French doors were installed to open onto the gardens, but then the garden plan was scrapped. The doors leaked air, creating drafts strong enough to blow papers off desks. Some of them eventually had to be welded shut. Many of the desks, which were custom designed, had to be repaired shortly after installation. The office and hotel wings each had courtyards with imported Italian marble benches and olive trees flown in from California. Two of the trees were so big they had to be lifted in with cranes. The landscapers had neglected to note, however, that North Texas winters are too cold for olive trees. The trees died.

Every office had stark white walls enlivened only by a work from Braniff's collection of 54 paintings by Alexander Calder (whom Lawrence also commissioned to decorate two of the airline's jets). No personal artifacts or mementos were allowed. Each desk held two phones, one a normal telephone, the other an intercom that allowed any executive, including Lawrence, to speak directly into any office, even if the phone was not taken off the hook. Frequently, a vice-president would be in the middle of a meeting in his office when Lawrence's voice would interrupt. The executive could shut the device off, but only at the risk of enraging Lawrence. Some referred to the instruments as Gestapo phones and to the office complex as Fort Lawrence.

The back section of the top floor in the executive wing was Harding Lawrence's apartment, which he rented from the company for $1,775 a month. Furnished and decorated at airline expense, it was a sumptuous exercise in white and off-white. Paintings from Lawrence's private collection hung on the walls. In the living room, a neon sculpture adorned a glass coffee table, a large antique birdcage occupied one corner, a polar bear rug lay in front of the fireplace. All these objects belonged to the airline. With a restaurant-size kitchen, the living room, a sitting room, two bedrooms, two and a half baths done in Italian marble, and a small swimming pool on the terrace out back, the apartment was well worth what the big boss paid for it.

Lawrence lived in his suite alone. He had a full-time personal valet and a housekeeper. They were provided at company expense, and most employees knew it. They saw the valet pick up Lawrence's rawhide luggage when he flew on the airline. (A special handler made sure his luggage was always last on and first off the plane and was carried to him directly at the baggage claim, which tended to draw the interest of the other passengers.)

There were other fringe benefits that the employees knew less about: a three-story house in London and a villa in Mexico. The latter was maintained at a cost, according to Braniff's 1978 proxy statement, of $92,000 a year. (That would rise to $172,000 a year in 1980.) Like top executives of many corporations, Lawrence also had a stock option plan. It gave him thousands of shares of company stock at a fixed value, which he could sell back to the company at the market price. If the market price increased, he could make a lot of money. In 1977 Lawrence exercised options on more than 78,000 shares, netting $236,000. In 1978 he sold another 200,000 shares, netting $1.4 million. He also received $871,794 in "salaries, fees, directors' fees, commissions, bonuses, and incentive compensation" during those two years.

THE STORM GATHERS

Even in those flush days, however, there was serious trouble in paradise. In December 1978 a high-ranking financial officer told Lawrence privately that Braniff's prospects for survival were nil. The airline was at the height of its expansion, and Lawrence was ginning out copious projections on the profits the coming months would bring. But he had already committed himself to spend so much on new planes and new routes that Braniff wasn't going to be able to bring in enough money to pay its bills. When the executive spoke to him, however, Lawrence insisted that everything would work out just as he predicted, that the executive "just didn't know about airlines." As the months passed and profits evaporated, the big boss talked to the man less and less.

Fuel costs, which represented about one fourth of the carrier's operating expenses, were fast becoming a critical drain on profits. They rose from 40¢ a gallon in 1978 to 62¢ in 1979, making the delicate economics of expansion more delicate still. Many of Braniff's new domestic routes were "add-ons" to old ones. Service to Milwaukee, for example, could be added because the airline had a plane in Chicago late in the evening. A 727 could be flown from there to Milwaukee less than half full without losing money. If more than half the seats could be filled, the flight

would turn a profit. But as the price of fuel rose, the break-even load factor, the number of passengers needed to make the flight pay for itself, also rose. Soon the flight might have to be two-thirds full to be profitable, and who wants to go from Chicago to Milwaukee in the late evening? Not that many people, the airline found.

On international flights, where the operating costs were multiplied over vast distances, the stage was set for huge losses. Some of the bolder executives advised Lawrence to delay inaugurating Braniff's new foreign routes, but the expansion moved on. In June 1979 came the four European cities. A month later, four destinations in the Pacific—Seoul, Hong Kong, Singapore, and Guam—were added over the protests of those who warned Lawrence that price cutting among nationally owned airlines in the Pacific is vicious and the volume of travelers small. Who wants to go to Seoul, South Korea, regardless of the time of day? Not that many people, the airline found.

At the same time all this was happening, the CAB was unexpectedly speeding up deregulation instead of slowing it. Route access was loosened even further. The franchise to fly from one city to another, that valuable commodity that in the past had been so difficult to acquire, had almost no value at all. The analysis of each route's cost and yield potential, which previously had been performed as part of the CAB route certification process, was no longer routine. The agency that had acted as a restraint to overzealous airlines was no longer a barrier to them. Decisions had to be based on economics, not chauvinism.

Airlines that made their decisions on the basis of economics have little sympathy with the course Braniff took. At the March 1982 stockholders' meeting of Continental Airlines in Los Angeles, Frank Lorenzo, president of Continental's parent company, Texas Air, which also owns Texas International Airlines, took pains to distinguish Continental from Braniff. "It's important to note that Continental took a fundamentally different approach to deregulation than the management of Braniff took," Lorenzo said. "The management of Braniff had a basic belief that deregulation was an opportunity to become more aggressive; Continental looked upon deregulation as a time of extreme caution. Time will tell who was right."

GOING DOWN

In fact, time had already told. In late 1979 Lawrence began receiving news that might have shaken the confidence of another executive. His new routes, particularly those in the Pacific, were losing millions a month. The company's total operating expenses were 92% higher than they had been two years earlier. Braniff lost $9.8 million in the third quarter. But chauvinism won out over economics: the jumbo jets kept flying.

As costs rose, fares were falling. On June 1, 1979, the very same day that Braniff was serving strudel to the Dallas-Fort Worth city fathers, Texas International trotted out a brass band in its DFW terminal to inaugurate service to New Orleans. It was selling round-trip tickets for 35¢ that day, as a promotion, and would soon be selling one-way "peanuts fare" tickets for $35. A ticket to New Orleans on Braniff cost twice as much. Price was now a selling point in a business where it never had been before. To compete on price, airlines would have to trim profits, and Braniff's profits were already nonexistent.

By the end of 1979 the company had lost $44.3 million. In the first quarter of 1980 its losses exceeded $21 million. Lawrence's tirades at staff meetings continued. The big boss seemed unable to fully admit to himself the severity of Braniff's illness. He dispatched two executives to Los Angeles to inquire about the possibility of purchasing Continental—which at that time was an independent company. They returned with the answer that no, it was Continental that wanted to buy Braniff.

The big boss lived at Braniff Place, needing only to step through a door in his living room to be in the Braniff boardroom, and yet another door to be in his office. Employees called Lawrence's sanctuary the Howard Hughes suite because they rarely saw him outside of it. He was occasionally spied padding about the halls of the headquarters building late at night in his stocking feet, but he was cut off from the outside world. He never had to leave Fort Lawrence even to go to the 7-11 to buy a quart of milk or a newspaper. His valet did that.

His insularity was only compounded by his dealings with upper management. Occasionally an executive working late in the evening would be summoned to Lawrence's flat to thrash out one problem or another with the big boss. But Lawrence usually did most of the talking, sometimes until the early hours of the morning, pacing back and forth, drink in hand, in the all-white living room. One did not speak unless spoken to or voice an opinion unless asked; it was so much easier to find ways of agreeing with Lawrence than to tell him the truth.

As 1980 progressed, however, the truth became inescapable. The red ink was a hemorrhage—second-quarter losses were more than $48 million.

The Pacific routes were consuming millions every month. Fuel prices were still headed upward. The economy edged into a recession, eroding the base of potential customers. And inflation continued to bloat expenses. Eventually, even Lawrence was compelled to acknowledge the need to cut costs. A labor relations expert was hired to help negotiate pay concessions with employee groups. Braniff was forced to do something it had never done much of: talk to its employees. On two occasions Lawrence was persuaded to attend the meetings to stress the urgency of Braniff's predicament. The very prospect sent ripples through the rank and file. Here was the man who threw food at his workers asking them to do him a favor. At the first gathering with the flight attendants, the big boss had the temerity to arrive in his chauffeur-driven Mercedes. "There was," says an executive who attended, "a broad-based feeling of contempt for Harding."

THE FINAL DAYS

With his airline in a nose dive, Lawrence became even more unpredictable. He singled out certain executives for early-morning phone calls. Awakened at 3 A.M., they would have to endure harangues about their "mistakes." The big boss was frustrated: at himself, at events, at the staff of incompetents who had let him down. Still, most employees stayed loyal; they felt a need to help the firm through its bad times. Moreover, after years of being told they were incompetent, many had come to believe it. "He had them believing they were so dumb they couldn't get a job anywhere else," says one who lived through this period. Two executives regularly sat in their offices and wept. Another concocted a series of business trips that kept him away from headquarters continuously; by staying away, he avoided the misery of the disintegration.

Lawrence sequestered himself in his apartment, which became known as the bunker. "He was out of touch with reality," says one vice-president. "He said we were gonna line up this loan and that loan, but he was dreaming. The numbers he talked about were much different from what was really happening. The airline was falling apart, but people were still running around trying to figure out how to deal with Harding. He had us moving armies we didn't have."

The employees who dealt with the public every day only heard rumors of this disintegration. But they had been whipsawed by the airline's growth and contraction. They had seen their ranks swell from

11,500 in 1977 to 15,200 in 1979 and then shrink back to 11,500 the very next year as the airline finally pared its unsuccessful routes. Never among the best-trained personnel in the industry, they tended to take their long-festering frustration with management out on the ticket buyers. At the same time, the company was in the midst of a "We Better Be Better" advertising campaign that in the eyes of Sam Coats, who later became senior vice-president for marketing, conveyed a sense of arrogance. It was as if all the company's difficulties—its financial problems, its management style, its public image—were converging at once to seal its destruction.

Lawrence met with financial reporters in August, during Braniff's last profitable quarter, to convince them of the airline's good health. "Braniff is a financially sound company," he said. "Braniff is not a company that is in financial trouble." But even he seemed to know the end was near. "My board, my stockholders, and all those people, I have a responsibility to them," he said. "I will be here as long as they require my services." He gave his home phone number to reporters, urging them to call him at any time with their questions. Indeed, it was not unusual for reporters to receive calls from Lawrence during this period—calls accusing them of biased reporting.

In the last quarter of 1980 the airline lost $77 million. In December the board of directors, at the mandate of the lenders, had no choice but to call for Lawrence's resignation. With a pension of $306,969 guaranteed for each year of the rest of his life, the big boss resigned without putting up a fight. (Now that Braniff is bankrupt, he may get less.) Quietly, on the night of December 30, 1980, Lawrence climbed the outside stairs of a Braniff gate at DFW, avoiding reporters waiting for him inside the terminal. He was boarding a jet for Mexico, for what he has since described as retirement. He keeps an office at his wife's advertising agency in New York, but there employees say he is traveling and unavailable for interviews.

AMONG THE RUINS

John Casey, vice-chairman under Lawrence, was promoted to fill the big boss's shoes. He succeeded in lessening the flow of red ink somewhat in 1981, but to reverse the airline's fortunes, he decided, new talent was needed. In September, Casey hired Howard Putnam as president for finance. Both men were lured away from Southwest Airlines, which had been the wunderkind of the industry in the '70s, compiling the highest profit margin of any U.S. airline. Even with their impressive credentials, Putnam and Guthrie would need a huge chunk of luck to succeed at Braniff: the airline had a demoralized work force, a degenerating public image, debts totaling well over $700 million, and creditors growling at the door. But Putnam was known for being tough, unpretentious, and unorthodox, and Guthrie had a reputation for financial expertise.

So it was with some optimism that the two of them drove out to the Braniff offices in Putnam's Oldsmobile last fall. Neither had ever seen Braniff Place before, and as they drove across the treeless grassland north of the airport, it loomed up in all its sparkling white glory. It was entirely different from Southwest's spartan offices in a converted airline terminal at Love Field. As they drew closer, they could see 28 flagpoles, which had been placed at the entrance to the complex at Harding Lawrence's direction. Originally there had been only two, but Lawrence had ordered the number increased as the airline expanded, so that the flag of every Braniff nation would fly above his office. Now, with the routes dropped to save money, the poles were empty. "My God," said Putnam, gazing at them, "they look just like masts of a sunken ship."

DISCUSSION QUESTIONS

1. What was Lawrence's leadership style? What effect did his leadership style have on Braniff Airlines? Did Lawrence exhibit any of the charismatic qualities described in the reading by Bass (1983)? Discuss these questions.

2. How did Lawrence make decisions? What effect did this have on Braniff Airlines?

3. What was it about Lawrence's leadership and decision-making style that caused the demise of Braniff Airlines?

4. Would a different leadership and decision-making style have led to a different outcome for Braniff? How? What should Lawrence have done?

Exercise: Vanatin—Group Decision Making and Ethics

PURPOSE

The purpose of this exercise is to help you understand group decision making and ethics. By the time you finish this exercise you will:

1. Understand the factors that contribute to decision making about ethical practices.

2. Participate in making a group decision about an ethical issue.

3. Explore the aspects of group dynamics and leadership that affect ethical decisions.

INTRODUCTION

The Vanatin case provides an opportunity for group members to struggle with questions of social responsibility and ethics in decision making. The case is constructed around a medical product, considered by experts to be injurious to the health of consumers—even to the point of possibly causing death. These consequences must be evaluated against the potential economic losses to the company, which would be substantial if sale of the drug were discontinued. The decision—not an easy one—is nevertheless common to many corporate and governmental groups that must consider both their own interest and the overall interests of society and public welfare.

INSTRUCTIONS

1. Your instructor will divide the class into groups and assign you to one of seven roles.

2. Read the Background Information for the Vanatin Case.

3. Read *only* your own role description and make notes on what you want to emphasize in the group discussion.

4. Read the directions for and complete the Vanatin role-play.

5. Participate in a class discussion.

This exercise was adapted by Roy J. Lewicki, Duke University, from an exercise developed by J. Scott Armstrong, University of Pennsylvania. It is reprinted from Douglas T. Hall, Donald D. Bowen, Roy J. Lewicki, and Francine S. Hall, *Experiences in Management and Organizational Behavior,* 2nd ed. (New York: John Wiley & Sons, 1982).

BACKGROUND INFORMATION FOR THE VANATIN CASE

You are a member of the Booth Pharmaceutical Corporation Board of Directors. You have been called to a special board meeting to discuss what should be done with the product Vanatin.

Vanatin is a "fixed-ratio" antibiotic sold by prescription. That is, it contains a combination of drugs. On the market for more than 13 years, it has been highly successful. It now accounts for about $18 million per year, which is 12 percent of Booth Company's gross income in the United States (and a greater percentage of net profits). Profits from foreign markets, where Booth is marketed under a different name, is roughly comparable to that in the United States.

Over the past 20 years, numerous medical scientists (such as the AMA's Council on Drugs) have objected to the sale of most fixed-ratio drugs. The arguments have been that (1) there is no evidence that these fixed-ratio drugs have improved benefits over single drugs, and (2) the possibility of detrimental side effects, including death, is at least double. For example, scientists have estimated that Vanatin is causing about 30 to 40 unnecessary deaths per year (that is, deaths that could be prevented if the patients had used a substitute made by a competitor of Booth). Despite recommendations to remove fixed-ratio drugs from the market, doctors have continued to use them. They offer a shotgun approach for doctors who are unsure of their diagnoses.

Recently, a National Academy of Science–National Research Council panel, a group of impartial scientists, carried out extensive research studies and recommended unanimously that the Food and Drug Administration (FDA) ban the sale of Vanatin. One of the members of the panel, Dr. Peterson of the University of Texas, was quoted by the press as saying, "There are few instances in medicine when so many experts have agreed unanimously and without reservation [about banning Vanatin]." This view was typical of comments made by other members of the panel. In fact, it was typical of comments that had been made about fixed-ratio drugs over the past 20 years. These impartial experts, then, believe that, while all drugs have some possibility of side effects, the costs associated with Vanatin far exceed the possible benefits.

The special board meeting has arisen out of an emergency situation. The FDA has told you that it plans to ban Vanatin in the United States and wants to give Booth time for a final appeal to them. Should the ban become effective, Booth would have to stop all sales of Vanatin and attempt to remove inventories from the market. Booth has no close substitutes to Vanatin, so that consumers will be switched to close substitutes currently marketed by rival firms. (Some of these substitutes apparently have no serious side effects.) It is extremely unlikely that bad publicity from this case would have any significant effect on the long-term profits of other products made by Booth.

The Board is meeting to review and make decisions on two issues:

1. What should be done with Vanatin in the U.S. market (the immediate problem)?

2. Assuming that Vanatin is banned from the U.S. market, what should Booth do in the foreign markets? (No government action is anticipated overseas.)

Decisions on each of these issues must be reached at today's meeting. The Chairman of the Board has sent out this background information, and he also wanted you to give some thought as to which of the following alternatives you would prefer for the domestic market:

1. Recall Vanatin immediately and destroy it.

2. Stop production of Vanatin immediately, but allow what's been made to be sold.

3. Stop all advertising and promotion of Vanatin, but provide it for doctors who request it.

4. Continue efforts to most effectively market Vanatin until its sale is actually banned.

5. Continue efforts to most effectively market Vanatin and take legal, political, and other necessary actions to prevent the authorities from banning Vanatin.

A similar decision must also be made for the foreign market *under the assumption that the sale is banned in the United States.*

VANATIN ROLES

(Read only the role to which you have been assigned.)

Role of Elmer B. Parker, Ombudsman and Consumer Advocate

You have been hired by the Board to represent the interests of the consumers of Booth's products, which in this case means both the doctors who prescribe the drugs and the patients who ultimately consume them. While you are aware that Vanatin makes life easier for some doctors, you feel that these doctors ought to know better. Any difficulty doctors might have if the drug is removed from the market is far outweighed by the deaths stemming from the use of the drug. Except for your vote, your ultimate weapon is to "blow the whistle" and give the Vanatin story to the newspapers. This would, however, cost you your job so that you could not continue to have the "moderating effect" that you have previously been able to exercise on Board decisions.

Role of Cyrus Booth, M.D., Chairman of the Board

As Chairman of the Board, it is your job to have the Board reach a decision on the two issues within the time allowed. You *must* reach a decision by the end of that time, since some of the Board members have to leave to catch a plane.

Your general philosophy about meetings is to try to allow various sides of the issues to be discussed before a decision is reached. Legally speaking, a majority vote is required to reach a decision. You prefer a consensus decision, but a formal vote may be used at the end of the meeting if necessary. At the end of the meeting, you are to record the decision on the group decision form and hand it to the instructor.

Personally, while you are concerned about the effect that a cut in the sale of Vanatin will have on earnings, you are also concerned that this company, which you have led through its period of greatest growth, also maintain its image of honesty and integrity. This is more than just "corporate image." Booth must be devoted to the maintenance of health and prevention of sickness, for in the last analysis that is how you and your family will be judged in history. You will make every effort to ensure that the decision reached today reflects a unified consensus of the Board.

Role of Philip Brown, President, and Vice Chairman of the Board

You were the President of Booth when Vanatin was introduced into the market. Naturally, you feel that Vanatin was, and still is, a good product for both Booth and for the people who have used it. If you didn't feel this way, you wouldn't have put Vanatin on the market in the first place. A cut in the sales of Vanatin would bring about managerial dislocations and threaten to reverse the strong growth of profits under your command. Furthermore, it has become increasingly difficult to develop new products because of extensive testing requirements of the FDA. On the other hand, as chief executive officer of Booth, you are concerned about the kind of company that you lead.

Role of Jack Booth, Son of Cyrus Booth, President, Booth Associates, Consultants

You and your two brothers manage a consulting firm that does most of its business with the Booth Company. You and your brothers control approximately 20 percent of Booth stock, and you are concerned with the potential effects of the proposed ban on corporate earnings. You have become increasingly disturbed recently at the responsiveness of management to the demands of labor, community, and governmental groups. You feel that management is hired by the stockholders, and that management through the Board should be primarily responsive to them. In a well publicized statement to *The Wall Street Journal*, you stated that "management seems to be more concerned with its own comfort and security than with corporate profits."

A suggestion was recently sent to you by the corporate lobbyist in Washington. He suggests that it might be possible to bring political pressure to bear on the FDA by securing the cooperation of the current Secretary of Health and Welfare. The Secretary might be willing to overrule a proposed ban by the FDA, since the ban would represent a major precedent that increases the power of the FDA at the expense of drug companies and their rights to free enterprise. Getting the Secretary to go along might require some major financial contributions to the President's reelection campaign.

Role of James Vance, Corporate Legal Counsel

You would prefer not to fight the FDA on Vanatin because you are convinced in the long run that Booth will lose. The FDA has respected research data to support its claim. Other legal tactics are necessary.

You have been checking out various ways of handling the problem with friends. One suggestion has been sent to you by another Booth attorney. He has seen the Vanatin issue develop over the past few years, and he thinks that it would be possible legally to delay any action by the FDA. He suggests that Judge Kent of Kalamazoo (a man whom you know personally) would be willing to serve an injunction on the FDA. This would prohibit the FDA from banning Vanatin until such time as a formal hearing can be held. The results of this hearing, if unfavorable, could then be appealed. In effect, the case could be tied up in the courts for three to five years. A similar move in international courts would not be likely to have an impact on Vanatin sales for five to ten years.

Role of John C. Gauntlett, M.D., Board of Directors

You have been aware of the bad publicity on Vanatin. As a practicing physician, you have been prescribing Vanatin for years, and you have seen nothing wrong with it. At the last AMA meeting, other doctors to whom you talked reported similar findings. Your thought is that an appeal should be sent to all doctors to protest the FDA, on the grounds that a ban by the FDA would be violating the physician's right to prescribe the most effective drugs. The fact that some of the doctors you talked to have been using Vanatin for 13 years indicated that it must have some value.

You have been a member of the Board of Directors for eight years and own 150,000 shares of Booth stock.

Role of Herb Phillips, M.D., Ph.D.

As head of Booth's research division, you are very aware of the deaths caused by Vanatin. Although it is the best product of its kind that Booth produces, products produced by Booth's competitors are just as effective and have fewer negative after-effects. It is because of Booth's superior marketing, advertising, and drug distribution system that Vanatin has fared so well competitively. Still, the profits of drugs like Vanatin help finance new drug research, and maintain your large and highly productive research laboratories.

VANATIN ROLE PLAY

Directions: The Chairman of the Board will conduct the discussion of the Vanatin problem. By the end of 45 minutes, the group should reach a decision on what to do about *both* domestic and international distribution of Vanatin. At the end of the meeting, each Chairman should record the decisions of the group on the Recording Form.

Recording Form

Group Decision on Vanatin

1. Check the category that most closely approximates your position with regard to the U.S. market (circle one letter only):
    a. Recall Vanatin immediately and destroy it.
    b. Stop production of Vanatin immediately, but allow what's been made to be sold.
    c. Stop all advertising and promotion of Vanatin, but provide it for doctors who request it.

d. Continue efforts to most effectively market Vanatin until sale is actually banned by the FDA.

e. Continue efforts to most effectively market Vanatin and take legal, political, and other necessary action to prevent the FDA from banning Vanatin.

2. Assume that the FDA did succeed in banning Vanatin but that it was still legal to sell Vanatin in foreign countries. What category most closely approximates your position with regard to foreign markets? (Circle one letter only.)

a. Recall Vanatin immediately and destroy it.

b. Stop production of Vanatin immediately, but allow what's been made to be sold.

c. Stop all advertising and promotion of Vanatin, but provide it for doctors who request it.

d. Continue efforts to most effectively market Vanatin until sale is banned in each particular country.

e. Continue efforts to most effectively market Vanatin and take legal, political, and other necessary action to prevent the banning of Vanatin.

TABULATION OF RESULTS

Directions: The instructor will tabulate the types of decisions made by all the groups for the U.S. and foreign markets. You may record the decisions on the table below.

1. Record in columns 1 and 2 the actual decisions made by the discussion groups.

2. *Privately* note to yourself what you think Booth actually did in this case. The instructor will tally the predictions, and you may record these predictions in columns 3 and 4.

3. Record in columns 5 and 6 what Booth actually did.

Decision	Decisions Made By Groups*		What Do You Think Happened?		What Actually Happened?	
	U.S.	Foreign	U.S.	Foreign	U.S.	Foreign
a. Recall immediately						
b. Stop production						
c. Stop advertising and promotion						
d. Continue to market						
e. Block FDA						
	(1)	(2)	(3)	(4)	(5)	(6)

*Record the letter designation of the group decision in the proper place.

1. What factors in your group's discussion affected the way the decision was arrived at? Did the nature of leadership in your group affect the decision-making process?

2. Did you use the "root" or the "branch" method of decision making? Did this affect how ethical your decision was?

3. Do you think the ethical nature of the decision affected the decision-making process?

4. How similar or different is this decision from other decisions you have made in a group? What kinds of decision situations in organizations have elements in common with this exercise?

Memo: Leadership

Effective leadership involves a complex interaction between the situation, the person, and the decision-making climate of the organization. Managers not only must make decisions effectively, but they must demonstrate the kinds of leadership qualities as expressed by Bass (1983) for those decisions to be effectively implemented.

Think about the managers you have encountered who have impressed you with their abilities as leaders and as decision makers. To what extent did these leaders:

1. Evidence charisma and create enthusiasm?

2. Delegate tasks and activities effectively?

3. Possess effective communication skills?

4. Organize effectively?

5. Evidence a developmental attitude toward subordinates?

6. Set high levels of intellectual standards to effectively stimulate subordinates?

7. Encourage subordinate participation in decisions that directly affected them?

8. Utilize the root or branch method of decision making?

9. Exhibit transformational behaviors and qualities?

Think about the managers you have observed who in your opinion have failed miserably as managers. What qualities does this group of managers have in common? What behaviors did they fail to demonstrate?

Based upon your analysis, identify a list of skills that are necessary for effective leadership and decision-making abilities. Once you have completed your list, review the list to determine which skills you have already demonstrated effectively, and those that require improvement. Develop an action plan to help you achieve the skills you lack to help you to improve your leadership and decision-making abilities.

ACTION PLAN

Effective Leadership and Decision-Making Skills	Skills I Demonstrate	Skills I Lack	How I Can Achieve Improvements in My Skills
1.	1.	1.	1.
2.	2.	2.	2.
3.	3.	3.	3.
4.	4.	4.	4.
5.	5.	5.	5.
6.	6.	6.	6.
7.	7.	7.	7.
8.	8.	8.	8.

CHAPTER FIVE

Power and Politics

INTRODUCTION

Power. The use and misuse of power are endemic to organizational life. But the dynamics that underlie the process and mechanics of power seem mysterious to many managers. Most of us are aware of those who have it—and those who don't. To be effective as managers, we need to understand how to gain and use power productively. As you will see, the productive use of power is vital for managerial effectiveness.

Power and politics are different parts of the same process. While power results from your position, politics are tactics used to wield power in organizational settings. Sometimes these tactics can be used to assume greater power or to lessen another's. For this reason power and politics often carry a manipulative connotation. The negative side of power is most clearly epitomized by people who use power to aggrandize themselves at the expense of greater organizational goals. When this occurs, misuses of power through political game playing may interfere with the organization's overall productivity.

But there is a positive side to power. Power can be used as both a tool and a resource, a means and an end. As Rosabeth Kanter says, power is the ability to get things done. Those in power are able to marshal their resources in a way that helps them achieve their goals. They are able to be effective in their jobs and productive in their work. Having power as a resource can help you gain support, information, supplies—everything and anything that is needed to be productive in your job. Without sufficient "productive power," you will be unable to be effective as a manager.

In this chapter, the dynamics of power will be explored at three levels: (1) interpersonal uses of power, (2) job sources that contribute to powerlessness, and (3) departmental or intergroup power.

READINGS

The first article, "Power, Dependence and Effective Management" by John P. Kotter, describes how important it is for managers to develop power strategies to cope with situations in which they are dependent. He argues that managers are unusually dependent in their jobs, and this makes the use of power crucial for managerial effectiveness. Recognizing the sources of dependency in managers' jobs and developing strategies to cope with those dependencies are critical for managerial success.

In "Power Failures in Management Circuits," Rosabeth Moss Kanter suggests that power is not as much a function of the individual as the position. She argues that certain situational factors, such as visibility, centrality, and a variety of task assignments, enhance position power, while the lack of these factors diminishes that power. Power, she maintains, is not directly related to authority—even upper-level executives can be rendered powerless when the lines of information, supply, and support are no longer effective in their jobs. Sharing power, rather than hoarding power, may help managers eliminate the sources of powerlessness and improve overall organizational effectiveness.

The third article, by Gerald Salancik and Jeffrey Pfeffer, "Who Gets Power and How They Hold on to It—A Strategic Contingency Model of Power," explains departmental or intergroup sources of power. These authors studied the differences among departmental resource allocations and attributed power in a university setting. They found, surprisingly, that departmental power is a function of how dependent the organization as a whole is on a department's ability to deal with critical problems affecting that organization. When a department is considered critical to the overall functioning of the organization, resource allocation monies flow to that department to enhance its effectiveness. But, once in power, such departments will do whatever it takes to distort reality to maintain their power. In short, the powerful get more, while the weak remain powerless. Salancik and Pfeffer show how these dynamics work in organizational settings using several examples to support their arguments.

The three readings in this chapter demonstrate the dynamics of power in organizational settings. Power is derived from position, as Kanter notes, and from departmental criticality, as Salancik and Pfeffer argue. Kotter suggests that managers must cope with the sources of dependency in their jobs and use power and political strategies effectively to improve their success as managers. Power, therefore, is a necessary tool of organizational life. When power is used productively, it can change the world; when used in a negative way, to dominate and control others, it can be destructive. Power is not as much mysterious as misunderstood.

EXERCISES AND CASES

The exercises provide an opportunity for you to understand and use power productively and effectively. The first exercise, "Dependency Situations," helps you determine how you might react to situations in which you find yourself dependent. Following Kotter's lead, it is important to learn how to manage situations in which you may find yourself dependent as a manager. Understanding your reactions to dependency will help you to determine the type of political style you adopt when you need to achieve a particular goal.

The second exercise, "Power Failures," provides an opportunity to apply what you have learned about power and powerlessness. Three scenarios are presented about managers in powerless job situations. Each manager has become turf-conscious, authoritarian, and rules-minded in his or her management style as a response to powerlessness. By serving as a consultant in this exercise, you will learn why jealously guarding your power is not always the most effective response to situations of powerlessness.

A third exercise, "Power Lab," explores intergroup power relationships. A simulated group situation will be created to allow you to experience how it feels to be in control, powerless, or caught in the middle. Managers are often caught in the middle in the management hierarchy. This exercise tests your myths and assumptions about power dynamics in organizational settings, and helps you to determine how it feels to wield power—or lose it—as a manager.

MEMO

To round out the chapter, the memo assignment asks you to consider the structural and interpersonal sources of power that affect you personally in your job. Where do you stand in the political network of your department? Where does your department fit in the political network of your organization? What strategies, if any, can be used to empower yourself, given the constraints of your position and your department? What are the structural sources of power that are contributing—or not contributing—to your current job?

By the time you finish this chapter, you will have a better understanding of power dynamics in organizational settings. You will also have an opportunity to assess your own empowerment profile and your reactions to authority. Finally, you will be able to understand the impact of power in your organization and how politics affects you personally in your job.

Power, Dependence, and Effective Management

John P. Kotter

Americans, as a rule, are not very comfortable with power or with its dynamics. We often distrust and question the motives of people who we think actively seek power. We have a certain fear of being manipulated. Even those people who think the dynamics of power are inevitable and needed often feel somewhat guilty when they themselves mobilize and use power. Simply put, the overall attitude and feeling toward

Reprinted by permission of *Harvard Business Review*. "Power, Dependence, and Effective Management," by John P. Kotter, 55(4). Copyright © 1977 by the President and Fellows of Harvard College; all rights reserved.

Author's note: This article is based on data from a clinical study of a highly diverse group of 26 organizations including large and small, public and private, manufacturing and service organizations. The study was funded by the Division of Research at the Harvard Business School. As part of the study process, the author interviewed about 250 managers.

power, which can easily be traced to the nation's very birth, is negative. In his enormously popular *Greening of America*, Charles Reich reflects the views of many when he writes, "It is not the misuse of power that is evil; the very existence of power is evil."[1]

One of the many consequences of this attitude is that power as a topic for rational study and dialogue has not received much attention, even in managerial circles. If the reader doubts this, all he or she need do is flip through some textbooks, journals, or advanced management course descriptions. The word *power* rarely appears.

This lack of attention to the subject of power merely adds to the already enormous confusion and misunderstanding surrounding the topic of power and

1. Charles A. Reich, *The Greening of America: How the Youth Revolution Is Trying to Make America Liveable* (New York: Random House, 1970).

management. And this misunderstanding is becoming increasingly burdensome because in today's large and complex organizations the effective performance of most managerial jobs requires one to be skilled at the acquisition and use of power.

From my own observations, I suspect that a large number of managers—especially the young, well-educated ones—perform significantly below their potential because they do not understand the dynamics of power and because they have not nurtured and developed the instincts needed to effectively acquire and use power.

In this article I hope to clear up some of the confusion regarding power and managerial work by providing tentative answers to three questions:

1. Why are the dynamics of power necessarily an important part of managerial processes?

2. How do effective managers acquire power?

3. How and for what purposes do effective managers use power?

I will not address questions related to the misuse of power, but not because I think they are unimportant. The fact that some managers, some of the time, acquire and use power mostly for their own aggrandizement is obviously a very important issue that deserves attention and careful study. But that is a complex topic unto itself and one that has already received more attention than the subject of this article.

RECOGNIZING DEPENDENCE IN THE MANAGER'S JOB

One of the distinguishing characteristics of a typical manager is how dependent he is on the activities of a variety of other people to perform his job effectively.[2] Unlike doctors and mathematicians, whose performance is more directly dependent on their own talents and efforts, a manager can be dependent in varying degrees on superiors, subordinates, peers in other parts of the organization, the subordinates of peers, outside suppliers, customers, competitors, unions, regulating agencies, and many others.

2. See Leonard R. Sayles, *Managerial Behavior: Administration in Complex Organization* (New York: McGraw-Hill, 1964) as well as Rosemary Stewart, *Managers and Their Jobs* (London: Macmillan, 1967) and *Contrasts in Management* (London: McGraw-Hill, 1976).

These dependency relationships are an inherent part of managerial jobs because of two organizational facts of life: division of labor and limited resources. Because the work in organizations is divided into specialized divisions, departments, and jobs, managers are made directly or indirectly dependent on many others for information, staff services, and cooperation in general. Because of their organization's limited resources, managers are also dependent on their external environments for support. Without some minimal cooperation from suppliers, competitors, unions, regulatory agencies, and customers, managers cannot help their organizations survive and achieve their objectives.

Dealing with these dependencies and the manager's subsequent vulnerability is an important and difficult part of a manager's job because, while it is theoretically possible that all of these people and organizations would automatically act in just the manner that a manager wants and needs, such is almost never the case in reality. All the people on whom a manager is dependent have limited time, energy, and talent, for which there are competing demands.

Some people may be uncooperative because they are too busy elsewhere, and some because they are not really capable of helping. Others may well have goals, values, and beliefs that are quite different and in conflict with the manager's and may therefore have no desire whatsoever to help or cooperate. This is obviously true of a competing company and sometimes of a union, but it can also apply to a boss who is feeling threatened by a manager's career progress or to a peer whose objectives clash with the manager's.

Indeed, managers often find themselves dependent on many people (and things) whom they do not directly control and who are not "cooperating." This is the key to one of the biggest frustrations managers feel in their jobs, even in the top ones, which the following example illustrates:

After nearly a year of rumors, it was finally announced in May 1974 that the president of ABC Corporation had been elected chairman of the board and that Jim Franklin, the vice president of finance, would replace him as president. While everyone at ABC was aware that a shift would take place soon, it was not at all clear before the announcement who would be the next president. Most people had guessed it would be Phil Cook, the marketing vice president.

Nine months into his job as chief executive officer, Franklin found that Phil Cook (still the marketing vice president) seemed to be fighting him in small and subtle ways. There was never anything blatant, but Cook just did not cooperate with Franklin as the other vice presidents did. Shortly after being elected, Franklin had tried to bypass what he saw as a potential conflict with Cook by telling him that he would understand if Cook would prefer to move somewhere else where he could be a CEO also. Franklin said that it would be a big loss to the company but that he would be willing to help Cook in a number of ways if he wanted to look for a presidential opportunity elsewhere. Cook had thanked him but had said that family and community commitments would prevent him from relocating and all CEO opportunities were bound to be in a different city.

Since the situation did not improve after the tenth and eleventh months, Franklin seriously considered forcing Cook out. When he thought about the consequences of such a move, Franklin became more and more aware of just how dependent he was on Cook. Marketing and sales were generally the keys to success in their industry, and the company's sales force was one of the best, if not the best, in the industry. Cook had been with the company for 25 years. He had built a strong personal relationship with many of the people in the sales force and was universally popular. A mass exodus just might occur if Cook were fired. The loss of a large number of salesmen, or even a lot of turmoil in the department, could have a serious effect on the company's performance.

After one year as chief executive officer, Franklin found that the situation between Cook and himself had not improved and had become a constant source of frustration.

As a person gains more formal authority in an organization, the areas in which he or she is vulnerable increase and become more complex rather than the reverse. As the previous example suggests, it is not at all unusual for the president of an organization to be in a highly dependent position, a fact often not apparent to either the outsider or to the lower level manager who covets the president's job.

A considerable amount of the behavior of highly successful managers that seems inexplicable in light of what management texts usually tell us managers do becomes understandable when one considers a manager's need for, and efforts at, managing his or her relationships with others.[3] To be able to plan, orga-

nize, budget, staff, control, and evaluate, managers need some control over the many people on whom they are dependent. Trying to control others solely by directing them and on the basis of the power associated with one's position simply will not work— first, because managers are always dependent on some people over whom they have no formal authority, and second, because virtually no one in modern organizations will passively accept and completely obey a constant stream of orders from someone just because he or she is the "boss."

Trying to influence others by means of persuasion alone will not work either. Although it is very powerful and possibly the single most important method of influence, persuasion has some serious drawbacks too. To make it work requires time (often lots of it), skill, and information on the part of the persuader. And persuasion can fail simply because the other person chooses not to listen or does not listen carefully.

This is not to say that directing people on the basis of the formal power of one's position and persuasion are not important means by which successful managers cope. They obviously are. But, even taken together, they are not usually enough.

Successful managers cope with their dependence on others by being sensitive to it, by eliminating or avoiding unnecessary dependence, and by establishing power over those others. Good managers then use that power to help them plan, organize, staff, budget, evaluate, and so on. *In other words, it is primarily because of the dependence inherent in managerial jobs that the dynamics of power necessarily form an important part of a manager's processes.*

An argument that took place during a middle management training seminar I participated in a few years ago helps illustrate further this important relationship between a manager's need for power and the degree of his or her dependence on others:

Two participants, both managers in their thirties, got into a heated disagreement regarding the acquisition and use of power by managers. One took the position that power was absolutely central to managerial work, while the other argued that it was virtually irrelevant. In support of their positions, each described a very "successful" manager with whom he worked. In one of these examples, the manager seemed to be constantly developing and using power, while in the other, such behavior was rare. Subsequently, both seminar participants were asked to describe their successful managers' jobs in terms of the dependence *inherent* in those jobs.

---

3. I am talking about the type of inexplicable differences that Henry Mintzberg has found; see his article "The Manager's Job: Folklore and Fact," HBR July-August 1975, p. 49.

The young manager who felt power was unimportant described a staff vice president in a small company who was dependent only on his immediate subordinates, his peers, and his boss. This person, Joe Phillips, had to depend on his subordinates to do their jobs appropriately, but, if necessary, he could fill in for any of them or secure replacement for them rather easily. He also had considerable formal authority over them; that is, he could give them raises and new assignments, recommend promotions, and fire them. He was moderately dependent on the other four vice presidents in the company for information and cooperation. They were likewise dependent on him. The president had considerable formal authority over Phillips but was also moderately dependent on him for help, expert advice, the service his staff performed, other information, and general cooperation.

The second young manager—the one who felt power was very important—described a service department manager, Sam Weller, in a large, complex, and growing company who was in quite a different position. Weller was dependent not only on his boss for rewards and information, but also on 30 other individuals who made up the divisional and corporate top management. And while his boss, like Phillips's, was moderately dependent on him too, most of the top managers were not. Because Weller's subordinates, unlike Phillips's, had people reporting to them, Weller was dependent not only on his subordinates but also on his subordinates' subordinates. Because he could not himself easily replace or do most of their technical jobs, unlike Phillips, he was very dependent on all these people.

In addition, for critical supplies, Weller was dependent on two other department managers in the division. Without their timely help, it was impossible for his department to do its job. These departments, however, did not have similar needs for Weller's help and cooperation. Weller was also dependent on local labor union officials and on a federal agency that regulated the division's industry. Both could shut his division down if they wanted.

Finally, Weller was dependent on two outside suppliers of key materials. Because of the volume of his department's purchase relative to the size of these two companies, he had little power over them.

Under these circumstances, it is hardly surprising that Sam Weller had to spend considerable time and effort acquiring and using power to manage his many dependencies, while Joe Phillips did not.

As this example also illustrates, not all management jobs require an incumbent to be able to provide the same amount of successful power-oriented behavior. But most management jobs today are more like Weller's than Phillips's. And, perhaps more important, the trend over the past two or three decades is away from jobs like Phillips's and toward jobs like Weller's. So long as our technologies continue to become more complex, the average organization continues to grow larger, and the average industry continues to become more competitive and regulated, that trend will continue; as it does so, the effective acquisition and use of power by managers will become even more important.

ESTABLISHING POWER IN RELATIONSHIPS

To help cope with the dependency relationships inherent in their jobs, effective managers create, increase, or maintain four different types of power over others.[4] Having power based in these areas puts the manager in a position both to influence those people on whom he or she is dependent when necessary and to avoid being hurt by any of them.

Sense of Obligation

One of the ways that successful managers generate power in their relationships with others is to create a sense of obligation in those others. When the manager is successful, the others feel that they should—rightly—allow the manager to influence them within certain limits.

Successful managers often go out of their way to do favors for people who they expect will feel an obligation to return those favors. As can be seen in the following description of a manager by one of his subordinates, some people are very skilled at identifying opportunities for doing favors that cost them very little but that others appreciate very much:

"Most of the people here would walk over hot coals in their bare feet if my boss asked them to. He has an incredible capacity to do little things that mean a lot to people. Today, for example, in his junk mail he

---

4. These categories closely resemble the five developed by John R.P. French and Bertram Raven; see "The Base of Social Power" in *Group Dynamics: Research and Theory,* Dorwin Cartwright and Alvin Zandler, eds. (New York: Harper & Row, 1968), Chapter 20. Three of the categories are similar to the types of "authority"-based power described by Max Weber in *The Theory of Social and Economic Organization* (New York: Free Press, 1947).

came across an advertisement for something that one of my subordinates had in passing once mentioned that he was shopping for. So my boss routed it to him. That probably took 15 seconds of his time, and yet my subordinate really appreciated it. To give you another example, two weeks ago he somehow learned that the purchasing manager's mother had died. On his way home that night, he stopped off at the funeral parlor. Our purchasing manager was, of course, there at the time. I bet he'll remember that brief visit for quite a while."

Recognizing that most people believe that friendship carries with it certain obligations ("A friend in need. . . ."), successful managers often try to develop true friendships with those on whom they are dependent. They will also make formal and informal deals in which they give something up in exchange for certain future obligations.

Belief in a Manager's Expertise

A second way successful managers gain power is by building reputations as "experts" in certain matters. Believing in the manager's expertise, others will often defer to the manager on those matters. Managers usually establish this type of power through visible achievement. The larger the achievement and the more visible it is, the more power the manager tends to develop.

One of the reasons that managers display concern about their "professional reputations" and their "track records" is that they have an impact on others' beliefs about their expertise. These factors become particularly important in large settings, where most people have only secondhand information about most other people's professional competence, as the following shows:

Herb Randley and Bert Kline were both 35-year-old vice presidents in a large research and development organization. According to their closest associates, they were equally bright and competent in their technical fields and as managers. Yet Randley had a much stronger professional reputation in most parts of the company, and his ideas generally carried much more weight. Close friends and associates claim the reason that Randley is so much more powerful is related to a number of tactics that he has used more than Kline has.

Randley has published more scientific papers and managerial articles than Kline. Randley has been more selective in the assignments he has worked on, choosing those that are visible and that require his

strong suits. He has given more speeches and presentations on projects that are his own achievements. And in meetings in general, he is allegedly forceful in areas where he has expertise and silent in those where he does not.

Identification with a Manager

A third method by which managers gain power is by fostering others' unconscious identification with them or with ideas they "stand for." Sigmund Freud was the first to describe this phenomenon, which is most clearly seen in the way people look up to "charismatic" leaders. Generally, the more a person finds a manager both consciously and (more important) unconsciously an ideal person, the more he or she will defer to that manager.

Managers develop power based on others' idealized views of them in a number of ways. They try to look and behave in ways that others respect. They go out of their way to be visible to their employees and to give speeches about their organizational goals, values, and ideals. They even consider, while making hiring and promotion decisions, whether they will be able to develop this type of power over the candidates:

One vice president of sales in a moderate-size manufacturing company was reputed to be so much in control of his sales force that he could get them to respond to new and different marketing programs in a third of the time taken by the company's best competitors. His power over his employees was based primarily on their strong identification with him and what he stood for. Emigrating to the United States at age 17, this person worked his way up "from nothing." When made a sales manager in 1965, he began recruiting other young immigrants and sons of immigrants from his former country. When made vice president of sales in 1970, he continued to do so. In 1975, 85% of his sales force was made up of people whom he hired directly or who were hired by others he brought in.

Perceived Dependence on a Manager

The final way that an effective manager often gains power is by feeding others' beliefs that they are dependent on the manager either for help or for not being hurt. The more they perceive they are dependent, the more most people will be inclined to cooperate with such a manager.

There are two methods that successful managers often use to create perceived dependence.

Finding & Acquiring Resources. In the first, the manager identifies and secures (if necessary) resources that another person requires to perform his job, that he does not possess, and that are not readily available elsewhere. These resources include such things as authority to make certain decisions; control of money, equipment, and office space; access to important people; information and control of information channels; and subordinates. Then the manager takes action so that the other person correctly perceives that the manager has such resources and is willing and ready to use them to help (or hinder) the other person. Consider the following extreme—but true—example.

When young Tim Babcock was put in charge of a division of a large manufacturing company and told to "turn it around," he spent the first few weeks studying it from afar. He decided that the division was in disastrous shape and that he would need to take many large steps quickly to save it. To be able to do that, he realized he needed to develop considerable power fast over most of the division's management and staff. He did the following:

☐ He gave the division's management two hours' notice of his arrival.

☐ He arrived in a limousine with six assistants.

☐ He immediately called a meeting of the 40 top managers.

☐ He outlined briefly his assessment of the situation, his commitment to turn things around, and the basic direction he wanted things to move in.

☐ He then fired the four top managers in the room and told them that they had to be out of the building in two hours.

☐ He then said he would personally dedicate himself to sabotaging the career of anyone who tried to block his efforts to save the division.

☐ He ended the 60-minute meeting by announcing that his assistants would set up appointments for him with each of them starting at 7:00 A.M. the next morning.

Throughout the critical six-month period that followed, those who remained at the division generally cooperated energetically with Mr. Babcock.

Affecting Perceptions of Resources. A second way effective managers gain these types of power is by influencing other persons' perceptions of the manager's resources.[5] In settings where many people are involved and where the manager does not interact continuously with those he or she is dependent on, those people will seldom possess "hard facts" regarding what relevant resources the manager commands directly or indirectly (through others), what resources he will command in the future, or how prepared he is to use those resources to help or hinder them. They will be forced to make their own judgments.

Insofar as a manager can influence people's judgments, he can generate much more power than one would generally ascribe to him in light of the reality of his resources.

In trying to influence people's judgments, managers pay considerable attention to the "trappings" of power and to their own reputations and images. Among other actions, they sometimes carefully select, decorate, and arrange their offices in ways that give signs of power. They associate with people or organizations that are known to be powerful or that others perceive as powerful. Managers selectively foster rumors concerning their own power. Indeed, those who are particularly skilled at creating power in this way tend to be very sensitive to the impressions that all their actions might have on others.

Formal Authority

Before discussing how managers use their power to influence others, it is useful to see how formal authority relates to power. By *formal authority,* I mean those elements that automatically come with a managerial job—perhaps a title, an office, a budget, the right to make certain decisions, a set of subordinates, a reporting relationship, and so on.

Effective managers use the elements of formal authority as resources to help them develop any or all of the four types of power previously discussed, just as they use other resources (such as their education). Two managers with the same formal authority can have very different amounts of power entirely because of the way they have used that authority. For example:

---

5. For an excellent discussion of this method, see Richard E. Neustadt, *Presidential Power* (New York: John Wiley, 1960).

☐ By sitting down with employees who are new or with people who are starting new projects and clearly specifying who has the formal authority to do what, one manager creates a strong sense of obligation in others to defer to his authority later.

☐ By selectively withholding or giving the high-quality service his department can provide other departments, one manager makes other managers clearly perceive that they are dependent on him.

On its own, then, formal authority does not guarantee a certain amount of power; it is only a resource that managers can use to generate power in their relationships.

EXERCISING POWER
TO INFLUENCE OTHERS

Successful managers use the power they develop in their relationships, along with persuasion, to influence people on whom they are dependent to behave in ways that make it possible for the managers to get their jobs done effectively. They use their power to influence others directly, face to face, and in more indirect ways.

Face-to-Face Influence

The chief advantage of influencing others directly by exercising any of the types of power is speed. If the power exists and the manager correctly understands the nature and strength of it, he can influence the other person with nothing more than a brief request or command:

☐ Jones thinks Smith feels obliged to him for past favors. Furthermore, Jones thinks that his request to speed up a project by two days probably falls within a zone that Smith would consider legitimate in light of his own definition of his obligation to Jones. So Jones simply calls Smith and makes his request. Smith pauses for only a second and says yes, he'll do it.

☐ Manager Johnson has some power based on perceived dependence over manger Baker. When Johnson tells Baker that he wants a report done in 24 hours, Baker grudgingly considers the costs of compliance, of noncompliance, and of complaining to higher authorities. He decides that doing the report is the least costly action and tells Johnson he will do it.

☐ Young Porter identifies strongly with Marquette, an older manager who is not his boss. Porter thinks Marquette is the epitome of a great manager and tries to model himself after him. When Marquette asks Porter to work on a special project "that could be very valuable in improving the company's ability to meet new competitive products," Porter agrees without hesitation and works 15 hours per week above and beyond his normal hours to get the project done and done well.

When used to influence others, each of the four types of power has different advantages and drawbacks. For example, power based on perceived expertise or on identification with a manager can often be used to influence attitudes as well as someone's immediate behavior and thus can have a lasting impact. It is very difficult to influence attitudes by using power based on perceived dependence, but if it can be done, it usually has the advantage of being able to influence a much broader range of behavior than the other methods do. When exercising power based on perceived expertise, for example, one can only influence attitudes and behavior within that narrow zone defined by the "expertise."

The drawbacks associated with the use of power based on perceived dependence are particularly important to recognize. A person who feels dependent on a manager for rewards (or lack of punishments) might quickly agree to a request from the manager but then not follow through—especially if the manager cannot easily find out if the person has obeyed or not. Repeated influence attempts based on perceived dependence also seem to encourage the other person to try to gain some power to balance the manager's. And perhaps most important, using power based on perceived dependence in a coercive way is very risky. Coercion invites retaliation.

For instance, in the example in which Tim Babock took such extreme steps to save the division he was assigned to "turn around," his development and use of power based on perceived dependence could have led to mass resignation and the collapse of the division. Babcock fully recognized this risk, however, and behaved as he did because he felt there was simply *no other way* that he could gain the very large amount of quick cooperation needed to save the division.

Effective mangers will often draw on more than one form of power to influence somone, or they will combine power with persuasion. In general, they do so because a combination can be more potent and less risky than any single method, as the following description shows:

EXHIBIT

Methods of Influence.

Face-to-Face Methods	What They Can Influence	Advantages	Drawbacks
Exercise obligation-based power.	Behavior within zone that the other perceives as legitimate in light of the obligation.	Quick. Requires no outlay of tangible resources.	If the request is outside the acceptable zone, it will fail; if it is too far outside, others might see it as illegitimate.
Exercise power based on perceived expertise.	Attitudes and behavior within the zone of perceived expertise.	Quick. Requires no outlay of tangible resources.	If the request is outside the acceptable zone, it will fail; if it is too far outside, others might see it as illegitimate.
Exercise power based on identification with a manager.	Attitudes and behavior that are not in conflict with the ideals that underlie the identification.	Quick. Requires no expenditure of limited resources.	Restricted to influence attempts that are not in conflict with the ideals that underlie the identification.
Exercise power based on perceived dependence.	Wide range of behavior that can be monitored.	Quick. Can often succeed when other methods fail.	Repeated influence attempts encourage the other to gain power over the influencer.
Coercively exercise power based on perceived dependence.	Wide range of behavior that can be easily monitored.	Quick. Can often succeed when other methods fail.	Invites retaliation. Very risky.
Use persuasion.	Very wide range of attitudes and behavior.	Can produce internalized motivation that does not require monitoring. Requires no power or outlay of scarce material resources.	Can be very time-consuming. Requires other person to listen.
Combine these methods.	Depends on the exact combination.	Can be more potent and less risky than using a single method.	More costly than using a single method.

Indirect Methods	What They Can Influence	Advantages	Drawbacks
Manipulate the other's environment by using any or all of the face-to-face methods.	Wide range of behavior and attitudes.	Can succeed when face-to-face methods fail.	Can be time-consuming. Is complex to implement. Is very risky, especially if used frequently.
Change the forces that continuously act on the individual: Formal organizational arrangements. Informal social arrangements. Technology. Resources available. Statement of organizational goals.	Wide range of behavior and attitudes on a continuous basis.	Has continuous influence, not just a one-shot effect. Can have a very powerful impact.	Often requires a considerable power outlay to achieve.

"One of the best managers we have in the company has lots of power based on one thing or another over most people. But he seldom if ever just tells or asks someone to do something. He almost always takes a few minutes to try to persuade them. The power he has over people generally induces them to listen carefully and certainly disposes them to be influenced. That, of course, makes the persuasion process go quickly and easily. And he never risks getting the other person mad or upset by making what that person thinks is an unfair request or command."

It is also common for managers not to coercively exercise power based on perceived dependence by itself, but to combine it with other methods to reduce the risk of retaliation. In this way, managers are able to have a large impact without leaving the bitter aftertaste of punishment alone.

Indirect Influence Methods

Effective managers also rely on two types of less direct methods to influence those on whom they are dependent. In the first way, they use any or all of the face-to-face methods to influence other people, who in turn have some specific impact on a desired person.

Product manager Stein needed plant manager Billings to "sign off" on a new product idea (Product X) which Billings thought was terrible. Stein decided that there was no way he could logically persuade Billings because Billings just would not listen to him. With time, Stein felt, he could have broken through that barrier. But he did not have that time. Stein also realized that Billings would never, just because of some deal or favor, sign off on a product he did not believe in. Stein also felt it not worth the risk of trying to force Billings to sign off, so here is what he did:

☐ On Monday, Stein got Reynolds, a person Billings respected, to send Billings two market research studies that were very favorable to Product X, with a note attached saying, "Have you seen this? I found them rather surprising. I am not sure if I entirely believe them, but still. . . ."

☐ On Tuesday, Stein got a representative of one of the company's biggest customers to mention casually to Billings on the phone that he had heard a rumor about Product X being introduced soon and was "glad to see you guys are on your toes as usual."

☐ On Wednesday, Stein had two industrial engineers stand about three feet away from Billings

as they were waiting for a meeting to begin and talk about the favorable test results on Product X.

☐ On Thursday, Stein set up a meeting to talk about Product X with Billings and invited only people whom Billings liked or respected and who also felt favorably about Product X.

☐ On Friday, Stein went to see Billings and asked him if he was willing to sign off on Product X. He was.

This type of manipulation of the environments of others can influence both behavior and attitudes and can often succeed when other influence methods fail. But it has a number of serious drawbacks. It takes considerable time and energy, and it is quite risky. Many people think it is wrong to try to influence others in this way, even people who, without consciously recognizing it, use this technique themselves. If they think someone is trying, or has tried, to manipulate them, they may retaliate. Furthermore, people who gain the reputation of being manipulators seriously undermine their own capacities for developing power and for influencing others. Almost no one, for example, will want to identify with a manipulator. And virtually no one accepts, at face value, a manipulator's sincere attempts at persuasion. In extreme cases, a reputation as a manipulator can completely ruin a manager's career.

A second way in which managers indirectly influence others is by making permanent changes in an individual's or a group's environment. They change job descriptions, the formal systems that measure performance, the extrinsic incentives available, the tools, people, and other resources that the people or groups work with, the architecture, the norms or values of work groups, and so on. If the manager is successful in making the changes, and the changes have the desired effect on the individual or group, that effect will be sustained over time.

Effective managers recognize that changes in the forces that surround a person can have great impact on that person's behavior. Unlike many of the other influence methods, this one doesn't require a large expenditure of limited resources or effort on the part of the manager on an ongoing basis. Once such a change has been successfully made, it works independently of the manager.

This method of influence is used by all managers to some degree. Many, however, use it sparingly simply because they do not have the power to change the forces acting on the person they wish to influence. In many organizations, only the top managers have the power to change the formal measurement systems, the extrinsic incentives available, the architecture, and so on.

GENERATING & USING POWER SUCCESSFULLY

Managers who are successful at acquiring considerable power and using it to manage their dependence on others tend to share a number of common characteristics.

1. They are sensitive to what others consider to be legitimate behavior in acquiring and using power. They recognize that the four types of power carry with them certain "obligations" regarding their acquisition and use. A person who gains a considerable amount of power based on his perceived expertise is generally expected to be an expert in certain areas. If it ever becomes publicly known that the person is clearly not an expert in those areas, such a person will probably be labeled a "fraud" and will not only lose his power but will suffer other reprimands too.

A person with whom a number of people identify is expected to act like an ideal leader. If he clearly lets people down, he will not only lose that power, he will also suffer the righteous anger of his ex-followers. Many managers who have created or used power based on perceived dependence in ways that their employees have felt unfair, such as in requesting overtime work, have ended up with unions.

2. They have good intuitive understanding of the various types of power and methods of influence. They are sensitive to what types of power are easiest to develop with different types of people. They recognize, for example, that professionals tend to be more influenced by perceived expertise than by other forms of power. They also have a grasp of all the various methods of influence and what each can accomplish, at what costs, and with what risks. (See the *Exhibit* on page 224.) They are good at recognizing the specific conditions in any situation and then at selecting an influence method that is compatible with those conditions.

3. They tend to develop all the types of power, to some degree, and they use all the influence methods mentioned in the exhibit. Unlike managers who are not very good at influencing people, effective managers usually do not think that only some of the methods are useful or that only some of the methods

are moral. They recognize that any of the methods, used under the right circumstances, can help contribute to organizational effectiveness with few dysfunctional consequences. At the same time, they generally try to avoid those methods that are more risky than others and those that may have dysfunctional consequences. For example, they manipulate the environment of others only when absolutely necessary.

4. They establish career goals and seek out managerial positions that allow them to successfully develop and use power. They look for jobs, for example, that use their backgrounds and skills to control or manage some critically important problem or environmental contingency that an organization faces. They recognize that success in that type of job makes others dependent on them and increases their own perceived expertise. They also seek jobs that do not demand a type or a volume of power that is inconsistent with their own skills.

5. They use all of their resources, formal authority, and power to develop still more power. To borrow Edward Banfield's metaphor, they actually look for ways to "invest" their power where they might secure a high positive return.[6] For example, by asking a person to do him two important favors, a manager might be able to finish his construction program one day ahead of schedule. That request may cost him most of the obligation-based power he has over that person, but in return he may significantly increase his perceived expertise as a manager of construction projects in the eyes of everyone in his organization.

Just as in investing money, there is always some risk involved in using power this way; it is possible to get a zero return for a sizable investment, even for the most powerful manager. Effective managers do not try to avoid risks. Instead, they look for prudent risks, just as they do when investing capital.

6. Effective managers engage in power-oriented behavior in ways that are tempered by maturity and self control.[7] They seldom, if ever, develop and use power in impulsive ways or for their own aggrandizement.

7. Finally, they also recognize and accept as legitimate that, in using these methods, they clearly

---

6. See Edward C. Banfield, *Political Influence* (New York: Free Press, 1965), Chapter II.

influence other people's behavior and lives. Unlike many less effective managers, they are reasonably comfortable in using power to influence people. They recognize, often only intuitively, what this article is all about—that their attempts to establish power and use it are an absolutely necessary part of the successful fulfillment of their difficult managerial role.

———————

7. See David C. McClelland and David H. Burnham, "Power Is the Great Motivator," HBR March-April 1976, p. 100.

Power Failure in Management Circuits

Rosabeth Moss Kanter

Power is America's last dirty word. It is easier to talk about money—and much easier to talk about sex— than it is to talk about power. People who have it deny it; people who want it do not want to appear to hunger for it; and people who engage in its machinations do so secretly.

Yet, because it turns out to be a critical element in effective managerial behavior, power should come out from undercover. Having searched for years for those styles or skills that would identify capable organization leaders, many analysts, like myself, are rejecting individual traits or situational appropriateness as key and finding the sources of a leader's real power.

Access to resources and information and the ability to act quickly make it possible to accomplish more and to pass on more resources and information to subordinates. For this reason, people tend to prefer bosses with "clout." When employees perceive their manager as influential upward and outward, their status is enhanced by association and they generally have high morale and feel less critical or resistant to their boss.[1] More powerful leaders are also more likely to delegate (they are too busy to do it all themselves), to reward talent, and to build a team that places subordinates in significant positions.

Powerlessness, in contrast, tends to breed bossiness rather than true leadership. In large organizations, at least, it is powerlessness that often creates ineffective, desultory management and petty, dictatorial, rules-minded managerial styles. Accountability without power—responsibility for results without the resources to get them—creates frustration and failure. People who see themselves as weak and powerless and find their subordinates resisting or discounting them tend to use more punishing forms of influence. If organizational power can "ennoble," then, recent research shows, organizational powerlessness can (with apologies to Lord Acton) "corrupt."[2]

So perhaps power, in the organization at least, does not deserve such a bad reputation. Rather than connoting only dominance, control, and oppression, *power* can mean efficacy and capacity—something managers and executives need to move the organization toward its goals. Power in organizations is analogous in simple terms to physical power: it is the ability to mobilize resources (human and material) to get things done. The true sign of power, then, is accomplishment—not fear, terror, or tyranny. Where the power is "on," the system can be productive; where the power is "off," the system bogs down.

But saying that people need power to be effective in organizations does not tell us where it comes from or why some people, in some jobs, systematically seem to have more of it than others. In this article I want to show that to discover the sources of productive power, we have to look not at the *person*—as conventional classifications of effective managers and employees do—but at the *position* the person occupies in the organization.

WHERE DOES POWER COME FROM?

The effectiveness that power brings evolves from two kinds of capacities: first, access to the resources, information, and support necessary to carry out a task; and, second, ability to get cooper-

1. Donald C. Pelz, "Influence: A Key to Effective Leadership in the First-Line Supervisor," *Personnel,* November 1952, p. 209.

———————

2. See my book, *Men and Women of the Corporation* (New York: Basic Books, 1977), pp. 164-205; and David Kipnis, *The Powerholders* (Chicago: University of Chicago Press, 1976).

ation in doing what is necessary. (*Exhibit I* identifies some symbols of an individual manager's power.)

Both capacities derive not so much from a leader's style and skill as from his or her location in the formal and informal systems of the organization— in both job definition and connection to other important people in the company. Even the ability to get cooperation from subordinates is strongly defined by the manager's clout outward. People are more responsive to bosses who look as if they can get more for them from the organization.

We can regard the uniquely organizational sources of power as consisting of three "lines":

1. *Lines of supply.* Influence outward, over the environment, means that managers have the capacity to bring in the things that their own organizational domain needs—materials, money, resources to distribute as rewards, and perhaps even prestige.

2. *Lines of information.* To be effective, managers need to be "in the know" in both the formal and the informal sense.

3. *Lines of support.* In a formal framework, a manager's job parameters need to allow for nonordinary action, for a show of discretion or exercise of judgment. Thus managers need to know that they can assume innovative, risk-taking activities without having to go through the stifling multi-layered approval process. And, informally, managers need the backing of other important figures in the organization whose tacit approval becomes another resource they bring to their own work unit as well as a sign of the manager's being "in."

Note that productive power has to do with *connections* with other parts of a system. Such systemic aspects of power derive from two sources—job activities and political alliances:

1. Power is most easily accumulated when one has a job that is designed and located to allow *discretion* (nonroutinized action permitting flexible, adaptive, and creative contributions), *recognition* (visibility and notice), and *relevance* (being central to pressing organizational problems).

2. Power also comes when one has relatively close contact with *sponsors* (higher-level people who confer approval, prestige, or backing), *peer networks* (circles of acquaintanceship that provide reputation and information, the grapevine often being faster than formal communication channels), and *subordinates* (who can be developed to relieve managers of some

of their burdens and to represent the manager's point of view).

When managers are in powerful situations, it is easier for them to accomplish more. Because the tools are there, they are likely to be highly motivated and, in turn, to be able to motivate subordinates. Their activities are more likely to be on target and to net them successes. They can flexibly interpret or shape policy to meet the needs of particular areas, emergent situations, or sudden environmental shifts. They gain the respect and cooperation that attributed power brings. Subordinates' talents are resources rather than threats. And, because powerful managers have so many lines of connection and thus are oriented outward, they tend to let go of control downward, developing more independently functioning lieutenants.

The powerless live in a different world. Lacking the supplies, information, or support to make things happen easily, they may turn instead to the ultimate weapon of those who lack productive power—oppressive power: holding others back and punishing with whatever threats they can muster.

Exhibit II summarizes some of the major ways in which variables in the organization and in job design contribute to either power or powerlessness.

POSITIONS OF POWERLESSNESS

Understanding what it takes to have power and recognizing the classic behavior of the powerless can immediately help managers make sense out of a number of familiar organizational problems that are usually attributed to inadequate people:

☐ The ineffectiveness of first-line supervisors.

☐ The petty interest protection and conservatism of staff professionals.

☐ The crises of leadership at the top.

Instead of blaming the individuals involved in organizational problems, let us look at the positions people occupy. Of course, power or powerlessness in a position may not be all of the problem. Sometimes incapable people *are* at fault and need to be retrained or replaced. (See the ruled insert on page 231 for a discussion of another special case, women.) But where patterns emerge, where the troubles associated with some units persist, organizational power failures could be the reason. Then, as Volvo Presi-

EXHIBIT I

Some Common Symbols of a Manager's Organizational Power
(Influence Upward and Outward)

To what extent a manager can—

Intercede favorably on behalf of someone in trouble with the organization

Get a desirable placement for a talented subordinate

Get approval for expenditures beyond the budget

Get above-average salary increases for subordinates

Get items on the agenda at policy meetings

Get fast access to top decision makers

Get regular, frequent access to top decision makers

Get early information about decisions and policy shifts.

EXHIBIT II

Ways Organizational Factors Contribute to Power or Powerlessness

Factors	Generates Power When Factor Is	Generates Powerlessness When Factor Is
Rules inherent in the job	few	many
Predecessors in the job	few	many
Established routines	few	many
Task variety	high	low
Rewards for reliability/predictability	few	many
Rewards for unusual performance/innovation	many	few
Flexibility around use of people	high	low
Approvals needed for nonroutine decisions	few	many
Physical location	central	distant
Publicity about job activities	high	low
Relation of tasks to current problems areas	central	peripheral
Focus of tasks	outside work unit	inside work unit
Interpersonal contact in the job	high	low
Contact with senior officials	high	low
Participation in programs, conferences, meetings	high	low
Participation in problem-solving task forces	high	low
Advancement prospects of subordinates	high	low

dent Pehr Gyllenhammar concludes, we should treat the powerless not as "villains" causing headaches for everyone else but as "victims."[3]

First-Line Supervisors

Because an employee's most important work relationship is with his or her supervisor, when many of them talk about "the company," they mean their immediate boss. Thus a supervisor's behavior is an important determinant of the average employee's relationship to work and is in itself a critical link in the production chain.

Yet I know of no U.S. corporate management entirely satisfied with the performance of its supervisors. Most see them as supervising too closely and not training their people. In one manufacturing company where direct laborers were asked on a survey how they learned their job, on a list of seven possibilities "from my supervisor" ranked next to last. (Only company training programs ranked worse.) Also, it is said that supervisors do not translate company policies into practice—for instance, that they do not carry out the right of every employee to frequent performance reviews or to career counseling.

In court cases charging race or sex discrimination, first-line supervisors are frequently cited as the "discriminating official."[4] And, in studies of innovative work redesign and quality of work life projects, they often appear as the implied villains; they are the ones who are said to undermine the program or interfere with its effectiveness. In short, they are often seen as "not sufficiently managerial."

The problem affects white-collar as well as blue-collar supervisors. In one large government agency, supervisors in field offices were seen as the source of problems concerning morale and the flow of information to and from headquarters. "Their attitudes are negative," said a senior official. "They turn people against the agency; they put down senior management. They build themselves up by always complaining about headquarters, but prevent their staff from getting any information directly. We can't afford to have such attitudes communicated to field staff."

Is the problem that supervisors need more management training programs or that incompetent people are invariably attracted to the job? Neither explanation suffices. A large part of the problem lies in the position itself—one that almost universally creates powerlessness.

First-line supervisors are "people in the middle," and that has been seen as the source of many of their problems.[5] But by recognizing that first-line supervisors are caught between higher management and workers, we only begin to skim the surface of the problem. There is practically no other organizational category as subject to powerlessness.

First, these supervisors may be at a virtual dead end in their careers. Even in companies where the job used to be a stepping stone to higher-level management jobs, it is now common practice to bring in MBAs from the outside for those positions. Thus moving from the ranks of direct labor into supervision may mean, essentially, getting "stuck" rather than moving upward. Because employees do not perceive supervisors as eventually joining the leadership circles of the organization, they may see them as lacking the high-level contacts needed to have clout. Indeed, sometimes turnover among supervisors is so high that workers feel they can outwait—and outwit—any boss.

Second, although they lack clout, with little in the way of support from above, supervisors are forced to administer programs or explain policies that they have no hand in shaping. In one company, as part of a new personnel program supervisors were required to conduct counseling interviews with employees. But supervisors were not trained to do this and were given no incentives to get involved. Counseling was just another obligation. Then managers suddenly encouraged the workers to bypass their supervisors or to put pressure on them. The personnel staff brought them together and told them to demand such interviews as a basic right. If supervisors had not felt powerless before, they did after that squeeze from below, engineered from above.

The people they supervise can also make life hard for them in numerous ways. This often happens when a supervisor has himself or herself risen up from the ranks. Peers that have not made it are resentful or derisive of their former colleague, whom

3. Pehr G. Gyllenhammar, *People at Work* (Reading, Mass.: Addison-Wesley, 1977), p. 133.

4. William E. Fulmer, "Supervisory Selection: The Acid Test of Affirmative Action," *Personnel,* November-December 1976, p. 40.

5. See my chapter (coauthor, Barry A. Stein), "Life in the Middle: Getting In, Getting Up, and Getting Along," in *Life in Organizations,* eds. Rosabeth M. Kanter and Barry A. Stein (New York: Basic Books, 1979).

they now see as trying to lord it over them. Often it is easy for workers to break rules and let a lot of things slip.

Yet first-line supervisors are frequently judged according to rules and regulations while being limited by other regulations in what disciplinary actions they can take. They often lack the resources to influence or reward people; after all, workers are guaranteed their pay and benefits by someone other than their supervisors. Supervisors cannot easily control events; rather, they must react to them.

In one factory, for instance, supervisors complained that performance of their job was out of their control: they could fill production quotas only if they had the supplies, but they had no way to influence the people controlling supplies.

The lack of support for many first-line managers, particularly in large organizations, was made dramatically clear in another company. When asked if contact with executives higher in the organization who had the potential for offering support, information, and alliances diminished their own feelings of career vulnerability and the number of headaches they experienced on the job, supervisors in five out of seven work units responded positively. For them *contact* was indeed related to a greater feeling of acceptance at work and membership in the organization.

But in the two other work units where there was greater contact, people perceived more, not less, career vulnerability. Further investigation showed that supervisors in these business units got attention only when they were in trouble. Otherwise, no one bothered to talk to them. To these particular supervisors, hearing from a higher-level manager was a sign not of recognition or potential support but of danger.

It is not surprising, then, that supervisors frequently manifest symptoms of powerlessness: overly close supervision, rules-mindedness, and a tendency to do the job themselves rather than to train their people (since job skills may be one of the few remaining things they feel good about). Perhaps this is why they sometimes stand as roadblocks between their subordinates and the higher reaches of the company.

Staff Professionals

Also working under conditions that can lead to organizational powerlessness are the staff specialists. As advisers behind the scenes, staff people must sell their programs and bargain for resources, but unless they get themselves entrenched in organizational power networks, they have little in the way of favors to exchange. They are seen as useful adjuncts to the primary tasks of the organization but inessential in a day-to-day operating sense. This disenfranchisement occurs particularly when staff jobs consist of easily routinized administrative functions which are out of the mainstream of the currently relevant areas and involve little innovative decision making.

Furthermore, in some organizations, unless they have had previous line experience, staff people tend to be limited in the number of jobs into which they can move. Specialists' ladders are often very short, and professionals are just as likely to get "stuck" in such jobs as people are in less prestigious clerical or factory positions.

Staff people, unlike those who are being groomed for important line positions, may be hired because of a special expertise or particular background. But management rarely pays any attention to developing them into more general organizational resources. Lacking growth prospects themselves and working alone or in very small teams, they are not in a position to develop others or pass on power to them. They miss out on an important way that power can be accumulated.

Sometimes staff specialists, such as house counsel or organization development people, find their work being farmed out to consultants. Management considers them fine for the routine work, but the minute the activities involve risk or something problematic, they bring in outside experts. This treatment says something not only about their expertise but also about the status of their function. Since the company can always hire talent on a temporary basis, it is unclear that the management really needs to have or considers important its own staff for these functions.

And, because staff professionals are often seen as adjuncts to primary tasks, their effectiveness and therefore their contribution to the organization are often hard to measure. Thus visibility and recognition, as well as risk taking and relevance, may be denied to people in staff jobs.

Staff people tend to act out their powerlessness by becoming turf-minded. They create islands within the organization. They set themselves up as the only ones who can control professional standards and judge their own work. They create sometimes false distinctions between themselves as experts (no one else could possibly do what they do) and lay people, and this continues to keep them out of the mainstream.

One form such distinctions take is a combination of disdain when line managers attempt to act in areas the professionals think are their preserve and of subtle refusal to support the managers' efforts. Or staff groups battle with each other for control of new "problem areas," with the result that no one really handles the issue at all. To cope with their essential powerlessness, staff groups may try to elevate their own status and draw boundaries between themselves and others.

When staff jobs are treated as final resting places for people who have reached their level of competence in the organization—a good shelf on which to dump managers who are too old to go anywhere but too young to retire—then staff groups can also become pockets of conservatism, resistant to change. Their own exclusion from the risk-taking action may make them resist *anyone's* innovative proposals. In the past, personnel departments, for example, have sometimes been the last in their organization to know about innovations in human resource development or to be interested in applying them.

Top Executives

Despite the great resources and responsibilities concentrated at the top of an organization, leaders can be powerless for reasons that are not very different from those that affect staff and supervisors: lack of supplies, information, and support.

We have faith in leaders because of their ability to make things happen in the larger world, to create possibilities for everyone else, and to attract resources to the organization. These are their supplies. But influence outward—the source of much credibility downward—can diminish as environments change, setting terms and conditions out of the control of the leaders. Regardless of top management's grand plans for the organization, the environment presses. At the very least, things going on outside the organization can deflect a leader's attention and drain energy. And, more detrimental, decisions made elsewhere can have severe consequences for the organization and affect top management's sense of power and thus its operating style inside.

In the go-go years of the mid-1960s, for example, nearly every corporation officer or university president could look—and therefore feel—successful. Visible success gave leaders a great deal of credibility inside the organization, which in turn gave them the power to put new things in motion.

In the past few years, the environment has been strikingly different and the capacity of many organization leaders to do anything about it has been severely limited. New "players" have flexed their power muscles: the Arab oil bloc, government regulators, and congressional investigating committees. And managing economic decline is quite different from managing growth. It is no accident that when top leaders personally feel out of control, the control function in corporations grows.

As powerlessness in lower levels of organizations can manifest itself in overly routinized jobs where performance measures are oriented to rules and absence of change, so it can at upper levels as well. Routine work often drives out nonroutine work. Accomplishment becomes a question of nailing down details. Short-term results provide immediate gratifications and satisfy stockholders or other constituencies with limited interests.

It takes a powerful leader to be willing to risk short-term deprivations in order to bring about desired long-term outcomes. Much as first-line supervisors are tempted to focus on daily adherence to rules, leaders are tempted to focus on short-term fluctuations and lose sight of long-term objectives. The dynamics of such a situation are self-reinforcing. The more the long-term goals go unattended, the more a leader feels powerless and the greater the scramble to prove that he or she is in control of daily events at least. The more he is involved in the organization as a short-term Mr. Fix-it, the more out of control of long-term objectives he is, and the more ultimately powerless he is likely to be.

Credibility for top executives often comes from doing the extraordinary: exercising discretion, creating, inventing, planning, and acting in nonroutine ways. But since routine problems look easier and more manageable, require less change and consent on the part of anyone else, and lend themselves to instant solutions that can make any leader look good temporarily, leaders may avoid the risky by taking over what their subordinates should be doing. Ultimately, a leader may succeed in getting all the trivial problems dumped on his or her desk. This can establish expectations even for leaders attempting more challenging tasks. When Warren Bennis was president of the University of Cincinnati, a professor called him when the heat was down in a classroom. In writing about this incident, Bennis commented, "I suppose he expected me to grab a wrench and fix it."[6]

People at the top need to insulate themselves from the routine operations of the organization in

---

6. Warren Bennis, *The Unconscious Conspiracy: Why Leaders Can't Lead* (New York: AMACOM, 1976).

order to develop and exercise power. But this very insulation can lead to another source of powerlessness—lack of information. In one multinational corporation, top executives who are sealed off in a large, distant office, flattered and virtually babied by aides, are frustrated by their distance from the real action.[7]

At the top, the concern for secrecy and privacy is mixed with real loneliness. In one bank, organization members were so accustomed to never seeing the top leaders that when a new senior vice president went to the branch offices to look around, they had suspicion, even fear, about his intentions.

Thus leaders who are cut out of an organization's information networks understand neither what is really going on at lower levels nor that their own isolation may be having negative effects. All too often top executives design "beneficial" new employee programs or declare a new humanitarian policy (e.g., "Participatory management is now our style") only to find the policy ignored or mistrusted because it is perceived as coming from uncaring bosses.

The information gap has more serious consequences when executives are so insulated from the rest of the organization or from other decision makers that, as Nixon so dramatically did, they fail to see their own impending downfall. Such insulation is partly a matter of organizational position and, in some cases, of executive style.

For example, leaders may create closed inner circles consisting of "doppelgängers," people just like themselves, who are their principal sources of organizational information and tell them only what they want to know. The reasons for the distortions are varied: key aides want to relieve the leader of burdens, they think just like the leader, they want to protect their own positions of power, or the familiar "kill the messenger" syndrome makes people close to top executives reluctant to be the bearers of bad news.

Finally, just as supervisors and lower-level managers need their supporters in order to be and feel powerful, so do top executives. But for them sponsorship may not be so much a matter of individual endorsement as an issue of support by larger sources of legitimacy in the society. For top executives the problem is not to fit in among peers; rather, the question is whether the public at large and other organization members perceive a common interest which they see the executives as promoting.

If, however, public sources of support are withdrawn and leaders are open to public attack or if inside constituencies fragment and employees see their interests better aligned with pressure groups than with organizational leadership, then powerlessness begins to set in.

When common purpose is lost, the system's own politics may reduce the capacity of those at the top to act. Just as managing decline seems to create a much more passive and reactive stance than managing growth, so does mediating among conflicting interests. When what is happening outside and inside their organizations is out of their control, many people at the top turn into decline managers and dispute mediators. Neither is a particularly empowering role.

Thus when top executives lose their own lines of supply, lines of information, and lines of support, they too suffer from a kind of powerlessness. The temptation for them then is to pull in every shred of power they can and to decrease the power available to other people to act. Innovation loses out in favor of control. Limits rather than targets are set. Financial goals are met by reducing "overhead" (people) rather than by giving people the tools and discretion to increase their own productive capacity. Dictatorial statements come down from the top, spreading the mentality of powerlessness farther until the whole organization becomes sluggish and people concentrate on protecting what they have rather than on producing what they can.

When everyone is playing "king of the mountain," guarding his or her turf jealously, then king of the mountain becomes the only game in town.

TO EXPAND POWER, SHARE IT

In no case am I saying that people in the three hierarchical levels described are always powerless, but they are susceptible to common conditions that can contribute to powerlessness. *Exhibit III* summarizes the most common symptoms of powerlessness for each level and some typical sources of that behavior.

I am also distinguishing the tremendous concentration of economic and political power in large corporations themselves from the powerlessness that can beset individuals even in the highest positions in such organizations. What grows with organizational position in hierarchical levels is not necessarily the power to accomplish—productive power—but the power to punish, to prevent, to sell off, to reduce, to fire, all without appropriate concern for consequences.

---

7. See my chapter, "How the Top is Different," in *Life in Organizations.*

EXHIBIT III

Common Symptoms and Sources of Powerlessness for Three Key Organizational Positions

Position	Symptoms	Sources
First-line supervisors	Close, rules-minded supervision	Routine, rules-minded jobs with little control over lines of supply
	Tendency to do things oneself, blocking of subordinates' development and information	Limited lines of information
	Resistant, underproducing subordinates	Limited advancement or involvement prospects for oneself/subordinates
Staff professionals	Turf protection, information control	Routine tasks seen as peripheral to "real tasks" of line organization
	Retreat into professionalism	Blocked careers
	Conservative resistance to change	Easy replacement by outside experts
Top executives	Focus on internal cutting, short-term results, "punishing"	Uncontrollable lines of supply because of environmental changes
	Dictatorial top-down communications	Limited or blocked lines of information about lower levels of organization
	Retreat to comfort of like-minded lieutenants	Diminished lines of support because of challenges to legitimacy (e.g., from the public or special interest groups)

It is that kind of power—oppressive power—that we often say corrupts.

The absence of ways to prevent individual and social harm causes the polity to feel it must surround people in power with constraints, regulations, and laws that limit the arbitrary use of their authority. But if oppressive power corrupts, then so does the absence of productive power. In large organizations, powerlessness can be a bigger problem than power.

David C. McClelland makes a similar distinction between oppressive and productive power:

"The negative . . . face of power is characterized by the dominance-submission mode: if I win, you lose. . . . It leads to simple and direct means of feeling powerful [such as being aggressive]. It does not often lead to effective social leadership for the reason that such a person tends to treat other people as pawns. People who feel they are pawns tend to be passive and useless to the leader who gets his satisfaction from dominating them. Slaves are the most inefficient form of labor ever devised by man. If a leader wants to have far-reaching influence, he must make his followers feel powerful and able to accomplish things on their own. . . . Even the most dictatorial leader does not succeed if he has not instilled in at least some of his followers a sense of power and the strength to pursue the goals he has set."[8]

Organizational power can grow, in part, by being shared. We do not yet know enough about new organizational forms to say whether productive power is infinitely expandable or where we reach the point of diminishing returns. But we do know that sharing power is different from giving or throwing it away. Delegation does not mean abdication.

Some basic lessons could be translated from the field of economics to the realm of organizations and management. Capital investment in plants and equipment is not the only key to productivity. The productive capacity of nations, like organizations, grows if the skill base is upgraded. People with the tools, information, and support to make more informed decisions and act more quickly can often accomplish more. By empowering others, a leader does not decrease his power; instead he may increase it—especially if the whole organization performs better.

This analysis leads to some counterintuitive conclusions. In a certain tautological sense, the principal problem of the powerless is that they lack power. Powerless people are usually the last ones to

---

8. David C. McClelland, *Power: The Inner Experience* (New York: Irvington Publishers, 1975), p. 263. Quoted by permission.

whom anyone wants to entrust more power, for fear of its dissipation or abuse. But those people are precisely the ones who might benefit most from an injection of power and whose behavior is likely to change as new options open up to them.

Also, if the powerless bosses could be encouraged to share some of the power they do have, their power would grow. Yet, of course, only those leaders who feel secure about their own power outward—their lines of supply, information, and support—can see empowering subordinates as a gain rather than a loss. The two sides of power (getting it and giving it) are closely connected.

There are important lessons here for both subordinates and those who want to change organizations, whether executives or change agents. Instead of resisting or criticizing a powerless boss, which only increases the boss's feeling of powerlessness and need to control, subordinates instead might concentrate on helping the boss become more powerful. Managers might make pockets of ineffectiveness in the organization more productive not by training or replacing individuals but by structural solutions such as opening supply and support lines.

Similarly, organizational change agents who want a new program or policy to succeed should make sure that the change itself does not render any other level of the organization powerless. In making changes, it is wise to make sure that the key people in the level or two directly above and in neighboring functions are sufficiently involved, informed, and taken into account, so that the program can be used to build their own sense of power also. If such involvement is impossible, then it is better to move these people out of the territory altogether than to leave behind a group from whom some power has been removed and who might resist and undercut the program.

In part, of course, spreading power means educating people to this new definition of it. But words alone will not make the difference; managers will need the real experience of a new way of managing.

Here is how the associate director of a large corporate professional department phrased the lessons that he learned in the transition to a team-oriented, participatory, power-sharing management process:

"Get in the habit of involving your own managers in decision making and approvals. But don't abdicate! Tell them what you want and where you're coming from. Don't go for a one-boss grass roots 'democracy.' Make the management hierarchy work for you in participation. . . .

"Hang in there, baby, and don't give up. Try not to 'revert' just because everything seems to go sour on a particular day. Open up—talk to people and tell them how you feel. They'll want to get you back on track and will do things to make that happen—because they don't really want to go back to the way it was. . . . Subordinates will push you to 'act more like a boss,' but their interest is usually more in seeing someone else brought to heel than getting bossed themselves."

Naturally, people need to have power before they can learn to share it. Exhorting managers to change their leadership styles is rarely useful by itself. In one large plant of a major electronics company, first-line production supervisors were the source of numerous complaints from managers who saw them as major roadblocks to overall plant productivity and as insufficiently skilled supervisors. So the plant personnel staff undertook two pilot programs to increase the supervisors' effectiveness. The first program was based on a traditional competency and training model aimed at teaching the specific skills of successful supervisors. The second program, in contrast, was designed to empower the supervisors by directly affecting their flexibility, access to resources, connections with higher-level officials, and control over working conditions.

After an initial gathering of data from supervisors and their subordinates, the personnel staff held meetings where all the supervisors were given tools for developing action plans for sharing the data with their people and collaborating on solutions to perceived problems. But then, in a departure from common practice in this organization, task forces of supervisors were formed to develop new systems for handling job and career issues common to them and their people. These task forces were given budgets, consultants, representation on a plantwide project steering committee alongside managers at much higher levels, and wide latitude in defining the nature and scope of the changes they wished to make. In short, lines of supply, information, and support were opened to them.

As the task forces progressed in their activities, it became clear to the plant management that the hoped-for changes in supervisory effectiveness were taking place much more rapidly through these structural changes in power than through conventional management training; so the conventional training was dropped. Not only did the pilot groups design useful new procedures for the plant, astonishing senior management in several cases with their knowledge and capabilities, but also, significantly, they learned to manage their own people better.

Several groups decided to involve shop-floor workers in their task forces; they could now see from their own experience the benefits of involving subordinates in solving job-related problems. Other supervisors began to experiment with ways to implement "participatory management" by giving subordinates more control and influence without relinquishing their own authority.

Soon the "problem supervisors" in the "most troubled plant in the company" were getting the highest possible performance ratings and were considered models for direct production management. The sharing of organizational power from the top made possible the productive use of power below.

One might wonder why more organizations do not adopt such empowering strategies. There are standard answers: that giving up control is threatening to people who have fought for every shred of it; that people do not want to share power with those they look down on; that managers fear losing their own place and special privileges in the system; that "predictability" often rates higher than "flexibility" as an organizational value; and so forth.

But I would also put skepticism about employee abilities high on the list. Many modern bureaucratic systems are designed to minimize dependence on individual intelligence by making routine as many decisions as possible. So it often comes as a genuine surprise to top executives that people doing the more routine jobs could, indeed, make sophisticated decisions or use resources entrusted to them in intelligent ways.

In the same electronics company just mentioned, at the end of a quarter the pilot supervisory task forces were asked to report results and plans to senior management in order to have their new budget requests approved. The task forces made sure they were well prepared, and the high-level executives were duly impressed. In fact, they were so impressed that they kept interrupting the presentations with compliments, remarking that the supervisors could easily be doing sophisticated personnel work.

At first the supervisors were flattered. Such praise from upper management could only be taken well. But when the first glow wore off, several of them became very angry. They saw the excessive praise as patronizing and insulting. "Didn't they think we could think? Didn't they imagine we were capable of doing this kind of work?" one asked. "They must have seen us as just a bunch of animals. No wonder they gave us such limited jobs."

As far as these supervisors were concerned, their abilities had always been there, in latent form perhaps, but still there. They as individuals had not changed—just their organizational power.

Women Managers Experience Special Power Failures

The traditional problems of women in management are illustrative of how formal and informal practices can combine to engender powerlessness. Historically, women in management have found their opportunities in more routine, low-profile jobs. In staff positions, where they serve in support capacities to line managers but have no line responsibilities of their own, or in supervisory jobs managing "stuck" subordinates, they are not in a position either to take the kinds of risks that build credibility or to develop their own team by pushing bright subordinates.

Such jobs, which have few favors to trade, tend to keep women out of the mainstream of the organization. This lack of clout, coupled with the greater difficulty anyone who is "different" has in getting into the information and support networks, has meant that merely by organizational situation women in management have been more likely than men to be rendered structurally powerless. This is one reason those women who have achieved power have often had family connections that put them in the mainstream of the organization's social circles.

A disproportionate number of women managers are found among first-line supervisors or staff professionals; and they, like men in those circumstances, are likely to be organizationally powerless. But the behavior of other managers can contribute to the powerlessness of women in management in a number of less obvious ways.

One way other managers can make a woman powerless is by patronizingly overprotecting her: putting her in "a safe job," not giving her enough to do to prove herself, and not suggesting her for high-risk, visible assignments. This protectiveness is sometimes born of "good" intentions to give her every chance to succeed (why stack the deck against her?). Out of managerial concerns, out of awareness that a woman may be up against situations that men simply do not have to face, some very well-meaning managers protect their female managers ("It's a jungle, so why send her into it?").

Overprotectiveness can also mask a manager's fear of association with a woman should she fail. One senior bank official at a level below vice president told me about his concerns with respect to a high-performing, financially experienced woman reporting to him. Despite *his* overwhelmingly positive work experiences with her, he was still afraid to recommend her for other assignments because he felt it was a personal risk. "What if other managers are not as accepting of women as I am?" he asked. "I know I'd be sticking my neck out; they would take her more because of my endorsement than her qualifications. And what if she doesn't make it? My judgment will be on the line."

Overprotection is relatively benign compared with rendering a person powerless by providing obvious signs of lack of managerial support. For example, allowing someone supposedly in authority to be bypassed easily means that no one else has to take him or her seriously. If a woman's immediate supervisor or other managers listen willingly to criticism of her and show they are concerned every time a negative comment comes up and that they assume she must be at fault, then they are helping to undercut her. If managers let other people know that they have concerns about this person or that they are testing her to see how she does, then they are inviting other people to look for signs of inadequacy or failure.

Furthermore, people assume they can afford to bypass women because they "must be uninformed" or "don't know the ropes." Even though women may be respected for their competence or expertise, they are not necessarily seen as being informed beyond the technical requirements of the job. There may be a grain of historical truth in this. Many women come to senior management positions as "outsiders" rather than up through the usual channels.

Also, because until very recently men have not felt comfortable seeing women as businesspeople (business clubs have traditionally excluded women), they have tended to seek each other out for informal socializing. Anyone, male or female, seen as organizationally naive and lacking sources of "inside dope" will find his or her own lines of information limited.

Finally, even when women are able to achieve some power on their own, they have not necessarily been able to translate such personal credibility into an organizational power base. To create a network of supporters out of individual clout requires that a person pass on and share power, that subordinates and peers be empowered by virtue of their connection with that person. Traditionally, neither men nor women have seen women as capable of sponsoring others, even though they may be capable of achieving and succeeding on their own. Women have been viewed as the *recipients* of sponsorship rather than as the sponsors themselves.

(As more women prove themselves in organizations and think more self-consciously about bringing along young people, this situation may change. However, I still hear many more questions from women managers about how they can benefit from mentors, sponsors, or peer networks than about how they themselves can start to pass on favors and make use of their own resources to benefit others.)

Viewing managers in terms of power and powerlessness helps explain two familiar stereotypes about women and leadership in organizations: that no one wants a woman boss (although studies show that anyone who has ever had a woman boss is likely to have had a positive experience), and that the reason no one wants a woman boss is that women are "too controlling, rules-minded, and petty."

The first stereotype simply makes clear that power is important to leadership. Underneath the preference for men is the assumption that, given the current distribution of people in organizational leadership positions, men are more likely than women to be in positions to achieve power and, therefore, to share their power with others. Similarly, the "bossy woman boss" stereotype is a perfect picture of powerlessness. All of those traits are just as characteristic of men who are powerless, but women are slightly more likely, because of circumstances I have mentioned, to find themselves powerless than are men. Women with power in the organization are just as effective—and preferred—as men.

Recent interviews conducted with about 600 bank managers show that, when a woman exhibits the petty traits of powerlessness, people assume that she does so "because she is a woman." A striking difference is that, when a man engages in the same behavior, people assume the behavior is a matter of his own individual style and characteristics and do not conclude that it reflects on the suitability of men for management.

Who Gets Power and How They Hold Onto It: A Strategic Contingency Model of Power

Gerald R. Salancik

Jeffrey Pfeffer

Power is held by many people to be a dirty word or, as Warren Bennis has said, "It is the organization's last dirty secret."

This article will argue that traditional "political" power, far from being a dirty business, is, in its most naked form, one of the few mechanisms available for aligning an organization with its own reality. However, institutionalized forms of power—what we prefer to call the cleaner forms of power: authority, legitimization, centralized control, regulations, and the more modern "management information systems"—tend to buffer the organization from reality and obscure the demands of its environment. Most great states and institutions declined, not because they played politics, but because they failed to accommodate to the political realities they faced. Political processes, rather than being mechanisms for unfair and unjust allocations and appointments, tend toward the realistic resolution of conflicts among interests. And power, while it eludes definition, is easy enough to recognize by its consequences—the ability of those who possess power to bring about the outcomes they desire.

The model of power we advance is an elaboration of what has been called strategic-contingency theory, a view that sees power as something that accrues to organizational subunits (individuals, departments) that cope with critical organizational problems. Power is used by subunits, indeed, used by all who have it, to enhance their own survival through control of scarce critical resources, through the placement of allies in key positions, and through the definition of organizational problems and policies. Because of the processes by which power develops and is used, organizations become both more aligned and more misaligned with their environments. This contradiction is the most interesting aspect of organizational power, and one that makes administration one of the most precarious of occupations.

WHAT IS ORGANIZATIONAL POWER?

You can walk into most organizations and ask without fear of being misunderstood, "Which are the powerful groups or people in this organization?" Although many organizational informants may be *unwilling* to tell you, it is unlikely they will be *unable* to tell you. Most people do not require explicit definitions to know what power is.

Power is simply the ability to get things done the way one wants them to be done. For a manager who wants an increased budget to launch a project that he thinks is important, his power is measured by his ability to get that budget. For an executive vice-president who wants to be chairman, his power is evidenced by his advancement toward his goal.

People in organizations not only know what you are talking about when you ask who is influential but they are likely to agree with one another to an amazing extent. Recently, we had a chance to observe this in a regional office of an insurance company. The office had 21 department managers; we asked ten of these managers to rank all 21 according to the influence each one had in the organization. Despite the fact that ranking 21 things is a difficult task, the managers sat down and began arranging the names of their colleagues and themselves in a column. Only one person bothered to ask, "What do you mean by influence?" When told "power," he responded, "Oh," and went on. We compared the rankings of all ten managers and found virtually no disagreement among them in the managers ranked among the top five or the bottom five. Differences in the rankings came from department heads claiming more influence for themselves than their colleagues attributed to them.

Such agreement on those who have influence, and those who do not, was not unique to this insurance company. So far we have studied over 20 very different organizations—universities, research firms, factories, banks, retailers, to name a few. In each one we found individuals able to rate themselves and their peers on a scale of influence or power. We have done this both for specific decisions and for general impact on organizational policies. Their agreement was unusually high, which suggests that distributions of influence exist well enough in everyone's mind to be referred to with ease—and we assume with accuracy.

WHERE DOES ORGANIZATIONAL POWER COME FROM?

Earlier we stated that power helps organizations become aligned with their realities. This hopeful prospect follows from what we have dubbed the strategic-contingencies theory of organizational power. Briefly, those subunits most able to cope with the organization's critical problems and uncertainties acquire power. In its simplest form, the strategic-contingencies theory implies that when an organization faces a number of lawsuits that threaten its existence, the legal department will gain power and influence over organizational decisions. Somehow other organizational interest groups will recognize its critical importance and confer upon it a status and power never before enjoyed. This influence may extend beyond handling legal matters and into decisions about product design, advertising production, and so on. Such extensions undoubtedly would be accompanied by appropriate, or acceptable, verbal justifications. In time, the head of the legal department may become the head of the corporation, just as in times past the vice-president for marketing had become the president when market shares were a worrisome problem and, before him, the chief engineer, who had made the production line run as smooth as silk.

Stated in this way, the strategic-contingencies theory of power paints an appealing picture of power. To the extent that power is determined by the critical uncertainties and problems facing the organization and, in turn, influences decisions in the organization, the organization is aligned with the realities it faces. In short, power facilitates the organization's adaptation to its environment—or its problems.

We can cite many illustrations of how influence derives from a subunit's ability to deal with critical contingencies. Michael Crozier described a French cigarette factory in which the maintenance engineers had a considerable say in the plantwide operation. After some probing he discovered that the group possessed the solution to one of the major problems faced by the company, that of troubleshooting the elaborate, expensive, and irascible automated machines that kept breaking down and dumbfounding everyone else. It was the one problem that the plant manager could in no way control.

The production workers, while troublesome from time to time, created no insurmountable problems; the manager could reasonably predict their absenteeism or replace them when necessary. Production scheduling was something he could deal with since, by watching inventories and sales, the demand for cigarettes was known long in advance. Changes in demand could be accommodated by slowing down or speeding up the line. Supplies of tobacco and paper were also easily dealt with through stockpiles and advance orders.

The one thing that management could neither control nor accommodate to, however, was the seemingly happenstance breakdowns. And the foremen couldn't instruct the workers what to do when emergencies developed since the maintenance department kept its records of problems and solutions locked up in a cabinet or in its members' heads. The breakdowns were, in truth, a critical source of uncertainty for the organization, and the maintenance engineers were the only ones who could cope with the problem.

The engineers' strategic role in coping with breakdowns afforded them a considerable say on plant decisions. Schedules and production quotas were set in consultation with them. And the plant manager, while formally their boss, accepted their decisions about personnel in their operation. His submission was to his credit, for without their cooperation he would have had an even more difficult time in running the plant.

Ignoring Critical Consequences

In this cigarette factory, sharing influence with the maintenance workers reflected the plant manager's awareness of the critical contingencies. However, when organizational members are not aware of the critical contingencies they face, and do not share influence accordingly, the failure to do so can create havoc. In one case, an insurance company's regional office was having problems with the performance of one of its departments, the coding department. From the outside, the department looked like a disaster area. The clerks who worked in it were somewhat dissatisfied; their supervisor paid little attention to them, and they resented the hard work. Several other departments were critical of this manager, claiming that she was inconsistent in meeting deadlines. The person most critical was the claims manager. He resented having to wait for work that was handled by her department, claiming that it held up his claims adjusters. Having heard the rumors about dissatisfaction among her subordinates, he attributed the situation to poor supervision. He was second in command in the office and therefore took up the issue with her immediate boss, the head of administrative services. They consulted with the personnel manager and the three of them concluded that the manager needed leadership training to improve her relations with her subordinates. The coding manager objected, saying it was a waste of time, but agreed to go along with the training and also agreed to give more priority to the claims department's work. Within a week after the training, the results showed that her workers were happier but that the performance of her department had decreased, save for the people serving the claims department.

About this time, we began, quite independently, a study of influence in this organization. We asked the administrative services director to draw up flow charts of how the work of one department moved on to the next department. In the course of the interview, we noticed that the coding department began or interceded in the work flow of most of the other departments and casually mentioned to him, "The coding manager must be very influential." He said "No, not really. Why would you think so?" Before we could reply he recounted the story of her leadership training and the fact that things were worse. We then told him that it seemed obvious that the coding department would be influential from the fact that all the other departments depended on it. It was also clear why productivity had fallen. The coding manager took the training seriously and began spending more time raising her workers' spirits than she did worrying about the problems of all the departments that depended on her. Giving priority to the claims area only exaggerated the problem, for their work was getting done at the expense of the work of the other departments. Eventually the company hired a few more clerks to relieve the pressure in the coding department and performance returned to a more satisfactory level.

Originally we got involved with this insurance company to examine how the influence of each manager evolved from his or her department's handling of critical organizational contingencies. We reasoned that one of the most important contingencies faced by all profit-making organizations was that of generating income. Thus we expected managers would be influential to the extent to which they contributed to this function. Such was the case. The underwriting managers, who wrote the policies that committed the premiums, were the most influential; the claims managers, who kept a lid on the funds flowing out, were a close second. Least influential were the

managers of functions unrelated to revenue, such as mailroom and payroll managers. And contrary to what the administrative services manager believed, the third most powerful department head (out of 21) was the woman in charge of the coding function, which consisted of rating, recording, and keeping track of the codes of all policy applications and contracts. Her peers attributed more influence to her than could have been inferred from her place on the organization chart. And it was not surprising, since they all depended on her department. The coding department's records, their accuracy and the speed with which they could be retrieved, affected virtually every other operating department in the insurance office. The underwriters depended on them in getting the contracts straight; the typing department depended on them in preparing the formal contract document; the claims department depended on them in adjusting claims; and accounting depended on them for billing. Unfortunately, the "bosses" were not aware of these dependencies, for unlike the cigarette factory, there were no massive breakdowns that made them obvious, while the coding manager, who was a hard-working but quiet person, did little to announce her importance.

The cases of this plant and office illustrate nicely a basic point about the source of power in organizations. The basis for power in an organization derives from the ability of a person or subunit to take or not take actions that are desired by others. The coding manager was seen as influential by those who depended on her department, but not by the people at the top. The engineers were influential because of their role in keeping the plant operating. The two cases differ in these respects: The coding supervisor's source of power was not as widely recognized as that of the maintenance engineers, and she did not use her source of power to influence decisions; the maintenance engineers did. Whether power is used to influence anything is a separate issue. We should not confuse this issue with the fact that power derives from a social situation in which one person has a capacity to do something and another person does not, but wants it done.

POWER SHARING IN ORGANIZATIONS

Power is shared in organizations; and it is shared out of necessity more than out of concern for principles of organizational development or participatory democracy. Power is shared because no one person controls all the desired activities in the organization. While the factory owner may hire people to operate his noisy machines, once hired they have some control over the use of the machinery. And thus they have power over him in the same way he has power over them. Who has more power over whom is a mooter point than that of recognizing the inherent nature of organizing as a sharing of power.

Let's expand on the concept that power derives from the activities desired in an organization. A major way of managing influence in organizations is through the designation of activities. In a bank we studied, we saw this principle in action. This bank was planning to install a computer system for routine credit evaluation. The bank, rather progressive-minded, was concerned that the change would have adverse effects on employees and therefore surveyed their attitudes.

The principal opposition to the new system came, interestingly, not from the employees who performed the routine credit checks, some of whom would be relocated because of the change, but from the manager of the credit department. His reason was quite simple. The manager's primary function was to give official approval to the applications, catch any employee mistakes before giving approval, and arbitrate any difficulties the clerks had in deciding what to do. As a consequence of his role, others in the organization, including his superiors, subordinates, and colleagues, attributed considerable importance to him. He, in turn, for example, could point to the low proportion of credit approvals, compared with other financial institutions, that resulted in bad debts. Now, to his mind, a wretched machine threatened to transfer his role to a computer programmer, a man who knew nothing of finance and who, in addition, had ten years less seniority. The credit manager eventually quit for a position at a smaller firm with lower pay, but one in which he would have more influence than his redefined job would have left him with.

Because power derives from activities rather than individuals, an individual's or subgroup's power is never absolute and derives ultimately from the context of the situation. The amount of power an individual has at any one time depends, not only on the activities he or she controls, but also on the existence of other persons or means by which the activities can be achieved and on those who determine what ends are desired and, hence, on what activities are desired and critical for the organization. One's own power always depends on other people for these two reasons. Other people, or groups or organizations, can determine the definition of what is a critical contingency for the organization and can also undercut the uniqueness of the individual's personal contribution to the critical contingencies of the organization.

Perhaps one can best appreciate how situationally dependent power is by examining how it is distributed. In most societies, power organizes around scarce and critical resources. Rarely does power organize around abundant resources. In the United States, a person doesn't become powerful because he or she can drive a car. There are simply too many others who can drive with equal facility. In certain villages in Mexico, on the other hand, a person with a car is accredited with enormous social status and plays a key role in the community. In addition to scarcity, power is also limited by the need for one's capacities in a social system. While a racer's ability to drive a car around a 90° turn at 80 mph may be sparsely distributed in a society, it is not likely to lend the driver much power in the society. The ability simply does not play a central role in the activities of the society.

The fact that power revolves around scarce and critical activities, of course, makes the control and organization of those activities a major battleground in struggles for power. Even relatively abundant or trivial resources can become the bases for power if one can organize and control their allocation and the definition of what is critical. Many occupational and professional groups attempt to do just this in modern economies. Lawyers organize themselves into associations, regulate the entrance requirements for novitiates, and then get laws passed specifying situations that require the services of an attorney. Workers had little power in the conduct of industrial affairs until they organized themselves into closed and controlled systems. In recent years, women and blacks have tried to define themselves as important and critical to the social system, using law to reify their status.

In organizations there are obviously opportunities for defining certain activities as more critical than others. Indeed, the growth of managerial thinking to include defining organizational objectives and goals has done much to foster these opportunities. One sure way to liquidate the power of groups in the organization is to define the need for their services out of existence. David Halberstam presents a description of how just such a thing happened to the group of correspondents that evolved around Edward R. Murrow, the brilliant journalist, interviewer, and war correspondent of CBS News. A close friend of CBS chairman and controlling stockholder William S. Paley, Murrow, and the news department he directed, were endowed with freedom to do what they felt was right. He used it to create some of the best documentaries and commentaries ever seen on television. Unfortunately, television became too large, too powerful, and too suspect in the eyes of the federal government that licensed it. It thus became, or at least the top executives believed it had become, too dangerous to have in-depth, probing commentary on the news. Crisp, dry, uneditorializing headliners were considered safer. Murrow was out and Walter Cronkite was in.

The power to define what is critical in an organization is no small power. Moreover, it is the key to understanding why organizations are either aligned with their environments or misaligned. If an organization defines certain activities as critical when in fact they are not critical, given the flow of resources coming into the organization, it is not likely to survive, at least in its present form.

Most organizations manage to evolve a distribution of power and influence that is aligned with the critical realities they face in the environment. The environment, in turn, includes both the internal environment, the shifting situational contexts in which particular decisions get made, and the external environment that it can hope to influence but is unlikely to control.

THE CRITICAL CONTINGENCIES

The critical contingencies facing most organizations derive from the environmental context within which they operate. This determines the available needed resources and thus determines the problems to be dealt with. That power organizes around handling these problems suggests an important mechanism by which organizations keep in tune with their external environments. The strategic-contingencies model implies that subunits that contribute to the critical resources of the organization will gain influence in the organization. Their influence presumably is then used to bend the organization's activities to the contingencies that determine its resources. This idea may strike one as obvious. But its obviousness in no way diminishes its importance. Indeed, despite its obviousness, it escapes the notice of many organizational analysts and managers, who all too frequently think of the organization in terms of a descending pyramid, in which all the departments in one tier hold equal power and status. This presumption denies the reality that departments differ in the contributions they are believed to make to the overall organization's resources, as well as to the fact that some are more equal than others.

Because of the importance of this idea to organizational effectiveness, we decided to examine it carefully in a large mid-western university. A university offers an excellent site for studying power. It is composed of departments with nominally equal power and is administered by a central executive structure much like other bureaucracies. However, at the same time it is a situation in which the departments have clearly defined identities and face diverse external environments. Each department has its own bodies of knowledge, its own institutions, its own sources of prestige and resources. Because the departments operate in different external environments, they are likely to contribute differentially to the resources of the overall organization. Thus a physics department with close ties to NASA may contribute substantially to the funds of the university; and a history department with a renowned historian in residence may contribute to the intellectual credibility or prestige of the whole university. Such variations permit one to examine how these various contributions lead to obtaining power within the university.

We analyzed the influence of 29 university departments throughout an 18-month period in their history. Our chief interest was to determine whether departments that brought more critical resources to the university would be more powerful than departments that contributed fewer or less critical resources.

To identify the critical resources each department contributed, the heads of all departments were interviewed about the importance of seven different resources to the university's success. The seven included undergraduate students (the factor determining size of the state allocations by the university), national prestige, administrative expertise, and so on. The most critical resource was found to be contract and grant monies received by a department's faculty for research or consulting services. At this university, contract and grants contributed somewhat less than 50 percent of the overall budget, with the remainder primarily coming from state appropriations. The importance attributed to contract and grant monies, and the rather minor importance of undergraduate students, was not surprising for this particular university. The university was a major center for graduate education; many of its departments ranked in the top ten of their respective fields. Grant and contract monies were the primary source of discretionary funding available for maintaining these programs of graduate education, and hence for maintaining the university's prestige. The prestige of the university itself was critical both in recruiting able students and attracting top-notch faculty.

From university records it was determined what relative contributions each of the 29 departments made to the various needs of the university (national prestige, outside grants, teaching). Thus, for instance, one department may have contributed to the university by teaching 7 percent of the instructional units, bringing in 2 percent of the outside contracts and grants, and having a national ranking of 20. Another department, on the other hand, may have taught one percent of the instructional units, contributed 12 percent to the grants, and be ranked the third best department in its field within the country.

The question was: Do these different contributions determine the relative power of the departments within the university? Power was measured in several ways; but regardless of how measured, the answer was "Yes." Those three resources together accounted for about 70 percent of the variance in subunit power in the university.

But the most important predictor of departmental power was the department's contribution to the contracts and grants of the university. Sixty percent of the variance in power was due to this one factor, suggesting that the power of departments derived primarily from the dollars they provided for graduate education, the activity believed to be the most important for the organization.

THE IMPACT OF ORGANIZATIONAL POWER ON DECISION MAKING

The measure of power we used in studying this university was an analysis of the responses of the department heads we interviewed. While such perceptions of power might be of interest in their own right, they contribute little to our understanding of how the distribution of power might serve to align an organization with its critical realities. For this we must look to how power actually influences the decisions and policies of organizations.

While it is perhaps not absolutely valid, we can generally gauge the relative importance of a department of an organization by the size of the budget allocated to it relative to other departments. Clearly it is of importance to the administrators of those departments whether they get squeezed in a budget crunch or are given more funds to strike out after new opportunities. And it should also be clear that when those decisions are made and one department can go ahead and try new approaches while another

must cut back on the old, then the deployment of the resources of the organization in meeting its problems is most directly affected.

Thus our study of the university led us to ask the following question: Does power lead to influence in the organization? To answer this question, we found it useful first to ask another one, namely: Why should department heads try to influence organizational decisions to favor their own departments to the exclusion of other departments? While this second question may seem a bit naive to anyone who has witnessed the political realities of organizations, we posed it in a context of research on organizations that sees power as an illegitimate threat to the neater rational authority of modern bureaucracies. In this context, decisions are not believed to be made because of the dirty business of politics but because of the overall goals and purposes of the organization. In a university, one reasonable basis for decision making is the teaching workload of departments and the demands that follow from that workload. We would expect, therefore, that departments with heavy student demands for courses would be able to obtain funds for teaching. Another reasonable basis for decision making is quality. We would expect, for that reason, that departments with esteemed reputations would be able to obtain funds both because their quality suggests they might use such funds effectively and because such funds would allow them to maintain their quality. A rational model of bureaucracy intimates, then, that the organizational decisions taken would favor those who perform the stated purposes of the organization—teaching undergraduates and training professional and scientific talent—well.

The problem with rational models of decision making, however, is that what is rational to one person may strike another as irrational. For most departments, resources are a question of survival. While teaching undergraduates may seem to be a major goal for some members of the university, developing knowledge may seem so to others; and to still others, advising governments and other institutions about policies may seem to be the crucial business. Everyone has his own idea of the proper priorities in a just world. Thus goals rather than being clearly defined and universally agreed upon are blurred and contested throughout the organization. If such is the case, then the decisions taken on behalf of the organization as a whole are likely to reflect the goals of those who prevail in political contests, namely, those with power in the organization.

Will organizational decisions always reflect the distribution of power in the organization? Probably not. Using power for influence requires a certain expenditure of effort, time, and resources. Prudent and judicious persons are not likely to use their power needlessly or wastefully. And it is likely that power will be used to influence organizational decisions primarily under circumstances that both require and favor its use. We have examined three conditions that are likely to affect the use of power in organizations: scarcity, criticality, and uncertainty. The first suggests that subunits will try to exert influence when the resources of the organization are scarce. If there is an abundance of resources, then a particular department or a particular individual has little need to attempt influence. With little effort, he can get all he wants anyway.

The second condition, criticality, suggests that a subunit will attempt to influence decisions to obtain resources that are critical to its own survival and activities. Criticality implies that one would not waste effort, or risk being labeled obstinate, by fighting over trivial decisions affecting one's operations.

An office manager would probably balk less about a threatened cutback in copying machine usage than about a reduction in typing staff. An advertising department head would probably worry less about losing his lettering artist than his illustrator. Criticality is difficult to define because what is critical depends on people's beliefs about what is critical. Such beliefs may or may not be based on experience and knowledge and may or may not be agreed upon by all. Scarcity, for instance, may itself affect conceptions of criticality. When slack resources drop off, cutbacks have to be made—those "hard decisions," as congressmen and resplendent administrators like to call them. Managers then find themselves scrapping projects they once held dear.

The third condition that we believe affects the uses of power is uncertainty: When individuals do not agree about what the organization should do or how to do it, power and other social processes will affect decisions. The reason for this is simply that, if there are no clear-cut criteria available for resolving conflicts of interest, then the only means for resolution is some form of social process, including power, status, social ties, or some arbitrary process like flipping a coin or drawing straws. Under conditions of uncertainty, the powerful manager can argue his case on any grounds and usually win it. Since there is no real consensus, other contestants are not likely to develop counter arguments or amass sufficient opposition. Moreover, because of his power and their need for access to the resources he controls, they are more likely to defer to his arguments.

Although the evidence is slight, we have found that power will influence the allocations of scarce and critical resources. In the analysis of power in the university, for instance, one of the most critical resources needed by departments is the general budget. First granted by the state legislature, the general budget is later allocated to individual departments by the university administration in response to requests from the department heads. Our analysis of the factors that contribute to a department getting more or less of this budget indicated that subunit power was the major predictor, overriding such factors as student demand for courses, national reputations of departments, or even the size of a department's faculty. Moreover, other research has shown that when the general budget has been cut back or held below previous uninflated levels, leading to monies becoming more scarce, budget allocations mirror departmental powers even more closely.

Student enrollment and faculty size, of course, do themselves relate to budget allocations, as we would expect since they determine a department's need for resources, or at least offer visible testimony of needs. But departments are not always able to get what they need by the mere fact of needing them. In one analysis it was found that high-power departments were able to obtain budget without regard to their teaching loads and, in some cases, actually in inverse relation to their teaching loads. In contrast, low-power departments could get increases in budget only when they could justify the increases by a recent growth in teaching load, and then only when it was far in excess of norms for other departments.

General budget is only one form of resource that is allocated to departments. There are others such as special grants for student fellowships or faculty research. These are critical to departments because they affect the ability to attract other resources, such as outstanding faculty or students. We examined how power influenced the allocations of four resources department heads had described as critical and scarce.

When the four resources were arrayed from the most to the least critical and scarce, we found that departmental power best predicted the allocations of the most critical and scarce resources. In other words, the analysis of how power influences organizational allocations leads to this conclusion: Those subunits most likely to survive in times of strife are those that are more critical to the organization. Their importance to the organization gives them power to influence resource allocations that enhance their own survival.

HOW EXTERNAL ENVIRONMENT IMPACTS EXECUTIVE SELECTION

Power not only influences the survival of key groups in an organization, it also influences the selection of individuals to key leadership positions, and by such a process further aligns the organization with its environmental context.

We can illustrate this with a recent study of the selection and tenure of chief administrators in 57 hospitals in Illinois. We assumed that since the critical problems facing the organization would enhance the power of certain groups at the expense of others, then the leaders to emerge should be those most relevant to the context of the hospitals. To assess this we asked each chief administrator about his professional background and how long he had been in office. The replies were then related to the hospitals' funding, ownership, and competitive conditions for patients and staff.

One aspect of a hospital's context is the source of its budget. Some hospitals, for instance, are run much like other businesses. They sell bed space, patient care, and treatment services. They charge fees sufficient both to cover their costs and to provide capital for expansion. The main source of both their operating and capital funds is patient billings. Increasingly, patient billings are paid for, not by patients, but by private insurance companies. Insurers like Blue Cross dominate and represent a potent interest group outside a hospital's control but critical to its income. The insurance companies, in order to limit their own costs, attempt to hold down the fees allowable to hospitals, which they do effectively from their positions on state rate boards. The squeeze on hospitals that results from fees increasing slowly while costs climb rapidly more and more demands the talents of cost accountants or people trained in the technical expertise of hospital administration.

By contrast, other hospitals operate more like social service institutions, either as government healthcare units (Bellevue Hospital in New York City and Cook County Hospital in Chicago, for example) or as charitable institutions. These hospitals obtain a large proportion of their operating and capital funds, not from privately insured patients, but from government subsidies or private donations. Such institutions rather than requiring the talents of a technically efficient administrator are likely to require the savvy of someone who is well integrated into the social and political power structure of the community.

Not surprisingly, the characteristics of administrators predictably reflect the funding context of the hospitals with which they are associated. Those hospitals with larger proportions of their budget obtained from private insurance companies were most likely to have administrators with backgrounds in accounting and least likely to have administrators whose professions were business or medicine. In contrast, those hospitals with larger proportions of their budget derived from private donations and local governments were most likely to have administrators with business or professional backgrounds and least likely to have accountants. The same held for formal training in hospital management. Professional hospital administrators could easily be found in hospitals drawing their incomes from private insurance and rarely in hospitals dependent on donations or legislative appropriations.

As with the selection of administrators, the context of organizations has also been found to affect the removal of executives. The environment, as a source of organizational problems, can make it more or less difficult for executives to demonstrate their value to the organization. In the hospital we studied, long-term administrators came from hospitals with few problems. They enjoyed amicable and stable relations with their local business and social communities and suffered little competition for funding and staff. The small city hospital director who attended civic and Elks meetings while running the only hospital within a 100-mile radius, for example, had little difficulty holding on to his job. Turnover was highest in hospitals with the most problems, a phenomenon similar to that observed in a study of industrial organizations in which turnover was highest among executives in industries with competitive environments and unstable market conditions. The interesting thing is that instability characterized the industries rather than the individual firms in them. The troublesome conditions in the individual firms were attributed, or rather misattributed, to the executives themselves.

It takes more than problems, however, to terminate a manager's leadership. The problems themselves must be relevant and critical. This is clear from the way in which an administrator's tenure is affected by the status of the hospital's operating budget. Naively we might assume that all administrators would need to show a surplus. Not necessarily so. Again, we must distinguish between those hospitals that depend on private donations for funds and those that do not. Whether an endowed budget shows a surplus or deficit is less important than the hospital's relations with benefactors. On the other hand, with a budget dependent on patient billing, a surplus is almost essential; monies for new equipment or expansion must be drawn from it, and without them quality care becomes more difficult and patients scarcer. An administrator's tenure reflected just these considerations. For those hospitals dependent upon private donations, the length of an administrator's term depended not at all on the status of the operating budget but was fairly predictable from the hospital's relations with the business community. On the other hand, in hospitals dependent on the operating budget for capital financing, the greater the deficit the shorter was the tenure of the hospital's principal administrators.

CHANGING CONTINGENCIES AND ERODING POWER BASES

The critical contingencies facing the organization may change. When they do, it is reasonable to expect that the power of individuals and subgroups will change in turn. At times the shift can be swift and shattering, as it was recently for powerholders in New York City. A few years ago it was believed that David Rockefeller was one of the ten most powerful people in the city, as tallied by *New York* magazine, which annually sniffs out power for the delectation of its readers. But that was before it was revealed that the city was in financial trouble, before Rockefeller's Chase Manhattan Bank lost some of its own financial luster, and before brother Nelson lost some of his political influence in Washington. Obviously David Rockefeller was no longer as well positioned to help bail the city out. Another loser was an attorney with considerable personal connections to the political and religious leaders of the city. His talents were no longer in much demand. The persons with more influence were the bankers and union pension fund executors who fed money to the city; community leaders who represent blacks and Spanish-Americans, in contrast, witnessed the erosion of their power bases.

One implication of the idea that power shifts with changes in organizational environments is that the dominant coalition will tend to be that group that is most appropriate for the organization's environment, as also will the leaders of an organization. One can observe this historically in the top executives of industrial firms in the United States. Up until the early 1950s, many top corporations were headed by former production line managers or engineers who gained prominence because of their abilities to cope with the problems of production. Their success, however, only spelled their demise. As production

became routinized and mechanized, the problem of most firms became one of selling all those goods they so efficiently produced. Marketing executives were more freqeuently found in corporate boardrooms. Success outdid itself again, for keeping markets and production steady and stable requires the kind of control that can only come from acquring competitors and suppliers or the invention of more and more appealing products—ventures that typically require enormous amounts of capital. During the 1960s, financial executives assumed the seats of power. And they, too, will give way to others. Edging over the horizon are legal experts, as regulation and antitrust suits are becoming more and more frequent in the 1970s, suits that had their beginnings in the success of the expansion generated by prior executives. The more distant future, which is likely to be dominated by multinational corporations, may see former secretaries of state and their minions increasingly serving as corporate figureheads.

THE NONADAPTIVE CONSEQUENCES OF ADAPTATION

From what we have said thus far about power aligning the organization with its own realities, an intelligent person might react with a resounding ho-hum, for it all seems too obvious: Those with the ability to get the job done are given the job to do.

However, there are two aspects of power that make it more useful for understanding organizations and their effectiveness. First, the "job" to be done has a way of expanding itself until it becomes less and less clear what the job is. Napoleon began by doing a job for France in the war with Austria and ended up Emperor, convincing many that only he could keep the peace. Hitler began by promising an end to Germany's troubling postwar depression and ended up convincing more people than is comfortable to remember that he was destined to be the savior of the world. In short, power is a capacity for influence that extends far beyond the original bases that created it. Second, power tends to take on institutionalized forms that enable it to endure well beyond its usefulness to an organization.

There is an important contradiction in what we have observed about organizational power. On the one hand we have said that power derives from the contingencies facing an organization and that when those contingencies change so do the bases for power. On the other hand we have asserted that subunits will tend to use their power to influence organizational decisions in their own favor, particularly when their own survival is threatened by the scarcity of critical resources. The first statement implies that an organization will tend to be aligned with its environment since power will tend to bring to key positions those with capabilities relevant to the context. The second implies that those in power will not give up their positions so easily; they will pursue policies that guarantee their continued domination. In short, change and stability operate through the same mechanism, and, as a result, the organization will never be completely in phase with its environment or its needs.

The study of hospital administrators illustrates how leadership can be out of phase with reality. We argued that privately funded hospitals needed trained technical administrators more so than did hospitals funded by donations. The need as we perceived it was matched in most hospitals, but by no means in all. Some organizations did not conform with our predictions. These deviations imply that some administrators were able to maintain their positions independent of their suitability for those positions. By dividing administrators into those with long and short terms of office, one finds that the characteristics of longer-termed administrators were virtually unrelated to the hospital's context. The shorter-termed chiefs on the other hand had characteristics more appropriate for the hospital's problems. For a hospital to have a recently appointed head implies that the previous administrator had been unable to endure by institutionalizing himself.

One obvious feature of hospitals that allowed some administrators to enjoy a long tenure was a hospital's ownership. Administrators were less entrenched when their hospitals were affiliated with and dependent upon larger organizations, such as governments or churches. Private hospitals offered more secure positions for administrators. Like private corporations, they tend to have more diffused ownership, leaving the administrator unopposed as he institutionalizes his reign. Thus he endures, sometimes at the expense of the performance of the organization. Other research has demonstrated that corporations with diffuse ownership have poorer earnings than those in which the control of the manager is checked by a dominant shareholder. Firms that overload their boardrooms with more insiders than are appropriate for their context have also been found to be less profitable.

A word of caution is required about our judgment of "appropriateness." When we argue some capabilities are more appropriate for one context than another, we do so from the perspective of an outsider

and on the basis of reasonable assumptions as to the problems the organization will face and the capabilities they will need. The fact that we have been able to predict the distribution of influence and the characteristics of leaders suggests that our reasoning is not incorrect. However, we do not think that all organizations follow the same pattern. The fact that we have not been able to predict outcomes with 100 percent accuracy indicates they do not.

MISTAKING CRITICAL CONTINGENCIES

One thing that allows subunits to retain their power is their ability to name their functions as critical to the organization when they may not be. Consider again our discussion of power in the university. One might wonder why the most critical tasks were defined as graduate education and scholarly research, the effect of which was to lend power to those who brought in grants and contracts. Why not something else? The reason is that the more powerful departments argued for those criteria and won their case, partly because they were more powerful.

In another analysis of this university, we found that all departments advocate self-serving criteria for budget allocation. Thus a department with large undergraduate enrollments argued that enrollments should determine budget allocations, a department with a strong national reputation saw prestige as the most reasonable basis for distributing funds, and so on. We further found that advocating such self-serving criteria actually benefited a department's budget allotments but, also, it paid off more for departments that were already powerful.

Organizational needs are consistent with a current distribution of power also because of a human tendency to categorize problems in familiar ways. An accountant sees problems with organizational performance as cost accountancy problems or inventory flow problems. A sales manager sees them as problems with markets, promotional strategies, or just unaggressive salespeople. But what is the truth? Since it does not automatically announce itself, it is likely that those with prior credibility, or those with power, will be favored as the enlightened. This bias, while not intentionally self-serving, further concentrates power among those who already possess it, independent of changes in the organization's context.

INSTITUTIONALIZING POWER

A third reason for expecting organizational contingencies to be defined in familiar ways is that the current holders of power can structure the organization in ways that institutionalize themselves. By institutionalization we mean the establishment of relatively permanent structures and policies that favor the influence of a particular subunit. While in power, a dominant coalition has the ability to institute constitutions, rules, procedures, and information systems that limit the potential power of others while continuing their own.

The key to institutionalizing power always is to create a device that legitimates one's own authority and diminishes the legitimacy of others. When the "Divine Right of Kings" was envisioned centuries ago it was to provide an unquestionable foundation for the supremacy of royal authority. There is generally a need to root the exercise of authority in some higher power. Modern leaders are no less affected by this need. Richard Nixon, with the aid of John Dean, reified the concept of executive privilege, which meant in effect that what the President wished not to be discussed need not be discussed.

In its simpler form, institutionalization is achieved by designating positions or roles for organizational activities. The creation of a new post legitimizes a function and forces organization members to orient to it. By designating how this new post relates to older, more established posts, moreover, one can structure an organization to enhance the importance of the function in the organization. Equally, one can diminish the importance of traditional functions. This is what happened in the end with the insurance company we mentioned that was having trouble with its coding department. As the situation unfolded, the claims director continued to feel dissatisfied about the dependency of his functions on the coding manager. Thus he instituted a reorganization that resulted in two coding departmemts. In so doing, of course, he placed activities that affected his department under his direct control, presumably to make the operation more effective. Similarly, consumer-product firms enhance the power of marketing by setting up a coordinating role to interface production and marketing functions and then appoint a marketing manager to fill the role.

The structures created by dominant powers sooner or later become fixed and unquestioned features of the organization. Eventually, this can be devastating. It is said that the battle of Jena in 1806 was lost by Frederick the Great, who died in 1786. Though the great Prussian leader had no direct hand in the disaster, his imprint on the army was so thorough, so embedded in its skeletal underpinnings, that the organization was inappropriate for others to lead in different times.

Another important source of institutionalized power lies in the ability to structure information systems. Setting up committees to investigate particular organizational issues and having them report only to particular individuals or groups, facilitates their awareness of problems by members of those groups while limiting the awareness of problems by the members of other groups. Obviously, those who have information are in a better position to interpret the problems of an organization, regardless of how realistically they may, in fact, do so.

Still another way to institutionalize power is to distribute rewards and resources. The dominant group may quiet competing interest groups with small favors and rewards. The credit for this artful form of co-optation belongs to Louis XIV. To avoid usurpation of his power by the nobles of France and the Fronde that had so troubled his father's reign, he built the palace at Versailles to occupy them with hunting and gossip. Awed, the courtiers basked in the reflected glories of the "Sun King" and the overwhelming setting he had created for his court.

At this point, we have not systematically studied the institutionalization of power. But we suspect it is an important condition that mediates between the environment of the organization and the capabilities of the organization for dealing with that environment. The more institutionalized power is within an organization, the more likely an organization will be out of phase with the realities it faces. President Richard Nixon's structuring of his White House is one of the better documented illustrations. If we go back to newspaper and magazine descriptions of how he organized his office from the beginning in 1968, most of what occurred subsequently follows almost as an afterthought. Decisions flowed through virtually only the small White House staff; rewards, small presidential favors of recognition, and perquisites were distributed by this staff to the loyal; and information from the outside world—the press, Congress, the people on the streets—was filtered by the staff and passed along only if initialed "bh." Thus it was not surprising that when Nixon met war protestors in the early dawn, the only thing he could think to talk about was the latest football game, so insulated had he become from their grief and anger.

One of the more interesting implications of institutionalized power is that executive turnover among the executives who have structured the organizations is likely to be a rare event that occurs only under the most pressing crisis. If a dominant coalition is able to structure the organization and interpret the meaning of ambiguous events like declining sales and profits or lawsuits, then the "real" problems to emerge will easily be incorporated into traditional molds of thinking and acting. If opposition is designed out of the organization, the interpretations will go unquestioned. Conditions will remain stable until a crisis develops, so overwhelming and visible that even the most adroit rhetorician would be silenced.

IMPLICATIONS FOR THE MANAGEMENT OF POWER IN ORGANIZATIONS

While we could derive numerous implications from this discussion of power, our selection would have to depend largely on whether one wanted to increase one's power, decrease the power of others, or merely maintain one's position. More important, the real implications depend on the particulars of an organizational situation. To understand power in an organization one must begin by looking outside it— into the environment—for those groups that mediate the organization's outcome but are not themselves within its control.

Instead of ending with homilies, we will end with a reversal of where we began. Power, rather than being the dirty business it is often made out to be, is probably one of the few mechanisms for reality testing in organizations. And the cleaner forms of power, the institutional forms, rather than having the virtues they are often credited with, can lead the organization to become out of touch. The real trick to managing power in organizations is to ensure some-how that leaders cannot be unaware of the realities of their environments and cannot avoid changing to deal with those realities. That, however, would be like designing the "self-liquidating organization," an un-likely event since anyone capable of designing such an instrument would be obviously in control of the liquidations.

Management would do well to devote more attention to determining the critical contingencies of their environments. For if you conclude, as we do, that the environment sets most of the structure influencing organizational outcomes and problems, and that power derives from the organization's activ-ities that deal with those contingencies, then it is the environment that needs managing, not power. The first step is to construct an accurate model of the environment, a process that is quite difficult for most organizations. We have recently started a project to aid administrators in systematically understanding their environments. From this experience, we have learned that the most critical blockage to perceiving an organization's reality accurately is a failure to incorporate those with the relevant expertise into the process. Most organizations have the requisite ex-perts on hand but they are positioned so that they can be comfortably ignored.

One conclusion you can, and probably should, derive from our discussion is that power—because of the way it develops and the way it is used—will always result in the organization suboptimizing its performance. However, to this grim absolute, we add a comforting caveat: If any criteria other than power were the basis for determining an organization's decisions, the results would be even worse.

Exercise: Dependency Situations

PURPOSE

The purpose of this exercise is to help you understand how you cope with being dependent. By the time you complete this exercise you will be able to:

1. Diagnose your empowerment strategy profile.

2. Understand a set of conditions that cause managers to be rendered powerless on the job.

3. Develop an action plan designed to help you recognize and deal with dependency situations at work.

INTRODUCTION

As discussed in the article by Kotter on "Power, Dependence, and Effective Management," managers frequently are dependent upon a variety of individuals in their jobs. How they cope with such situations may make the difference between effective and ineffective management practices. Recognizing the sources of dependency and understanding the strategies that are available to you in coping with those sources of dependency in your job are important first steps.

This exercise provides you with an opportunity to determine how you would react to several hypothetical situations in which you are dependent. Once you identify those strategies that you commonly use, you will be asked to reflect upon actual dependency situations that affect your job, and to develop an action plan for dealing with such situations.

INSTRUCTIONS

Part I

1. Complete the questionnaire on dependency situations as directed by your instructor.

2. Score your results to determine your typical empowerment strategy profile.

3. Read the enclosed reading insert, "Empowerment Strategies and Dependency Situations."

4. Participate in a classroom tabulation of the class results (if directed to do so by your instructor).

This exercise was developed from the ideas in the article by Lisa A. Mainiero, "Coping with Powerlessness: The Relationship of Gender and Job Dependency to Empowerment Strategy Usage," *Administrative Science Quarterly,* December 1986, Vol. 31(4), 633-653.

Part II

1. Reflect upon a recent situation in which you found yourself dependent on someone (a co-worker, teacher, boss, roommate, or someone). On the enclosed worksheet, briefly describe the situation and the strategies used.

2. Answer the questions that apply to Part II on the Empowerment Strategy Profile. Then determine an action plan to help you meet your goals.

3. In a group, share your experiences with others. You may want to reflect upon your questionnaire score to determine whether or not your questionnaire results are consistent with how you behaved in actual situations.

4. Participate in a class discussion.

PART I: THE DEPENDENCY SITUATION QUESTIONNAIRE

Directions: The following cases represent problematic situations that require employees to be dependent on others for information, resources, or support. Please read each case carefully and indicate which strategies you might employ if you were faced with the situation described.

Rank the strategies described below. Indicate a (1) for the strategy you would use first, a (2) for the strategy you would use second, a (3) for the strategy you would use third in the situation, and so on until you reach (6), the last strategy you would attempt. If you would *never* attempt a particular strategy in the hypothetical situation described, leave a blank space to indicate your lack of usage of that strategy. Please read each description carefully before you complete your rankings.

Situation #1. You have been serving in your present job for over three years, and you have recently decided that it is time for a change. A position in another department, for which you are qualified, has become available, and you would very much like to take the position. The new job would provide you with additional visibility and recognition, since you would have the chance to work on a "hot" new project. Last week you went to your boss to discuss the possibility of a transfer, but your boss seemed unwilling to let you move at the present time. It is true that you are currently working on a project that needs your special expertise, but it could be handled in a short period (if you did some overtime). The other department needs to fill the position quickly, and the manager of the department would very much like to hire you for the job. You are dependent on your boss to release you from your present position; you need the support of your boss.

If you were in this situation, what would you do? How would you handle the situation?

a. _____ Ask the manager of the new department to discuss the situation with your boss on your behalf.

b. _____ Discuss the situation with your boss, explaining your reasons for wanting the job transfer.

c. _____ Try to do your boss a favor by putting in a few weeks overtime on the special project so you could ask for your release a second time.

d. _____ Find another way to obtain the transfer by bypassing bureaucratic channels and asking higher-ups to grant your release.

e. _____ Put pressure on your boss by threatening to leave the company unless he or she supports your transfer.

f. _____ Accept the situation, decide that it is not the right time, wait for the next opportunity and hope for the best.

Situation #2. You have been working on a project for a few months that requires you to interact with members of another department to gain the information that you need. In particular, you need information from a peer in the other department who has the necessary expertise to help you solve some of the problems on the project. This individual has a tendency to put off your requests for information because he/she has a great deal of work of his/her own to accomplish. You are dependent on this individual because he/she is the only person who has the necessary information readily available to help you do your work. A deadline for your project is approaching fast, and you really need your colleague to give you some critical information in the next few days.

If you were involved in this situation, what would you do? How would you handle the situation?

a. _____ Put pressure on this individual by threatening to go to his/her boss if help is not forthcoming.

b. _____ Try to do this individual a favor early in the week so that he/she will be more willing to do the work you need when you ask him/her later in the week.

c. _____ Discuss the situation with this individual, letting him/her know how important the information is to you and the fast-approaching deadline.

d. _____ Try to find another individual in the same department who may be able to provide some of the information.

e. _____ Accept the situation, wait for the next opportunity, face up to the situation with your boss, and hope for the best.

f. _____ Ask your peers in the department to support your cause by discussing your situation with this individual at the next opportunity.

Situation #3. Your boss has just been handed the assignment of heading up a task force on a coveted project, and you want very much to become a member of the task force. Your boss will be making selections of candidates for the task force shortly, and you very much would like to get on the list. It is a project in which you have a great deal of interest, and your background and qualifications show that you have expertise that may be helpful in assessing the project. You are dependent on your boss to get on the task force, for your boss is the only person who will be making the selection decisions.

If you were involved in this situation, what would you do? How would you handle the situation?

a. _____ Discuss your desire to become a member of the task force with your boss, highlighting your qualifications and interest.

b. _____ Do your boss a favor by finishing some extra work ahead of time to put you in the right position to discuss the task force assignment.

c. _____ Put pressure on your boss by threatening to leave the company if you can't get on the task force.

d. _____ Ask another manager who has been supporting your career to suport your cause in a meeting with your boss.

e. _____ Find another way to get on the task force by accessing valuable information the task force members will need. This way, regardless of whether or not you are selected, they will need you to be part of the task force.

f. _____ Accept the situation, wait it out, and hope for the best.

Situation #4. To complete a special project, you need to use a piece of equipment in another department. Your manager had told you that you have permission to use the equipment at any time, but every time you try to use the equipment, someone else is on the machine. You are dependent upon your peers in the other department to let you use the machine, for you are not a direct member of their group. A deadline is fast approaching, and your career hinges on meeting that deadline.

If you were involved in this situation, what strategy would you use? How would you handle the situation?

a. _____ Discuss the situation with your peers, explaining why you must use the equipment in short order.

b. _____ Put pressure on your peers by threatening to go to their boss.

c. _____ Find another way to use the equipment by working overtime and using it at night and in the early morning hours.

d. _____ Accept the situation, wait it out, and hope for the best.

e. _____ Do your peers a favor by helping them with something they need; then ask them to help you.

f. _____ Ask your boss to talk to the manager of the department to ensure that you have sufficient time to use the equipment.

Situation #5. You are a manager of a group of production workers, and your boss has just given you a deadline that must be met by the end of the month. Lately, a subset of your group of subordinates has been working more slowly than usual, and they are taking longer coffee breaks and lunches. You have not mentioned anything to them about this issue, because they are generally a good group of workers characterized by a strong sense of camaraderie and friendship. However, you are dependent upon them to work steadily until the end of the month in order to meet the deadline set by your boss. You feel this may be a test set by your boss to determine whether or not you should be promoted to the next level.

If you were involved in this situation, what would you do? How would you handle the situation?

a. _____ Discuss the deadline with your total group of subordinates, highlighting its importance and necessity.

b. _____ Ask some of your other subordinates (not members of the problematic group) to do some voluntary overtime work.

c. _____ Put pressure on your problematic group of subordinates by threatening that, if they don't shape up, there will be some repercussions by the end of the month.

d. _____ Ask your other subordinates to outline your need to make the deadline to the problematic group.

e. _____ Do your problematic group of subordinates a favor by saying that you won't report their recent behavior if they will work to capacity until the end of the month.

f. _____ Accept the situation, decide you don't want to rock the boat, and hope for the best.

Situation #6. You are the manager of a staff engineering group involved in several active projects. A conflict in your schedule for next week requires you to be in New York for a meeting, and you also are scheduled to meet with another client in Boston at the same time. Neither meeting can be rescheduled to a different day, and your boss has requested your participation at the Boston meeting. The only subordinate who is capable of representing you at the New York meeting has been traveling a lot lately and does not want to go. You are dependent upon her to represent you since she is the only one with the expertise from your group to serve the New York customer.

If you were involved in this situation, how would you handle the situation? What would you do?

a. _____ Discuss with your subordinate your need to have her represent you at the New York meeting.

b. _____ Do your subordinate a favor by giving her a few days off to compensate her upon returning.

c. _____ Fine another less qualified subordinate from your group to attend the New York meeting.

d. _____ Ask other subordinates in your group to impress upon her how important it is that she attend the New York meeting regardless of her concerns.

e. _____ Put pressure on your subordinate by saying that if she doesn't attend the meeting, there will be repercussions later.

f. _____ Accept the situation, talk to your boss about the meeting conflicts, and hope for the best.

Empowerment Strategies and Dependency Situations

Contrary to popular opinion, managers are frequently dependent on a variety of sources to accomplish their tasks and manage their careers. And, as indicated in the reading by Kotter on "Power, Dependency, and Organizational Effectiveness," how managers cope with such dependency relationships may have an enormous effect on their careers. Managers frequently find themselves dependent upon their bosses for career support, dependent upon subordinates to get their job tasks done on time, and dependent upon peers to provide the information or resources that is needed. The problem is, when you are dependent on someone else, that individual has power over you. Power has little to do with formal line authority. Instead, research suggests it has everything to do with the dependency of others derived from that formal line authority.

Dependency creates a power imbalance. When managers find themselves dependent, they are rendered vulnerable and powerless. Under such conditions, it is necessary to employ empowerment strategies to restore the balance of power. By taking action to empower themselves, managers are able to gain control over the situation once more. In this way, they are able to be effective and productive in their jobs.

Which strategies, therefore, might an individual employ to restore the balance of power when dependent? There are a multitude of available strategies. The use of particular strategies will depend on the situation at hand and the choices made by the manager.

For the purposes of this exercise, six typical strategies have been chosen:

1. *Assertion:* Describing the reasons for being dependent and requesting help from the high-power target.

2. *Ingratiation:* Offering concessions or favors to the high-power target to achieve what is desired.

3. *Alternatives:* Searching for an alternative person or route to obtain what is needed.

4. *Coalition Formation:* Joining with at least one other individual or set of individuals to put pressure on the target to achieve the goal.

5. *Coercion:* Using threats to put pressure on the high-power target.

6. *Acquiescence:* Accepting the situation and giving into the demands of the high-power target.

The types of strategies you use may be influenced by the target of the situation. Kipnis, Schmidt, Swaffin-Smith, and Wilkinson (1984)

argue that the exercise of influence is a fundamental activity for all managers, and they have researched the pattern of responses that managers use with superiors and subordinates. They found that managers they used:

- ☐ Reasoning/assertive tactics first.
- ☐ Then coalition formation.
- ☐ Friendly/ingratiation.
- ☐ Bargaining/alternatives.
- ☐ Further assertive tactics.
- ☐ Appeals to higher authorities.

For subordinates:

- ☐ Reasoning and assertive tactics first.
- ☐ Then friendliness/ingratiation.
- ☐ Coalition formation.
- ☐ Bargaining/alternatives.
- ☐ Appeals to higher authorities.
- ☐ Finally coercion/sanctions.[1]

Kipnis, Schmidt, Swaffin-Smith, and Wilkinson (1984) further identified three categories of managers based on their study of influence attempts:

☐ "Shotgun" managers were high on the use of all six influence strategies across the board.

☐ "Tactician" managers were high on the use of reason/assertion more so than the other strategies.

☐ "Bystander" managers were low on the use of influence strategies across the board.

Managers categorized as tacticians were found to be the highest on organizational power, were most successful in achieving their own objectives, and most satisfied in their jobs.

Shotgun mangers generally were inexperienced on the job; bystander managers were the most dissatisfied.

Which of the strategies best describes your actions and responses? What is your empowerment strategy profile?

---

[1]The titles Kipnis, et al. (1984) use in their research are slightly different from the titles of the strategies used in this exercise. For this reason the (/) slash bar is used in the insert to describe conceptually similar strategies between the terms used in the exercise versus those employed in the research study. For further clarification, see Kipnis, et al., "Patterns of Managerial Influence: Shotgun Managers, Tacticians, and Bystanders," *Organizational Dynamics*, Winter 1984, 58-67.

SCORING KEY

Part I: Primary Strategy Style

Directions: Write in your rankings for each case. Total the number of points per strategy. Your *lowest* score is your primary strategy style.

Assertion	Ingratiation	Alternatives
Case 1. b _____	1. c _____	1. d _____
Case 2. c _____	2. b _____	2. d _____
Case 3. a _____	3. b _____	3. e _____
Case 4. a _____	4. e _____	4. c _____
Case 5. a _____	5. e _____	5. b _____
Case 6. a _____	6. b _____	6. c _____
Totals _____	_____	_____
_____	_____	_____

Coalition Formation	Coercion	Acquiescence
Case 1. a _____	1. e _____	1. f _____
Case 2. f _____	2. a _____	2. e _____
Case 3. d _____	3. c _____	3. f _____
Case 4. f _____	4. b _____	4. d _____
Case 5. d _____	5. c _____	5. f _____
Case 6. d _____	6. e _____	6. f _____
Totals _____	_____	_____
_____	_____	_____

Primary strategy style (lowest score) = _____

EMPOWERMENT STRATEGY PROFILE

Directions:

I. Identify your empowerment strategy pattern:

Most commonly used strategy: _____

Second most commonly used strategy: _____

Third most commonly used strategy: _____

II. Determine the sequence of strategy usage across time for the six hypothetical dependency situations. How do your responses differ depending upon the target (boss, subordinate, or peer) of the situation?

Strategy Diagram Directions:

Diagram your strategies over time on the graph below. For each situation, which strategy did you use first, second, and third? To graphically display your results, use a single line (_____) for situations 1 and 3 (superior target), a dotted line (. . . . . .) for situations 2 and 4 (peer target), and a dashed line (————) for situations 5 and 6 (subordinate target).

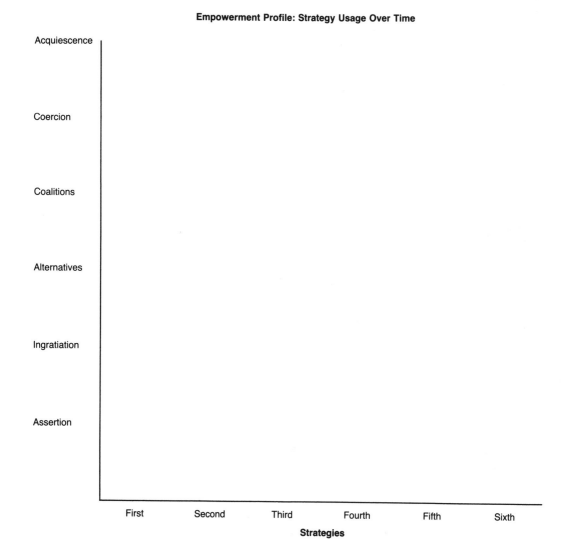

Empowerment Profile: Strategy Usage Over Time

PART II: ACTUAL DEPENDENCY SITUATIONS

Directions:

I. Reflect upon two recent situations in which you found yourself dependent. Using the worksheets on the following two pages, describe each of these situations, including the target of the situation (whether a boss, subordinate, or peer), and the actions you took in the situation to overcome your dependency on that individual.

II. What are the implications of your profile? How do you behave in actual dependency situations?

a. Are you a Tactician, employing primarily assertive strategies; a Shotgun Manager, using a multitude of strategies; or a Bystander, low on influence attempts in general?

b. How does your strategy profile differ depending upon the target of the situation (superior/boss, subordinate, peer/colleague)?

c. Which strategies did you *omit* using in the situation? Are there other strategies that you could be using (but have chosen not to) in your relationships with superiors, subordinates, and peers upon whom you are dependent?

DEPENDENCY SITUATION WORKSHEET

Summary of the Situation: _____

_____

_____

_____

_____

_____

_____

_____

_____

_____

_____

_____

_____

_____

_____

_____

_____

_____

_____

_____

Primary Target in the Situation
(Superior, Subordinate, or Peer): _____

Actions Taken in the Situation: _____

_____

_____

_____

_____

_____

_____

_____

DEPENDENCY SITUATION WORKSHEET

Summary of the Situation: _____

_____

_____

_____

_____

_____

_____

_____

_____

_____

_____

_____

_____

_____

_____

_____

_____

_____

_____

_____

Primary Target in the Situation
(Superior, Subordinate, or Peer): _____

Actions Taken in the Situation: _____

_____

_____

_____

_____

_____

_____

_____

III. Develop an action plan that describes how you will handle future dependency situations at work. Identify two dependency situations that you anticipate will cause you to employ empowerment strategies in the future, and focus your action plan on dealing with these situations.

DEPENDENCY SITUATION ACTION PLAN

Anticipated Situation	Target of the Situation	Recommended Actions	Estimated Probability of Success	Contingency Plan
Situation #1: _____ _____ _____ _____	Circle one: Boss Peer Subordinate	First Choice Strategy— _____ _____ Second Choice Strategy— _____ Third Choice Strategy— _____	_____ _____ _____ _____ _____	_____ _____ _____ _____ _____ _____ _____
Situation #2: _____ _____ _____ _____	Circle one: Boss Peer Subordinate	First Choice Strategy— _____ _____ Second Choice Strategy— _____ Third Choice Strategy— _____	_____ _____ _____ _____	_____ _____ _____ _____ _____

DEPENDENCY SITUATION DECISION TREE

Diagnosis of the Situation

Strategy Usage Over Time

Who am I dependent upon in this situation?

—Superior

—Peer

—Subordinate

For what reason am I dependent?
—Task Reasons
—Career Reasons

Which strategies would I feel most comfortable using *first* in this situation?

assertion
ingratiation
alternatives
coalition formation
coercion
acquiescence

Which strategies would I feel most comfortable using *second* in this situation?

assertion
ingratiation
alternatives
coalition formation
coercion
acquiescence

Which strategies would I feel most comfortable using *third* in this situation?

assertion
ingratiation
alternatives
coalition formation
coercion
acquiescence

For what reason am I dependent?
—Task Reasons
—Career Reasons

Which strategies would I feel most comfortable using *first* in this situation?

assertion
ingratiation
alternatives
coalition formation
coercion
acquiescence

Which strategies would I feel most comfortable using *second* in this situation?

assertion
ingratiation
alternatives
coalition formation
coercion
acquiescence

Which strategies would I feel most comfortable using *third* in this situation?

assertion
ingratiation
alternatives
coalition formation
coercion
acquiescence

For what reason am I dependent?
—Task Reasons
—Career Reasons

Which strategies would I feel most comfortable using *first* in this situation?

assertion
ingratiation
alternatives
coalition formation
coercion
acquiescence

Which strategies would I feel most comfortable using *second* in this situation?

assertion
ingratiation
alternatives
coalition formation
coercion
acquiescence

Which strategies would I feel most comfortable using *third* in this situation?

assertion
ingratiation
alternatives
coalition formation
coercion
acquiescence

1. What is your empowerment strategy profile? To what extent did your questionnaire results model your actions in "real life"?

2. Which strategies were more commonly used for superior relationships? Peer relationships? Subordinates? What does this say about the use of formal authority (or lack thereof) and the kinds of strategies you must employ in your work relationships?

3. Under what conditions are stronger, more definitive strategies preferable?

Exercise: Power Failures

PURPOSE

The purpose of this exercise is to sensitize you to the consequences of structural powerlessness. By the time you finish this exercise, you will:

1. Understand the conditions that cause structural powerlessness.

2. Learn why powerless job situations have a negative impact on management practice.

3. Identify strategies for overcoming powerlessness in the context of three organizational situations.

INTRODUCTION

In her article, "Power Failures in Management Circuits," Rosabeth Moss Kanter argues that much of what is labeled poor management is simply the result of insufficient power. Power, as she defines it, is the ability to get things done. Without sufficient power, individuals are rendered ineffective in their jobs because they are unable to gather the resources, information, support, or supplies to accomplish their job task. Those who are powerless are caught in a downward spiral, constantly seeking whatever "crumbs" of information, resources, or support they can find.

One reaction to this type of situation is the practice of authoritarian or territorial management styles, designed to retain whatever little power or

The three role play scenarios in this exercise are from *Developing Management Skills* by David Whetten and Kim Cameron. Copyright © 1984 by Scott, Foresman and Company. Reprinted by permission. The original idea for this exercise is derived from Rosabeth M. Kanter's article, "Power Failures in Management Circuits," *Harvard Business Review*, 1979, 57(4).

authority that can be exercised. As Kanter says, "Absolute power corrupts, but powerlessness corrupts absolutely." Instead of criticizing such managers as incompetent, Kanter argues that we should empower these individuals so that they can truly "get things done."

However, it can be very difficult to encourage those in power to give up some of their power and *share* it rather than protect it in a turf-minded, territorial manner. By empowering others, greater sharing of resources, information, sources of supply, and support can take place, helping all to be optimally effective in their jobs. When power is shared, organizations can become much more productive.

In this exercise, you will have the opportunity to experience two different roles: a) a manager in a structurally powerless position, and b) a consultant who must provide suggestions and recommendations to the powerless manager.

INSTRUCTIONS

1. Read the article by Rosabeth Kanter, "Power Failures in Management Circuits" prior to participating in this exercise.

2. Choose a partner with whom you will work during this exercise.

3. Read the three scenarios on the following pages and, with your partner, select the two that you will use for the role plays.

4. Decide who will play the consultant for the first situation you have chosen.

5. If you are in the consultant role, take ten minutes to identify possible strategies that the manager in the scenario you selected could use to increase his or her power and influence in the organization. (Use the chart on powerless vs. powerful jobs in the Kanter reading for additional information.)

6. If you are in the manager role, take this time to think about how you would feel in the situation described. How would you react? How will you respond to the consultant?

7. Participate in the role play. Feel free to embellish on the information provided.

8. When the first situation is completed, switch roles (the consultant in the first role play will now play the manager and the manager will play the consultant).

9. Complete steps 5 through 7 for the second scenario you have chosen.

10. Participate in a class discussion.

Power Failure Scenarios

Situation 1: *First Line Supervisor*

Judy Butler had been a first line supervisor for six months. She had thought her new position was a promotion, but she found instead that it made her feel completely powerless. She felt at a dead end in her career, and she didn't see any way to get promoted out of the job. She was not in a central part of the organization, and she felt that no one ever noticed her unless she messed up. She was expected to be supportive of her subordinates, but they never returned the favor. She was expected to absorb the flack without any recognition. Her job was extremely rule-bound, so she had little discretion in what she did or how she did it. She didn't control the pay or benefits of her subordinates, so she felt powerless to reward or punish them in ways that really mattered.

As a result, she found she was more and more apt to impose rules to get subordinates to do what she wanted. She became more and more jealous of any successes and recognition achieved by her subordinates, so she tended to isolate them from people higher up in the organization and from complete information. She lost her penchant for informality and became fairly rigid in following standard operating procedures. Unfortunately, her subordinates were becoming more resentful and less productive.

Situation 2: Staff Professional

Jake Butler had come to the organization a year ago as a staff professional. He had thought it might be a way for him to achieve a lot of visibility with the top brass, but instead he found that he felt completely powerless. As a staff officer, he had almost no decision making authority except in his narrow area of expertise. Most of what went on in the organization occurred without his involvement. Innovation and entrepreneurial activity were completely out of his realm. While some of the line officers were given opportunities for professional development, no one seemed to care about his becoming more experienced and capable. They only saw him as a specialist. Because his job didn't require that he work with others, he had little opportunity to cultivate relationships that might lead to contacts with someone near the top.

What hurt was that a consultant had been hired a few times to work on projects that were part of his area. In consultants could be brought in to do his work, he thought he must not be very indispensable to the organization.

Jake found himself being more and more turf-conscious. He didn't want others encroaching on his area of expertise. He tried to demonstrate his competence to others, but the more he did so, the more he became defined as a specialist, outside the mainstream of the organization. He felt that he was losing ground in his professional career, rather than gaining ground.

Situation 3: Top Executive

Jodie Butler had been a top executive for three years now. When she had been given the position, she had felt that her ultimate career goal had been achieved. Now she was not so sure. She had begun to sense her power-lessness. For example, the job had so many demands and details associated with it that she never had time to engage in any long-term planning. There always seemed to be one more crisis that demanded her attention.

Unfortunately, most of them were from sources she couldn't control—government regulations, stockholder's demands, union relationships, equal opportunity statutes, and so on. She had built her reputation as a successful manager on being entrepreneurial, creative, and non-routine, but none of those qualities were desirable in this job. Furthermore, because she was so mired in operations, she had become more and more out of touch with the information flows in the organization. Some things had to remain confidential with her, but her secrecy led to others being unwilling to share information with her. She had assistants who were supposed to be monitoring the organization and providing her with information, but she often felt they only told her what she wanted to hear.

Jodie had begun to hear rumors about certain special interest groups' demanding her removal from the top job. She responded by becoming more dictatorial and defensive, with the result that the organization was becoming more control oriented and conservative. She felt she was on a downward spiral, but she couldn't find a way to reverse the trend.

DISCUSSION QUESTIONS

1. How realistic were the strategies that the consultant recommended in each scenario? Could these strategies really be used in actual organizational situations?

2. Why is it so difficult to empower yourself once you have been placed in a position of structural powerlessness?

3. How should organizations be designed so that power can be shared rather than protected in the context of "fiefdoms" of authoritarianism throughout the organization?

4. What policies should companies adopt to facilitate power-sharing? How might this change the culture of most organizations? To what extent is this realistic?

Exercise: Power Lab

PURPOSE

The purpose of this exercise is to help you understand groups within organizations power dynamics that occur among authority. By the time you finish this exercise you will:

This exercise is adapted from a version entitled, "A Simple But Powerful Simulation" that appeared in Dorthea Hai's book, *Organizational Behavior: Experiences and Cases* (New York: West Publishers, 1986). This exercise originally appeared in an article by Lee Bolman and Terence Deal in *Exchange*, Vol. 4(3), 38-42. Teaching notes have also been adapted from these sources. All have been used with permission of the publishers.

1. Experience intergroup power dynamics firsthand.

2. Understand the intersection of resource allocation decisions and power dynamics across departments and groups with an organization.

3. Explore different perspectives on power and authority.

INTRODUCTION

As discussed in the Salancik and Pfeffer article, power can have a significant effect on organizational functioning. Those in power can alter the resource allocations to remain in power, while those who lack power remain powerless. Upper management holds the most power by virtue of the authority present in their management positions. Those at the lower levels must fight for recognition and resources, and those at the middle management level often are caught between both groups.

In this exercise, you will participate in a three-tiered intergroup simulation that is designed to simulate the power dynamics among these three groups. Some of you will experience what it is like to be Tops, controlling the resources of the organization. Others will serve as Bottoms, serving the most menial tasks of the organization. Still others will experience a liaison role as Middles, negotiating between both groups.

INSTRUCTIONS

1. Prior to this exercise, read the article by Salancik and Pfeffer, "Who Gets Power and How They Hold onto It: A Strategic-Contingency Model of Power."

2. Your instructor will ask you to bring a one dollar bill to class for the purpose of this exercise. Turn in your one dollar bill to the instructor upon entering the class.

3. At the start of class, you will be assigned to serve as a participant in one of the three groups: Tops, Middles, and Bottoms. Read the *Power Lab Description and Rules* that follow.

4. Begin the simulation. Complete the tasks that you are assigned.

5. Participate in a class discussion. Your instructor will request that you elect a representative from your group to speak for your group about your feelings and attitudes throughout the exercise.

6. Summary and wrap-up.

POWER LAB DESCRIPTION AND RULES

In this simulation, there are three groups with the following responsibilities:

1. *The Top Group:* Responsible for the overall effectiveness and learning from the simulation, as well as for determining resource allocation decisions.

2. *The Middle Group:* Responsible for assisting the Tops in providing for the overall welfare of the organization, and for serving as a liaison between the Tops and Middles.

3. *The Bottom Group:* Responsible for the identification of the organization's resources, and for producing the goods and services for the organization.

The rules for the simulation are as follows:

1. The Bottoms will produce the goods for the organization, namely the construction of rectangular buildings out of index cards, staples, and tape as provided by your instructor.

2. The Middles will supervise the construction of the rectangular buildings.

3. The Tops will determine the design of the buildings and are free to reject any buildings they deem unfit for sale.

4. The Tops retain all the money. They may determine what portion can be doled out to the Middles for the procurement of additional supplies and resources, and the Bottoms as payment for their labor.

5. Members of the Top Group are free to enter the space of either of the other groups and to communicate whatever they wish, whenever they wish. Members of the Middle Group may enter the space of the lower group whenever they wish but must request permission to enter the Top Group's space (a request the Top Group may refuse). Members of the Bottom Group may not disturb the Top Group in any way unless specifically invited by the Tops to do so. The Bottom Group does have the right to knock on the door of the Middle Group and reqest permision to communicate with them (though that permission may be refused).

6. The Bottoms must remain in their assigned space unless told to do otherwise.

DISCUSSION QUESTIONS

1. How did you feel as a member of your particular group? How would you expect the members of the other groups to feel during the simulation?

2. Did your feelings grow stronger or weaker throughout the simulation?

3. Were you satisfied with the amount of power you were allocated?

4. Did you attempt to exercise or gain more power (or reduce and share your power) during the exercise?

5. What parallels can be drawn between this exercise and real-life organizational situations?

REFERENCES

Oshry, Barry. *Power and Position.* Boston: Power Systems, 1979.

Memo: Power and Politics

Think about your current job—or a job you have held in the past. Analyze the relative structural power of that job using the following questions as a guide:

1. To what extent are you dependent on others for the information and support necessary to perform the tasks associated with your job?

2. On whom are you dependent for this information and support?

3. How dependent are you on each source of information and support?

4. How dependent are others on you for the information and support necessary to perform the tasks associated with their jobs?

5. Relative to other jobs within your department, how important is your job?

6. How aware is upper management of the work that you do in your job?

7. To what extent is the way you perform your job limited by company policies and procedures?

8. To what extent does your job allow you to exercise your own initiative in carrying out your assignments?

9. How critical is your department's work to the success of your organization?

10. Which departments in your organization have the most people and/or the largest budgets?

11. Is your department one of them?

12. How important does upper management consider the work of your department?

Based on this analysis:

1. Determine the structural power of your job.

2. Identify the aspects of your job that provide the lines of support and information that contribute to your ability to exercise power in your job.

3. Identify the aspects of your job that interfere with the lines of support and information that would help you exercise greater power in your job.

4. Develop a strategy for increasing the structural power of your job.

CHAPTER SIX

Group and Intergroup Behavior

INTRODUCTION

"Why do we have to study groups?" "What do groups have to do with management practice?" "Groups are such a pain!" These are some of the common reactions of management students to this subject. However, groups are one of the most important subjects for managers to study because many managerial activities take place in group settings—in task force meetings, in developing a team of subordinates, in group presentations, and in meetings of peers. Thus an understanding of group dynamics can help managers become more effective performers.

Group decision making is an increasingly popular practice in corporate settings. However, many managers find working in groups to be a frustrating experience. This negative reaction to groups is the result of diverse factors. For example, groups take longer than individuals to make decisions. Groups can also fall prey to negative interpersonal dynamics and destructive conflict that distort the decision-making process. Further, groups sometimes go off on a tangent and are unable to make realistic and effective decisions.

However, group decision making need not be a negative experience. When effectively managed, groups can make higher-quality decisions that are more widely accepted. The challenge for managers is to understand the dynamics that contribute to effective group decision making.

Managers should also understand intergroup, or between-group, behavior— that is, the dynamics occurring between two or more groups when they interact. Because groups or departments within organizations often pursue different goals, engage in different activities, enjoy different status and covet the same resources, intergroup behavior is commonly characterized by conflict. This conflict can have either positive or negative effects for the organization and the group.

On the positive side, intergroup conflict can result in increased motivation through competition which may have some positive outcomes for the organization. As a result, managers have sometimes encouraged groups to maintain their competitive stance. Sometimes this works to the benefit of the organization; sometimes it does not. When competition escalates into destructive conflict, "winning" becomes more important than reaching the organization's goals and any performance gains for the organization are lost.

Intergroup conflict also affects within-group behavior. This too can have both positive and negative consequences. It *binds* the members of each group together, which may result in increased motivation, but it *blinds* each group to the realities of its own and the other group's performance. Thus it creates a distortion of reality such that what "we" do is judged much more positively than what "they" do. In its most extreme form, "they" become the symbol for everything that is wrong or bad and "we" become the image of everything that is right or good.

Learning how to recognize the conditions that contribute to intergroup conflict and developing skills to deal with such conflict effectively are important ingredients in managerial success. Where there are groups there is usually intergroup conflict. In Chapter Two, Ware and Barnes assert that interpersonal conflict is a fact of organizational life. Intergroup conflict is no less pervasive, and learning effective coping skills no less important.

READINGS

This chapter contains three articles that articulate different aspects of group and intergroup dynamics. The first article, Norman Maier's "Assets and Liabilities in Group Problem Solving," focuses on some of the benefits and problems associated with group decision-making processes. Maier outlines the advantages and disadvantages of group problem-solving methods. For example, one well-known advantage of group decision making is the opportunity to generate more alternatives. An equally well-known disadvantage is pressure for social conformity which can decrease the breadth of alternatives presented. By reading this article, you will be better able to discern the conditions under which a group decision may be warranted versus the conditions under which it should be avoided.

The second article, "Groupthink" by Irving Janis, is considered a classic by many. "Groupthink" is a term that describes a mindset to which some groups fall victim as they make decisions of consequence. Janis uses examples of policy formulation in the Kennedy and Johnson administrations, such as the Bay of Pigs fiasco and the Vietnam war, to illustrate the dynamics and processes of groupthink. When groups believe they are invulnerable, righteous, and inherently moral, they override self-censorship to create an illusion of assumed consensus. When this occurs, groups usually make ineffective decisions. They are unable to complete a thorough survey of alternatives. Often, such groups take risks that are out of proportion to the problems at hand. Groups that fall victim to groupthink take on a life of their own and the quality of their decisions often suffer as a consequence.

In the third reading, "Managing Conflict Among Groups," L. Dave Brown cogently explores the basics of intergroup conflict and argues for the importance of effectively managing it in organizations. He presents the notion that there can be too little or too much conflict, and neither of these situations is optimally effective. He feels that managers should strive for a balance rather than just assuming that conflict is always destructive. He presents practical models for diagnosing symptoms of too much and too little conflict, as well as for intervening based on the diagnosis. Both of these models are broken down by areas of concern: attitudes, behavior, and structure. He also looks at the varieties of intergroup conflict that are typical of organizations: functional differences, power differences, and societal differences, exploring ways of coping effectively with each.

EXERCISES AND CASES

The first exercise in the chapter, "Group Decision Making and Effectiveness," gives you the opportunity to determine the effectiveness of group versus individual decisions. Then you will be asked to reflect upon the decision-making process that occurred in your group. Were the decisions based on consensus or majority rule? How was the disagreement handled? Did the group fall victim to groupthink? These and other issues are the focus of the exercise.

The second exercise, "The NASA/Challenger Incident," asks you to apply groupthink concepts to an analysis of the NASA/Challenger Space Shuttle disaster. Many of us were shocked and surprised when the Rogers Commission issued its report on the Challenger crash. The Rogers Commission, in one of its findings, highlighted ineffective decision-making processes as one of the many causes of the crash. Groupthink may have been a part of the problem. By reading this case, you will have an opportunity to debate the issues and determine whether or not groupthink was at fault.

The final exercise, "Labor Relations and Intergroup Conflict," is an opportunity for you to experience a specific variety of intergroup dynamic—labor negotiations. A labor negotiation is an example of power differences identified by Brown in his article, "Managing Conflict Among Groups." During the exercise you will be a member of a team negotiating a simulated labor contract. This is an occasion for you to explore the problems and opportunities inherent in this type of negotiation.

MEMO

The memo assignment, "Group and Intergroup Behavior," asks you to reflect upon a group of which you are currently a member—a task force, your department, or any intact group. The questions presented in the assignment direct you to analyze the dynamics within your group or department and the relationship between your group and a group with which you interact frequently. After you have completed this analysis you will develop a plan for improvement. By understanding group and intergroup dynamics in a real-life situation, you will be able to apply the concepts and skills from this chapter to improve group effectiveness and to increase the likelihood of working cooperatively with other groups to achieve organizational goals.

By the time you finish this chapter, you will have a greater understanding of group dynamics and decision-making processes. You will also be able to identify and diagnose the intergroup dynamics that may be: (a) affecting the relationship among the departments and groups in your organization and (b) affecting the behavior within your group. In addition, you will learn how to monitor, understand, and intervene to improve decision making practices and intergroup relations.

Assets and Liabilities in Group Problem Solving: The Need for an Integrative Function

Norman R. F. Maier

A number of investigations have raised the question of whether group problem solving is superior, inferior, or equal to individual problem solving. Evidence can be cited in support of each position so that the answer to this question remains ambiguous. Rather than pursue this generalized approach to the question, it seems more fruitful to explore the forces that influence problem solving under the two conditions (see reviews by Hoffman, 1965; Kelley & Thibaut, 1954). It is hoped that a better recognition of these forces will permit clarification of the varied dimensions of the problem solving process, especially in groups.

The forces operating in such groups include some that are assets, some that are liabilities, and some that can be either assets or liabilities, depending upon the skills of the members, especially those of the discussion leader. Let us examine these three sets of forces.

GROUP ASSETS

Greater Sum Total of Knowledge and Information

There is more information in a group than in any of its members. Thus problems that require the utilization of knowledge should give groups an advantage over individuals. Even if one member of the group (e.g., the leader) knows much more than anyone else, the limited unique knowledge of lesser-informed individuals could serve to fill in some gaps in knowledge. For example, a skilled machinist might contribute to an engineer's problem solving and an ordinary workman might supply information on how a new machine might be received by workers.

Greater Number of Approaches to a Problem

It has been shown that individuals get into ruts in their thinking (Duncker, 1945; Maier, 1930; Wertheimer, 1959). Many obstacles stand in the way

of achieving a goal, and a solution must circumvent these. The individual is handicapped in that he tends to persist in his approach and thus fails to find another approach that might solve the problem in a simpler manner. Individuals in a group have the same failing, but the approaches in which they are persisting may be different. For example, one researcher may try to prevent the spread of a disease by making man immune to the germ, another by finding and destroying the carrier of the germ, and still another by altering the environment so as to kill the germ before it reaches man. There is no way of determining which approach will best achieve the desired goal, but undue persistence in any one will stifle new discoveries. Since group members do not have identical approaches, each can contribute by knocking others out of ruts in thinking.

Participation in Problem Solving Increases Acceptance

Many problems require solutions that depend upon the support of others to be effective. Insofar as group problem solving permits participation and influence, it follows that more individuals accept solutions when a group solves the problem than when one person solves it. When one individual solves a problem he still has the task of persuading others. It follows, therefore, that when groups solve such problems, a greater number of persons accept and feel responsible for making the solution work. A low-quality solution that has good acceptance can be more effective than a higher-quality solution that lacks acceptance.

Better Comprehension of the Decision

Decisions made by an individual, which are to be carried out by others, must be communicated from the decision-maker to the decision-executors. Thus individual problem solving often requires an additional stage—that of relaying the decision reached. Failures in this communication process detract from the merits of the decision and can even cause its failure or create a problem of greater magnitude than the initial problem that was solved. Many organizational problems can be traced to inadequate communication of decisions made by superiors and transmitted to sub-

From *Psychological Review*, 1967, Vol. 74 (4), pp. 239–249. Copyright © 1967 by the American Psychological Association. Reprinted by permission of the publisher and author.

ordinates, who have the task of implementing the decision.

The chances for communication failures are greatly reduced when the individuals who must work together in executing the decision have participated in making it. They not only understand the solution because they saw it develop, but they are also aware of the several other alternatives that were considered and the reasons why they were discarded. The common assumption that decisions supplied by superiors are arbitrarily reached therefore disappears. A full knowledge of goals, obstacles, alternatives, and factual information is essential to communication, and this communication is maximized when the total problem-solving process is shared.

GROUP LIABILITIES

Social Pressure

Social pressure is a major force making for conformity. The desire to be a good group member and to be accepted tends to silence disagreement and favors consensus. Majority opinions tend to be accepted regardless of whether or not their objective quality is logically and scientifically sound. Problems requiring solutions based upon facts, regardless of feelings and wishes, can suffer in group problem-solving situations.

It has been shown (Maier & Solem, 1952) that minority opinions in leaderless groups have little influence on the solution reached, even when these opinions are the correct ones. Reaching agreement in a group often is confused with finding the right answer, and it is for this reason that the dimensions of a decision's acceptance and its objective quality must be distinguished (Maier, 1963).

Valence of Solutions

When leaderless groups (made up of three or four persons) engage in problem solving, they propose a variety of solutions. Each solution may receive both critical and supportive comments, as well as descriptive and explorative comments from other participants. If the number of negative and positive comments for each solution are algebraically summed, each may be given a *valence index* (Hoffman & Maier, 1964). The first solution that receives a positive valence value of 15 tends to be adopted to the satisfaction of all participants about 85% of the time, regardless of its quality. Higher quality solutions introduced after the critical value for one of the

solutions has been reached have little chance of achieving real consideration. Once some degree of consensus is reached, the jelling process seems to proceed rather rapidly.

The critical valence value of 15 appears not to be greatly altered by the nature of the problem or the exact size of the group. Rather, it seems to designate a turning point between the idea-getting process and the decision-making process (idea evaluation). A solution's valence index is not a measure of the number of persons supporting the solution, since a vocal minority can build up a solution's valence by actively pushing it. In this sense, valence becomes an influence in addition to social pressure in determining an outcome.

Since a solution's valence is independent of its objective quality, this group factor becomes an important liability in group problem solving, even when the value of a decision depends upon objective criteria (facts and logic). It becomes a means whereby skilled manipulators can have more influence over the group process than their proportion of membership deserves.

Individual Domination

In most leaderless groups a dominant individual emerges and captures more than his share of influence on the outcome. He can achieve this end through a greater degree of participation (valence), persuasive ability, or stubborn persistence (fatiguing the opposition). None of these factors is related to problem-solving ability, so that the best problem solver in the group may not have the influence to upgrade the quality of the group's solution (which he would have had if left to solve the problem by himself).

Hoffman and Maier (1967) found that the mere fact of appointing a leader causes this person to dominate a discussion. Thus, regardless of his problem-solving ability a leader tends to exert a major influence on the outcome of a discussion.

Conflicting Secondary Goal: Winning the Argument

When groups are confronted with a problem, the initial goal is to obtain a solution. However, the appearance of several alternatives causes individuals to have preferences and once these emerge the desire to support a position is created. Converting those with neutral viewpoints and refuting those with opposed viewpoints now enters into the problem-solving process. More and more the goal becomes that of winning the decision rather than finding the best solution. This new goal is unrelated to the quality of the problem's solution and therefore can result in lowering the quality of the decision (Hoffman & Maier, 1966).

FACTORS THAT SERVE AS ASSETS OR LIABILITIES, DEPENDING LARGELY UPON THE SKILL OF THE DISCUSSION LEADER

Disagreement

The fact that discussion may lead to disagreement can serve either to create hard feelings among members or lead to a resolution of conflict and hence to an innovative solution (Hoffman, 1961; Hoffman, Harburg, & Maier, 1962; Hoffman & Maier, 1961; Maier, 1958, 1963; Maier & Hoffman, 1965). The first of these outcomes of disagreement is a liability, especially with regard to the acceptance of solutions; while the second is an asset, particularly where innovation is desired. A leader can treat disagreement as undesirable and thereby reduce the probability of both hard feelings and innovation, or he can maximize disagreement and risk hard feelings in his attempts to achieve innovation. The skill of a leader requires his ability to create a climate for disagreement which will permit innovation without risking hard feelings. The leader's perception of disagreement is one of the critical factors in this skill area (Maier & Hoffman, 1965). Others involve permissiveness (Maier, 1953), delaying the reaching of a solution (Maier & Hoffman, 1960b; Maier & Solem, 1962), techniques for processing information and opinions (Maier, 1963; Maier & Hoffman, 1960a; Maier & Maier, 1957), and techniques for separating idea-getting from idea-evaluation (Maier, 1960, 1963; Osborn, 1953).

Conflicting Interests Versus Mutual Interests

Disagreement in discussion may take many forms. Often participants disagree with one another with regard to solutions, but when issues are explored one finds that these conflicting solutions are designed to solve different problems. Before one can rightly expect agreement on a solution, there should be agreement on the nature of the problem. Even before this, there should be agreement on the goal,

as well as on the various obstacles that prevent the goal from being reached. Once distinctions are made between goals, obstacles, and solutions (which represent ways of overcoming obstacles), one finds increased opportunities for cooperative problem solving and less conflict (Hoffman & Maier, 1959; Maier, 1960, 1963; Maier & Solem, 1962; Solem, 1965).

Often there is also disagreement regarding whether the objective of a solution is to achieve quality or acceptance (Maier & Hoffman, 1964b), and frequently a stated problem reveals a complex of separate problems, each having separate solutions so that a search for a single solution is impossible (Maier, 1963). Communications often are inadequate because the discussion is not synchronized and each person is engaged in discussing a different aspect. Organizing discussion to synchronize the exploration of different aspects of the problem and to follow a systematic procedure increases solution quality (Maier & Hoffman, 1960a; Maier & Maier, 1957). The leadership function of influencing discussion procedure is quite distinct from the function of evaluating or contributing ideas (Maier, 1950, 1953).

When the discussion leader aids in the separation of the several aspects of the problem-solving process and delays the solution-mindedness of the group (Maier, 1958, 1963; Maier & Solem, 1962), both solution quality and acceptance improve; when he hinders or fails to facilitate the isolation of these varied processes, he risks a deterioration in the group process (Solem, 1965). His skill thus determines whether a discussion drifts toward conflicting interests or whether mutual interests are located. Cooperative problem solving can only occur after the mutual interests have been established and it is surprising how often they can be found when the discussion leader makes this his task (Maier, 1952, 1963; Maier & Hayes, 1962).

Risk Taking

Groups are more willing than individuals to reach decisions involving risks (Wallach & Kogan, 1965); Wallach, Kogan, & Bem, 1962). Taking risks is a factor in acceptance of change, but change may either represent a gain or a loss. The best guard against the latter outcome seems to be primarily a matter of a decision's quality. In a group situation this depends upon the leader's skill in utilizing the factors that represent group assets and avoiding those that make for liabilities.

Time Requirements

In general, more time is required for a group to reach a decision than for a single individual to reach one. Insofar as some problems require quick decisions, individual decisions are favored. In other situations acceptance and quality are requirements, but excessive time without sufficient returns also represent a loss. On the other hand, discussion can resolve conflicts, whereas reaching consensus has limited value (Wallach & Kogan, 1965). The practice of hastening a meeting can prevent full discussion, but failure to move a discussion forward can lead to boredom and fatigue-type solutions, in which members agree merely to get out of the meeting. The effective utilization of discussion time (a delicate balance between permissiveness and control on the part of the leader), therefore, is needed to make the time factor an asset rather than a liability. Unskilled leaders tend to be too concerned with reaching a solution and therefore terminate a discussion before the group potential is achieved (Maier & Hoffman, 1960b).

Who Changes

In reaching consensus or agreement, some members of a group must change. Persuasive forces do not operate in individual problem solving in the same way they operate in a group situation; hence, the changing of someone's mind is not an issue. In group situations, however, who changes can be an asset or a liability. If persons with the most constructive views are induced to change the end-product suffers; whereas if persons with the least constructive points of view change the end-product is upgraded. The leader can upgrade the quality of a decision because his position permits him to protect the person with a minority view and increase his opportunity to influence the majority position. This protection is a constructive factor because a minority viewpoint influences only when facts favor it (Maier, 1950, 1952; Maier & Solem, 1952).

The leader also plays a constructive role insofar as he can facilitate communications and thereby reduce misunderstandings (Maier, 1952; Solem, 1965). The leader has an adverse effect on the end-product when he suppresses minority views by holding a contrary position and when he uses his office to promote his own views (Maier & Hoffman, 1960b, 1962; Maier & Solem, 1952). In many problem-solving discussions the untrained leader plays

a dominant role in influencing the outcome, and when he is more resistant to changing his views than are the other participants, the quality of the outcome tends to be lowered. This negative leader-influence was demonstrated by experiments in which untrained leaders were asked to obtain a second solution to a problem after they had obtained their first one (Maier & Hoffman, 1960a). It was found that the second solution tended to be superior to the first. Since the dominant individual had influenced the first solution, he had won his point and therefore ceased to dominate the subsequent discussion which led to the second solution. Acceptance of a solution also increases as the leader sees disagreement as idea-producing rather than as a source of difficulty or trouble (Maier & Hoffman, 1965). Leaders who see some of their participants as trouble-makers obtain fewer innovative solutions and gain less acceptance of decisions made than leaders who see disagreeing members as persons with ideas.

THE LEADER'S ROLE FOR INTEGRATED GROUPS

Two Differing Types of Group Process

In observing group problem solving under various conditions it is rather easy to distinguish between cooperative problem-solving activity and persuasion or selling approaches. Problem-solving activity includes searching, trying out ideas on one another, listening to understand rather than to refute, making relatively short speeches, and reacting to differences in opinion as stimulating. The general pattern is one of rather complete participation, involvement, and interest. Persuasion activity includes the selling of opinions already formed, defending a position held, either not listening at all or listening in order to be able to refute, talking dominated by a few members, unfavorable reactions to disagreement, and a lack of involvement of some members. During problem solving the behavior observed seems to be that of members interacting as segments of a group. The interaction pattern is not between certain individual members, but with the group as a whole. Sometimes it is difficult to determine who should be credited with an idea. "It just developed," is a response often used to describe the solution reached. In contrast, discussions involving selling or persuasive behavior seem to consist of a series of interpersonal interactions with each individual retaining his identity. Such groups do not function as integrated units but as separate individuals, each with an agenda.

In one situation the solution is unknown and is sought; in the other, several solutions exist and conflict occurs because commitments have been made.

The Starfish Analogy

The analysis of these two group processes suggests an analogy with the behavior of the rays of a starfish under two conditions; one with the nerve ring intact, the other with the nerve ring sectioned (Hamilton, 1922; Moore, 1924; Moore & Duodoroff, 1939; Schneirla & Maier, 1940). In the intact condition, locomotion and righting behavior reveal that the behavior of each ray is not merely a function of local stimulation. Locomotion and righting behavior reveal a degree of coordination and interdependence that is centrally controlled. However, when the nerve ring is sectioned, the behavior of one ray still can influence others, but internal coordination is lacking. For example, if one ray is stimulated, it may step forward, thereby exerting pressure on the sides of the other four rays. In response to these external pressures (tactile stimulation), these rays show stepping responses on the stimulated side so that locomotion successfully occurs without the aid of neural coordination. Thus integrated behavior can occur on the basis of external control. If, however, stimulation is applied to opposite rays, the specimen may be "locked" for a time, and in some species the conflicting locomotions may divide the animal, thus destroying it (Crozier, 1920; Moore & Duodoroff, 1939).

Each of the rays of the starfish can show stepping responses even when sectioned and removed from the animal. Thus each may be regarded as an individual. In a starfish with a sectioned nerve ring the five rays become members of a group. They can successfully work together for locomotion purposes by being controlled by the dominant ray. Thus if uniformity of action is desired, the group of five rays can sometimes be more effective than the individual ray in moving the group toward a source of stimulation. However, if "locking" or the division of the organism occurs, the group action becomes less effective than individual action. External control, through the influence of a dominant ray, therefore can lead to adaptive behavior for the starfish as a whole, but it can also result in a conflict that destroys the organism. Something more than external influence is needed.

In the animal with an intact nerve ring, the function of the rays is coordinated by the nerve ring. With this type of internal organization the group is always superior to that of the individual actions. When the rays function as a part of an organized unit, rather than as a group that is physically together, they become a higher type of organization—a single intact organism. This is accomplished by the nerve ring, which in itself does not do the behaving. Rather, it receives and processes the data which the rays relay to it. Through this central organization, the responses of the rays become part of a larger pattern so that together they constitute a single coordinated total response rather than a group of individual responses.

The Leader as the Group's Central Nervous System

If we now examine what goes on in a discussion group we find that members can problem-solve as individuals, they can influence others by external pushes and pulls, or they can function as a group with varying degrees of unity. In order for the latter function to be maximized, however, something must be introduced to serve the function of the nerve ring. In our conceptualization of group problem solving and group decision (Maier, 1963), we see this as the function of the leader. Thus the leader does not serve as a dominant ray and produce the solution. Rather, his function is to receive information, facilitate communications between the individuals, relay messages, and integrate the incoming responses so that a single unified response occurs.

Solutions that are the product of good group discussions often come as surprises to discussion leaders. One of these is unexpected generosity. If there is a weak member, this member is given less to do, in much the same way as an organism adapts to an injured limb and alters the function of other limbs to keep locomotion on course. Experimental evidence supports the point that group decisions award special consideration to needy members of groups (Hoffman & Maier, 1959). Group decisions in industrial groups often give smaller assignments to the less gifted (Maier, 1952). A leader could not effectually impose such differential treatment on group members without being charged with discriminatory practices.

Another unique aspect of group discussion is the way fairness is resolved. In a simulated problem of how to introduce a new truck into a group of drivers, the typical group solution involves a trading of trucks so that several or all members stand to profit. If the leader makes the decision the number of persons who profit is often confined to one (Maier & Hoffman, 1962; Maier & Zerfoss, 1952). In industrial practice, supervisors assign a new truck to an individual member of a crew after careful evaluation of needs. This practice results in dissatisfaction, with the charge of *unfair* being leveled at him. Despite these repeated attempts to do justice, supervisors in the telephone industry never hit upon the notion of a general reallocation of trucks, a solution that crews invariably reach when the decision is theirs to make.

In experiments involving the introduction of change, the use of group discussion tends to lead to decisions that resolve differences (Maier, 1952, 1953; Maier & Hoffman, 1961, 1964a, 1964b). Such decisions tend to be different from decisions reached by individuals because of the very fact that disagreement is common in group problem solving and rare in individual problem solving. The process of resolving difference in a constructive setting causes the exploration of additional areas and leads to solutions that are integrative rather than compromises.

Finally, group solutions tend to be tailored to fit the interests and personalities of the participants; thus group solutions to problems involving fairness, fears, face-saving, etc., tend to vary from one group to another. An outsider cannot process these variables because they are not subject to logical treatment.

If we think of the leader as serving a function in the group different from that of its membership, we might be able to create a group that can function as an intact organism. For a leader, such functions as rejecting or promoting ideas according to his personal needs are out of bounds. He must be receptive to information contributed, accept contributions without evaluating them (posting contributions on a chalk board to keep them alive), summarize information to facilitate integration, stimulate exploratory behavior, create awareness of problems of one member by others, and detect when the group is ready to resolve differences and agree to a unified solution.

Since higher organisms have more than a nerve ring and can store information, a leader might appropriately supply information, but according to our model of a leader's role, he must clearly distinguish between supplying information and promoting a solution. If his knowledge indicates the desirability of a particular solution, sharing this knowledge might lead the group to find this solution, but the solution should be the group's discovery. A leader's contributions do not receive the same treatment as those of a member of the group. Whether he likes it or not, his position is different. According to our conception of the leader's contribution to discussion, his role not only differs in influence, but gives him an entirely different function. He is to serve much as the nerve ring in the

starfish and to further refine this function so as to make it a higher type of nerve ring.

This model of a leader's role in group process has served as a guide for many of our studies in group problem solving. It is not our claim that this will lead to the best possible group function under all conditions. In sharing it we hope to indicate the nature of our guidelines in exploring group leadership as a function quite different and apart from group membership. Thus the model serves as a stimulant for research problems and as a guide for our analyses of leadership skills and principles.

CONCLUSIONS

On the basis of our analysis, it follows that the comparison of the merits of group versus individual problem solving depends on the nature of the problem, the goal to be achieved (high quality solution, highly accepted solution, effective communication and understanding of the solution, innovation, a quickly reached solution, or satisfaction), and the skill of the discussion leader. If liabilities inherent in groups are avoided, assets capitalized upon, and conditions that can serve either favorable or unfavorable outcomes are effectively used, it follows that groups have a potential which in many instances can exceed that of a superior individual functioning alone, even with respect to creativity.

This goal was nicely stated by Thibaut and Kelley (1961) when they

> wonder whether it may not be possible for a rather small, intimate group to establish a problem solving process that capitalizes upon the total pool of information and provides for great interstimulation of ideas without any loss of innovative creativity due to social restraints [p. 268].

In order to accomplish this high level of achievement, however, a leader is needed who plays a role quite different from that of the members. His role is analogous to that of the nerve ring of the starfish which permits the rays to execute a unified response. If the leader can contribute the integrative requirement, group problem solving may emerge as a unique type of group function. This type of approach to group processes places the leader in a particular role in which he must cease to contribute, avoid evaluation, and refrain from thinking about solutions or group *products.* Instead he must concentrate on the group *process,* listen in order to understand rather than to appraise or refute, assume responsibility for accurate communication between members, be sensitive to unexpressed feelings, protect minority points of view, keep the discussion moving, and develop skills in summarizing.

REFERENCES

Crozier, W. J. Notes on some problems of adaptation. *Biological Bulletin,* 1920, 39, 116–129.

Duncker, K. On problem solving. *Psychological Monographs,* 1945, 58 (5, Whole No. 270).

Hamilton, W. F. Coordination in the starfish. III. The righting reaction as a phase of locomotion (righting and locomotion). *Journal of Comparative Psychology,* 1922, 2, 81–94.

Hoffman, L. R. Conditions for creative problem solving. *Journal of Psychology,* 1961, 52, 429–444.

Hoffman, L. R. Group problem solving. In L. Berkowitz (Ed.), *Advances in experimental social psychology,* Vol. 2. New York: Academic Press, 1965. Pp. 99–132.

Hoffman, L. R., Harburg, E., & Maier, N. R. F. Differences and disagreement as factors in creative group problem solving. *Journal of Abnormal and Social Psychology,* 1962, 64, 206–214.

Hoffman, L. R., & Maier, N. R. F. The use of group decision to resolve a problem of fairness. *Personnel Psychology,* 1959, 12, 545–559.

Hoffman, L. R., & Maier, N. R. F. Quality and acceptance of problem solutions by members of homogeneous and heterogeneous groups. *Journal of Abnormal and Social Psychology,* 1961, 62, 401–407.

Hoffman, L. R. & Maier, N. R. F. Valence in the adoption of solutions by problem-solving groups: Concept, method, and results. *Journal of Abnormal and Social Psychology,* 1964, 69, 264–271.

Hoffman, L. R., & Maier, N. R. F. Valence in the adoption of solutions by problem-solving groups: II. Quality and acceptance as goals of leaders and members. Unpublished manuscript, 1967. (Mimeo)

Kelley, H. H., & Thibaut, J. W. Experimental studies of group problem solving and process. In G. Lindzey (Ed.), *Handbook of social psychology.* Cambridge, Mass.: Addison Wesley, 1954. Pp. 735–785.

Maier, N. R. F. Reasoning in humans. I. On direction. *Journal of Comparative Psychology,* 1930, 10, 115–143.

Maier, N. R. F. The quality of group decisions as influenced by the discussion leader. *Human Relations,* 1950, 3, 155–174.

Maier, N. R. F. *Principles of human relations.* New York: Wiley, 1952.

Maier, N. R. F. An experimental test of the effect of training on discussion leadership. *Human Relations,* 1953, 6, 161–173.

Maier, N. R. F., *The appraisal interview.* New York: Wiley, 1958.

Maier, N. R. F. Screening solutions to upgrade quality: A new approach to problem solving under conditions of uncertainty. *Journal of Psychology,* 1960, 49, 217–231.

Maier, N. R. F. *Problem solving discussions and conferences: Leadership methods and skills.* New York: McGraw-Hill, 1963.

Maier, N. R. F., & Hayes, J. J. *Creative management.* New York: Wiley, 1962.

Maier, N. R. F., & Hoffman, L. R. Using trained "developmental" discussion leaders to improve further the quality of group decisions. *Journal of Applied Psycholology,* 1960, 44, 247–251. (a)

Maier, N. R. F., & Hoffman, L. R. Quality of first and second solutions in group problem solving. *Journal of Applied Psychology,* 1960, 44, 278–283. (b)

Maier, N. R. F., & Hoffman, L. R. Organization and creative problem solving. *Journal of Applied Psychology,* 1961, 45, 277–280.

Maier, N. R. F., & Hoffman, L. R. Group decision in England and the United States. *Personnel Psychology,* 1962, 15, 75–87.

Maier, N. R. F., & Hoffman, L. R. Financial incentives and group decision in motivating change. *Journal of Social Psychology,* 1964, 64, 369–378. (a)

Maier, N. R. F., & Hoffman, L. R. Types of problems confronting managers. *Personnel Psychology,* 1964, 17, 261–269. (b)

Maier, N. R. F., & Hoffman, L. R. Acceptance and quality of solutions as related to leaders' attitudes toward disagreement in group problem solving. *Journal of Applied Behavioral Science,* 1965, 1, 373–386.

Maier, N. R. F., & Maier, R. A. An experimental test of the effects of "developmental" vs. "free" discussions on the quality of group decisions. *Journal of Applied Psychology,* 1957, 41, 320–323.

Maier, N. R. F., & Solem, A. R. The contribution of a discussion leader to the quality of group thinking: The effective use of minority opinions. *Human Relations,* 1952, 5, 277–288.

Maier, N. R. F., & Solem, A. R. Improving solutions by turning choice situations into problems. *Personnel Psychology,* 1962, 15, 151–157.

Maier, N. R. F., & Zerfoss, L. F. MRP: A technique for training large groups of supervisors and its potential use in social research. *Human Relations,* 1952, 5, 177–186.

Moore, A. R. The nervous mechanism of coordination in the

crinoid *Antedon rosaceus. Journal of Genetic Psychology,* 1924, 6, 281–288.

Moore, A. R., & Duodoroff, M. Injury recovery and function in an aganglionic central nervous system. *Journal of Comparative Psychology,* 1939, 28, 313–328.

Osborn, A. F. *Applied Imagination.* New York: Scribner's, 1953.

Schneirla, T. C., & Maier, N. R. F. Concerning the status of the starfish. *Journal of Comparative Psychology,* 1940, 30, 103–110.

Solem, A. R. 1965: Almost anything I can do, we can do better. *Personnel Administration,* 1965, 28, 6–16.

Thibaut, J. W., & Kelley, H. H. *The social psychology of groups.* New York: Wiley, 1961.

Wallach, M. A., & Kogan, N. The roles of information, discussion and concensus in group risk taking. *Journal of Experimental and Social Psychology,* 1965, 1, 1–19.

Wallach, M. A., Kogan, N., & Bem, D. J. Group influence on individual risk taking. *Journal of Abnormal and Social Psychology,* 1962, 65, 75–86.

Wertheimer, M. *Productive thinking.* New York: Harper, 1959.

Groupthink

Irving L. Janis

"How could we have been so stupid?" President John F. Kennedy asked after he and a close group of advisers had blundered into the Bay of Pigs invasion. For the last two years I have been studying that question, as it applies not only to the Bay of Pigs decision-makers but also to those who led the United States into such other major fiascos as the failure to be prepared for the attack on Pearl Harbor, the Korean War stalemate and the escalation of the Vietnam War.

Stupidity certainly is not the explanation. The men who participated in making the Bay of Pigs decision, for instance, comprised one of the greatest arrays of intellectual talent in the history of American Government—Dean Rusk, Robert McNamara, Douglas Dillon, Robert Kennedy, McGeorge Bundy, Arthur Schlesinger Jr., Allen Dulles and others.

It also seemed to me that explanations were incomplete if they concentrated only on disturbances in the behavior of each individual within a decision-making body: temporary emotional states of elation, fear, or anger that reduce a man's mental efficiency, for example, or chronic blind spots arising from a man's social prejudices or idiosyncratic biases.

I preferred to broaden the picture by looking at the fiascos from the standpoint of group dynamics as it has been explored over the past three decades, first by the great social psychologist Kurt Lewin and

later in many experimental situations by myself and other behavioral scientists. My conclusion after poring over hundreds of relevant documents—historical reports about formal group meetings and informal conversations among the members—is that the groups that committed the fiascos were victims of what I call "groupthink."

"GROUPY"

In each case study, I was surprised to discover the extent to which each group displayed the typical phenomena of social conformity that are regularly encountered in studies of group dynamics among ordinary citizens. For example, some of the phenomena appear to be completely in line with findings from social-psychological experiments showing that powerful social pressures are brought to bear by the members of a cohesive group whenever a dissident begins to voice his objections to a group consensus. Other phenomena are reminiscent of the shared illusions observed in encounter groups and friendship cliques when the members simultaneously reach a peak of "groupy" feelings.

Above all, there are numerous indications pointing to the development of group norms that bolster morale at the expense of critical thinking. One of the most common norms appears to be that of remaining loyal to the group by sticking with the policies to which the group has already committed itself, even when those policies are obviously working out badly and have unintended consequences that disturb the

Reprinted with permission from *Psychology Today Magazine.* Copyright © 1971 American Psychological Association.

conscience of each member. This is one of the key characteristics of groupthink.

1984

I use the term groupthink as a quick and easy way to refer to the mode of thinking that persons engage in when *concurrence-seeking* becomes so dominant in a cohesive ingroup that it tends to override realistic appraisal of alternative courses of action. Groupthink is a term of the same order as the words in the newspeak vocabulary George Orwell used in his dismaying world of *1984*. In that context, groupthink takes on an invidious connotation. Exactly such a connotation is intended, since the term refers to a deterioration in mental efficiency, reality testing and moral judgments as a result of group pressures.

The symptoms of groupthink arise when the members of decision-making groups become motivated to avoid being too harsh in their judgments of their leaders' or their colleagues' ideas. They adopt a soft line of criticism, even in their own thinking. At their meetings, all the members are amiable and seek complete concurrence on every important issue, with no bickering or conflict to spoil the cozy, "we-feeling" atmosphere.

KILL

Paradoxically, soft-headed groups are often hard-hearted when it comes to dealing with outgroups or enemies. They find it relatively easy to resort to dehumanizing solutions—they will readily authorize bombing attacks that kill large numbers of civilians in the name of the noble cause of persuading an unfriendly government to negotiate at the peace table. They are unlikely to pursue the more difficult and controversial issues that arise when alternatives to a harsh military solution come up for discussion. Nor are they inclined to raise ethical issues that carry the implication that *this fine group of ours, with its humanitarianism and its high-minded principles, might be capable of adopting a course of action that is inhumane and immoral.*

NORMS

There is evidence from a number of social-psychological studies that as the members of a group feel more accepted by the others, which is a central feature of increased group cohesiveness, they display less overt conformity to group norms. Thus we would expect that the more cohesive a group becomes, the

less the members will feel constrained to censor what they say out of fear of being socially punished for antagonizing the leader or any of their fellow members.

In contrast, the groupthink type of conformity tends to increase as group cohesiveness increases. Groupthink involves nondeliberate suppression of critical thoughts as a result of internalization of the group's norms, which is quite different from deliberate suppression on the basis of external threats of social punishment. The more cohesive the group, the greater the inner compulsion on the part of each member to avoid creating disunity, which inclines him to believe in the soundness of whatever proposals are promoted by the leader or by a majority of the group's members.

In a cohesive group, the danger is not so much that each individual will fail to reveal his objections to what the others propose but that he will think the proposal a good one, without attempting to carry out a careful scrutiny of the pros and cons of the alternatives. When groupthink becomes dominant, there also is considerable suppression of deviant thoughts, but it takes the form of each person's deciding that his misgivings are not relevant and should be set aside, that the benefit of the doubt regarding any lingering uncertainties should be given to the group consensus.

STRESS

I do not mean to imply that all cohesive groups necessarily suffer from groupthink. All ingroups may have a mild tendency toward groupthink, displaying one or another of the symptoms from time to time, but it need not be so dominant as to influence the quality of the group's final decision. Neither do I mean to imply that there is anything necessarily inefficient or harmful about group decisions in general. On the contrary, a group whose members have properly defined roles, with traditions concerning the procedures to follow in pursuing a critical inquiry, probably is capable of making better decisions than any individual group member working alone.

The problem is that the advantages of having decisions made by groups are often lost because of powerful psychological pressures that arise when the members work closely together, share the same set of values and, above all, face a crisis situation that puts everyone under intense stress.

The main principle of groupthink, which I offer in the spirit of Parkinson's Law, is this: *The more amiability and esprit de corps there is among the members of a policy-making ingroup, the greater the danger that independent critical thinking will be replaced by groupthink, which is likely to result in irrational and dehumanizing actions directed against outgroups.*

SYMPTOMS

In my studies of high-level governmental decision-makers, both civilian and military, I have found eight main symptoms of groupthink.

1. Invulnerability

Most or all of the members of the ingroup share an *illusion* of invulnerability that provides for them some degree of reassurance about obvious dangers and leads them to become over-optimistic and willing to take extraordinary risks. It also causes them to fail to respond to clear warnings of danger.

The Kennedy ingroup, which uncritically accepted the Central Intelligence Agency's disastrous Bay of Pigs plan, operated on the false assumption that they could keep secret the fact that the United States was responsible for the invasion of Cuba. Even after news of the plan began to leak out, their belief remained unshaken. They failed even to consider the danger that awaited them: a worldwide revulsion against the U.S.

A similar attitude appeared among the members of President Lyndon B. Johnson's ingroup, the "Tuesday Cabinet," which kept escalating the Vietnam War despite repeated setbacks and failures. "There was a belief," Bill Moyers commented after he resigned, "that if we indicated a willingness to use our power, they [the North Vietnamese] would get the message and back away from an all-out confrontation . . . There was a confidence—it was never bragged about, it was just there—that when the chips were really down, the other people would fold."

A most poignant example of an illusion of invulnerability involves the ingroup around Admiral H. E. Kimmel, which failed to prepare for the possibility of a Japanese attack on Pearl Harbor despite repeated warnings. Informed by his intelligence chief that radio contact with Japanese aircraft carriers had been lost, Kimmel joked about it: "What, you don't know where the carriers are? Do you mean to say that they could be rounding Diamond Head (at Honolulu) and you wouldn't know it?" The carriers were in fact moving full-steam toward Kimmel's command post at the time. Laughing together about a danger signal, which labels it as a purely laughing matter, is a characteristic manifestation of groupthink.

2. Rationale

As we see, victims of groupthink ignore warnings; they also collectively construct rationalizations in order to discount warnings and other forms of negative feedback that, taken seriously, might lead the group members to reconsider their assumptions each time they recommit themselves to past decisions. Why did the Johnson ingroup avoid reconsidering its escalation policy when time and again the expectations on which they based their decisions turned out to be wrong? James C. Thompson Jr., a Harvard historian who spent five years as an observing participant in both the State Department and the White House, tells us that the policymakers avoided critical discussion of their prior decisions and continually invented new rationalizations so that they could sincerely recommit themselves to defeating the North Vietnamese.

In the fall of 1964, before the bombing of North Vietnam began, some of the policymakers predicted that six weeks of air strikes would induce the North Vietnamese to seek peace talks. When someone asked, "What if they don't?" the answer was that another four weeks certainly would do the trick.

Later, after each setback, the ingroup agreed that by investing just a bit more effort (by stepping up the bomb tonnage a bit, for instance), their course of action would prove to be right. *The Pentagon Papers* bear out these observations.

In *The Limits of Intervention,* Townsend Hoopes, who was acting Secretary of the Air Force under Johnson, says that Walt W. Rostow in particular showed a remarkable capacity for what has been called "instant rationalization." According to Hoopes, Rostow buttressed the group's optimism about being on the road to victory by culling selected scraps of evidence from news reports or, if necessary, by inventing "plausible" forecasts that had no basis in evidence at all.

Admiral Kimmel's group rationalized away their warnings, too. Right up to December 7, 1941, they convinced themselves that the Japanese would never dare attempt a full-scale surprise assault against Hawaii because Japan's leaders would realize that it would precipitate an all-out war which the United States would surely win. They made no attempt to look at the situation through the eyes of the Japanese leaders—another manifestation of groupthink.

3. Morality

Victims of groupthink believe unquestioningly in the inherent morality of their ingroup; this belief inclines the members to ignore the ethical or moral consequences of their decisions.

Evidence that this symptom is at work usually is of a negative kind—the things that are left unsaid in group meetings. At least two influential persons had doubts about the morality of the Bay of Pigs adventure. One of them, Arthur Schlesinger Jr., presented his strong objections in a memorandum to President Kennedy and Secretary of State Rusk but suppressed them when he attended meetings of the Kennedy team. The other, Senator J. William Fulbright, was not a member of the group, but the President invited him to express his misgivings in a speech to the policymakers. However, when Fulbright finished speaking the President moved on to other agenda items without asking for reactions of the group.

David Kraslow and Stuart H. Loory, in *The Secret Search for Peace in Vietnam,* report that during 1966 President Johnson's ingroup was concerned primarily with selecting bomb targets in North Vietnam. They based their selections on four factors—the military advantage, the risk to American aircraft and pilots, the danger of forcing other countries into the fighting, and the danger of heavy civilian casualties. At their regular Tuesday luncheons, they weighed these factors the way school teachers grade examination papers, averaging them out. Though evidence on this point is scant, I suspect that the group's ritualistic adherence to a standardized procedure induced the members to feel morally justified in their destructive way of dealing with the Vietnamese people—after all, the danger of heavy civilian casualties from U.S. air strikes was taken into account on their checklists.

4. Stereotypes

Victims of groupthink hold stereotyped views of the leaders of enemy groups: they are so evil that genuine attempts at negotiating differences with them are unwarranted, or they are too weak or too stupid to deal effectively with whatever attempts the ingroup makes to defeat their purposes, no matter how risky the attempts are.

Kennedy's groupthinkers believed that Premier Fidel Castro's air force was so ineffectual that obsolete B-26s could knock it out completely in a surprise attack before the invasion began. They also believed that Castro's army was so weak that a small Cuban-exile brigade could establish a well-protected beachhead at the Bay of Pigs. In addition, they believed that Castro was not smart enough to put down any possible internal uprisings in support of the exiles. They were wrong on all three assumptions. Though much of the blame was attributable to faulty intelligence, the point is that none of Kennedy's advisers even questioned the CIA planners about these assumptions.

The Johnson advisers' sloganistic thinking about "the Communist apparatus" that was "working all around the world" (as Dean Rusk put it) led them to overlook the powerful nationalistic strivings of the North Vietnamese government and its efforts to ward off Chinese domination. The crudest of all stereotypes used by Johnson's inner circle to justify their policies was the domino theory ("If we don't stop the Reds in South Vietnam, tomorrow they will be in Hawaii and next week they will be in San Francisco," Johnson once said). The group so firmly accepted this stereotype that it became almost impossible for any adviser to introduce a more sophisticated viewpoint.

In the documents on Pearl Harbor, it is clear to see that the Navy commanders stationed in Hawaii had a naive image of Japan as a midget that would not dare to strike a blow against a powerful giant.

5. Pressure

Victims of groupthink apply direct pressure to any individual who momentarily expresses doubts about any of the group's shared illusions or who questions the validity of the arguments supporting a policy alternative favored by the majority. This gambit reinforces the concurrence-seeking norm that loyal members are expected to maintain.

President Kennedy probably was more active than anyone else in raising skeptical questions during the Bay of Pigs meetings, and yet he seems to have encouraged the group's docile, uncritical acceptance of defective arguments in favor of the CIA's plan. At every meeting, he allowed the CIA representatives to dominate the discussion. He permitted them to give their immediate refutations in response to each tentative doubt that one of the others expressed, instead of asking whether anyone shared the doubt or wanted to pursue the implications of the new worrisome issue that had just been raised. And at the most crucial meeting, when he was calling on each member to give his vote for or against the plan, he did not call on Arthur Schlesinger, the one man there who was known by the President to have serious misgivings.

Historian Thomson informs us that whenever a member of Johnson's ingroup began to express doubts, the group used subtle social pressures to "domesticate" him. To start with, the dissenter was made to feel at home, provided that he lived up to two restrictions: 1) that he did not voice his doubts to outsiders, which would play into the hands of the opposition; and 2) that he kept his criticisms within the bounds of acceptable deviation, which meant not challenging any of the fundamental assumptions that went into the group's prior commitments. One such "domesticated dissenter" was Bill Moyers. When Moyers arrived at a meeting, Thomson tells us, the President greeted him with, "Well, here comes Mr. Stop-the-Bombing."

6. Self-Censorship

Victims of groupthink avoid deviating from what appears to be group consensus; they keep silent about their misgivings and even minimize to themselves the importance of their doubts.

As we have seen, Schlesinger was not at all hesitant about presenting his strong objections to the Bay of Pigs plan in a memorandum to the President and the Secretary of State. But he became keenly aware of his tendency to suppress objections at the White House meetings. "In the months after the Bay of Pigs I bitterly reproached myself for having kept so silent during those crucial discussions in the cabinet room," Schlesinger writes in *A Thousand Days*. "I can only explain my failure to do more than raise a few timid questions by reporting that one's impulse to blow the whistle on this nonsense was simply undone by the circumstances of the discussion."

7. Unanimity

Victims of groupthink share an *illusion* of unanimity within the group concerning almost all judgments expressed by members who speak in favor of the majority view. This symptom results partly from the preceding one, whose effects are augmented by the false assumption that any individual who remains silent during any part of the discussion is in full accord with what the others are saying.

When a group of persons who respect each other's opinions arrives at a unanimous view, each member is likely to feel that the belief must be true. This reliance on consensual validation within the group tends to replace individual critical thinking and reality testing, unless there are clear-cut disagreements among the members. In contemplating a course of action such as the invasion of Cuba, it is painful for the members to confront disagreements within their group, particularly if it becomes apparent that there are widely divergent views about whether the preferred course of action is too risky to undertake at all.

Such disagreements are likely to arouse anxieties about making a serious error. Once the sense of unanimity is shattered, the members no longer can feel complacently confident about the decision they are inclined to make. Each man must then face the annoying realization that there are troublesome uncertainties and he must diligently seek out the best information he can get in order to decide for himself exactly how serious the risks might be. This is one of the unpleasant consequences of being in a group of hardheaded, critical thinkers.

To avoid such an unpleasant state, the members often become inclined, without quite realizing it, to prevent latent disagreements from surfacing when they are about to initiate a risky course of action. The group leader and the members support each other in playing up the areas of convergence in their thinking, at the expense of fully exploring divergencies that might reveal unsettled issues.

"Our meetings took place in a curious atmosphere of assumed consensus," Schlesinger writes. His additional comments clearly show that, curiously, the consensus was an illusion—an illusion that could be maintained only because the major participants did not reveal their own reasoning or discuss their idiosyncratic assumptions and vague reservations. Evidence from several sources makes it clear that even the three principals—President Kennedy, Rusk and McNamara—had widely differing assumptions about the invasion plan.

8. Mindguards

Victims of groupthink sometimes appoint themselves as mindguards to protect the leader and fellow members from adverse information that might break the complacency they shared about the effectiveness and morality of past decisions. At a large birthday party for his wife, Attorney General Robert F. Kennedy, who had been constantly informed about the Cuban invasion plan, took Schlesinger aside and asked him why he was opposed. Kennedy listened coldly and said, "You may be right or you may be wrong, but the President has made his mind up. Don't push it any further. Now is the time for everyone to help him all they can."

Rusk also functioned as a highly effective mindguard by failing to transmit to the group the strong objections of three "outsiders" who had learned of the invasion plan—Undersecretary of State Chester Bowles, USIA Director Edward R. Murrow, and Rusk's intelligence chief, Roger Hilsman. Had Rusk done so, their warnings might have reinforced

Schlesinger's memorandum and jolted some of Kennedy's ingroup, if not the President himself, into reconsidering the decision.

PRODUCTS

When a group of executives frequently displays most or all of these interrelated symptoms, a detailed study of their deliberations is likely to reveal a number of immediate consequences. These consequences are, in effect, products of poor decision-making practices because they lead to inadequate solutions to the problems under discussion.

First, the group limits its discussions to a few alternative courses of action (often only two) without an initial survey of all the alternatives that might be worthy of consideration.

Second, the group fails to reexamine the course of action initially preferred by the majority after they learn of risks and drawbacks they had not considered originally.

Third, the members spend little or no time discussing whether there are nonobvious gains they may have overlooked or ways of reducing the seemingly prohibitive costs that made rejected alternatives appear undesirable to them.

Fourth, members make little or no attempt to obtain information from experts within their own organizations who might be able to supply more precise estimates of potential losses and gains.

Fifth, members show positive interest in facts and opinions that support their preferred policy; they tend to ignore facts and opinions that do not.

Sixth, members spend little time deliberating about how the chosen policy might be hindered by bureaucratic inertia, sabotaged by political opponents, or temporarily derailed by common accidents. Consequently, they fail to work out contingency plans to cope with foreseeable setbacks that could endanger the overall success of their chosen course.

SUPPORT

The search for an explanation of why groupthink occurs has led me through a quagmire of complicated theoretical issues in the murky area of human motivation. My belief, based on recent social psychological research, is that we can best understand the various symptoms of groupthink as a mutual effort among the group members to maintain self-esteem and emotional equanimity by providing social support to each other, especially at times when they share responsibility for making vital decisions.

Even when no important decision is pending, the typical administrator will begin to doubt the wisdom and morality of his past decisions each time he receives information about setbacks, particularly if the information is accompanied by negative feedback from prominent men who originally had been his supporters. It should not be surprising, therefore, to find that individual members strive to develop unanimity and esprit de corps that will help bolster each other's morale, to create an optimistic outlook about the success of pending decisions, and to reaffirm the positive value of past policies to which all of them are committed.

PRIDE

Shared illusions of invulnerability, for example, can reduce anxiety about taking risks. Rationalizations help members believe that the risks are really not so bad after all. The assumption of inherent morality helps the members to avoid feelings of shame or guilt. Negative stereotypes function as stress-reducing devices to enhance a sense of moral righteousness as well as pride in a lofty mission.

The mutual enhancement of self-esteem and morale may have functional value in enabling the members to maintain their capacity to take action, but it has maladaptive consequences insofar as concurrence-seeking tendencies interfere with critical, rational capacities and lead to serious errors of judgment.

While I have limited my study to decision-making bodies in Government, groupthink symptoms appear in business, industry and any other field where small, cohesive groups make the decisions. It is vital, then, for all sorts of people—and especially group leaders—to know what steps they can take to prevent groupthink.

REMEDIES

To counterpoint my case studies of the major fiascos, I have also investigated two highly successful group enterprises, the formulation of the Marshall Plan in the Truman Administration and the handling of the Cuban missile crisis by President Kennedy and his advisers. I have found it instructive to examine the steps Kennedy took to change his group's decision-making processes. These changes ensured that the mistakes made by his Bay of Pigs ingroup were not repeated by the missile-crisis ingroup, even though the membership of both groups was essentially the same.

The following recommendations for preventing groupthink incorporate many of the good practices I discovered to be characteristic of the Marshall Plan and missile-crisis groups:

1. The leader of a policy-forming group should assign the role of critical evaluator to each member, encouraging the group to give high priority to open airing of objections and doubts. This practice needs to be reinforced by the leader's acceptance of criticism of his own judgments in order to discourage members from soft-pedaling their disagreements and from allowing their striving for concurrence to inhibit critical thinking.

2. When the key members of a hierarchy assign a policy-planning mission to any group within their organization, they should adopt an impartial stance instead of stating preferences and expectations at the beginning. This will encourage open inquiry and impartial probing of a wide range of policy alternatives.

3. The organization routinely should set up several outside policy-planning and evaluation groups to work on the same policy questions, each deliberating under a different leader. This can prevent the insulation of an ingroup.

4. At intervals before the group reaches a final consensus, the leader should require each member to discuss the group's deliberations with associates in his own unit of the organization—assuming that those associates can be trusted to adhere to the same security regulations that govern the policymakers—and then to report back their reactions to the group.

5. The group should invite one or more outside experts to each meeting on a staggered basis and encourage the experts to challenge the views of the core members.

6. At every general meeting of the group, whenever the agenda calls for an evaluation of policy alternatives, at least one member should play devil's advocate, functioning as a good lawyer in challenging the testimony of those who advocate the majority position.

7. Whenever the policy issue involves relations with a rival nation or organization, the group should devote a sizable block of time, perhaps an entire session, to a survey of all warning signals from the rivals and should write alternative scenarios on the rivals' intentions.

8. When the group is surveying policy alternatives for feasibility and effectiveness, it should from time to time divide into two or more subgroups to meet separately, under different chairmen, and then come back together to hammer out differences.

9. After reaching a preliminary consensus about what seems to be the best policy, the group should hold a "second-chance" meeting at which every member expresses as vividly as he can all his residual doubts, and rethinks the entire issue before making a definitive choice.

HOW

These recommendations have their disadvantages. To encourage the open airing of objections, for instance, might lead to prolonged and costly debates when a rapidly growing crisis requires immediate solution. It also could cause rejection, depression and anger. A leader's failure to set a norm might create cleavage between leader and members that could develop into a disruptive power struggle if the leader looks on the emerging consensus as anathema. Setting up outside evaluation groups might increase the risk of security leakage. Still, inventive executives who know their way around the organizational maze probably can figure out how to apply one or another of the prescriptions successfully, without harmful side effects.

They also could benefit from the advice of outside experts in the administrative and behavioral sciences. Though these experts have much to offer, they have had few chances to work on policy-making machinery within large organizations. As matters now stand, executives innovate only when they need new procedures to avoid repeating serious errors that have deflated their self-images.

In this era of atomic warheads, urban disorganization and ecocatastrophes, it seems to me that policymakers should collaborate with behavioral scientists and give top priority to preventing groupthink and its attendant fiascos.

Managing Conflict Among Groups

L. Dave Brown

Conflict among groups is extremely common in organizations, although it often goes unrecognized. Managing conflict among groups is a crucial skill for those who would lead modern organizations. To illustrate:

> Maintenance workers brought in to repair a production facility criticize production workers for overworking the machinery and neglecting routine maintenance tasks. The production workers countercharge that the last maintenance work was improperly done and caused the present breakdown. The argument results in little cooperation between the two groups to repair the breakdown, and the resulting delays and misunderstandings ultimately inflate organization-wide production costs.

> A large manufacturing concern has unsuccessful negotiations with a small independent union, culminating in a bitter strike characterized by fights, bombings, and sabotage. The angry workers, aware that the independent union has too few resources to back a protracted battle with management, vote in a powerful international union for the next round of negotiations. Management prepares for an even worse strike, but comparatively peaceful and productive negotiations ensue.

> Top management of a large bank in a racially mixed urban area commits the organization to system-wide integration. Recruiters find several superbly qualified young black managers, after a long and highly competitive search, to join the bank's prestigious but all-white trust division and yet, subsequently, several leave the organization. Since virtually all the managers in the trust division are explicitly willing to integrate, top management is mystified by the total failure of the integration effort.

These cases are all examples of conflict or potential conflict among organizational groups that influence the performance and goal attainment of the organization as a whole. The cases differ in two important ways.

First, the extent to which the potential conflict among groups is *overt* varies across cases: conflict is all too obvious in the labor-management situation; it is subtle but still evident in the production-maintenance relations; it is never explicit in the attempt to integrate the bank's trust division. It is clear that *too much* conflict can be destructive, and much attention has been paid to strategies and tactics for reducing escalated conflict. Much less attention has been paid to situations in which organizational performance suffers because of *too little* conflict, or strategies and tactics for making potential conflicts more overt.

Second, the cases also differ in the *defining characteristics* of the parties: the production and maintenance groups are functionally defined; the distribution of power is critical to the labor and management conflict; the society's history of race relations is important to the black-white relations in the bank. Although there has been much examination of organizational conflict among groups defined by function, there has been comparatively little attention to organizational conflicts among groups defined by *power differences* (e.g., headquarters-branch relations, some labor-management relations) or by *societal history* (e.g., religious group relations, black-white relations, male-female relations).

It is increasingly clear that effective management of modern organizations calls for dealing with various forms of intergroup conflict: too little as well as too much conflict, and history-based and power-based as well as function-based conflicts. This paper offers a framework for understanding conflict among groups in the next section, and suggests strategies and tactics for diagnosing and managing different conflict situations.

CONFLICT AND INTERGROUP RELATIONS

Conflict: Too Much or Too Little?

Conflict is a form of interaction among parties that differ in interests, perceptions, and preferences. Overt conflict involves adversarial interaction that ranges from mild disagreements through various degrees of fighting. But it is also possible for parties with substantial differences to act as if those differ-

---

Reprinted by permission of the author from D. A. Kolb, I. M. Rubin, and I. N. McIntyre (eds.), *Organizational Psychology: Readings on Human Behavior in Organizations,* 4th ed. (Englewood Cliffs, N.J.: Prentice Hall, 1984).

ences did not exist, and so keep potential conflict from becoming overt.

It is only too clear that it is possible to have *too much* conflict between or among groups. Too much conflict produces strong negative feelings, blindness to interdependencies, and uncontrolled escalation of aggressive action and counteraction. The obvious costs of uncontrolled conflict have sparked a good deal of interest in strategies for conflict reduction and resolution.

It is less obvious (but increasingly clear) that it is possible to have *too little* conflict. Complex and novel decisions, for example, may require pulling together perspectives and information from many different groups. If group representatives are unwilling to present and argue for their perspectives, the resulting decision may not take into account all the available information. The Bay of Pigs disaster during the Kennedy Administration may have been a consequence of too little conflict in the National Security Council, where critical information possessed by representatives of different agencies was suppressed to preserve harmonious relations among them (Janis, 1972).

In short, moderate levels of conflict—in which differences are recognized and extensively argued—are often associated with high levels of energy and involvement, high degrees of information exchange, and better decisions (Robbins, 1974). Managers should be concerned, in this view, with achieving levels of conflict that are *appropriate* to the task before them, rather than concerned about preventing or resolving immediately all intergroup disagreements.

Conflict among Groups

Conflict in organizations takes many forms. A disagreement between two individuals, for example, may be related to their personal differences, their job definitions, their group memberships, or all three. One of the most common ways that managers misunderstand organizational conflict, for example, is to attribute difficulties to "personality" factors, when it is, in fact, rooted in group memberships and organizational structure. Attributing conflict between production and maintenance workers to their personalities, for example, implies that the conflict can be reduced by replacing the individuals. But if the conflict is, in fact, related to the differing goals of the two groups, *any* individual will be under pressure to fight with members of the other group, regardless of their personal preferences. Replacing individuals in such

situations without taking account of intergroup differences will *not* improve relations.

Groups are defined in organizations for a variety of reasons. Most organizations are differentiated horizontally, for example, into functional departments or product divisions for task purposes. Most organizations also are differentiated vertically into levels or into headquarters and plant groups. Many organizations also incorporate in some degree group definitions significant in the larger society, such as racial and religious distinctions.

A good deal of attention has been paid to the relations among groups of relatively equal power, such as functional departments in organizations. Much less is known about effective management of relations between groups of unequal power or those having different societal histories. But many of the most perplexing intergroup conflicts in organizations include all three elements—functional differences, power differences, and historical differences. Effective management of the differences between a white executive from marketing and a black hourly worker from production is difficult indeed, because so many issues are likely to contribute to the problem.

Intergroup relations, left to themselves, tend to have a regenerative, self-fulfilling quality that makes them extremely susceptible to rapid escalation. The dynamics of escalating conflict, for example, have impacts within and between the groups involved. *Within* a group (i.e., within the small circles in Figure 1), conflict with another group tends to increase cohesion and conformity to group norms (Sherif, 1966; Coser, 1956) and to encourage a world view that favors "us" over "them" (Janis, 1972; Deutsch, 1973). Simultaneously, *between*-groups (i.e., the relations between the circles in Figure 1) conflict promotes negative stereotyping and distrust (Sherif, 1966), increased emphasis on differences (Deutsch, 1973), decreased communications (Sherif, 1966) and increased distortion of communications that do take place (Blake and Mouton, 1961). The *combination* of negative stereotypes, distrust, internal militance, and aggressive action creates a vicious cycle: "defensive" aggression by one group validates suspicion and "defensive" counteraggression by the other, and the conflict escalates (Deutsch, 1973) unless it is counteracted by external factors. A less well understood pattern, in which positive stereotypes, trust, and cooperative action generate a benevolent cycle of increasing cooperation, may also exist (Deutsch, 1973).

To return to one of the initial examples, both the maintenance concern with keeping the machines

FIGURE 1
Varieties of Intergroup Conflict.

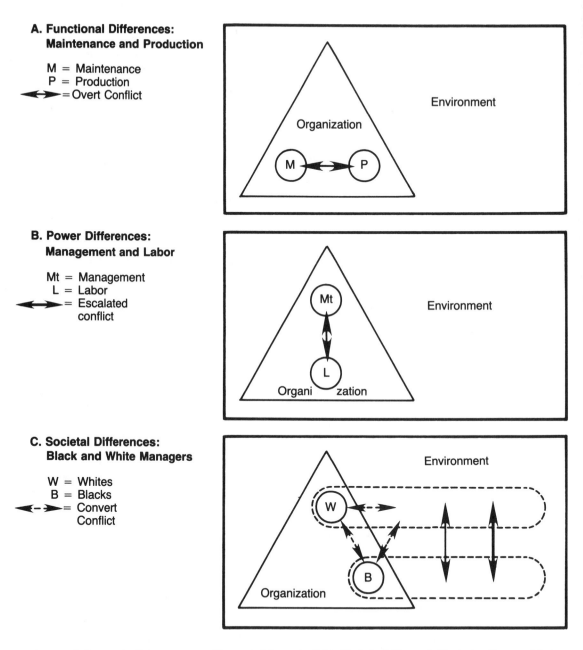

A. Functional Differences:
Maintenance and Production

M = Maintenance
P = Production
◄——►= Overt Conflict

Organization
Environment
M ◄——► P

B. Power Differences:
Management and Labor

Mt = Management
L = Labor
◄——►= Escalated
conflict

Mt
Environment
L
Organi zation

C. Societal Differences:
Black and White Managers

W = Whites
B = Blacks
◄--►= Convert
Conflict

Environment
W
B
Organization

clean and the production concern with maximizing output were organizationally desirable. But those concerns promoted a negative maintenance stereotype of production ("too lazy to clean machines") and a production stereotype of maintenance ("want us to polish the machine, not use it") that encouraged them

to fight. Part A of Figure 1 illustrates the overt but not escalated conflict between the parties.

Introducing power differences into intergroup relations further suppresses communications among the groups. The low-power group is vulnerable, and so must censor communication—such as dissatisfaction—that might elicit retaliation from the high-power group. In consequence, the high-power group remains ignorant of information considered sensitive by the low-power group. The long-term consequences of this mutually reinforcing fear and ignorance can be either escalating oppression—a peculiarly destructive form of too little conflict—or sporadic eruptions of intense and unexpected fighting (Brown, 1978).

The fight between the small independent union and the large corporation described at the outset illustrates the potential for outbursts of violent conflict when the parties are separated by large differences in power. The small union felt unable to influence the corporation at the bargaining table, and so used violence and guerrilla tactics to express its frustration and to influence management without exposing the union to retaliation. Part B of Figure 1 illustrates the positions of the parties and the quality of their conflict.

Conflicts among groups that involve societal differences may be even more complicated. Differences rooted in societal history are likely to be expressed in a network of mutually reinforcing social mechanisms—political, economic, geographic, educational—that serve to *institutionalize* the differences. Societal differences do not necessarily imply power differences between the groups, but very frequently the effect of institutionalization is to enshrine the dominance of one party over another. Relations among such groups within organizations are strongly influenced by the larger society. Organizational tensions may be the result of environmental developments that the organization cannot control. In addition, differences associated with histories of discrimination or oppression may involve strong feelings and entrenched stereotypes that can lead to explosive conflict. Societal differences in organizations call for careful management that permits enough overt conflict so the differences are understood, but not so much that they are exacerbated.

The failure to integrate the trust division illustrates the problem of managing institutionalized racism. The black recruits had all the technical skills for success, but they could not join the all-white clubs or buy a house in the all-white suburbs where their colleagues lived, played, and learned the social ropes of the trust business. Nor could they challenge top-level decisions to keep them away from the oldest (and richest) clients ("who might be racist and so take their business elsewhere"). But the failure to face the potential conflicts—among members of the organization and between the organization and its clients—in essence made it impossible for the black managers to become full members. This situation is diagrammed in Part C of Figure 1.

Diagnosing the Conflict

Diagnosis is a crucially important and often-neglected phase of conflict management. Since conflict problems are often not recognized until after they have become acute, the need for immediate relief may be intense. But intervention in a poorly understood situation is not likely to produce instant successes. On the contrary, it may make the situation worse.

The manager of conflict should at the outset answer three questions about the situation:

1. At what level or levels is the conflict rooted (e.g., personal, interpersonal, intergroup, etc.)?

2. What role does s/he play in the relations among the parties?

3. What is a desirable state of relations among the parties?

A conflict may be the result of an individual, an interpersonal relationship, an intergroup relationship, or a combination of the three. If the manager understands the contributions of different levels, s/he can respond appropriately. It is generally worthwhile to examine the conflict from *each* of these perspectives early in the diagnosis.

The position of the manager vis-a-vis the parties is also important. Managers who are themselves parties to the dispute are likely to be biased, and almost certainly will be perceived by their opponents as biased. Actual bias requires that the manager be suspicious of his/her own perceptions and strive to empathize with the other party; perceived bias may limit the manager's ability to intervene credibly with the other party until the perception is dealt with. Conflict managers who are organizationally superior to the parties may not be biased in favor of either, but they are likely to have poor access to information about the conflict. For such persons special effort to understand the parties' positions may be necessary. Third parties that are respected and seen as neutral by both sides are in perhaps the best position to intervene, but they are a rare luxury for most situations. In any case, awareness of one's position vis-a-vis the parties can help the manager avoid pitfalls.

Finally, a conflict manager needs to develop a sense of what is too much and what is too little conflict among the parties—when is intervention merited, and should it increase or decrease the level of conflict? Relations among groups may be diagnosed in terms of attitudes, behavior, and structure, and each of those categories have characteristic patterns associated with too much and too little conflict.

Attitudes include the orientations of groups and group members to their own and other groups—the extent to which they are aware of group interdependencies, the sophistication of group representatives about intergroup relations, and the quality of feelings and stereotypes within groups. Too much conflict is characterized by blindness to interdependencies, naiveté about the dynamics and costs of conflict, and strong negative feelings and stereotypes. Too little conflict, in contrast, is marked by blindness to conflicts of interests, naiveté about the dynamics and costs of collusion, and little awareness of group differences.

Behaviors include the ways in which groups and their members act—the levels of cohesion and conformity within groups, the action strategies of group representatives, the extent to which interaction between the groups is marked by escalating conflict or cooperation. Too much conflict often involves monolithically conforming groups, rigidly competitive action strategies, and escalating aggression among the groups. Too little conflict is associated with undefined or fragmented groups, unswervingly cooperative action strategies, and collusive harmony and agreement in place of examination of differences.

Structures are underlying factors that influence interaction in the long term—the larger systems in which parties are embedded, structural mechanisms that connect the parties, group boundaries and long-term interests, and regulatory contexts that influence interaction. Too much conflict is promoted by undefined or differentiated larger systems, lack of integrative mechanisms that link the groups, clearly defined and conflicting group interests and identities, and few rules or regulations to limit conflict. Too little conflict is encouraged by a shared larger system that suppresses conflict, no mechanisms to promote examination of differences, vague definitions of conflicting group interests and identities, and regulations that discourage overt conflict.

These diagnostic categories and the earmarks of too much and too little conflict are summarized in Table 1. Attitudinal, behavioral, and structural aspects of intergroup relations tend to interact with and support one another. The result is a tendency to escalate either the conflict or the collusion until some external force exerts a moderating effect. Thus,

intergroup relations are volatile and capable of rapid escalatory cycles, but they also offer a variety of leverage points at which their self-fulfilling cycles may be interrupted by perceptive managers.

Intervention

Intervention to promote constructive conflict may involve *reducing* conflict in relations with too much or *inducing* conflict in relations with too little. In both cases, intervention involves efforts to disrupt a cyclical process produced by the interaction of attitudes, behavior, and structure. Interventions may start with any aspect of the groups' interaction, although long-term change will probably involve effects in all of them. More work has been done on the problem of reducing conflict than on inducing it—but conflict-reduction strategies often have the seeds of conflict induction within them.

Changing *attitudes* involves influencing the ways in which the parties construe events. Thus *altering group perceptions of their differences or similarities* may influence their interaction. Sherif (1966), for example, reports reduction in intergroup conflicts as a consequence of introducing superordinate goals that both groups desired but whose achievement required cooperation; emphasizing interdependencies may reduce escalated conflict. On the other hand, inducing conflict may require deemphasizing interdependencies and emphasizing conflicts of interest. Attitudes may also be changed by *changing the parties' understanding of their relations.* Increased understanding of the dynamics of intergroup conflict and its costs, for example, may help participants reduce their unintentional contributions to escalation (e.g., Burton, 1969). By the same token, increased understanding may help parties control the development of collusion (Janis, 1972). *Feelings and stereotypes may also be changed* by appropriate interventions. Sharing discrepant perceptions of each other has helped depolarize negative stereotypes and reduce conflict in a number of intergroup conflicts (e.g., Blake, Shepard, and Mouton, 1964), and consciousness raising to clarify self and other perceptions may help to increase conflict in situations where there is too little. Attitude-change interventions, in short, operate on the ways in which the parties understand and interpret the relations among the groups.

Changing *behaviors* requires modifying ways in which group members act. *Altering within-group behavior,* for example, may have a substantial impact on the ways in which the groups deal with each other. When members of a highly cohesive group confront

TABLE 1
Diagnosing Conflict Among Groups.

Area of Concern	General Issue	Symptoms of Too Much Conflict	Symptoms of Too Little Conflict
Attitudes	Awareness of similarities and differences	Blind to interdependence	Blind to conflicts of interest
	Sophistication about intergroup relations	Unaware of dynamics and costs of conflict	Unaware of dynamics and costs of collusion
	Feelings and perceptions of own and other group	Elaborated stereotypes favorable to own and unfavorable to other group	Lack of consciousness of own group and differences from other group
Behavior	Behavior within groups	High cohesion and conformity; high mobilization	Fragmentization; mobilization
	Conflict management style of groups	Overcompetitive style	Overcooperative style
	Behavior between groups	Aggressive, exploitative behavior; preemptive attack	Avoidance of conflict; appeasement
Structure	Nature of larger system	Separate or underdefined common larger system	Shared larger system that discourages conflict
	Regulatory context for interaction	Few rules to limit escalation	Many rules that stifle differences
	Relevant structural mechanisms	No inhibiting third parties available	No third parties to press differences
	Definition of groups and their goals	Impermeably bounded groups obsessed with own interests	Unbounded groups aware of own interests

explicitly differences that exist *within* the group, their enthusiasm for fighting with outside groups may be reduced. Similarly, an internally fragmented group that becomes more cohesive may develop an increased appetite for conflict with other groups (Brown, 1977). A second behavior-changing strategy is to *train group representatives to manage conflict more effectively.* Where too much conflict exists, representatives can be trained in conflict-reduction strategies, such as cooperation induction (Deutsch, 1973) or problem solving (Filley, 1975). Where the problem is too little conflict, the parties might benefit from training in assertiveness or bargaining skills. A third alternative is to *monitor between-group behavior,* and so influence escalations. Third parties trusted by both sides can control escalative tendencies or lend credibility to reduction initiatives by the parties that might otherwise be distrusted (Walton, 1969). Similarly, conflict induction may be an outcome of third-party "process consultation" that raises questions about collusion (Schein, 1969). Behavior-change strategies, in summary, focus on present activities as an influence on levels of conflict, and seek to move those actions into more constructive patterns.

Changing structures involves altering the underlying factors that influence long-term relations among groups. A common alternative is to *invoke larger system interventions.* Conflict between groups in the same larger system is often reduced through referring the question at issue to a higher hierarchical level (Galbraith, 1971). A similar press for conflict induction may be created when too little conflict results in lowered performance that catches the attention of higher levels. A related strategy for managing conflict is to *develop regulatory contexts* that specify appropriate behaviors. Such regulatory structures can limit conflict by imposing rules on potential fights, as collective bargaining legislation does on labor-management relations. Changes in regulatory structures can also loosen rules that stifle desirable conflict. A third strategy is the *development of new interface mechanisms* that mediate intergroup relations. Integrative roles and departments may help to reduce conflict among organizational departments

(Galbraith, 1971), while the creation of ombudsmen or "devil's advocates" can help surface conflict that might otherwise not become explicit (Janis, 1972). Another possibility is *redefinition of group boundaries and goals,* so the nature of the parties themselves is reorganized. Redesigning organizations into a matrix structure, for example, in effect locates the conflicted interface within an individual to ensure that effective management efforts are made (Galbraith, 1971). Alternatively, too little conflict may call for clarifying group boundaries and goals so the differences among them become more apparent and more likely to produce conflict. Structural interventions typically demand heavier initial investments of time and energy, and they may take longer to bear fruit than attitudinal and behavioral interventions. But they are also more likely to produce long-term changes.

These strategies for intervention are summarized in Table 2. This sample of strategies is not exhaustive, but it is intended to be representative of interventions that have worked with groups that are relatively equal in power and whose differences are primarily related to the organization's task. The

introduction of power differences and societal differences raises other issues.

Power Differences

Relations between high-power and low-power groups are worth special examination because of their potential for extremely negative outcomes. The poor communications that result from fear on the part of the low-power group and ignorance on the part of the high-power group can result in either extreme oppression (too little conflict) or unexpected explosions of violence (too much).

It is understandable that high-power groups prefer too little conflict to too much, and that low-power groups are anxious about the risks of provoking conflict with a more powerful adversary. But organizations that in the short run have too little conflict often have too much in the long term. Inattention to the problems of low-power groups requires that they adopt highly intrusive influence strategies in order to be heard (e.g., Swingle, 1967). So the comfort of avoiding conflict between high- and low-power groups may have high costs in the long run.

TABLE 2
Intervening in Conflict Among Groups.

Area of Concern	General Issue	Strategies for Too Much Conflict	Strategies for Too Little Conflict
Attitudes	Clarify differences and similarities	Emphasize interdependencies	Emphasize conflict of interest
	Increased sophistication about intergroup relations	Clarify dynamics and costs of escalation	Clarify costs and dynamics of collusion
	Change feelings and perceptions	Share perceptions to depolarize stereotypes	Consciousness raising about group and others
Behavior	Modify within-group behavior	Increase expression of within-group differences	Increase within-group cohesion and consensus
	Train group representatives to be more effective	Expand skills to include cooperative strategies	Expand skills to include assertive, confrontive strategies
	Monitor between-group behavior	Third-party peacemaking	Third-party process consultation
Structure	Invoke larger system interventions	Refer to common hierarchy	Hierarchical pressure for better performance
	Develop regulatory contexts	Impose rules on interaction that limit conflict	Deemphasize rules that stifle conflict
	Create new interface mechanisms	Develop integrating roles of groups	Create "devil's advocates" or ombudsmen
	Redefine group boundaries and goals	Redesign organization to emphasize task	Clarify group boundaries and goals to increase differentiation

Managing conflict between high- and low-power groups requires dealing in some fashion with their power differences, since those differences drastically affect the flow of information and influence among the parties. A prerequisite to conflict management interventions may well be *evening the psychological odds,* so that both groups feel able to discuss the situation without too much risk. Evening the odds does not necessarily mean power equalization, but it does require trustworthy protection (to reduce the fear of low-power groups) and effective education (to reduce the ignorance of high-power groups). Given psychological equality, interventions related to attitudes, behavior, and structure that have already been discussed may be employed to promote constructive levels of conflict (e.g., Brown, 1977). It should be noted that for differently powerful groups the boundary between too much and to little conflict is easily crossed. Managers may find themselves oscillating rapidly between interventions to induce and interventions to reduce conflict between such groups.

To return once again to an initial example, the history of fighting and violence between the small union and the corporation led the latter's managers to expect even worse conflict when faced by the international union. But voting in the international in effect evened the odds between labor and management. Violent tactics considered necessary by the small union were not necessary for the international, and the regulatory structure of collective bargaining proved adequate to manage the conflict subsequently.

Societal Differences

Organizations are increasingly forced to grapple with societal differences. These differences are typically not entirely task-related; rather, they are a result of systematic discrimination in the larger society. Group members enter the organization with sets toward each other with which the organization must cope to achieve its goals. Societal differences are most problematic when they involve histories of exploitation (e.g., blacks by whites, women by men), and successful conflict management of such differences requires more than good intentions.

Managing societal differences in organizations may call for evening the odds, as in managing power differences, since societal differences so often include an element of power asymmetry. But coping with societal differences may also require more, since the effect of institutionalization is to ensure that the differences are preserved. *Invoking pressures from the environment* may be required even to get mem-

bers of some groups into the organization at all. External forces such as federal pressure for "equal opportunity" and expanding educational opportunities for minorities can be used to press for more attention to societally based conflicts within organizations. Organizations may also develop *internal counterinstitutions* that act as checks and balances to systemic discrimination. A carefully designed and protected "communications group," which includes members from many groups and levels, can operate as an early warning system and as a respected third party for managing societal intergroup tensions in an organization (Alderfer, 1977).

The bank's failure to integrate the trust department turned largely on institutionalized racism. The decision to hire black managers was made partly in response to environmental pressure, and so overcame the initial barrier to letting blacks into the division at all. But once into the division, no mechanisms existed to press for overt discussion of differences. Without that discussion, no ways could be developed for the black managers to scale the insurmountable barriers facing them. The bank colluded with its supposedly racist clients by protecting them from contact with the new recruits. Although the first step—recruiting the black managers—was promising, trust division managers were unable to make the differences discussable or to develop the mechanisms required for effective management of the black-white differences in the division.

CONCLUSION

It may be helpful to the reader to summarize the major points of this argument and their implications. It has been argued that relations among groups in organizations can be characterized by too much or too little conflict, depending on their task, the nature of their differences, and the degree to which they are interdependent. This proposition suggests that *conflict managers should strive to maintain some appropriate level of conflict,* rather than automatically trying to reduce or resolve all disagreements. Effective management of intergroup conflict requires both understanding and appropriate action. Understanding integroup conflict involves diagnosis of attitudes, behaviors, structures, and their interaction. *Effective intervention to increase or decrease conflict requires action to influence attitudes, behaviors, and structures grounded in accurate diagnosis.*

Power differences between groups promote fear and ignorance that result in reduced exchange of information between groups and the potential for either explosive outbursts of escalated conflict or escalating oppression. Evening the odds, at least in psychological terms, may be a prerequisite to effective intervention in such situations. *Managers must cope with fear, ignorance, and their consequences to effectively manage conflicts between unequally powerful groups.*

Societal differences institutionalized in the larger society may further complicate relations among groups in organizations by introducing environmental events and long histories of tension. Managing such differences may require invocation of environmental pressures and the development of counterinstitutions that help the organization deal with the effects of systemic discrimination in the larger society. *Environmental developments produce the seeds for organizational conflicts, but they also offer clues to their management.*

The importance of effective conflict management in organizations is increasing, and that development is symptomatic of global changes. We live in a rapidly shrinking, enormously heterogeneous, increasingly interdependent world. The number of interfaces at which conflict may occur is increasing astronomically, and so are the stakes of too much or too little conflict at those points. If we are to survive—let alone prosper—in our onrushing future, we desperately need skilled managers of conflict among groups.

REFERENCES

Alderfer, C. P. Improving Organizational Communication Through Long-Term Intergroup Intervention. *Journal of Applied Behavioral Science, 13,* 1977, 193–210.

Blake, R. R., and Mouton, J. S. Reactions to Intergroup Competition Under Win-Lose Conditions. *Management Science, 4,* 1961.

Blake, R. R., Shepard, H. A., and Mouton, J. S. *Managing Intergroup Conflict in Industry.* Ann Arbor, Mich.: Foundation for Research on Human Behavior, 1964.

Brown, L. D. Can Haves and Have-Nots Cooperate? Two Efforts to Bridge a Social Gap. *Journal of Applied Behavioral Science, 13,* 1977, 211–224.

Brown, L. D. Toward a Theory of Power and Intergroup Relations, in *Advances in Experiential Social Process,* edited by C. A. Cooper and C. P. Alderfer. London: Wiley, 1978.

Burton, J. W. *Conflict and Communication: The Use of Controlled Communication in International Relations.* London: Macmillan, 1969.

Coser, L. A. *The Functions of Social Conflict.* New York: Free Press, 1973.

Deutsch, M. *The Resolution of Conflict.* New Haven, Conn.: Yale University Press, 1973.

Filley, A. C. *Interpersonal Conflict Resolution.* Glenview, Ill.: Scott, Foresman, 1975.

Galbraith, J. R. *Designing Complex Organizations.* Reading, Mass.: Addison-Wesley, 1971.

Janis, I. *Victims of Groupthink.* Boston: Houghton-Mifflin, 1972.

Lawrence, P. R., and Lorsch, J. W. *Organization and Environment.* Boston: Harvard Business School, 1967.

Robbins, S. P. *Managing Organizational Conflict.* Englewood Cliffs, N.J.: Prentice Hall, 1974.

Exercise: Group Decision Making and Effectiveness

PURPOSE

The purpose of this exercise is to help you better understand group process and group effectiveness. By the time you finish this exercise you will:

1. Identify the pros and cons of group versus individual decision making.

2. Experience a group decision-making situation.

3. Practice diagnosing work group effectiveness.

INTRODUCTION

Much of the work that takes place in organizations is done in groups. In fact, the more important a task, the more likely it is to be assigned to a group. There is a tendency to believe that groups make better decisions and are better at solving problems than individuals. However, the evidence on this subject is contradictory and seems to suggest that "it depends." Groups are more effective under some circumstances and individuals under others. There are assets and liabilities associated with both (Maier, 1967). Because so much important work is done in groups, it is necessary for group members to learn to minimize the liabilities and capitalize on the assets of group problem solving.

This two-part exercise is designed to give you the opportunity to work with a group to solve a problem and then reflect on that experience. In Part I you will have the opportunity to find out whether your group was able to minimize the liabilities and capitalize on the assets of group problem solving. In Part II you will evaluate the process that your group used to solve the problem.

INSTRUCTIONS

Part I

1. Read the directions and complete the Wilderness Survival Worksheet.

2. Form groups of five to seven people.

3. In groups, read the directions for and complete the Wilderness Survival Group Consensus Task.

Wilderness Survival is reprinted from: J. William Pfeiffer and John E. Jones (Eds.), *1976 Annual Handbook for Group Facilitators,* San Diego, CA: University Associates, Inc., 1976). Used with permission. The Group Effectiveness Checklist is based on the ideas presented in I. L. Janis, "Groupthink," *Psychology Today,* 1971, November; N. R. F. Maier, "Assets and Liabilities in Group Problem Solving: The Need for an Integrative Function," *Psychological Review,* 1967, *74,* 239–249.

4. Calculate your scores according to the directions in the Wilderness Survival Scoring Sheet.

5. Interpret your score.

6. Participate in a class discussion.

Part II

1. Read the directions and evaluate your group using the Group Effectiveness Checklist.

2. Fill out the Group Effectiveness Worksheet.

3. Meet in your group to discuss the Worksheets.

4. Develop a plan for improving group effectiveness.

5. Participate in a class discussion.

PART I: WILDERNESS SURVIVAL WORKSHEET

Directions: Here are twelve questions concerning personal survival in a wilderness situation. Your first task is to *individually* select the best of the three alternatives given under each item. Try to imagine yourself in the situation depicted. Assume that you are alone and have a minimum of equipment, except where specified. The season is fall. The days are warm and dry, but the nights are cold.

After you have completed the task individually, you will again consider each question as a member of a small group. Both the individual and group solutions will later be compared with the "correct" answers provided by a group of naturalists who conduct classes in woodland survival.

	Your Answer	*Your Group's Answer*	*Expert Answer*
1. You have strayed from your party in trackless timber. You have no special signaling equipment. The best way to attempt to contact your friends is to: a. Call for "help" loudly but in a low register. b. Yell or scream as loud as you can. c. Whistle loudly and shrilly.	_____	_____	_____
2. You are in "snake country." Your best action to avoid snakes is to: a. Make a lot of noise with your feet. b. Walk softly and quietly. c. Travel at night.	_____	_____	_____
3. You are hungry and lost in wild country. The best rule for determining which plants are safe to eat (those you do not recognize) is to: a. Try anything you see the birds eat. b. Eat anything except plants with bright red berries. c. Put a bit of the plant on your lower lip for five minutes; if it seems all right, try a little more.	_____	_____	_____
4. The day becomes dry and hot. You have a full canteen of water (about one liter) with you. You should: a. Ration it—about a capful a day. b. Not drink until you stop for the night, then drink what you think you need. c. Drink as much as you think you need when you need it.	_____	_____	_____
5. Your water is gone; you become very thirsty. You finally come to a dried-up watercourse. Your best chance of finding water is to: a. Dig anywhere in the stream bed. b. Dig up plant and tree roots near the bank. c. Dig in the stream bed at the outside of a bend.	_____	_____	_____

	Your Answer	*Your Group's Answer*	*Expert Answer*

6. You decide to walk out of the wild country by following a series of ravines where a water supply is available. Night is coming on. The best place to make camp is:
   a. Next to the water supply in the ravine.
   b. High on a ridge.
   c. Midway up the slope.

7. Your flashlight glows dimly as you are about to make your way back to your campsite after a brief foraging trip. Darkness comes quickly in the woods and the surroundings seem unfamiliar. You should:
   a. Head back at once, keeping the light on, hoping the light will glow enough for you to make out landmarks.
   b. Put the batteries under your armpits to warm them, and then replace them in the flashlight.
   c. Shine your light for a few seconds, try to get the scene in your mind, move out in the darkness, and repeat the process.

8. An early snow confines you to your small tent. You doze with your small stove going. There is danger if the flame is:
   a. Yellow.
   b. Blue.
   c. Red.

9. You must ford a river that has a strong current, large rocks, and some white water. After carefully selecting your crossing spot, you should:
   a. Leave your boots and pack on.
   b. Take your boots and pack off.
   c. Take off your pack, but leave your boots on.

10. In waist-deep water with a strong current, when crossing the stream, you should face:
    a. Upstream.
    b. Across the stream.
    c. Downstream.

11. You find yourself rimrocked; your only route is up. The way is mossy, slippery rock. You should try it:
    a. Barefoot.
    b. With boots on.
    c. In stocking feet.

	Your Answer	*Your Group's Answer*	*Expert Answer*

12. Unarmed and unsuspecting, you surprise a large bear prowling around your campsite. As the bear rears up about ten meters from you, you should:
   a. Run.
   b. Climb the nearest tree.
   c. Freeze, but be ready to back away slowly.

Individual Score _____

WILDERNESS SURVIVAL GROUP CONSENSUS TASK

Directions: You have just completed an individual solution to Wilderness Survival. Now your small group will decide on a group solution to the same dilemmas. A decision by consensus is difficult to attain, and not every decision may meet with everyone's unqualified approval. There should be, however, a general feeling of support from all members before a group decision is made. Do not change your individual answers, even if you change your mind in the group discussion.

SCORING SHEET

Directions:

1. As your instructor reads the experts' answers, record these in the Expert Answer column of the Wilderness Survival Worksheet.

2. Compare these "correct" answers with your individual answers and record the number of questions you answered correctly in the Individual Score space provided at the end of the Wilderness Survival Worksheet.

3. Compare the experts' answers with your group's answers, and record the number of questions the group answered correctly in the Group Score space provided on the chart below.

4. Compute your group's Average Individual Score by adding the Individual Scores of all group members and dividing by the number of members in your group. Record the result on the chart below.

5. Compute your Asset/Liability Score by subtracting the Average Individual Score from the Group Score, and record the result on the chart. If the result is positive, your group was more effective than the individual group members would have been working independently. In other words, the group capitalized on the "assets" of group problem solving. If the result is negative, your group did not capitalize on its assets, but fell prey to the "liabilities" of group problem solving.

6. Poll your group to find the highest and lowest individual scores. Record this range on the chart below. If any of the group members scored higher than the group, that individual would have performed better working alone than with the group. That individual was also unable to adequately influence the group.

7. Select a spokesperson to report your (a) Range of Individual Scores, (b) Average Individual Score, (c) Group Score, and (d) Asset/Liability Score.

Scoring Chart

Range of Individual Scores	
Average Individual Score	
Group Score	
Asset/Liability Score	

PART II: GROUP EFFECTIVENESS CHECKLIST

Directions: Reflect on your group experience. Carefully read each of the following statements and decide whether it is *Mostly True* or *Mostly False*. Put a check in the corresponding space beside each statement. If you do not have enough information to answer any of the questions, leave it blank. When you complete the checklist, fill out the Group Effectiveness Worksheet according to the directions.

Mostly True	Mostly False	
_____	_____	1. We listened to each other and considered each other's opinions.
_____	_____	2. During the discussion, objective quality was more important than majority rule.
_____	_____	3. Disagreements led to a more innovative solution.
_____	_____	4. Members felt comfortable expressing their opinions.
_____	_____	5. Disagreements did not cause hard feelings.
_____	_____	6. We all felt that we were working toward a common goal.
_____	_____	7. No one dominated the conversation.
_____	_____	8. People listened to understand rather than to refute.
_____	_____	9. Members' efforts were acknowledged and rewarded.
_____	_____	10. We openly discussed how we were going to perform the task.
_____	_____	11. Finding the best solution was more important to people than winning the argument.
_____	_____	12. We analyzed the task before beginning to perform it.
_____	_____	13. Individuals freely shared their knowledge and information.
_____	_____	14. The group carried out a careful critical scrutiny of the pros and cons of the alternatives.
_____	_____	15. The group seriously considered minority viewpoints.
_____	_____	16. We surveyed all of the alternatives before deciding on a solution.
_____	_____	17. We spent time trying to look beyond the obvious.
_____	_____	18. The group tried to get everyone's input.
_____	_____	19. Group members showed positive interest in facts and opinions that did not support their ideas.

GROUP EFFECTIVENESS WORKSHEET

Directions: With your group, go over the questions on the checklist. The items that you checked as *Mostly True* are the things that your group did that contributed to its effective performance. The items that you checked as *Mostly False* are the things that your group did that got in the way of its effective performance. Under the *Mostly True* column, list all of the items that the entire group agreed were mostly true. Do the same thing for the Mostly False column. List the items on which the group did not agree in the *Differences* column. Discuss the items for which there was disagreement and try to come to a consensus decision. Write these items in the appropriate column (*Mostly True* or *Mostly False*).

Mostly True	*Mostly False*	*Differences*

ACTION PLAN

Directions: As a group, review the Mostly False column of your Group Effectiveness Worksheet and decide on a plan for improvement.

Problem Areas	Plan for Improvement

1. Does your diagnosis of your group's interaction process help explain how well you did on the Wilderness Survival Exercise? How?

2. What were some of the items from the Group Effectiveness Checklist that your group disagreed on? What were the reasons for the differences in perception?

3. Were there any problem areas for which you were unable to identify any improvement strategies? Why?

4. If your group did a similar exercise tomorrow, do you think you would be more effective? Why?

5. Do you plan to use what you have learned about group effectiveness the next time you are in a task group? What are some of the difficulties that you may face implementing your plan? How do you plan to overcome these difficulties?

REFERENCES

Janis, I. L. "Groupthink," *Psychology Today,* November, 1971.

Maier, N. R. F. "Assets and Liabilities in Group Problem Solving: the Need for an Integrative Function," *Psychology Review,* 1967, *74,* 239–249.

Exercise: The NASA/Challenger Incident

PURPOSE

The purpose of this exercise is to provide you with an opportunity to analyze groupthink dynamics as they affect group decision-making processes. By the time you finish this exercise, you will:

1. Apply the concepts of groupthink to a recent news event.

2. Identify the pressures that caused groupthink to occur in this situation.

3. Determine the ways in which groupthink processes could be averted.

INTRODUCTION

As Maier (1967) states, there are as many disadvantages as advantages in group decision making. One disadvantage is the phenomenon of groupthink, described by Irving Janis. Groupthink is a mindset that causes the group to misread the decision situation. Because of some of the disadvantages of group decision-making processes, poor judgments sometimes are made, often with far-reaching consequences. Managers need to be aware of the pressures that cause groupthink *and* the ways in which it can be averted.

The case of the NASA/Challenger disaster provides a fruitful ground from which to understand groupthink processes at work. The Rogers Commission, when it published its report on the NASA/Challenger disaster, indicated that much of what went wrong concerned NASA's "flawed" decision-making processes. Read this case to determine what you think.

INSTRUCTIONS

1. Read the articles by Irving Janis, "Groupthink," and by Maier, "Assets and Liabilities in Group Problem Solving," as preparation for this case.

2. Read the insert, "Anatomy of a Tragedy."

3. Complete the discussion questions at the end of the case.

4. Participate in a class discussion.

Anatomy of a Tragedy

Six days after the Challenger disaster, on Feb. 3, 1986, President Reagan appointed a commission and charged it with reviewing the accident's circumstances, determining its probable cause, and recommending measures toward preventing another such disaster. Known as the Rogers commission after its chairman, former Secretary of State William P. Rogers, it had 120 days to work.

On June 6, the commission announced its conclusion: The immediate physical cause of Challenger's destruction was "a failure in the joint between the two lower segments of the right Solid Rocket Motor," the report said. "The specific failure was the destruction of the seals that are intended to prevent hot gases from leaking through the joint during the propellant burn. . . ."

But contributing to the accident was, in the commission's now-famous words, the fact that "the decision to launch the Challenger was flawed." The report continued: "Those who made that decision were unaware of the recent history of problems concerning the O-rings and the joint and were un-

© 1987 IEEE. Reprinted, with permission, from *IEEE Spectrum*, Vol. 24 (2), February, 1987, pp. 44–51.

aware of the initial written recommendation of the contractor advising against the launch at temperatures below 53 degrees Fahrenheit and the continued opposition of the engineers at Thiokol after the management reversed its position." It faulted the management structure of both Thiokol and NASA for not allowing such information to flow to the people who needed to know it.

After the Rogers commission report was released, the U.S. House of Representatives' Committee on Science and Technology spent two months conducting its own hearings and reached its own conclusions in November 1986. Although the House committee agreed with several of the Rogers commission's conclusions, it also stated that "the fundamental problem was poor technical decision-making over a period of several years by top NASA and contractor personnel."

The House committee pointed out that ". . . information on the flaws in the joint design and on the problem encountered in missions prior to 51-L was widely available and had been presented to all levels of Shuttle management." But the committee's report continued: "The NASA and Thiokol technical managers failed to understand or to fully accept the seriousness of the problem. There was no sense of urgency on their part to correct the design flaws in the SRB. No one suggested grounding the fleet. . . . Rather NASA chose to continue to fly with a flawed design and to follow a measured, 27-month corrective program," leading to a new type of joint proposed for later missions—the capture joint. The committee came to the conclusion that the problem surrounding the field-joint O-rings had been recognized soon enough for it to have been corrected, but that no correction was made, because "meeting flight schedules and cutting cost were given a higher priority than flight safety."

The findings both of the Rogers commission and of the House committee suggest a fundamental question that neither investigation addressed: just how could NASA—an organization with a reputation for ingenuity, good design, meticulous engineering, reliability, and safety—have found itself in a position where it repeatedly overlooked the obvious until disaster struck?

WHY WASN'T THE DESIGN FIXED?

Design of the joint was not changed, say Thiokol and NASA engineers and managers, because it was assumed the joint would behave like the similar joints on the Titan boosters. "In an overall sense," said Thiokol's Joe Kilminster last December, "the comfort zone, if you will, was expanded because of the fact that the shuttle joint was so similar to the Titan joint, and its many uses had shown successful operation. That's why a lot of—I guess 'faith' is the right word—was based on the fact that the Titan had had all these tests and successful experience."

Furthermore, Boisjoly pointed out: "The working troops—and I consider myself one of the working troops—had no knowledge of the thing being changed to a Criticality 1. So far as we were concerned, we had two seals that were redundant. . . . So either you believe that you fly, or you don't believe it and shut the program down."

WHY WASN'T EROSION SEEN AS A DANGER SIGN?

By 1985, erosion and blow-by had come to be accepted as normal—to the point where, in the Level I flight-readiness review for STS 51-L that analyzed the results of the preceding flight STS 61-C, NASA's Mulloy noted there were "no 61-C flight anomalies" and "no major problems or issues," in spite of the fact that there had been erosion or blow-by in three joints. Although some engineers were beginning to be

alarmed about the frequency of the erosion—especially after an analysis of the results of STS 51-B in April 1985 disclosed that the secondary O-ring of a nozzle joint had been eroded as well as its primary—they received little support from NASA or Thiokol.

In July 1985, for example, Thiokol's unofficial task force was told to solve the O-ring erosion problems for both the short and long term. But in a memorandum of July 31, Boisjoly noted the group's "essential nonexistence" and asked that it be officially endorsed. He wrote that the consequences of not dealing with the seal problems "would be a catastrophe of the highest order—loss of human life."

By October, however, one task-force member was dismayed enough to write a note to Allan McDonald: "HELP! The seal task force is constantly being delayed by every possible means. . . . This is a red flag." And around the same time Boisjoly went to Kilminster and, as he now recalls, "pleaded for help." But remembering that meeting, Boisjoly said: "And quite frankly, when we were leaving the room he [Kilminster] said, 'Well, it was a good bullshit session anyway.' And that was the end of it." Boisjoly now says he didn't use exactly those words when describing, in his weekly activity report of Oct. 4, 1985, his problem in obtaining support from Kilminster. "But I had it in my notebook. I was really ticked because we were pleading for help and we couldn't get it. We were fighting all the major inertia in the plant, just like everybody else, and yet we were supposed to be this tiger team to get a very severe problem solved." Kilminster, Boisjoly now says, "just didn't basically understand the problem. We were trying to explain it to him, and he just wouldn't hear it. He felt, I guess, that we were crying wolf."

OPERATIONAL: AND THEN WHAT?

"There's just no way that I can understand in God's green earth that an airline could undertake with its normal procedures the operation of the space shuttle," said former Apollo astronaut Frank Borman, now vice-chairman of Texas Air Corp. in Las Cruces, N.M. "When NASA came out with the request for a proposal from airlines to run the shuttle like it was a [Boeing] 727, I called them and I told them they were crazy. The shuttle is an experimental vehicle, and will remain an experimental, highly sophisticated vehicle on the edge of technology."

In the early 1980s there was much discussion about whether it made sense for NASA, a research and development agency, to run what was already being viewed as a common carrier, and proposals were solicited from airlines for operating agreements. "NASA's highest priority is to make the Nation's Space Transportation System (STS) fully operational and cost-effective in providing routine access to space." So stated National Security Decision Directive 42, in 1982, and Directive 144, in 1984. The directives set as a goal "a flight schedule of up to 24 flights per year with margins for routine contingencies attendant with a flight-surge capability."

The goal of being operational also changed NASA's philosophy on crew safety, as is seen from a 1985 report produced by Rockwell International for NASA's Langley Research Center, in Hampton, Va., titled "Space Station Crew Safety Alternatives Study." Wrote the Rockwell authors: "It is interesting to trace the evolution of crew safety philosophy [from Apollo through shuttle] and to understand the reasons for this evolution. The emphasis has gone historically in two directions: (1) a tendency to go from escape and rescue measure (e.g. abort systems) toward obtaining inherent safety (i.e., reduce/eliminate threats); and (2) an increasing interest in saving not only the crew, but also the very valuable space systems. We expect these trends to continue as space operations mature and become more routine."

This emphasis on eliminating or controlling threats rather than escaping from them is consistent with airline mentality. "You don't put parachutes on airlines because the margin of safety is built into the machine," said Borman, for 17 years president of Eastern Airlines. But, he pointed out, "The 727 airplanes that we fly are proven vehicles with levels of safety and redundancy built in"—levels, he said, that the space shuttle comes nowhere near to. The way Borman sees it, the shuttle is "a hand-made piece of experimental gear."

Nevertheless, people both within and outside NASA began to treat the shuttle like an airplane, with an attendant psychological casualness about its mechanical safety. Harold Finger, formerly NASA's associate administrator for organization and management and now president of the U.S. Committee for Energy Awareness in Washington, D.C., said the NASA successes may have led to a lack of vigilance and high-level knowledge of potential danger.

WHY NO SECOND SOURCES?

Ever since the start of the shuttle program, other manufacturers had been after NASA to let them be second sources for the boosters, the largest market anywhere for solid-fuel rocket motors. Congress had also wanted a second source, for national

security reasons, so that the shuttles would be available for military payloads in the event of a work stoppage or accident at Thiokol.

Obedient to the U.S. Competition in Contracting Act, NASA announced on Dec. 26, 1985—less than a month before Challenger's original launch date—a set of rules under which other manufacturers could bid to become a second source for the boosters. Although the bidding rules favored Thiokol in many ways, the announcement, Levin said, still threatened "a very fat contract. . . . Why did Thiokol management surrender on the night of Jan. 27? They didn't have to," he said—except for the fact that they were in the midst of negotiating the next production buy, and they were being threatened with a second source in connection with that buy, "Thus, keeping this customer happy was very important," Levin said.

THE NASA/CHALLENGER INCIDENT

NASA and Thiokol were aware of the likely impact of redesigning the booster joint from the ground up at least six months before Challenger's last flight. On July 23,1985, NASA budget analyst Richard C. Cook sent a memorandum to his superior, Michael Mann. It was clear that the booster seal threatened flight safety, Cook wrote. If the cause of the problems required a major redesign, it "would lead to the suspension of Shuttle flights, redesign of the SRB [solid-fuel rocket booster], and scrapping of existing stockpiled hardware. The impact on the FY 1987-8 budget could be immense."

Within Thiokol, Boisjoly wrote in his weekly report of July 22, 1985, that the company needed to focus attention on the problem. Otherwise, "We stand in danger of having one of our competitors solve our problem via an unsolicited proposal. This thought is almost as horrifying as having a flight failure before a solution is implemented to prevent O-ring erosion."

HOW DID NASA AND THIOKOL VIEW THE ODDS?

"No data conclusively showed that low temperatures would increase the risk," said NASA's Mulloy. "I agree with the House committee that continually taking that risk was bad engineering judgment, but that bad judgment started long before the teleconference that night of Jan. 27, and had the highest levels of NASA management participating in it."

Marshall propulsion engineer Ben Powers said that, at the time, "my understanding was that the [booster] motor was qualified [down] to 31° [F]."

However, he recalled little surprise in finding that the Thiokol engineers were now stating that it should not be flown in conditions that cold. The Jan. 27 teleconference, he said, was the first time his attention had been directed to it. "The emphasis was not enough earlier on."

According to Thiokol's Kilminster, "All the tests that showed that the resiliency of the [primary] O-ring was lower at low temperature did not include the effects of pressure acting on it during the motor-ignition pressure rise. This pressure acting on the O-ring tended to move it into a sealing position," he said. "We felt—based on all the test experience we had to that point, plus flight experience—that pressure caused the O-ring to operate as it was designed to operate, even in some of the static tests that were relatively cold—40° F."

Mulloy, in recalling his own reasoning about the launch conditions, said he argued: "We've been addressing this problem of O-ring erosion *every* launch. What is *different* this time? What was different was temperature. What is the effect of temperature? Our conclusion was that there is no correlation between low temperature and O-ring erosion—in fact, our worst erosion was at one of the highest temperatures.

"I concluded that we're taking a risk every time," Mulloy said. "We all signed up for that risk. And the conclusion was, there was *no* significant difference in risk from previous launches. We'd be taking essentially the same risk on Jan. 28 that we have been every since we first saw O-ring erosion," he said.

The fact that data linking low temperature to increased O-ring problems were uncertain may have had an underappreciated role. "In the face of uncertainty, people's preferences take over," said Dennis Mileti, professor of sociology and director of Colorado State University's Hazards Assessments Laboratory at Fort Collins, Colo. The risk is denied, discounted, and the chance is taken. . . . "This is not unique. It's just like any of us getting on an airplane— we all know that airplanes crash, but in our hearts we don't believe that the one we get on will crash."

Uncertainty over the affect of cold on the seal came about in several ways. There was no launch-commit criterion for the booster joint with regard to temperature. Also, Boisjoly later noted, there was "no graph plotting flights, with or without erosion as a function of temperature," that might have enabled the engineers to assess whether or not there was a correlation.

Moreover, there was, and continues to be, uncertainty over what temperatures had been speci-fied in the design criteria for the entire shuttle. McDonald and Lund of Thiokol both now say that the only specification they knew of called for the booster to operate between 40 and 90° F—although even what those limits referred to was unclear: Did it apply to the ambient temperature or to the propellant's mean bulk temperature inside each booster? Thiokol engineers say they never knew of a "higher-level spec," set at Johnson Space Center that called for the entire shuttle system to function at ambient temperatures from 31 to 99° F.

Mulloy calls that uncertainty "nonsense." Thiokol wrote the end-item specifications, he said, with 40 to 90° set for the propelant's mean bulk temperature, 31 to 99° for the ambient temperature, 21° for the external tank-booster strut interface, and 25° for the joint between the booster's aft and aft-center sections—the joint that failed on Challenger. Nonetheless, everyone at NASA up to Jesse Moore seems to have assumed that because specifications did exist, the entire shuttle met them. There also seems to have been confusion over the establishment of launch-commit criteria, as well as over when the criteria could be waived.

No one either at Thiokol or at NASA knew for sure how the O-rings would respond to cold, said Mulloy. He pointed out that the Viton rubber O-rings had never been tested below 50° F, mainly because the material had been designed to withstand the heat of combustion gases rather than the chill of winter launches. The Viton was formulated to military specifications for use between –30 and +500° F, but NASA did no tests of its own to see whether the O-rings met those specifications.

Even opposition by several Thiokol engineers to sending up the shuttle in freezing weather was not, in itself, seen as sufficient reason to scrub the launch, because experience itself is an uncertain guide. "When I was working as [NASA's] deputy administrator, I don't think there was a single launch where there was some group of subsystem engineers that didn't get up and say 'Don't fly,' " said Hans Mark, now chancellor of the University of Texas system in Austin. "You always have arguments.'

WHAT ROLE DID NASA's SAFETY OFFICE PLAY?

The Rogers commission noted the absence of safety personnel in making the decision to launch Challenger. Arnold Aldrich told the commission of five distinct failures that contributed to the decision, four of them relating to safety, reliability, and quality assurance. There was, he said, a lack of problem-reporting requirements, and a failure to involve NASA's safety office in critical discussions.

Inded, NASA's own corporate architecture contributed to those problems. Safety, reliability, and quility assurance was the reponsibility of NASA's chief engineer, Milton Silveira, at headquarters in Washington. As NASA's hub, the headquarters directs the 16 field centers and facilities all over the country. According to the Rogers commission, one of Silveira's headquarters staff of 20 devoted one-quarter of his time to space-shuttle concerns; another spent only one-tenth of his time on flight-safety issues.

"In the early days of the space program we were so damned uncertain of what we were doing that we always got everbody's opinion," said Silveira. "We would ask for continual reviews, continual scrutiny by anybody we had respect for, to look at this thing and mnake sure we were doing it right. As we started to fly the shuttle again and again, I think the system developed false confidence in itself and didn't do the same thing."

WAS NASA OR THIOKOL PRESSURED TO LAUNCH?

The push was on for 15 launches in 1986 and 24 launches a year by 1990. "That can't help but influence the degree of risk that one would take," said Mulloy. "But to me that is a self-imposed thing. You make a commitment and you try your damnedest to meet it. It's probably self-imposed professional pride—doing what you, by God, said you were going to do."

But the House committee report stressed the likely result of such a punishing schedule: "The pressure on NASA to achieve planned flight rates was so pervasive that it undoubtedly adversely affected attitudes regarding safety. . . . Operating pressures were causing an increase in unsafe practices," such as shortcuts in established launch-preparation procedures to save time.

The very day of the disaster brought speculation about pressure from the White House to have Challenger launched in time for President Reagan's State of the Union message, scheduled for that evening. NASA officials told the Rogers commission, however, that there was no such outside pressure and after a short discussion, the commission concluded that "the decision to launch the Challenger was made solely by the appropriate NASA officials without any outside intervention or pressure."

"I don't have any personal first-hand knowledge about presidential pressure, but circumstances and events were suggestive of pressure from the White House," said Traficant in August. "Whether or not there was any direct intent to apply pressure to have [the shuttle] launched in a timely way to orchestrate it with the State of the Union message, I believe NASA *perceived* that these types of timetable are important."

Richard C. Cook, the former NASA budget analyst who wrote the memorandum of July 23, 1985, warning of the possible effects of the joint's design, believes there was political pressure. In a 137-page report Cook stated: "The reason NASA overruled contractor engineers and lost Challenger was because they wanted to get the shuttle into the air by the time of the President's State of the Union Message, which mentioned the teacher in space. I believe that without political motivation, the accident would not have happened," he stated, adding: "I believe that the reason the White House formed its Presidential commission was to cover that up . . . and that there is perjury by NASA officials in the commission hearings."

In support of Dennis Mileti's theory that in the face of uncertainty people opt for their preferences, Levin said: "None of these folks that decided to fly Challenger wanted those people to die. None of them in their hearts would acknowledge that they were doing something stupid, evil, or rotten. We're not talking about murderers. We're talking about people who took a desperately high risk with other people's money, other people's lives—hoping like hell that the good luck that had always attended NASA activities would hold."

WHY DIDN'T THEY TALK TO EACH OTHER?

The Rogers commission perceived a lack of communication between engineers doing technical work at Thiokol and the top NASA managers who made the launch decisions. This breakdown meant that no information flowed on known problems with the booster joint—not only during the decision to launch Challenger, but also during the entire design and development process.

Hans Mark, widely regarded for his insight and skill in technology management, has observed: "The only criticism that I have of the [Rogers commission] report is that they laid more blame on the lower-level engineers and less blame on the upper-level management than they should have. As with most of those commissions, the guys on the bottom took the rap. They quote [associate administrator for space flight Jesse] Moore and [administrator James] Beggs and a few others saying they didn't know about the O-ring problems, which I find awfully hard to believe. I mean, hell, I knew about it two years before the accident and even wrote a memo about it. I just find it very hard to believe."

Robert Boisjoly at Thiokol, Ben Powers at NASA, and other technical people assert they did as much as they felt they could to air their concerns about the joint, short of risking being fired. They saw themselves as loyal employees, believing in the chain of command. Boisjoly told the Rogers commission: "I must emphasize, I had my say, and I never take [away] any management right to take the input out of an engineer and then make a decision based upon that input, and I truly believe that. . . . So there was no point in me doing anything any further."

And Powers said in an interview: "You don't override your chain of command. My boss was there; I made my position known to him; he did not choose to pursue it. At that point it's up to him; he doesn't have to give me any reasons; he doesn't work for me; it's his prerogative." And at least two others, asked by the Rogers commission why they did not voice their concerns to someone other than their immediate superior, replied in virtually identical language: "That would not be my reporting channel."

Following the chain of command is regarded favorably by managers and organizational theorists. But Harold Finger of the Committee for Energy Awareness warned: "You must organize for multiple lines of communication. You cannot be in a situation of any nature where you are limited by the requirement for a single reportage. In my mind, that's exactly what happened in the shuttle accident. There was no deliberate built-in system of multiple communications. Therefore, when objections were registered to somebody at Marshall or Houston or Kennedy, and he determined it didn't have to go up, it didn't go up."

Furthermore, even if the lower-level managers do pass the technical staff's concerns up the chain, they may make crucial modifications. "The fact that people are in a hierarchy tends to amplify misperceptions," said William H. Starbuck, ITT professor of creative management at New York University's Graduate School of Business Administration. "A low-level person has a fear that something might happen and reports it to a higher level. As it goes up the hierarchy, information gets distorted, usually to reflect the interests of the bosses."

WHAT ABOUT NASA'S SUCCESS STORY?

It is human nature to believe that success breeds success, when in some situations success may lead directly to failure. One of those situations is when people in an organization feel they have a problem licked. Said NYU's Starbuck: "As a company goes along and is successful, it assumes that success is inevitable. NASA had a history of 25 years of doing the impossible.

"My speculation is that this history made NASA come to have two points of view," Starbuck said. "First, risks as presented by engineers are always overstated—the actual risk is much smaller than it appears. Second, there is something magical about this group of people at NASA that can somehow surmount these risks. I think they developed a feeling of invulnerability."

Otto Lerbinger, professor of communications at Boston University, characterized this feeling that nothing can go wrong as "the Titanic syndrome." On the Titanic, he said, everyone felt that safety had been taken care of. "They even felt they didn't need lifeboats for everyone because the ship was unsinkable." It was the kind of situation where Lerbinger would see complacency setting in. "People make convenient assumptions because they want to move on. They note risks involved, but forget their assumptions and forget the risks they originally recognized," he said.

Starbuck, Lerbinger and Colorado State University's Dennis Mileti all sense that such feelings of invulnerability can gradually lead an organization to take greater chances. Starbuck mentioned a cut in the number of NASA inspectors assigned to oversee contractor's work, and the decrease in the safety, reliability, and quality assurance staff, disproportionate to other NASA staff cuts over the 15-year shuttle program.

All three experts mentioned NASA's shaving safety margins to increase shuttle payloads. "You build a bridge and it works, and so you figure on the next one you can trim it," said Starbuck. "That exceeds expectations, so you trim a bit more on the next one, until you build one that collapses." With the shuttle, he said, increasing amounts of O-ring erosion came to be accepted as normal.

John Hodge, who recently retired as NASA's acting associate administrator for space stations, said: "The problem is everybody thinks of engineering as an exact science. I think one of the real problems that we've had at NASA is that the more successful we are, the more people believe it's an exact science—and it isn't. There's a great deal of trade-off on design, and a great deal of judgment involved in engineering, and there always will be."

WHAT LESSONS HAVE BEEN LEARNED?

For Lawrence Mulloy, there are two major lessons to be learned from Challenger. "The paramount lesson is to assure that a product one sets the specs for and procures is designed, qualified, and certified to actually meet the design requirements," he said. "The fact that the booster was to function in 31° F ambient temperatures was flat missed. Whether that caused the accident is academic, but the fact was that it was missed."

Second, said Mulloy, "Be very, very careful in using subscale tests and analytical techniques to justify continuing operations on a flight vehicle where the component is not operating as you designed it to operate. Be careful in rationalizing the acceptance of anomalies you didn't expect."

According to Boston University's Lerbinger, corporate cultures try to ignore the unpleasant, and this has to be counteracted by deliberately creating a culture that encourages people to bring up unpleasant information. "In a group trying to move ahead with a decision, you find that those people that have anything negative to say are unpopular," said Lerbinger. "So a manager deliberately has to *encourage* people taking the devil's advocate position. In a crisis situation, somebody has got to think about the possibility of something going wrong, and to use a worst-case scenario approach."

Erasmus Kloman, retired consultant for the National Academy of Public Administration in Washington, has written six management studies of NASA. "The way to minimize uncertainty is to have an environment where bad news can travel up," he said. "Where there's that, there's trust and confidence."

Time and again there is the tendency to kill the messenger bringing bad news, rather than punish the wrongdoers. This was pointed out by NYU's Starbuck as well as by Myron Peretz Glazer, professor of sociology at Smith College in Northampton, Mass.

After the Challenger disaster Roger Boisjoly found he was ostracized within Thiokol and no longer allowed to work with NASA. In July he was put on permanent leave. Allan McDonald was initially stripped of his staff; later Thiokol sent out a press release that he was in charge of redesigning the booster joint. "They made it sound as if Al was heading up the whole thing, but that's a bunch of baloney," said Boisjoly. "He got his old job back, period."

"That's a very normal story," said Starbuck. "It's very typical for a whistleblower to be punished by an organization." Lerbinger agreed, pointing out that objections to Thiokol's determination to launch would be seen as "organizational treason."

On the other hand, as far as Thiokol and NASA were concerned, "The price was not nearly as heavy as one would have expected," said Glazer. "If one looks at the costs involved and the risks people took, it was the most disastrous thing that could have happened, yet they walked away okay." Glazer pointed out that William Lucas retired, by no means in disgrace, as director of Marshall Space Flight Center, shortly after the Challenger disaster. Research by Glazer and Penina Migdal Glazer for a book on whistleblowers shows, Glazer said, that "People who hung tough with their organization managed to do very well. Hanging in there and not protesting is valued highly. They manage to survive because of their fundamental and correct belief that the organization will protect them."

In fact, Starbuck said, "Thiokol's management worries me even more than NASA's. It's Thiokol where one manager said to another, 'Take off your engineering hat and put on your management hat.' They are the ones who should have looked into the questions surrounding the O-ring."

When no penalty is foreseen for being careless or doing wrong, the very behavior that should be prevented is actually enforced. Thus penalties have to be clarified and exacted, said attorney Robert Levin. "One of the things that's clear to me is that engineers do not speak the same language as managers," he said. "And engineers as a group are not politically savvy. What I would very much like to come out of all this— legislatively or otherwise—is that the next time this kind of dispute comes up, one of these engineers can day 'Damn it! Look what it *cost* Thiokol.' Now you're talking the language those folks understand."

Levin pointed out that not only is Thiokol reluctant to pay the $10 million penalty to NASA stipulated in its contract in the event of such a disaster, but "Thiokol has received millions of dollars as a result of this disaster; they're getting paid for the redesign."

The fact that there are few real penalties to organizations that commit avoidable errors also concerns Boston University's Lerbinger. "It's almost political law," he said. "Public memory is short. That puts managers in a position where they can *ignore* safety unless there is some reinforcement that gets public opinion aroused again."

DISCUSSION QUESTIONS

1. In your opinion, in what ways is the Challenger disaster a result of groupthink processes operating at NASA? At Morton Thiokol?

2. What antecedent conditions led to groupthink in the NASA and Morton Thiokol decision situation?

3. Could groupthink have been averted using Janis' principles for overcoming groupthink?

4. Is the groupthink explanation too simplistic to explain the faulty decision-making processes that affected the launch decision? What other processes (communication difficulties, strategic priorities, and the like) were operating in this situation?

Exercise: Labor Relations and Intergroup Conflict

PURPOSE

The purpose of this exercise is to provide an opportunity for you to experience intergroup dynamics through a forced labor negotiation. By the time you finish this exercise you will:

1. Determine an actual position for a labor negotiations dispute.

2. Develop an understanding of intergroup dynamics as they affect labor negotiations.

3. Identify ways to solve within-group conflict as well as between-group conflicts.

INTRODUCTION

At some point in your career, you may find yourself in the middle of a labor negotiations dispute—either on the side of management or on the side of labor. Labor negotiations, by their very nature, are a good example of intergroup dynamics. Each side must take a position, and each side must negotiate a final solution. Ideally, the solution achieved should be win-win.

This exercise was revised by Bonita L. Betters-Reed and Judith A. Babcock, 1986, from an original exercise by Arthur A. Whately and Nelson Lane Kelley in *Personnel Management in Action: Skill Building Experiences* (St. Paul: West Publishing Co., 1977).

In this exercise, you will have an opportunity to participate in a labor negotiations dispute. As a member of the negotiating team, you will need to identify a position and negotiate a solution. Your abilities to negotiate and solve the conflict will have a direct bearing upon the quality of the final solution.

INSTRUCTIONS

1. Your instructor will assign you to a negotiating team with four to six other members. Half of the groups will play the role of the union negotiators, while the other half will play the role of the management negotiators.

2. Read the P&M Manufacturing Company and Rules for Negotiations. All class members should study the Bargaining Issues and Table 1 on Labor–Management Agreements Among Competitors in the New England Area.

3. If playing the role of a union negotiator, read *only* the Negotiator's Role for TWA. If playing the role of a management negotiator, read *only* the Negotiator's Role for P&M.

4. Each team should meet separately to make the following decisions:
    a. Rank order the bargaining issues in terms of importance to the team.
    b. For each bargaining issue, determine three positions: the minimum for which you will settle, the maximum you will request, and a midpoint.
    c. Select a spokesperson and agree on a time-out signal.

5. Hold the negotiating session. If issues are not settled by the end of the session (25 minutes), a strike will be called.

6. Participate in a class discussion on the questions at the end of the exercise.

P&M MANUFACTURING COMPANY

P&M Manufacturing Company, located in Providence, Rhode Island, produces small toy cars for distribution and sales nationally. Employing about 300 manufacturing workers, it is much smaller than its competitors because P&M is not diversified in its operations. It has been able to meet its competition by emphasizing high production quality and personalized marketing techniques. It has the best reputation in the industry for quality.

In the early 1960s the employees at P&M were organized by the Toy Workers of America (TWA), and relations between the union and management have been very good. No time has ever been lost due to a work stoppage or strike. In the last year one of P&M's largest competitors dropped its market operation, which gave P&M a tremendous opportunity to increase its market share from 20 percent to 30 and perhaps 40 percent. Management is excited about the possibilities and wants to increase its production as soon as possible.

The current union contract expires in a week. Representatives from management and the union have been negotiating the new contract for several days, but no agreements have been reached.

Company Demographics

☐ In the past 10 years the male/female ratio has shifted from 80/20 to 50/50.

☐ Of all the workers, 20 percent are single; 80 percent are married or are heads of household (i.e., usually divorced or widowed mothers; approximately 100 have preschool children). [A survey has shown that 50 percent of the absenteeism is related to baby-sitter problems. There is considerable sentiment among the workers (88 percent surveyed) favoring benefits to help pay for day care of preschool children of workers.]

☐ Thirty percent do not have a U.S. high school diploma (some are recent immigrants), 50 percent have finished high school, and 20 percent have had some college education.

BARGAINING ISSUES*

1. Blue Cross and Blue Shield, RIGHA, or Ocean State
   Past contract agreement:

   > 1985–1986: P&M made a 90 percent contribution, employee paid 10 percent of full premiums for individuals only at group rates

   Present bargaing positions:

   > TWA: P&M should pay full cost

   > P&M: Employee should pay 10 percent of cost for individual coverage

Company Contribution

P&M	90 percent Individual	Full Individual	Full Family	Full Medical + Vision	Full Medical, Vision + Dental	TWA
	0	$37,000	$213,000	$321,000	$471,000	

Costs

2. Establishment of a third shift
   Past contract agreement:

   > 1985–1986: Third shift can be unilaterally established at any time with no allowances for difference in pay (150 on 3rd shift, costs include wages + increase in Soc. Sec.)

   Present bargaining positions:

   > TWA: $.50 more per hour

   > P&M: No increase

Per Hour Increases

P&M	0	$.10	$.20	$.30	$.40	$.50	TWA
	0	$32,130	$64,260	$96,390	$128,520	$160,650	

Costs

3. Wage Increases
   Past contract agreements:

   > 1985–1986: $4.50 per hour

   Present bargaining Positions:

   > TWA: $.80 more per hour

   > P&M: No increase

Per Hour Increases

P&M	0	$.10	$.20	$.30	$.40	$.50	$.60	$.70	$.80	TWA
	0		$128,520		$257,040		$385,560		$514,080	
		$64,260		$192,780		$321,300		$449,820		

Costs

---

*These bargaining issues are conceptualized here in terms of "trading points." This approach is described in A. A. Sloane and F. Whitney, *Labor Relations*, 2nd ed. (Englewood Cliffs, NJ: Prentice Hall, 1972), pp. 194–195.

4. One additional employee per crew
   Past contract agreement:

        1985–1986: 10 persons per crew (15 crews)
   Present bargaining positions:

           TWA: 1 additional person at a cost of $10,500 each

           P&M: No increase

Increase Per Crew

	0 person		1 person	
P&M				TWA
	0		$157,500	
		Costs		

5. Vacation Benefits
   Past contract agreements:

        1985–1986: One week for the first year, two weeks for all employees with two years of service
   Present bargaining positions:

           TWA: Four weeks for twenty years of service

           P&M: No change

	2 weeks after 2 years	2 weeks after 1 year	4 weeks after 30 years	4 weeks after 25 years	4 weeks after 20 years	
P&M						TWA
	0	$9,000	$12,000	$15,000	$20,000	
			Costs			

6. Child care (75 out of the 100 with pre-school children would use child care benefits)
   Past contract agreement:

        1985–1986: Not included in contract
   Present bargaining positions:

           TWA: $100 per week

           P&M: None

	0	25/week	50/week	75/week	100/week	
P&M						TWA
	0	$93,750	$187,500	$281,250	$375,000	
			Costs			

7. Personal days (cumulative, unused days carried over)
   Past contract agreement,

        1985–1986: None included in contract
   Present bargaining positions:

           TWA: 2 days

           P&M: 0 days

	0	.5	1	1.5	2	
P&M						TWA
	0	$5,400	$10,800	$16,200	$21,600	
			Costs			

TABLE 1: LABOR–MANAGEMENT AGREEMENTS AMONG COMPETITORS IN THE NEW ENGLAND AREA

	Competitor A (Boston)	Competitor B (Hartford)	Competitor C (Lowell)	Competitor D (Bangor)	Competitor E (Providence)
Company Contribution					
Medical	full medical + vision + dental	medical + dental	medical + dental	individual only	full family only
Third Shift Pay Differential	yes	no	yes	no	no
Hourly Wage Rate	$5.45	$4.75	$5.05	$4.50	$4.60
No. of Workers per Crew	10	10	10	11	10
Vacation Benefits	2 weeks after 1 year, 4 weeks after 15 years	2 weeks after 1 year, 4 weeks after 20 years	2 weeks after 1 year, 3 weeks after 20 years	2 weeks after 1 year	2 weeks after 2 years, 3 weeks after 20 years
Personal Days (Annual)	3	2	1	0	1
Child Care	100/week	25/week	no	no	no
Current Contract Expiration Date	12 months	9 months	15 months	1 month	3 months

Read only the role to which you have been assigned.

Negotiator's Role for P&M

You are the negotiator for P&M Manufacturing Company. The union demands for the new contract are viewed by you and the management as being extremely unrealistic. If the company meets the union demands at this time, the price of P&M's product will have to be increased and thus will prevent P&M from taking advantage of the opportunity to improve its market share brought about by a large competitor dropping out of the market. The union's stance is hard-nosed and you feel that, for the first time, a strike is a possibility. It has been estimated that a strike will cost P&M $50,000 per day in lost revenue.

Budgeting Information

Your financial vice president projects that with expansion and increased productivity you can afford $900,000 in a union settlement without raising prices. If you settle for more than this, you will have to raise prices and are likely to lose market share as well as being unable to tap into the market share of the dropped competitor. (*Note:* Union negotiators do not have this information.)

Negotiator's Role for TWA

As the negotiator for the union in the current contract dispute with P&M Manufacturing Company, you are expected to take a hard position regarding the proposals your union has placed before management. The sentiment of the union membership is that P&M is on the verge of expansion and as a result has a very favorable chance of improving its profitability. The membership wants part of the action.

The union also feels that some personnel policies and practices of P&M lag behind those of its competitors. For example, since a third of the workers are mothers with preschool children, who are also heads of households, there is strong sentiment that the company should provide day care or funds for that purpose to be used for public or private day care centers. Also, since 80 percent of the workers are married or unmarried women who are heads of households (with children) and the company only pays medical insurance equivalent to 90 percent of the premium for individuals, many workers must pay extra to cover their families. These workers resent this extra cost. Employees feel so strongly about this issue that the possibility of a strike exists. A strike will cost the membership $12,000 per day in lost wages and benefits.

You are to get as much for the union as you can.

RULES FOR NEGOTIATIONS

1. One person on a team is to be designated as the team spokesperson. Only the spokesperson may talk during negotiations. During negotiations, the team may decide to designate another person as spokesperson. If so, the other team must be informed of the change.

2. Whenever a team member wishes a timeout for a team conference, that person signals the spokesperson who must initiate the timeout. Timeouts do not count towards the 25-minute deadline, but they must be restricted to 3 minutes each.

3. Any tactic is acceptable but keep in mind that time is important. If a contract is not approved in 25 minutes, a strike occurs—costing each side dearly.

4. During negotiations, record agreements that are reached on the form below:

Final Agreement

Medical_____

Third Shift Differential_____

Wage Increases_____

Enlarging Work Crew_____

Vacation Benefits_____

Personal Days_____

Child Care_____

5. Once an agreement on an issue is reached, it cannot be renegotiated. Issues may be linked together into a "package" but only if agreement has not been reached on the issues to be linked.

DISCUSSION QUESTIONS

1. Discuss the feelings and emotions of team members. How did those of you who were not the spokesperson feel? The spokesperson?

2. What approach to labor negotiations was most successful in terms of reaching an agreement? How did the goals of each side differ? Why?

3. Given that there was conflict between the two teams, was there also conflict within the teams? How was it resolved?

4. What preceding and current situational factors contribute positively to the resolution of conflict? What factors have a negative effect?

REFERENCES

For the bargaining issues on trading points, see A. A. Sloane and F. Whitney, *Labor Relations,* 2nd ed. (Englewood Cliffs, N.J.: Prentice Hall, 1972), pp. 194–195.

Memo: Group and Intergroup Behavior

The purpose of this memo is to help you analyze and identify your group's interaction process and identify the sources of conflict that may affect intergroup relations where you work. Think about a group that you know well and that is important to you (if possible a work group such as your group or task force), and answer the following questions:

1. What impairs the group's effectiveness? What contributes to the group's effectiveness?

2. Do members within the group communicate openly and honestly? Are conflicts aired without prejudgments?

3. Does the composition of the group affect the group's effectiveness? How?

4. How does the group normally make decisions? Majority rule, minority rule, apathy, or complete consensus? What are the consequences of this decision-making style?

5. Does the group capitalize on the assets of group problem solving? Does the group minimize the liabilities of group problem solving? If not, why not?

6. Does the group fall into the trap of groupthink? How does this manifest itself?

7. With which groups are the members of your group most frequently in contact? For what reasons?

8. What are the goals and priorities of your group? How do they differ from the goals and priorities of the groups you identified above?

9. What are the attitudes of your group toward the groups with which you must work most frequently? What do you think the attitudes of these groups are toward your group?

10. How do resource allocations (such as staff, budget, and the like) differ between your group and the groups with which you must most frequently work?

11. What are the most common conflicts that emerge between your group and the groups on which you have focused?

Use this analysis to formulate a plan for improving the effectiveness of your group and the relationship of your group and the groups with which you are in conflict. Be sure to include:

1. What your group must do, both internally and in relation to the other group.

2. How you plan to influence your group.

3. How you expect your group to respond.

4. What you expect the other groups to do.

5. The support the organization must provide.

6. What obstacles you may encounter.

7. How you plan to overcome these obstacles.

8. Potential consequences—both positive and negative—for your group, the other groups, and your organization.

Organization Design, Structure, And Environment

INTRODUCTION

Managers frequently ask how to design their organizations for maximum effectiveness. Groups of similar jobs must be organized into departments, departments with similar functions must be organized into divisions, and the relationships among divisions and departments must be specified.

Complicating these decisions is the fact that organizations are open systems that interact with, and depend on, their environment for survival. Organizations take in resources from the environment, transform these resources and export the results back to the environment. For example, an automobile manufacturer brings steel and other raw materials into the organization, cuts, screws, welds, and paints these raw materials to create a car, which is then shipped to a dealer's showroom. A university recruits students, whom it transforms through educational activities into graduates and sends out into the world to make money to contribute to its alumni fund.

Because an organization must continually interact with its environment, the most appropriate design will depend, to a large extent, on that environment. The part of an organization's environment that must be considered in design decisions includes all of the conditions outside of its boundaries that could affect it. For example, it might be important for an organization to consider government regulation, economic conditions, competition, availability of raw materials or customers. The specific elements that will be of interest to a particular organization will depend to a great degree on the strategic choices that the organization has made.

As the organization grows or the environment changes, the critical elements of the environment will also change. Organizations must be constantly alert to changes in their environment. When organizational structure is not matched to the demands of the environment, it will be difficult if not impossible for the organization to operate effectively. Thus, learning how to align an organization's structure with the demands of its environment is an important managerial skill and the purpose of this chapter.

READINGS

The first reading, "What is the Right Organization Structure? Decision Tree Analysis Provides the Answer" by Robert Duncan, presents a decision tree to

help managers choose the right organizational structure. This article is a rare combination of solid theoretical background and useful advice for managers who find themselves involved in designing their organization. Duncan reviews the objectives of organizational design, which he sees as: (1) facilitating the flow of information within the organization to reduce the uncertainty in decision making and (2) achieving effective coordination between departments. He examines two of the predominant organizational structures—functional and decentralized—and discusses the critical interaction between the design of an organization and its environment. By the time you finish this reading you will understand what organization structure is, why the careful design of structure is so critical to organizational success, and what factors must be considered for a design to be effective.

In the second reading, "Mechanistic and Organic Systems of Management," T. Burns and G. M. Stalker present the idea of mechanistic and organic systems that are polar extremes suited to different rates of technical and commercial change. Mechanistic systems, which are bureaucratic in nature, are adapted to relatively stable conditions, while organic systems, which are less rigid and hierarchical, are adapted to conditions of change. Although their perspective is different from Duncan's, they agree that matching structure to the demands of the environment is of primary importance.

The last reading, "Evolution and Revolution as Organizations Grow" by Larry Greiner, describes the developmental phases that companies pass through as they grow and develop into mature organizations. According to Greiner, an organization's structure should match its stage of development as well as the demands of its environment. Thus, as an organization grows, its structure should change to keep pace with this development. He posits five developmental phases: creativity, direction, delegation, coordination, and collaboration. Each of these phases is associated with a different management focus, organization structure, top management style, control system, and management reward emphasis.

EXERCISES AND CASES

The exercises in this chapter are designed to give you the opportunity to begin developing your skills at environmental analysis and organization design. In the first exercise, "Environmental Analysis," you will analyze the task environment of different organizations. Because the most appropriate structure for an organiza- tion will depend, to a great degree, on its environment, the first step in any organization design is an analysis of that environment. In this exercise you will first determine the degree of environmental uncertainty, then you will use the decision tree presented by Duncan to determine the most appropriate structure for each of several organizations.

In the second exercise, "Small Business Design: The Case of a Publishing Firm," you will have the opportunity to design a new, small organization. The *Job-Getter Enterprise* is a small local publication that lists jobs. It was founded by a young entrepreneur, Martin Manicot, who is beginning to experience problems with his growing organization. You are given all of the necessary information and

placed in the position of a consultant to whom Manicot has come for help in structuring and organizing his enterprise.

The "Rondell Data Corporation" presents the problems faced by the director of engineering and engineering services, Frank Forbus. Frank's problem is the lack of cooperation he is getting from other departments. This lack of cooperation is making it impossible for him to get a new piece of equipment off the drawing board. What he fails to recognize is that the real problem lies not in the personalities involved, but in the way the organization is structured. Misattributing organizational problems to personalities is a common mistake. This case will broaden your perspective, enable you to formulate alternative hypotheses when faced with organizational problems, and thus develop effective solutions.

MEMO

The organization design memo gives you the opportunity to apply the theories and skills that you have learned to your organization. You are asked to diagnose the structure of your organization by answering a series of questions concerning your organization's environment, current structure, and developmental stage. Using this information you will determine what—if any—changes should be made in the structure of your organization.

Looking at organizational behavior from the perspective of organization design and structure may seem strange at first. Most managers are more accustomed to focusing on people or groups as the source of organizational difficulties. However, an ineffective structure can often be the primary cause of problems that, on the surface, seem to be the result of difficult individuals or groups. By the time you finish this chapter you will have gained an appreciation for the critical role structure plays in organizational effectiveness. You will also have increased your skills at designing the most appropriate structure for an organization based on its environment, goals, and developmental stage.

What Is the Right Organization Structure?
Decision Tree Analysis Provides the Answer

Robert Duncan

Organization design is a central problem for managers. What is the "best" structure for the organization? What are the criteria for selecting the "best" structure? What signals indicate that the organization's existing structure may not be appropriate

Reprinted, by permission of the publisher, from *Organizational Dynamics,* Winter, 1979. Copyright, © 1979 American Management Association, New York. All rights reserved.

to its tasks and its environment? This article discusses the purposes of organization structure and presents a decision tree analysis approach to help managers pick the right organization structure.

THE OBJECTIVES OF ORGANIZATIONAL DESIGN

What is organization structure and what is it supposed to accomplish? Organization structure is

more than boxes on a chart; it is a pattern of interactions and coordination that links the technology, tasks, and human components of the organization to ensure that the organization accomplishes its purpose.

An organization's structure has essentially two objectives: First, it facilitates the flow of information within the organization in order to reduce the uncertainty in decision making. The design of the organization should facilitate the collection of the information managers need for decision making. When managers experience a high degree of uncertainty—that is, when their information needs are great—the structure of the organization should not be so rigid as to inhibit managers from seeking new sources of information or developing new procedures or methods for doing their jobs. For example, in developing a new product, a manufacturing department may need to seek direct feedback from customers on how the new product is being accepted; the need to react quickly to customer response makes waiting for this information to come through normal marketing and sales channels unacceptable.

The second objective of organization design is to achieve effective coordination—integration. The structure of the organization should integrate organizational behavior across the parts of the organization so it is coordinated. This is particularly important when the units in the organization are interdependent. As James Thompson had indicated, the level of interdependence can vary. In *pooled interdependence* the parts of the organization are independent and are linked together only in contributing something to the same overall organization. In many conglomerates, the divisions are really separate organizations linked only in that they contribute profits to the overall organization. Simple rules—procedures—can be developed to specify what the various units have to do. In *sequential interdependence*, however, there is an ordering of activities, that is, one organizational unit has to perform its function before the next unit can perform its. For example, in an automobile plant manufacturing has to produce the automobiles before quality control can inspect them. Now such organizations have to develop plans to coordinate activities; quality control needs to know when and how many cars to expect for inspection.

Reciprocal interdependence is the most complex type of organizational interdependence. Reciprocal interdependence is present when the output of Unit A become the inputs of Unit B and the outputs of B cycle back to become the inputs of Unit A. The relationship between the operations and maintenance

in an airline is a good example of this type of interdependence. Operations produces "sick" airplanes that need repair by maintenance. Maintenance repairs these planes and the repaired planes become inputs to the operations division to be reassigned to routes. When reciprocal interdependence between organization units is present, a more complex type of coordination is required. This is coordination by feedback. Airline operations and maintenance must communicate with one another so each one will know when the planes will be coming to them so they can carry out their respective functions.

Organizational design, then, is the allocation of resources and people to a specified mission or purpose and the structuring of these resources to achieve the mission. Ideally, the organization is designed to fit its environment and to provide the information and coordination needed.

It is useful to think of organization structure from an information-processing view. The key characteristic of organizational structure is that it links the elements of the organization by providing the channels of communication through which information flows. My research has indicated that when organizational structure is formalized and centralized, information flows are restricted and, as a consequence, the organization is not able to gather and process the information it needs when faced with uncertainty. For example, when an organization's structure is highly centralized, decisions are made at the top and information tends to be filtered as it moves up the chain of command. When a decision involves a great deal of uncertainty, it is unlikely therefore that the few individuals at the top of the organization will have the information they require to make the best decision. So decentralization, that is, having more subordinates participate in the decision-making process, may generate the information needed to help reduce the uncertainty and thereby facilitate a better decision.

ALTERNATIVE ORGANIZATIONAL DESIGNS

The key question for the manager concerned with organization design is what are the different structures available to choose from. Contingency theories of organization have shown that there is no one best structure. However, organization theorists have been less clear in elaborating the decision process managers can follow in deciding which structure to implement.

In discussing organization design, organization theorists describe structure differently from the way managers responsible for organization design do.

Organizational theorists describe structure as more or less formalized, specialized, centralized, or hierarchical. However, managers tend to think of organizational structure in terms of two general types, the *functional* and the *decentralized*. Most organizations today are either functional or decentralized or some modification or combination of these two general types. Therefore, if we are to develop a heuristic for helping managers make decisions about organization structure, we need to think of structures as functional or decentralized and not in terms of the more abstract dimensions of formalization, centralization, and so on, that organizational theorists tend to use.

ORGANIZATIONAL ENVIRONMENT AND DESIGN: A CRITICAL INTERACTION

In deciding on what kind of organization structure to use, managers need to first understand the characteristics of the environment they are in and the demands this environment makes on the organization in terms of information and coordination. Once the environment is understood, the manager can proceed with the design process.

The first step in designing an organization structure, therefore, is to identify the organization's environment. The task environment constitutes that part of the environment defined by managers as relevant or potentially relevant for organizational decision making. Figure 1 presents a list of environmental components managers might encounter. Clearly, no one organization would encounter all these components in decision making, but this is the master list from which organizational decision makers would identify the appropriate task environments. For example, a manager in a manufacturing division could "define an environment consisting of certain personnel, certain staff units and suppliers, and perhaps certain technological components. The usefulness of the list in Figure 1 is that it provides a guide for decision makers, alerting them to the elements in the environment they might consider in decision making.

Once managers have defined the task environment, the next step is to understand the state of that

FIGURE 1
Environmental Components List.

Internal Environment	External Environment
Organizational personnel component	Customer component
—Educational and technological background and skills	—Distributors of product or service
—Previous technological and managerial skill	—Actual users of product or service
—Individual member's involvement and commitment to attaining system's goals	Suppliers component
—Interpersonal behavior styles	—New materials suppliers
—Availability of manpower for utilization within the system	—Equipment suppliers
	—Product part suppliers
Organizational functional and staff units component	—Labor supply
—Technological characteristics of organizational units	Competitor component
—Interdependence of organizational units in carrying out their objectives	—Competitors for suppliers
—Intraunit conflict among organizational functional and staff units	—Competitors for customers
	Sociopolitical component
Organizational level component	—Government regulatory control over the industry
—Organizational objectives and goals	—Public political attitude toward industry and its particular product
—Integrative process integrating individuals and groups into contributing maximally to attaining organizational goals	—Relationship with trade unions with jurisdiction in the organization
—Nature of the organization's product service	Technological component
	—Meeting new technological requirements of own industry and related industries in production of product or service
	—Improving and developing new products by implementing new technological advances in the industry

FIGURE 2

Classification of Organizational Environments.

	Simple	Complex
Static	*Low Perceived Uncertainty* Small number of factors and components in the environment Factors and components are somewhat similar to one, another Factors and components remain basically the same and are not changing **1** *Example:* Soft drink industry	*Moderately Low Perceived Uncertainty* Large number of factors and components in the environment Factors and components are not similar to one another Factors and components remain basically the same **2** *Example:* Food products
Dynamic	*Moderately High Perceived Uncertainty* Small number of factors and components in the environment Factors and components are somewhat similar to one another Factors and components of the environment are in a continual process of change *Example:* Fast food industry	**3 4** *High Perceived Uncertainty* Large number of factors and components in the environment Factors and components are not similar to one another Factors and components of environment are in a continual process of change *Examples:* Commercial airline industry Telephone communications (AT&T)

environment. What are its key characteristics? In describing organizational environments, we empha-size two dimensions: simple-complex and static-dynamic.

The simple-complex dimension of the environ-ment focuses on whether the factors in the environ-ment considered for decision making are few in num-ber and similar or many in number and different. An example of a *simple* unit would be a lower-level pro-duction unit whose decisions are affected only by the parts department and materials department, on which it is dependent for supplies, and the marketing de-partment, on which it is dependent for output. An example of a *complex* environment would be a pro-gramming and planning department. This group must consider a wide variety of environmental factors when making a decision. It may focus on the marketing and materials department, on customers, on suppliers, and so on. Thus this organizational unit has a much more heterogeneous group of environmental factors to deal with in decision making—its environment is more complex than that of the production unit.

The static-dynamic dimension of the environ-ment is concerned with whether the factors of the environment remain the same over time or change. A *static* environment, for example, might be a produc-tion unit that has to deal with a marketing department whose requests for output remain the same and a materials department that is able to supply a steady rate of inputs to the production unit. However, if the marketing department were continually changing its requests and the materials department were incon-sistent in its ability to supply parts, the production unit would be operating in a more *dynamic* envi-ronment.

Figure 2 provides a four-way classification of organizational environments and some examples of organizations in each of these environments. Complex-dynamic (Cell 4) environments are probably the most characteristic type today. These environ-ments involve rapid change and create high uncer-tainty for managers. The proper organizational struc-ture is critical in such environments if managers are to have the information necessary for decision making. Also, as organizations move into this turbulent envi-ronment, it may be necessary for them to modify their structures. For example, AT&T has moved from a functional organization to a decentralized structure

organized around different markets to enable it to cope with more competition in the telephone market and in communications. This change in structure was in response to the need for more information and for a quicker response time to competitive moves.

STRATEGIES FOR ORGANIZATIONAL DESIGN

Once the organization's environment has been diagnosed, what type of structure the organization should have becomes the key question.

Simple Design Strategy

When the organization's environment is relatively simple, that is, there are not many factors to consider in decision making, and stable, that is, neither the make-up of the environment nor the demands made by environmental components are changing, the information and coordination needs for the organization are low. In such circumstances, a *functional organization structure* is most appropriate. A key characteristic of the functional organization is specialization by functional areas. Figure 3 presents a summary of this structure's strengths and weaknesses. The key strengths of the functional organization are that it supports in-depth skill development and a simple decision-communication network. However, when disputes or uncertainty arises among managers about a decision, they get pushed up the hierarchy to be resolved. A primary weakness of the functional organization, therefore, is that when the organization's environment becomes more dynamic and uncertainty tends to increase many decisions move to the top of the organization. Lower-level managers do not have the information required for decision making so they push decisions upward. Top-level managers become overloaded and are thus slow to respond to the environment.

Organizational Design Dilemma

The organizational designer faces a dilemma in such situations. Designs can be instituted that *reduce* the amount of information required for decision making. Decentralization is the principal strategy indicating. Or organizations can develop more lateral relations to *increase* the amount of information available. A decentralized organization is possible when-ever an organization's tasks are self-contained. Decentralized organizations are typically designed around products, projects, or markets. The decentralized healthcare organization in Figure 4 is organized around product areas (Medical and Dental) and market area (International). Each division has all the resources needed to perform its particular task. For example, Medical Products (Figure 4) has its own functional organization consisting of production, marketing, and R&D to carry out its mission. The information needed by Medical Products Division's manager's is reduced

FIGURE 3

Characteristics of the Functional Organization.

Organizational Functions	*Accomplished in Functional Organization*
Goals	Functional subgoal emphasis (projects lag)
Influence	Functional heads
Promotion	By special function
Budgeting	By function or department
Rewards	For special capability

Strengths	*Weaknesses*
1. Best in *stable* environment	1. Slow response time
2. Colleagueship ("home") for technical specialists	2. Bottlenecks caused by sequential tasks
3. Supports in-depth skill development	3. Decisions pile at top
4. Specialists freed from administrative/coordinating work	4. If multiproduct, product priority conflict
5. Simple decision/communication network excellent in small, limited-output organizations	5. Poor interunit coordination
	6. Stability paid for in less innovation
	7. Restricted view of whole

because they have organized around a set of common medical products, and they don't have to worry about dental, pharmaceutical, or hospital support services or products.

In the decentralized organization, managers only have to worry about their own products or services; they have the resources to carry out these activities, and they don't have to compete for shared resources or schedule shared resources. There is also a full-time commitment to a particular product line. The decentralized structure is particularly effective when the organization's environment is very complex, that is, there are a large number of factors to be considered in decision making, and the environment can be segmented or broken down into product or market areas around which the organization can structure itself. For example, the health products organization (Figure 4) probably started out as a functional organization. However, as its product line increased, it undoubtedly became more difficult for one manufacturing unit to have the expertise to produce such a wide range of products efficiently and to handle the diversity of information needed to do it. It would also be difficult for one marketing unit to market such a diverse group of products; different kinds of information and skills would be required to sell the different products. Segmenting this complex environment into product areas facilitates increased specialization. As a result, divisional managers need less information than if they had to deal with all the products and services of the corporation.

Figure 5 summarizes the characteristics and the strengths and weaknesses of the decentralized organization. Decentralized organizations face several problems. For example, it is sometimes difficult to decide what resources are to be pooled in a corporate staff to be used to service the entire organization. If the divisions are very different from one another in terms of products, customers, technology, and so on, however, it becomes very difficult to staff a corporate services unit with the diverse knowledge needed to be able to help the divisions. A restricted approach to innovation is another problem decentralized organizations may encounter. Because each division is organized around a particular product or geographic area, each manager's attention is focused on his or her special area. As a result, their innovations focus on their particular specialties. Managers don't have the diverse information needed to produce radical innovations.

One major liability of decentralized organizations is their relative inability to provide integration or coordination among the divisions, even when their interdependence increases. When divisions are relatively autonomous and have only pooled interdependence, there is not much need for coordination. However, when uncertainty increases and the divisions have to work together because of increased either sequential or reciprocal interdependence between the units, decentralized organizations have no formal mechanisms to coordinate and resolve the increased needs for information.

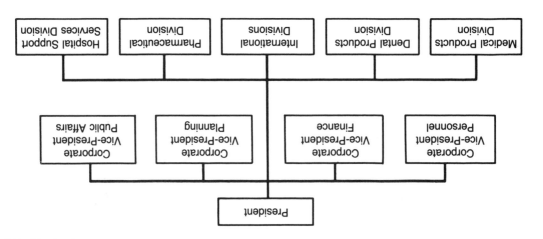

FIGURE 4
Decentralized Organization.

FIGURE 5
Characteristics of the Decentralized Organization.

Organizational Functions	Accomplished in Decentralized Organization
Goals	Special product emphasis (technologies lag)
Influence	Product, project heads
Promotion	By product management
Budgeting	By product, project, program
Rewards	For integrative capability

Strengths	Weaknesses
1. Suited to fast change	1. Innovation/growth restricted to existing project areas
2. High product, project, or program visibility	2. Tough to allocate pooled resources (i.e., computer, lab)
3. Full-time task orientation (i.e., dollars, schedules, profits)	3. Shared functions hard to coordinate (i.e., purchasing)
4. Task responsibility, contact points clear to customers or clients	4. Deterioration of in-depth competence—hard to attract technical specialists
5. Processes multiple tasks in parallel, easy to cross functional lines	5. Possible internal task conflicts, priority conflicts
	6. May neglect high level of integration required in organization

Since today's organizational environments are becoming more complex and interdependent, large decentralized corporations are finding that the need to integrate has increased for at least five reasons:

1. The increased level of regulation organizations face requires more and more coordination across divisions to be sure that all regulatory requirements are being met. For example, crackdowns by the SEC on illegal foreign payments and the increased liabilities of boards of directors have required organizations to have better control systems and information sources to enable their headquarters staff groups to know what's going on in the divisions. Affirmative action requirements have required that divisions share information on how they are doing and where possible pools of affirmative action candidates may be found.

2. Organizational environments are changing, and this can lead to a requirement of more coordination across divisions. New customer demands may require what were previously autonomous divisions to coordinate their activities. For example, if the International Group in the health products company mentioned earlier faces a demand to develop some new products for overseas, it may be necessary to provide a means by which the Medical Products and Pharmaceutical Divisions can work in a coordinated and integrated way with International to develop these new products.

3. Technological changes are placing more emphasis on increased interaction among divisions. More and more, computer systems and R&D services are being shared thus compelling the divisions to interact more with one another.

4. The cost of making "wrong" strategic decisions is increasing in terms of both sunk costs and losses because of failure to get market share. Since such "wrong" decisions sometimes result from a lack of contact between divisions, it emphasizes the need to have more coordination across divisions and more sharing of information. For example, AT&T has just recently begun to market telephone and support equipment to counter the competition of other suppliers of this equipment that have entered the market. To do this AT&T has organized around markets. It has also increased the opportunities for interaction among these market managers so they can share information, build on one another's expertise and competence, and ensure required coordination.

5. Scarce resources—for example, capital and raw materials—will require more interaction among divisions to set overall priorities. Is a university, for

example, going to emphasize its undergraduate arts program or its professional schools? By setting up task forces of the deans of the schools, the university might be able to identify opportunities for new inno-vative programs that could benefit the entire organi-zation. New programs in management of the arts—museums, orchestras, and so on—could draw on the expertise of the arts department and the business school and would not require a lot of new venture capital.

For a number of reasons, then, there is a need for increased coordination among divisions in decen-tralized organizations. Given the decentralized orga-nization's weakness, organizational designers need to implement the second general design strategy, in-creasing the information flow to reduce uncertainty and facilitate coordination.

Lateral Relations: Increasing Information Available for Decision Making

Lateral relations is really a process that is overlaid on an existing functional or decentralized structure. Lateral relations as a process moves deci-sion making down to where the problem is in the organization. It differs from decentralization in that no self-contained tasks are created.

Jay Galbraith has identified various types of lateral relations. *Direct contact*, for example, can be used by managers of diverse groups as a mechanism to coordinate their different activities. With direct contact, managers can meet informally to discuss their common problems. *Liaison roles* are a formal communication link between two units. Engineering liaison with the manufacturing department is an ex-cellent example of the liaison role. The engineer serving in the liaison role may be located in the production organization as a way of coordinating engineering and production activities.

When coordination between units becomes more complex, an *integrator role* may be established. Paul Lawrence and Jay Lorsch have indicated that the integrator role is particularly useful when organiza-tional units that must be coordinated are differenti-ated from one another in terms of their structure, subgoals, time, orientation, and so on. In such situ-ations, there is the possibility of conflict between the various units. For example, production, marketing, and R&D units in an organization may be highly differentiated from one another. Marketing, for ex-ample, is primarily concerned with having products to sell that are responsive to customer needs. R&D, on the other hand, may be concerned with developing innovative products that shape customer needs. Pro-duction, for its part, may want products to remain unchanged so that manufacturing setups don't have to be modified. Obviously there are differences among the three units in terms of their subgoals. The integrator roles is instituted to coordinate and mod-erate such diverse orientations. The integrator could be a materials manager or a group executive whose additional function would be to coordinate and inte-grate the diverse units in ways that meet the organi-zation's common objectives.

To be effective as an *integrator*, a manager needs to have certain characteristics. First, he needs wide contacts in the organization so that he possesses the relevant information about the different units he is attempting to integrate. Second, the integrator needs to understand and share, at least to a degree, the goals and orientations of the different groups. He cannot be seen as being a partisan of one particular group's perspective. Third, the integrator has to be rather broadly trained technically, so that he can talk the language of the different groups. By being able to demonstrate that he has some expertise in each area, he will be viewed as more credible by each group and will also be better able to facilitate information ex-change between the units. The integrator can in effect become an interpreter of each group's position to the others. Fourth, the groups that the integrator is working with must trust him. Again, the integrator is trying to facilitate information flow and cooperation between the groups and thus the groups must believe that he is working toward a solution acceptable to all the groups. Fifth, the integrator needs to exert influence on the basis of his expertise rather than through formal power. The integrator can provide information and identify alternative courses of action for the different units as they attempt to coordinate their activities. The more he can get them to agree on solutions and courses of action rather than having to use his formal power, the more committed they will be to implementing the solution. Last, the integra-tor's conflict resolution skills are important. Because differentiation between the units exists, conflict and disagreement are inevitable. It is important, there-fore, that confrontation is used as the conflict reso-lution style. By confrontation we mean that parties to the conflict identify the causes of conflict and are committed to adopting a problem-solving approach to finding a mutually acceptable solution to the conflict. The parties must also be committed, of course, to work to implement that solution.

When coordination involves working with six or

seven different units, then task forces can be established. Task forces involve a group of managers working together on the coordination problems of their diverse groups. For example, in a manufacturing organization, the marketing, production, R&D, finance, and engineering managers may meet twice a week (or more often when required) to discuss problems of coordination that they may be having that require their cooperation to solve. In this use a task force is a problem-solving group formed to facilitate coordination.

The matrix type of structure is the most complex form of lateral relations. The matrix is typically a formal structure in the organization; it is not a structure that is often added temporarily to an existing functional or decentralized structure. As Lawrence, Kolodny, and Davis have indicated in their article "The Human Side of the Matrix" (*Organizational Dynamics*, Summer 1977), there are certain key characteristics of a matrix structure. The most salient is that there is dual authority, that is, both the heads of the functions and the matrix manager have authority over those working in the matrix unit.

The matrix was initially developed in the aerospace industry where the organization had to be responsive to products/markets as well as technology. Because the matrix focuses on a specific product or market, it can generate the information and concentrate the resources needed to respond to changes in that product or market rapidly. The matrix is now being used in a variety of business, public, and health organizations. Figure 6 provides a summary of the characteristics and strengths and weaknesses of the matrix form of organization.

The matrix structure is particularly useful when an organization wants to focus resources on producing a particular product or service. The use of the matrix in the aerospace industry, for example, allowed these organizations to build manufacturing units to produce particular airplanes, thus allowing in-depth attention and specialization of skills.

Matrix organizations, however, are complicated to manage. Because both project managers and traditional functional area managers are involved in matrix organizations, personnel in the matrix have two bosses, and there is an inherent potential for conflict under such circumstances. As a result, the matrix form of lateral relations should only be used in those situations where an organization faces a unique problem in a particular market area or in the technological requirements of a product. When the informational and technological requirements are such that a

full-time focus on the market or product is needed, a matrix organization can be helpful. Citibank, for example, has used a matrix structure in its international activity to concentrate on geographic areas. Boeing Commercial Airplane has used the matrix to focus resources on a particular product.

Lateral relations require a certain organizational design and special interpersonal skills if this process for reducing uncertainty by increasing the information available for improving coordination is going to be effective. From a design perspective, four factors are required:

1. The organization's reward structure must support and reward cooperative problem solving that leads to coordination and integration. Will a manager's performance appraisal, for example, reflect his or her participation in efforts to achieve coordination and integration? If the organization's reward does not recognize joint problem-solving efforts, then lateral relations will not be effective.

2. In assigning managers to participate in some form of lateral relations, it is important that they have responsibility for implementation. Line managers should be involved since they understand the problems more intimately than staff personnel and, more importantly, they are concerned about implementation. Staff members can be used, but line managers should be dominant since this will lead to more commitment on their part to implementing solutions that come out of lateral relations problem-solving efforts.

3. Participants must have the authority to commit their units to action. Managers who are participating in an effort to resolve problems of coordination must be able to indicate what particular action their units might take in trying to improve coordination. For example, in the manufacturing company task force example mentioned earlier, the marketing manager should be able to commit his group to increasing the lead time for providing information to production on deadlines for delivering new products to customers.

4. Lateral processes must be integrated into the vertical information flow. In the concern for increasing information exchange *across* the units in the organization there must be no loss of concern for vertical information exchange so that the top levels in the organization are aware of coordination efforts.

Certain skills are also required on the part of participants for lateral relations to work:

1. Individuals must deal with conflict effectively, in the sense of identifying the sources of

conflict and then engaging in problem solving to reach a mutually acceptable solution to the conflict situation.

2. Participants need good interpersonal skills. They must be able to communicate effectively with one another and avoid making other participants defensive. The more they can learn to communicate with others in a descriptive, nonevaluative manner, the more open the communication process will be.

3. Participants in lateral relations need to understand that influence and power should be based on expertise rather than formal power. Because of the problem-solving nature of lateral relations, an individual's power and influence will change based on the particular problem at hand and the individual's ability to provide key information to solve the problem. At various times different members will have more influence because of their particular expertise.

Lateral relations, then, is a process that is overlaid onto the existing functional or decentralized organization structure. Lateral relations requires various organization structure, so it is imperative that an organization never adopts this approach without training the people involved. Before implementing lateral relations, team building might be used to develop the interpersonal skills of the participating managers. These managers might spend time learning how to operate more effectively in groups, how to improve communication skills, and how to deal with conflict in a positive way so that it does not become disruptive to the organization.

The Organizational Design Decision Tree

We have discussed the different kinds of organization structure that managers can implement. We are now prepared to identify the decision-making process the manager can use in selecting the appropriate structure to "fit" the demands of the environment. Figure 7 presents a decision tree analysis for selecting either the functional or decentralized organization structure. This decision tree analysis also indicates when the existing functional or decentralized organization structure should be supplemented with some form of lateral relations in the form of a task force or a matrix. In general, an organization should use one of the simpler forms of lateral relations rather than the more complex and expensive matrix. In using this decision tree, there are a number of questions that the designer needs to ask. The first question is whether the organization's environment is simple, that is, there are few factors to consider in the environment, or complex, that is,

FIGURE 6
Characteristics of the Matrix Organization.

Organizational Functions	Accomplished in Matrix Organization
Goals	Emphasis on production/market
Influence	Matrix manager and functional heads
Promotion	By function or into matrix manager job
Budgeting	By matrix organization project
Rewards	By special functional skills and performance in matrix

Strengths	Weaknesses
1. Full-time focus of personnel on project of matrix	1. Costly to maintain personnel pool to staff matrix
2. Matrix manager is coordinator of functions for single project	2. Participants experience dual authority of matrix manager and functional area managers
3. Reduces information requirements as focus is on single product/market	3. Little interchange with functional groups outside the matrix so there may be duplication of effort, "reinvention of the wheel"
4. Masses specialized technical skills to the product/market	4. Participants in matrix need to have good interpersonal skills in order for it to work

there are a number of different environmental factors to be considered in decision making. If the environment is defined as *simple*, the next question focuses on whether the environmental factors are *static*, that is, remain the same over time, or are *dynamic*, that is, change over time. If we define the environment as static, there is likely to be little uncertainty associated with decision making. In turn, information requirements for decision making are low. In this simple-static environment, the functional organization is most efficient. It can most quickly gather and process the information required to deal with this type of environment.

At this point the question might be raised, are there any organizational environments that are in fact both simple and static or is this a misperception on the part of the managers that oversimplifies the environment? There may be environments like this, but the key is that these environments may change,

that is, they may become more dynamic as the marketplace changes, as resources become scarce, or the organization's domain is challenged. For example, the motor home/recreational vehicle industry was very successful in the early 1970s. Its market was relatively homogeneous (simple) and there was a constantly high demand (static) for its products. Then the oil embargo of 1973 hit, and the environment suddenly became dynamic. The industry had a very difficult time changing because it had done no contingency planning about "what would happen if" demand shifted, resources became scarce, and so on. The important point is that an organization's environment may be simple and static today but change tomorrow. Managers should continually scan the environment and be sensitive to the fact that things can change and contingency planning may be useful.

If this simple environment is defined as dynamic, with some components in the environment

FIGURE 7

Organizational Design Decision Tree Heuristic.

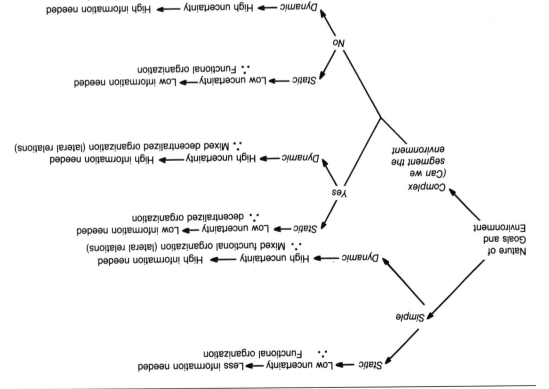

changing, some uncertainty may be experienced by decision makers. Thus information needs will be greater than when the environment was static. Therefore, in this simple—dynamic environment the mixed functional organization with lateral relations is likely to be the most effective in gathering and processing the information required for decision making. Because the organization's environment is simple, the creation of self-contained units would not be efficient. It is more economical to have central functional areas responsible for all products and markets as these products and markets are relatively similar to one another. However, when uncertainty arises and there is need for more information, some form of lateral relations can be added, to the existing functional organization.

Figure 8 shows the functional organization of a manufacturing organization. The organization suddenly may face a problem with its principal product. Competitors may have developed an attractive re-placement. As a result of this unique problem, the president of the firm may set up a task force chaired by the vice-president of sales to develop new products. The task force consists of members from manufacturing, sales, research, and engineering services. Its function, obviously, will be to develop and evaluate suggestions for new products.

If the organization's environment is defined by the managers as complex, that is, there are a large number of factors and components that need to be considered in decision making, the next question to ask is, can the organization *segment* its environment into geographic areas, market, or product areas? If the environment is defined as segmentable, then the next question focuses on whether the environment is static or dynamic. If the environment is defined as static, there is going to be low uncertainty and thus information needs for decision making are not going to be high. Thus, in the complex-segmentable-static environment, the decentralized organization is most

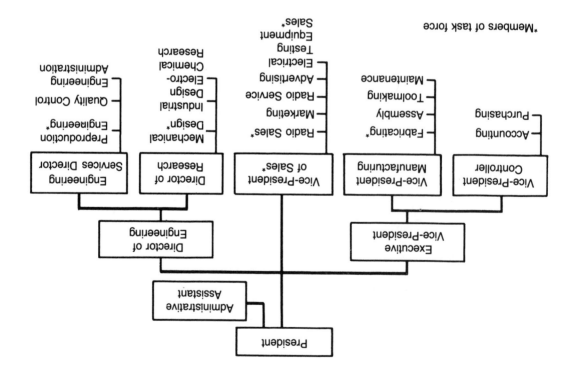

FIGURE 8
Functional Organization with Task Force.

appropriate, and the health products organization discussed earlier is a good example of this. The organization can break the environment apart in the sense that it can organize around products or markets, for example, and thus information, resources, and so forth, are only required to produce and market these more homogeneous outputs of the organization.

In the complex-segmentable-dynamic environment there is a change in the components of the environment and the demands they are making on the organization, or in fact the organization has to now consider different factors in the environment that it had not previously considered in decision making. Uncertainty and coordination needs may be higher. The result is that decision makers need more information to reduce uncertainty and provide information to facilitate coordination. The mixed decentralized organization with lateral relations is the appropriate structure here.

Figure 9 presents the design of a multidivision decentralized health products organization. Some form of lateral relations may be added to this structure to help generate more information. For example, the International Division may be attempting to develop new products but may be encountering problems, with the result that the entire organization, stimulated by the president's concern, may be experiencing uncertainty about how to proceed. In such a situation, a task

force of the manager of the International Group and the Dental Group and the Pharmaceutical Group might work together in developing ideas for new products in the International Division. The lateral relations mechanism of the task force facilitates information exchange *across* the organization to reduce uncertainty and increase coordination of the efforts of the divisions that should be mutually supportive. By working together, in the task force, the division managers will be exchanging information and will be gaining a better understanding of their common problems and how they need to work and coordinate with one another in order to solve these problems.

If the organization's complex environment is defined by managers as nonsegmentable, the functional organization will be appropriate because it is not possible to break the environment up into geographic or product/service areas.

In effect, there simply might be too much interdependence among environmental components, or the technology of the organization may be so interlinked, that it is not possible to create self-contained units organized around components of the environment.

A hospital is a good example of this organization type. The environment is clearly complex. There are numerous and diverse environmental components that have to be considered in decision making (for example, patients, regulatory groups, medical societ-

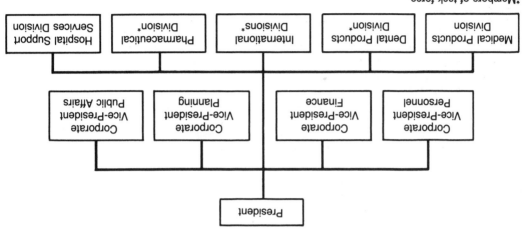

FIGURE 9
Decentralized Organization with Lateral Relations.

* Members of task force

FIGURE 10
Functional Organization with Matrix.

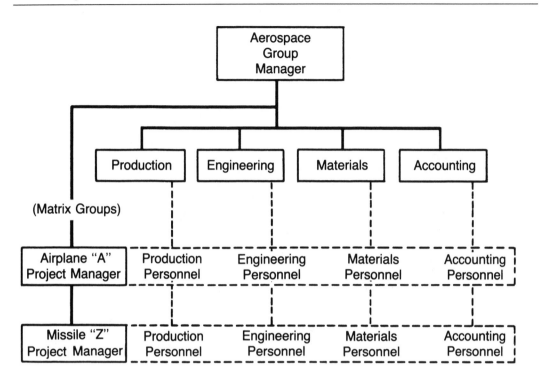

ies, third-party payers, and suppliers). In the complex—nonsegmentable—static environment, environmental components are rather constant in their demands. Thus here the functional organization is most apropriate.

However, the functional organization, through its very specific rules, procedures, and channels of communication, will likely be too slow in generating the required information. Therefore, some form of lateral relations may be added to the functional organization. Figure 10 presents an example of an aerospace functional organization that uses a matrix structure for its airplane and missile products divisions. The matrix structure provides in-depth concentration of personnel and resources on these different product areas, each of which has its own very unique information and technological requirements.

SYMPTOMS OF INAPPROPRIATE ORGANIZATIONAL STRUCTURE

The key question at this point is "So what?" What are the costs to an organization if it is using the wrong structure, given its product/service and the environment in which it operates? In order to be effective, an organization needs to attain its goals and objectives, it needs to adapt to the environment, and last, it should be designed in such a way that its managers experience low role conflict and ambiguity.

Therefore, there are certain kinds of information the manager responsible for organizational design should be sensitive to in monitoring whether the appropriate structure is being used. While using the appropriate structure may have some direct impact on the organization's ability to attain its goals, its biggest impact will probably be on the adaptability of the organization and the role behavior of its managers.

Certain kinds of symptoms regarding ineffective adaptability may occur. For example:

● Organizational decision makers may not be able to anticipate problems before they occur. There may be a tendency in the organization to wait until problems occur and then react to them because the organization simply does not have enough information to develop contingency plans.

• Decision makers may err in trying to predict trends in their decision environment. Without proper coordination across divisions, the organization may lose control over the relationship between its internal functioning and its environment.

• The organization may not be able to get key information for decision making to the right place for effective decision making. For example, division managers from different product groups have information that quality and liability standards on their respective products are unrealistically high. However, because of decentralization and lack of effective coordination through some form of lateral relations, this information may not get to the staff groups in the organization that are responsible for setting corporate policy in this area.

• The organization, having identified a problem vis-à-vis its environment, may simply not be able to take corrective action quickly enough.

Symptoms of poor fit between structure and environment may also show at the level of the individual in terms of some increase in either role conflict or role ambiguity. It is important, therefore, that the organization monitor the level of role conflict and role ambiguity among its managers and the resulting stress they experience so the system has a baseline for comparison. If there is a significant increase from this baseline in conflict and ambiguity and stress, then the organization may consider that the increase is a symptom of an organizational design problem. For example:

• Individuals may be experiencing increased role conflict. This may occur when the organization is implementing a functional organization in a dynamic environment. The environment may be changing and the individuals may be required to make quick responses to this changing environment. Having to wait for new policy changes to come down the hierarchy may delay the organization from responding appropriately. Decision makers at the top of the organization will also suffer from role conflict when the environment is changing rapidly. In the functional organization, when new situations occur they are referred to higher levels of the organization for decision and action. The result is that top-level decision makers become overloaded and the organization's response to the environment slows down. In a dynamic environment, the functional organization constrains the decision-making adaptation process.

• Individuals in the organization also may experience increased role ambiguity—they may be unclear as to what is expected of them in their roles. For example, role ambiguity is likely to occur when

the decentralized organization is implemented without some effective use of lateral relations. Individuals may feel they don't have the information needed for decision making. Divisional managers may not know what the corporate staff's policy is on various issues, and corporate staff may have lost touch with the divisions.

These are the kinds of information managers should be aware of as indicators of dysfunctional organization design. These data can be collected in organizational diagnosis surveys that we have developed so that a more systemic monitoring of structure exists just as we monitor organizational climate. As fine tuning the organization's design to its environment becomes more critical, organizations will begin to monitor their organizational design more systematically.

SUMMARY

What are the advantages to managers in using the design decision tree? There appear to be several:

1. It provides a *broad framework* for identifying the key factors a manager should think about in considering an organizational design. For example: What is our environment? What different structural options do we have?

2. It forces the manager to *diagnose* the decision environment. What is our environment like? How stable is it? How complex is it? Is it possible to reduce complexity by segmenting the environment into product or geographical subgroups?

3. It causes managers to think about *how much interdependence* there is among segments of the organization. How dependent on one another are different parts of the organization in terms of technology, services, support, help in getting their tasks completed? The decision points in the heuristic forces managers to question themselves about what other parts of the organization they need to coordinate their activities with, and then to think about how to do it.

4. Once the organization is in either a functional or decentralized structure, the decision tree points out what can be done to meet *the increased needs for information* through the use of lateral relations. Lateral relations provide a mechanism for supplementing the existing structure to facilitate dealing with the organization's increased needs for information and coordination.

Managers in a variety of organizations have commented that the decision tree gives them ". . . a handle for thinking about organizational design so we can tinker with it, fine tune it and make it work better. We don't have to be coerced by structure. We now have a better feel for when certain structures should be used and for the specific steps we can take to make a given structure work."

Mechanistic and Organic Systems of Management

T. Burns

G. M. Stalker

Recently, with G.M. Stalker, I made an attempt to elucidate the situation of firms in the electronics industry that were confronted with rapidly changing commercial circumstances and a much faster rate of technical progress. I found it necessary to posit two "ideal types" of working organization, the one mechanistic, adapted to relatively stable conditions, the other organic, adapted to conditions of change.

In mechanistic systems, the problems and tasks that face the firm are, typically, broken down into specialties. Each individual carries out his or her assigned task apart from the overall purpose of the company as a whole. "Somebody at the top" is responsible for seeing that each individual's work is relevant to that of others. The technical methods, duties, and powers attached to each post are precisely defined, and a high value is placed on precision and demarcation. Interaction within the working organization follows vertical lines—i.e., between superiors and subordinates. How people operate and what they do is prescribed by their functional roles and governed by instructions and decisions issued from superiors. This hierarchy is maintained by the assumption that the only person who knows—or should know—all about the company is the boss at the top. This person is the only one, therefore, who knows exactly how the human resources should be properly disposed. The management system, usually visualized as the complex hierarchy familiar in organization charts, operates as a simple control system, with information flowing upwards through a succession of filters, and decisions and instructions flowing downwards through a succession of amplifiers.

Mechanistic systems are, in fact, the "rational bureaucracy" of an earlier generation of students of organization. For the individual, it provides an ordered world of work in which decisions and actions occur within a stable constellation of jobs, skills, specialized knowledge, and sectional responsibilities. In a textile mill, or in any factory that sees itself turning out any standardized product for a familiar and steady market, one finds decision-making at all levels prescribed by the familiar.

As one descends through the levels of management, one finds more limited information and less understanding of the human capacities of other members of the firm. One also finds each person's task more and more clearly defined by a superior. Beyond a certain limit the individual has insufficient authority, insufficient information, and usually insufficient technical ability to be able to make decisions. He or she is informed quite clearly when this limit occurs; beyond it, there is one course open—report to one's superior.

Organic systems are adapted to unstable conditions, when new and unfamiliar problems and requirements continually arise that cannot be broken down and distributed among specialists roles within a hierarchy. Jobs lose much of their formal definition. The definitive and enduring demarcation of functions becomes impossible. Responsibilities and functions, and even methods and powers, have to be constantly redefined through interaction with others participating in common tasks or in the solution of common problems. Members have to do their jobs with knowledge of overall purpose and the situation of the company as a whole. Interaction runs laterally as much as vertically, and communication between people of different rank tends to resemble lateral consul-

---

Combined excerpts taken from T. Burns, "Industry in a New Age," *New Society, London, The Weekly Review of the Social Sciences,* 31 January 1963, London: New Science Publications; and T. Burns and G. M. Stalker, "Mechanistic and Organic Systems of Management," *The Management of Innovation,* London: Associated Book Publishers Ltd., 1961.

tation rather than vertical command. Omniscience can no longer be imputed to the boss at the top.

The head of one successful electronics concern, at the very beginning of the first inteview of the whole study, attacked the idea of the organization chart as inapplicable in his concern and as a dangerous method of thinking. The first requirement of management, according to him, was that it should make the fullest use of the capacities of its members; any individual's job should be as little defined as possible, so that it would "shape itself" to his or her special abilities and initiative.

In this company, insistence on the least possible specification for managerial positions was much more in evidence than devices for insuring adequate interaction within the system. This did occur, but it was often due to physical conditions rather than to order by top management. A single-storyed building housed the entire company, two thousand strong, from laboratories to canteen. Access to anyone was therefore physically simple and direct; it was easier to walk across to the laboratory door, the office door, or the factory door and look for the person one wanted than even to telephone. Written communication inside the factory was actively discouraged. More important than the physical set-up however was the need of all managers for interaction with others in order to get their functions defined, since these were not specified from above.

For the individuals, the important part of the difference between the mechanistic and the organic is in the degree of commitment to the working organization. Mechanistic systems tell individuals what has to be attended to, and how, and also what does *not* have to be bothered with, what is not their affair, what is *not* expected of them—what is the responsibility of others. In organic systems, such boundaries disappear. Individuals are expected to regard themselves as fully implicated in the discharge of any task appearing over their horizon. They have not merely to exercise a special competence, but to commit themselves to the success of the concern's undertakings as a whole.

We are now at the point at which we may set down the outline of the two management systems that represent for us the two polar extremities of the forms that such systems can take when they are adapted to a specific rate of technical and commercial change.

Both types represent a "rational" form of organization, in that they may both, in our experience, be explicitly and deliberately created and maintained to exploit the human resources of a concern in the most efficient manner feasible in the circumstances of the firm.

A *mechanistic* management system is appropriate to stable conditions. It is characterized by:

1. The specialized differentiation of functional tasks into which the problems and tasks facing the concern as a whole are broken down;

2. The abstract nature of each individual task, which is pursued with techniques and purposes more or less distinct from those of the concern as a whole, i.e., the functionaries tend to pursue the technical improvement of means, rather than the accomplishment of the ends of the concern;

3. The reconciliation, for each level in the hierarchy, of these distinct performances by immediate superiors, who are in turn responsible for seeing that each is relevant in his or her own special part of the main task;

4. The precise definition of rights and obligations and technical methods attached to each functional role;

5. The translation of rights and obligations and methods into the responsibilities of a functional position;

6. Hierarchic structure of control, authority, and communication;

7. A reinforcement of the hierarchic structure by the location of knowledge of actualities exclusively at the top of the hierarchy, where the final reconciliation of distinct tasks and assessment of relevance is made;

8. A tendency for interaction between members of the concern to be vertical, i.e., between superior and subordinate;

9. A tendency for operations and working behavior to be governed by the instructions and decisions issued by superiors;

10. Insistence on loyalty to the firm and obedience to superiors as a condition of membership;

11. A greater importance and prestige attaching to internal (local) than to general (cosmopolitan) knowledge, experience and skill.

The *organic* form is appropriate to changing conditions, which give rise constantly to fresh problems and unforeseen requirements for action that cannot be broken down or distributed automatically, arising from the functional roles defined within a hierarchic structure. It is characterized by:

1. The contributive nature of special knowledge and experience to the common task of the firm;

2. The "realistic" nature of the individual task, which is seen as set by the total situation of the firm;

3. The adjustment and continual redefinition of individual tasks through interaction with others;

4. The sheding of "responsibility" as a limited field of rights, obligations, and methods (problems may not be posted upwards, downwards, or sideways as being someone else's responsibility);

5. The spread of commitment to the firm beyond any technical definition;

6. A network structure of control, authority, and communication. The sanctions that apply to the individual's conduct in his or her working role derive more from presumed community of interest with the rest of the working organization in the survival and growth of the firm and less from a contractual relationship betweeen the individual and a nonpersonal corporation, represented by an immediate superior;

7. Omniscience no longer imputed to the head of the company; knowledge about the technical or commercial nature of the here and now task may be located anywhere in the network, this location, becoming the ad hoc center of control, authority, and communication;

8. A lateral rather than a vertical direction of communication through the organization, communication between people of different rank, also, resembling consultation rather than command;

9. A content of communication that consists of information and advice rather than instructions and decisions;

10. Commitment to the concern's tasks and to the "technological ethos" of material progress and expansion is more highly valued than loyalty and obedience;

11. Importance and prestige attach to affiliations and expertise valid in the industrial and technical and commercial milieu external to the firm.

One important corollary to be attached to this account is that while organic systems are not hierarchic in the same sense as are mechanistic systems, they remain stratified. Positions are differentiated according to seniority, i.e., greater expertise. The lead in joint decisions is frequently taken by seniors, but it is an essential presumption of the organic system that the lead, i.e., authority, is taken by whoever is the most informed and capable, i.e., the "best authority." The location of authority is settled by consensus.

A second observation is that the area of commitment to the firm—the extent to which individuals yield themselves as resources to be used by the working organization—is far more extensive in organic than in mechanistic systems. Commitment, in fact, is expected to approach that of professional scientists to their work, and frequently does. One further consequence of this is that it becomes far less feasible to distinguish informal from formal organization.

Thirdly, the emptying out of significance from the hierarchic command system, by which cooperation is insured and that serves to monitor the working organization under a mechanistic sytem, is countered by the development of shared beliefs about the values and goals of the company. The growth and accretion of institutionalized values, beliefs, and conduct, in the form of commitments, ideology, and manners, around an image of the firm in its industrial and commercial setting make good the loss of formal structure.

Finally, the two forms of system represent a polarity, not a dichotomy; there are, as we have tried to show, intermediate stages between the extremities empirically known to us. Also, the relation of one form to the other is elastic, so that a firm oscillating between relative stability and relative change may also oscillate between the two forms. A company may (and frequently does) operate with a management system that includes both types.

The organic form, by departing from the familiar clarity and fixity of the hierarchic structure, is often experienced by the individual manager as an uneasy, embarrassed, or chronically anxious quest for knowledge about what should be done, or what is expected, and similar apprehensiveness about what others are doing. Indeed, as we shall see later, this kind of response is necessary if the organic form of organization is to work effectively. Understandably, such anxiety finds expression in resentment when the apparent confusion besetting the manager is not explained. In these situations, all managers some of the time, and many managers all the time, yearn for more definition and structure.

On the other hand, some managers recognize a rationale of non-definition, a reasoned basis for the practice of those successful firms in which designation of status, function, and line of responsibility and authority has been vague or even avoided.

The desire for more definition is often in effect a wish to have the limits of one's task more neatly defined—to know what and when one doesn't have to bother about, as much as to know what one does have to. It follows that the more definition is given, the more omniscient the management must be, so that no functions are left wholly or partly undischarged, no persons are overburdened with undelegated responsibility, or left without the authority to do their jobs properly. To do this, to have all the separate functions attached to individual roles fitting together and comprehensively, to have communication between persons constantly maintained on a level adequate to the needs of each functional role, requires rules or traditions of behavior proved over a long time and an equally fixed, stable task. The omniscience that may then be credited to the head of the firm is expected throughout its body through the lines of command, extending in a clear, explicitly titled hierarchy of officers and subordinates.

The whole mechanistic form is instinct with this twofold principle of definition and dependence that acts as the frame within which action is conceived and carried out. It works, unconsciously, almost in the smallest minutiae of daily activity. "How late is late?" The answer to this question is not to be found in the rule book, but in the superior. Late is when the boss thinks it is late. Is the boss the kind of person who thinks 8:00 is the time, and 8:01 is late? Does the boss think 8:15 is all right occasionally if it is not a regular thing or that everyone should be allowed five minutes' grace after 8:00 but after that they are late?

One other feature of mechanistic organization needs emphasis. It is a necessary condition of its operation that individuals "work on their own," functionally isolated, that they "know their jobs," "and are responsible for seeing them done." They work at jobs that are in a sense artificially abstracted from the realities of the situation the company is dealing with, the accountant dealing with the cost side, the works manager pushing production, and so on. In practice, the rest of the organization becomes part of the problem situation the individual has to deal with in order to perform successfully, i.e., difficulties and problems arising from work or information that has been handed over the "responsibility barrier" between two jobs or departments are regarded as "really" the responsibility of the person from whom they were received. As a design engineer put it, "When you get designers handing over designs completely to production, it's 'their responsibility' now. And you get tennis games played with the responsibility for anything that goes wrong. What happens is that you're constantly getting unsuspected faults arising from characteristics which you didn't think important in the design. If you get to hear of these through a sales person, or a production person, or somebody to whom the design was handed over to in the dim past, then, instead of being a design problem, it's an annoyance caused by that particular person, who can't do the job—because you'd thought you were finished with that one, and you're on to something else now."

When the assumptions of the form of organization make for preoccupation with specialized tasks, the chances of career success, or of greater influence, depend rather on the relative importance that may be attached to each special function by the superior whose task it is to reconcile and control a number of them. And, indeed, to press the claims of one's job or department for a bigger share of the firm's resources is in many cases regarded as a mark of initiative, of effectiveness, and even of loyalty to the firm's interests. This state of affairs thus engenders an aloof detachment similar to a court of appeal. The ordinary relationship prevailing between individual managers "in charge of" different functions is one of rivalry, a rivalry that may be rendered innocuous to the persons involved by personal friendship or the norms of sociability, but that turns discussion about the situations that constitute the real problems of the firm—how to make products more cheaply, how to sell more, how to allocate resources, whether to curtail activity in one sector, whether to risk expansion in another, and so on—into an arena of conflicting interests.

The distinctive feature of the second, organic system is the pervasiveness of the working organization as an institution. In concrete terms, this makes itself felt in a preparedness to combine with others in serving the general aims of the company. Proportionate to the rate and extent of change, the less can the omniscience appropriate to command organizations be ascribed to the head of the organization; for executives, and even operatives, in a changing firm it is always theirs to reason why. Furthermore, the less definition can be given to status, roles, and modes of communication, the more do the activities of each member of the organization become determined by the real tasks of the firm than by instruction and routine. The individual's job ceases to be self-contained; the only way in which one's job can be done is by participating continually with others in the solution of problems that are real to the firm, and put in a language of requirements and activities meaningful to them all. Such methods of working place much heavier demands on the individual.

We have endeavored to stress the appropriateness of each system to its own specific set of conditions. Equally, we desire to avoid the suggestion that either system is superior under all circumstances to the other. In particular, nothing in our experience justifies the assumption that mechanistic systems should be superseded by organic systems in conditions of stability. The beginning of administrative wisdom is the awareness that there is no one optimum type of management system.

Evolution and Revolution as Organizations Grow

Larry E. Greiner

A small research company chooses too complicated and formalized an organization structure for its young age and limited size. It flounders in rigidity and bureaucracy for several years and is finally acquired by a larger company.

Key executives of a retail store chain hold on to an organization structure long after it has served its purpose, because their power is derived from this structure. The company eventually goes into bankruptcy.

A large bank disciplines a "rebellious" manager who is blamed for current control problems, when the underlying cause is centralized procedures that are holding back expansion into new markets. Many younger managers subsequently leave the bank, competition moves in, and profits are still declining.

The problems of these companies, like those of many others, are rooted more in past decisions than in present events or outside market dynamics. Historical forces do indeed shape the future growth of organizations. Yet management, in its haste to grow, often overlooks such critical developmental questions as: Where has our organization been? Where is it now? And what do the answers to these questions mean for where we are going? Instead, its gaze is fixed outward toward the environment and the future—as if more precise market projections will provide a new organizational identity.

Companies fail to see that many clues to their future success lie within their own organizations and their evolving states of development. Moreover, the inability of management to understand its organization development problems can result in a company becoming "frozen" in its present stage of evolution or,

ultimately, in failure, regardless of market opportunities.

My position in this article is that the future of an organization may be less determined by outside forces than it is by the organization's history. In stressing the force of history on an organization, I have drawn from the legacies of European psychologists (their thesis being that individual behavior is determined primarily by previous events and experiences, not by what lies ahead). Extending this analogy of individual development to the problems of organization development, I shall discuss a series of developmental phases through which growing companies tend to pass. But, first, let me provide two definitions:

1. The term *evolution* is used to describe prolonged periods of growth where no major upheaval occurs in organization practices.

2. The term *revolution* is used to describe those periods of substantial turmoil in organization life.

As a company progresses through developmental phases, each evolutionary period creates its own revolution. For instance, centralized practices eventually lead to demands for decentralization. Moreover, the nature of management's solution to each revolutionary period determines whether a company will move forward into its next stage of evolutionary growth. As I shall show later, there are at least five phases of organization development, each characterized by both an evolution and a revolution.

KEY FORCES IN DEVELOPMENT

During the past few years a small amount of research knowledge about the phases of organization

Reprinted by permission of *Harvard Business Review.* "Evolution and Revolution as Organizations Grow" by Larry E. Greiner, Vol. 50(4). Copyright © 1972 by the President and Fellows of Harvard College; all rights reserved.

development has been building. Some of this research is very quantitative, such as time-series analyses that reveal patterns of economic performance over time.[1] The majority of studies, however, are case-oriented and use company records and interviews to reconstruct a rich picture of corporate development.[2] Yet both types of research tend to be heavily empirical without attempting more generalized statements about the overall process of development.

A notable exception is the historical work of Alfred D. Chandler, Jr., in his book *Strategy and Structure*.[3] This study depicts four very broad and general phases in the lives of four large U.S. companies. It proposes that outside market opportunities determine a company's strategy, which in turn determines the company's organization structure. This thesis has a valid ring for the four companies examined by Chandler, largely because they developed in a time of explosive markets and technological advances. But more recent evidence suggests that organization structure may be less malleable than Chandler assumed; in fact, structure can play a critical role in influencing corporate strategy. It is this reverse emphasis on how organization structure affects future growth which is highlighted in the model presented in this article.

From an analysis of recent studies,[4] five key dimensions emerge as essential for building a model of organization development:

1. Age of the organization.
2. Size of the organization.
3. Stages of evolution.
4. Growth rate of the industry.

I shall describe each of these elements separately, but first note their combined effect as illustrated in *Exhibit I*. Note especially how each dimension influences the other over time; when all five elements begin to interact, a more complete and dynamic picture of organizational growth emerges.

After describing these dimensions and their interconnections, I shall discuss each evolutionary/revolutionary phase of development and show (a) how each stage of evolution breeds its own revolution, and (b) how management solutions to each revolution determine the next state of evolution.

Age of the Organization

The most obvious and essential dimension for any model of development is the life span of an organization (represented as the horizontal axis in *Exhibit I*). All historical studies gather data from various points in time and then make comparisons. From these observations, it is evident that the same organization practices are not maintained throughout a long time span. This makes a most basic point: management problems and principles are rooted in time. The concept of decentralization, for example, can have meaning for describing corporate practices at one time period but loses its descriptive power at another.

The passage of time also contributes to the institutionalization of managerial attitudes. As a result, employee behavior becomes not only more predictable but also more difficult to change when attitudes are outdated.

Size of the Organization

This dimension is depicted as the vertical axis in *Exhibit I*. A company's problems and solutions tend to change markedly as the number of employees and sales volume increase. Thus, time is not the only determinant of structure; in fact, organizations that do not grow in size can retain many of the same management issues and practices over lengthy periods. In addition to increased size, however, problems of coordination and communication magnify, new functions emerge, levels in the management hierarchy multiply, and jobs become more interrelated.

[1]See, for example, William H. Starbuck, "Organizational Metamorphosis," in *Promising Research Directions,* edited by R. W. Millman and M. P. Hottenstein (Tempe, Arizona, Academy of Management, 1968), p. 113.

[2]See, for example, the *Grangesberg* case series, prepared by C. Roland Christensen and Bruce R. Scott, Case Clearing House, Harvard Business School.

[3]*Strategy and Structure: Chapters in the History of the American Industrial Enterprise* (Cambridge, Massachusetts, The M.I.T. Press, 1962).

[4]I have drawn on many sources for evidence: (a) numerous cases collected at the Harvard Business School; (b) *Organization Growth and Development,* edited by William H. Starbuck (Middlesex, England, Penguin Books, Ltd., 1971), where several studies are cited; and (c) articles published in journals, such as Lawrence E. Fouraker and John M. Stopford, "Organization Structure and the Multinational Strategy," *Administrative Science Quarterly,* Vol. 13, No. 1, 1968, p. 47; and Malcolm S. Salter, "Management Appraisal and Reward Systems," *Journal of Business Policy,* Vol. 1, No. 4, 1971.

EXHIBIT I
Model of Organization Development.

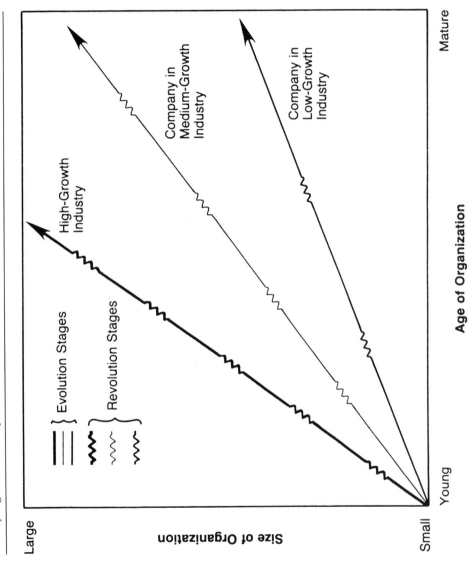

Stages of Evolution

As both age and size increase, another phenomenon becomes evident: the prolonged growth that I have termed the evolutionary period. Most growing organizations do not expand for two years and then retreat for one year; rather, those that survive a crisis usually enjoy four to eight years of continuous growth without a major economic setback or severe internal disruption. The term evolution seems appropriate for describing these quieter periods because only modest adjustments appear necessary for maintaining growth under the same overall pattern of management.

Stages of Revolution

Smooth evolution is not inevitable; it cannot be assumed that organization growth is linear. *Fortune*'s "500" list, for example, has had significant turnover during the last 50 years. Thus we find evidence from numerous case histories which reveals periods of substantial turbulence spaced between smoother periods of evolution.

I have termed these turbulent times the periods of revolution because they typically exhibit a serious upheaval of management practices. Traditional management practices, which were appropriate for a smaller size and earlier time, are brought under scrutiny by frustrated top managers and disillusioned lower-level managers. During such periods of crisis, a number of companies fail—those unable to abandon past practices and effect major organization changes are likely either to fold or to level off in their growth rates.

The critical task for management in each revolutionary period is to find a new set of organization practices that will become the basis for managing the next period of evolutionary growth. Interestingly enough, these new practices eventually sow their own seeds of decay and lead to another period of revolution. Companies therefore experience the irony of seeing a major solution in one time period become a major problem at a latter date.

Growth Rate of the Industry

The speed at which an organization experiences phases of evolution and revolution is closely related to the market environment of its industry. For example, a company in a rapidly expanding market will have to add employees rapidly; hence, the need for new organization structures to accommodate large staff increases is accelerated. While evolutionary periods tend to be relatively short in fast-growing industries, much longer evolutionary periods occur in mature or slowly growing industries.

Evolution can also be prolonged, and revolutions delayed, when profits come easily. For instance, companies that make grievous errors in a rewarding industry can still look good on their profit and loss statements; thus they can avoid a change in management practices for a longer period. The aerospace indusry in its infancy is an example. Yet revolutionary periods still occur, as one did in aerospace when profit opportunities began to dry up. Revolutions seem to be much more severe and difficult to resolve when the market environment is poor.

PHASES OF GROWTH

With the foregoing framework in mind, let us now examine in depth the five specific phases of evolution and revolution. As shown in *Exhibit II*, each evolutionary period is characterized by the dominant *management style* used to achieve growth, while each revolutionary period is characterized by the dominant *management problem* that must be solved before growth can continue. The patterns presented in *Exhibit II* seem to be typical for companies in industries with moderate growth over a long time period; companies in faster growing industries tend to experience all five phases more rapidly, while those in slower growing industries encounter only two or three phases over many years.

It is important to note that *each phase is both an effect of the previous phase and a cause for the next phase.* For example, the evolutionary management style in Phase 3 of the exhibit is "delegation," which grows out of, and becomes the solution to, demands for greater "autonomy" in the preceding Phase 2 revolution. The style of delegation used in Phase 3, however, eventually provokes a major revolutionary crisis that is characterized by attempts to regain control over the diversity created through increased delegation.

The principal implication of each phase is that management actions are narrowly prescribed if growth is to occur. For example, a company experiencing an

EXHIBIT II
The Five Phases of Growth.

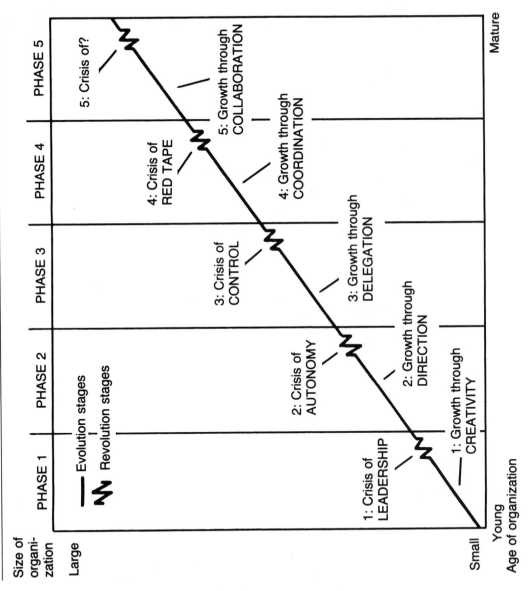

Size of
organi-
zation

Large

—— Evolution stages
∿ Revolution stages

| PHASE 1 | PHASE 2 | PHASE 3 | PHASE 4 | PHASE 5 |

5: Crisis of?

5: Growth through
COLLABORATION

4: Crisis of
RED TAPE

4: Growth through
COORDINATION

3: Crisis of
CONTROL

3: Growth through
DELEGATION

2: Crisis of
AUTONOMY

2: Growth through
DIRECTION

1: Crisis of
LEADERSHIP

1: Growth through
CREATIVITY

Small

Young
Age of organization

Mature

343

autonomy crisis in Phase 2 cannot return to directive management for a solution—it must adopt a new style of delegation in order to move ahead.

Phase 1: Creativity . . .

In the birth stage of an organization, the emphasis is on creating both a product and a market. Here are the characteristics of the period of creative evolution:

☐ The company's founders are usually technically or entrepreneurially oriented, and they disdain management activities; their physical and mental energies are absorbed entirely in making and selling a new product.

☐ Communication among employees is frequent and informal.

☐ Long hours of work are rewarded by modest salaries and the promise of ownership benefits.

☐ Control of activities comes from immediate marketplace feedback; the management acts as the customers react.

. . . & *the leadership crisis:* All of the foregoing individualistic and creative activities are essential for the company to get off the ground. But therein lies the problem. As the company grows, larger production runs require knowledge about the efficiencies of manufacturing. Increased numbers of employees cannot be managed exclusively through informal communication; new employees are not motivated by an intense dedication to the product or organization. Additional capital must be secured, and new accounting procedures are needed for financial control.

Thus the founders find themselves burdened with unwanted management responsibilities. So they long for the "good old days," still trying to act as they did in the past. And conflicts between the harried leaders grow more intense.

At this point a crisis of leadership occurs, which is the onset of the first revolution. Who is to lead the company out of confusion and solve the managerial problems confronting it? Quite obviously, a strong manager is needed who has the necessary knowledge and skill to introduce new business techniques. But this is easier said than done. The founders often hate to step aside even though they are probably temperamentally unsuited to be managers. So here is the first critical development choice—to locate and install a strong business manager who is

acceptable to the founders and who can pull the organization together.

Phase 2: Direction . . .

Those companies that survive the first phase by installing a capable business manager usually embark on a period of sustained growth under able and directive leadership. Here are the characteristics of this evolutionary period:

☐ A functional organization structure is introduced to separate manufacturing from marketing activities, and job assignments become more specialized.

☐ Accounting systems for inventory and purchasing are introduced.

☐ Incentives, budgets, and work standards are adopted.

☐ Communication becomes more formal and impersonal as a hierarchy of titles and positions builds.

☐ The new manager and his key supervisors take most of the responsibility for instituting direction, while lower-level supervisors are treated more as functional specialists than as autonomous decision-making managers.

. . . & *the autonomy crisis:* Although the new directive techniques channel employee energy more efficiently into growth, they eventually become inappropriate for controlling a larger, more diverse and complex organization. Lower-level employees find themselves restricted by a cumbersome and centralized hierarchy. They have come to possess more direct knowledge about markets and machinery than do the leaders at the top; consequently, they feel torn between following procedures and taking initiative on their own.

Thus the second revolution is imminent as a crisis develops from demands for greater autonomy on the part of lower-level managers. The solution adopted by most companies is to move toward greater delegation. Yet it is difficult for top managers who were previously successful at being directive to give up responsibility. Moreover, lower-level managers are not accustomed to making decisions for themselves. As a result, numerous companies flounder during this revolutionary period, adhering to centralized methods while lower-level employees grow more disenchanted and leave the organization.

Phase 3: Delegation . . .

The next era of growth evolves from the successful application of a decentralized organization structure. It exhibits these characteristics:

☐ Much greater responsibility is given to the managers of plants and market territories.

☐ Profit centers and bonuses are used to stimulate motivation.

☐ The top executives at headquarters restrain themselves to managing by exception, based on periodic reports from the field.

☐ Management often concentrates on making new acquisitions which can be lined up beside other decentralized units.

☐ Communication from the top is infrequent, usually by correspondence, telephone, or brief visits to field locations.

The delegation stage proves useful for gaining expansion through heightened motivation at lower levels. Decentralized managers with greater authority and incentive are able to penetrate larger markets, respond faster to customers, and develop new products.

. . . & the control crisis: A serious problem eventually evolves, however, as top executives sense that they are losing control over a highly diversified field operation. Autonomous field managers prefer to run their own shows without coordinating plans, money, technology, and manpower with the rest of the organization. Freedom breeds a parochial attitude.

Hence, the Phase 3 revolution is under way when top management seeks to regain control over the total company. Some top managements attempt a return to centralized management, which usually fails because of the vast scope of operations. Those companies that move ahead find a new solution in the use of special coordination techniques.

Phase 4: Coordination . . .

During this phase, the evolutionary period is characerized by the use of formal systems for achieving greater coordination and by top executives taking responsibility for the initiation and administration of these new systems. For example:

☐ Decentralized units are merged into product groups.

☐ Formal planning procedures are established and intensively reviewed.

☐ Numerous staff personnel are hired and located at headquarters to initiate company-wide programs of control and review for line managers.

☐ Capital expenditures are carefully weighed and parceled out across the organization.

☐ Each product group is treated as an investment center where return on invested capital is an important criterion used in allocating funds.

☐ Certain technical functions, such as data processing, are centralized at headquarters, while daily operating decisions remain decentralized.

☐ Stock options and companywide profit sharing are used to encourage identity with the firm as a whole.

All of these new coordination systems prove useful for achieving growth through more efficient allocation of a company's limited resources. They prompt field managers to look beyond the needs of their local units. While these managers still have much decision-making responsibility, they learn to justify their actions more carefully to a "watchdog" audience at headquarters.

. . . & the red tape crisis: But a lack of confidence gradually builds between line and staff, and between headquarters and the field. The proliferation of systems and programs begins to exceed its utility; a red-tape crisis is created. Line managers, for example, increasingly resent heavy staff direction from those who are not familiar with local conditions. Staff people, on the other hand, complain about uncooperative and uninformed line managers. Together both groups criticize the bureaucratic paper system that has evolved. Procedures take precedence over problem solving, and innovation is dampened. In short, the organization has become too large and complex to be managed through formal programs and rigid systems. The Phase 4 revolution is underway.

Phase 5: Collaboration . . .

The last observable phase in previous studies emphasizes strong interpersonal collaboration in an attempt to overcome the red-tape crisis. Where Phase 4 was managed more through formal systems and procedures, Phase 5 emphasizes greater spontaneity in management action through teams and the skillful confrontation of interpersonal differences. Social control and self-discipline take over from formal control. This transition is especially difficult for those experts who created the old systems as well as for those line managers who relied on formal methods for answers.

The Phase 5 evolution, then builds around a more flexible and behavioral approach to management. Here are its characteristics:

☐ The focus is on solving problems quickly through team action.

☐ Teams are combined across functions for task-group activity.

☐ Headquarters staff experts are reduced in number, reassigned, and combined in interdisciplinary teams to consult with, not to direct, field units.

☐ A matrix-type structure is frequently used to assemble the right teams for the appropriate problems.

☐ Previous formal systems are simplified and combined into single multipurpose systems.

☐ Conferences of key managers are held frequently to focus on major problem issues.

☐ Educational programs are utilized to train managers in behavioral skills for achieving better teamwork and conflict resolution.

☐ Real-time information systems are integrated into daily decision making.

☐ Economic rewards are geared more to team performance than to individual achievement.

☐ Experiments in new practices are encouraged throughout the organization.

. . . & the ? crisis: What will be the revolution in response to this stage of evolution? Many large U.S. companies are now in the Phase 5 evolutionary stage, so the answers are critical. While there is little clear evidence, I imagine the revolution will center around the "psychological saturation" of employees who grow emotionally and physically exhausted by the intensity of teamwork and the heavy pressure for innovative solutions.

My hunch is that the Phase 5 revolution will be solved through new structure and programs that allow employees to periodically rest, reflect, and revitalize themselves. We may even see companies with dual organization structures: a "habit" structure for getting the daily work done, and a "reflective" structure for stimulating perspective and personal enrichment. Employees could then move back and

forth between the two structures as their energies are dissipated and refueled.

One European organization has implemented just such a structure. Five reflective groups have been established outside the regular structure for the purpose of continuously evaluating five task activities basic to the organization. They report directly to the managing director, although their reports are made public throughout the organization. Membership in each group includes all levels and functions, and employees are rotated through these groups on a six-month basis.

Other concrete examples now in practice include providing sabbaticals for employees, moving managers in and out of "hot spot" jobs, establishing a four-day workweek, assuring job security, building physical facilities for relaxation *during* the working day, making jobs more interchangeable, creating an extra team on the assembly line so that one team is always off for reeducation, and switching into longer vacations and more flexible working hours.

The Chinese practice of requiring executives to spend time periodically on lower-level jobs may also be worth a nonideological evaluation. For too long U.S. management has assumed that career progress should be equated with an upward path toward title, salary, and power. Could it be that some vice presidents of marketing might just long for, and even benefit from, temporary duty in the field sales organization?

IMPLICATIONS OF HISTORY

Let me now summarize some important implications for practicing managers. First, the main features of this discussion are depicted in *Exhibit III,* which shows the specific management actions that characterize each growth phase. These actions are also the solutions which ended each preceding revolutionary period.

In one sense, I hope that many readers will react to my model by calling it obvious and natural for depicting the growth of an organization. To me this type of reaction is a useful test of the model's validity.

But at a more reflective level I imagine some of these reactions are more hindsight than foresight. Those experienced managers who have been through a developmental sequence can empathize with it now, but how did they react when in the middle of a stage of evolution or revolution? They can probably recall the limits of their own developmental understanding at that time. Perhaps they resisted desirable changes or were even swept emotionally

EXHIBIT III
Organization Practices During Evolution in the Five Phases of Growth.

Category	PHASE 1	PHASE 2	PHASE 3	PHASE 4	PHASE 5
MANAGEMENT FOCUS	Make & Sell	Efficiency of operations	Expansion of market	Consolidation of organization	Problem solving & innovation
ORGANIZATION STRUCTURE	Informal	Centralized & functional	Decentralized & geographical	Line-staff & product groups	Matrix of teams
TOP MANAGEMENT STYLE	Individualistic & entrepreneurial	Directive	Delegative	Watchdog	Participative
CONTROL SYSTEM	Market results	Standards & cost centers	Reports & profit centers	Plans & Investment centers	Mutual goal setting
MANAGEMENT REWARD EMPHASIS	Ownership	Salary & merit increases	Individual bonus	Profit sharing & stock options	Team bonus

into a revolution without being able to propose constructive solutions. So let me offer some explicit guidelines for managers of growing organizations to keep in mind.

Know where you are in the developmental sequence.

Every organization and its component parts are at different stages of development. The task of top management is to be aware of these stages; otherwise, it may not recognize when the time for change has come, or it may act to impose the wrong solution.

Top leaders should be ready to work with the flow of the tide rather than against it; yet they should be cautious, since it is tempting to skip phases out of impatience. Each phase results in certain strengths and learning experiences in the organization that will be essential for success in subsequent phases. A child prodigy, for example, may be able to read like a teenager, but he cannot behave like one until he ages through a sequence of experiences.

I also doubt that managers can or should act to avoid revolutions. Rather, these periods of tension provide the pressure, ideas, and awareness that afford a platform for change and the introduction of new practices.

Recognize the limited range of solutions.

In each revolutionary stage it becomes evident

that this stage can be ended only by certain specific solutions; moreover, these solutions are different from those which were applied to the problems of the preceding revolution. Too often it is tempting to choose solutions that were tried before, which makes it impossible for a new phase of growth to evolve.

Management must be prepared to dismantle current structures before the revolutionary stage becomes too turbulent. Top managers, realizing that their own managerial styles are no longer appropriate, may even have to take themselves out of leadership positions. A good Phase 2 manager facing Phase 3 might be wise to find another Phase 2 organization that better fits his talents, either outside the company or with one of its newer subsidiaries.

Finally, evolution is not an automatic affair; it is a contest for survival. To move ahead, companies must consciously introduce planned structure that not only are solutions to a current crisis but also are fitted to the *next* phase of growth. This requires considerable self-awareness on the part of top management, as well as great interpersonal skill in persuading other managers that change is needed.

Realize that solutions breed new problems.

Managers often fail to realize that organizational solutions create problems for the future (i.e., a decision to delegate eventually causes a problem of control). Historical actions are very much determinants of what happens to the company at a much later date.

An awareness of this effect should help managers to evaluate company problems with greater historical understanding instead of "pinning the blame" on a current development. Better yet managers should be in a position to *predict* future problems, and thereby to prepare solutions and coping strategies before a revolution gets out of hand.

A management that is aware of the problems ahead could well decide *not* to grow. Top managers may, for instance, prefer to retain the informal practices of a small company, knowing that this way of life is inherent in the organization's limited size, not in their congenial personalities. If they choose to grow, they may do themselves out of a job and a way of life they enjoy.

And what about the managements of very large organizations? Can they find new solutions for continued phases of evolution? Or are they reaching a stage where the government will act to break them up because they are too large.

CONCLUDING NOTE

Clearly, there is still much to learn about processes of development in organizations. The phases outlined here are only five in number and are still only approximations. Researchers are just beginning to study the specific developmental problems of structure, control, rewards, and management style in different industries and in a variety of cultures.

One should not, however, wait for conclusive evidence before educating managers to think and act from a developmental perspective. The critical dimension of time has been missing for too long from our management theories and practices. The intriguing paradox is that by learning more about history we may do a better job in the future.

Exercise: Environmental Analysis

PURPOSE

The purpose of this exercise is to help you understand organization environments. By the time you finish this exercise you will:

1. Understand the concept of environmental uncertainty.

2. Analyze the task environment of different organizations.

3. Understand the effect of environmental uncertainty on organization structure.

INTRODUCTION

Organizations are open systems. They operate in an environment and are dependent on that environment for survival. Organizations depend on the environment as a place from which to import the resources they need and as a place to which they can export the resources they produce. Without this constant interaction with the environment, organizations would be unable to survive.

Because of this interdependence, an organization must be responsive to the demands of the environment in which it operates. As Duncan (1979) points out, one of the critical aspects of this responsiveness is the structure of the organization. Thus the structure of an organization should be a direct response to the demands of its environment. Stated another way, an organization must understand its environment before it can decide on an appropriate structure.

The degree of uncertainty present in an organization's environment is a primary determinant of organization-environment compatibility. Environmental uncertainty is comprised of two dimensions: simple/complex and static/dynamic (Duncan, 1979). In this exercise you will use these two dimensions to diagnose the environment of a variety of organizations. You will then use Duncan's decision tree to determine the most appropriate structure for each of these organizations.

INSTRUCTIONS

1. Read Duncan's article, "What is the Right Organization Structure? Decision Tree Analysis Provides the Answer."

2. Form groups of five to seven people.

3. In groups, complete the Environmental Analysis Worksheets for the organizations assigned by your instructor.

This exercise is based on the ideas presented in R. D. Duncan, "What Is the Right Organization Structure? Decision Tree Analysis Provides the Answer," *Organizational Dynamics,* 1979, Winter, 59-79.

4. Appoint a spokesperson and report your analyses to the class.

5. Participate in a class discussion.

ENVIRONMENTAL ANALYSIS WORKSHEETS

Directions: For each of the organizations assigned by your instructor determine:

☐ The task environment [see Figure 1 (Duncan, 1979)].

☐ Whether the environment is simple or complex.

☐ Whether the environment is static or dynamic.

☐ The degree of uncertainty present in the environment [see Figure 2 (Duncan, 1979)].

☐ The most appropriate structure for that environment [see Figure 7 (Duncan, 1979)].

ENVIRONMENTAL ANALYSIS WORKSHEET I

1. Organization:

Task Environment

Internal Environment   External Environment

Simple or Complex? _____

Static or Dynamic? _____

Degree of Uncertainty? _____

Most Appropriate Structure? _____

2. Organization:

Task Environment

Internal Environment   External Environment

Simple or Complex? _____

Static or Dynamic? _____

Degree of Uncertainty? _____

Most Appropriate Structure? _____

ENVIRONMENTAL ANALYSIS WORKSHEET I

3. Organization:

Task Environment

Internal Environment   External Environment

Simple or Complex? _____

Static or Dynamic? _____

Degree of Uncertainty? _____

Most Appropriate Structure? _____

4. Organization:

Task Environment

Internal Environment   External Environment

Simple or Complex? _____

Static or Dynamic? _____

Degree of Uncertainty? _____

Most Appropriate Structure? _____

DISCUSSION QUESTIONS

1. Did you have difficulty determining the task environment? The degree of environmental uncertainty? The most appropriate structure?

2. Were there differences between your analyses and those of the other groups? Why do you think this happened?

3. Do you think that this is a feasible task for managers to undertake when considering the structure of their organizations? Why or why not?

4. Consider your university. Is it structured according to the demands of its environment? If not, what are some of the consequences?

REFERENCES

Duncan, R. D. "What Is the Right Organization Structure? Decision Tree Analysis Provides the Answer." *Organizational Dynamics,* 1979, Winter, 59-79.

Exercise: Small Business Design: The Case Of a Publishing Firm

PURPOSE

The purpose of this exercise is to provide you with the experience of designing a new organization. By the time you complete this exercise you will:

1. Identify the differences between the product, functional, geographic, and matrix forms of organization.

2. Determine an appropriate design for an emergent organization.

3. Design job descriptions for the new functions in this organization.

INTRODUCTION

The topic of organizational design is very complex, entailing many variables. The appropriate form of organization will depend upon the size of the company, its

This case is based on original material. All names in the case are ficticious. This case was prepared as a basis for class discussion rather than to illustrate effective or ineffective approaches to management. The reading insert is based on material presented in Chapter 11, "Organizing and Coordinating Work Units" in Arthur Bedeian and William Gluck, *Management,* 3rd ed. (New York: The Dryden Press, 1984).

environment, its product or services, its technological demands, its requirements for integration and differentiation, and its stage of growth.

The *pure* forms of organizational design each have their own advantages and disadvantages. Some of the pure forms (such as the product form of organization) enhance interdepartmental coordination but create redundancies and duplication of efforts. Others (such as the functional design) maintain efficiency but focus upon short- rather than long-term horizons for product development. As indicated in the article by Duncan, the organizational environment and rate of change is another key factor that must be considered in determining organizational designs.

In this exercise you will have an opportunity to test these considerations while designing a new organization. In addition, you will also be developing job descriptions for the primary functions of the company.

INSTRUCTIONS

1. Read the readings in the chapter.

2. Read the enclosed insert, "Advantages and Disadvantages of Organizational Forms."

3. Read the case material on The Job-Getter Enterprise.

4. In small groups of four to six people, design an organizational structure for the Job-Getter Enterprise.

5. Draw an organizational chart depicting the reporting relationships of key players and departments.

6. Write job descriptions for the key positions in the Job-Getter Enterprise.

7. Choose a spokesperson from your group who will present your organizational design to the class.

8. Participate in a class discussion.

ADVANTAGES AND DISADVANTAGES OF ORGANIZATIONAL FORMS

Functional Departmentalization (see page 357)

Functional departmentalization is the most widely used basis for grouping activities. The functionally structured firm groups its activities into departments, each of which undertakes a distinctive function.

Advantages	*Disadvantages*
Maximizes functional interests within departmental units	Difficulty in achieving coordination between functional areas
Simple communication and decision network	Fosters parochial emphasis on functional objectives
Results in efficient use of resources	Cost of coordination between departments can be high

Facilitates measurement of functional outputs and results	Employee identification with specialist groups makes change difficult
Simplifies training of functional specialists	Limits development of broadly trained managers
Gives status to major functional areas	Encourages interdepartmental rivalry and conflict
Preserves strategic control at top management level	Client satisfaction can be low

Product Departmentalization (see page 358)

Grouping of activities along product lines was pioneered by DuPont and General Motors in the 1920s. Following a product arrangement, each major product line is administered through a separate and semi-autonomous division. In this regard, product specialists are grouped to perform all the duties necessary to produce an individual product or service.

Advantages	Disadvantages
Evaluates departments as autonomous profit centers	Increases coordination between specialized product areas
Facilitates coordination between functions for rapid response	Leads to decreased communication between functional specialists
Adds flexibility to a firm's structure	Contributes to a lack of clarity of functional area responsibilities and a duplication of sevices
Focuses on client needs	
Develops broadly trained managers	

Territorial Departmentalization (see page 359)

Also known as geographic or area departmentalization, territorial departmentalization is especially appropriate for large firms whose activities have become physically or geographically dispersed.

Advantages	Disadvantages
Allows units to adapt to local circumstances	Requires a large number of general managers
Takes advantages of local legal, political, and cultural differences	Leads to possible duplication of staff services
Provides territories as a training ground for general managers	Presents problems for top management control over local operations

Customer Departmentalization (see page 360)

This form of structural design is often used when a firm's clients have very different needs. Rather than structuring departments around products, activities are grouped on the basis of customer needs. This form of departmentalization is typically used by firms with a diverse clientele in an effort to cater to the specific requirements of different buyer segments.

Advantages	*Disadvantages*
Responds to customer needs	Increases difficulty of establishing uniform companywide practices
Ties performance to requirements of key market segments	Leads to pressure for special treatment of various buyer segments
	Contributes to customer groups developing at an unequal pace leading to underutilization of resources

Matrix Organization (see page 361)

This form of design attempts to cross the product and functional approaches to departmentalization in order to get the best (and avoid the worst) of both. The distinguishing feature of this approach is that functional and product lines of authority are overlaid (to form a grid or matrix). As a consequence, many employees belong simultaneously to two groups, a functional group and a product or project group. They report to two or more superiors—a permanent boss in a functional area unit and one or more temporary bosses representing various project groups. Although matrix is a still evolving organizational form, its users include such firms as General Electric, Lockheed Aircraft, Dow Corning, Procter & Gamble, and Texas Instruments.

Advantages	*Disadvantages*
Adapts to fluctuating work loads	Places a premium on teamwork
Establishes one person as focal point for all matters pertaining to an individual project	Leads to possible conflict with existence of two separate operating systems
Permits maximum use of limited pool of functional specialists	Creates possible power struggles between project managers and functional area heads
Provides a home base for functional specialists between projects	Slows decision making and increases costs in certain instances
Makes it possible to respond to several environmental sectors simultaneously	Promotes narrow management viewpoint

FUNCTIONAL DEPARTMENTALIZATION

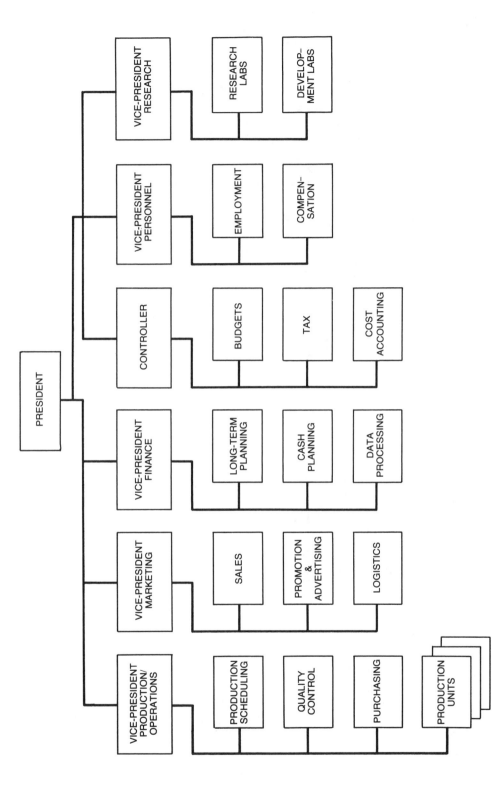

PRODUCT DEPARTMENTALIZATION

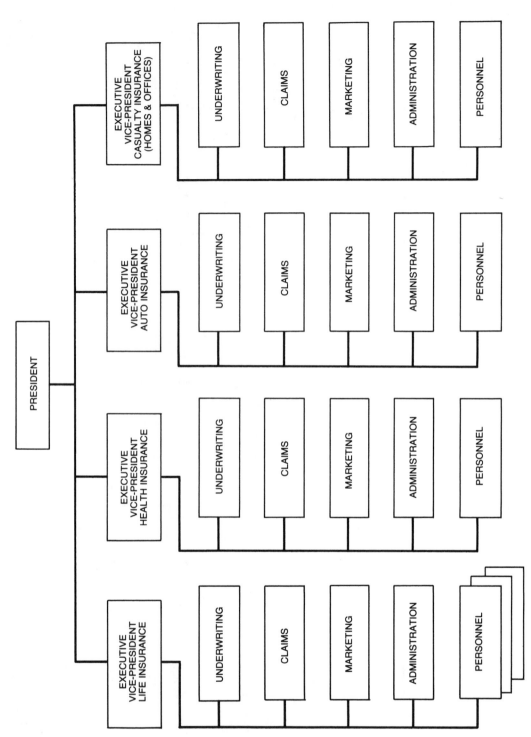

TERRITORIAL DEPARTMENTALIZATION

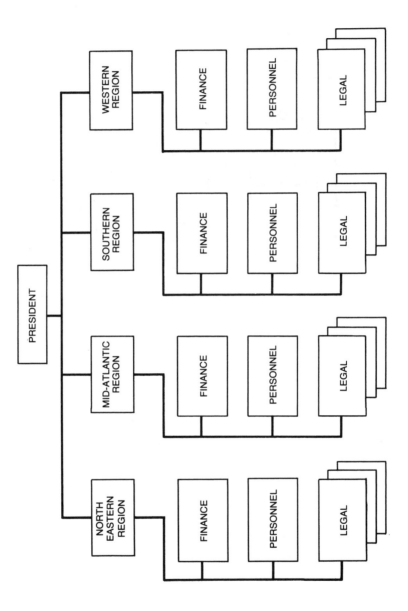

CUSTOMER DEPARTMENTALIZATION

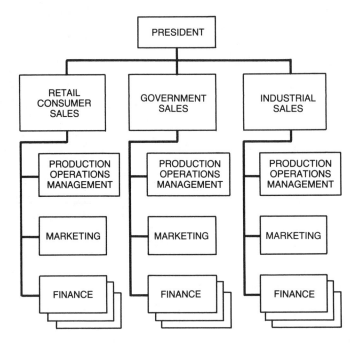

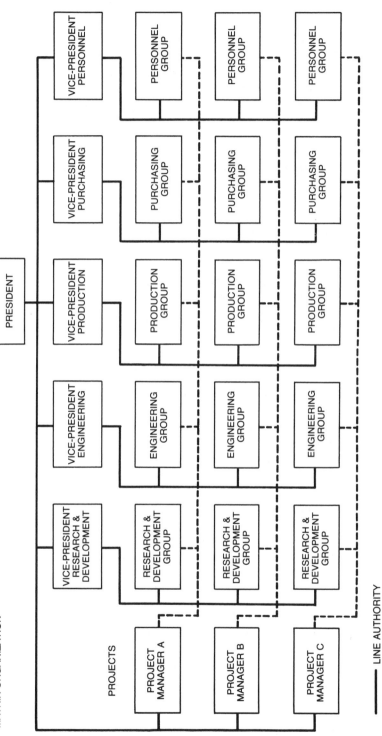

MATRIX ORGANIZATION

THE JOB-GETTER ENTERPRISE

The Job-Getter Enterprise is a new organization in the San Francisco-San Jose-Monterey Bay area, founded by Martin Manicot, a new entrepreneur. In 1981, Manicot arrived in San Jose with a degree in engineering from MIT, and went to work for a technological start-up company in CAD-CAM design. Three years later, he matriculated at Stanford University in the Graduate Schools of Business. After completing his degree, Manicot settled in the Silicon Valley area. He decided to start his own business.

Manicot spent four months planning his new enterprise. His idea was to create a bimonthly publication that would list local job opportunities in the San Francisco-San Jose-Monterey Bay area. He realized he could sell such a publication in local convenience stores, as well as campus bookstores, and reap a tidy profit.

Market research indicated that many people would pay at least $1 for a small local publication of this type. Two types of information would be included in the publication:

1. *Job Listings*—simply a description of the job, salary requirements, experience required, and location.

2. *Advertising Listings*—paid for by employment agencies, and corporations who seek help.

Manicot's forecasts showed that with a minimal amount of advertising space sold (such as sixteen full-page ads per 50 page issue) and by selling the publication for $1 (a price his market research indicated most people would be happy to pay for such a publication), the business would break even within a year to eighteen months. If successful, the business could be later expanded into other metropolitan areas along the West Coast, such as Los Angeles and San Diego, as well as Denver and Las Vegas.

Three key problems plagued this entrepreneurial venture. *First,* obtaining timely information for job listings for the publication was a potential problem. If the job listings were not timely, then repeat sales for the publication would be low. Customers would be unwilling to purchase the publication unless they perceived that the job listings met their needs, were timely, and were local.

A *second* issue involved breaking into the market. Local distributors were not very willing to carry an untested publication on their newsracks. Circulation was low because the number of locations in which the new publication was sold were few. This was a potential problem because circulation is traditionally a key factor in attracting advertising for the publication.

Third, the success of the publication would depend upon the number of advertisements sold. Full-page advertisements account for the bulk of revenue. Advertisements could not be sold until distribution and circulation within the San Francisco-San Jose-Monterey Bay area was sufficiently widespread. Because local distributors were unwilling to carry an untested product, this could take some time. It was the task of the new publication to identify and publish timely job listings, while simultaneously increasing circulation and distribution to be able to attract competitive advertising space.

The key functions of the new enterprise could be summarized as follows:

1. Sales (job listings and advertising space).

2. Circulation and distribution.

3. Production of the publication.

Sales encompassed two categories: (a) job listings, which were listed for free in the publication, and (b) advertising space, for companies who wished to advertise particular positions or continual employment needs. Job listings were gathered via telemarketing (calling local companies to determine if they wanted to list a job opening). Advertising space was sold via on-site personal visits to firms.

At present, seven people are employed in sales jobs in the general San Francisco-San Jose-Monterey Bay area. Salespeople have been hired on a mostly part-time basis, with only the sales manager, Jennifer, and one other salesperson hired full-time. Full-time salespeople are expected to equally emphasize job listing and advertising sales. They are paid part salary ($100 per week) and part commission (25 percent of advertising space sold) for on-site sales or telemarketing sales. Part-time salespeople concentrate primarily on telemarketing sales; they are paid minimum wage on an hourly basis ($4.25 per hour) and receive a 10-percent commission.

The sales manager was expected to: (1) contribute to sales, (2) promote the magazine (name recognition through free copies, radio advertising, and the like), and (3) train new sales personnel.

Circulation and distribution involved visiting prospective convenience store owners and asking them to carry the publication in their stores. Every two weeks, the publication would be distributed to each store that agreed to carry the product. Store owners received a small percentage (10 percent) of every issue sold.

The publication is carried by approximately 700 outlets; there is potential for as many as 1,500 outlets or more. In addition, newsracks could be utilized in urban areas, just like newspaper stands, as additional outlets to sell the publication. The cost of newsracks is small ($100 each) but maintaining them requires additional effort and cost. It is the circulation manager's responsibility to purchase and maintain newsracks, to oversee distribution, and to increase the number of outlets throughout the San Francisco-San Jose-Monterey Bay area.

Currently, one employee, Greg, serves as the circulation manager. He is responsible for increasing circulation by improving the number of outlets in the San Francisco-San Jose-Monterey Bay area.

Another employee, Alfred, has been hired on a part-time basis as a distribution manager responsible for the bimonthly distribution and collection of the publication from the assigned locations.

The circulation manager is a salaried position, paid $325 per week with no commission. The distribution manager is paid a single sum for the distribution and collection of each issue during the month. The distribution manager reports to the circulation manager.

Production involved printing the bimonthly publication, inputting the job listings into a personal computer, designing advertisements, and proofreading each issue. Once the current issue is completed with the aid of a simple Apple computer, it is output on an Apple Laserwriter and sent to a local print shop for presswork and binding. The individuals responsible for production are two part-time secretaries, Barbara and Judy, who input the job listings. Production is paid on an hourly basis at $4.25 minimum wage per hour.

Manicot has found that his current organizational design is not working. There's a problem with sales; the salespeople are concentrating on telemarketing (which can be done easily from home), rather than on-site visits to sell advertising space. Three months into the publication, advertising sales are much lower than projected. For those salespeople who have attempted on-site visits to sell advertising space, much of their activity has centered around locations close to their homes, rather than the larger targeted sales areas. In addition, Manicot is concerned that the job listing information is less timely than needed. This may present a problem with repeat sales business.

The geographical span includes a territory over 200 miles, with the Monterey Bay area as one geographical location, Sacramento and points east as another area, San Francisco and the Silicon Valley-San Jose basin as a third. Manicot would like to expand into the Napa Valley area north of San Francisco, as well, but he can't seem to get his salespeople to concentrate on that area.

The sales manager, Jennifer, complains that she cannot concentrate on sales, telemarketing, training new salespeople, and promotion all at the same time. She recognizes that in a small business it is often necessary to perform more than one task, but the combination of all four is simply too time-consuming. As a result, her job performance suffers. Because her pay is directly tied to her sales, she spends most of her time selling rather than training or working on promotional activities.

The circulation manager, Greg, complains that his territory is too large for one individual. This is complicated by his other responsibilities, particularly while he is battling major distributors who sell publications en masse to local stores and newsracks. The geographic area for circulation is as dispersed as the sales territory. Additionally, he maintains he cannot sell the publication to new vendors until it is proven via circulation. Circulation will not be boosted until customers get to know the product, and are willing to purchase it on a repeat sales basis.

The distribution manager, Alfred, reports in only once every two weeks. He seems to want to do more than simple distribution and collection tasks, but Manicot is unclear what that could be. Alfred is motivated, interested in earning more money, and a good coworker. He has mentioned an interest in developing circulation or helping with sales from time to time, but as a part-time worker, it is unclear how much he really could contribute. The production staff works primarily at home, and Manicot is displeased with the quality of their proofreading and listings. Some of the listings for the last publication were actually omitted by mistake, causing delays in the timeliness of the job listing information.

Turnover has plagued the sales ranks. Four part-timers and one full-timer have left the company during its first three months of operation. Over the past six months, Manicot has lost a circulation manager and two other members of his production staff. Although turnover is to be expected in a small business, each time someone leaves, a new person must be trained properly. New employees they have been cannot work to full capacity until they have been on the job at least two full months. As a result, Manicot always seems to be running behind on his sales and circulation objectives.

Furthermore, Manicot is doing virtually everything himself—training new salespeople, performing on-site visits, proofreading and job listing production, manning the phones, and obtaining new vendors for distribution. He feels he needs to create clear-cut jobs that specify the functions and responsibilities so that he can do what he really needs to do for the business—on-site visits to obtain additional financing to capitalize the business. If he could get additional financing, he could afford to pay his personnel more competitively and reduce turnover. At the moment, he is not paying benefits to his employees beyond what is required by the law. With additional financing, he could increase benefit coverage, pay more competitively, and hire more personnel to increase sales and circulation.

Manicot is convinced that this new enterprise will be a success if he can obtain sufficient financing and organize the business properly. Sales of the publication have been promising, and the $1 price tag seems to attract customers. He has received a great deal of positive feedback on the publication from local distributors and customers, and he has investors ready to invest in the business, provided that he cleans up some of his current organizational and staffing dilemmas.

Manicot has come to you to help him define and organize his enterprise. To increase sales, he needs to hire new people to fill as yet undefined positions, because his organization is growing at a rapid rate. He is looking to you as a consultant to help him define his organization and determine the job descriptions for the functions of the new enterprise.

CURRENT ORGANIZATIONAL CHART: THE JOB-GETTER ENTERPRISE

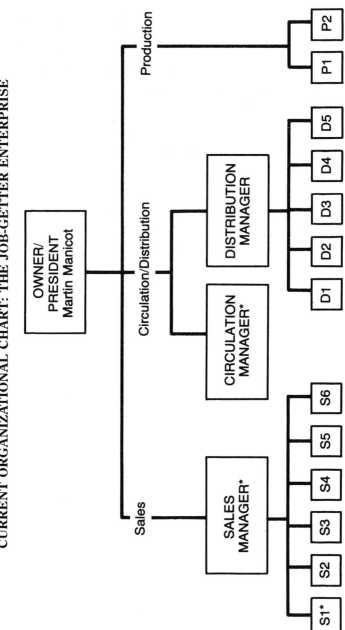

FINANCIAL INFORMATION: THE JOB-GETTER ENTERPRISE

Revenue per month:

Approximately 4,000 issues sold at $1 per issue: @ .70 return*	$2,800
Approximately 10 full pages of advertising space sold per month at $350 per page (after commissions paid)	$3,500
Total Revenue	$6,300

Expenses per month:

Office expenses (including office rental, five telephone lines, supplies	$2,000
Production costs per issue for printing (20,000 issues printed)	$1,400

Compensation Costs:

Sales: $100 per week plus 20% commission	400
Telemarketing: Minimum wage ($4.25 per hour) plus 10% commission. Total $2600 per month	$2600
Circulation: $325 per week, no commission/$1400 per month	$1400
Production: Minimum wage ($4.25 per hour)/$200 per month	$200
Delivery: Minimum wage ($4.25 per hour)/$1100 per month	$1100
Total month expenses:	$9,800
Net loss	$3,500

Number of current locations: 800

*.30 cents goes to vendors

BANKING/FINANCIAL

ADMINISTRATIVE SECRETARY - See "Office-Administn."

BOOKKEEPER - Work for a rapidly growing, Independent bank. We are seeking qualified & competent personnel. Conveniently located near BART. An E.O.E. Please send resume or contact.

Pay Rge:.....D.O.E.
Co:..........Bank of
Jb Loc:......Oakland.....................#Emp: 22-30
Contact......Mrs. Van Dycke.........................

AUTOMOTIVE

AUTO MACHANIC - Exp. brake & exhaust Specialist F/T. Trainee positions also avail. @ all locations. Discover the possibilities for a life time position w/ Paid vacations, medical, advancement oppt.

Exp.Req:..... 1yr.
Pay Rge:.... $20K & up
Co:..........
Jb Loc:......Fremont, Dublin Fairfield, San Bruno, San Francisco, Newark
Contact......Chet Gould.........................

RISE ABOVE THE CROWD

$20,000 TO START

Student Loan
Portfolio Manager

The Job As A Portfolio Manager

has openings for Portfolio Managers of delinquent student loans. This challenging job allows a wide use of your own discretion and involves negotiating the repayment of loans for our clients which include colleges, universities & state guarantee agencies. You will learn how to locate borrowers, work with attorneys, negotiate loan payments, and become familiar with all aspects of loan portfolio management. You will be thoroughly trained in handling all aspects of the job.

Qualifications
* Must be hardworking, self-motivated & career minded.
* Good communication skills.
* Minimum 4 years general work experience.
* College helpful but not required.

Employee Benefits
* Medical Plan
* Dental Plan
* Vision Care Plan
* Wealth Accumulation Program
* Child Care Assistance
* 9 1/2 Holidays plus one week Holiday Break
* Vacations
* In-House Legal Services
* Educational Reimbursement Program

FOR AN OPEN HOUSE TOUR AND INTERVIEW

CALL

A VALUE DRIVEN COMPANY WITH
A COMMITMENT TO EXCELLENCE

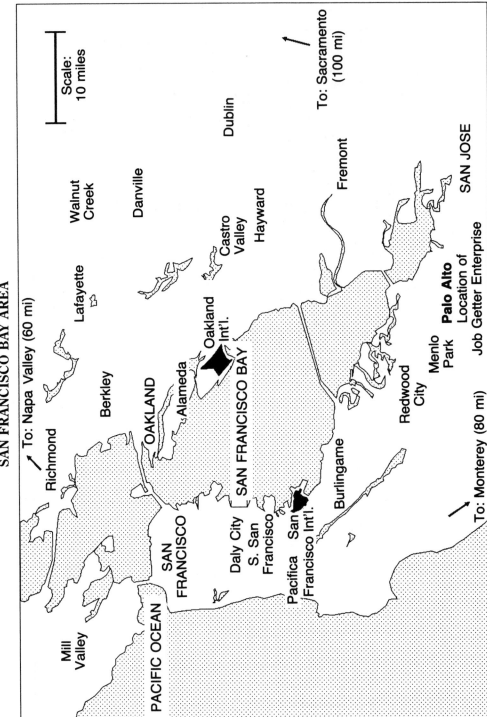

SAN FRANCISCO BAY AREA

Scale:
10 miles

To: Sacramento
(100 mi)

To: Napa Valley (60 mi)

Richmond

Dublin

Walnut
Creek

Danville

Lafayette

Fremont

Berkley

Castro
Valley

Hayward

OAKLAND

Oakland
Int'l.

Alameda

SAN FRANCISCO BAY

SAN
FRANCISCO

SAN JOSE

Daly City
S. San
Francisco

Menlo
Park

Palo Alto
Location of
Job Getter Enterprise

Redwood
City

Pacifica   San
Francisco Int'l.

Burlingame

To: Monterey (80 mi)

PACIFIC OCEAN

Mill
Valley

The Job-Getter Enterprise Organizational Chart

Directions: After reading the insert "Advantages and Disadvantages of Organizational Forms," choose a form that you feel is most appropriate for the Job-Getter Enterprise. Then draw the chart, complete with reporting relationships and functions, that describe how you feel the Job-Getter Enterprise should be organized.

The Job-Getter Enterprise Job Descriptions

Descriptions: Once you have determined the most effective form of organization for the Job-Getter Enterprise, write out job descriptions for the key positions listed on your chart. Be certain to specify the job functions, responsibilities, activities, and tasks to the extent possible.

DISCUSSION QUESTIONS

1. Which organizational design did you choose for the Job-Getter Enterprise? What are the advantages and disadvantages of this design?

2. What state of evolution/revolution does the Job-Getter Enterprise represent in its current state of growth?

3. Are most young entrepreneurial companies organic in form? Should they be?

4. How would you characterize the environment of the Job-Getter Enterprise? Which variables did you consider in your design?

Case: Rondell Data Corporation

PURPOSE

The case of Rondell Data Corporation highlights the complexities of organizational design. By the time you finish this case assignment you will:

1. Recognize the problems that can occur with improper organizational designs.

2. Identify the environmental conditions that can affect the appropriateness of an organizational design.

3. Understand how dysfunctional organizational structures can impair work effectiveness among departmental functions.

INTRODUCTION

Frank Forbus, the new director of engineering at Rondell, is having a number of problems managing the transition from design to production. Forbus appears to believe that many of the problems are personality-based, rather than the result of inadequate organizational design and structure. His inability to conceptualize the problems associated with organizational design and structure lead to his downfall.

As you read this case, identify the problems from an organizational design and structure point of view. What should Frank Forbus have recognized about the structure and design of his department? What needs to be changed about the current structure to minimize conflict in the future?

INSTRUCTIONS

1. Read the readings in the chapters.

2. Read the case "Rondell Data Corporation."

3. Consider the following questions:
   a. What is your analysis of the problems at Rondell?
   b. What changes should the new manager who takes over the Director of Engineering job consider?

4. Participate in a class discussion.

Rondell Data Corporation

"God damn it, he's done it again!"

Frank Forbus threw the stack of prints and specifications down on his desk in disgust. The Model 802 wide-band modulator, released for production the previous Thursday, had just come back to Frank's Engineering Services Department with a caustic note that began, "This one can't be produced, either . . ." It was the fourth time Production had kicked the design back.

Frank Forbus, director of engineering for Rondell Data Corp., was normally a quiet man. But the Model 802 was stretching his patience; it was beginning to look just like other new products that had hit delays and problems in the transition from design to production during the eight months Frank had worked for Rondell. These problems were nothing new at the sprawling old Rondell factory; Frank's predecessor in the engineering job had run afoul of them too, and had finally been fired for protesting too vehemently about the other departments. But the Model 802 should have been different. Frank had met two months before (July 3, 1978) with the firm's president, Bill Hunt, and with factory superintendent Dave Schwab to smooth the way for the new modulator design. He thought back to the meeting . . .

"Now we all know there's a tight deadline on the 802," Bill Hunt said, "and Frank's done well to ask us to talk about its introduction. I'm counting on both of you to find any snags in the system, and to work together to get that first production run out by October second. Can you do it?"

"We can do it in Production if we get a clean design two weeks from now, as scheduled," answered Dave Schwab, the grizzled factory superintendent. "Frank and I have already talked about that, of course. I'm setting aside time in the card room and the machine shop, and we'll be ready. If the design goes over schedule, though, I'll have to fill in with other runs, and it will cost us a bundle to break in for the 802. How does it look in Engineering, Frank?"

"I've just reviewed the design for the second

time," Frank replied. "If Ron Porter can keep the salesmen out of our hair, and avoid any more last minute changes, we've got a shot. I've pulled the draftsmen off three other overdue jobs to get this one out. But, Dave, that means we can't spring engineers loose to confer with your production people on manufacturing problems."

"Well, Frank, most of those problems are caused by the engineers, and we need them to resolve the difficulties. We've all agreed that production bugs come from both of us bowing to sales pressure, and putting equipment into production before the designs are really ready. That's just what we're trying to avoid on the 802. But I can't have 500 people sitting on their hands waiting to have *some* engineering support."

Bill Hunt broke in, "So long as you two can talk calmly about the problem I'm confident you can resolve it. What a relief it is, Frank, to hear the way you're approaching this. With Kilmann (the previous director of engineering) this conversation would have been a shouting match. Right, Dave?" Dave nodded and smiled.

"Now there's one other thing you should both be aware of," Hunt continued. "Doc Reeves and I talked last night about a new filtering technique, one that might improve the signal-to-noise ratio of the 802 by a factor of two. There's a chance Doc can come up with it before the 802 reaches production, and if it's possible, I'd like to use the new filters. That would give us a real jump on the competition."

Four days after that meeting, Frank found that two of his key people on the 802 design had been pulled to Production for emergency consultation on a bug found in final assembly: two halves of a new data transmission interface wouldn't fit together because recent changes in the front end required a different chassis design for the back end.

Another week later, Doc Reeves walked into Frank's office, proud as a new parent, with the new filter design. "This won't affect the other modules of the 802 much," Doc had said. "Look, it takes three new cards, a few connectors, some changes in the wiring harness, and some new shielding, and that's all."

Frank had tried to resist the last-minute design changes, but Bill Hunt had stood firm. With a lot of overtime by the engineers and draftsmen, Engineering Services should still be able to finish the prints in time.

Two engineers and three draftsmen went onto 12-hour days to get the 802 ready, but the prints were still five days late reaching Dave Schwab. Two days later, the prints came back to Frank, heavily annotated in red. Schwab had worked all day Saturday to review the job, and had found more than a dozen discrepancies in the prints—most of them caused by the new filter design and insufficient checking time before release. Correction of those design faults had brought on a new generation of discrepancies; Schwab's cover note on the second return of the prints indicated he'd had to release the machine capacity he'd been holding for the 802. On the third iteration, Schwab committed his photo and plating capacity to another rush job. The 802 would be at least one month late getting into production. Ron Porter, Vice President for Sales, was furious. His customer needed 100 units *NOW,* he said. Rondell was the customer's only late supplier.

"Here we go again," thought Frank Forbus.

COMPANY HISTORY

Rondell Data Corp. traced its lineage through several generations of electronics technology. Its original founder, Bob Rondell, had set the firm up in 1920 as "Rondell Equipment Co." to manufacture several electrical testing devices he had invented as an engineering faculty member at a large university. The firm branched into radio broadcasting equipment in 1947, and into data transmission equipment in the early 1960s. A well-established corps of direct sales people, mostly engineers, called on industrial, scientific and government accounts, but concentrated heavily on original equipment manufacturers. In this market, Rondell had a long-standing reputation as a source of high-quality, innovative designs. The firm's salespeople fed a continual stream of challenging problems into the Engineering Department, where the creative genius of Ed "Doc" Reeves and several dozen other engineers "converted problems to solutions" (as the sales brochure bragged). Product design formed the spearhead of Rondell's growth.

By 1978, Rondell offered a wide range of products in its two major lines. Broadcast equipment sales had benefitted from the growth of UHF TV and FM radio; it now accounted for 35% of company sales. Data transmission had blossomed, and in this field an increasing number of orders called for unique specifications, ranging from specialized display panels to entirely untried designs.

The company had grown from 100 employees in 1947 to over 800 in 1978 (Exhibit 4-1 shows the current organization chart of key employees.) Bill Hunt, who had been a student of the company's

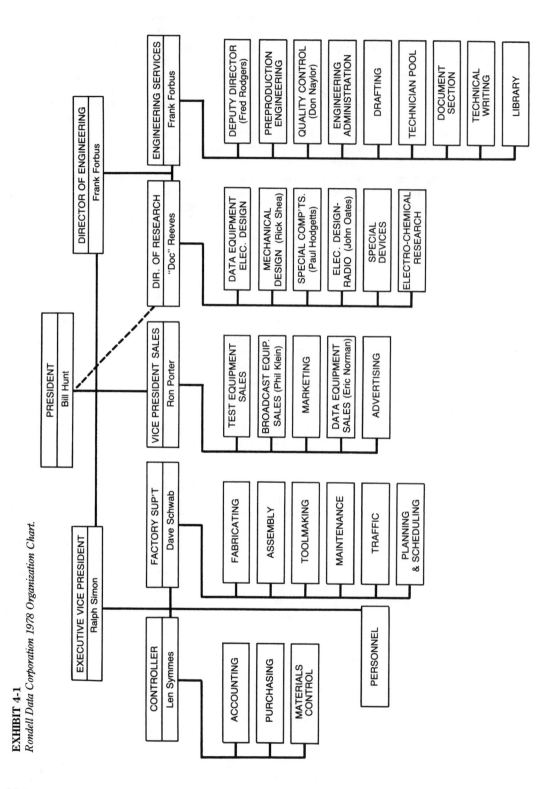

EXHIBIT 4-1
Rondell Data Corporation 1978 Organization Chart.

PRESIDENT
Bill Hunt

EXECUTIVE VICE PRESIDENT
Ralph Simon

DIRECTOR OF ENGINEERING
Frank Forbus

ENGINEERING SERVICES
Frank Forbus

- DEPUTY DIRECTOR (Fred Rodgers)
- PREPRODUCTION ENGINEERING
- QUALITY CONTROL (Don Naylor)
- ENGINEERING ADMINISTRATION
- DRAFTING
- TECHNICIAN POOL
- DOCUMENT SECTION
- TECHNICAL WRITING
- LIBRARY

DIR. OF RESEARCH
"Doc" Reeves

- DATA EQUIPMENT ELEC. DESIGN
- MECHANICAL DESIGN (Rick Shea)
- SPECIAL COMP'TS. (Paul Hodgetts)
- ELEC. DESIGN-RADIO (John Oates)
- SPECIAL DEVICES
- ELECTRO-CHEMICAL RESEARCH

VICE PRESIDENT SALES
Ron Porter

- TEST EQUIPMENT SALES
- BROADCAST EQUIP. SALES (Phil Klein)
- MARKETING
- DATA EQUIPMENT SALES (Eric Norman)
- ADVERTISING

FACTORY SUP'T
Dave Schwab

- FABRICATING
- ASSEMBLY
- TOOLMAKING
- MAINTENANCE
- TRAFFIC
- PLANNING & SCHEDULING

CONTROLLER
Len Symmes

- ACCOUNTING
- PURCHASING
- MATERIALS CONTROL

- PERSONNEL

founder, had presided over most of that growth, and took great pride in preserving the "family spirit" of the old organization. Informal relationships between Rondell's veteran employees formed the backbone of the firm's day-to-day operations; all the managers relied on personal contact, and Hunt often insisted that the absence of bureaucratic red tape was a key factor in recruiting outstanding engineering talent. The personal management approach extended throughout the factory. All exempt employees were paid on a straight salary plus a share of the profits. Rondell boasted an extremely loyal group of senior employees, and very low turnover in nearly all areas of the company.

The highest turnover job in the firm was Frank Forbus's. Frank had joined Rondell in January of 1978, replacing Jim Kilmann, who had been director of engineering for only 10 months. Kilmann, in turn, had replaced Tom MacLeod, a talented engineer who had made a promising start, but had taken to drink after a year in the job. MacLeod's predecessor had been a genial old timer who retired at 70 after 30 years in charge of engineering. (Doc Reeves had refused the directorship in each of the recent changes, saying, "Hell, that's no promotion for a bench man like me. I'm no administrator.")

For several years, the firm had experienced a steadily increasing number of disputes between research, engineering, sales, and production people—disputes generally centered on the problem of new product introduction. Quarrels between departments became more numerous under MacLeod, Kilmann, and Forbus. Some managers associated those disputes with the company's recent decline in profitability—a decline that, inspite of higher sales and gross revenues, was beginning to bother people in 1977. President Bill Hunt commented:

Better cooperation, I'm sure, could increase our output by 5-10%. I'd hoped Kilmann could solve the problems, but pretty obviously he was too young, too arrogant. People like him—that conflict type of personality—bother me. I don't like strife, and with him it seemed I spent all my time smoothing out arguments. Kilmann tried to tell everyone else how to run their departments, without having his own house in order. That approach just wouldn't work, here at Rondell. Frank Forbus, now, seems much more in tune with our style of organization. I'm really hopeful now.

Still, we have just as many problems now as we did last year. Maybe even more. I hope Frank can get a handle on Engineering Services soon . . .

THE ENGINEERING DEPARTMENT: RESEARCH

According to the organization chart (see Exhibit 4-1), Frank Forbus was in charge of both research (really the product development function) and engineering services (which provided engineering support). To Forbus, however, the relationship with research was not so clear-cut.

Doc Reeves is one of the world's unique people, and none of us would have it any other way. He's a creative genius. Sure, the chart says he works for me, but we all know Doc does his own thing. He's not the least bit interested in management routines, and I can't count on him to take any responsibility in scheduling projects, or checking budgets, or what-have-you. But as long as Doc is director of research, you can bet this company will keep on leading the field. He has more ideas per hour than most people have per year, and he keeps the whole engineering staff fired up. Everybody loves Doc—and you can count me in on that, too. In a way, he works for me, sure. But that's not what's important.

"Doc" Reeves—unhurried, contemplative, casual, and candid—tipped his stool back against the wall of his research cubicle and talked about what *was* important:

Development engineering. That's where the company's future rests. Either we have it there, or we don't have it.

There's no kidding ourselves that we're anything but a bunch of Rube Goldbergs here. But that's where the biggest kicks come from—from solving development problems, and dreaming up new ways of doing things. That's why I so look forward to the special contracts we get involved in. We accept them not for the revenue they represent, but because they subsidize the basic development work which goes into all our basic products.

This is a fantastic place to work. I have a great crew and they can really deliver when the chips are down. Why, Bill Hunt and I (he gestured toward the neighboring cubicle, where the president's name hung over the door) are likely to find as many people here at work at ten p.m. as at three in the afternoon. The important thing here is the relationships between people; they're based on mutual respect, not on policies and procedures.

Administrative red tape is a pain. It takes away from development time.

Problems? Sure, there are problems now and then. There are power interests in production, where they sometimes resist change. But I'm not a fighting man, you know. I suppose if I were, I might go in there and push my weight around a little. But I'm an engineer, and can do more for Rondell sitting right here, or working with my own people. That's what brings results.

Other members of the Research Department echoed Doc's views and added some additional sources of satisfaction with their work. They were proud of the personal contacts they built up with customers' technical staffs—contacts that increasingly involved travel to the customers' factories to serve as expert advisors in preparation of overall system design specifications. The engineers were also delighted with the department's encouragement of their personal development, continuing education, and independence on the job.

But there were problems, too. Rich Shea, of the mechanical design section, noted.

In the old days I really enjoyed the work—and the people I worked with. But now there's a lot of irritation. I don't like someone breathing down my neck. You can be hurried into jeopardizing the design.

John Oates, head of the radio electronic design section, was another designer with definite views:

Production engineering is almost nonexistent in this company. Very little is done by the preproduction section in engineering services. Frank Forbus has been trying to get preproduction into the picture, but he won't succeed because you can't start from such an ambiguous position. There have been three directors of engineering in three years. Frank can't hold his own against the others in the company. Kilmann was too aggressive. Perhaps no amount of tact would have succeeded.

Paul Hodgetts was head of special components in the R & D department. Like the rest of the department he valued bench work. But he complained of engineering services.

The services don't do things we want them to do. Instead, they tell us what they're going to

do. I should probably go to Frank, but I don't get any decisions there. I know I should go through Frank, but this holds things up, so I often go direct.

THE ENGINEERING DEPARTMENT: ENGINEERING SERVICES

The Engineering Services Department provided ancillary services to R & D, and served as liaison between engineering and the other Rondell departments. Among its main functions were drafting; management of the central technicians' pool; scheduling and expediting engineering products; documentation and publication of parts lists and engineering orders; preproduction engineering (consisting of the final integration of individual design components into mechanically compatible packages); and quality control (which included inspection of incoming parts and materials, and final inspection of subassemblies and finished equipment). Top management's description of the department included the line, "ESD is responsible for maintaining cooperation with other departments, providing services to the development engineers, and freeing more valuable people in R & D from nonessential activities which are diversions from and beneath their main competence."

Many of Frank Forbus's 75 employees were located in other departments. Quality control people were scattered through the manufacturing and receiving areas, and technicians worked primarily in the research area or the prototype fabrication room. The remaining ESD personnel were assigned to leftover nooks and crannies near production or engineering sections.

Frank Forbus described his position:

My biggest problem is getting acceptance from the people I work with. I've moved slowly rather than risk antagonism. I saw what happend to Kilmann, and I want to avoid that. But although his precipitate action had won over a few of the younger R & D people, he certainly didn't have the department's backing. Of course it was the resentment of other departments which eventually caused his discharge. People have been slow accepting me here. There's nothing really overt, but I get a negative reaction to my ideas.

My role in the company has never been well defined, really. It's complicated by Doc's unique position, of course, and also by the fact that ESD sort of grew by itself over the years, as the design engineers concentrated more and more on the creative parts of product development. I wish I could be more involved in the technical side. That's been my training, and it's a lot of fun. But in our setup, the technical side is the least necessary for me to be involved in.

Schwab (production head) is hard to get along with. Before I came and after Kilmann left, there were six months intervening when no one was really doing any scheduling. No work loads were figured, and unrealistic promises were made about releases. This puts us in an awkward position. We've been scheduling way beyond our capacity to manufacture or engineer.

Certain people within R & D, for instance John Oates, head of the radio electronic design section, understand scheduling well and meet project deadlines, but this is not generally true of the rest of the R & D department, especially the mechanical engineers who won't commit themselves. Most of the complaints come from sales and production department heads because items— like the 802—are going to production before they are fully developed, under pressure from sales to get out the unit, and this snags the whole process. Somehow, engineering services should be able to intervene and resolve these complaints, but I haven't made much headway so far.

I should be able to go to Hunt for help, but he's too busy most of the time, and his major interest is the design side of engineering, where he got his own start. Sometimes he talks as though he's the engineering director as well as president. I have to put my foot down; there are problems here that the front office just doesn't understand.

Sales people were often observed taking their problems directly to designers, while production frequently threw designs back at R & D, claiming they could not be produced and demanding the prompt attention of particular design engineers. The latter were frequently observed in conference with production supervisors on the assembly floor. Frank went on:

The designers seem to feel they're losing something when one of us tries to help. They feel it's a reflection on them to have someone take over what they've been doing. They seem to want to carry a project right through to the final stages, particularly the mechanical people. Consequently, engineering services people are used below their capacity to contribute and our department is de-

nied functions it should be performing. There's not as much use made of engineering services as there should be.

Frank Forbus's technician supervisor added his comments:

Production picks out the engineer who'll be the "bum of the month." They pick on every little detail instead of using their heads and making the minor changes that have to be made. The fifteen-to-twenty-year people shouldn't have to prove their ability any more, but they spend four hours defending themselves and four hours getting the job done. I have no one to go to when I need help. Frank Forbus is afraid. I'm trying to help him but he can't help me at this time. I'm responsible for fifty people and I've got to support them.

Fred Rodgers, who Frank had brought with him to the company as an assistant, gave another view of the situation:

I try to get our people in preproduction to take responsibility but they're not used to it and people in our departments don't usually see them as best qualified to solve the problem. There's a real barrier for a newcomer here. Gaining people's confidence is hard. More and more, I'm wondering whether there really is a job for me here.

(Rodgers left Rondell a month later.) Another of Forbus's subordinates gave his view:

If Doc gets a new product idea you can't argue. But he's too optimistic. He judges that others can do what he does—but there's only one Doc Reeves. We've had 900 production change orders this year—they changed 2,500 drawings. If I were in Frank's shoes I'd put my foot down on all this new development. I'd look at the reworking we're doing and get production set up the way I wanted it. Kilmann was fired when he was doing a good job. He was getting some system in the company's operations. Of course, it hurt some people. There is no denying that Doc is the most important person in the company. What gets overlooked is that Hunt is a close second, not just politically but in terms of what he contributes technically and in customer relations.

This subordinate explained that he sometimes went out into the production department but that

Schwab, the production head, resented this. Personnel in production said that Kilmann had failed to show respect for oldtimers and was always meddling in other departments' business. This was why he had been fired, they contended.

Don Taylor was in charge of quality control. He commented:

> I am now much more concerned with administration and less with work. It is one of the evils you get into. There is tremendous detail in this job. I listen to everyone's opinion. Everybody is important. There shouldn't be distinctions—distinctions between people. I'm not sure whether Frank has to be a fireball like Kilmann. I think the real question is whether Frank is getting the job done. I know my job is essential. I want to supply service to the more talented people and give them information so they can do their jobs better.

THE SALES DEPARTMENT

Ron Porter was angry. His job was supposed to be selling, he said, but instead it had turned into settling disputes inside the plant and making excuses to waiting customers. He jabbed a finger toward his desk:

> You see that telephone? I'm actually afraid nowadays to hear it ring. Three times out of five, it will be a customer who's hurting because we've failed to deliver on schedule. The other two calls will be from production or ESD, telling me some schedule has slipped again.
>
> The Model 802 is typical. Absolutely typical. We padded the delivery date by six weeks, to allow for contingencies. Within two months the slack had evaporated. Now it looks like we'll be lucky to ship it before Christmas. (It was now November 28.) We're ruining our reputation in the market. Why, just last week one of our best customers—people we've worked with for 15 years—tried to hang a penalty clause on their latest order.
>
> We shouldn't have to be after the engineers all the time. They should be able to see what problems they create without our telling them.

Phil Klein, head of broadcast sales under Porter, noted that many sales decisions were made by top management. Sales was understaffed, he thought, and had never really been able to get on top of the job.

We have grown further and further away from engineering. The director of engineering does not pass on the information that we give him. We need better relationships there. It is very difficult for us to talk to customers about development problems without technical help. We need each other. The whole of engineering is now too isolated from the outside world. The morale of ESD is very low. They're in a bad spot—they're not well organized.

People don't take much to outsiders here. Much of this is because the expectation is built up by top management that jobs will be filled from the bottom. So it's really tough when an outsider like Frank comes in.

Eric Norman, order and pricing coordinator for data equipment, talked about his own relationship with the production department:

> Actually, I get along with them fairly well. Oh, things could be better, of course, if they were more cooperative generally. They always seem to say, "It's my bat and my ball, and we're playing by my rules." People are afraid to make production mad; there's a lot of power in there. But you've got to understand that production has its own set of problems. And nobody in Rondell is working any harder than Dave Schwab to try to straighten things out.

THE PRODUCTION DEPARTMENT

Dave Schwab had joined Rondell just after the Korean War, in which he had seen combat duty (at the Yalu River) and intelligence duty at Pyong Yang. Both experiences had been useful in his first year of civilian employment at Rondell's: the wartime factory superintendent and several middle managers had been, apparently, indulging in highly questionable side deals with Rondell's suppliers. Dave Schwab had gathered evidence, revealed the situation to Bill Hunt, and had stood by the president in the ensuing unsavory situation. Seven months after joining the company, Dave was named Factory Superintendent.

His first move had been to replace the fallen managers with a new team from outside. This group did not share the traditional Rondell emphasis on informality and friendly personal relationships, and had worked long and hard to install systematic manufacturing methods and procedures. Before the reorganization, production had controlled purchasing, stock control, and final quality control (where final assembly of products in cabinets was accomplished). Because of the wartime events, management decided on a check-and-balance system of organization and removed these three departments from production jurisdiction. The new production managers felt they had been unjustly penalized by this reorganization, particularly since they had uncovered the behavior that was detrimental to the company in the first place.

By 1978, the production department had grown to 500 employees, of whom 60% worked in the assembly area—an unusually pleasant environment that had been commended by *Factory* magazine for its colorful decoration, cleanliness, and low noise level. An additional 30% of the work force, mostly skilled machinists, staffed the finishing and fabrication department. About 60 others performed scheduling, supervisory, and maintenance duties. Production workers were non-union, hourly-paid, and participated in both the liberal profit-sharing program and the stock purchase plan. Morale in production was traditionally high, and turnover was extremely low. Dave Schwab commented:

To be efficient, production has to be a self-contained department. We have to control what comes into the department and what goes out. That's why purchasing, inventory control, and quality ought to run out of this office. We'd eliminate a lot of problems with better control there. Why, even Don Naylor in QC, would rather work for me than for ESD; he's said so himself. We understand his problems better.

The other departments should be self-contained, too. That's why I always avoid the underlings, and go straight to the department heads with any questions. I always go down the line.

I have to protect my people from outside disturbances. Look what would happen if I let unfinished, half-baked designs in here—there'd be chaos. The bugs have to be found before the drawings go into the shop, and it seems I'm the one who has to find them. Look at the 802, for example. (Dave had spent most of Thanksgiving Day (it was now November 28) red-pencilling the latest set of prints.) ESD should have found every one of those discrepancies. They just don't check drawings properly. They change most of the things I flag, but then they fail to trace through the impact of those changes on the rest of the design. I shouldn't have to do that.

And those engineers are tolerance crazy. They want everything to a millionth of an inch. I'm

the only one in the company who's had any experience with actually machining things to a millionth of an inch. We make sure that the things that engineers say on their drawings actually have to be that way and whether they're obtainable from the kind of raw material we buy.

That shouldn't be production's responsibility, but I have to do it. Accepting bad prints wouldn't let us ship the order any quicker. We'd only make a lot of junk that had to be reworked. And that would take even longer.

This way, I get to be known as the bad guy, but I guess that's just part of the job. (He paused with a wry smile.) Of course, what really gets them is that I don't even have a degree.

Dave had fewer bones to pick with the sales department because, he said, they trusted him.

When we give Ron Porter a shipping date, he knows the equipment will be shipped *then*.

You've got to recognize, though, that all of our new product problems stem from sales making absurd commitments on equipment that hasn't been fully developed. That always means trouble. Unfortunately, Hunt always backs sales up, even when they're wrong. He always favors them over us.

Ralph Simon, age 65, executive vice president of the company, had direct responsibility for Rondell's production department. He said:

There shouldn't really be a dividing of departments among top management in the company. The president should be czar over all. The production people ask me to do something for them, and I really can't do it. It creates bad feelings between engineering and production, this special attention that they [R & D] get from Bill. But then Hunt likes to dabble in design. Schwab feels that production is treated like a poor relation.

THE EXECUTIVE COMMITTEE

At the executive committee meeting of December 6, it was duly recorded that Dave Schwab had accepted the prints and specifications for the Model 802 modulator, and had set Friday, December 29, as the shipping date for the first 10 pieces. Bill Hunt, in the chairperson's role, shook his head and changed the subject quickly when Frank tried to open the agenda to a discussion of interdepartmental coordination.

The executive committee itself was a brainchild of Rondell's controller, Len Symmes, who was well aware of the disputes that plagued the company. Symmes had convinced Bill Hunt and Ralph Simon to meet every two weeks with their department heads, and the meetings were formalized with Hunt, Simon, Ron Porter, Dave Schwab, Frank Forbus, Doc Reeves, Symmes, and the personnel director attending. Symmes explained his intent and the results:

Doing things collectively and informally just doesn't work as well as it used to. Things have been gradually getting worse for at least two years now. We had to start thinking in terms of formal organization relationships. I did the first organization chart, and the executive committee was my idea too—but neither idea is contributing much help, I'm afraid. It takes top management to make an organization click. The rest of us can't act much differently until the top people see the need for us to change.

I had hoped the committee especially would help get the department managers into a constructive planning process. It hasn't worked out that way because Mr. Hunt really doesn't see the need for it. He uses the meetings as a place to pass on routine information.

MERRY CHRISTMAS

"Frank, I didn't know whether to tell you now, or after the holiday." It was Friday, December 22, and Frank Forbus was standing awkwardly in front of Bill Hunt's desk.

"But, I figured you'd work right through Christmas Day if we didn't have this talk, and that just wouldn't have been fair to you. I can't understand why we have such poor luck in the engineering director's job lately. And I don't think it's entirely your fault. But . . ."

Frank only heard half of Hunt's words, and said nothing in response. He'd be paid through February 28 . . . He should use the time for searching . . . Hunt would help all he could . . . Jim Kilmann was supposed to be doing well at his own new job, and might need more help . . .

Frank cleaned out his desk, and numbly started home. The electronic carillon near his house was playing a Christmas carol. Frank thought again of Hunt's rationale: conflict still plagued Rondell—and Frank had not made it go away. Maybe somebody else could do it.

"And what did Santa Claus bring you, Frankie?" he asked himself.

"The sack. Only the empty sack."

DISCUSSION QUESTIONS

1. In what ways does the current structure of Rondell make sense? What doesn't make sense?

2. What stage of evolution/revolution is Rondell experiencing at the present time?

3. To what extent are personal conflicts exacerbating the design issues?

4. What should be done to reorganize and change this organization?

Memo: Organization Design

Diagnose the structure of your organization and determine what changes—if any—you would make. Use the answers to the following questions to guide your analysis:

1. What are the internal and external components of your organization's task environment?

2. Is the environment simple or complex? Static or dynamic? How much uncertainty is there in the environment?

3. Is your organization more mechanistic or more organic? Explain.

4. How large is the organization?

5. What is the organization's stage of evolution/revolution?

6. What is the growth rate in the industry?

Using the information derived from these questions, analyze your organization and write a brief description of the changes you think should be made in its structure. Be specific and support your decisions.

CHAPTER EIGHT

Organizational Culture and Planned Change

INTRODUCTION

Organizational cultures comprise the shared values, beliefs, and assumptions that guide—often unconsciously—the behavior of members of organzations. When we say things like, "That's just the way we do things around here," we are expressing our view of the culture "around here." The more widely these values, beliefs, and assumptions are shared, the stronger the culture is said to be and the greater is its ability to control behavior.

In Chapter Seven the importance of shared goals for organizational effectiveness was discussed. Goals and culture have a mutually reinforcing relationship. One of the assets and outcomes of a strong culture is that the goals of the organization are widely shared. However, they can also be one of the methods for creating a stronger culture.

Because the culture guides so much of the behavior that occurs in organizations, it has become an increasingly common target for change. Further, since the culture provides the context within which organizational behavior occurs, understanding context is important before attempting any type of organizational change.

The purpose of this chapter is to help you understand what culture is, why it is important, and how to more effectively manage and change it.

READINGS

The first article, "Strong Cultures: The New 'Old Rule' for Business Success" by Terrence Deal and Allan Kennedy, is taken from their book *Corporate Cultures: The Rites and Rituals of Corporate Life.* The authors make a persuasive statement for the positive effect of a strong culture on organizational success and outline the elements that comprise it: (1) a close fit between the organization's culture and its business environment, (2) a rich and complex system of shared values, (3) a well specified and routine set of behavioral rituals, and (4) an articulated cultural network.

Hypothesizing that a major reason for Japanese business success is the strength and cohesiveness of their national culture, they urge a return to the ideas of America's early leaders of business who believed that a strong culture brought success. Deal and Kennedy assert that a strong culture leads to success because it not only provides a system of informal rules that helps employees know what is expected of them, but also increases motivation by making people feel better about what they do.

In the second reading, "Implications of Corporate Culture: A Manager's Guide to Action," Vijay Sathe effectively combines basic concepts and practical implications. The author argues that, to effectively manage culture, we must first develop a better understanding of it. To this end he presents a framework for cultural diagnosis and examines the effect of culture on five behavioral processes: communication, cooperation, commitment, decision making, and implementation.

Unlike Deal and Kennedy, Sathe finds that a strong culture can be a liability as well as an asset. The author asserts that a more thorough understanding of culture can help managers capitalize on the strengths of a culture and minimize the liabilities. Specifically he addresses action implications: (1) how to more effectively enter an unfamiliar culture, (2) how to operate more successfully in an existing culture and deviate from it with positive results, and (3) how to change culture to increase organizational effectiveness.

The third reading, "Operational Components: The Nature of Organization Development" by Wendell French and Cecil Bell, discusses a specific type of organizational change, organization development (OD). In a chapter from their book, *Organization Development: Behavioral Science Interventions for Organization Improvement,* the authors describe the basic operational components of organization development:

☐ *Diagnosis* includes two steps. The first occurs at the beginning of the OD process when information is gathered about the strengths and problem areas of the system. The second step takes place later in the process when information is gathered to determine if the interventions used had the desired effect.

☐ *Action* entails the planning of these interventions using the technology of OD. The goals of the action plan are to maintain the strengths and to correct the weaknesses identified in the diagnosis.

☐ *Process maintenance* involves making sure that the values that underlie all OD are being adhered to throughout the entire change project.

These three readings explore a range of organizational culture and change issues. Deal and Kennedy's article is prescriptive in nature. They argue that organizations need strong cultures to be successful. Sathe takes a different approach: A strong culture can be either an asset or a liability, and to effectively manage or change a culture we must first understand it. French and Bell describe one type of organizational change process, organization development. These authors take Sathe's argument for diagnosis one step farther. OD's focus is the process of change, not its content. Sometimes this involves changing an organization's culture, sometimes it does not. The diagnosis of the organization determines its strengths and weaknesses, and thus the focus of the change.

EXERCISES AND CASES

The exercises in this chapter are designed to help you develop skills at diagnosing and changing culture.

The first case, "Managing by Mystique," is the story of Tandem Computers. Tandem has a unique and strong corporate culture. This case is an opportunity for you to practice diagnosing culture and to come to some conclusions about whether there are liabilities associated with a strong culture and—if there are—how they can be minimized.

In the second exercise, "Tapemaster Company," you will practice goal setting as a part of an organizational change strategy. Tapemaster has recently undergone a period of growth that has led to massive confusion. There seem to be few shared assumptions or beliefs, except that no one knows what they are supposed to be doing. The first job in reshaping the culture of Tapemaster is formulate a set of goals around which the company can begin to regroup.

The third exercise, "An OD Change Project," is an opportunity for you to develop skills at organizational diagnosis. You are placed in the position of an external consultant and given the interview transcriptions of the employees of a small travel agency. Your assignment is to analyze the data and prepare a presentation for the agency's owner. When you are done with this exercise you should have a better understanding of some of the complexities, ambiguities, and surprises that are always part of a change project.

MEMO

The memo asks you to diagnose the culture of your company. It is important for your job satisfaction that the values of your organization are not in conflict with your personal values. If they are, you may find yourself unhappy with your job and not know why. The first step—as with any change project—is to do a diagnosis. Once you know where conflicts exist—if they do—you can begin to formulate a plan of action.

By the time you finish this chapter, you will have gained a better understanding of the elements of corporate culture. You will know how to diagnose an organization's culture and have an improved understanding of what is involved in an organizational change project.

Strong Cultures: The New "Old Rule" for Business Success

Terrence E. Deal
Allan A. Kennedy

S. C. Allyn, a retired chairman of the board, likes to tell a story about his company—the National Cash Register Corporation. It was August 1945, and Allyn was among the first allied civilians to enter Germany at the end of the war. He had gone to find out what had happened to an NCR factory built just before the war but promptly confiscated by the German military command and put to work on the war effort. He arrived via military plane and traveled through

Reprinted by permission from *Corporate Cultures: The Rites and Rituals of Corporate Life* (Reading, Mass: Addison-Wesley, 1982).

burned-out buildings, rubble, and utter desolation until he reached what was left of the factory. Picking his way through bricks, cement, and old timbers, Allyn came upon two NCR employees whom he hadn't seen for six years. Their clothes were torn and their faces grimy and blackened by smoke, but they were busy clearing out the rubble. As he came closer, one of the men looked up and said, "We knew you'd come!" Allyn joined them in their work and together the three men began cleaning out the debris and rebuilding the factory from the devastation of war. The company had even survived the ravages of a world war.

A few days later, as the clearing continued, Allyn and his co-workers were startled as an American tank rumbled up to the site. A grinning GI was at its helm. "Hi," he said, "I'm NCR, Omaha. Did you guys make your quota this month?" Allyn and the GI embraced each other. The war may have devastated everything around them, but NCR's hard driving, sales-oriented culture was still intact.

This story may sound unbelievable, but there are hundreds like it at NCR and every other company. Together they make up the myths and legends of American business. What do they mean? To us these stories mean that businesses are human institutions, not plush buildings, bottom lines, strategic analysis, or five-year plans. NCR was never just a factory to the three men who dug it out of the rubble. Nor was it to others like them. Rather it was a living organization. The company's real existence lay in the hearts and minds of its employees. NCR was, and still is, a corporate culture, a cohesion of values, myths, heroes, and symbols that has come to mean a great deal to the people who work there.

Culture, as *Webster's New Collegiate Dictionary* defines it, is "the integrated pattern of human behavior that includes thought, speech, action, and artifacts and depends on man's capacity for learning and transmitting knowledge to succeeding generations." Marvin Bower, for years managing director of McKinsey & Company and author of *The Will to Manage,* offered a more informal definition—he described the informal culture elements of a business as "the way we do things around here."

Every business—in fact every organization—has a culture. Sometimes it is fragmented and difficult to read from the outside—some people are loyal to their bosses, others are loyal to the union, still others care only about their colleagues who work in the sales territories of the Northeast. If you ask employees why they work, they will answer "because we need the money." On the other hand,

sometimes the culture of an organization is very strong and cohesive; everyone knows the goals of the corporation, and they are working for them. Whether weak or strong, culture has a powerful influence throughout an organization; it affects practically everything—from who gets promoted and what decisions are made, to how employees dress and what sports they play. Because of this impact, we think that culture also has a major effect on the success of the business.

Today, everyone seems to complain about the decline in American productivity. The examples of industries in trouble are numerous and depressing. Books proclaim that Japanese management practices are the solution to America's industrial malaise. But we disagree. We don't think the answer is to mimic the Japanese. Nor do we think the solution lies with the tools of "scientific" management: MBA's analyses, portfolio theories, cost curves, or economic models. Instead we think the answer is as American as apple pie. American business needs to return to the original concepts and ideas that made institutions like NCR, General Electric, International Business Machines (IBM), Procter & Gamble, 3M, and others great. We need to remember that people make businesses work. And we need to relearn old lessons about how culture ties people together and gives meaning and purpose to their day-to-day lives.

The early leaders of American business such as Thomas Watson of IBM, Harley Procter of Procter & Gamble, and General Johnson of Johnson & Johnson believed that strong culture brought success. They believed that the lives and productivity of their employees were shaped by where they worked. These builders saw their role as creating an environment—in effect, a culture—in their companies in which employees could be secure and thereby do the work necessary to make the business a success. They had no magic formulas. In fact, they discovered how to shape their company's culture by trial and error. But all along the way, they paid almost fanatical attention to the culture of their companies. The lessons of these early leaders have been passed down in their own companies from generation to generation of managers; the cultures they were so careful to build and nourish have sustained their organizations through both fat and lean times. Today these corporations still have strong cultures and still are leaders in the marketplace.

We think that anyone in business can learn a lot from these examples. A major reason the Japanese have been so successful, we think, is their continuing ability to maintain a very strong and cohesive culture throughout the entire country. Not only do individual businesses have strong cultures, but the links among business, the banking industry, and the government are also cultural and also very powerful. Japan, Inc., is actually an expansion of the corporate culture idea on a national scale. Although this homogenization of values would not fit American culture on a national scale, we do think that it has been very effective for individual companies. In fact, a strong culture has almost always been the driving force behind continuing success in American business.

We came to this conclusion through our work and study—Kennedy at McKinsey & Company and Deal at Harvard's Graduate School of Education. The idea had several origins. One was at a meeting at Stanford. A group of sociologists was puzzling over the absence of relationships among variables that organizational theory said should be related. If the structure of an organization doesn't control work activities, what does it do? These questions led to new theories and views: structure and strategy may be more symbolic than substantive. The other was a McKinsey meeting. We were talking about the problems of organizations, and someone asked, "What makes for consistently outstanding company performance?" Another person offered the hypothesis that the companies that did best over the long haul were those that believed in something. The example was, "IBM means service." Others chimed in, and soon the table was full of examples:

☐ GE: "Progress is our most important product."

☐ DuPont: "Better things for better living through chemistry."

☐ Chubb Insurance: "Excellence in underwriting."

While the focus at that point was on slogan-like evidence of a paramount belief—which we later called a "superordinate goal"—we were struck by the fact that each of the companies named had an impressive track record in the marketplace.

Intrigued by this initial evidence of support for our somewhat unconventional hypothesis, we conducted an informal survey over the next several months by interviewing McKinsey consultants about companies or organizations* they knew on a firsthand basis. The questions we asked were:

☐ Does Company X have one or more visible beliefs?

☐ If so, what are they?

☐ Do people in the organization know these beliefs? If so, who? And how many?

☐ How do these beliefs affect day-to-day business?

☐ How are the beliefs communicated to the organization?

☐ Are the beliefs reinforced—by formal personnel processes, recognition, rewards?

☐ How would you characterize the performance of the company?

In total, over a period of about six months, we developed profiles of nearly eighty companies. Here's what we found out:

☐ Of all the companies surveyed, only about one third (twenty-five to be precise) had clearly articulated beliefs.

☐ Of this third, a surprising two-thirds had qualitative beliefs, or values, such as "IBM means service." The other third had financially oriented goals that were widely understood.

☐ Of the eighteen companies with qualitative beliefs, all were uniformly outstanding performers; we could find no correlations of any relevance among the other companies—some did okay, some poorly, most had their ups and downs. We characterized the consistently high performers as strong culture companies.**

---

*Our survey covered both profit-making companies and a few non-profit organizations we found particularly intriguing. For simplicity we refer in the text to all of these as "companies."

**These were: Caterpillar Tractor, General Electric, DuPont, Chubb Insurance, Price Waterhouse & Co., 3M, Jefferson-Smurfit, The Training Services Administration Agency of the British government, Digital Equipment Corporation, International Business Machines, Dana Corporation, Procter and Gamble, Hewlett-Packard, Leo Burnett Advertising Agency, Johnson & Johnson, Tandem Computer, Continental Bank, and the Rouse Corporation.

These strong culture companies, we thought, were on to something. And so were we. Although this was far from a scientific survey, we did have evidence that the impact of values and beliefs on company performance was indeed real. We decided to follow up this "finding" by trying to figure out how these values got there and how they were transmitted throughout the corporation. We wanted to see what had made America's great companies not merely organizations, but successful, human institutions.

Here we stumbled onto a goldmine of evidence. Biographies, speeches, and documents from such giants of business as Thomas Watson of IBM, John Patterson (the founder of NCR), Will Durant of General Motors, William Kellogg of Kellogg's, and a host of others show a remarkable intuitive understanding of the importance of a strong culture in the affairs of their companies.

We read about Edwin Land, who built Polaroid into a successful $1 billion company (before losing control and having the company fall on hard times) and who developed a whole theory for Polaroid's culture; he called it "Semi-Topia" after the theories of Utopia. We also learned about Alfred Sloan, the manager who built General Motors into a monolith, who spent three full days every quarter reviewing person-by-person the career progression of his top 1,000 managers. And about Charles Steinmetz, the crippled Austrian dwarf who brought alternating current into electrical systems of the world while at GE, but who also adopted his lab assistant and the man's entire family. These, and many more stories, led us to one unmistakable conclusion: the people who built the companies for which America is famous all worked obsessively to create strong cultures within their organizations.

In our own research and consulting, we also found that many of the exciting, new, high-tech businesses springing up around Route 128 in Boston and Silicon Valley in California seem obsessed with culture. Consider the case of Tandem.

THE BUSINESS OF CULTURE

The Tandem Corporation, one of Silicon Valley's most highly publicized companies, is a company whose president deliberately manages the "informal," human side of the business. Founded by four former Hewlett-Packard employees, Tandem had built a highly successful company by solving a simple problem: the tendency of computers to break down. By yoking two computers together in one mainframe, Tandem offers customers the assurance that they will always have computer power available. If one of the processors breaks down, the other will carry on.

"Tandem is saying something about the product and people working together. Everything here works together. People with people; product with product; even processor with processor, within the product. Everything works together to keep us where we are." The quotation is not from Jim Treybig, Tandem's chief executive officer. It came from one of Tandem's managers, and the same sentiment is echoed through the ranks of the employees:

"I feel like putting a lot of time in. There is a real kind of loyalty here. We are all working in this together—working a process together. I'm not a workaholic—it's just the place. I love the place."

"I don't want anything in the world that would hurt Tandem. I feel totally divorced from my old company, but not Tandem."

These employees seem to be describing an ideal corporation, one most managers would give their eyeteeth to create. And by most standards, Tandem is enormously successful. It is growing at the rate of 25 percent per quarter, with annual revenues over $100 million. The turnover rate is nearly three times below the national average for the computer industry. Tandem's loyal employees like their jobs and the company's product. They are led by a talented group of experienced managers, a group which so far has been able to handle the phenomenal growth of the company.

Only time will tell whether Tandem can maintain its pattern of high performance. While it is easy to attribute the success of the company to fast growth and lack of competition, other things at work internally at Tandem suggest an interesting rival explanation—that the strong culture of Tandem produces its success. Here is how.

A Widely Shared Philosophy

Tandem is founded on a well-ordered set of management beliefs and practices. The philosophy of the company emphasizes the importance of people: "that's Tandem's greatest resource—its people, creative action, and fun." This ethic is widely shared and exemplified by slogans that everyone knows and believes in:

"It's so nice, it's so nice, we do it twice."
"It takes two to Tandem."
"Get the job done no matter what it takes."
"Tandemize it—means make it work."

The slogans are broadcast by T-shirts, bulletin boards, and word of mouth.

Top management spends about half of its time in training and in communicating the management philosophy and the essence of the company. Work is underway on a book that will codify the philosophy for future generations of workers at Tandem. "The philosophy is our future," one senior manager notes:

> "It mostly tells the 'whats' and 'hows' for selecting people and growing managers. Even though everything else around here changes, I don't want what we believe in and what we want to change."

At Tandem the management philosophy is not an afterthought, it's a principle preoccupation.

The Importance of People

Tandem has no formal organizational chart and few formal rules. Its meetings and memos are almost non-existent. Jobs are flexible in terms of duties and hours. The absence of name tags and reserved parking spaces suggests a less well-defined hierarchy than is typical in the corporate world. Despite this, the organization works and people get their jobs done.

What keeps employees off each other's toes and working in the same direction? One possibility is the unwritten rules and shared understandings. As one person put it: "There are a lot of unwritten rules. But there is also a lot of freedom to make a jerk out of yourself. Most of the rules are philosophical rules." Another is dispersed authority:

> "The open door policy gives me access to anyone—even the president."
> "Everyone here, managers, vice-presidents, and even janitors, communicate on the same level. No one feels better than anyone else."

Tandem seems to maintain a balance between autonomy and control without relying heavily on centralized or formalized procedures, or rigid status hierarchies.

Heroes: The President and the Product

Jim Treybig is a hero at Tandem, and his employees confirm it:

"Jimmy is really a symbol here. He's a sign that every person here is a human being. He tries to make you feel part of the organization from the first day you are here. That's something people talk about."

"The one thing you have to understand about the company—Treybig's bigger than life."

Treybig shares the hero's limelight with the Tandem Continuous 10 Computer—the backbone product of the company. The computer design is the company's logo and provides the metaphor for the "working together" philosophy.

> "The product is phenomenal, everyone is proud to be part of it."
> "When a big order was shipped, everyone in the plant was taking pictures. There were 'oh's' and 'ah's'. People were applauding. Can you believe it? For a computer."

Treybig and the computer share the main spotlight. But there were countless other heroes at Tandem—people whose achievements are regularly recognized on bulletin boards as "Our Latest Greatests."

Ritual and Ceremony

Tandem is renowned for its Friday afternoon "beer-busts" which everyone attends. But the ritual does more than help people wind down after a busy work week. It serves as an important vehicle for informal communication and mingling across groups.

Tandem's emphasis on ritual, ceremony, and play is not confined to beer-busts, however. There is a golf course, exercise room, and swimming pool. Company-wide celebrations are staged on important holidays. These provide opportunities for employees to develop a spirit of "oneness" and symbolize that Tandem cares about employees.

Tandem's attention to ritual and ceremony begins in its personnel selection interviews. During the hiring process, potential employees are called back two or three times for interviews and must accept the position before salary negotiations take place. The interviews have been likened to an "inquisition." The message conveyed to prospective employees is "we take longer, and take care of people we hire—because we really care." The impact of this process is significant.

"They had me here for four interviews. That's about four hours, for a position of stock clerk. It was clear that they were choosy about the people they hired. That said something about what they thought I was. They thought I was good."

Treybig personally appears at each orientation to welcome new employees and to explain the company's motivation and commitment philosophy. His appearance reinforces the honor of being accepted to work at Tandem. It's no surprise that people at Tandem feel special—after all, they were made to feel that way before they were hired. Moreover, they feel special because the company and its product are special. And their feelings are expressed in an unusual display of loyalty and commitment to the company.

"My goals follow the company's. It's the company and I. I think that's pretty true of everyone. We all want to see it work. You have to have it all or don't have any of it."

Employees see their work as linked to Tandem's success:

"My job is important, and if I don't do it, Tandem doesn't make a buck."

Tandem is a unique company. And much of its success appears as intimately tied to its culture as to its product and marketplace position. The company has explicit values and beliefs which its employees share. It has heroes. It has storytellers and stories. It has rituals and ceremonies on key occasions. Tandem appears to have a strong culture which creates a bond between the company and employees, and inspires levels of productivity unlike most other corporations. Established heroes, values, and rituals are crucial to a culture's continued strength, and Tandem has kept them. The trick is in sustaining the culture so that it in turn drives the company.

Will Tandem's culture last? Although Tandem is neither big enough nor old enough to judge whether or not it will ultimately take a place in the annals of great American business, we think it is off to a good start. Indeed, other companies like IBM and P&G have already succeeded in sustaining and evolving culture over generations. These strong culture companies truly are the giants of American industry. Yet, their cultures began taking shape in a way that was very similar to Tandem.

THE ELEMENTS OF CULTURE

What is it about Tandem's organization that exerts such a grip on its employees? Why do other strong culture companies seem to inspire such loyalty? As we continued our research, we delved into the organizational literature to understand better the elements that make up a strong culture. What is it that determines the kind of culture a company will have in the first place? And how will that culture work in the day-to-day life of a company? Although we examine each one in depth later in the book, let's summarize the elements now:

Business Environment

Each company faces a different reality in the marketplace depending on its products, competitors, customers, technologies, government influences, and so on. To succeed in its marketplace, each company must carry out certain kinds of activities very well. In some markets that means selling; in others, invention; in still others, management of costs. In short, the environment in which a company operates determines what it must do to be a success. This business environment is the single greatest influence in shaping a corporate culture. Thus, companies that depend for success on their ability to sell an undifferentiated product tend to develop one type of culture—what we call a work hard/play hard culture—that keeps its sales force selling. Companies that spend a great deal of research and development money before they even know if the final product will be successful or not tend to develop a different culture—one that we call a bet-your-company culture—designed to make sure decisions are thought through before actions are taken.

Values

These are the basic concepts and beliefs of an organization; as such they form the heart of the corporate culture. Values define "success" in concrete terms for employees—"if you do this, you will be a success"—and establish standards of achievement within the organization. The strong culture companies that we investigated all had a rich and complex system of values that were shared by the employees. Managers in these companies talked about these beliefs openly and without embarrassment, and they didn't tolerate deviance from the company standards.

Heroes

These people personify the culture's values and as such provide tangible role models for employees to follow. Some heroes are born—the visionary institution builders of American business—and some are "made" by memorable moments that occur in day-to-day corporate life. Smart companies take a direct hand in choosing people to play these heroic roles, knowing full well that others will try to emulate their behavior. Strong culture companies have many heroes. At General Electric, for instance, the heroes include Thomas Edison, the inventor; Charles Steinmetz, the compleat engineer; Gerald Swope and now Jack Welch, the CEO entrepreneurs; and a legion of lesser-known but equally important internal figures: the inventor of the high-torque motor that powered the electric toothbrush; the chief engineer of the turbine works; the export salesman who survived two overseas revolutions; the international manager who had ghosts exorcised from a factory in Singapore; and many others. These achievers are known to virtually every employee with more than a few months' tenure in the company. And they show every employee "here's what you have to do around here."

The Rites and Rituals

These are the systematic and programmed routines of day-to-day life in the company. In their mundane manifestations—which we call rituals—they show employees the kind of behavior that is expected of them. In their extravaganzas—which we call ceremonies—they provide visible and potent examples of what the company stands for. Strong culture companies go to the trouble of spelling out, often in copious detail, the routine behavior rituals they expect their employees to follow.

The Cultural Network

As the primary (but informal) means of communication within an organization, the cultural network is the "carrier" of the corporate values and heroic mythology. Storytellers, spies, priests, cabals, and whisperers form a hidden hierarchy of power within the company. Working the network effectively is the only way to get things done or to understand what's really going on.

THE IMPORTANCE OF UNDERSTANDING CULTURE

Companies that have cultivated their individual identities by shaping values, making heroes, spelling out rites and rituals, and acknowledging the cultural network have an edge. These corporations have values and beliefs to pass along—not just products. They have stories to tell—not just profits to make. They have heroes whom managers and workers can emulate—not just faceless bureaucrats. In short, they are human institutions that provide practical meaning for people, both on and off the job.

We think that people are a company's greatest resource, and the way to manage them is not directly by computer reports, but by subtle cues of a culture. A strong culture is a powerful lever for guiding behavior; it helps employees do their jobs a little better, especially in two ways:

A strong culture is a system of informal rules that spells out how people are to behave most of the time. By knowing what exactly is expected of them, employees will waste little time in deciding how to act in a given situation. In a weak culture, on the other hand, employees waste a good deal of time just trying to figure out what they should do and how they should do it. The impact of a strong culture on productivity is amazing. In the extreme, we estimate that a company can gain as much as one or two hours of productive work per employee per day.

A strong culture enables people to feel better about what they do, so they are more likely to work harder. When a sales representative can say "I'm with IBM," rather than "I peddle typewriters for a living," he will probably hear in response, "Oh, IBM is a great company, isn't it?" He quickly figures out that he belongs to an outstanding company with a strong identity. For most people, that means a great deal. The next time they have the choice of working an extra half hour or sloughing off, they'll probably work. Overall, this has an impact on productivity too.

Unlike workers ten or twenty years ago, employees today are confused. According to psychologist Frederick Herzberg, they feel cheated by their jobs; they allow special interests to take up their time; their life values are uncertain; they are blameful and cynical; they confuse morality with ethics. Uncertainty is at the core of it all. Yet strong culture companies remove a great degree of that uncertainty because they provide structure and standards and a value system in which to operate. In fact, corporations may be among the last institutions in America that can effectively take on the role of shaping values. We think that workers, managers, and chief executive officers should recognize this and act on it.

People at all stages of their careers need to understand culture and how it works because it will likely have a powerful effect on their work lives. People just starting their careers may think a job is just a job. But when they choose a company, they often choose a way of life. The culture shapes their responses in a strong, but subtle way. Culture can make them fast or slow workers, tough or friendly managers, team players or individuals. By the time they've worked for several years, they may be so well conditioned by the culture they may not even recognize it. But when they change jobs, they may be in for a big surprise.

Take an up-and-coming executive at General Electric who is being wooed by Xerox—more money, a bigger office, greater responsibility. If his first reaction is to grab it, he's probably going to be disappointed. Xerox has a totally different culture than GE. Success (and even survival) at Xerox is closely tied to an ability to maintain a near frenetic pace, the ability to work and play hard, Xerox-style.

By contrast, GE has a more thoughtful and slow-moving culture. The GE culture treats each business activity seriously—almost as though each activity will have an enormous impact on the company. Success at GE is a function of being able to take work seriously, a strong sense of peer group respect, considerable deference for authority, and a sense of deliberateness. A person of proven success at GE will bring these values to Xerox because past experience in GE's culture has reinforced them. But these same values may not be held in high esteem elsewhere.

Bright young comers at GE could, for example, quickly fizzle out at Xerox—and not even understand why. They'll be doing exactly what they did to succeed at GE—maybe even working harder at it—but their deliberate approach to issues large and small will be seen by insiders at Xerox as a sign that they "lack smarts." Their loss of confidence, self-esteem, and ability will be confusing to them and could significantly derail their careers. For Xerox, the loss of productivity could be appreciable.

This is no imaginary scenario. It happens again and again at Xerox, General Electric, and many other companies when managers ignore the influence of culture on individual approaches to work. Culture shock may be one of the major reasons why people supposedly "fail" when they leave one organization for another. Where they fail, however, is not necessarily in doing the job, but in not reading the culture correctly.

People who want to get ahead within their own companies also need to understand—at least intuitively—what makes their culture tick. If product quality is the guiding value of your company, then you'd better be thinking about getting into manufacturing where you can contribute to the work on quality control teams. If you're a marketing whiz in a company where all of the heroes are number crunchers, then you have a problem. You can start taking accounting courses, or you can start trying to find a more compatible environment. Unless the culture itself is in a state of change—shifting, say, from a financial emphasis to a marketing orientation—then the chances are very slim for any single person who is out of step with the culture to make it to the very top.

Aside from considerations of personal success, managers must understand very clearly how the culture works if they want to accomplish what they set out to do. If you're trying to institute a competitive, tough approach to marketing in a company that is full of hail-fellow-well-met salesmen, then you have your work cut out for you. Even if everyone agrees with what you want to do, you must know how to manage the culture—for instance, create new role model heroes—in order to teach your legion of easy-going salesmen the new rules of the game.

Finally, senior executives and especially chief executive officers may be missing out on one of the key ingredients for their companies' eventual success by ignoring either the influence of culture on corporate success or their own central role in shaping it. Their culture may be rich with lore or starved for shared values and stories. It may be coherent and cohesive, or fragmented and poorly understood. It may create meaning or contribute to blind confusion. It may be rich, fiery, focused, and strong; or weak, cold, and diffuse. Understanding the culture can help senior executives pinpoint why their company is succeeding or failing. Understanding how to build and manage the culture can help the same executives make a mark on their company that lasts for decades.

Can every company have a strong culture? We think it can. But to do that, top management first has to recognize what kind of culture the company already has, even if it is weak. The ultimate success of a chief executive officer depends to a large degree on an accurate reading of the corporate culture and the ability to hone it and shape it to fit the shifting needs of the marketplace.

In reading this book, we can imagine that many managers will ask themselves, is culture too "soft"? Can serious managers actually take the time to deal with it? Indeed, we believe that managers must. Management scientists sometimes argue that corporations are so complex and vulnerable to diverse external and internal forces that managers' freedom to act and lead is limited. Their argument is plausible, but our experience does not support it. By and large, the most successful managers we know are precisely those who strive to make a mark through creating a guiding vision, shaping shared values, and otherwise providing leadership for the people with whom they work.

It all comes down to understanding the importance of working with people in any organization. The institution builders of old knew the value of a strong culture and they worked hard at it. They saw themselves as symbolic players-actors in their corporations. They knew how to orchestrate, even dramatize events to drive their lessons home. They understood how corporations shape personal lives and were not shy about suggesting the standards that people should live by. If we are to have such great institutions tomorrow, the managers of today will have to take up this challenge again.

Implications of Corporate Culture: A Manager's Guide to Action

Vijay Sathe

Corporate culture, which plays a subtle but pervasive role in organizational life, has important implications for managerial action. Consider these examples:

☐ Bob Drake accepted a lucrative, challenging job with a profitable company only to discover, six months later, that he could not operate successfully in a company whose managers shared such deep faith in the virtues of cutthroat competition. He resigned.

☐ Doug Mills had innovative ideas for growing his business, but these went against the grain of his company's culture of risk-aversion. Doug was frustrated and demotivated, feeling that both he and the company were losing out.

☐ Matt Holt, whose company had been buffeted by shifting market forces, was convinced profitability would improve dramatically if a new shared commitment to technology could be created among the organization's key managers. Two years later, Matt felt he had been unsuccessful in this effort and wasn't sure what he could have done to accomplish his objective.

Although it is now generally agreed that corporate culture has a powerful impact on managers and

their organizations, it is not equally clear why this is the case, and what can be done about it. For many people culture remains an elusive and fuzzy concept. Here I will attempt to show how the concept of culture can provide important insights for understanding and dealing appropriately with various managerial situations. Specifically, the following questions, which will cover both basic concepts and their action implications, will be addressed:

Basic Concepts

1. What is corporate culture?

2. Why does culture have such a subtle but powerful influence on organizational life?

Implications for Action

1. What can be done to better anticipate and more effectively enter a new corporate culture, avoiding problems such as those encountered by Bob Drake?

2. How can one better operate within the existing corporate culture, and successfully deviate from it when necessary, to overcome obstacles such as those faced by Doug Mills?

3. How can managers influence change in the prevailing culture to realize gains such as those hoped for by Matt Holt?

BASIC CONCEPTS

What is culture? Unfortunately, there isn't one unanimously accepted definition. I will not go into all of the ways in which culture has been interpreted (one scholarly study in the field of anthropology, from which the concept derives, has listed 164 definitions), but I will illustrate the principal ways in which culture can be described.

One view of culture, preferred by the "cultural adaptationist" school in anthropology, is based on what is directly observable about the members of a community—that is, their patterns of behavior, speech, and use of material objects. Another view, favored by the "ideational school," looks at what is shared in community members' minds.

This is one reason the subject is confusing: Different people think of different slices of reality when they talk about culture. It is pointless to argue about which view is correct because, like other concepts, "culture" does not have some true and sacred meaning that is to be discovered. Each view has its place, depending on what one is interested in. I will argue that both perspectives on culture are important for managers, and that both views are interrelated but sufficiently distinct so that it is not analytically advantageous to combine them.

For the purposes of this article, the term *culture* will be used to denote the "ideational view"; the term *behavior* will refer to the "cultural adaptationist" view and both views will be considered simultaneously. Specifically, the following definition of culture will be adopted: *Culture is the set of important understandings (often unstated) that members of a community share in common.*

This definition limits the concept of culture to what is shared in the minds of community members; the phrase "often unstated" in the definition is crucial because members of a culture are frequently unaware of many of these mutual understandings. Thus the advantage of this definition of culture is that it forces us to pay attention to an important organizational reality that is otherwise easily missed because it is "invisible."

Diagnosing Culture

In order to decipher a culture, one cannot simply rely on what people say about it. Other evidence, both historical and current, must be taken into account to infer what the culture is. The example spelled out below illustrates one systematic procedure for doing this. It must be pointed out, however,

that reading a culture is an interpretive, subjective activity. There are no exact answers, and two observers may come up with somewhat different descriptions of the same culture. The validity of the diagnosis must be judged by the utility of the insights it provides, not by its "correctness" as determined by some objective criteria.

A diagnostic framework for culture's important shared understandings is presented in Figure 1, and its use is illustrated with information on Company X in Figure 2. Each important shared understanding listed in Figure 2 is inferred from one or more shared things, shared sayings, shared doings, and shared feelings. One may come up with a somewhat different list, but the point is to distill from the "laundry list" of shared things, shared sayings, shared doings, and shared feelings (that is, from the *manifestations* of the culture) a much shorter list of important shared understandings (that is, the culture's content).

Beliefs and Values

In describing culture, we will talk about two principal types of shared understandings: beliefs and values. (A glossary of terms commonly used in discussing culture is provided in the box on page 397.) Beliefs are basic assumptions about the world and how it works. Because many facets of physical and social reality are difficult or impossible to experience personally or to verify, people rely on others they identify with and trust to help them decide what to believe and what not to believe. (One of these, for example, is: "Money is the most powerful motivator"—item 4 in Figure 2.)

Like beliefs, values are also basic assumptions, but ones with an *ought to* implicit in them. The term *norms* is sometimes used interchangeably with *values,* but there is an important distinction. Although both have an *ought to* implicit in them, norms are more tactical and procedural than are values. Norms are standards of expected behavior, speech, and "presentation of self"—that is, being on time, disagreeing politely, dressing conservatively. Values, on the other hand, represent preferences for more ultimate end states—that is, striving to be no. 1, or avoiding debt at all costs (see items 1, 2, 3, and 5 in Figure 2).

Beliefs and values that have been held for a long time without being violated or challenged may become taken so much for granted that people are no longer aware of them. This is why organizational members frequently fail to realize what a profound influence culture has on them.

FIGURE 1
Framework for Diagnosing Culture.

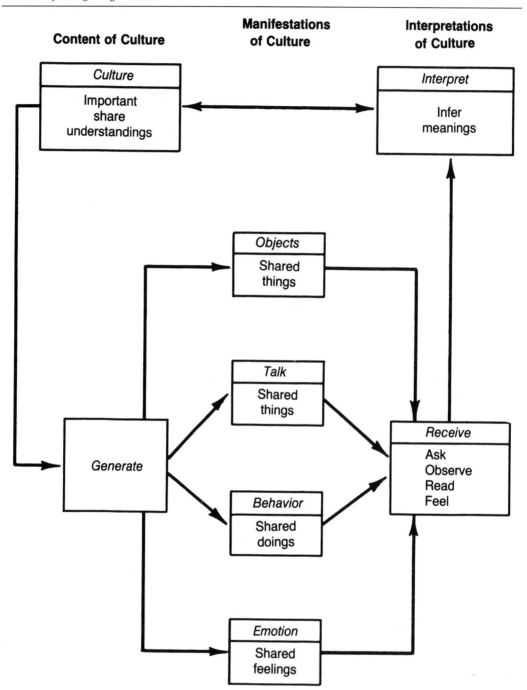

FIGURE 2

Inferring Important Shared Understanding from Shared Things,
Shared Sayings, Shared Doings, and Shared Feelings (Company X).

Important Shared Understandings	*Shared Things*
1. Provide highly responsive, quality customer service (SS1, SS2, SD2, SD5).	ST1. Shirt sleeves.
	ST2. One-company town.
	ST3. Open offices.

Shared Sayings

2. Get things done well and quickly ("expediting") (SS1, SD1, SD4, SD5).	SS1. "Get out there" to understand the customer. (Belief in travel)
3. Operate informally (ST1, SS3, SD3, SD6).	SS2. "We cannot rely on systems" to meet customer needs. (Highly responsive customer service)
	SS3. "We don't stand on rank." (No parking privileges)

Shared Doings

4. Perceive company as part of the family (ST2, SD6, SF1, SF2, SF3).	SD1. Participate in lots of meetings.
	SD2. Make sure organization is detail-oriented to provide quality customer service.
5. Encourage constructive disagreement (ST3, SD1).	SD3. Engage in personal relationships and communications.
	SD4. Rally to meet customer needs in a crisis.
	SD5. Expedite jobs to deliver highly responsive service.
	SD6. Maintain close relationship with union.

Shared Feelings

SF1. The company is good to me.
SF2. We like this place.
SF3. We care about this company because it cares about us as individuals.

Corporate Culture or Cultures?

Although the term "corporate culture" is widely used in management circles, not everyone uses it in the same way. Some use the term to denote the culture of the corporation as a whole. Others use it to refer to the culture of any community within the corporate context. It is in this latter sense that the term will be used here—in other words, a work unit culture, a department culture, a division culture, and so forth. Each is viewed as a corporate culture in the sense that each refers to the culture of an organization within the corporate context. Depending on the circumstances, one or more of these organizational units and their cultures may have to be considered in addressing the problem at hand. For convenience of discussion, the term *culture* will be used here without reference to a particular organizational entity.

Let us now turn to the question of why culture has such a profound influence on organizational life.

Culture's Influence on Behavior

Culture is both an asset and a liability. It is an asset because shared beliefs ease and economize communications, and shared values generate higher levels of cooperation and commitment than is otherwise possible. This is highly efficient.

Efficiency, however, does not imply effectiveness. Efficiency is achieved when something is done with a minimum expenditure of resources (time, money, and so forth). The extent to which the something being done is the appropriate thing to do is a question of effectiveness. If culture guides behavior in inappropriate ways, we have efficiency but not effectiveness. Culture is a liability when the shared beliefs and values are not in keeping with the needs of the organization, its members, and its other constituencies.

To take a closer look at how culture affects behavior, let us examine five basic processes—communication, cooperation, commitment, decision making, and implementation—that lie at the heart of any organization. We will then be able to draw some generalizations about culture's influence on organizational behavior.

Communication

Miscommunication is common in organizations and in everyday life. Even two-person, face-to-face communication is fraught with dangers of misunderstanding the other person's meaning. Communication problems are even more complex when one organization member tries to communicate with someone in a different organizational unit or location, or when a corporate senior executive tries to reach "the masses."

Although culture does not do away with the basic difficulty, it reduces the dangers of miscommunication in two ways. First, there is no need to communicate items about which shared beliefs and values exist: Certain things go without saying. Second, such sharing provides guidelines and cues to help the receiver interpret messages.

The beliefs and values about what to communicate, and how openly to communicate, are crucial. In some organizations, the culture values open communications ("bad news is bad, but withholding it is worse"). In others, it doesn't. Withholding of information beyond that specifically asked for, secrecy, and outright distortion may prevail.

Cooperation

Assuming that communications are interpreted as intended, the question is: What will ensure that organizational members will act as intended by the communications? The answer seems obvious. Failure to do so could bring sanctions. But this merely begs the question, for it implies that organizational members are motivated to act only according to the "letter of the law," not necessarily in the "spirit of the law." The latter would mean true cooperation. The former could mean worse than no cooperation; it could mean subtle sabotage as illustrated by the "work-to-rule" tactic used by, for example, the air controllers, who have on occasion made their grievances known by following the rules too strictly (that is, more conservatively than demanded by the prevailing situation) to

create bottlenecks and slowdowns at airports. The effect of adhering to the literal wording of a contract can be as devastating as an open violation of the contract—if not more so.

The point is that true cooperation cannot be "legislated." Management can resort to carefully worded employment contracts, spell out detailed expectations, and devise clever, complicated incentive schemes to reward just the right behavior. But such procedures, however well-thought-out, cannot anticipate all the contingencies that can conceivably arise. When one of these does, the organization is at the mercy of the employee to act in the "spirit of the law." Interpreting the spirit of the law is a problem of communication. Acting according to the spirit of the law is a question of intent, goodwill, and mutual trust. The degree of true cooperation is influenced by the shared beliefs and values in these areas.

Commitment

People feel a sense of commitment to an organization's objectives when they identify with those objectives and experience some emotional attachment to them. The shared beliefs and values that compose culture help generate such identification and attachment. In making decisions and taking actions, people who feel a sense of commitment automatically evaluate alternatives in terms of their impact on the organization.

Decision Making

Culture affects the decision-making process because shared beliefs and values give organizational members a consistent set of basic assumptions and preferences. This leads to a more efficient decision-making process, because there are fewer disagreements about which premises should prevail. This does not mean that there is necessarily less overall conflict in a stronger culture than in a weaker one. That would depend on the shared beliefs and values about the role of conflict in organizational life. Where constructive dissent is a shared value, for instance, there would be greater conflict than where this is not a shared value—all other things being equal. All that is implied is that there are fewer areas of disagreement in a stronger culture because of the greater sharing of beliefs and values, and that this is efficient.

As pointed out earlier, however, efficiency does not imply effectiveness. If the shared beliefs and values are not in keeping with the needs of business,

GLOSSARY OF CULTURAL TERMS

The following terms are commonly used in describing culture. The items in parenthesis refer to Company X, whose culture is diagnosed in the text. (See page 393 and Figures 1 and 2). The illustrative items can be found in Figure 2.

Beliefs. These are the basic assumptions concerning the world and how it works (see, for example, item 4).

Values. Like beliefs, values are also basic assumptions, but they have an "ought to" implicit in them (for example, items 1, 2, 3, and 5).

Identity. This includes the understandings that members share concerning who they are and what they stand for as a community (for example, item 4).

Image. This is the community's identity as understood by members of another community.

Attitudes. These are the set of understandings that members of a community share about a specific object or situation (for example, Company X's attitude about working relationships is that informality and confrontation are preferred—that is, items 3 and 5; and the attitude of Company X toward its customers is to do everything possible to provide superb service—that is, item 1).

Climate. This includes the understandings that members share about what it is like to work in the community. Climate surveys report aggregated perceptions on such dimensions as clarity (how well members understand goals and policies), responsibility (degree to which members feel personally responsible for their work), and teamwork (how well members believe they work together).

Pivotal Value. This is the most important corporate value (that is, item 1). All other corporate values "revolve around" the pivotal value.

Norms. These are the standards of expected behavior, speech, and "presentation of self" (for example, those items from the list of shared things, shared sayings, shared doings, and shared feelings in Figure 2 that imply such standards). Note the distinction between norms and values. Although both have an "ought to" implicit in them, norms are more tactical and procedural than are values.

Ideology. This is the dominant set of interrelated ideas that explain to members of a community why the important understandings they share "make sense." An ideology gives meaning to the content of a culture (for example, for Company X the ideology is: "Expediting behavior is valued because we believe it is critical to our competitive edge of highly responsive, quality customer service. Further, informal operation and constructive disagreement are encouraged because we believe these behaviors help bring about such service.")

---

the organization, and its members, dysfunctional consequences will result.

Implementation

One of the difficulties commonly encountered when implementing organizational policy and decisions is this: What should be done when unforeseen difficulties arise? There are times when immediate action is called for in a more or less ambiguous situation where it is not possible to check with others concerning the appropriate response. Under these conditions, culture is a compass that helps point people in the right direction. Consider this situation:

An important overseas customer was demanding immediate help from the company's local contact in connection with certain reciprocal arrangements involving a third party that did business with both the company and this customer. Such arrangements were not tolerated by the company. Despite the importance of the account, and the company's emphasis on customer service, the company's local contact declined this "urgent request."

In this case, two company values were in conflict: customer service and ethical sales practices. Although the customer was important, ethical corporate behavior was the company's pivotal value. ("Use every honorable means to satisfy the customer.") Culture provides such "guiding principles" that employees can rely on when close calls are to be made without consultation.

Strength of Culture

As we have seen, culture has a powerful influence on organizational behavior because the shared beliefs and values represent basic assumptions and preferences that guide such behavior. Further, the influence is subtle because many of these underlying premises have a taken-for-granted quality and tend to remain outside people's awareness. Thus the irony of culture (and the reason it can be so treacherous) is that, like the air people breathe, its powerful effects normally escape the attention of those it most affects.

However, not all cultures have an equally strong influence on behavior. The following conditions make a difference. First, cultures with more shared beliefs and values have a stronger influence on behavior because there are more basic assumptions guiding behavior. IBM, for example, has a "thick" culture with several deeply held beliefs and values (for example: respect for the individual, encouragement of constructive rebellion, an emphasis on doing what is right). "Thin" cultures have few such shared assumptions, and thus a weaker influence on organizational life. Second, cultures whose beliefs and values are more widely shared have a more pervasive impact because a larger number of people are guided by them. At IBM, the values mentioned are very widely shared.

Finally, cultures whose beliefs and values are more clearly ordered (that is, where the relative importance of the various basic assumptions are well known) have a more profound effect on behavior because there is less ambiguity about which beliefs and values prevail when there is a conflict. IBMers know the pivotal importance of the values mentioned. Thicker, more widely shared, and more ordered cultures have a more profound influence on organizational behavior, and are therefore referred to as "stronger" cultures.

Why are some cultures stronger than others? The number of employees in the organization and their geographical dispersion are two important factors that make a difference. All other things being equal, smaller operations that are more localized facilitate the growth of a stronger culture because it is easier for shared beliefs and values to become widely shared. But larger organizations with worldwide operations can also have a strong culture, as IBM has, if there has been a continuity of strong leadership that has emphasized the same beliefs and values, and a relatively stable and long-tenured workforce. Under these conditions, there is time for a consistent set of beliefs and values to take hold and become widely shared and more clearly ordered.

To return to the illustration in Figure 2, Company X has several important beliefs and values that are widely shared and fairly well ordered. The pivotal value of highly responsive, quality customer service (item 1 in Figure 2) is tied directly to the value placed on expediting and informality (items 2 and 3), which in turn are supported by the belief in a family spirit (item 4). The value of constructive disagreement (item 5) is not as directly interconnected with the others. Thus Company X has a fairly strong culture because it has several widely shared and rather well-ordered beliefs and values.

Why does Company X have such a strong culture? History, leadership, organizational size, and the stability of its membership all have had an impact. Company X is a medium-size firm with low employee turnover. In its 60-year history, there have been only two generations of top management; the former chief executive officer and the former chief operating officer continue to serve as chairman of the board and chairman of the executive committee, respectively.

What we say about culture thus needs to be moderated by its strength. Stronger cultures produce more powerful effects than weaker cultures do. For convenience, I will not refer to this qualification during the rest of this discussion, but it is an important facet of culture to keep in mind.

IMPLICATIONS FOR ACTION

How does the view of culture developed here help managers deal more effectively with problems of the type mentioned at the beginning of this article? Let us begin with problems associated with entry into a new culture, which is typically accompanied by one or more surprises, rude awakenings, or painful revelations.

Culture Shock

Consider the following vignette from Bob Drake's experience:

The first unpleasant surprise for Bob came on his third day with the company when he heard two senior colleagues arguing "in public," cursing and shouting at each other. Within the next few weeks he realized this wasn't aberrant behavior in the company. He was also struck by the very long hours, the few group meetings, and the unusually high amount of rumor and gossip. Bob had previously worked for a company where more polite public behavior, shorter hours, more "team play," and more openness prevailed. He was disturbed, but reasoned: "It's too bad they operate this way, but I can live with that without becoming a part of it." The next shock was of higher voltage. After about two months with the company, Bob was called into his boss's office and told he was not being "tough enough." To "really contribute in this environment," he was told, he would have to "be more aggressive." Bob was upset, but tried to keep his cool. For one who prided himself on his managerial competence, the last thing he felt he needed was "advice on management style."

Bob decided he would redouble his efforts "to show these people what I can contribute." A large part of Bob's job involved dealings with peers in another department, and he decided to communicate his willingness and ability to contribute by putting in hours with them, and going out of his way to help them. What Bob experienced, however, was fierce internal competition, with such tactics as "memo battles," information withholding, and "end running" apparently condoned; appeals to various parties were of no avail. At the six months' performance review Bob's boss told him that he had failed to learn from the feedback given earlier. This was open competition, he was told, and he was not measuring up. Bob got an unsatisfactory rating and was given the option to resign. He did.

Such entry experiences are certainly not uncommon. What can the new manager do to handle these situations better? Presented first are some suggestions for one's recruitment phase, followed by guidelines for the period just after entry—during one's "liability of newness," to borrow a phrase that refers to a similarly treacherous period faced by new businesses.

Before making the decision to join, it is important to try to determine whether there are irreconcilable mismatches between the prospective corporate culture and one's personal beliefs and values. Needed are self-insight and culture-foresight. Constructive introspection and a willingness to learn from one's experience can facilitate the former; regarding the latter, it is best to anticipate that culture cannot be *fully* anticipated. However, everything that can be done should be done to explore major misfits before accepting a company's offer. It helps to approach encounters with the prospective culture in a spirit of adventure, with an inquisitive rather than an evaluative attitude, and to look and listen for underlying meanings. The common human tendency to rationalize, to inadequately test one's assumptions, and to confuse hopes with expectations must be avoided to the extent possible.

Bob Drake, for instance, might have profited by pursuing several early clues. Phrases such as these were used by company executives recruiting him: "We need people like you." "We play to win." "This is a rough place, but a fun place." "You will have to fight here to get your points across." Bob might have thought about, and perhaps asked: "Why *me?*" and "Whom are you playing *against?*" Given his background as a former star college basketball player, Bob thought that *team* play and a winning *team* were being alluded to. Apparently what was being communicated, however, was the importance of *internal individual* competition. Other probing by Bob might have included: "Why is it a *rough* place?" and "What do you mean you have to *fight* to get your point across?"

Whatever the assessment before entry, one or more culture shocks of greater or lesser intensity are typically experienced after joining any organization. To turn these episodes to one's advantage, they are best viewed as painful but timely invitations to learn the new culture, for they indicate that the novice has not as yet understood it. Bob reacted to these shocks with increased determination to overcome the hurdles encountered. Had equal attention been paid to their underlying significance, he might have realized that he had not really understood the ordering of two cultural values. While cooperation prevailed over competition where he had worked previously, it was just the reverse in his current company. Having grasped this, Bob might have been able to take appropriate action.

One might also look upon these early surprises, however unpleasant, as opportunities to better understand oneself. Like body fever, they are symptoms that all is not well and that additional investigation is needed. The self-insight that may result could spur personal growth. For instance, consideration of the following questions about one's perceived misfit with the prevailing culture may be appropriate: Am I resisting the culture because of implied new behaviors and skills that I'm afraid I won't be able to learn? Or is it that the beliefs and values embodied in the culture are basically incompatible with my own?

As the foregoing indicates, it is important to avoid irreconcilable mismatches, but it is usually neither possible nor necessarily desirable in the long run for either the individual or the organization to try to avoid culture/person misfits altogether. What is needed, therefore, is a way of thinking about them so as to facilitate both individual and organizational development. Such an approach is presented here.

Deviating from Culture

Figure 3, which is based on the distinction between culture and behavior emphasized earlier, derives from the fact that cultural beliefs and values are seldom completely shared—that is, not everyone believes and behaves as prescribed by the culture. The scheme can be viewed from either the individual or the organizational perspective, and the following questions are asked. First, to what extent does the individual behave as prescribed by the culture? The answer could range from "a great deal" (that is, behavior conformity) to "not at all" (that is, behavior nonconformity). Second, to what extent does the individual hold the beliefs and values of the culture? The answer could similarly vary from culture confor-

mity to culture nonconformity. The answers to these two questions place an individual somewhere on the culture-prescribed behavior space shown in Figure 3. The four corners of the space are labeled *maverick, good soldier, adapter,* and *rebel.* These culture caricatures are intended to be memory and discussion aids for use in analysis; one should not fall into the trap of stereotyping flesh-and-blood people with these terms.

It is possible for one to be a misfit on the prescribed behavior dimension as well as on the culture dimension. However, such nonconformity requires sensitivity to resulting pressures, and the willingness and ability to overcome them. In general, the greater the distance from the "good soldier" corner, the greater the imagination, determination, and marshalling of personal and organizational resources needed to be effective.

Doug Mill's problems in the second vignette opening this article may now be more clearly understood. He had bought into most of the company's basic beliefs and values: business professionalism, social responsibility, and respect for the individual.

FIGURE 3
Culture Caricatures: Analytical Scheme for Studying Cultural Nonconformity.

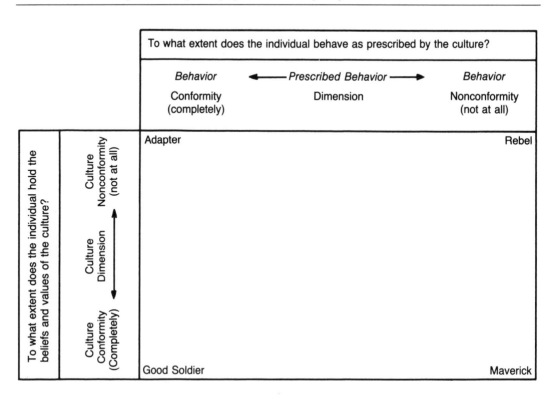

One that he had not bought was risk-aversion. Since Doug was a near conformist on the prescribed behavior dimension, this placed him somewhere between good soldier and adapter in Figure 3. What he needed to do, if he wanted to implement the courage of his convictions, was to "go East" on this map.

Two basic strategies are available to successfully deviate from culture in this way: cultural insurance and self-insurance. The first calls for the support of powerful others—particularly those close to the good-soldier corner. This spreads the risk of nonconformity among the culture's old faithful. It works because behavior deviance by culture conformists is more tolerated than is such nonconformity by others.

The second strategy—self-insurance—is to deviate from culture on the basis of one's own track record, personal power, and credibility within the system. Here one must cash in on one's existing resources and credit. Effective continued use of this strategy requires that one continue to replenish the pile of "chits" from which one draws each time one deviates. If this is done successfully over a period of time, one can acquire the reputation of "a nonconformist who gets away with murder around here"— an image that can enhance one's ability to buck the culture.

Culture Change vs. Behavior Change

Let us now turn to the question of culture change by taking a closer look at the problems faced by Matt Holt in the third vignette at the beginning of this article.

Buffeted by shifting market forces and management turnover, the corporate business strategy had lacked coherent direction. Matt Holt's mandate was to take a longer-term view of the business and to create a technology-driven organization. Analysis conducted with the help of outside consultants indicated that a "cultural metamorphosis" was needed to accomplish this. A reorganization followed, including changes in the measurement and reward system to "encourage the required behavior."

Matt realized there would be a "wait-and-see" period while people tried to figure out "whether they really mean it." He knew that his "true intentions" would be judged on the basis of what he did, not just what he said. Accordingly, he tried to ensure that the management systems inspected and rewarded the required behavior, and he conducted his own affairs (that is, use of his time, visits, "pats on the back") to reinforce and support what the new formal systems were signalling.

Two years later, there had been some improvements. People appeared to be "doing the right things," allocating their time and resources as prescribed by the new systems. Missing, however, was the "missionary zeal"—the sense of excitement and commitment—that Matt had hoped to inject into the life of the company as people came to identify with and share his vision of the mission.

What happened here? This change was more carefully orchestrated than most. Particularly impressive was Matt's sensitivity to "By your actions shall ye be judged," and his resolve to "put his money where his mouth was." Put simply, the problem was that the important distinction between culture change and behavior change had not been recognized and addressed. The "cultural metamorphosis" was directed at changes in people's behavior patterns, and failed to pay attention to their shared beliefs and values—that is, culture as defined in this article. Had this been done, results might have been different.

I am not arguing that managers should always strive to create culture change. There are times when only behavior change is appropriate or is all that is possible—for instance, when culture change would take too long or when only a temporary change in behavior is required to cope with a transient situation. However, be aware that behavior change without culture change requires constant monitoring of behavior to ensure compliance and the continued use of rewards and punishments to sustain it. Without such constant "payoff," the new behavior dies out. This is not the case, however, when behavior change is accompanied by culture change. Although more difficult to accomplish, such change is also more enduring because it is self-sustaining.

What I am saying, then, is that managers should assess what kind of change is needed and ensure that the methods they use are appropriate to the task. In the case just mentioned, Matt Holt was trying to inject a "missionary zeal" into the organization. This clearly required a change in shared beliefs and values—that is, a cultural change, not just the behavior change that his methods were directed at. Before turning to the question of how this can be done, let us pause to ask an important question that managers engaged in culture change will sooner or later confront.

Ethics of Culture Change

Do managers have any business trying to change people's beliefs and values? The following points may be made in addressing this issue. First, questions about changing people's beliefs and values are laden with emotion because they connote "brainwashing." Especially in the United States, born of the quest for religious and political freedom, any hint of this raises eyebrows as well as adrenalin levels. Second, such questions are personally threatening because a lot is at stake for the individual. One's beliefs and values are not a random assembly; changes in one or more of them require changes in related others. Such reorganization is painful and frequently resisted because the learning of new skills and behaviors is implied.

Finally, it is important to note that we are talking here about organization-related beliefs and values, not such private beliefs and values as religious or political ones. The problem is that the two sets are interrelated. Changes in one set most likely affect the other; more theoretical and empirical work is needed to better understand the interrelationship between people's organization-related beliefs and values and their private ones.

Despite these reservations, most people I have talked to have argued that, just as it is in the nature of the manager's job to influence organizational behavior in a responsible and professional manner, so it is his or her job to conscientiously shape organizational beliefs and values in the appropriate direction. I tend to agree and would now like to show how this can be done.

INFLUENCING CULTURE CHANGE

Managers interested in producing culture change must understand and intervene in each of the basic processes that cause culture to perpetuate itself (Figure 4). Let us consider each of them in turn.

Behavior

The process by which culture influences behavior was described earlier in this article, and it is consistent with the conventional wisdom—that is, that beliefs and values influence behavior. However, the opposite is also true. A considerable body of social science literature indicates that, under certain conditions to be discussed shortly, one of the most effective ways of changing people's beliefs and values is to first change their behavior. (The techniques for creating behavior change—Process 1, Figure 4—are well covered in the existing management literature and will not be dealt with here.)

Justifications of Behavior

Behavior change does not necessarily produce culture change, because of the intervening process of justification (Process 2, Figure 4). This is what happened in the case of Matt Holt. People were behaving as called for by the new formal systems, but they continued to share the old beliefs and values in common and "explained" their behavior to themselves by noting the external justifications for it—for example, "We are doing it because it is required of us." "We are doing it because of the incentives." There was behavior compliance, not culture commitment. In a very real sense, people in this case were behaving the way they were because they felt they had no real choice, not because they fundamentally believed in it or valued it.

Thus managers seeking to produce culture change must work on two related fronts simultaneously. First, they must remove external justifications for the new behavior. This means, essentially, that they cannot place too great an emphasis on financial incentives and other extrinsic forms of motivation, but must rely instead on more intrinsic forms to motivate the new behavior—that is, getting people to see the inherent worth of what it is they are being asked to do. A combination of gentle incentives to engage in the new behavior and compelling persuasion is what is needed. Second, and closely related, managers engaged in culture change must communicate the new beliefs and values and get people to adopt them. Because both of these endeavors entail communications, let us now turn to this process.

Cultural Communications

Culture is communicated via both explicit and implicit forms (Process 3, Figure 4). The former include announcements, pronouncements, memos, and other explicit communications. The latter include rituals, ceremonies, stories, metaphors, heroes, logos, decor, dress, and other symbolic forms of communication. Both explicit and implicit communications must be relied on to nullify external justifications for the new behavior and persuade people to adopt new cultural beliefs and values.

If the new beliefs and values being communicated are already intrinsically appealing to the audience, the main problem is the communicator's cred-

FIGURE 4
How Culture Perpetuates Itself.

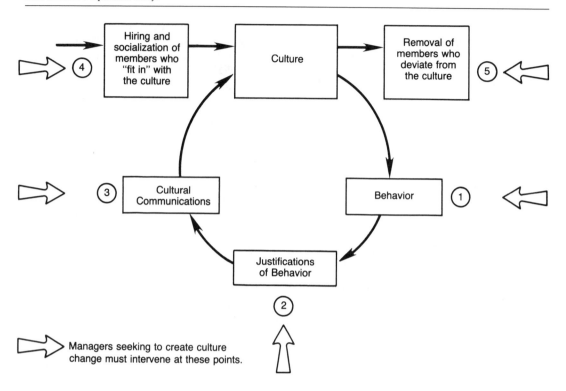

ibility, as in much political campaign rhetoric ("I like what I am hearing, but is this what the communicator really believes?"). How can communications be made more credible? Given their nature, explicit communications about beliefs and values—"We believe people are our most important asset"—are likely to fall on deaf ears, or to be received as corporate propaganda, unless they are made credible by consistent action. Interestingly, research shows that communications are not only more memorable but also more believable—that is, credible—if more implicit forms are used, such as the telling of stories and anecdotes from company history or individual experience to make a point.

As one example, consider the ways in which T.J. Watson, Jr., tried to mold the IBM culture when he took over its leadership from his father. A case in point is his attempt to instill in the organization the virtues of constructive rebellion. One way in which he

tried to do this was directly stating it as an important value in his speeches to company employees: "I just wish somebody would stick his head in my office and say (to me) 'you're wrong.' I would really like to hear that. I don't want yes-men around me." Reportedly, such pronouncements were met with skepticism, and as mere corporate propaganda, by many employees.

Much more credible were Watson's attempts to communicate this value by telling a variety of stories, including this one:

Early in 1961, in talking to our sales force, I attempted to size up the then new Kennedy Administration as I saw it. It was not a political talk. I urged no views on them. It was an optimistic assessment, nothing more. But at the close of the meeting, a number of salesmen came up front. They would listen to what I had to say about business, they said, but they didn't want to hear about the new Administration in a company meeting.

On my return to New York, I found a few letters in the same vein. Lay off, they seemed to say, you're stepping on our toes in something that's none of your business.

At first I was a bit annoyed at having been misunderstood. But when I thought about it, I was pleased, for they had made it quite clear they were no man's collar and they weren't at all hesitant to tell me so. From what I have read of organization men, that is not the way they are supposed to act.

Why are stories more credible? Essentially, it is their concreteness, as well as the fact that the moral of the story is not explicitly stated. Because the listener draws his or her own conclusions, he or she is more likely to believe them. The problem with such communications is that the moral inferred may be different from the one intended; however, for some stories the moral is less open to "misinterpretation."

What if the new beliefs and values being communicated are *not* intrinsically appealing to the audience? In this case, credible communications about the new beliefs and values results in their being believed to be true intentions rather than mere corporate propaganda (for example, "I think management is really serious about this."), but this doesn't mean the new values have been accepted as the audience's own. Without such acceptance the audience is aware of the important beliefs and values that are being communicated, but they don't internalize and share them.

If new beliefs and values are to be internalized and shared, communications about them must be not only emphatic and credible, but persuasive as well. Such "culture persuasion" cannot rely on statistics and other "facts" alone, for beliefs and values are not necessarily accepted and internalized on the basis of "hard evidence." Research and common observation indicate that it is no easy matter to get people to change their beliefs and values. When this key point is overlooked, and persuasion is based on a pile of facts alone, results are often disappointing. There are two basic approaches to effective culture persuasion: identification and "Try it, you'll like it."

Identification. This approach relies on the audiences's identification with one or more persons who credibly communicate their attachment or conversion to the specific beliefs and values in question. Such a person could be the manager directing the culture change, or it could be anyone else whom the audience not only believes, but identifies with. Here is one example:

In a company with a long tradition of authoritarian management, a new CEO with a strong belief in participative management was having a great deal of difficulty getting managers to do more than "go through the motions." One of the senior executives from "the old school," who was widely respected and admired as a company "folk hero" who would never say or do anything he didn't really believe in, then began to come around. As word of his "conversion" spread informally, others began to change their beliefs. It got to the point that this "idol's" department became a model of the intended culture. The beliefs in participative management began to "seep" to the rest of the company and gradually became more widely shared.

Try It, You'll Like It. The following account of how this "folk hero" came to change his belief in participatory management in the first place indicates the second approach to effective culture persuasion:

He began to try the approach being advocated because he was a company loyalist who had an even stronger value: "I owe the new boss a fair shake." He was skeptical at first but then came a few fairly dramatic changes having to do with the improved morale of certain valued but difficult employees, changes that he attributed to the "new philosophy." Gradually, he changed his mind about the participative management. Advocacy followed, and eventually he became a "culture champion."

If people can be persuaded to "give it a fair chance," and they like the experience that they attribute to it, the new beliefs and values may become accepted and eventually internalized. As mentioned previously, such persuasion to try the new behavior must be based on gentle incentives—that is, it must not rely too heavily on financial and other extrinsic forms of motivation if it is to be effective at producing culture change. Otherwise the incentive will serve as external justification for the new behavior and will produce no changes in the prevailing beliefs and values. Both appeals and challenges can be tools in effective persuasion.

In the case just cited, the "folk hero" decided to "give it a try" because the appeal was to his higher value ("I owe the new boss a fair shake."). A more general form of this appeal is one that asks people to "give it a try" in more tentative, exploratory, and relatively nonthreatening ways. Another general form of appeal is one that draws on dormant beliefs and values that are part of the heritage of the people in question, but not part of their current tradition. For instance, this is one of the things AT&T management is currently doing to try to create a more marketing-driven organization. The appeal to engage in the new way of doing things is based on references to the company's heritage—for example, "This isn't new for us, we have done this before." In effect, the activation of dormant beliefs and values "gently induces" people and gives them the confidence "to give it a try."

Another way to get people to try the new behavior without heavy reliance on incentives is to challenge them to do so.

Hiring and Socializing Newcomers and Removing Deviants

A final set of processes that are important to consider if culture change is being attempted is (1) the hiring and socialization of newcomers to fit into the intended culture and (2) the "weeding out" and removal of existing members who do not (Processes 4 and 5, Figure 4).

First, as pointed out earlier, a "perfect" culture/person fit is not usually possible or even desirable, as we shall presently see. However, it is important to avoid irreconcilable mismatches between the person being hired and the intended culture. Both the individual and the organization bear responsibility for ensuring this; suggestions from the individual's standpoint were made previously when discussing culture shock. From the organization's standpoint, one danger to guard against is the common human tendency to place undue emphasis on surface manifestations—such as dress, physical appearance, and background characteristics—in inferring another's beliefs and values. This can seriously undermine a reasoned determination based on all the evidence available.

Second, careful attention must be paid to the socialization process: how new members learn and are taught, the important corporate realities, including culture. It may be added that informal socialization is more effective than formal socialization programs perhaps because the spontaneity with which the latter takes place bestows on it somewhat greater credibility. Socialization does not end with the newcomer's having survived culture shock and the "liability of newness." It continues as members become more aware of the full scope of the culture and feel progressively more committed to it. Mentors play an important role in this continuing socialization.

Cultural Blindspots

Although it is difficult to make and usually takes longer to accomplish than behavior change, culture change can be made. Unfortunately, however, the need for such change often goes unrecognized—until it is too late. It typically takes new leadership to see the extent to which culture has become a liability, and the need to change it.

One way in which enlightened managers can avoid being blindsided by culture is to accommodate a certain degree of nonconformity in their organizations, especially in the case of individuals whose exceptional talents make them invaluable. People who believe and behave differently are difficult to deal with and retain, but they help keep others "honest" by demonstrating alternate ways of thinking and acting. Although this may cause some loss of cultural efficiency, it is an insurance against culture's becoming so firmly entrenched that people can no longer see its blindspots. Some important questions that organizational leaders must therefore ask are: What does the distribution of our membership look like on the culture-prescribed behavior space shown in Figure 3? Is it what it should be in light of our situation? How many people do we have close to the maverick, good soldier, adapter, and rebel corners? Are we losing capable and talented people who are close to one or more of these corners? Why?

Another way in which managers can help prevent a dysfunctional culture from perpetuating itself unheeded is to deviate from it themselves when necessary. How to do so was discussed earlier.

CONCLUSION

While its importance is generally accepted, culture remains an elusive and fuzzy concept for many people. I have tried to show how the approach to understanding culture developed here provides important insights for dealing with various managerial situations.

First, it is possible to see more clearly why culture has such a profound influence on organizational life. Shared beliefs and values represent important common assumptions that guide organizational thinking and action. Further, the influence is subtle, because people are not typically aware of their basic beliefs and values until those beliefs and values are violated or challenged.

Second, the distinction between culture nonconformity and behavior nonconformity can be examined and taken into account in entering and deviating from culture (Figure 3). Third, the dynamics in Figure 4 explain why culture's efficiency and durability are both an asset and a liability. The challenge for leaders is to harness culture's benefits while remaining alert to the dangers of perpetuating a culture that is out of tune with the needs of the business, the organization, and its members. Enlightened leadership can avoid cultural blindspots by accommodating selective nonconformity in their organizations, and by themselves deviating from culture when the situation calls for it.

Finally, the critical difference between culture change and behavior change can be recognized and addressed. It is possible to see why behavior change does not necessarily produce culture change and to determine what is needed to influence culture change, if this is deemed appropriate.

In sum, the approaches to understanding, entering, deviating from, and changing culture presented here can help enhance both organizational efficiency and organizational effectiveness.

SELECTED BIBLIOGRAPHY

A comprehensive review of the concept of culture, including 164 definitions, is contained in A.L. Kroeber and Clyde Kluckhohn's *Culture: A Critical Review of Concepts and Definitions* (Vintage Books, 1952).

The definition adopted in this article belongs to the "ideational" school, which views culture as a system of shared ideas, knowledge, and meanings. The rival school, the "cultural adaptationists," view culture as a system of socially transmitted behavior patterns that serve to relate human communities to their ecological settings. See Roger M. Keesing's "Theories of Culture" in *Annual Review of Anthropology* (1974).

Clifford Geertz's *The Interpretation of Cultures* (Basic Books, 1973), suggests that broad, all-encompassing definitions of culture, such as E.B. Taylor's original one that includes "knowledge, belief, art, law, morals, custom, and other capabilities and habits," obscure a good deal more than they reveal. Geertz argues that a narrower, more specialized definition is theoretically more powerful,

a view that is consistent with the approach taken in this article.

The analytical benefits gained by separating culture from behavior are cogently articulated by Marc Swartz and David Jordan's *Culture: An Anthropological Perspective* (John Wiley, 1980).

The definitions of beliefs and values follow Milton Rokeach's *Beliefs, Attitudes, and Values* (Jossey-Bass, 1968) and Daryl J. Bem's *Beliefs, Attitudes, and Human Affairs* (Brooks/Cole, 1970). The definitions of identity and image in the glossary of cultural terms follow Renato Tagiuri's "Managing Corporate Identity: The Role of Top Management" (Harvard Business School Working Paper 82-68, March 1982) and the definition of ideology is consistent with George C. Lodge's *The New American Ideology* (Alfred A. Knopf, 1980).

An insightful analysis of culture shock and the socialization process is provided by Edgar H. Schein's "Organizational Socialization and the Profession of Management" (*Industrial Management Review,* Winter 1968). His *Career Dynamics* (Addison-Wesley, 1978) contains additional valuable information on this topic. John Van Maanen's "Breaking In: Socialization to Work" in Robert Dubin's (ed.) *Handbook of Work, Organization, and Society* (Rand McNally, 1976) is an excellent, comprehensive review of the literature on entry into a new organization. See also Meryl Louis's "Surprise and Sense Making: What Newcomers Experience in Entering Unfamiliar Organizational Settings" (*Administrative Science Quarterly,* June, 1980).

On culture/person misfits and the notion that some degree of misfit can ultimately benefit both the individual and the organization see Chris Argyris's *Personality and Organization* (Harper, 1957), and Edgar H. Schein's "Organizational Socialization and the Profession of Management," cited above.

Research linking type of communication with its perceived credibility is reported in Joanne Martin's "Stories and Scripts in Organizational Settings," in A. Hastorf and A. Isen's (eds.) *Cognitive Social Psychology* (Elsevier-North Holland Publishing Co., 1982). An early account which demonstrates that beliefs and values may continue to be held despite disconforming evidence is the classic study of a group of "doomsday prophets" by Leon Festinger, H.W. Riecken, and S. Shacter, *When Prophecy Fails* (The University of Minnesota Press, 1956). If people can point to external justifications for new behavior, changes in attitudes, beliefs, and values may not necessarily follow. See Daryl J. Bem's *Beliefs, Attitudes, and Human Affairs,* cited above, and Elliot Aronson's *The Social Animal,* Third Edition (W.H. Freeman, 1980).

The IBM stories in this article and their general analysis is from Joanne Martin and Melanie E. Powers's "Truth on Corporate Propaganda: The Value of a Good War Story," in L. Pondy, P. Frost, G. Morgan, and T. Dandridge, (eds.) *Organizational Symbolism* (JAI Press, 1983). The actual quotes are from R. Malik, *And tomorrow . . . the world? Inside IBM* (Mullington HD, 1975), and T.J. Watson, Jr.'s *A Business and Its Beliefs: The Ideas That Helped Build IBM* (McGraw-Hill, 1963).

Three excellent sources on the topic of organizational change are John P. Kotter and Leonard A. Schlesinger's "Choosing Strategies for Change"

(*Harvard Business Review*, March-April 1979), Michael Beer's *Organization Change and Development* (Goodyear Publishing Co., 1980), and Edgar H. Schein's *Organizational Psychology* (Prentice-Hall, 1965, Third Edition, 1980).

ACKNOWLEDGMENT

The author wishes to thank Mark Rhodes, doctoral candidate in psychology and social relations at Harvard University, for suggesting the addition of "shared feelings" to the diagnostic framework in Figure 1.

Operational Components: The Nature of Organization Development

Wendell L. French

Cecil H. Bell, Jr.

Organization development [as defined earlier] was differentiated from other organizational and educational interventions as a unique process for improving organizational functioning. In this chapter and the next, we continue and extend that earlier discussion by focusing attention on the nature of OD. The efficacy of organization development is due largely to the nature of the OD process itself. The nature of OD—what it is, what it tries to accomplish, what characteristics and components it has, and what its theoretical underpinnings are—that is the scope of this discussion.

The nature of OD could be presented in several ways. As shown in Figure 6-1, we have chosen to characterize it in terms of the foundations of the OD process and the *components of the OD process in operation*. The outer ellipse describes the foundation characteristics we consider important; the inner ellipse describes the basic components or operations found in any OD program. We will discuss the basic operational components of OD in this chapter (the inner ellipse) and the characteristics and foundations of the OD process in the next chapter (the outer ellipse).

There are three basic components of the OD process in operation; any OD program will contain these elements of *diagnosis, action,* and *process maintenance.* In the next chapter the major characteristics and the theoretical underpinnings of organization development are explored; these might be considered the foundation upon which the process is built. The characteristics we want particularly to emphasize are that organization development is an ongoing interactive process, is data based (built on an action research model), is experience based, is goal oriented, constitutes a normative-reeducative strategy of changing, is both a form of and a result of applied behavioral science, uses a systems approach, and has a work team emphasis. . .

OVERVIEW OF THE OPERATIONAL COMPONENTS OF ORGANIZATION DEVELOPMENT

Implementation of an OD program requires attention to three operations that we call the basic components or elements of an OD program in operation: the diagnostic component, representing a continuous collection of system data, focuses on the total system, its subsystems, and system processes; the action (or intervention) component consists of all the activities of consultants and system members designed to improve the organization's functioning;[1] and

Wendell L. French and Cecil H. Bell, Jr., *Organization Development: Behavioral Science Interventions for Organization Improvement*, 3rd ed. (Englewood Cliffs, NJ: Prentice Hall, Inc., 1984), pp. 63-84.

FIGURE 6-1
The Nature of Organization Development.

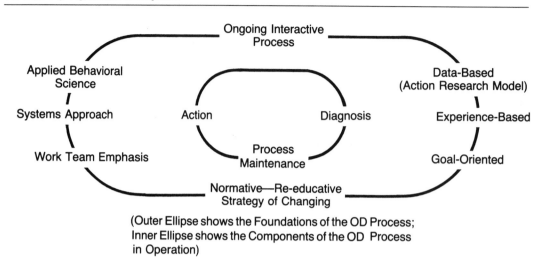

Ongoing Interactive Process

Applied Behavioral Science

Systems Approach

Work Team Emphasis

Action

Diagnosis

Process Maintenance

Data-Based (Action Research Model)

Experience-Based

Goal-Oriented

Normative—Re-educative Strategy of Changing

(Outer Ellipse shows the Foundations of the OD Process; Inner Ellipse shows the Components of the OD Process in Operation)

the process-maintenance component encompasses the activities oriented toward the maintenance and management of the OD process itself. The first two elements relate to the OD process vis-à-vis the organization; the third element relates to the OD process vis-à-vis itself.

Figure 6-2 shows what we mean when we describe the OD process in terms of diagnosis, action, and process-maintenance components.

The first step in organization development is to diagnose the state of the system: What are its strengths? What are its problem areas? As we indicated in the preceding chapter, the system can be conceptualized as having various subsystems, such as the goal, task, technological, structural, human-social, and external interface subsystems. The diagnosis (step 1) will focus on any or all of these subsystems. From the diagnosis comes identification of strengths and problem areas. Action plans are then developed to correct the problem areas and maintain the areas of strength. These action plans usually result from various interventions that constitute the OD technology. Interventions have been developed to correct problems at the levels of individual effectiveness, team effectiveness, intergroup relations, and so forth and also to correct problems at the levels of the various subsystems, such as human-social, goal, and structural. Step 2 then consists of fact-finding concerning the results of the corrective actions taken. Did the actions have the desired effects? Is the problem solved? If the answer is yes, the organization members move on to new

and different problems; if the answer is no, the organization members initiate new action plans and interventions to correct the problem (step 4). Often when problems remain unsolved after an initial attack on them, steps 3 and 4 entail redefining and reconceptualizing the problem areas. There may be steps 5, 6, 7, and so on for some problems, but further steps are just iterations of the basic sequence of diagnosis-action-evaluation-action.

During the entire sequence attention must be paid simultaneously to the OD process itself. Energy is expended to ensure that the program is supported by the organization members, that the program is relevant to the organization's priority concerns, and that the program is making discernible progress.

THE DIAGNOSTIC COMPONENT: DIAGNOSING THE SYSTEM AND ITS PROCESSES

Organization development is at heart an action program based on valid information about the status quo, current problems and opportunities, and effects of actions as they relate to goal achievement. An OD program thus starts with diagnosis and continuously employs data collecting and data analyzing throughout. The requirement for diagnostic activities—activities designed to provide an accurate account of things as they really are—stems from two needs: the first is to know the state of things or "what is"; the second is to know the effects or consequences of actions.

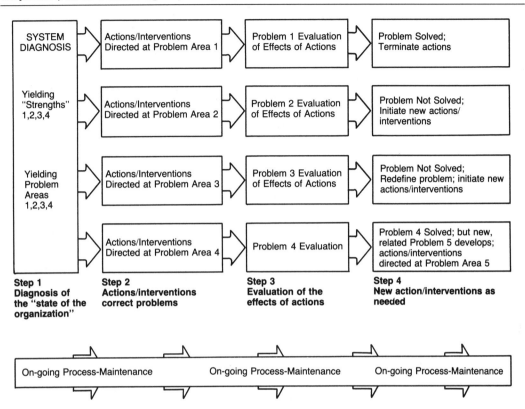

The importance of diagnostic activities is emphasized by Beckhard as follows:

> The development of a strategy for systematic improvement of an organization demands an examination of the present state of things. Such an analysis usually looks at two broad areas. One is a diagnosis of the various subsystems that make up the total organization. These subsystems may be natural "teams" such as top management, the production department, or a research group; or they may be levels such as top management, middle management, or the work force.
>
> The second area of diagnosis is the organization processes that are occurring. These include decision-making processes, communications patterns and styles, relationships between interfacing groups, the management of conflict, the setting of goals, and planning methods.[2]

Table 6-1 shows how one would proceed to diagnose a system and its subsystems (the whole and its subunits). For each of the major targets or subsystems in an organization, the typical information desired and common methods of obtaining the information are given. The OD practitioner may be interested in all these target groups or in only one or two of them; he or she may work with one subsystem during one phase of the program and other subsystems during subsequent phases. Frequently, the improvement strategy (the overall OD intervention strategy) calls for concentrating on different organizational targets in a planned sequence. For example, the program may start at an important subsystem, move to another subsystem, and then extend to the total organization; or the initial focus could be on the total organization and then move to selected subsystems. . . .

An alternative way to conceptualize the diagnostic components emphasizes the organization's principal processes rather than its primary target groups. Such a scheme is presented in Table 6-2 showing the principal organization processes, the typical desired information concerning the processes, and the common methods of obtaining the information.

In practice the OD consultant works from both tables simultaneously. Although interested in some specific target group from Table 6-1 and the information about that group, the consultant is also interested in the processes found in that group and would rely on Table 6-2. Organizational processes are the *what* and the *how* of the organization, that is, What is going on? and How is it being accomplished? To know about the organization's processes is to know about the organization in its dynamic and complex reality. Organiza-

tion development practitioners typically pay special attention to the processes listed in Table 6-2 because of their centrality for effective organization functioning, because of their ubiquitous nature in organizations, and because significant organizational problems often stem from them. Careful examination of the two tables will give a good sense of the inner workings of an OD program and its thrusts, emphases, and mechanics.

TABLE 6-1
Diagnosing Organizational Subsystems.

Diagnostic Focus or Target	Explanation and Identifying Examples	Typical Information Sought	Common Methods of Diagnosis
The total organization (having a common "charter" or mission and a common power structure)	The total system is the entity assessed and analyzed. The diagnosis might also include, if relevant, extra-system (environmental) organizations, groups, or forces, such as customers, suppliers, and governmental regulations. Examples are a manufacturing firm, a hospital, a school system, a department store chain, or a church denomination.	What are the norms ("cultural oughts") of the organization? What is the organization's culture? What are the attitudes, opinions, and feelings of system members toward various "cognitive objects" such as compensation, organization goals, supervision, and top management? What is the organizational climate—open vs. closed, authoritarian vs. democratic, repressive vs. developmental, trusting vs. suspicious, cooperative vs. competitive? How well do key organizational processes, such as decision making and goal setting, function? What kind and how effective are the organization's "sensing mechanisms" to monitor internal and external demands? Are organization goals understood and accepted?	Questionnaire surveys are most popular with a large organization. Interviews, both group and individual, are useful for getting detailed information, especially if based on effective sampling techniques. A panel of representative members who are surveyed or interviewed periodically is useful to chart changes over time. Examination of organizational "potsherds"—rules, regulations, policies, symbols of office and/or status, etc., yields insight into the organization's culture. Diagnostic meetings held at various levels within the organization yield a great amount of information in a short time period.

TABLE 6–1 *(cont.)*

Diagnostic Focus or Target	Explanation and Identifying Examples	Typical Information Sought	Common Methods of Diagnosis
Large subsystems that are by nature complex and heterogeneous	This target group stems from making different "slices" of the organization, such as by hierarchical *level, function,* and geographical *location.* Two criteria help to identify this set of subsystems: first they are viewed as a subsystem by themselves or others; and second, they are heterogeneous in	All of the above, plus: How does this subsystem view the whole and vice versa? How do the members of this subsystem get along together? What are the unique demands on this subsystem? Are organization structures and processes related to the unique demands? Are there makeup, that is, the members have some things in common, but many differences from each other, too. Examples would be the middle-management group, consisting of managers from diverse functional groups; the personnel department members of an organization that has widely dispersed operations with a personnel group at each location; everyone in 1 plant in a company that has 10 plants; a division made up of several functional groups.	If the subsystems are large or widely dispersed, questionnaire and survey techniques are recommended. Interviews and observations may be used to provide additional supporting or hypothesis-testing information. "high" and "low" subunits within the subsystem in terms of performance. Why? What are the major problems confronting this subsystem and its subunits? Are the subsystem's goals compatible with organization goals? Does the heterogeneity of role demands and functional identity get in the way of effective subsystem performance?
Small subsystems that are simple and relatively homogeneous	These are typically formal work groups or teams that have frequent face-to-face interaction. They may be permanent groups, temporary task forces, or newly constituted groups (e.g., the group Charged with "start-up" of a new operation, or the group formed by an	The questions on culture, climate, attitudes, and feelings are relevant here, plus: What are the major problems of the team? How can team effectiveness be improved? What do people do that gets in the way of others? Are member/leader relations those that are	Typical methods include the following: individual interviews followed by a group meeting to review the interview data; short questionnaires; observation of staff meetings and other day-to-day operations; and a family group meeting for self-diagnosis.

TABLE 6–1 *(cont.)*

Diagnostic Focus or Target	Explanation and Identifying Examples	Typical Information Sought	Common Methods of Diagnosis
	acquisition or merger). Examples are the top-management team, any manager and his or her key subordinates, committees of a permanent or temporary nature, task force teams, the work force in an office, the teachers in a single school, etc.	desired? Do individuals know how their jobs relate to group and organizational goals? Are the group's working processes, i.e., the way they get things done as a group, effective? Is good use made of group and individual resources?	tions; and a family group meeting for self-diagnosis.
Small, total organizations that are relatively simple and homogeneous	An example would be a local professional organization. Typical problems as seen by officers might be declining membership, low attendance, or difficulty in manning special task forces.	How do the officers and the members see the organization and its goals? What do they like and dislike about it? What do they want it to be like? What is the competition like? What significant external forces are impacting on the organization?	Questionnaires or interviews are frequently used. Descriptive adjective questionnaires can be used to obtain a quick reading on the culture, "tone," and health of the organization. Diagnostic family group meetings can be useful.
Interface or intergroup subsystems	These consist of subsets of the total system that contain members of two subsystems, such as a matrix organizational structure requiring an individual or a group to have two reporting lines. But more often this target consists of members of one subsystem having common problems and responsibilities with members of another subsystem. We mean to include subsystem with common problems and responsibilities	How does each subsystem see the other? What problems do the two groups have in working together? In what ways do the subsystems get in each other's way? How can they collaborate to improve the performance of both groups? Are goals, subgoals, areas of authority and responsibility clear? What is the nature of the climate between the groups?	Confrontation meetings between both groups are often the method for data gathering and planning corrective actions. Organization mirroring meetings are used when three or more groups are involved. Interviews of each subsystem followed

TABLE 6–1 *(cont.)*

Diagnostic Focus or Target	Explanation and Identifying Examples	Typical Information Sought	Common Methods of Diagnosis
	such as production and maintenance overlaps, marketing and sales overlaps.	What do the members want it to be?	by a "sharing the data" meeting or observation of interactions can be used.
Dyads and/or triads	Superior/subordinate pairs, interdependent peers, linking pins—i.e., persons who have multiple group memberships—all these are subsystems worthy of analysis.	What is the quality of the relationship? Do the parties have the necessary skills for task accomplishment? Are they collaborative or competitive? Are they effective as a subsystem? Does the addition of a third party facilitate or inhibit their progress? Are they supportive of each other?	Separate interviews followed by a meeting of the parties to view any discrepancies in the interview data are often used. Checking their perceptions of each other through confrontation situations may be useful. Observation is an important way to assess the dynamic quality of the interaction.
Individuals	Any individual within the organization, such as president, division heads, key occupants of positions in a work flow process, e.g., quality control, R&D. In school systems, this would be students, teachers, or administrators.	Do people perform according to the organization's expectations? How do they view their place and performance? Do certain kinds of problems typically arise? Do people meet standards and norms of the organization? Do they need particular knowledge, skills, or ability? What career development opportunities do they have/want/need? What pain are they experiencing?	Interviews, information derived from diagnostic work team meetings, or problems identified by the personnel department are sources of information. Self-assessment growing out of team or subsystem interventions is another source.

TABLE 6–1 *(cont.)*

Diagnostic Focus or Target	Explanation and Identifying Examples	Typical Information Sought	Common Methods of Diagnosis
Roles	A role is a set of behaviors enacted by a person as a result of his occupying a certain position within the organization. All persons in the organization have roles requiring certain behaviors, such as the secretaries, production supervisiors, accountants.	Should the role behaviors be added to, subtracted from, or changed? Is the role defined adequately? What is the "fit" between the person and role? Should the role performer be given special skills and knowledge? Is this the right person for this role?	Usually information comes from observations, interviews, role analysis technique, a team approach to "management by objectives." Career planning activities yield this information as an output.
Between organization systems constituting a suprasystem	An example might be the system of law and order in a region, including local, county, state, federal police or investigative enforcement agencies, courts, prisons, parole agencies, prosecuting officers and grand juries. Most such suprasystems are so complex that change efforts tend to focus on a pair or a trio of subparts.	How do the key people in one segment of the suprasystem view the whole and the subparts? Are there frictions or incongruities between subparts? Are there high-performing and low-performing subunits? Why?	Organizational monitoring, or developing lists of how each group sees each other, is a common method of joint diagnosis. Questionnaires and interviews are useful in extensive, long-range interventions.

TABLE 6-2

Diagnosing Organizational Processes.

Organizational Process	Identifying Remarks and Explanation	Typical Information Sought	Common Methods of Diagnosis
Communications patterns, styles and flows	Who talks to whom, for how long, about what? Who initiates the interaction? Is it two-way or one-way? Is it top-down; down-up; lateral?	Is communication directed upward, downward, or both? Are communications filtered? Why? In what way? Do communications patterns "fit" the nature of the jobs to be accomplished? What is the "climate" of communications? What is the place of written communications vs. oral?	Observations, especially in meetings; questionnaires for large-sized samples; interviews and discussions with group members—all these methods may be used to collect the desired information. Analysis of video-taped sessions by all concerned is especially useful.
Goal setting	Setting task objectives and determining criteria to measure accomplishment of the objectives takes place at all organizational levels.	Do they set goals? How is this done? Who participates in goal setting? Do they possess the necessary skills for effective goal setting? Are they able to set long-range and short-range objectives?	Questionnaires, interviews, and observation all afford ways of assessing goal-setting ability of individuals and groups within the organization.
Decision making, problem solving, and action planning	Evaluating alternatives and choosing a plan of action are integral and central functions for most organization members. This includes getting the necessary information, establishing priorities, evaluating alternatives, and choosing one alternative over all others.	Who makes decisions? Are they effective? Are all available sources utilized? Are additional decision-making skills needed? Are additional problem-solving skills needed? Are organization members satisfied with the problem-solving and decision-making processes?	Observation of problem-solving meetings at various organizational levels is particularly valuable in diagnosing this process. Analysis of videotaped sessions by all concerned is especially useful.
Conflict resolution and management	Conflict—interpersonal, intrapersonal, and intergroup—frequently exists in organizations. Does the organization have effective ways of dealing with conflict?	Where does conflict exist? Who are the involved parties? How is it being managed? What are the system norms for dealing with conflict? Does the reward system promote conflict?	Interviews, third-party observations, and observation meetings are common methods for diagnosing these processes.

TABLE 6–2 *(cont.)*

Organizational Process	Identifying Remarks and Explanation	Typical Information Sought	Common Methods of Diagnosis
Managing interface relations	Interfaces represent these situations wherein two or more groups (subsystems) face common problems or overlapping responsibility. This is most often seen when members of two separate groups are interdependently related in achieving an objective but have separate accountability.	What is the nature of the relations between two groups? Are goals clear? Is responsibility clear? What major problems do the two groups face? What structural conditions promote/inhibit effective interface management?	Interviews, third-party observations, and observation of group meetings are common methods for diagnosing these processes.
Superior-subordinate relations	Formal hierarchical relations in organizations dictate that some people lead and others follow: these situations are often a source of many organizational problems.	What are the extant leadership styles? What problems arise between superiors and subordinates?	Questionnaires can show overall leadership climate and norms. Interviews and questionnaires reveal the desired leadership behaviors.
Technological and engineering systems	All organizations rely on multiple technologies—for production and operations, for information processing, for planning, for marketing, etc., to produce goods and services.	Are the technologies adequate for satisfactory performance? What is the state of the art and how does this organization's technology compare with that? Should any changes in technology be planned and implemented?	Generally this is not an area of expertise of the OD consultant. He or she must then seek help from "experts" either inside the organization or outside. Interviews and group discussions focused on technology are among the best ways to determine the adequacy of technological systems. Sometimes outside experts conduct an audit and make recommendations; sometimes inside experts do so.

TABLE 6–2 *(cont.)*

Organizational Process	Identifying Remarks and Explanation	Typical Information Sought	Common Methods of Diagnosis
Strategic management and long-range planning	Monitoring the environment, adding and deleting "products," predicting future events, and making decisions that affect the long-term viability of the organization must occur for the organization to remain competitive and effective.	Who is responsible for "looking ahead" and for making long-range decisions? Do they have adequate tools and support? Have recent long-range decisions been effective? What is the nature of current and future environmental demands? What are the unique strengths and competencies of the organization? What are the threats to the organization?	Interviews of key policymakers, group discussions, and examination of historical records give insights to this dimension.

These tables are intended as heuristic tools for operational diagnosis. As an illustration, suppose that the personnel director in conjunction with a manager of a large, complex, heterogeneous subsystem is interested in OD efforts primarily directed to improving the functioning of significant pairs and individuals within the subsystem. It is helpful to know what information is typically needed and what methods are available for getting an accurate picture of the *status quo* of the large complex unit. And it is helpful to know what different kinds of information and data-gathering techniques are indicated when attention is focused on the pairs and individuals. This knowledge facilitates designing the diagnostic phases of the organization development program.

Continual diagnosis is thus a necessary ingredient of any planned change effort. Such diverse activities as getting rich, managing your time, and losing weight, for example, all begin with an audit of "what is"—the status quo—and then require continual monitoring of the changing status quo over time. From a comparison of "what is" with "what should be" comes a discovery of the gap between actual and desired conditions. Action plans are then developed to close the gap between the actual and the desired conditions; and the effects (consequences) of these action plans are continuously monitored to measure progress or movement toward the goal.[3] Diagnostic activities are therefore basic to all goal-seeking behaviors.

Organization development, with its emphasis on moving the organization from "what is" to "what should be," requires continuous generation of system data.[4] In this regard, Argyris states that the consultant ("interventionist" in his terms) has three "primary intervention tasks": to help the client system generate valid data; to enable the client system to have free, informed choice; and to help the client system generate internal commitment to the choices made.[5] Argyris says: "One condition that seems so basic as to be defined axiomatic is the generation of *valid information*. Without valid information it would be difficult for the client to learn and for the interventionist to help. . . . Valid information is that which describes the factors, plus their interrelationships, that create the problem for the client system."[6]

Granted that diagnosis is a sine qua non of effective organization development, two issues remain. First, is the diagnosis systematically planned and structured in advance so that it follows an extensive category system and structured question format, or is the diagnosis more emergent—following the data wherever they may lead? Second, what diagnostic categories are to be used? Practice varies widely on these two dimensions. We tend to be about in the middle of the "structured in advance—emergent" continuum. We have some structured questions but follow up on leads as they develop in the course of the diagnosis. We also tend to use the diagnostic categories of Tables 6-1 and 6-2 because we focus on system and subsystem cultures and processes.

Roger Harrison uses somewhat different categories (see Figure 6-3) and an emergent diagnostic approach.[7] In his words, "I approach the system with my antennae waving, and as data are produced I probably slot them into these different categories; and then if one or another of them seems predominant as a focus for the system members, then that's the one I'm likely to use as entry."[8]

Probably the most thorough and systematic diagnostic activities in OD are done as a part of Grid OD, the six-phase organization development program used by Robert Blake and Jane Mouton.[9]. . . In addition to being thorough, Blake and Mouton extend the diagnostic categories to include financial considerations, general business strategy, and general business logic. In their view a corporation has six major areas of activities—human resources, financial management, operations (production/manufacturing), marketing, research and development, and corporate. Each of these areas must be managed effectively if the corporation is to achieve corporate excellence, and each of these areas is measured/assessed in depth and detail. This extension of diagnosis to the business logic of the organization, in addition to the more usual focus of most OD practitioners on the human and social dynamics of the organization, represents a significant positive feature of Grid OD.

Finally, in an OD program, not only are the *results* of diagnostic activities important, but *how the information is collected* and *what is done with the information* are also significant aspects of the process. There is active collaboration between the OD practitioner and the organization members about such issues as what target groups are to be diagnosed, how the diagnosis is best accomplished, what processes and dynamics should be analyzed, what is to be done with the information, how the data will be worked with, and how the information will be used to aid action planning. Usually information is collected through a variety of methods—interviews, observations, questionnaires, and organization records. Information is generally considered to be the property of those persons who generated it; the data serve as the foundation for planning actions. This is basically an action research model consisting of the following steps: (1) data collection, (2) data feedback to the people who supplied the data, (3) identification of problem areas based on the data, (4) planning corrective action steps, (5) implementing the action steps, and (6) collecting data to evaluate the effects of the actions. Therefore the diagnostic component and the action component are intimately related in organization development.

THE ACTION COMPONENT: INTERVENING IN THE CLIENT SYSTEM

As we have seen, organization development may be viewed as a process designed to improve an organization's adapting, coping, problem-solving, and goal-setting processes. The assumptions are made that the organization is not doing these processes as well as it could or should be doing them and that the organization can improve. Improvement requires, first, knowing what processes are inadequate—gained through diagnosis—and, second, doing something to make the inadequate processes more effective—accomplished by taking corrective actions. Taking corrective actions is achieved through activities in the client system called *interventions,* which we define . . . as "*sets of structured activities* in which selected organizational units (target groups or individuals) engage with a task or sequence of tasks where the task goals are related *directly or indirectly to organizational improvement.*"

To intervene in the client system is to interpose or interject activities into the normal activities of the organization in such a way that the intervention activities are done *in addition to* the normal activities or are done *instead of* the normal activities. An example of an "in addition to" intervention would be for a staff group to include a "process critique" at the end of each staff meeting. This simply means that a few minutes are set aside to look at "how we worked"—the process—during the meeting. Critiquing "how we worked" can enable the group to correct any deficient processes and become more effective in its deliberations. An example of an "instead of" intervention would be getting a key service department of an organization to hold an "organization mirroring" workshop with its user-clients to determine how the clients view the services provided and how they want the services changed or improved. In this case, instead of the normal activities of begging, cajoling, or coercing the user-clients to utilize the staff services, a problem-solving workshop called the organization mirror is convened in which the clients give feedback to the service group regarding services and a two-way dialogue is established between service providers and service users. Such a meeting would probably not be a normal activity in the organization.

FIGURE 6-3
Harrison's Model for Organizational Diagnosis: Categories and Subcategories.

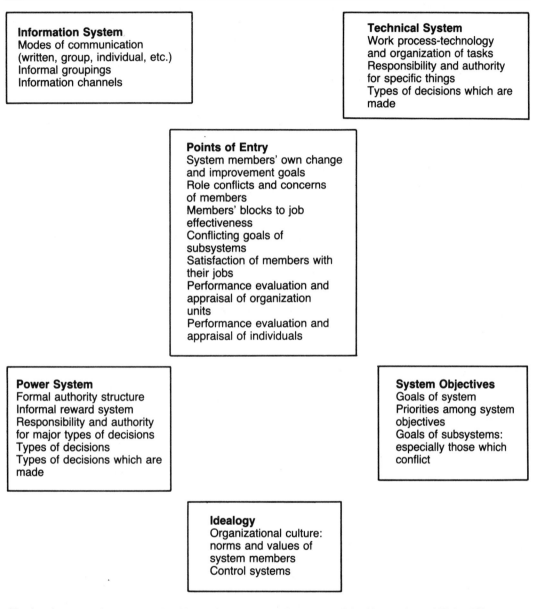

Information System
Modes of communication
(written, group, individual, etc.)
Informal groupings
Information channels

Technical System
Work process-technology
and organization of tasks
Responsibility and authority
for specific things
Types of decisions which are
made

Points of Entry
System members' own change
and improvement goals
Role conflicts and concerns
of members
Members' blocks to job
effectiveness
Conflicting goals of
subsystems
Satisfaction of members with
their jobs
Performance evaluation and
appraisal of organization
units
Performance evaluation and
appraisal of individuals

Power System
Formal authority structure
Informal reward system
Responsibility and authority
for major types of decisions
Types of decisions
Types of decisions which are
made

System Objectives
Goals of system
Priorities among system
objectives
Goals of subsystems:
especially those which
conflict

Idealogy
Organizational culture:
norms and values of
system members
Control systems

Harrison's categories were derived from his response to a portion of the Hornstein and Tichy "Change Agent Survey" questionnaire which instructed respondents to: (1) indicate what information (from a list including such things as formal reward structure, goals, control system, individual satisfactions, etc.) they would seek in order to diagnose and understand an organization; and (2) arrange the items into categories.

Source: Reproduced by special permission from *The Journal of Behavioral Science,* "An interview with Roger Harrison," by Noel Tichy, Vol. 9, No. 6, p. 707. Copyright 1973 NTL Institute for Applied Behavioral Science.

The range of OD interventions is quite extensive. Structured activities have been developed to solve most organizational problems. For example, there are interventions that focus on most of the target groups in Table 6-1 and most of the organizational processes of Table 6-2. Thus, if problems exist in a particular organizational system or subsystem or in a particular organizational process, intervention activities can be initiated to remedy the problems. . . .

A well-designed OD program unfolds according to a strategy or game plan, called the *overall OD strategy*. This strategy may be planned in advance or may emerge over time as events dictate. The strategy is based on answers to such questions as the following: What are the overall change/ improvement goals of the program? What parts of the organization are most ready and receptive to the OD program? What are the key leverage points (individuals and groups) in the organization? What are the most pressing problems of the client organization? What resources are available for the program in terms of client time and energy and internal and external facilitators? Answers to these questions lead the practitioner to develop a game plan for where to intervene in the system, what to do, the sequencing of interventions, and so forth.

It can be seen that planning actions, executing actions, and evaluating the consequences of actions are an integral and essential part of organization development. This emphasis on action planning and action taking is a powerful feature of OD and, in some respects, is a distinguishing one. In many traditional educational and training activities, learning and action taking are separated in that the knowledge and skills are "learned" in one setting, say, in a classroom, and are then taken back to the organization with the learner being admonished to practice what he or she has learned, that is, to take actions. This artificial separation is minimized in most OD interventions in several ways. First, in many intervention activities there are two goals: a learning or educational goal and an accomplishing-a-task goal. Second, OD problem-solving interventions tend to focus on real organization problems that are central to the needs of the organization rather than on hypothetical, abstract problems that may or may not fit the members' needs. Third, OD interventions utilize several learning models, not just one. Let us examine these three points in more detail.

The dual aspect of OD interventions can be clarified with an illustration. Let us say that the top executives of an organization spend three days to-gether in a workshop in which they do the following things: (1) explore the need for and desirability of a long-range strategy plan for the organization; (2) learn how to formulate such a strategy by analyzing other strategies, determining what the strategic variables are, being shown sequence of steps for preparing a comprehensive plan, and so forth; and (3) actually make a three-year strategy plan for the organization.[10] This intervention combines the dual features of learning and action: the executives engaged in activities in which they learned about strategy planning, and they then generated a strategy. In some OD interventions, the "learning aspect" predominates, and in others, the "action aspect" predominates; but both aspects are present in most interventions.

Organization development interventions tend to focus on real problems rather than on abstract problems. The problems facing organization members are real, not hypothetical; the problems members get rewarded for solving are real, not hypothetical; and the problems central to the needs of organization members are real, not hypothetical. Developing the skills and knowledge to solve real problems as they arise in their "natural state" means that the educational problem of "transfer of learning" from one situation to another is minimized (although the problem of generalization, that is, knowing the appropriate times and places to apply this particular set of skills and knowledge, is still present).

An additional feature of working on real problems as found in some OD interventions, is that the real set of individuals involved in the problem is the group that the problem solvers work with. For example, in a human relations class, if a manager were having trouble understanding and working with disadvantaged subordinates, he or she would perhaps "role play" the situation with the instructor or fellow students. In OD the manager would probably interact with the disadvantaged employees with whom he or she was having difficulties—but would do so in carefully structured activities that have a high probability of resulting in learning for both parties and a high probability of being a "success experience" for both parties.

Organization development programs rely on several learning models. For example if "learning how to" do something precedes "doing" it, then we have a somewhat traditional approach to learning that most people are familiar with. If the "doing" preceded the "learning how to," then we have a "deficiency" model of learning in which the learning comes primarily from critiquing the actions after the fact to see how they could have been done differently and, presumably, better. Both models are viable learning modes, and both are used extensively in organization development. Even the traditional model of "learning how to" and "doing" becomes nontraditional as performed in OD, however, since the OD approach would be for a formal work team to be learning and doing *together* with the help of a change agent.

Action programs in OD are closely linked with explicit goals and objectives. Careful attention is given to the problem of translating goals into observable, explicit, and measurable actions or behaviors, and equal care is given to the related problem of ensuring that actions are relevant to and instrumental for goal attainment. Such questions as the following thus become an integral part of organizational life: How does this action relate to the goal we have established? What are the action implications of that goal for me, my subordinates, my group? When we say we want to achieve a certain goal, what do we really mean by that, in measurable terms? Given several alternative forms of action, which one seems most appropriate to achieve the goal we have set?

Diagnosis, action taking, and goal setting are inextricably related in an OD program. Diagnostic activities are precursors to action programs; that is, fact-finding is done to provide a foundation for action. Actions are continuously evaluated for their contribution to goal accomplishment. Goals are continuously evaluated in terms of their appropriateness—whether or not they are attainable and whether or not they can be translated into action programs. Organizational development is a continuous process of the cycling of setting goals and objectives, collecting data about the status quo, planning and taking actions based on hypotheses and on the data, and evaluating the effects of action through additional data collection.

THE PROCESS-MAINTENANCE COMPONENT: MAINTAINING AND MANAGING THE OD PROCESS ITSELF

Just as OD practitioners apply behavioral science principles and practices to ongoing complex systems to improve the system's functioning, ideally they apply these same principles and practices to their own work. The OD process and the practitioner group typically model the techniques being proposed for the organization; both the program and the prac-

titioners practice what they preach. Diagnosing and evaluating are an integral part of managing the OD process, similarly so is treating the organization from a systems viewpoint with the OD program being a component force within a wider field of system forces. Practitioners would find the client system probably resisting their teaching and preaching about the desirability and feasibility of managing interpersonal conflict if it were known that conflict was not being managed within the OD group; teaching others to manage against measurable objectives would appear hollow if the OD group did not know where it was going and how; reverberations will occur throughout the total organization as a result of an OD program in one subsystem and this fact must be taken into account.

Among other things, managing the OD process means actively seeking answers to the following questions:

☐ Are we being timely and relevant in our interventions?

☐ Are our activities producing the effects we intended and wanted? If not, why not; if so, why?

☐ Is there continued "ownership," that is, involvement, commitment, and investment, in the program by the clients?

☐ What are the total system ramifications of our efforts? Did we anticipate these? Are any of the ramifications undesirable? If yes, what do we do about them?

☐ What about the culture of our own OD group? Must it be changed in any ways? Are we solving problems effectively, managing against clearly understood goals, and modeling the kinds of interpersonal climate we think is desirable in an organization?

To summarize, the process-maintenance element is designed to accomplish several objectives: to model self-analysis and self-reflection as means of self-improvement; to model the action research principles of goal setting coupled with data feedback loops to guide and evaluate actions; to work to ensure ownership of the interventions and the entire program by organization members; to model the ability to detect and cope with problems and opportunities in the internal and external environment; to test the effectiveness of interventions by utilizing feedback from the system; to test for relevancy of the program to the organization's needs; to test for timeliness of interventions; and to ensure that intended and unintended consequences do not obviate the organization's and the OD program's goals.

The importance of this component can hardly be overstated. Managing the OD process effectively can spell the difference between success and failure for the improvement effort. This component, maintenance and management of the OD process, may help to explain why there are many aborted OD efforts and few long-range, successful ones. The practicing-what-you-preach aspect probably contributes significantly to bringing about real, genotypic, lasting change in the organization instead of apparent, phenotypic, or "pasted on" change. . . .

OD, ACTION RESEARCH, AND THE ANALYSIS OF DISCREPANCIES

Diagnosis, action taking, and process maintenance have been emphasized as major operational components of organization development programs, and the central role of problem solving in OD has been described. OD is much more than just problem solving, but certainly such activities are of paramount importance.

A useful underlying model for this discussion of problem solving could be termed discrepancy analysis—examination of the discrepancies or gaps between what is happening and what should be happening and discrepancies between where one is and where one wants to be. Discrepancies therefore, define both problems and goals. Discrepancies require *study* (diagnosis and planning) and *action* if the gaps are to be eliminated. We believe that a good part of OD is problem solving, hence, discrepancy analysis. Action research . . . describes an iterative problem-solving process that is essentially discrepancy analysis—the study of problems and opportunities (goals) or the study of discrepancies between where one is and where one wants to be. Organization development provides technologies for studying and closing gaps.

This simple but powerful analytical model is presented clearly and effectively by Charles Kepner and Benjamin Tregoe in *The Rational Manager.*[11] Their ideas have been translated into training seminars to improve problem-solving and decision-making skills. Kepner and Tregoe state, "The problem analyzer has an expected standard of performance, a 'should' against which to compare actual performance. . . . A problem is a deviation from a standard of performance."[12] According to these authors, a problem is a gap; problem solving is discovering the

cause of the gap; decision making is discovering the *solution*—a set of actions—to close the gap.

In *Analyzing Performance Problems,* Robert Mager and Peter Pipe use a discrepancy or gap model to great advantage.[13] Beginning with a "performance discrepancy," they show how to discover the source of the discrepancy and how to correct it. By focusing first on precisely defined performance discrepancies, then determining whether or not the cause is related to a skill deficiency, they show how performance problems can be quickly analyzed and corrected. The basic model is discrepancy analysis. This method of analyzing performance discrepancies is readily applicable to many day-to-day problems found in organizations.

In *The New Science of Management Decision,* Herbert Simon proposed a discrepancy model of problem analysis.[14] He stated that a problem is a deviation from an expected standard and a cause of a problem is a *change* of some sort. Simon's conclusions were derived from his studies of human cognitive processes and computer science. His model is one of analyzing gaps. Kepner and Tregoe call Simon's book "the best statement of problem-solving theory to be found in the literature on the subject."[15]

Goals also represent gaps—gaps between where we are and where we want to be. Goal setting is the process of defining or imposing a gap; goal accomplishment is made possible by taking actions to close the gap.

We have said that organization development is more than just problem solving and goal seeking. But a large part of any OD program is devoted to these two critical activities. The discrepancy analysis approach is a fruitful way in which to conceptualize problems and goals.

SUMMARY

We have identified three major components of an operational OD program as follows: the diagnostic component; the intervention, or action-taking, component; and the OD process-maintenance component. All three components are necessary for success. The diagnostic component has two facets: finding out about the state of the system and evaluating the effects of remedial action plans. The action/intervention component represents the range of OD interventions designed to improve the functioning of the organization. The process-maintenance component directs attention to keeping the process itself viable and relevant. Finally, it has been suggested that there is considerable value in conceptualizing problems and goals within a framework of discrepancy analysis, where gaps between where one is and where one wants to be are examined and systematically eliminated.

NOTES

1. In fact, all three components represent actions or interventions in the system and thus fall into an action category. Diagnostic activities, for example, have a powerful "action impact" on an organization. We have artificially separated the three components here for analytical purposes only.

2. Richard Beckhard, *Organization Development: Strategies and Models* (Reading, Mass.: Addison-Wesley, 1969), p. 26. Beckhard's use of subsystem synonymously with *subunit* is congruent with our usage in Chapter 5. However, we develop a supplemental conceptual scheme in that chapter that also permits viewing the organization in terms of subsystems that are common to all subunits: goal, technological, task, structural, human-social, and external interface.

3. This "actual condition" versus "ideal condition" discrepancy model is an integral feature of Kurt Lewin's force field analysis [Kurt Lewin, *Field Theory in Social Science* (New York: Harper & Bros., 1951)] and appears, in fact, to be basic to all human goal-seeking and problem-solving activities. See, for example, George A. Miller, Eugene Galanter, and Karl H. Pribram, *Plans and the Structure of Behavior* (New York: Holt, Rinehart and Winston, 1960).

4. The movement of the organization from "what is" to "what should be" is the explicit underlying dynamic in Grid OD. See Robert R. Blake and Jane Srygley Mouton, *Corporate Excellence Through Grid Organization Development* (Houston: Gulf, 1968).

5. Chris Argyris, *Intervention Theory and Method: A Behavioral Science View* (Reading, Mass.: Addison-Wesley, 1970).

6. Ibid., pp. 16–17.

7. Noel Tichy, "An Interview with Roger Harrison," *Journal of Applied Behavioral Science* 9, No. 6 (1973), pp. 701-711. This figure is taken from page 707 and is used by permission.

8. Ibid., pp. 706, 708.

9. Robert R. Blake and Jane Srygley Mouton, *Building a Dynamic Corporation Through Grid Organization Development* (Reading, Mass.: Addison-Wesley, 1969); and R. R. Blake and J. S. Mouton, *Corporate Excellence Diagnosis: The Phase 6 Instrument* (Austin, Tex.: Scientific Methods, 1968).

10. Actually, in a real strategy planning session steps 1 and 2 might take place during the first session, with that session concluding with some "homework" assignments to the members in order that the necessary information for the strategy plan could be available. Then, in a second session, step 3 would be finalized. This kind of separation in time is not the artificial one just described but, rather, a separation in time designed to facilitate step 3.

11. Charles H. Kepner and Benjamin B. Tregoe, *The Rational Manager* (New York: McGraw-Hill, 1965). This book is highly recommended for OD practitioners.

12. Ibid., p. 44.

13. Robert F. Mager and Peter PIpe, *Analyzing Performance Problems or "You Really Oughta Wanna"* (Belmont, Calif.: Fearon, 1970).

14. Herbert A. Simon, *The New Science of Management Decision* (New York: Harper & Row, 1960).

15. Kepner and Tregoe, *The Rational Manager,* p. 252.

Case: Managing by Mystique

PURPOSE

The purpose of this case assignment is to introduce the concepts of metanorms, rituals, myths, and heroes as they apply to corporate cultures. By the time you finish this case assignment you will:

1. Diagnose a unique corporate culture.

2. Determine the impact a founder can have on corporate culture.

3. Understand the impact a corporate culture can have on employee behavior.

INTRODUCTION

Organizational cultures comprise the shared values, beliefs, and assumptions that guide the behavior of the members of an organization. In the same way that people develop different personalities, corporations also create their own unique personalities, as reflected by the rites and rituals of daily company life. For example, in some firms, it always may be expected of you as an employee to attend meetings promptly, to never contradict your boss, and to avoid conflict. In other firms, advocating your own unique perspective to generate conflict may be not only encouraged, but expected.

Tandem Computers, headquartered in the Silicon Valley area of California's technology belt, has a unique corporate culture. As you read this case, reflect upon what makes this particular company's culture unique, meaningful, and distinct from others.

INSTRUCTIONS

1. Read the case, "Managing By Mystique."

2. Read the excerpted chapter from Deal and Kennedy's book, "Corporate Cultures: The Rites and Rituals of Corporate Life."

3. Diagnose the elements of this company's culture by completing the questions on the Corporate Cultures Worksheet in this exercise.

4. Participate in a class discussion.

It's 4:30 on Friday afternoon, and the weekly beer bust is in full swing at Tandem Computers' Cupertino, California, headquarters. Sun shines on the basketball court beyond the corporate patio and sparkles on the company swimming pool. Programmer A, bearded like a mountain man, is discussing stock options and tax-law changes while dancing in place to the secret music he hears in his own conversation. Earnest Programmer B, clinching his point about Silicon Valley culture by noting that the Programmer Bs have more married than single friends, turns to greet with a soulful kiss a convivial employee his visitor mistakes for Mrs. B.

Five hundred cheerfully bibulous souls, mostly young and casual-looking, are talking animatedly, glass in hand; and the same genial scene is being reenacted on a smaller scale at Tandem offices as far afield as Omaha or Kowloon. Every week 60 percent of the company drops in at the beer bust for an hour, joined sometimes by visiting customers or suppliers, who take away indelible memories. Says the representative of one satisfied user, a stately major bank, "When the president comes down in a cowboy hat and boots and swills beer—that's different!"

The fun's not confined to Fridays. Take the company's last Halloween costume party, which filled most of a gigantic warehouse. The merriment was heightened by the granting of a 100-share stock option to every employee. Another big event has left its mark, too, on a sunny, modest office belonging to the vice-president of software development, who's one of Tandem's phalanx of mid-thirtyish millionaires. With nondescript steel furniture and a humid display of potted plants, it's indistinguishable from any other Tandem executive's office, including the president's—except for the red satin sash on the wall, bearing the legend "Incredible Hunk," won a while ago by the vice-president himself. He and another Tandemite outshone thirty-odd gym-shorts-clad male opponents in a headquarters-wide beauty contest sponsored by the company's female employees.

GROWTH WITHOUT A HICCUP

Can this company be serious? Meteoric growth and surging profits say it is. Only 7½ years old and already a more than $300-million-a-year operation, it's one of the bright stars of the *Fortune* "Second 500" list and seems inexorably growing to "First 500" magnitude. This isn't only because its Nonstop II system—the computer that's never down—is an estimable machine, commanding a market only recently contested. As Ulric Weil, a Morgan Stanley

security analyst, puts it, "No company could be as successful as Tandem is—without a hiccup—unless its management were gifted and kept its finger on the tiller."

Indeed, all the corporate high jinks play their part in an elaborate management scheme conceived largely by Tandem's founder-president, James G. Treybig (pronounced *Try*-big), a 41-year-old Texan whose hands-in-pockets slouch and untucked shirttail give him the incongruous air of a teenager hanging out on Main Street. Freewheeling theorizing comes naturally to Jimmy T., as Tandemites call him. Yet he's no idle daydreamer. Before he started Tandem he fleshed out his engineering BS and Stanford MBA with several years in sales and marketing at Texas Instruments and Hewlett-Packard and in venture capital at San Francisco's high-flying Kleiner Perkins Caufield & Byers partnership. He speaks, in his lovingly preserved Texas twang, from experience.

"Jim Treybig sometimes likes to shock people," says Samuel Wiegand, 50, Tandem's former marketing VP. The result, according to software-development VP Dennis McEvoy (the aforementioned Hunk), is that "a lot of people when they meet Jim for the first time think he's a bullshitter, just shuckin' and jivin'." Certainly getting to the heart of his management theory requires pushing through an exotic tangle of rhetoric about how the company represents "the convergence of capitalism and humanism" or how it tries to foster not just its employees but also their spouses and "spouse equivalents." What's more, Treybig (himself married and the father of three) is given to reducing complexity to a simplicity more elegant than true, as in his five cardinal points for running a company, beginning with the at least debatable assertion that "all people are good".

Is there anything in this provocative talk that other CEOs should be listening to? The answer comes down to yes, but. Behind the verbiage is a cluster of hard-headed policies, many of them familiar in high-tech companies, especially in the Bay Area, and some of them applicable to other businesses. But the swaggering tone also points to something in Tandem that's far out, even for California, and that every company wouldn't want.

Generous stock options aimed at riveting employees' attention on the business's success are nothing new in high-tech companies, though perhaps none has gone so far as Tandem, where *every* employee gets gift options. This can mean real money: Tandem's stock has risen steeply from the start, and each employee with the company since it went public in 1977 has drawn options theoretically worth almost

$100,000. So raptly attentive to corporate performance have employees become that Tandem now posts the stock price three times a day on its work-station screens; formerly too many people were monopolizing the telex machines to find out. A forceful promotion-from-within policy, so diligently observed that three out of five new managers have risen from the ranks, similarly concentrates the mind.

Unrevolutionary too is Tandem's easy-going flexibility about working hours. As Michael Green, a company founder, puts it, "We don't want to pay people for attendance but for output." So time clocks are out, and managers often don't know just how long their subordinates toil, though indicators like the position of an employee's car in the democratically first-come, first-served parking lot speak volumes to the discerning. As for jogging trails, space for dance-exercise, and yoga classes, and periodic company-supplied weekend barbecues for employees working overtime—amenities like these are not unheard of in other companies.

Treybig argues that the swimming pool, to take one example, improves productivity by giving single parents an agreeable place to park their kids, thus enabling them to work on weekends. Perhaps so—if only because all such appurtenances help spark the so-called Hawthorne effect, an increase in productivity that appears to result from *any* new attention paid to employees' working conditions or amenities. Even the beer bust, in terms of the current fashion for fostering unstructured communication across an institution's vertical and horizontal boundaries, is arguably a productivity ploy.

THE TANDEM GOSPEL

Also hardly novel is soaking employees in an endless stream of company-boosting propaganda urging loyalty, hard work, self-esteem, and respect for co-workers. But Tandem's indoctrination effort goes so far beyond the ordinary as to make clear how radical a departure the company's managerial style, taken as a whole, really is. First, there's its sheer quantity—from orientation lectures and breakfasts, newsletters, and a glossy magazine that some Tandemites call "Propaganda Quarterly" to a fat tome (standard issue to all employees) called *Understanding Our Philosophy,* supplemented by a two-day course on its finer points. This is mandatory for all employees, notes James Katzman, a company founder, though mandatory is a taboo word, for it "goes against the culture." A lavish facility to house these so-called philosophy seminars and other programs is in the planning stage.

Then there's the content, in which conventional pieties, by their vehemence of expression, take on new meaning. For instance, here's "all employees should be treated with respect" rendered in Treybigese: "You never have the right at Tandem to screw a person or to mistreat them. It's not allowed. . . . No manager mistreats a human without a fear of their job." An aggrieved employee's ready access to anyone in the company gives this provision teeth: managers have been fired. Or take the idea that everyone in a company is essential to its success. In the Tandem ideology this platitude takes on a more egalitarian tinge than usual: Treybig dismisses with indulgent but characteristic sarcasm some German productivity experts who "had never danced with an assembly worker."

Yet the indoctrination goes further, for Tandem, in its "philosophy" book and seminars, takes pains to give each employee an understanding of the essence of the company's business and five-year plan. Folded into the philosophy book is a labyrinthine chart the size of a road map—it took two weeks of Treybig's time to draft—showing how a push on this spot of the complex system will have repercussions everywhere else. Several computers shipped late, for instance, can drop quarterly profits enough to lower the stock price, which makes raising capital more expensive, which leaves less money for research and incentives, which . . . You get the idea.

THE ONCE-A-MONTH MANAGER

Letting employees see the big picture and peek at strategic secrets boosts loyalty. "People really get a great kick out of being part of the team and trusted with the corporate jewels," as Jim Katzman says. But the deeper purpose is to lessen the need for management by pointing everybody in the right direction and explaining what's happening on all sides of him. "Most companies are overmanaged," Treybig believes. "Most people need less management than you think." Thus at Tandem, says marketing director Gerald Peterson, stating the company's fundamental managerial principle, "the controls are not a lot of reviews or meetings or reports, but rather the control is understanding the basic concept and philosophy." What this means in practice, says one software designer, is that "I speak to my manager about once a month—that's how often my manager manages me."

Not everyone can work this way, so hiring is crucial at Tandem. The philosophy, aiming to curb the all-too-human tendency of institutions to clog themselves with unthreatening mediocrities and yes-men, nags managers to choose smarter or more qualified people than themselves and not to "hire in their own image." Normally, only proved and experienced applicants get considered—which incidentally insures Tandem a steady flow of new ideas from other companies—and grueling interviews, sometimes twenty hours of them, put candidates through the wringer. Tandem's managers, not its essentially administrative personnel office, do all the hiring; prospective co-workers interview applicants too. "A manager will never hire somebody his people don't think is good," says a programmer. "Basically, he says will you work with this person, and you say yes or no." As a result, new employees are on their way to integration into the community even before their first day on the job.

Without question this system works. Tandem's productivity figures are among the highest in the industry; even shipping clerks don't seem just to go through the motions by rote. As to imbuing employees with zeal for the company's success—one satisfied customer speaks of a service technician who gladly gave out his home phone number, cheerfully took an emergency call at 2:30 in the morning, and turned up, toolbox in hand, at 6 A.M.

Yet this managerial style can't be applied indiscriminately to all businesses. What makes it work at Tandem is its close fit to that company's special circumstances. For instance, aiming everybody in the same direction and keeping supervision light makes sense in a company with one basic product and one clearly defined market, but it could spell chaos in a complex, diversified corporation. Lean management works well, too, in an operation with so many functions farmed out. Tandem buys most of its components from subcontractors and gets cleaned by a contract janitorial service. For all its talk about equality, the whole company is an elite, leaving the lowest functions to others.

What manufacturing Tandem does itself—in quiet, airy rooms more like labs than factories—is high-level assembly and massive testing. This requires skilled workers, self-disciplined and intelligent enough to dispense with a supervisor over each shoulder. Rare everywhere, such workers are especially hard to hire in Silicon Valley, where demand is so high that "assembly people and operators can literally walk across the street and find work the next day," as Gordon Campbell, president of neighboring

Seeq Technology, puts it. Stoking employee loyalty with every conceivable amenity thus becomes a matter of urgency, particularly when sky-high Valley housing costs make an influx of new assembly workers most unlikely.

But the real competition is the battle for engineering talent among the Valley's high-tech companies, all constantly making passes at each other's technical staffs. "Once you have one of these guys," says Stanford computer-science Professor Edward Feigenbaum, "you don't want to lose him. You have to coddle these people." Hence the Tandem swimming pool (which competes with the health clubs and hot tubs of nearby companies), the six-week sabbaticals every four years that have sent Tandemites up the mountains of Nepal or into London's Cordon Bleu cooking school, and the stock options, some of them carefully calibrated to make leaving the company before four years very expensive. Such emoluments not only stay the footloose; they've also largely kept unions out of Silicon Valley.

"The most creative computer people are the semi-freakies," Feigenbaum notes, and—especially in the case of the software designers who breathe the soul into Tandem's machines—they need freedom and solitude to perform their occult art. After all, the continual refining and extending of the system's intelligence, not the bolting together of components, is the essence of Tandem's business and the key to its future. "When you have a good systems-development shop, things always look to the outside observer as if they're out of control—and to some extent they are," explains John Brodie, a software consultant who writes programs for some of Tandem's customers. "It's semi-channeled chaos." Tandem's loose, flexible style reflects this industry reality.

It reflects, too, the youth of its staff, many of whom went to college in the Sixties and early Seventies, when they were at least touched by the values of the counter-culture. "I used to call those development people down at Tandem pseudo-hippies," ex-VP Wiegand says with a chuckle, "but they were terribly hard workers." That statement sums up a tension common enough in people of that generation, especially in northern California, between the claims of openness, spontaneity, non-judgmental acceptance, brotherhood, freedom, and expressiveness on the one hand, and technical proficiency coupled with personal ambition on the other. Tandem, with its youthful style, beer-bust rap sessions, high-flown egalitarianism, engineering excellence, and hefty financial incentives, resolves that conflict.

Asked if this is the right way to run a company, one personnel officer, not quite 30, sounds the authentic Tandem tone: "It's progressive. It's ahead of the times. I don't know that it's right. I don't know what's right or wrong. I know that it's very unique. It sure feels right to me: it fits in with the way I like to see people treated."

Tandemites do have a way of growing vague when they try to make sense of the company mystique. Often enough, they are reduced to quoting *Understanding Our Philosophy* as if it were Chairman Mao's Little Red Book. "Some people might call it brainwashing," says corporate-materials VP Jerald Reaugh, "but I don't think it is. I don't think it's immoral or illegal." Treybig himself, half jokingly, makes a different analogy. "I know this sounds like religion or something," he says, adding, "It's almost like religion."

THE BOSS LIKES THAT NOISE

Certainly it resembles religion, at least of the sect or cult variety, in the premium it puts on inner dedication. As a programmer remarks, "I don't think someone who thought Tandem was just a job would work out, because Tandem expects commitment." Accordingly, ordeals like the prolonged interviews serve not just to hire good people but also to build loyalty by making employees feel tried and specially chosen by an exacting community. And such initiations boost dedication simply by being ordeals, for, in the economy of the emotions, people value what has cost them a lot.

All sects need a charismatic leader, and Tandem's is, of course, Treybig. "Jimmy gets almost like an evangelist when he talks about the basic people issues of running a company," says marketing director Peterson, and McEvoy allows that seeing Treybig address the Tandem staff in a huge tent in the parking lot brings unwelcome thoughts of religion to his mind. Venture capitalist Franklin "Pitch" Johnson, Jr., a Tandem director, describes the "muttering that builds up into a roar of approval" that greets Treybig at such events. "It's an acknowledgment that they believe in him and they support him," Johnson says. "Jimmy likes it when he stands up there and hears that noise—that Tandem noise—of approval." Says Yale

management professor Rosabeth Moss Kanter of companies like these, "Their success makes it feel magical." Their employees, she says, feel that "we must be touched by some special gift."

Tandemites explain how all this has affected them by endless talk about how the company has helped them "grow." Like many Tandem values, this one, much emphasized in the corporate creed, is a little vague. "I can't describe it," says Richard Bixler, the company's engineering-operations manager, "but it feels pretty good. I feel like I'm accomplishing something with myself." Certainly the rich opportunities for promotion, learning, and initiative, added to the corporate culture's hold on the self-image of employees, gives them a sense of moving toward the full development of all their human potentialities. To convince employees that they are amply filling their innermost goals of self-realization as they advance the company's interest is almost a miraculous feat in itself. But the sense of self-realization Tandem's mystique produces may prove illusory, for the radiance of mystiques is, like the glow of moonshine, notoriously liable to fade.

It's on a less ineffable kind of growth—explosive corporate growth—that Tandem's system ultimately rests. This creates not only the big profits and lavish benefits, but also the acute need for new managers, rapid promotion, and the ability of employees to manage themselves that gives Tandemites their sense of personal growth and freedom. With nearly half the employees at the company for less than six months, hierarchies are not fully defined, roles are relatively unfixed, and there's potential power and opportunity for all.

"The haunting question," says Johnson, "is, if we have a hickey on our growth rate, will this fantastic morale we've built hold up?" He foresees no such blemish, but Tandem management is working to institutionalize and codify the magic. Such devices as those philosophy seminars are preparation for the fast-approaching day when the company is too big for Treybig to dance with every employee and the day, sometime after that, when the amazing growth inevitably starts to slow. Meanwhile Treybig, by announcing plans to expand a $300-million-a-year company with 3,000-odd employees into a $1-billion one with 11,000 employees over the next three years, has promised his next faith-inspiring wonder.

CORPORATE CULTURES WORKSHEET

Directions: Diagnose the elements of this company's culture by answering the following questions:

1. What values and beliefs do employees espouse?

_____

_____

_____

2. Which metanorms or standards of behavior apply to all employees?

_____

_____

_____

3. What rites and rituals are expected behavior in which company employees must participate?

_____

_____

_____

4. Who are the heroes and what are the legends of the culture?

_____

_____

_____

5. What impact has the company founder had on the development of the culture?

_____

_____

_____

6. How would you describe this company's external environment?

_____

_____

_____

DISCUSSION QUESTIONS

1. To what extent do you believe that Tandem can maintain this particular culture over time?

2. Are loosely coupled corporate cultures a characteristic of young, growing organizations?

3. To what extent has the company's external environment influenced the development of this culture? How likely is it that a company operating in the staid Wall Street environment would develop a similar culture?

4. Which metanorms and values have the potential for being more dysfunctional than productive over time? Why? Explain.

REFERENCES

Deal, T. E. and A. A. Kennedy. "Strong Cultures: The New/Old Rule for Business Success," in *Corporate Cultures: The Rituals of Corporate Life.* Reading, Mass.: Addison-Wesley, Inc., 1982.

Exercise: Tapemaster Company

PURPOSE

The purpose of this exercise is to help you understand how to use organization goals as a change strategy. By the time you finish this exercise you will:

    1. Understand how goal clarification can be used as part of an organizational change strategy.

    2. Practice goal setting in a simulated organizational setting.

    3. Identify some of the major problems faced by managers when they attempt to set organizational goals as part of an organizational change project.

INTRODUCTION

You have undoubtedly been involved in goal setting on the individual level, determining goals for your personal life, your education, and your career. Because most definitions of the term "organization" include the idea that an organization is goal-directed, many writers in the field of organizational behavior and management have focused on goals, goal setting, and goal achievement, rather than on the goals of individuals within the organization.

Organizational goals are of two major types: official and operative. *Official goals*, which are usually value-based and not specific, are the formal mission statement of the organization. *Operative goals* are specific and outline how the organization will operate on a day-to-day basis.

As already indicated, organizations are goal-directed. In other words, the goals of an organization propel it in a given direction. Decisions about organizational goals underlie the eight attributes of a well run firm described by Peters (1980). Further, Deal and Kennedy (1982) point out that a strong cohesive culture, which they see as leading to organizational success, involves the organization's goals and how it works toward them. Thus, the goals are inexorably interwoven with organizational effectiveness and organizational culture.

Because of the critical role goals play in organizational effectiveness, a clear, shared understanding of them is a necessary first step in a program of organizational change. Unclear goals can make coherent strategy formulation impossible. Before an organization can decide what needs to be changed, it must first understand where it wants to go and what it wants to be. Many change efforts have resulted in failure because the organization had no shared understanding of where it wanted the change to lead. Thus learning to establish shared organizational goals is the necessary first step in many change projects. Further, the process of establishing shared goals often leads to changes in the way the organization operates. For example, when an organization establishes a clear and

Adapted from an exercise developed in 1987 by Judith A. Babcock of Rhode Island College.

shared set of goals, conflict is often reduced, coordination is improved, and communication is enhanced.

In this exercise you will have the opportunity to participate in setting goals for an organization and/or a subunit of that organization as part of an organizational change project. You will then analyze the goals set by the subunits and by the top management of the company.

INSTRUCTIONS

Option 1

1. Your instructor will assign you to a functional department or to the top management group of the Tapemaster Company (TC).

2. Read the General Information about the Tapemaster Company and The Goal-Setting Meeting directions.

3. Meet in your group to complete the goal-setting exercise.

4. Each group will appoint a spokesperson to report its goals to the class.

5. Participate in a class discussion of results and Discussion Questions.

Option 2

1. Your instructor will assign you to a functional department or to the top management group of the Tapemaster Company.

2. The top managment group will include the vice president for each functional department as well as the CEO.

3. Read the General Information about the Tapemaster Company and The Goal-Setting Meeting directions.

4. Meet in your group to complete the goal-setting exercise. The vice presidents will meet with their respective departments and the CEO will work alone.

5. The vice presidents of each functional division and the CEO will meet to determine the goals for TC in a "fishbowl" setting with the other class members observing.

6. Each group will appoint a spokesperson to report its goals to the class.

7. Participate in a class discussion of results and Discussion Questions.

The Tapemaster Company (TC) manufactures three products: audiotapes, videotapes, and compact discs. TC is a functionally structured organization with the following departments: marketing, personnel, research and development, production, and finance and accounting.

During the last year TC has experienced a period of rapid growth, with its sales volume almost doubling. To keep pace with the current and projected growth, TC has been hiring every qualified person available, even before job descriptions have been developed. As a result many of the new employees are not sure what they are supposed to be doing. As one of the new employees in the Marketing Department put it:

> I was hired two months ago and I'm still not sure what my job is. Whenever I ask my supervisor where I fit into the department and the company, he just tells me not to worry about it and puts me on another project. I've been assigned to projects that I didn't even know how to do. Sometimes I feel like a ping pong ball. Like I'm just being batted back and forth across the table and I don't even know the rules of the game. I've talked to some of the other new hires in the other departments and they all say basically the same thing. It's really hard to do a good job when you don't know what you're supposed to be doing or why you're doing it.

There is little communication between the departments, and as a result there is often a duplication of effort and on occasion serious conflict. The Production Department feels squeezed between the Marketing Department and the Research and Development Department. As a production engineer described it:

> Those guys in Research and Development are always sending us designs that aren't ready for production yet. We end up having to do a lot of design rework before we can produce it, and that costs us a lot of time which we don't have enough of anyway. Then the other day, after we had spent three days reworking one of their designs, the guys from R&D came waltzing in and said they'd changed the design. How are we supposed to do our job? Sometimes it feels like they're trying to sabotage us. It makes me wonder whether we're even working for the same company. To make matters worse we've got the Marketing Department pushing us from the other side. They're always making promises to customers that we can't possibly keep and then pressuring us to meet their impossible deadlines. Sometimes quality has suffered as a result. I hate to send out a product that isn't right but sometimes it can't be helped. I have R&D sending me designs that are impossible to produce and Marketing telling me to produce them on an impossible schedule. It's no wonder things go wrong sometimes. It seems like the left hand has no idea what the right hand is doing and doesn't care.

Every department seems to have the same kinds of complaints about one or more of the other departments.

The general feeling at Tapemaster is one of chaos. One employee described it a "chicken with its head cut off, just running in circles, bumping into things with no sense of what it should or should not be doing." People are in a continual state of crisis. They run from one fire to another trying to put them out with no sense of direction. There also seems to be a leadership vacuum. People complain that when they ask for direction they are not given any, and every level seems to have the same complaint. One supervisor said that he felt completely out of control of the situation. He said:

> I can't get my boss to tell me what I should be doing, so it's hard for me to give my people any direction. I know it's not a good situation, but even if I knew what to tell my people I wouldn't have time to do it. Everyone around here is pretty much on their own.

The CEO of TC is worried because, although sales have almost doubled, profits have been falling steeply. He sees the chaos around him but he doesn't know what to do about it. As he said:

> When we started to grow so quickly everything just got out of control. We've always been very interested in innovation and growth, but this is ridiculous. We have a pretty informal climate around here which I think is important in our kind of business. I've always been the kind of boss who believed in letting people have as much autonomy as possible. But this is just not working. Sometimes I feel like that fellow who said about his subordinates, "There they go. I am their leader and I must follow them." The problem is that no one seems to know where we're going. Everything is just out of control. I hired a management consultant to help me figure out a way to manage the company's growth and improve the profit picture. He did a preliminary diagnosis and said that before we could do anything we had to develop a clear understanding of what our goals as a company are. He said that many of our problems stem from the fact that people don't share a sense of where the company is going or what it needs to do to get there. I've asked each of the departments and the top management group to meet and develop a set of operative goals.

THE GOAL-SETTING MEETING

Directions: Your group is to develop a set of operative goals for the unit and the company. These should include specific and realistic goals in the following areas:

- ☐ Profit.
- ☐ Volume.
- ☐ Growth.
- ☐ Resources (acquisition of material and financial resources).
- ☐ Market (market share, pricing, level of promotion, and so on).
- ☐ Employee development.
- ☐ Innovation.
- ☐ Productivity.

Following the meeting, each group should appoint a spokesperson to report its goals to the rest of the company.

DISCUSSION QUESTIONS

1. Did the goals you developed highlight any other problems that the company is having? What should be TC's next step in the change process? Discuss.

2. What changes do you expect your set of goals to achieve? To what extent do you think Tapemaster will achieve the goals set by your group? By other groups?

3. What are the similarities and differences between the goals set by your group and the goals set by other groups? Discuss.

4. Is the goal-setting process likely to be the same for all organizations? Discuss. If the CEO of TC were to make a clear statement of the official goals, what effect do you think such a statement would have on the goal-setting process?

Exercise: An OD Change Project

PURPOSE

The purpose of this exercise is to help you to understand the process of organization development. By the time you finish this exercise you will:

This exercise was developed for classroom discussion only.

1. Practice diagnosing organizational problems.

2. Develop a plan for presenting your diagnosis to top management.

3. Understand the complexities and difficulties that can occur during an organization development project.

INTRODUCTION

Organization development (OD) is a program of planned change involving the use of behavioral science principles to improve organizational effectiveness. OD has a broad focus. It is concerned with the entire system of interest (such as a company, a department, or a work group) rather than a single facet of a problem. In the context of the total system, some of the problems that OD addresses are communication, managerial strategy, cultural norms, structure, roles, intergroup competition, planning, motivation, career development, and goal setting.

One of the assumptions of OD is that, to improve organizational effectiveness, it is first necessary to develop a picture of the current state of the organization and what is interfering with its effectiveness. This diagnostic process—one of the most important features of OD—involves collecting data about the organization from interviews, observation, questionnaires, archival sources, or some combination of these. From this data an understanding of the current state of the organization can be developed. Thus OD does not involve a predetermined change strategy. Instead it is based on the individual nature of the system.

Another important aspect of an OD intervention is that it is collaborative. That is, the change agent and the organization work together to understand the data collected during the diagnosis and develop strategies for change based on that diagnosis.

One of the consequences of this diagnostic/collaborative approach to planned change is that the process is difficult to predict and control. There are always surprises—good and bad—and there are few if any simple answers. This exercise is an opportunity for you to experience one part of the OD process.

INSTRUCTIONS

1. Read the Diagnosis Meeting directions, General Information, and Interview Transcripts.

2. Form groups of five to seven people.

3. In groups, complete the Diagnosis Proposal Worksheets.

4. Appoint a spokesperson to report your group's proposal to the class.

5. Participate in a class discussion.

DIAGNOSIS MEETING

Directions: You are an external consulting group called in by the owner (Brenda Cortland) of a small travel agency (Worldwide) to improve organizational effectiveness. You have already completed interviews with all of the key personnel. At a meeting with Brenda scheduled for tomorrow, you plan to present her with your preliminary findings and, with her, develop a program of change based on your diagnosis. You are meeting to discuss the data that you have collected and decide on:

☐ What you see as the major problems in the organization.

☐ What data supports your view of the problems.

☐ How you plan to present the information that you have collected to Brenda.

☐ The problems you think you may encounter during your meeting with her.

☐ A proposed strategy for dealing with these problems.

Use the Diagnosis Proposal Worksheets as a guide for your discussion and as a way of summarizing your proposal.

DIAGNOSIS PROPOSAL WORKSHEET I

Major Organizational Problems	Supporting Data

DIAGNOSIS PROPOSAL WORKSHEET II

Presentation Plan:

_____

_____

_____

_____

_____

_____

_____

_____

Anticipated Problems:

_____

_____

_____

_____

_____

_____

_____

_____

Problem Strategy:

_____

_____

_____

_____

_____

_____

_____

_____

GENERAL INFORMATION

Worldwide, which is located in the suburb of a large Midwestern city, was started by Brenda Cortland ten years ago. Before starting Worldwide, Brenda worked for a large travel agency for eight years. Worldwide's business is divided about equally between corporate and individual clients. Because the profit on each ticket or tour package is so low, Worldwide must book a large volume of travel to make a profit. Because of this, Brenda spends three days each week out of the office visiting corporate clients.

In addition to Brenda, Worldwide has one part-time and three full-time employees.

Full-Time

1. *Joan Locke, Office Manager:* Joan oversees the day-to-day operation of the agency. Nominally she is in charge of the other employees. She also pitches in with the reservations when things are busy. She has been with the agency for three months.

2. *Susan Delacort, Reservation Clerk:* Susan is in charge of booking reservations and tours for the agency's corporate clients. Susan has been with the agency for nine months.

3. *Nancy Abrams, Reservation Clerk:* Nancy is in charge of booking the travel arrangements for private individuals. Nancy has been with the agency for four months.

Part-Time

1. *Theresa Slyker, Bookkeeper:* Theresa comes in twice a month. She has been with the agency for ten years.

When Brenda first contacted you, she was in a state of panic. She told you that her Office Manager and one of her Reservation Clerks was on the verge of quitting. You agreed to meet with her. The following is an edited transcript of that first meeting.

INTERVIEW TRANSCRIPTS

Brenda Cortland

My business is very low commission. I have to have a high volume. I have $10,000.00 per month overhead—you have to sell a lot of tickets to make that much. There's a lot of detail work. There are so many places to make mistakes. I have to be out of the office three days a week. I spend it in [the nearby city] talking with my corporate clients. I also go to other groups to try to sell them package tours. There is a lot of promotion associated with this business.

It's really hard for me to find employees. I can't pay very much and I need someone who is reliable, conscientious, and willing to work hard. I've had a lot of turnover. My last office manager was here for only six weeks. She got angry because I wasn't willing to pay for any sick days for the first three months so she just stopped coming to work. I had to get a temp to fill in and that made me really uncomfortable because she didn't know the job, the industry, or our clients. I had to watch her every minute. One of the last reservation clerks I had went to the unemployment board because she didn't like the policies . . . she knew what they were when I hired her. The office manager before the one who just stopped coming to work was really great. I hated to lose her. We had a blow up over something she did wrong—I don't remember what it was now. But she was wonderful, she gave a lot, she was a really good person and very conscientious. She always was willing to stay late, come in on the weekends, whatever it took. But as good as she was, she couldn't take any initiative. I had to tell her how to do everything. I don't really know what happened with her. I guess it was a combination of her expecting a lot of herself and having to put in more time than she wanted to even though I never asked her to do so. One night I asked her to stay late and she got upset. Things were never the same after that. She had some personal problems. She said that I was demanding, but I don't think I really was. By and large we got along great. She was fun, you know, and appreciative. She was not educated but she was very special.

My current office manager, Joan . . . I looked for three months and finally hired her because I needed someone. She's been here for three months now. I told her about the people who had had her job previously. I think she has a personality problem. She comes on very strong, definitive and defensive. She's very uncooperative and has a tendency to blow up. She seems to like Susan and Nancy a lot. I feel completely left out when I am in the office. They're very cliquish and it makes me feel uptight. They seem like they just can't wait for me to leave the office. Joan seems to like her job, but she doesn't seem to like me. Our values and ways of communicating are really different. I tried to talk to her about her feelings one Friday and she was very vindictive. She also makes a lot of mistakes and she never apologizes. When I'm out of the office I want them [Joan, Susan and Nancy] to keep a log of what they did so I can see what happened while I was gone. I then go over it with them when I get back. I don't think that I'm demanding. I have respect for my people. I don't shout or yell.

Joan is dependable and diligent but she doesn't invest herself in the business. She doesn't feel that she is being an office manager, she feels like she's being stifled, stymied, like she's in a box. Her disposition isn't what I feel comfortable with either and she sighs a lot. She has sort of a strange philosophy, i.e., make it easy for Joan, not for Brenda. My employees should be making it easier for me. I'm afraid to tell her anything because I'm afraid she'll get mad and I just can't face trying to find someone else. I want someone who is efficient, caring, and sensitive. Joan is qualified. In general she does a pretty good job, but her typing isn't too great. [Brenda gets up and opens the door to her office.] They're out there talking when they should be working and this is what kills me. Joan is so strong that she intimidates me. I don't want to pick on people so I figured with someone like Joan that wouldn't happen.

Susan [the reservation clerk in charge of the agency's corporate clients] is trying upward delegation, which I really resent because I am already working 12 to 14 hours a day and some weekends. She doesn't like me, which is alright, but she should respect me. Everyone in the office seems to be fighting for more control, they want to do their own thing more. Susan is also very obstinate and interrupts constantly. When I ask her to do something she'll day, "That's not necessary." I don't think that she's qualified to judge what is necessary and what is not.

Nancy [the Reservation Clerk in charge of individual travelers] just can't seem to do the work. She is so slow plus she makes a lot of mistakes. I like her temperament. She's very low key but she can't seem to get the work done. And then she complains that she has too much to do and is overworked. Plus she is very defensive, she can't take criticism well at all. Also her voice drives me crazy, it really grates on my nerves. But she does seem to care, I just wish she didn't make so many mistakes . . . she also has a tendency to blame me when something goes wrong.

It just seems like no one really cares. If someone is invested in their job they don't say, "I have to leave now, it's five o'clock." They always seem like they're trying to get me out of the office. I think that it's so they can slack off. They're not committed. I feel like people are working against me instead of with me. I use praise a lot. I think praise is very important.

Theresa [the part-time Bookkeeper] is wonderful. I wish that I could have her for a full-time employee. She is so easygoing and caring. I never have any problem with her. She's been my bookkeeper since I started Worldwide. She comes in and does her job and doesn't waste time. Why can't I find someone like her?

Joan Locke

I've been here for about three months. I handle everything that comes in—mail, billing, phoning, typing letters, filing. I don't feel like an office manager. I feel more like a private secretary. It's part of my own adjustment too. I came from a larger corporation where I was given some kind of responsibility and could set up my own schedule. Brenda constantly tells me what to do—every day, every step I take. And I am not told once, but five times. I find it very irritating. When I told Brenda that I was unhappy with the job and the situation she was surprised. I am unhappy. Brenda is a total autocrat. This is the first time that I've had difficulty in a relationship with someone I work with. Brenda wants someone who can be very accommodating. I can only be accommodating if there is give and take, and she just doesn't listen. Brenda needs me and at the same time she is afraid of me. I think she would like to like me but she is too afraid of me.

She does respect my abilities. She's always saying, "Just give me a little time to let go of things." I don't know how much longer I can wait. There has to be some give and take. I want to be treated like an adult. I don't really trust Brenda. She does things to be nice, but I feel like at this point it's self-serving. I would like her to like me and I don't think she does.

When she's not in the office she makes a tape for me telling me what to do and what Susan and Nancy should do. I have to transcribe it and she repeats things four or five times. This tape is incredibly repetitive and disorganized. Brenda is not at all organized and transcribing it takes an enormous amount of time and it's similar every day. It's so redundant it drives me up the wall. Then we have to check off everything on the tape that we do so she can check it. We also have to keep track of everything that we do, such as: "got mail," "did tape," "did billing."

It's a log of every move you make during the day including things like locking the door and turning on the answering machine. Also, everything you do goes into a folder for her to check. Plus on the days that she is out of the office she calls a minimum of two times to find out what's going on. So we have the tape—what to do, the log—what we did, and the folder—actual work.

Brenda wants me to come in early, but I refuse to because I think that it's a waste of time. She goes over everything, every step of the log and the folder, one question after another: "How did you do it?" "Why did you do it?" "Are you sure you did it?" If anything has to be redone it goes back to her. Some of these things are legitimate, but it's so extreme. I have tried to get her to organize things to make it easier for both of us. I have tried to simplify and organize things, but Brenda doesn't take advantage of it. There's lots of redundant work and I guess I rebel at redundant work.

If I could have any kind of responsibility and run with the job I would love it. While she was on vacation we had the office running smoothly, but that didn't seem to make an impression on her even though she said that she was pleased. Some of her clients told her, "Boy, that's some staff you have there. They really kept things rolling." She has no people skills. If she treated us like she does her clients everything would be great. She treats us like servants—"Someone go get my suitcase." It's impossible to get a feeling of accomplishment. Brenda just keeps giving you more and more and more to do. The more you do the more is put on you.

The business has a tremendous potential for growth. But if the business is going to grow, Brenda is going to have to let someone else assume some of the responsibility. There is nothing, nothing that doesn't go through her—nothing. But she tries, she really tries.

It's a very tentative situation. I told her that I want to make it work and I do. She isn't as tough on me as she is on Susan because I intimidate her. What she does give me she only does because she's afraid that I'll walk out. I don't want to upset her. Maybe me wanting to stay is not the right thing for her.

Brenda tries to trap you with her distrust. When I first started she would call at 5:25 or say, "I guess you left a little early yesterday." It feels like she's trying to entrap you whenever she's been out and comes back.

Sometimes I feel like I have another child. I don't think there are many people who would stick it out with her. I don't want to hurt her, but I'm not sure where I fit. I wish she could see me as I really am. She does not know the real me. I wish that she would allow me to be what I can be. She sees me as tough. She's right, that's the way I've come across to her in order to deal with her and that is really not like me and I don't like doing it. After almost three months there is no interest in me as a person beyond this place . . . no interest in you as a person beyond how it affects her.

Nancy Abrams

I feel like I am finally beginning to get familiar with the work. There is just so much to learn. I'm still a little unsure of some of the details plus sometimes Brenda will change what she wants. She forgets. I do have a problem with communication. I'll remember very clearly that she says things and she swears she didn't say them . . . "do such and so" and she doesn't remember. She thinks I'm in error and I think she's in error. She has it in her mind but relays it in an abbreviated fashion. It happens mostly at the end of the day when people are whipping around. I'm not good under pressure . . . rushing to do things, I make mistakes.

Brenda has been under a lot of pressure. I think we're getting along better . . . working better together. I have a big concern about my future with Brenda. I feel that I don't have far to go with Worldwide.

Brenda blows things out of proportion, so I end up making more mistakes. Brenda expects that I can work a lot of overtime for nothing. Our agreement was that she'd pay time and a half for overtime. I guess we have a different system of what we feel is expected.

Sometimes she seems to run hot and cold. I see more generosity coming through; it really does affect my attitude. I'm leery of putting in a lot of overtime if I don't feel that anything is going to come of it. This job can be so much fun when the work isn't overwhelming. I love the work. But sometimes I feel like I'm being bled dry. I know Brenda works really hard, but it's her business. She does get nervous, she can be snappy and unfair and unreasonable. She's really a perfectionist and she can be pushy. I try to understand it because it's her business and her personality, but sometimes it's a little hard to deal with.

She does tend to harp on mistakes no matter how big or small they are. She makes a big production over nothing. I feel like I have to defend myself and I feel embarrassed. I take it personally. I think her expectations are too high. I really do want to do a good job.

Susan Delacort

This job just fell into my lap and I was very happy to be able to learn. But things are getting so bad around here that I can't ignore it anymore. It is so subtle that you can easily miss it. Brenda is totally immersed in work and has no personal life. She expects people to succumb to every whim rather than to fill a responsibility. Brenda has told me that I'm overqualified for the job, but she sees the nitty-gritty of the job as demeaning. There's a lot of little things. I get so frustrated. I say things to her and she just ignores them. She makes me so defensive that I don't want to do anything. Plus there is so much repetition about such trivial things, "Did you empty the garbage? Did you sharpen the pencils?" No kidding. The job could really be a lot of fun, but I don't feel responsible for anything.

I think she's a nice person and tries to be a good person, but she's too involved with nonessentials. She wants to have hands on everything. She wants quick answers to things, which is understandable, but we can't give them to her because we're so bogged down in nonessentials. And she doesn't trust anyone. Everytime she comes back from a day away she counts the petty cash.

I'm efficient. In every recommendation that's ever been written about me they've said that. That seems to bug Brenda. Her priorities are the little details, the little piddling things. It's an aggravating situation. She keeps saying that she can't understand why she can't get people to stay late. A person wants to feel like they're in control, like they're important. But Brenda says, "This is my business." But we all want to feel important and responsible. She interferes in everything. One day I had all of my work sorted into piles. She walked by my desk and said, "This isn't neat," and put it into one big pile. She gets so involved in details that she misses what is important. She will spend an hour going over the list of office supplies that we need. She goes over every item, "Do we really need this? What is this?" One time Brenda called the post office to tell Joan to make sure to come home with a receipt. We're not stupid and we do care about the business. If you give me the responsibility I will assume it. I know I'm not perfect. I have the worst memory in the world.

It's like being in prison. I feel like I'm in a delinquent school and my main objective is to learn to follow directions. And she gets upset about the strangest things, she always blows things out of proportion, "I dropped a pencil on the floor and you didn't pick it up for me." She keeps repeating, "You are here to help me. You should be working with me rather than against me." She's right, and we do try to work with her, but nothing is ever good enough. She makes me feel like an idiot sometimes. Nobody wants to be somebody's lackey.

She really works hard. But if she would get off Joan's back and let her do her job, she would have less work. I do think she tries, I do think she wants to be a good person. People have to enjoy their work. This is not a sweat shop or an assembly line. I can't keep giving and giving and not getting anything.

Theresa Slyker

I really don't have much to say. I've been with Brenda ever since she started Worldwide. We're good friends, but I'm glad I don't work here full-time. All I can tell you is that the people who are here now say the same things that people have always said. It's Brenda's business and she feels like she needs to know everything that's going on. She works herself too hard and she expects everyone who works for her to care as much as she does about the business. I know that she is always worried about money. She has a lot of overhead and she spends a lot of time worrying about being able to pay the bills. She hired Joan to take things over for her, but she hasn't let her. Joan suggests things but Brenda doesn't pick up on them. If people know what they're doing, they're the ones that are keeping things under control. She just can't seem to trust anyone. Plus the kind of person she says she wants does not seem to be the kind of person she can get along with. She says she wants someone who is professional and willing to accept responsibility and take some of the load off her, but that isn't the kind of person she feels comfortable working with.

Things are usually better when Brenda isn't in the office. More seems to get done. People don't spend so much time repeating themselves, going over things that have already been gone over, and doing little things for Brenda that she could do for herself—sharpening pencils, getting things for her, copying personal things for her, making calls she could make, things like that.

The atmosphere around here has been really horrible lately. I hope that you can do something. I have the feeling that we're in for more turnover and I'm not sure that Brenda could handle that.

1. What did your group identify as the major problems at Worldwide?

2. What was your major concern about presenting your diagnosis to Brenda?

3. Do you think that things are likely to change at Worldwide? Why or why not?

4. What was the most difficult part of this exercise? Do you think that you would like to be the OD consultant? Why or why not?

Memo: Organizational Culture

Assess the culture of your organization using the following questions as a guide:

1. What is the primary business or mission of your company?

2. In what type of environment does your company do business? Is the environment of your company's industry fast-paced and growing, or slow-paced and static?

3. What are the greatest strengths of your company? What are the greatest weaknesses of your company?

4. What is the company's image of itself? What do you think the company's image is in the minds of competitors?

5. What is the general philosophy of management? Is management more oriented to human resource or budget objectives?

6. How much freedom do members of the organization have in doing their own work?

7. What rituals or ceremonies are characteristic of your company?

8. Who are your company's heroes? Why did they become so greatly admired?

9. How are status symbols used?

10. What rites of passage exist for progression up the career ladder?

Use your answers to these questions to describe your company's culture and how well these cultural values fit your personal values.

Index

Task significance:
  discussion of, 142
  as factor increasing motivation, 103
Territorial departmentalization:
  advantages, 355
  chart of, 359
  disadvantages, 355
Texas Instruments, 356
Theories of management, 2
Theory X, 29, 30, 31, 40
Theory Y, 29, 30, 31, 40
3M, 39
Timbering Act, 155
Time, Inc., 424
Traditional normative framework for effective management, 1
Transactional leaders, 160
Transcontinental Air Transport, 194
Transcripts, interview, organization development, 440–445
Transformational leaders, 160
Troublemakers, as over-generalized label, 86
Typological framework, illustrating components of manager's work, 1–3

U

Uncertainty, environmental, concept of, 349–353

Unfamiliar culture, effectively entering, 383

V

Value-based goals, 431
Values:
  promoting, 30–34
  shared as component of corporate culture, 425
  shared, effects on business environment, 382
Vanatin case, 202–208
Variety, as characterized in manager's workload, 1–3
Visibility, as factor influencing job content, 103
Volume, setting goals for, 435
Vroom and Yetton Model:
  applying, 189–192
  definition of, 161
Vroom, Victor H., 160, 162, 189

W

Wall Street Journal, The, 205
Wall Street, as external environment, 430
Ware, James, 48, 53, 265
Waterman, Robert, 39

Wilderness Survival Group Consensus Task, 291–300
Wilderness Survival Worksheet, 293–295
Within-group behavior, 265–266
  solving conflicts, 308–315
Work assignments:
  discussing with employees, 29–36
  making, 36
Work climate, as part of motivation for employees, 35–37
Work group, see Group decision making . . .
Working conditions, as factor influencing job context, 103
Workload, manager's composition of, 2
Worksheets, diagnosis proposal, for organization development, 438–439

Y

Yetton, Philip, 160, 162, 189